A Dictionary of Landscape Architecture

Soros residence, Long Island, New York. Design and photo by A. E. Bye.

A Dictionary of Landscape Architecture

Baker H. Morrow, ASLA

University of New Mexico Press
Albuquerque

Illustrations

Line drawings by Julia Morrow
Huchmala.
Additional drawings by Laura Lee
Toulouse, Lisa Flynn,
Elizabeth Grubb, and Patricia Davis
Willson.
All photographs are individually
credited to their sources.
The abbreviation BBMSL refers to the
Bainbridge Bunting Memorial
Slide Library, University of New
Mexico.

Frontispiece:
A. E. Bye. Soros estate, Long
Island, New York. Photo courtesy
A. E. Bye.

Library of Congress Cataloging in Publication Data

Morrow, Baker H., 1946—
    A dictionary of landscape architecture.

    Bibliography: p.
    1. Landscape architecture—Dictionaries.   I. Title.
SB469.25.M67   1987   712'.03'21   87-5847
ISBN 0-8263-0943-7
ISBN 0-8263-0944-5 (pbk.)

To my parents, Hazel B. Morrow and Findley H. Morrow,
and to my grandfather, the late Clint Morrow,
road showman, fisherman, butcher,
and gardener.

Acknowledgments

I worked on this dictionary for ten years, mostly in the evenings when the terms of landscape design and construction practice were still fresh in my ears. As the book was composed, many people contributed their ideas, reviews of entries, encouragement, and other kindnesses freely and with great generosity. I would like to thank, among others, Nancy Athene, Steve Borbas, A. E. Bye, Alice Carmona-Morgan, Etienne Cowper, Barbara Daniels, Barbara Dent, Garrett Eckbo, Peter Eller, Mark Eshelman, Frank Fuchs, Marty Furch, Paul Friedberg, Don Gillmore, Tafazzul Hussain, J. B. Jackson, Dan Kiley, Will Lee, Marleyne Levin, Mark Levine, Professor Sir Albert Lopes, Carl Mayfield, Carla McConnell, Roz Menton, R. Jack Meyers, Dolores Pizzola, Wolf Preiser, Fred Roach, John Rupley, Hideo Sasaki, Shelby Smith-Sanclare, Craig and Laura Sowers, Scott Taylor, Nancy Tertipes, Luther Wilson, and Regan Young.

The Canadian entry would not have been possible without the assistance of Mr. Ron Ehlert of Landplan Associates, Calgary, Alberta, and of Professor Sue Donaldson of the University of Calgary.

Mr. John Oldham of Perth graciously provided me detailed information from his researches into the history of Australian landscape architecture. I also appreciated the kind assistance of Dean George Seddon of the University of Melbourne and of Mr. Ralph Neale of *Landscape Australia.*

I am grateful to Mr. Boyden Evans and the staff of *The Landscape,* the publication of the New Zealand Institute of Landscape Architects, and to Mr. and Mrs. J. L. S. "Rory" Gordon and family of Galatea, New Zealand, for their help with the New Zealand entry.

Dr. Elisabeth MacDougall and the staff of Dumbarton Oaks and Zelda Richardson, director of the Bainbridge Bunting Slide Library at the University of New Mexico, provided first-rate assistance in technical research.

Fred Collatz, Professor Edward Cook, Guy R. Johns, ASLA, Professor Natasha Kolchevska, Jack Leaman, FASLA, Professor William Martin, Professor Tim McGinty, Professor Jonathan Porter, Professor Richard Robbins, Ray Trujillo, AIA, and Professor Robert Walters read all or part of the manuscript and offered invaluable advice and criticism.

Dean George Anselevicius, FAIA, of the School of Architecture and Planning, University of New Mexico, graciously offered administrative assistance and equipment for the production of the typescript. I am also grateful to Tina Taylor of the School of Architecture and Planning for her patient typing and reworking of a difficult manuscript.

I owe a debt to Beth Hadas, director of the University of New Mexico Press, for her lingering belief in this work; to Dana Asbury, my editor; to Emmy Ezzell, graphic designer; and to their staff. Vangie Mares of the UNM Printing Plant did an extraordinary job of typesetting the manuscript.

I extend my thanks to Mr. Gilles Stockton of Grass Range, Montana, for the series of conversations many years ago on the form of modern Paris that lie at the core of a number of the ideas expressed in this book.

JoAnn Strathman offered help and encouragement at every step as the manuscript took on its final form.

I would like to say, however, that none of these people is responsible for the accuracy of any entries. The shortcomings of this dictionary are entirely mine.

Notes on Sources

Nan Fairbrother's *The Nature of Landscape Design* (Knopf, 1974) is an excellent general introduction to modern landscape architecture. Michael Laurie's *An Introduction to Landscape Architecture* (Elsevier, 1975) and John Simonds's *Landscape Architecture, Second Edition* (McGraw-Hill, 1983) are also fine general accounts of the field. Norman Booth's *Basic Elements of Landscape Architectural Design* (Elsevier, 1973) is more specific, dealing with detailed design elements. *An Introduction to Urban Design* (Harper and Row, 1982) by Jonathan Barnett deals with the contributions of landscape architecture, architecture, and engineering to the making of a city.

In planning studies, Kevin Lynch's *Site Planning* (MIT, third edition 1984) and Edmund Bacon's *Design of Cities* (Viking Penguin, revised edition 1974) are immediately useful. *A Guide to Site and Environmental Planning, Second Edition* by Harvey Rubenstein (Wiley, 1980) deals with planning at a smaller scale and with the practical details of site development.

British histories of landscape and garden design are in general superior in content and readability. The English landscape and English writers about gardens, in particular, seem to have a long history of inspiring one another. Christopher Thacker's *The History of Gardens* (University of California Press, 1979) is among the best of a modern crop that also includes *The Garden: An Illustrated History* by Julia Berrall (Viking Penguin, 1978) and *The Landscape of Man* by Geoffrey and Susan Jellicoe (Thames and Hudson, 1975). *Park Maker* (Macmillan, 1977) by Elizabeth Stevenson is a biography of the Jovian American landscape architect Frederick Law Olmsted and a thoughtful study of nineteenth-century landscape design. The redoubtable *Design on the Land: The Development of Landscape Architecture* by Norman T. Newton (Harvard/Belknap, 1971) remains the fullest American work of landscape history. The American John B. Jackson, author of *The Necessity for Ruins* (University of Massachusetts Press, 1980), and the Englishman W. G. Hoskins, author of *The Making of the English Landscape* (Pelican, 1970), have created a new kind of landscape study and liberal art often termed *cultural geography*. In these and other books, Jackson and Hoskins emphasize the popular landscape and its many implications for landscape architecture. *Gardens in Time* (Lansdowne, 1980), by the Australians John and Ray Oldham, argues the case for greater historic Oriental influence in the Western landscape.

Several contemporary books serve as unequaled introductions to the study of Eastern landscapes. These include *Magic of Trees and Stones: Secrets of Japanese Gardening* by Katsuo Saito and Sadaji Wada (Japan Publications Trading Company, 1964), *Space and Illusion in the Japanese Garden* (Weatherhill/Tankosha, 1983) by Teiji Itoh, *The Chinese Garden* by Maggie Keswick (Rizzoli, 1978), *The Classical Gardens of China* (Van Nostrand Reinhold, 1982) by Yeng Hongxun, and Elizabeth Moynihan's *Paradise as a Garden* (George Braziller, 1979). A concise chapter in Derek Clifford's *A History of Garden Design* (Praeger, revised edition 1967) is a very clear account of the Islamic landscape and its continuing effects on the gardens of Europe and its former colonies.

Africa, the Soviet Union, and much of Latin America are utterly ignored by most landscape architectural historians. A fine short introduction to urban Africa is *African Cities and Towns before the European Conquest* by Richard W. Hull (Norton, 1976). Accurate Western studies of the landscape architecture of the Union of Soviet Socialist Republics are rare or nonexistent. Among the most informative sources on Soviet design are *The Art and Architecture of Russia* by George Heard Hamilton (Penguin, 1983) and *Pavlovsk Palace and Park* (Aurora Art Publishers, 1975). *Mexican Landscape Architecture* by Rosina Greene Kirby (Arizona, 1972), Emilio Ambasz's *The Architecture of Luis Barragan* (Museum of Modern Art, 1979), and Pietro Maria Bardi's *The Tropical Gardens of Burle Marx* (Reinhold, 1964) are probably the best contemporary accounts of Latin American landscape architecture.

Listings of landscape or landscape-related terms may be found in Warner Marsh's *Landscape Vocabulary* (Miramar, 1964), in J. Stewart Stein's *Construction Glossary* (Wiley, 1980), and in Cyril M. Harris's *Dictionary of Architecture and Construction* (McGraw-Hill, 1975), with landscape architectural entries by A. E. Bye. *Who's Who in Architecture* (Weidenfeld and Nicholson, 1977), edited by J. M. Richards, is a fine source of biographical information on designers from A.D. 1400 to the present.

There is a bewildering variety of garden books available to both amateur and professional gardeners. Among the most reliable of these is the massive *Hortus Third* (Macmillan, 1976), by the Liberty Hyde Bailey Hortorium, a standard reference on North American plants used in ornamental horticulture. Taylor's *Encyclopedia of Gardening* (Houghton Mifflin, 1976) and *Ortho's Complete Guide to Successful Gardening* (Ortho Books, 1983) are good one-volume references. For more detailed information, the *Time-Life Encyclopedia of Gardening* (Time-Life, 1971) and the *Marshall Cavendish Illustrated Encyclopedia of Gardening* (Marshall Cavendish, 1968–70) may be consulted. *Plant and Planet* (Penguin, 1978) by Anthony Huxley is a highly idiosyncratic and masterful introduction to plants, their distribution, and their habits of growth. Laura and Robert Rice's *Principles of Practical Horticulture* (Keston, 1986) is arguably the best contemporary overview of the field.

It would be hard to improve on Albe Munson's *Construction Design for Landscape Architects* (McGraw-Hill, 1974) for general utility in the field of landscape construction. The American Society of Landscape Architects and the Landscape Architecture Foundation have recently revised and updated their *Handbook of Landscape Architectural Construction* (Landscape Architecture Foundation, 1986). *Landscape Architecture Construction* (Elsevier, 1979) by Harlow C. Landphair and Fred Klatt, Jr., and *Urban Planning and Design Criteria* (Van Nostrand Reinhold, 1975) by Joseph De Chiara and Lee Koppelman also have instant applications in practical design. James A. Watkins's *Turf Irrigation Manual* (Telsco, 1977), though proprietary, crackles with good advice on systems design in this rapidly developing specialty.

Specification writing, even with modern machines, is learned only through hard practice under difficult deadlines. Good background books such as *Plants in the Landscape* (Freeman, 1975) by Philip L. Carpenter et al., and Robert W. Abbett's *Engineering Contracts and Specifications* (Wiley, 1963), which also serves as a first-rate introduction to design contracts, are useful to gain a footing.

To understand twentieth-century landscape architecture, the thoughtful student might well begin with *An Introduction to the Study of Landscape Design* (Hubbard Educational Trust, 1967) by Henry Hubbard and his wife, Theodora Kimball. Hubbard's book provides a very readable summary of nineteenth- and early twentieth-century design approaches. Garrett Eckbo's *The Landscape We See* (McGraw-Hill, 1969) and *Urban Landscape Design* (McGraw-Hill, 1964) are long, thoughtful essays on the mid-century designed landscape. However, the classic *Gardens Are for People* by Thomas Church (McGraw-Hill, revised edition 1983) is the most evocative account of the California or modern garden. Ian McHarg's *Design with Nature* (Doubleday, 1971) is a comprehensive product of the contemporary "ecological movement" in landscape architecture. Modern golf course architecture is well served by Geoffrey S. Cornish and Ronald E. Whitten in *The Golf Course* (Rutledge, 1981). And in the measured wisdom of Nan Fairbrother's *New Lives, New Landscapes* (Penguin, 1972), the art of landscape creation is gently prodded toward the twenty-first century.

A morning's walk through the courts of the Alhambra
and a book to remember them by.

Spencer MacInnes

Preface

There are the two eminent fields of architecture and horticulture influencing landscape architecture, neither of them dominant, of course, and both augmented to a greater or lesser degree by engineering, geography, planning, and other modern disciplines. Landscape architecture owes a debt to painting and sculpture, too, and it has been intimately connected to these arts for thousands of years. Yet it is more than these, more than the sum of its many contributing parts. Its ultimate charm and beauty and usefulness probably lie in the unusual power of its synthesis: when well done, it seems never to be finished, always evolving, always new or different with the passing seasons and years.

I have tried in this dictionary to identify its many small and large components and yet keep the threads that connect them to landscape architecture as a whole. The connecting links are themselves sometimes as important as what they tie together.

What we now call landscape architecture may be the subtlest of the fine arts, and it is among the oldest. Its beginnings in the West were in Sumer, at the head of the Persian Gulf, about 5,000 years ago. The Sumerian gods set up Utnapishtim, the survivor of the great flood and a seeker of immortality, in the garden of the sun in Dilmun. And nearby was the woman Siduri with her wine in a golden bowl in her own garden at the edge of the bright sea. It is an old story, a fable certainly, the first great linking of people and gardens, perhaps our own story as well.

Baker H. Morrow
Albuquerque
April 1986

A Dictionary of Landscape Architecture

AASHTO *American Association of State Highway and Transportation Officials,* q.v.

AB A common abbreviation for **Aggregate Base.** See also **Base course.**

ABC soil A soil with a profile of topsoil, subsoil, and a water (rock) stratum. See also **Soil horizon.**

Abcission The loosening and detachment of leaves, fruits, stems, or other plant parts.

Abeyance In real properties, a suspension of ownership lasting until the land in question is claimed or a settlement is reached.

Ablation Surface erosion by flowing water or glacial action.

Abrasion Surface erosion by means of the scouring action of particles suspended in air or water, or by moving ice.

ABS pipe In irrigation, a plastic (acrylonitrile butadiene styrene) pipe.

Absenker **Layering,** q.v.

Absolute humidity See **Humidity.**

Absolute pressure In irrigation pumps, all real pressure above zero—i.e., gauge plus atmospheric pressure.

Absorption A natural process in soils and plants by which liquid water or gases may be taken into tissue or soil structure.

Absorption rate (irrigation) In soils, the amount of water that will soak into the earth within a specific time. Absorption is fast in loose, gravelly, or sandy soils and slower in compact soils such as clay. See also **Precipitation rate.**

Abutment In landscape construction, a support wall engineered to withstand the thrust of a bridge or similar structure.

AC 1) A soil containing topsoil (A) and an underlying C horizon (bedrock or water-bearing stratum) but no subsoil. Often found on slopes. See also **Soil horizon.** 2) An abbreviation for **Asphaltic Concrete,** q.v.

A-C pipe See **Asbestos cement pipe.**

Acaricide A pesticide used to control spider mites.

Acarpous In botany, fruitless.

Acaulescent In botany, lacking a stalk above the soil surface. See also **Caulescent.**

ACB An abbreviation for **Asphalt Concrete Base.** See **Base course.**

Accent In landscape architecture, a feature that is included as an incidental complement to part or all of a design. Above-ground lamps along a garden path or an incidentally colorful tree in the midst of a uniform mass of trees are accents.

Accent stone A kind of **Bluestone,** q.v., with a rough or hammer-struck surface.

Acceptance, final See **Final acceptance.**

Acceptance (legal) See also **Conditional acceptance, Final acceptance,** and **Provisional acceptance.**

Access In landscape architecture, a means of approach or entry; specifically, a walkway, drive, path, series of stepstones, and the like.

Access, disabled or **handicapped** See **Handicapped access.**

Access road A road leading to and often paralleling a freeway or other limited-entry road. Also **Frontage road.**

Access structure A **Catch basin, Drop inlet,** or **Manhole,** q.q.v., allowing surface water to feed into an underground drainage system. An access structure also allows for maintenance of the drainage system.

Accidental colors
See **Complementary colors.**

Acclimation (acclimatization) A process of adaptation undergone by a plant as it becomes accustomed to a new (transplant) locale. See also **Hardening off.**

Accord and satisfaction A legal term indicating an acceptance by one party or changes of substitutions in the contract obligations of a second party.

Account, force See **Force account.**

Accretion 1) In streams and rivers, an increase in water volume derived from seep springs and the influx of tributaries. 2) In geology, the long-term building up of land by stream deposition, sea-wave deposition, and the like.

Acequia In the southwestern United States and in Spanish-speaking countries, a ditch or channel. The *Acequia madre* is the parent ditch which feeds smaller field-supplying channels.

Acerose In plants, a needlelike form. Also **Acicular.**

Achene In botany, a small fruit, generally dry, with its outer wall separating from the seed when ripe. Dandelion is an example.

Achromatic color See **Chromatic color.**

ACI American Concrete Institute, q.v.

Acicular (plants) See **Acerose.**

Acid rain A toxic form of rain caused by air pollution. Acid rain has been the cause of increasing damage to lakes and soil in the northeastern United States, eastern Canada, and elsewhere since the 1970s.

Acid soil A soil with a saturation pH reading of less than 7.0. A soil containing small amounts of lime. Acid soils are often found in regions with good to excessive rainfall and contain large amounts of humus-producing material. An extremely acidic soil is a **Sour soil,** q.v. See also **Alkaline soil, lime, pH factor.**

Acotyledon A plant with no seed lobes. A spore-producing plant, i.e., moss, fungus, and the like. See also **Cotyledon.**

ACP Asbestos cement pipe, q.v.

ACPA American Concrete Pipe Association, a manufacturers' organization promoting standards for materials and overall quality in concrete pipe construction.

Acre An English measurement of land encompassing 4,840 square yards (43,560 square feet) or .4047 hectare.

Acre foot The amount of water extending over one acre of land at a depth of one foot. A measurement of water often used in agriculture and for large-scale man-made landscapes.

Acreage An extended area of land, especially unenclosed or open area. A quantity of acres.

Acropolis 1) The highest portion of a Greek city upon which a temple to a principal local deity was located. 2) The location of the Parthenon in Athens, the most famous of all acropolises.

Action, capillary See **Capillary action.**

Action, frost See **Frost action.**

Activated sludge See **Sludge.**

Acuminate In leaves, a long form tapering to a tip.

AD An abbreviation for **Assessment district,** q.v..

Adapter (irrigation) See **Fitting.**

Adaptive radiation In biology, the divergent evolution of closely related plants or animals from a common form.

Addendum In landscape specifications, an addition, correction, or deletion made to construction documents before bids are opened. Plural: addenda or addendums. See also **Specifications.**

Addison, Joseph Eighteeenth-century English writer on naturalistic gardening. Addison, with **Alexander Pope,** q.v., and others, was influential in the development of a **Picturesque** approach to landscape architecture gardening. See also **English landscape architecture.**

Additional services (of the landscape architect) In contracts, subsidiary items of design and other consultation to be provided by a landscape architect to an owner for a consideration. See also **Design contract.**

Additive An item of enrichment such as manure, sawdust, peat moss, shredded bark, gypsum, straw, or chemical fertilizer that is mixed into a soil to reduce or increase pH, increase friability, improve drainage, add humus, or otherwise improve the quality of the earth being treated. See also **Soil amendment.**

Adobe. Making adobes, New Mexico, 1879. Photo courtesy BBMSL, UNM.

Additive alternate See **Alternate (bid).**

Additive, soil See **Soil amendment.**

Adhesion A phenomenon of molecular attraction, allowing a liquid such as water to cling to soil particles (**Hygroscopic water,** q.v.).

Adjustable riser In irrigation, a threaded riser (pipe) that can be modified in height for better coverage. See also **Riser.**

Adjusted net fill In landscape construction, the fill left after grading and compaction. See also **Cut and fill.**

Adjusted static pressure In irrigation, a design pressure calculated at 10% to 25% below a measured **Hydrostatic pressure,** q.v., to allow for great demand on the main supply line. The adjusted static pressure is also the maximum **Design pressure.** See also **Working pressure.**

Adjustor, flow (irrigation) See **Flow adjustor.**

Admixture In concrete construction, a material mixed with cement and aggregates to accelerate or retard curing, add color, or the like.

Admixture, air-entraining (concrete) See **Air-entraining agent.**

Admixture, pozzolanic (in concrete) See **Pozzolanic admixture.**

Adobe A mixture of clay, some sand, and straw or similar binder used in the making of sun-dried, form-cast brick. Also, a similar earthen mortar used to bind irregular stonework in walls or other structures. Adobe block is known in some regions as *Pise de terre* or **Soft mud brick.**

Adonis garden

Adonis garden In classical Greece, a small garden centered on a statue of Adonis, the handsome paramour of Aphrodite, whose death each fall and rebirth in spring were celebrated by the placement of small pots full of flowers or seeds at the base of his statue. The Adonis garden is the source of the Mediterranean courtyard garden of flowering pots ringing a fountain or statue. See also **Greek landscape architecture.**

Adsorption The covering of the surface of a solid particle by a thin layer of liquid—i.e., a soil granule by water.

ADT In traffic engineering and transportation studies, average daily traffic. See also **DHV.**

Adventitious bud, root In botany, a bud produced in an unusual place or under unusual circumstances. Any bud occurring on an abnormal part of a plant. Also adventitious roots, leaves, etc. An adventitious root is often produced by **Layering,** q.v.

Adventive plant A wild plant introduced outside its normal range—usually a temporarily established weed.

Adventure playground A supervised playground featuring creative indoor crafts for children (clay, drawing, and the like) combined with an active outdoor area in which crates, tires, boards, stones, ropes, and other materials are fashioned into play structures by the children themselves.

Advertisement for bids
   See **Invitation to bid.**

Aedicule A hollow or niche in a wall for a statue.

Aeolian Pertaining to wind or wind-borne deposits. From Aeolus, god of winds. See also **Loess.**

Aeolian harp A "harp" consisting of strings over a sounding board played by passing breezes. The Aeolian harp produced a kind of "natural" music that came to be very popular in the landscape gardens of the late eighteenth century. Its invention is traced to Athanasius Kircher (c. 1640). A remarkable Aeolian harp still exists in Pyatigorsk, Stavropol Region, Russian Federated S.S.R.

Aeration In lawn and shrub beds, the process of puncturing or loosening the soil so that water, fertilizer, and air may pass through more freely. Also **Aerification.** Also, a common treatment process leading to purification of sewage.

Aerenchyma Collectively, the fleshy tissue of wetland plants, exhibiting large air spaces between cells.

Aerial layering See **Air layering.**

Aerial perspective See **Perspective.**

Aerial photography The making of precise photographs from an airplane which are assembled stereoscopically to aid in the mapping of existing contours and other features. See also **Photogrammetry.**

Aerial (air) root See **Root.**

Aerification See **Aeration.**

Aerobic In botany, a plant directly dependent on free air. See also **Anaerobic.**

Aerology   The science of atmospheric study.

Aerophyte   A plant that is nourished by air.

Aesthetics (esthetics)   The quality of beauty.

Affidavit, collusion or noncollusion   See **Noncollusion affidavit.**

Affirmative Action   A civil rights program of the United States federal government actively pursued in the 1970s. In landscape construction, Affirmative Action required designers, contractors, and suppliers actively to acquire or use the goods or services of minorities and women. Percentage quotas were frequently established by statute and were incorporated in design and construction contracts.

Affluent   1) A tributary. 2) A stream flowing into a pond or lake. See also **Effluent, Influent.**

Afforestation   See **Forestation.**

African landscape architecture   In the savannas of Africa, the acacia is the most striking plant. It is an elegant, ubiquitous, thorny, thin-leafed tree, browsed by many animals. Among the most unusual of these is the giraffe, which can eat *down* into the crown of a tree of four or five meters, its tongue gingerly wrapping around the bits of foliage to miss the long white thorns.

These same spiny branches have been chopped from time immemorial to make the **Zaribas** or thorny enclosures that Africans throughout the continent use as folds for their grazing animals or as protection for their own houses at night. In sub-Saharan Africa, housing compounds or **Kraals** may also be enclosed by reed or pole fencing. The open spaces between these clusters of mud

and wattle rondavels or *mundels* are often beaten earth, and these serve cooking, weaving, playing, dancing, and general social purposes. African marketplaces often display the same tendency: a straightforward square or rectangle of beaten red earth will accommodate droves of sellers, buyers, and curious passers-by.

The general African landscape, if it is man-made, springs from an ancient pastoral or agricultural tradition. Even the largest of old African cities, such as Zimbabwe in the south, Timbuktu and Djenne of the old Mali and Songhai Empires in the northwest, and Mogadiscio and Brava in the Horn, have stayed strongly agrarian. Courtyards and gardens within compound walls and teashops set casually in the shade of sprawling trees remain popular city landscapes.

A sacred rock or grove in Africa, as in Europe and North America, has often been an important landscape element. In the twelfth-century city of Zimbabwe, monoliths, large altars, and stone birds set on pedestals were sited near a well-designed public marketplace. Zimbabwe itself was fashioned of and walled off in stone, and has survived reasonably intact into the twentieth century. The later Zulu "new towns" of South Africa and modern Zimbabwe were established under the rule of Shaka and his successor Dingaan in the nineteenth century. Shaka's settlements, consisting primarily of grass rondavels in extended kraals, were invariably constructed on hillsides, with good views and drainage. The largest Zulu settlement was probably Dingaan's capital Umgungundhlovu in Natal, burnt by the Boers in 1838.

The classic southern African kraal consists of a boys' hut or huts, girls' hut(s), wives' huts, cooking and storage areas, a wattle or other fence, a visitors' hut, and the

husband's hut. From this cluster planning for families came cluster-planned towns. Concentric walls in a series developing from palaces or market squares are common. Ibadan, Nigeria, the largest city in black Africa in the 1800s, had a thriving and famous marketplace. Gridiron towns are also traditionally found in Africa, as are settlements based on avenues radiating from a royal residence.

In both Saharan and sub-Saharan Africa, the village well is a landscape focal point, often used as a place for visiting and recreation. The ancient preeminence of the village square as a landscape feature was expanded with the coming of Islam. In Hausaland, Nigeria, the mosque squares of Sokoto were furnished with shade trees in 1809. Their builder, the caliph Mohammed Bello, felt that his improvements would allow Islam to be better observed. The rectangular interior courtyard with an **Impluvium** (water basin) was common in Yorubaland by the early nineteenth century.

The land itself remains sacred in rural West Africa. Tradition has always held it to be a living thing—something owned by the ancestors, and available to the living only for a limited period of good stewardship.

From the Greek historian Diodorus Siculus we know that the African countryside of the fourth century B.C. near Carthage would have been somewhat more familiar to Western eyes. The Carthaginian villas of what is now Tunisia were replete with orchards, streams, canals, vineyards, and market gardens. The Phoenician settlers kept cattle, horses, and other livestock grazing in well-tended pastures. Villa homes were stuccoed and sited to take good advantage of the mild Mediterranean climate. After the Third Punic War and the eclipse of Carthage by Rome, the villa tradition

African landscape architecture.
Square and courtyard of the Great
Mosque of Djenne', Mali, 1907.
Photo courtesy BBMSL, UNM.

was expanded to other parts of
North Africa. New Roman cities such
as Timgad and Leptis Magna in
Libya were developed in gridiron
fashion with amphitheatres, temple
squares, and forums as features. The
private house was normally designed
with an atrium, or central open
space, containing a pool and
surrounding plants and work areas.

But the Egyptians, predecessors of
both the Romans and the
Carthaginians, were probably the

earliest Mediterranean civilization to
influence the sub-Sahara. The
monumental public and religious
open spaces of Thebes and Memphis
were echoed at Axum, in Nubia,
and at Meroe, in Ethiopia. Egyptian-
inspired steles, temple grounds, and
pyramid groupings were also
common features in these cities.

The rise of Islam in the seventh
century A.D. had a profound effect
on African landscape architecture.
The **Chahar-bagh** or paradise

garden of four quadrants became a
commonplace in Egypt, Libya,
Tunisia, and the Maghreb. Fountains
for cleansing before prayers at
mosques, courtyard "color" gardens,
the hillside gardens of Morocco all
flourished under the Arabs. In
medieval East Africa, seafaring
Omani traders found ready clients in
the prosperous city-states of the
coast. Mogadiscio, Brava,
Mombasa, and other Swahili trading
towns maintained a vigorous
commerce from the twelfth to the
sixteenth centuries. At Kilwa, in what
is now Tanzania, the great palace
compound of Husani Kubwa was
completed c. 1245. It contained
courtyards, a sunken pool for
bathing, and a terrace garden. In
Kilwa, as in the other Swahili cities,
vegetable gardens for the production
of daily market produce were
commonplace. The general urban

liveliness of the coast declined with the coming of the Portuguese in 1488.

The vigorous African agrarian tradition has not been widely reinterpreted in twentieth-century landscape design. In South Africa, several of the Witwatersrand mine tips have recently been slated for landscape reclamation to stop blowing dust. Derek Lovejoy and Partners, British landscape architects, have developed a plan for shelterbelts that will also yield golf courses, tennis courts, and general park spaces around Johannesburg. In Cape Town, the Kirstenbosch National Botanical Garden, with its concentration on South African natives, sprawls over some 1,200 acres (about 486 hectares). Developed by the botanist H. W. Pearson after 1902, its land was donated by Cecil Rhodes. Its specialty gardens include protea and cycad collections and the Jan van Riebeeck Hedge, planted by early Dutch colonists in 1660. Cape Town's mild climate has also given rise recently to several new and dynamic offices of landscape architects, including those of Johan van Papendorp, Bernie Oberholzer, and others.

In East Africa, Melanie Schwenke, a landscape architect trained in England and the United States, developed a practice in the 1970s that concentrated heavily on the use of local plants. In contrast to the general continental trend, the Egyptian architect and urban planner Hassan Fathy has emphasized the imaginative use of traditional forms. His designs for housing masses include bathing pools, patios, and public squares well integrated with the living units themselves.

See also **Egyptian landscape architecture, Islamic landscape architecture, Roman landscape architecture.**

After-ripening   The phenomenon of mature seeds requiring further chemical or other changes before they will germinate. Apple seed is an example.

Agamic reproduction (in plants)   Vegetative or asexual reproduction. Also **Apomixis.** See also **Asexual reproduction.**

AGC   An abbreviation for Associated General Contractors of America, a professional organization for primarily general contractors rather than subcontractors.

Agency   A legal relationship in which an individual or group authorizes a second individual or group to act in its behalf. The party authorizing the action is the principal; the party empowered to act on behalf of another is the agent. See also **Agent, General agency, Limited agency,** and **Principal.**

Agency, contracting   See **Owner.**

Agency, planning   See **Planning agency.**

Agent   A person or group who acts on behalf of another individual or group. See also **Agency** and **Principal.**

Agent, agricultural extension   See **County agent.**

Agent, air-entraining (in concrete)   See **Air-entraining agent.**

Agent, county   See **County agent.**

Agent, extension   See **County agent.**

Agent, wetting   See **Wetting agent.**

Agger (Latin)   In ancient Rome, the constructed earthworks around the perimeters of camps or fortresses.

Aggradation   The natural process of the building up of a riverbed or surrounding lands through the deposition of stream-borne sediments. See also **Degradation.**

Aggregate   1) A neutral granular substance that, in combination with a matrix, forms concrete or mortar. Examples include sand, gravel, crushed stone, brick chips, perlite, vermiculite, and slag. See also **Coarse aggregate, Exposed aggregate, Fine aggregate.** 2) In botany, a fruit consisting of ripe, abutting ovaries.

Aggregate base   See **Base course.**

Aggregate, choker.   See **Choker aggregate.**

Aggregate, coarse   See **Coarse aggregate.**

Aggregate, combined   See **Combined aggregate.**

Aggregate, crusher-run   See **Crusher-run aggregate.**

Aggregate, exposed   See **Exposed aggregate.**

Aggregate, fine   See **Fine aggregate.**

Aggregate, graded   See **Graded aggregate.**

Aggregate seal (asphalt)   A type of **Asphalt sealer,** q.v.

Agora   An outdoor gathering or assembly place in ancient Greece, particularly a marketplace. A prototype for the Western **Square** or **Plaza,** q.q.v. See also **Forum.**

Agrarian   Referring to rural (especially agricultural) land or landscape.

Agreement   An understanding or contract between two or more parties.

Agreement, borrowed personnel   See **Borrowed personnel agreement.**

Agreement, hold harmless   See **Hold harmless agreement.**

Agreement, letter of   See **Letter of intent.**

Agreement between owner and contractor   See **Construction contract.**

Agreement between owner and landscape architect   See **Design contract.**

Agreement for site preparation   See **Construction contract.**

Agreement, stipulated sum   See **Flat fee.**

Agric horizon   In soils, the layer just below a plowed surface soil. Agric horizons normally have a considerable volume of clay and organic material.

Agriculture   Farming. The cultivation of plants and raising of livestock. Agriculture and landscape architecture are implicitly connected.

Agriculture, subsistence   See **Subsistence farming.**

Agrobiology   The study of the soils, plants, and productivity of croplands.

Agronomy   The science and management of land, especially rural, agricultural land.

A-horizon   See **Soil horizon.**

AIAP   The Asociazione Italiana di Architetti Paisagisti—Italian Association of Landscape Architects.

AILA   Australian Institute of Landscape Architects, founded 1966 in Sydney. Also, formerly, American Institute of Landscape Architects.

Air conditioning, outdoor   See **Outdoor air conditioning.**

Air layering (aerial layering)   In horticulture, a propagation technique used to produce roots along a stem by means of securing an airtight, moss-filled bag around the stem for several days or weeks. See also **Layering.**

Air plant   See **Epiphyte.**

Air pollution   Generated principally by the burning of fossil fuels, air pollution is composed of particulate emissions and, usually, many or all of the following gases: ozone, sulphur dioxide, fluorides, and PAN (Peroxyacetyl nitrate). Eroded soil lifted into the air by storms is also a major pollutant. See also **Smog, Water pollution.**

Air rights   A type of easement granting building rights over a street or structure to a project owner or developer.

Air (aerial) root   See **Root.**

Air-entraining agent (in concrete)   A chemical added to concrete at a maximum of 7% to aid in frost-resistance, increase plasticity, and reduce weight and compressive strength. Also **Air-entraining admixture.**

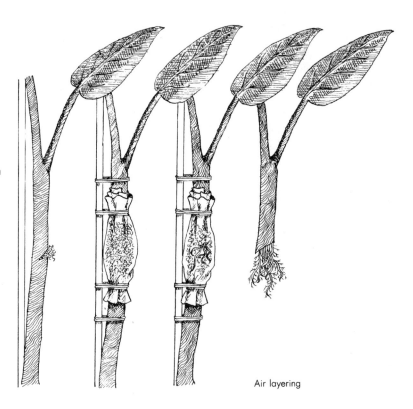

Air layering

Albedo The proportion of the sun's light and heat reflected from a surface.

Alberti, Leone Battista (1404–72) Alberti personifies the freewheeling quality of the early Renaissance. He was a writer, composer, athlete, architect, painter, and design theoretician. His *De Re Aedificatoria* (1452), codifies the planning and layout of the Italian villa. Basing his ideas on classical models (see **Pliny**), Alberti opened up the Renaissance estate by insisting on open views, free use of nearby "borrowed" landscape, consideration of winds, available waters and sun, and expansive, well-conceived gardens.

Alberti's use of Greek and Roman precedents was combined with the demands of site-specific design—a typically new Renaissance approach. He emphasized the need for integrating philosophy, mathematics, and archaeology in his architecture and site design. Another book, *Del Governo della Famiglia,* praised rural life and the hillslope as the ideal setting for the development of a villa. See also **Renaissance landscape architecture.**

Albic horizon A light-colored soil horizon or stratum in which most clay particles are absent or isolated.

Alburnum See **Sapwood.**

Alegretes Small Portuguese courtyard gardens, dating from the time of Phillip II and before (sixteenth century). See also **Portuguese landscape architecture.**

Alignment of streets Street layout in two planes. 1) **Horizontal alignment:** The layout of a road or street in plan view, including curve configurations. 2) **Vertical alignment:** Street profile or section alignment, showing downhill and uphill motion of the street across the surface of the land.

Alkali One of several active bases containing metallic soluble salts such as sodium and potassium. Found as constituent materials of concrete and mortar and often as highly concentrated deposits in arid soils. See also **Alkaline soil.**

Alkaline soil A soil in which excessive exchangeable sodium interferes with most plant growth. Any soil in which the saturation pH reading is higher than 7.0. It may contain some amounts of soluble salts. Alkaline soils are often found in arid regions and characteristically lack humus-producing material. Also **Basic soil, Solonez soil.** See **Acid soil, Alkali, pH.**

Allée (French) A shady lane or road with lines of overhanging trees on either side. A narrow, clearly bordered passageway.

Allee, pleached See **Pleached bower.**

Allelopathy In botany, the ability of a plant to secrete toxins directed at other plants—sometimes plants of the same species—to limit their growth or spreading. Allelopathy is the function of a type of plant territoriality. In the southwestern United States, the creosote (*Larrea tridentata*) and its habits are an example.

Alligator cracks In asphalt and concrete pavements, cracks on older surfaces with a pattern like an alligator's hide.

Allograft In horticulture, a graft in which the scion differs genetically from the rootstock. See **Grafting.**

Allometry In botany, differences in the size or appearance of birds, leaves, flowers, branches, stems or their parts among the individuals of a species. See also **Dimorphism.**

Allotment gardens Small gardens reserved for the use of apartment tenants or condominium owners.

Allowance, cash (contracting) See **Cash allowance.**

Allowance, shrinkage (earthwork) See **Shrinkage allowance.**

Alloy nails See **Nails.**

Alluvial fan A fan-shaped deposit of sediment at the mouth of a watercourse.

Alluvial soil Soil built up by flood deposition.

Alluvium A deposition of rock, rock particles, or soil left in an area after flooding.

Alphand, Jean Charles Nineteenth-century French engineer and urban designer. See **Von Haussmann.**

Alpine Pertaining to mountains, especially a high mountain system.

Alpine garden A man-made garden in which the predominant elements include carefully placed stones, mosses, low evergreens, flowers, and low-growing ground covers. Water in streams or pools may also be present. Trees may be limited to evergreen species such as bristlecone and limber pines, alpine (corkbark) fir, and the like. Alpine gardens are similar to rock gardens. Their character is derived from the high North American and European cold regions (Arctic-Alpine life zones). The overall effect of an alpine garden can be extremely subtle, and many of its elements may be years in maturing. Popularized by **William Robinson,** q.v., in the late nineteenth century. See also **Rock garden, Life zone.**

Alternate leaves

Alpine meadow soils A high mountain, intrazonal soil group of dark, wet meadow soils.

Alternate (bid) Added to or deducted from a **Base bid,** q.v., a specific amount indicated by a contractor in his **Bid proposal,** q.v., to be used if there is a change in project scope or in the methods or materials of construction. Commonly, **Additive alternates** and **Deductive alternates.**

Alternate leaves Leaves occurring in alternate sequence (at different intervals) on opposite sides of a stem.

Alternation of generations In plant reproduction, leap-frog generations of sexual and asexual plants.

Alternation work In landscape construction, an addition to or modification of existing construction features.

Altitude See **Elevation.**

Alumina An extremely common oxide of aluminum found in clay.

Aluminosilicates Common soil compounds containing aluminum and silica.

Aluminum-coated fabric In chainlink and other fencing construction, steel mesh plated with a thin, protective aluminum coating.

Ambient temperature Air temperature.

Ambulatory A cloistered walk or arcade in a monastery, usually constructed around a common or courtyard. See also **Cloister.**

Amendment (soil) See **Soil amendment.**

Amenity (site amenity) 1) An item of site furnishing, such as a bench, drinking fountain, kiosk, or the like. 2) A remarkable site feature—i.e., view, soil, trees, water, or the like.

Ament Catkin, q.v.

American Association of State Highway and Transportation Officials (AASHTO) An organization that, among other functions, determines construction material quality and standards for certain public works.

American Concrete Institute (ACI) A trade and materials organization that sets standards for concrete composition, quality, and handling.

American Concrete Pipe Association See **ACPA.**

American Farmland Trust A United States conservation organization that concentrates on the preservation and protection of farmlands.

American Institute of Landscape Architects (AILA) Formerly the second national organization of landscape architects. Founded in 1957 as the California Institute of Landscape Architects, the AILA was headquartered in Phoenix, Arizona until 1981, when it merged with the American Society of Landscape Architects (ASLA).

American landscape architecture See **United States landscape architecture.**

American Public Works Association (APWA) An organization composed largely of public officials concerned with standards for public works construction, including highways, bridges, sewers, and the like. The APWA composes standard specifications for construction and concerns itself with other public works issues.

American Society of Golf Course Architects A professional society founded in 1948 by Robert Trent Jones, Donald Ross, and others. See also **Golf course architecture.**

American Society of Landscape Architects See **ASLA.**

American Society for Testing and Materials (ASTM) A testing organization that sets standards for the quality and performance of asphalt concrete, Portland cement concrete, and the like. ASTM standards are often cited in CSI and APWA format specifications.

Ammonification The formation of ammonium compounds, or ammonia (fertilizers).

Ammonium compounds Fertilizers high in nitrogen, including, among others, ammonium nitrate, ammonium phosphate, and ammonium sulfate.

Amorphous Formless.

Amphitheatre A round or oval arena with tiered seating, usually recessed into a hillside. First devised by the Greeks as a setting for drama.

Anabolism   In living organisms, the creation (manufacture) of larger and more complex molecules from simpler ones. See also **Catabolism, Metabolism.**

Anaerobe   See **Anaerophyte.**

Anaerobic   In botany, referring to a plant surviving without the direct need of air. See also **Aerobic.**

Anaerophyte   In botany, any plant not directly dependent on air. Also **Anaerobe.**

Analysis, pollen   See **Pollen analysis.**

Analysis, site   See **Site analysis.**

Anandrous   In flowers, without **Stamens,** q.v.

Anastomosing   1) In botany, referring to a leaf with a network of veins. 2) In geology, a braided stream form.

Anchor bolt   A strong metal pin or stay used to anchor posts, cables, plates or similar items in modern landscape construction. Often embedded in concrete.

Anchor, ground (trees)   See **Dead man.**

Androecium   In flowers, the stamens or male reproductive organs collectively. See also **Gynoecium, Stamen.**

Androgynous   In plants, containing male and female parts in the same flower cluster. See also **Inflorescence.**

Androphore   See **Stamen.** See also **Pistil (gynophore).**

Anemophily   In flowers, wind fertilization. Adjective: anemophilous. See also **Entomophily, Wind pollution.**

Angiosperms   Flowering plants, one of the two primary subdivisions of seed-bearing plants (spermatophytes), comprising over 250,000 species worldwide. The angiosperms are highly sophisticated true seed-bearers. The typical angiosperm has broad leaves and conspicuous flowers and bears seed enclosed in a fruit. Angiosperms are further divided into **Dicotyledon(s)** and **Monocotyledon(s),** q.q.v. See also **Gymnosperms** and **Spermatophyte.**

Angle, central and deflection (road curves)   See **Central and deflection angle.**

Angle, clip (for steel member joining)   See **Clip angle.**

Angle iron brace   In irrigation, a common brace used to support a quick coupler assembly.

Angle of repose   A slope angle that cannot be exceeded without soil displacing and sliding downhill. Usual maximums fall between 30% and 80%, with a 3:1 slope (33%) as the norm. See also **Maximum slope, Slope ratio, Soil.**

Angle, slope   See **Gradient.**

Angle (angle-control) valve   In irrigation, a **Globe valve,** q.v., that emits water at a right angle to the water's entry. See also **Manual system, Valve.**

Anglo-Chinois garden   A French garden of the late 1700s done up in a vaguely Chinese and overly picturesque naturalism. A "fad" garden adapted by the French from the **Landscape gardening school** of **Brown** and **Repton,** q.q.v.

Annuals. Pansies (*Viola tricolor var.*). Photo by author.

Animal ecology   See **Zooecology.**

Animate landscape   See **Soft landscape.**

Anisotrophic soil   A soil of variable stress and permeability.

Annealed steel guy wire   Steel wire that is made stronger and more resistant by tempering with long-lasting, slowly-decreasing heat.

Annual   In botany, a plant which completes its growing cycle in a single season and must be planted anew each year. Typical temperate-zone annuals: petunias, pansies, sunflowers, snapdragons, cosmos, zinnias, and the like. See also **Biennial, Bulb, Perennial, Winter annual.**

Annual border   A garden accent developed from rows or masses of annual flowers placed along a path or at the edge of a planter. Annual borders can add great successional color when well conceived and maintained.

Aqueduct (modern). Sultanate of Oman. Photo courtesy Steve Borbas.

Annual rings   See **Growth rings.**

Annual, winter   See **Winter annual.**

Annular drainage   See **Trellis drainage.**

Annulment without fault of contractor   A provision sometimes included in construction agreements allowing an owner to invalidate a contract with just compensation for work performed upon giving written notice to the contractor.

Anodizing   A chemical-electrical process of aluminum finishing, as a result of which color and protection against the elements are added to the metal's surface.

Antecedent drainage   See **Inconsequent drainage.**

Anther   In botany, the pollen sac or sacs at the tip of the pollen-producing (male reproductive) portion (stamen) of a flower—i.e., the **Stamen,** q.v. See also **Theca.**

Anthesis   The act of flowering.

Anthocyanins   Red, purple, and blue pigments found in a plant's cell sap, responsible for flower, leaf, and bud colors. A specific anthocyanin tint is dependent on the acidity of the vascular solution in which it is present. See also **Plant pigments.**

Anthropic soil (anthropic epipedon)   A man-made soil, resulting from short or long-term cultivation and mulching or manuring. Anthropic soils do not follow the normal ABC sequence found in undisturbed natural soils. See also **Soil horizon.**

Anthropomorphism   The assignation of human attributes to inorganic objects, plants, animals, or the like.

Antidazzle   A kind of planting in a road median intended to reduce the reflected daytime glare of cars and buildings and to alleviate headlight glare at night.

Antidesiccant   A chemical agent sprayed on foliage during transplanting to prevent excessive loss of moisture through transpiration. Also called **Wilt-proof** or wilt-proofing.

Antisiphon valve   See **Vacuum breaker.**

Antrorse   In plant structures, a part pointing or growing up or forward. Usually refers to plant hairs.

Ap   In soils, a topsoil layer developed by grazing or plowing.

Apetalous   In flowers, without petals.

Aphyllous   Leafless.

Apical bud   See **Bud.**

Apiculate   In plant structures, displaying a short, abrupt point.

Apomixis   See **Vegetative reproduction.**

Apparent depth (landscape design)   See **Trompe l'oeil.**

Application for payment (landscape construction)   See **Pay request.**

Approval, landscape architect's   See **Landscape architect's approval.**

Approved equal   Any item or act of construction or type of construction equipment reviewed and endorsed by a project landscape architect as equivalent to specified material, equipment, or methods.

Appurtenance (irrigation)   Any pipe accessory item or device. Tees, ells, valves, and the like are examples.

APWA   American Public Works Association, q.v.

Aquatic   Of or pertaining to water. Aquatics are water plants.

Aqueduct   A man-made channel, usually lined but open on top, used to carry water. The Romans developed the most spectacular aqueducts, some of which are still in use in southern and western Europe.

Aquiclude In geography, an impervious stratum that prevents passage of groundwater.

Aquifer A water-bearing stratum (or strata), usually of sand, gravel, or permeable rock. See also **Water table.**

Arabesque An architectural, painting, or sculptural flourish or surface-design pattern of geometric flourishes. From medieval Moorish and Persian architectural design.

Arachnoid In plant structures, spider-like, or bearing inconsequential, messy hairs.

Arbitration A means of settling disputes, demands, or claims arising during design or construction by which an impartial, knowledgeable arbitrator or arbitrators hear evidence and reach a decision. Arbitration precludes litigation, and may or may not be binding on both parties.

Arbor 1) A group of intermediate or light trees, shrubs, or vines, clustered for shade. 2) A light trellis-like frame covered with shade-producing plants. Also **Bower, Herber** (antique English). See also **Overhead, Pergola, Trellis.**

Arbor Day An informal United States and Canadian holiday, observed on varying dates by individual states and provinces, in which trees are planted as an encouragement to conservation. Arbor Day was begun in Nebraska in 1872 by J. Sterling Morton, a journalist. School children are usually involved in Arbor Day plantings, which take place in the spring of the year.

Arboreal Having to do with or living in trees.

Arborescent Tree-like.

Arboretum A botanical garden in which trees and other woody plants may be grown for scientific or educational use and for strolling pleasure. A kind of **Botanic** or **Botanical garden,** q.q.v. See also **Public garden.**

Arboriculture The raising and care of trees, especially for uses not related to the production of lumber.

Arborist A person engaged in the professional practice of tree care. Also **Tree surgeon.**

Arc In irrigation, the land area served by a sprinkler head as measured in degrees of arc.

Arc welding See **Welding.**

Arcade A series of columns connected by arches. A covered passageway or path. See also **Colonnade, Peristyle, Portico.**

Arcadian Bucolic. Idealistically rural or rustic. See also **English landscape architecture, Picturesque.**

Arch An ancient, curved structural device at the top of two pillars or columns used as a support for a wall, roof, or other structure. A series of arches forms an **Arcade,** q.v.

Arch, pipe See **Pipe arch.**

Archaeobotany The emerging study of the use of plants by man as revealed by archaeological excavation and examination. See also **Pollen analysis.**

Archaeology, landscape See **Landscape archaeology.**

Archetype A first of its kind. A prototype.

Architect, golf course See **Golf course architect.**

Arbor

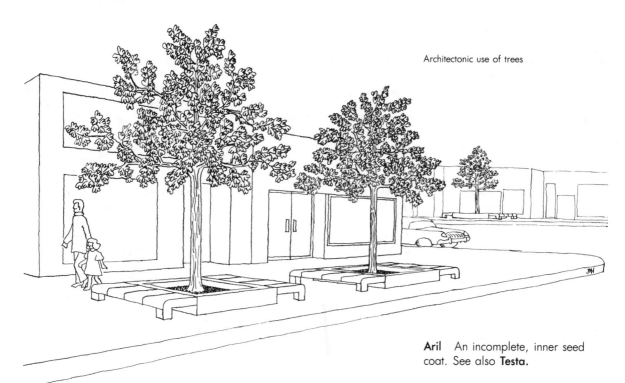

Architectonic use of trees   The use of trees for the specific purpose of space definition, especially as ceilings and walls for outdoor space. Tree architecture.

Architecture, garden   See **Garden architecture.**

Architecture, golf course   See **Golf course architecture.**

Arctic-Alpine (zone)   See **Life zone.**

Arcuate   In plants or geological structures, slightly arced or curving.

Arcuated   Referring to a structure developed with arches as a prime construction element. See also **Trabeation.**

Arcure training (fruit trees)   A system of fruit-tree training in which the trunk as well as selected upper branches are pruned to "arc" away from the vertical in successive, opposing semicircles.

Are   A metric measurement of 10 by 10 or 100 square meters (119.6 square yards). See also **Hectare.**

Area, meristem (plants)   See **Meristem area.**

Area, service or utility   See **Service area.**

Arena   An outdoor or indoor sporting court partially or fully surrounded by elevated seating. From the Latin *arena,* sand, sandy floor.

Argillaceous (argillic) limestone   Limestone (carbonate of lime) containing a high percentage of clay.

Arid region   In geography, any landscape area which receives approximately 10 inches or 25 centimeters of moisture per year.

Aridic soil   See **Pedocal soil.**

Aridisol   Any of several arid area or desert soils.

Aril   An incomplete, inner seed coat. See also **Testa.**

Aristate   In plant structures, bristly or bristle-like and generally inflexible.

Arm, bracket or mast   See **Bracket arm.**

Armed plant   Any plant protected by spines, thorns, or bristles.

Armillary sphere   A globe of intersecting rings used by the classical Greeks to indicate the coming of a seasonal equinox and related phenomena. The rings of the modern armillary sphere represent the Earth's equator, Arctic and Antarctic circles, the tropics, and the like. A common garden feature, usually mounted on a pedestal. See also **Sundial.**

Armoring   In streams, a reduction of suspended sediment resulting in the removal from the streambed of gravels and sand, leaving larger stones and boulders. Often occurring below dams or sedimentation ponds.

Arrester, water hammer (irrigation)   See **Water hammer arrester.**

Arris The "native" or acute edge of a building stone, concrete slab, or other building material. Often cleanly cut away by means of a **Chamfer**, q.v.

Arrissing tool In landscape construction, a concrete finish tool used to produce rounded edges.

Arroyo In the southwestern United States, a dry watercourse that turns into a roily torrent after thunderstorms. Much arroyo-cutting and severe run-off are due to overgrazing or other misuse and a subsequent lack of vegetative hold on the arid land. See also **Nullah** and **Wadi**.

Arterial street Any busy, important city street with limited or no streetside parking.

Article In specifications, a subdivision of a section. Sometimes divided into paragraphs, subparagraphs, and clauses.

Articulated plane See **Vertical plane.**

Armillary sphere

Articulation 1) The joint system of a plant stem and its branches, or of other plant parts. 2) In design, the clear expression of a plan idea in a drawing or note or in the executed work.

Artificial manure See **Chemical fertilizer.**

Aryk (Russian) A common, open, streetside irrigation channel in Soviet Central Asia.

Asbestos cement pipe A large-diameter pipe composed of asbestos, silica, and cement. Asbestos cement pipe is resistant to corrosion and is often used in mains, but it must be very carefully bedded and blocked at ells and tees for **Surge** or **Water hammer**, q.q.v. Abbreviated **ACP.** Also **AC pipe, Transite pipe.**

As-built drawings Modified working drawings for a project prepared by a landscape architect from records kept by the project contractor during construction. As-built drawings show important changes to the contract work made as the project is built. Also **Drawings of record, Record drawings.**

ASCA The American Society of Consulting Arborists, an organization of United States horticultural consultants.

ASCE American Society of Civil Engineers.

Asexual reproduction (in plants) Vegetative or **Agamic reproduction**, q.v. Also **Apomixis.**

ASGCA See **American Society of Golf Course Architects.**

Ashlar A kind of square-cut stone used in the construction of outdoor walls. Also **Dimension stone, Hewn stone.** See also **Rubble.**

Asian landscape architecture See **Central Asian landscape architecture, Indian landscape architecture, Russian landscape architecture.**

ASLA American Society of Landscape Architects, founded in 1899. The ASLA has concerned itself with bettering the practice of landscape architecture through its education, research, state registration, and other programs. It sponsors continuing professional education and curriculum certification. It publishes *Landscape Architecture* and *Garden Design* magazines and offers yearly awards to members for excellence in design.

ASME American Society of Mechanical Engineers.

Aspect 1) Of land, the lay, slope, or form of the Earth's surface in a given area. 2) Of buildings or other structures, the orientation of a wall surface or surfaces. 3) In landscape architecture, garden orientation.

Asperous In plant structures, rough to the touch.

Asphalt A dark cementitious binding material occurring naturally or refined from petroleum, and consisting principally of bitumen. It is combined with fine and/or coarse aggregates to form a common pavement. Also **Blacktop, Macadam.** See also **Asphaltic concrete** and **Bitumen.**

Asphalt base course See **Base course.**

Asphalt binder course In asphalt paving, a middle or intermediate course sometimes used between an asphalt **Base course** and an **Asphalt surface course**, q.q.v.

Asphalt block A preformed asphalt construction (pavement) block.

Asphalt cement   Any of several asphalt binder materials that are heated before use.

Asphalt concrete base (ACB)   See **Base course.**

Asphalt, cutback   See **Cutback asphalt.**

Asphalt, extruded   See **Extruded asphalt.**

Asphalt intermediate course   See **Asphalt binder course, Asphalt tack coat.**

Asphalt joint filler   An asphaltic expansion joint and crack-filling material.

Asphalt macadam   See **Macadam.**

Asphalt mastic   A mixture of asphalt and fine mineral aggregate applied either hot or cold to a surface as a filler or sealer.

Asphalt overlay   In landscape construction, one of two layers of new, reconditioning asphalt pavement placed on an existing (usually asphalt) pavement.

Asphalt prime coat   In pavement construction, viscous bitumen applied to a crushed base course to prepare it for an overlaying pavement.

Asphalt primer   A penetrating, lightly viscous liquid asphalt used to prepare a base course of crushed rock or other material for further pavement.

Asphalt sealer   A surface finish material consisting of pitch, bituminous, acrylic, or other substances whose principal function is to extend the life of an asphalt pavement by retarding ultraviolet decay, oxidation, acid breakdown, and other detrimental effects. **Aggregate seals** and **Emulsion slurry seals**, among others, are common. See **Asphalt seal coat.**

Asphalt soil stabilization   See **Dust palliative.**

Asphalt surface course   See **Asphalt wearing course, Wearing course.**

Asphalt surface treatment   In pavement construction, repairs to roads and other pavements consisting of an asphaltic mixture usually less than one inch or 2.4 centimeters in thickness.

Asphalt tack coat (binder)   In pavement construction, a light, sticky, diluted asphalt emulsion (spray) used to create a bond between a base course and a top or finish course of asphalt. Sometimes used with crushed gravel to create a binder course.

Asphalt wearing course   In pavement construction, a finish course consisting of asphalt and fine aggregates applied over foundation and base courses or prepared subgrade. See also **Asphaltic concrete, Asphalt sealer.**

Asphaltic (bituminous) concrete   A solid or semisolid pavement material consisting of coarse and/or fine aggregates mixed with hot bituminous matrix (asphalt cement) and laid over a base course or courses. Once laid as pavement, it must be constantly driven or walked on to maintain its quality. Also **Tarmac, Tarmacadam.** See also **Macadam.**

Asphaltic pavement   See **Asphaltic concrete.**

Asphalt-treated base   In asphalt pavements, a base-course mixture compounded in a commercial plant. Also **ATB.** See also **Base course.**

Assessed value   In real estate appraisal, a monetary value that in whole or part is used to fix the worth of a piece of land and its improvements.

Assessment district   A usually urban area in which property owners are charged a reckoned fee by a government agency for the installation of public utilities or conveniences such as sewers, streets, walks, street trees, and the like. Often abbreviated **AD.**

Assessment, site   See **Site analysis.**

Association of plants   See **Plant community.**

Association, soil   See **Soil association.**

ASTM   American Society for Testing and Materials, q.v.

Asymmetry   A design condition of imprecise balance. Irregularity. An asymmetrical design or object may often contain an occult or covert balance. See also **Occult balance, Symmetry.**

Atavism   A throw-back plant characteristic (old-fashioned).

ATB   Plan abbreviation for **Asphalt-treated base,** q.v.

Atmosphere   The air envelope or gaseous cover of the earth. The present atmosphere is an evolutionary product of the development of life. See also **Hydrosphere, Lithosphere.**

Atrio. San Esteban Mission Church,
Acoma, New Mexico, 1629–49.
Photo courtesy BBMSL, UNM.

Atmospheric perspective
  See **Perspective.**

Atmospheric pressure   A pressure
used in irrigation system calculations.
The weight in **PSI** or **KSMM**, q.q.v.,
of the Earth's atmosphere, calculated
at altitude above mean sea level.
The usual measurement for irrigation
systems is noted as **Standard
atmospheric pressure** for a project.

Atmospheric vacuum breaker   In
irrigation, a vacuum breaker with an
air vent placed on the unpressurized
side of a control valve. See also
**Backflow preventer, Vacuum
breaker.**

Atrio (Span.)   In Mexico and
elsewhere, an enclosed courtyard or
patio space in front of a church,
paved in stone and often lined with
trees, flowers, and other plants. See
also **Mexican landscape architecture.**

Atrium   In classical Roman houses,
an open central court. The atrium
has lasted to the present day as a
principal feature of Mediterranean
architecture.

Attenuate   In plants, pertaining to
narrowly tapering leaves, buds, or
other parts.

Attorney in fact   An individual
legally enabled to act on behalf of
another individual or organization
within the written limits of a Power
of Attorney. See also **Power of
Attorney.**

Attorney, power of   See **Power of
attorney.**

Auger   A large tool for boring
holes in the earth, hand- or engine-
powered, resembling an oversized
screw. An engine-driven auger,
mounted on the back of a tractor, is
often operated by two people and is
used to dig tree and shrub holes.

Auger, soil   See **Soil auger.**

Auger, water   See **Water auger.**

Auricle   In plants, an ear-like
protuberance or appendage.
Adjective: auriculate.

**Australian Institute of Landscape
Architects**   See **AILA.**

Australian landscape architecture

Australia is a very old continent, its ancient mountains and deserts worn thin and smooth by endless ages of erosion. Its aboriginal inhabitants, like those of other continents, developed sacred groves and grottoes in hospitable nooks for their religious rites, arranging the landscape to suit high purpose.

European gardens only began at the turn of the nineteenth century, when Governor Lachlan Macquarie's wife Elizabeth developed the grounds of Government House in Sydney. Elizabeth Macquarie's designs followed the informal lines of the English Landscape Garden School. Sir Joseph Banks, the English botanist of the *Endeavour*, Captain Cook's ship, had begun his study of Australian flora in the late eighteenth century and had an influence not only on Mrs. Macquarie's gardens but on other new Australian landscapes until his death in 1820.

The Australian fascination with botanical gardens was apparent as early as 1816, when Governor Macquarie hired Charles Fraser as the superintendent of the new botanical garden at Government House in Sydney. A botanical garden was developed in Tasmania in the 1820s by Daniel Bunce, a landscape gardener who later practiced in Melbourne. The Adelaide botanical gardens were founded in the 1830s. In Perth, the new botanical garden was started with the intent of acclimatizing exotics recently arrived in the country.

But it was the Royal Botanic Gardens in Melbourne, dating from 1845, that became the most spectacular in Australia. The early plant hunter and explorer Ferdinand J. H. von Mueller (1825–96) was the first director of these gardens. Von Mueller followed Banks's lead in popularizing Australian flora. He designed the gardens very formally, in an old-fashioned, north European

baroque style. Von Mueller was the first botanist to send eucalypts abroad and is recognized as the founder of botanical science in Victoria. But von Mueller was discharged in 1873, and the eminent landscape nurseryman and designer William Guilfoyle (1840–1912) took his place. Guilfoyle had come to Australia from Britain (c. 1849) with his father Michael, a plantsman who had trained in London nurseries. William Guilfoyle undertook the redesign of the Melbourne Botanic Gardens from 1873–1909 in the softer English Landscape Garden style, with a large part of the grounds open to the public as a park. Guilfoyle's hard work established Melbourne as one of the two best botanical gardens in the Southern Hemisphere—its contemporary, the Christchurch Botanical Gardens in New Zealand, sharing the honor. Other works by Guilfoyle singly or with his father include the Greenoaks estate, Werribee Park (another private commission), and the Mawallok and Turkeith gardens. Guilfoyle had become the preeminent Australian landscape designer of his day at the time of his death in 1912.

Publications on Australian landscape design had been issued as early as the 1830s. A collection of lectures by Thomas Shepherd on landscape gardening in the style of **Capability Brown,** q.v., was published in 1836, after Shepherd's untimely death. It was the first book to mention Australian growing conditions. Talented designers such as Alexander Macleay and James Sinclair took advantage of fine local prospects to produce the Elizabeth Bay landscape garden (1822) near Sydney and the Fitzroy Gardens at Melbourne, respectively. By the mid-1800s, many fine country estates and gardens had been established on the slopes of Mount Wilson in the Blue Mountains of New South Wales; some of these were destroyed by

great bushfires in 1983. The grounds of Government House, Perth, Western Australia—still in good repair—were laid out in 1860. Australia by the 1860s had begun to feel more conscious of civic design; travellers remarked on the well-tended orchards, grain fields, and landscape gardens of such big cities as Sydney and Melbourne throughout the second half of the century.

The American architect Walter Burley Griffin (1876–1936) won the commission to design the new national capital of Canberra in 1912. Griffin planned the entire city and maintained a private practice in Sidney until 1920. Parks, parkways, grand avenues, sports fields, lakes, residential suburbs, and a native-plant botanical garden were parts of Griffin's scheme. The essential plan made use of a large central axis carved out of the bush with a golf course and naturalistic plantings nearby. Lindsay Pryor and others of Griffin's successors continued to fill in his masterplan after 1920.

Several rather stiff formal gardens were produced in Melbourne and environs at the turn of the century by the architects Walter Butler and Robert Haddon. William Wilson and Leslie Wilkinson, also architects, developed a series of cottage gardens in the 1920s. Charles Luffman, the Principal of Burnley Horticultural College, laid out the grounds of the school in an enthusiastic, naturalistic style. Edna Walling (1896–1973), an English immigrant to Australia and graduate of Burnley College, became an influential designer and writer on Australian landscape themes. Strongly influenced by **Gertrude Jekyll,** q.v., her best-known works include Cruden Farm, Victoria, and the Markdale Estate in New South Wales. Edna Walling's assistant for many years, Ellis Stones, became a garden designer in his own right and

Australian landscape architecture. Open space at Perth Water Narrows Interchange, Perth, Western Australia. John Oldham, landscape architect. Photo courtesy John Oldham.

Australian landscape architecture. Detail of gardens at Perth Water, Perth, Western Australia. John Oldham, landscape architect. Photo courtesy John Oldham.

began to popularize the use of Australian native plants in his work. Stones, a former stonemason, created a series of particularly fine gardens at Eltham, Victoria.

National parks in Australia (begun in the 1870s) were well developed by mid-century. Among the best parks in the national system are Wyperfeld, Victoria; Royal and Blue Mountain National Parks, New South Wales; and the Flinders Ranges National Park in South Australia. Numerous modern botanical gardens

have been added to the national collection begun in the early nineteenth century: Darwin, the expanded Royal Gardens in Sydney, and Green Mountains near Brisbane are among the most prominent of these.

In the late twentieth century, Australian landscape architecture has responded to such influences as the **California garden,** q.v., which is well-suited to a mild climate, while maintaining a growing interest in the indigenous "bush garden." In the

cities, broad "urban-interest" plantings such as those in Queen Victoria Gardens, Alexandra Gardens, and along St. Kilda Road in Melbourne have become very popular. Aging Victorian parks have generated a growing charm in such cities as Adelaide and Brisbane. The architect and landscape architect **John Oldham,** q.v., has created a series of new dam-site landscapes in Western Australia. His work along the Swan River Estuary in Perth has also become a national model for

Australian landscape architecture.
Detail of gardens at Perth Water,
Perth, Western Australia. John
Oldham, landscape architect. Photo
courtesy John Oldham.

the comprehensive design and planning of city-scale, mixed-use sites. New urban water works, such as the El Alamein fountain in Sydney, Melbourne's Coles Fountain, and the Christchurch, New Zealand City Hall Fountain, all by Robert Woodward, have been typical of the 1960s and 1970s. The landscape architect Bruce McKenzie has established a practice in New South Wales that has made a specialty of "bush-oriented" parks. Botany Bay Park, near Sydney, is typical.

The country has developed degree programs in landscape architecture to meet the increasing demand for landscape architects and planners. Peter Spooner founded the first of these at the University of New South Wales in 1965. George Seddon established a full program in landscape architecture at the University of Melbourne shortly thereafter. The rise of interest in landscape architecture coincided with the worldwide "ecology movement" of the 1960s. A trilogy of recent books by Thistle Harris on Australian native flora has continued to popularize the use of many once-maligned species. The Australian Institute of Landscape Architects (AILA), founded in 1967 by Mervyn Davis, has recently become the national organ of landscape architects, promoting landscape preservation and professional practice throughout the country and publishing a quarterly journal, *Landscape Australia,* edited by Ralph Neale. See also **New Zealand landscape architecture.**

Austrian landscape architecture

The landscape architecture of Austria becomes particularly notable after 1720, when the gardens of the Austrian royal palace at Schonbrunn near Vienna were developed in the high French style of Louis XIV. Schonbrunn is not as large as Versailles, but its meticulous fountains, hornbeam hedges, strong vistas, and well-developed contrast of forest and open space are more accessible. Its near-contemporaries, the baroque gardens of the Belvedere in Vienna by F. Girard, and the Mirabelle and Hellbrunn gardens near Salzburg, are now considered national treasures.

The designer Ludwig Forster began the layout of Vienna's Ring about 1850. He also contributed to other urban development planning for the city. Late in the nineteenth century, the Austrian architect and town planner **Camilo Sitté,** q.v., theorized that closer attention to civic design detail rather than wholesale, radical change would improve urban Europe. His book, *Die Stadtebau,* is to some degree a reaction to the autocratic planning of Baron **von Haussmann** in Paris. Postwar Austria has been characterized by refined playground and recreation design. The Kurpark at Oberlaa, near Vienna, is a park built on a wasteland. Within its 95 hectares is a series of recreation gardens combined with a theme park. Its children's play area is particularly complete and exciting. The designer was the West German landscape architect Erich Hanke. See also **German landscape architecture.**

Autoecological optimum In horticulture, the best state of reproduction, spread of range, and growth habit achieved by a single plant species in a pure seeding.

Autoecology "Individual"ecology; the relationship between a single plant or animal and its surroundings. See also **Ecology, Synecology.**

Automated system (irrigation) See **Automatic system.**

Automatic clock (irrigation) See **Automatic controller.**

Austrian landscape architecture. Schonbrunn, Vienna. Photo courtesy Steve Johnson.

Automatic controller (irrigation)   In irrigation, a system of electric valve circuitry, housed in a metal or fiberglass casing (box), which opens and closes valves and controls the length of their operation at given intervals, thus assuring consistent and correct water coverage. Wall-mount, pedestal mount, and cast-in-place housing controllers are commonly used.

In larger systems, a **Primary controller** operates a number of **Satellite controllers**. A satellite controller operates a quantity of section or zone valves. Also **Automatic timer, Controller, Irrigation timer, Timer box,** others. See also **Hydraulic (automatic) controller, Manual system.**

Automatic drain valve   See **Drain valve.**

Automatic system (automated system, irrigation)   A self-operating irrigation system, run by means of an **Automatic controller,** q.v. See also **Hydraulic automatic controller, Manual system.**

Automatic timer (irrigation)   See **Automatic controller.**

Automatic valve   See **Remote control valve.**

Automatic venting   In irrigation lines, the use of air relief valves to prevent air pocketing and to alleviate water hammer.

Automobile   A metal or fiberglass petroleum-powered car used for urban and rural transportation. Of all human inventions, the automobile has had the most profound effect on the landscape with its insatiable demands for roads, parking bays, fuel, and components, and with the noxious products of its operation spread far and wide in the air.

Autophytic   In botany, pertaining to a plant that is capable of producing its own food. Any plant with chlorophyll.

Autotrophic plant   Soil bacteria or other simple plants able to ingest and use soil elements directly in their life functions. Also, generally, any plant capable of making its own food from inorganic substances. See also **Heterotrophic plant.**

Autumn color   See **Fall color.**

Autumn garden   A garden laid out to take advantage of the luxurious bronzes, yellows, and oranges of autumn-turning leaves. Late blooming flowers and background evergreens also are frequently found in the autumn garden. Also **Fall garden.**

Autumn wood   Incorrect term for summer wood, a component of the annual growth of woody plants. See **Growth rings.**

Auxin   An important plant hormone affecting terminal and lateral branching. Highly developed as a growth mechanism in tall trees; barely present in prostrate, horizontal shrubs and herbaceous plants. See also **Gibberellin, Hormone, Tropism.**

Available nutrient (for plants)   A chemical element present in the soil that can be readily taken up by a plant for use in its metabolism. Twenty-one elements are necessary for plant and animal growth and functioning. **Macronutrients,** q.v., are needed in large amounts, **Trace elements,** q.v., in lesser quantities. See also **Plant foods, Soil minerals.**

Available water   See **Capillary water.**

Aven   See **Sinkhole.**

Avenue   Originally, a wide roadway lined with trees.

Average end method   See **Cut and fill.**

Aviary   A large, meshed indoor or outdoor cage for birds. Large modern aviaries allow extensive flight, mating, and other bird activity.

Avulsion   A change in land ownership from one party to another as a result of a river shifting in its course.

Award, notice of   See **Notice of award.**

AWG   American wire gauge, a nonferrous wire measurement.

Awn   In botany, a bristle at the tip of a grass stalk.

AWPA   American Wood Preservers Association.

AWPI   American Wood Preservers Institute.

AWS   American Welding Society.

AWWA   American Water Works Association.

Axial design   An age-old method of landscape arrangement in which a linear axis predominates and lesser elements intersect it at right angles or take their essential form from it. See also **Axis.**

Axial load   In landscape construction, the amount of load expressed in pounds per square inch as applied vertically to a post.

Axial symmetry   See **Symmetry.**

Axil   In plants, the angular area between the base of a leaf stem and the plant stem or branch from which it grows; the point of branching. Axils contain latent buds, which will later form new leaves, flowers, or other growth. Adjective: axillary.

Axillary bud   See **Bud.**

Axis   1) In landscape design, a central, straight line about which portions of the design are more or less symmetrically located. 2) The central line of a plant structure, such as a leaf or conspicuous fruit, or the main trunk or stem of a plant. Adjective: axile. See also **Axial design.**

Axonometric projection   A design drawing, based on a true-to-scale plan, that projects a building or other structure vertically with some distortion. Roughly, a three-dimensional drawing.

Azimuth   A sky arc measured from a fixed object (the sun, for example) down to the horizon, which the arc line intercepts at right angles.

Azonal soil   A soil that lacks recognizable horizons. See also **Lithosol, Regosol.**

Azulejo (Spanish and Portuguese, ultimately Moorish)   Bright, multicolored, fired tile.

Axial design. Chateau and gardens of Chantilly, France, seventeenth century, by André Le Nôtre. Photo courtesy BBMSL, UNM.

B

B and B   See **Balled and burlapped.**

B or better lumber   The highest quality or grade of select lumber, perfect or near perfect in grain, form, finish, strength, and the like. See **Lumber.**

Baccate   In botany, berry-producing or berry-like.

Backcross   In botany, a hybrid bred back on one of its parents.

Backfill   1) In plant installation operations, the portion of existing or amended soil that is put back into a tree or shrub hole and compacted around plant roots. 2) Soil, usually amended, which is used to refill a previously excavated area. See also **Cut and fill.**

Backflow preventer   In irrigation, an antisiphon mechanism used to keep water from reentering a potable water system. Also backflow prevention device or **BFPD.** See also **Vacuum breaker.**

Backhoe   A mechanical spade and bucket attached to the back of a tractor for landscape excavation. Backhoes are hydraulically operated and useful for precision digging.

Backplaster   See **Parge.**

Back pressure valve   See **Check valve.**

Back siphonage   In underground irrigation systems, the flow of water from the heads or laterals back toward a source.

Backwash   In irrigation and pumps, a reverse of water flow to clear out a filter.

Bacteria   Tiny organisms that form the lowest order of plants. Bacteria contain no chlorophyll. They are found everywhere and are responsible for decomposition of organic matter, nitrogen fixation, and other functions in the soil.

Badland   A highly eroded, barren wasteland, usually occurring in arid regions afflicted with infrequent, heavy downpours.

Badminton   A lawn game played over a net with light racquets and a shuttlecock. The standard doubles play area is 20 × 44 ft.

Bagh   A Persian garden. See also **Chahar-bagh** and **Persian landscape architecture.**

Bailey   An exterior wall used to protect a medieval castle.

Balance, biotic   See **Biotic balance.**

Balance of nature   A series of plant, animal, climatic, and other processes that have evolved in response to each other, producing recognizable, traditional patterns in which environmental change is only a very slow constant and the general surroundings are, on the whole, "healthy."

Balance, occult (in landscape design)   See **Occult balance, Asymmetry.**

Balance of water   See **Waters balance.**

Ball and burlap   A common method in plant relocation of securing the root ball by retaining much of the existing soil around the roots in a roughly spherical form. The ball is secured by burlap or similar material wrapped with thin metal mesh or rope. Also **B and B.**

Ball and platform   A method of tree transplantation. The root ball is secured with burlap and then tightly fastened to a small wooden platform for moving. Ball and platform trees are often specified by the United States Park Service and other agencies.

Ball-driven head (sprinkler) In irrigation, a rotary head with a smoothly rotating nozzle. This sort of head is operated by a drive arm that is struck by a water-spun, internal metal ball. See also **Rotary head.**

"Ball-park" estimate A general estimate of construction costs for a project based on a broad analysis of area, volume, or similar requirements. An opinion of probable cost. See also **Detailed estimate of construction cost** and **Preliminary estimate.**

Ballast Gravel or coarse aggregate.

Balling 1) In transplanting, the digging of a tree or shrub and wrapping of its roots for protection with burlap or other material. See **Ball and burlap.** 2) In botany, lack of bud development due to thrip or other insect infestation.

Baluster A support post for a **Balustrade**, or railing.

Ball and burlap

Balustrade A railing. In landscape architecture, often found along a walk or around a pool or other garden feature.

Banco (Spanish) A seat formed in a wall, usually of adobe or concrete masonry units covered with stucco.

Band, belly (horticulture) See **Belly band.**

Bank 1) The land margin of a river, stream, or lake. 2) A built-up mound or abrupt grade change.

Bank yard A yard of undisturbed earth in position before cut and fill begins.

Banner The upper or back petal of a sweet pea or other leguminous flower. See also **Papilla.**

Bar, reinforcing See **Rebar.**

Bar, stretcher (chainlink fence construction) See **Stretcher bar.**

Barb In plants, a small hair or protuberance with a catch or hook.

Barbecue (Barbecue pit) A hollow metal or masonry structure fitted with a grille and used with charcoal for outdoor cooking. Also **BBQ.**

Barbed wire Two or more strands of wire twisted about each other with short, sharp, protruding metal wire lengths interwoven. Used for fencing of pastures, range, or stock pens.

Barchan dune See **Dune.**

Bareroot stock Deciduous trees or shrubs with no container or soil surrounding the roots; planted while dormant. See also **Collected stock, Container grown stock, Field grown stock.**

Bark 1) The protective outer covering or sheath of tree, shrub, and certain vine stems and roots. 2) Tree bark reduced to strips, chips, or shreds and placed thickly on top of the soil as a ground cover or mulch. Also **Cortex.**

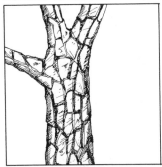

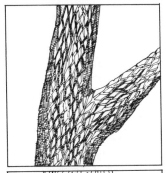

Bark

Baroque. Isola Bella, Lake Maggiore 17th century. Photo courtesy BBMSL, UNM.

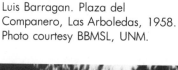

Luis Barragan. Plaza del Companero, Las Arboledas, 1958. Photo courtesy BBMSL, UNM.

Baroque An extravagant, sprawling, overly decorative style of art and design prominent in the seventeenth and eighteenth centuries, and influential in the development of modern landscape form. Baroque design, emerging in the late Renaissance, abandoned strict classical fitting of form to site and a clean use of specific landscape elements. Isola Bella (c. 1632–70), in the Lago Maggiore, Italy, at the foot of the Alps, is a prime example of baroque landscape form. See also **Renaissance landscape architecture** and **Rococo.**

Barragan, Luis (1901–) Mexican architect and landscape architect. Barragan's fascination with the play of clean, plane wall surfaces against foliage, water and sky made his landscape art world famous. His work at the Pedregal subdivision near Mexico City typifies this approach with its burly, rough lava masses, cubistic buildings, metal grilles, and bright green shrub accents.

Barragan was born in Jalisco State and is an engineer by training. The uncluttered feeling of his landscapes is all the more remarkable set against the overwhelmingly baroque Mexican tradition of garden design. Barragan places traditional landscape elements in his gardens; but the refinement of each item leaves no room for excess detail. His trademark *bebederos* (troughs) and elegant aqueducts contribute to Barragan's feeling that a protected garden should be a place to hear splashing water—"the music of the landscape."

In recent years, books and magazines have popularized Barragan's designs. He and the Brazilian **R. Burle Marx** remain Latin America's most influential landscape architects. See also **Latin American landscape architecture, Mexican landscape architecture.**

Barrens A geographical area in which extreme cold or aridity, or a combination of the two, creates a wasteland. A harsh, infertile, bleak region.

Barrier-free design The systematic design of landscape features and facilities that may be approached, enjoyed, and used by handicapped people. Currently mandated by law in the United States and elsewhere.

Barrow See **Tumulus.**

Barrow pit A hole dug by hand or machinery in a slope or bank to extract gravel or fill dirt for roadway and landscape construction. Also **Borrow pit.**

Barry, Sir Charles (1795–1860) British architect, responsible for the design of Parliament and for multiple neoclassical estates and other buildings in Victorian Britain. He frequently created strongly formal terraces and other geometric forms brightened by intense bedding plantings.

Barry often worked with the landscape gardener **W. A. Nesfield,** q.v. Among his best known projects are Trentham, Staffordshire; Cliveden, Buckinghamshire; and Shrubland Park in Suffolk. His work is described in *Formal Gardens in England and Scotland* (1902) by Inigo Trigg.

Bartram, William (1739–1823) American naturalist. Bartram travelled extensively through the eastern United States, collecting and studying flora and fauna. He introduced many European plant species to the United States and exported many American species to the Old World. Bartram published *Travels* (1791), a book noted in America and on the Continent.

Bas relief A type of sculpture often used in monumental landscape that features forms standing out slightly from a flat backdrop.

Basal break In botany, a **Sucker,** q.v.

Basal rot A variety of diseases affecting lower plant parts. Basal rot often affects bulbs or bulb-like plants.

Base bid The basic and essential portion of a proposal for landscape construction. Deductive alternates are subtracted from and additive alternates added to a base bid. See also **Alternate bid.**

Base bid specifications Specifications, q.v., in which the quality and performance as well as a manufacturer and model number are indicated for a product. Base bid specifications usually preclude substitutions.

Base course 1) In road construction, a first course of asphaltic concrete over which a top or finish course is laid down. Common synonym: **ACB (Asphalt Concrete Base).** See also **Asphalt-treated base.** 2) A first course of crushed stone or other material beneath a concrete slab.

Base, crusher-run See **Crusher-run base.**

Base level The lowest feasible point or plane of landscape erosion. Theoretically, mean sea level.

Base line 1) In surveying: (a) An east-west line used in conjunction with longitudinal meridians to establish townships. (b) An east-west line to which, along with a meridian reference, points on a plane survey are calculated. 2) In landscape drawing, a fenceline, building wall, or other "straight edge" from which distances to certain site features are plotted. 3) A known side of a survey triangle, used to plot the other sides. See also **Plane coordinates.**

Base map See **Base plan.**

Base plan In planning or design, an essential sheet showing site or general plan boundaries and significant items of interest, used as a basis for subsequent plan development. Also **Base map.**

Base plane A flat (plane) or inclined surface used as a reference for a field of vision and upon which objects rest and other planes depend. See also **Articulated plane, Overhead plane, Penetrable plane, Vertical plane.**

Base planting See **Foundation planting.**

Base pressure In irrigation, the pipe pressure required to operate a sprinkler head.

Bashi A bridge in a Japanese garden. See also **Japanese landscape architecture.**

Basic services (of the landscape architect)   The usual services offered by a landscape architect to his or her client include schematic design, design development, preparation of construction documents, supervision of bidding or negotiation, and contract administration.

Basic soil   See **Alkaline soil.**

Basifixed   In leaves, attached at the base.

Basin, catch   See **Catch basin.**

Basin, catchment   See **Watershed.**

Basin, earth   See **Earth basin.**

Basin irrigation   The watering of a more or less level plot of land closed off by banks or ridges.

Basin, leaching   See **Leaching basin.**

Basket, planting   See **Planting basket.**

Basketweave pattern (masonry)   See **Paver brick pattern.**

Bast (botanical)   See **Liber.**

Bastard trenching   In gardening, half or partial trenching.

Batch   A concrete mixture made up at one time.

Batha (Turkey and elsewhere)   See **Garigue.**

Batten   A lath-like, small strip of wood used for fence-finishing (board-and-batten construction), weather-stripping, or the like. A batten is normally placed over a joint of some kind.

Batter   In landscape construction, the ratio of deviation from the vertical in walls, step risers, and the like. A 3:1 batter equals a 3-inch deviation (tilt) in a one foot height of wall. Also **Rake.**

Batter boards   In construction, horizontal boards set with stakes to indicate the grade and foundation line of a building to be constructed.

Bay   1) A length of wall between two pilasters. 2) In an arcade, the space between two columns. 3) In open gardens, a mass of flowers or specimen plantings tucked into an evergreen or similar background. 4) A somewhat surrounded sea or lake inlet.

BBQ   Common abbreviation for **Barbecue,** q.v.

BC   An engineering abbreviation indicating **Bottom of curb,** q.v. 2) An abbreviation for back of curb. 3) An abbreviation for beginning of curve.

BCR   A plan abbreviation for back-of-curb radius or beginning of curb return.

BC soil   A soil with a profile of subsoil and a water stratum. See also **Soil horizon.**

Beach   A strand, or length of land by a sea or lake shore, composed of sand or pebbles and developed between high and low water reaches.

Beak   A bill-like protuberance in flowers, fruits, and the like.

Beam   In landscape construction, a structural timber bearing a considerable transverse load and measuring 5 × 8 inches (nominal dimensions) or more in thickness and width. 1) **Simple beam:** rests on one support at each end. 2) **Cantilevered beam:** extends beyond its support(s). 3) **Continuous beam:** lies upon three or more supports.

Beam and stringer lumber   See **Lumber.**

Bearded   In plant structures, equipped with lengthy, gathered hairs.

Bearing   In surveying, the angle between a determined point (a line point) and true north. A bearing is determined for purposes of site layout as the plane distance between two points calculated clockwise or counterclockwise off a north-south line in degrees, minutes, and seconds.

Bearing capacity   In soils, the maximum weight a given soil can withstand before it fails or gives way. Used as a gauge for building weighty structures. The **Ultimate bearing capacity** will produce a crumbling of the underlying earth mass.

Bearing plate   In landscape construction, a steel plate at the base of a post or other construction element that assumes or spreads a load.

Beauty bark   Decorative surface mulch. See also **Bark.**

Beaux Arts   The predominant school of nineteenth-century site and building design, often picturesque, emanating from the Ecole des Beaux Arts in Paris.

Beckford, William (1760—1844)   In his time, Beckford, an English country squire, may have been the richest man in the world. He developed his enormous Wiltshire estate, Fonthill, at the end of the eighteenth century. Beckford wanted a "huge paradise." Fonthill was the most sprawling English School landscape park ever built. It contained multiple lakes, forests, open fields, a lengthy surrounding wall, and the elaborate folly, Fonthill Abbey.

Beckford later moved to Bath, his Abbey fell down, and the landscape garden itself became a farm. See also **English School of Landscape Gardening.**

Bed, raised   See **Raised bed.**

Bed, warming   See **Coldframe** and **Warming bed.**

Bedding   The specially treated earthen or other area upon which a pipe is laid. Also **Bedding plant,** q.v.

Bedding, carpet or **massed**   See **Carpet bedding.**

Bedding plant   An annual flower or ground cover raised in coldframes or greenhouses and transplanted for seasonal effect to a public or private garden. Bedding plants date from the formal European gardens of the eighteenth century or earlier and are always laid out in masses. See also **Parterre.**

Bedding, ribbon   See **Ribbon bedding.**

Bedrock   The solid stone underlying all soil and subsoil; sometimes exposed on slopes, ledges, or in other areas.

Bedroom community   A suburban community easily reached by train, car, or bus that serves a larger urban center. See also **Satellite town.**

Beds, plunge   See **Plunging.**

Beeste   In an English Renaissance (Tudor) or derivative garden, a carved animal figure placed on a post as a curiosity.

Berm

Bell glass   In Renaissance England, a glass roughly the shape of a beehive placed over bedding plants or vegetables to "force" them in cold weather.

Belly band (horticulture)   In **Ball and burlap,** q.v., tree transplanting, a transverse metal band around the root ball serving as reinforcement.

Belt course   In masonry, a distinct course of flagstones or similar cut stones in a wall.

Belt, shelter   See **Shelter belt, Windbreak.**

Belt, thermal   See **Thermal belt.**

Belt walk   A walk around a central garden or landscape feature, such as a lawn, lake, or the like.

Belt, wheat   See **Wheat belt.**

Belvedere   A gazebo or summerhouse constructed on a hill in a garden to take advantage of good views. Also, a viewing room built on the roof of a palace.

Bema (Greek)   Classically, a raised speaker's platform (Athenian).

Bench   An outdoor seat for several people, usually of wood, metal, concrete or stone, with or without a back.

Benchmark (BM)   A surveyor's mark, usually cut in stone, used as a basis for determining the relative elevations of a given property. Normal appearance: ⏃ or ⊗. Benchmarks often show elevation above sea level. See also **Control points.**

Bench terrace   See **Terrace.**

Bender board   A thin (½ by 6 inch approximate dimensions), long board, often redwood, used as a temporary dividing strip between a lawn and planter or the like. See also **Header.**

Bending moment   In landscape construction, a direct stress applied to a beam and its uprights.

Bentgrass   See **Grasses.**

Benthic   Pertaining to the plant and animal life of the bottom of a sea or stream. From the Greek *benthos.*

Bentonite (clay)   A kind of clay often used in landscape architecture to line pool and lake bottoms.

Berm   1) Originally, a more or less level area separating a trench or ditch from a banked slope at a hillside fort. 2) A low, rolling, artificial hill often used in twentieth-century landscape design. The direct descendant of the medieval **Mount,** q.v.

Bermuda See **Grasses.**

Berry A small fruit, usually pulpy, composed of a thickened ripe ovary. Typical berries: tomato, banana, cranberry, blueberry, grape. See also **Fruit.**

Berso (Italian) Carpenter's work covering a walk (Renaissance or later). Designed for vines, climbing roses, and the like. French: **berseau.**

Beton brut (French) Rough-formed concrete, especially concrete with a surface pattern imprinted by wooden forms. See also **Concret brut.**

ᵇF **Board foot,** q.v.

BFPD Backflow prevention device. See **Backflow preventer.**

B-horizon See **Soil horizon.**

Biannual Twice-yearly. See also **Biennial.**

Biaxial In landscape design or plant form, composed of a double axis or two axes.

Bib A downward-turned faucet and connection for a garden hose. Also **Bibcock, Hosebib.**

Bible garden A specialty garden, usually small, featuring cultivated plants mentioned in the Bible.

Bicycle paths See **Cycleways.**

Bid A complete, signed proposal to execute a portion or all of a designed landscape for a designated sum, submitted to an owner or his representative by a contractor.

Bid, alternate See **Alternate (bid).**

Bid, base See **Base bid.**

Bid bond A legal guarantee in the form of a surety that a bidder has tendered a proposal in good faith and will enter into a contract for work if his bid is accepted. A bid bond normally does not exceed 5% of the total bid amount. Also **Bid guarantee.** See also **Bid security, Bond, Surety.**

Bid conditions In landscape construction, all the conditions the contractor must make note of and abide by as he prepares and submits a bid for contract construction. See also **Information for bidders, Instructions to bidders, Invitation to bid.**

Bid date A date specified by an owner and landscape architect for the opening of bids received for project construction.

Bid documents Construction drawings, an invitation to bid, instructions to bidders, specifications—including general conditions, special conditions, technical specifications and related items, a bid bond, a performance bond, a labor and materials payment bond, and the contract for contruction between owner and contractor, plus associated addenda and change orders, all prepared and issued to landscape contractors for purposes of preparation of competitive or negotiated bids. Also **Bidding documents.** See also **Construction documents, Specifications, Working drawings.**

Bid form A form provided to a bidder, including unit or lump-sum prices and alternates, if any, which is completed and submitted by a contractor as his bid according to the provisions of the construction documents.

Bid guarantee See **Bid bond.**

Bid item An item of construction clearly specified in construction documents as part of a contractor's bid for site improvements.

Bid item list See **Bid list.**

Bid list 1) A list of items of construction specified in construction documents as necessary for completion of a contractor's bid for site improvements. 2) A list of contractors bidding on a specific project. Also **Bid item list.**

Bid lot In landscape construction documents, a group of major items of work for which a definite proposal or bid submission is required.

Bid proposal A section of landscape architectural general specifications. The landscape contractor fills out the proposal form detailing items of construction and costs for a project and formally presents it to the project owner with his bonds and insurance. See also **Bond, Liability insurance,** and **Specifications.**

Bid security A submittal or deposit of cash, bank draft, money order, check, or bid bond accompanying a bid and serving as an assurance that a contractor will execute a project in accordance with construction documents if awarded a bid. See also **Bid bond.**

Bidder A contractor who submits a proposal for the installation of a project to an owner or his representative. See also **Subbidder.** A contract is normally awarded to a low bidder.

Bidders' information
  See **Information for bidders.**

Bidding See **Contract bidding.**

Bidding, closed   See **Invitational bidding.**

Bidding, contract   See **Contract bidding.**

Bidding documents   See **Bid documents.**

Bidding, invitational
   See **Invitational bidding.**

Bidding, open   See **Open bidding.**

Bidding, selective   See **Invitational bidding.**

Bidentate   In plants, a structure such as a seed coat equipped with two "teeth" at its tip.

Biennial   In botany, a plant that completes its life cycle in 2 years or 2 growing seasons. Normally, plant establishment occupies the first season and flowering occurs during the second. See also **Annual, Biannual, Bulb, Perennial.**

Bifid   In plants, two-lobed.

Bifoliolate   See **Foliolate.**

Bifurcation (of trees)   The division of a tree trunk into two distinct branches of main growth.

Bigelow, Dr. Joseph   Nineteenth-century United States designer of Mt. Auburn Cemetery (1831) near Cambridge, Massachusetts. Bigelow, also a horticulturist, followed the lead of the Scot, **J. C. Loudon,** q.v., in proposing multiple uses for cemeteries (picnicking, general open-space purposes).

Bigeneric hybrid   In horticulture, the cross of two botanic genera. Now, more commonly, intergeneric hybrid.

Bight   A crescent-shaped coastal indentation.

Bikepaths   See **Cycleways.**

Bikeways   See **Cycleways.**

Bilateral symmetry   See **Symmetry.**

Billabong (Australian)   A seasonal lake formed in the pinched meander of an old river. An **Ox-bow lake.**

Bin, soil   See **Soil bin.**

Binder (asphalt)   See **Asphalt tack coat.**

Binder course, asphalt   See **Asphalt binder course.**

Binder, sand   See **Sand binder.**

Binder, seed   See **Seed binder.**

Binders, soil   See **Soil binders.**

Binomial (classification or nomenclature)   The scientific two-part name of plants or animals. The first (generic) name gives the genus and is capitalized; the second (specific) name indicates species and is not capitalized. The two-name system was created by the botanist Linnaeus (Carl von Linne) in the eighteenth century, and is today standardized by the **International Code for Botanical Nomenclature** and the **International Code of Nomenclature for Cultivated Plants,** q.q.v. Example: Snapdragon/ *Antirrhinum majus,* Silk tree/*Albizzia julibrissin,* and Modesto ash/*Fraxinus velutina* "Modesto." The binomial is often set off in italics, with the exception of the name of the **Cultivar,** q.v. See also **Botanical classification.**

Biocenosis   Ecosystem, q.v.

Bioclimatology   The scientific study of climate and its effects on life and, especially, human existence.

Biodegradable   Capable of decomposition by bacteria.

Bioengineering   A kind of site engineering using live plants for erosion control and stabilization, soil improvement and restoration, or the like. Also **Structural planting.**

Biogenic   Pertaining to anything produced by living creatures.

Biogeography   The scientific study of plant and animal distribution. See also **Phytogeography.**

Biology   The science of living organisms.

Biome   A plant and animal combination typical of a large area. A pine forest, swamp, or temperate forest are examples. See also **Plant formation.**

Biomorphic   Taking form from nature.

Biopoiesis (Greek)   The generation of living matter from dead substance.

Biosphere   The part of the Earth inhabited by life. See also **Ecosphere.**

Biotic balance   A term describing the give and take of a healthy plant and animal environment.

Biotic climax   A climax or "ultimate" plant association in which a **Biotic factor,** q.v., is the limiting or key agent.

Biotic factor   An organic attribute or characteristic that affects environment. Also, more broadly, a particular kind of animal behavior that affects the animal's surroundings, such as human farming or elephants' stripping of tree-top branches. See also **Biotic climax, Climatic factor.**

Biotope In **Paleoecology**, q.v., a single aspect of the natural surroundings considered for study.

Birmingham wire gauge (BWG) An English wire measurement. See also **Wire gauge.**

Bisexual In botany, pertaining to a perfect flower. See **Flower.**

Bisymmetrical In landscape design, containing two cross-axes and their associated balanced elements.

Bitumen A mixture of hydrocarbons found in asphalt or tar. See also **Asphalt.**

Bituminous Containing tar or asphalt compounds.

Bituminous concrete Asphaltic concrete, q.v.

Bituminous down drain An asphalt valley gutter. See also **Valley gutter.**

Black earth A deep, rich soil consisting of loess, humus, and a quantity of lime. Extremely productive. Black earth is a **Prairie soil,** found in the Ukraine, Canada, and the United States. Also **Chernozem.** See also **Brown earth, Pedocal.**

Blacktop Asphalt, q.v.

Blade, leaf See **Leaf blade.**

Blading Earthwork in which the ground is planed off with a heavy metal tractor or bulldozer blade.

Blanching In gardening, a process designed to whiten asparagus, leek, and other vegetable stalks by means of heaping earth around the plant stems or otherwise keeping light from reaching them.

Blanket, gravel See **Gravel blanket.**

Blanket, rock See **Rock blanket.**

Bleeder stub A pavement underdrain positioned with its outlet discharging into a manhole or manholes. See also **Underdrain.**

Bleeding The oozing of tree or shrub sap at a wound or cut. The plant normally begins to heal or scar after a period of bleeding.

Blight Plant rot and wither from numerous organic or climatic sources.

BLM See **Bureau of Land Management.**

Block, asphalt See **Asphalt block.**

Block, cement See **Concrete masonry unit.**

Block, concrete See **Concrete masonry unit.**

Block holing A kind of stone demolition in which dynamite is set off in a drilled shaft.

Block, slump See **Slump block.**

Block, soil See **Soil block.**

Block, split face (CMU) See **Split face block.**

Block, system (irrigation) See **Section system.**

Blocking In landscape construction, a series of reinforcing members installed at right angles to overhead joists to prevent them from twisting and warping. See also **Bridging.**

Bloom 1) A blossom. 2) A powdery coating found on certain fruits or leaves. Also **Farina.** See also **Glaucous, Pruinose, Pubescence.**

Bloom, water See **Water bloom.**

Blowdown In irrigation, a strainer-cleaning mechanism consisting of a pipe and drain valve installed with the strainer at the vacuum breaker.

Blown-out lands Severely wind-eroded lands.

Blue garden A garden in which blue-tone flowers and blue-leaved plants are the dominant design feature. White or yellow flower masses are often found in a blue garden as accents.

Blue staking In landscape construction, location staking of existing utility lines or easements for the prevention of construction damage or errors.

Bluegrass See **Grasses.**

Blueprint In landscape architecture, a reproduction of an original plan made on sensitized paper (often through an ammonia process), used for review, reference, and construction. Originally, a print of white lines on a blue background. See also **Print.**

Bluestone A kind of cut-stone pavement (usually blue or blue-gray sandstone, gneiss, or schist) customarily set in a mortar bed over a concrete base with grouted mortar joints.

Bluff A sharp, precipitous slope, cliff, or headland.

Bluing The bluish shading of an aging red rose.

BM In surveying, an abbreviation indicating **Benchmark,** q.v.

Board foot A common measurement of lumber equal to 1 in. × 1 ft.–0 in. × 1 ft–0 in. Abbreviated **bF.**

Board, planning   See **Planning agency, Planning commission.**

Board-and-batten (fence)   See **Batten.**

Boards, batter   See **Batter boards.**

Bocage   In France, farmlands made by lines of trees and hedges into small fields.

Bog   A stretch of wet, spongy, low-lying ground, saturated with water, and containing a great amount of decomposing plant matter. Bogs are covered with highly acidic, low-oxygen water that is usually stagnant. See also **Marsh** and **Swamp.**

Bog garden   A "wet" garden usually found in a low-lying area, containing irises, cattails, mosses, or similar plants.

Bog, raised   See **Hochmoor.**

Bog soil   A mucky or peat soil developed in a marshy area. Usually low in oxygen and incompletely decomposed.

Boil, frost   See **Frost action.**

"Boilerplate" specifications   A common term for general (or nontechnical) project specifications. See also general specifications under **Specifications.**

Bole   1) The trunk of a tree. 2) A lump of red clay.

Bollard   1) A protruding pile at a wharf or dock to which boats and ships are moored. 2) A post used in landscape design to section off foot and vehicle traffic. A bollard is a friendly tool for limiting or preventing vehicular access to designated areas.

Bolson   In deserts and semideserts, a large shallow depression or basin covered with water at intervals. See also **Playa.**

Bolting   In plant growth, the production of seed rather than usual herbaceous growth. In general, premature growth. Bolting in vegetables often accompanies high temperatures and may involve unwanted flower production as well. See also **Breaking.**

Bolts   Metal fastening rods or pins, sometimes threaded. See **Anchor bolt, Carriage bolt,** under their own headings.

Bomanite   See **Impressed concrete pavement.**

Bond   1) A legal surety by means of which a first party warrants the financial soundness and performance of a second party. A bond is an essential part of a **Suretyship,** q.v. See also **Bid bond, Labor and materials payment bond, Performance bond, Specifications.** 2) A pattern of brick pavement. See also **Paver brick pattern.**

Bond, bid   See **Bid bond.**

Bond, common (masonry)   See **Common bond.**

Bond, completion   See **Performance bond.**

Bond, construction   See **Performance bond.**

Bond, contract   See **Performance bond.**

Bond, English (masonry)   See **Brick wall pattern.**

Bond, fidelity   See **Fidelity bond.**

Bond, Flemish (masonry)   See **Brick wall pattern.**

Bond, header (masonry)   See **Brick wall pattern.**

Bond, labor   See **Labor and materials payment bond.**

Bond, lien   See **Lien bond.**

Bond, materials payment   See **Labor and materials payment bond.**

Bollards. Photo courtesy Morrow and Company.

Bond, pattern   See **Pattern bond.**

Bond, performance
See **Performance bond.**

Bond, running (masonry)
See **Running bond** and **Paver brick pattern.**

Bond, stacked (walls)   See **Stacked bond.**

Bond stone   In wall facades, an anchor stone upon which a veneer may be based. The quantity of bond stones in a wall is often called out in a building code.

Bond, stretcher (masonry)
See **Running bond.**

Bond, stretching (masonry)
See **Running bond.**

Bond, structural (masonry)
See **Structural bond.**

Bond, supply   See **Supply bond.**

Bond, surety   See **Surety.**

Bond, tensile   See **Tensile bond.**

Bond, union wage   See **Union wage bond.**

Bonding company   A company or agency issuing bonds or assurances payable to the owner of a project that: 1) warrant the faithful execution of a contract by a contractor submitting a bid; and 2) warrant the contractor's job performance and payment of debts after a contract is awarded. Bonding companies largely control the size and quantity of jobs a contractor may pursue at any one time. See also **Bond.**

Bonds, dedicated tax, general obligation, and **revenue**
See **Financing for public works construction.**

Bonds, guaranty   See **Guaranty bonds.**

Bonds, municipal   See **Municipal bonds.**

Bone meal   Bones ground to a fine powder used as a fertilizer. Bone dust is even more finely pulverized.

Bonsai   A Japanese method of dwarfing full-sized trees and shrubs by stem and root pruning. A bonsai plant is grown in a container.

Bonus and penalty clause   In a construction contract, a stipulation giving an incentive amount of money to a contractor as a reward for early completion of a project, and providing for **Liquidated damages,** q.v., or other designated penalties for construction time overruns. Often found in the proposal form of the general specifications.

Book, garden   See **Garden book.**

Book, plat (surveying)   See **Plat book.**

Booster (pump)   In irrigation, a pump used to increase existing water pressure. Three basic types are common: 1) centrifugal, 2) submersible, 3) turbine. All these classes of booster pump use a bladed internal disc to force water into a line to be discharged. The booster makes possible the operation of heads that otherwise would be unusable due to insufficient and/or irregular pressure.

BOR   See **Bureau of Outdoor Recreation.**

Border   In a garden, an edging of paths, mowing strips, plantings, or the like at the margin of a lawn or yard.

Border, annual   See **Annual border.**

Bonsai

Border, herbaceous
See **Herbaceous border.**

Border, reserve   See **Reserve border.**

Border, stone   An edging stone in a garden or other landscape.

Border, tonal   See **Tonal border.**

Boreal   Pertaining to a northern (usually Continental) forest, especially an evergreen forest.

Boring, check (soils)   See **Check boring.**

Borings   1) Drillings made to determine the nature and composition of soil or rock strata. 2) Well drillings.

Boron   A nonmetallic element necessary in tiny amounts for plant (and animal) health and growth. A **Trace element,** q.v. See also **Available nutrient, Soil minerals.**

Borrow excavation
See **Excavation.**

Borrow pit   See **Barrow Pit.**

Borrowed landscape   See **Borrowed scenery.**

Borrowed personnel agreement   A form of contract between owner and

Boscage or Bosquet. Boston Fens, 1878, by Frederick L. Olmsted. Photo by the author.

landscape architect in which the owner (usually a government agency) temporarily "attaches" the services of the landscape architect to his office to accomplish a specific item of design or consultation.

Borrowed scenery   All or part of an adjacent landscape, the features of which figure in the composition of the landscape or garden at hand. Also **Borrowed landscape.** See also **Extensional landscape.**

Boscage (Boskage)   A thicket or grove of trees and/or shrubs, especially in a country setting.

Boscaresque   Displaying a picturesque woodland setting.

Bosco (Italian)   A mass of trees, shrubs, or undergrowth. In Renaissance Italy, a grove, one of the three principal parts of the villa garden. For **Sacro bosco,** see **Sacred grove.** See also **Renaissance landscape architecture.**

Bosquet (French)   A cluster or clump of trees or shrubs. Also bosket. A **Copse.** Also **Bosque (Spanish), Bosk, Bosco (Italian),** q.v.

Botanic or Botanical garden   A specialized public garden in which plants are grown for educational and scientific purposes and for general display. A plant museum.

The modern botanical garden has its origin in the medieval cultivation of cloistered herb beds (see **Physic garden**). The Renaissance garden dedicated to the study of plants, exemplified by the early botanical gardens of Padua, Pisa, Breslau, Leyden, Oxford, and elsewhere, is typical of the sixteenth and seventeenth centuries. It was developed to display and study the thousands of new plant species pouring into Europe from Africa, Asia, and the New World. In the New World itself, the botanical gardens of Huastepec, built by the Aztecs near Tenochtitlan between 1440 and 1460 A.D., rival the embryonic European gardens in age, complexity, and sophistication.

Botanical gardens were in a heyday by the mid-nineteenth century, with the great gardens at Kew, England, and Shaw's Gardens in St. Louis, Missouri as outstanding examples in numbers of species and extent of acreage. Renowned modern botanical gardens also include those at Edinburgh; Glasnevin, Ireland; the New York Botanical Garden; the Sydney and Melbourne Botanical Gardens; and others.

Botanical classification   The scientific system of codifying an individual plant by stating its relationship to larger groups of its relatives.

Carolus Linnaeus, q.v., in the book *Species Plantarum* (1753) laid the basis for modern scientific classification. Plant types are arranged in **Divisions,** q.v., or **Phyla** (see **Phylum**) indicating the degree of evolutionary complexity of the organisms involved:

A. Kingdom—plant
B. Division (phylum)
   1. Division I, Thallophyta
   2. Division II, Bryophyta
   3. Division III, Pteridophyta
   4. Division IV, Spermatophyta. Most plants used in landscape architecture are **Spermatophytes,** q.v., or seed-bearing plants.
C. Class
D. Order
E. Family
F. Genus
G. Species
H. Variety or subspecies.

Normal botanical classification indicates genus, species, and sometimes variety. Broader identification places an individual plant in its family, order, or higher category.

The common or popular name or names of a plant may often vary from region to region or among countries and may include as many as a dozen or more terms for a single species. However, only one current Latin name is recognized for each species.

A modern authority on scientific Latin used in plant nomenclature is *Botanical Latin* by W. T. Stearn. See also **Binomial.**

Botanical code   See **Cultivated plant code.**

Botanical name Commonly, the **Genus** and **Species**, q.q.v. (and **Subspecies** or **Variety**, q.q.v.), by which a plant is universally classified. Also **Binomial**. See also **Botanical classification**.

Botanical nomenclature Usually, the **Binomial**, q.v., or generic and specific names of a plant, but sometimes the entire family, order, class, and division as well. Botanical nomenclature refers to the highly descriptive Latin names of general plant classification. See also **Botanical classification**.

Botany The science of plant study, part of biology. Also **Phytology**. See **Histology, Morphology, Plant Physiology, Taxonomy,** and **Teratology** under their own headings. See also **Ecology**.

Botany, systematic See **Taxonomy**.

Bottle garden A **Terrarium**, q.v., arranged in a bottle rather than a tank.

Bottom of curb (BC) A basic point of mean elevation above sea level, useful as an indicator of water flow and curb height. See also **Flowline, Top of curb**.

Bottom heat A kind of uniform heat created by electrical wiring set up below propagation flats in a greenhouse.

Boulder clay See **Till**.

Boulder ditch See **French drain**.

Boulevard A wide street, especially a street bordered by commercial or government buildings. True boulevards are often set off by extensive tree plantings, wide pedestrian walks, and medians. French in origin.

Bound water See **Hygroscopic water**.

Boundary survey A kind of property survey in which a closed traverse of an area of land is made, with dimensions, angles, and bearings all indicated. Normally executed by a **Land surveyor**, q.v. See also **Survey**.

Bourne In Britain, an ephemeral or intermittent brook or spring, often dry in winter.

Bower An arbor or shady enclave. See also **Pleached bower**.

Bowling green See **Green**.

Box, controller (irrigation) See **Automatic controller**.

Box, junction (electrical) See **Junction box**.

Box, shadow See **Shadow box**.

Box, timer (irrigation) See **Automatic controller**.

Box, valve (irrigation) See **Valve box**.

Box, window See **Window box**.

Boxed plant See **Container plant**.

Boyceau, Jacques (c. 1600) French gardener and author of the *Traité du Jardinage*. Boyceau worked at the Tuileries gardens with **Claude Mollet**, q.v., for Henri IV, where he developed the **Parterre de broderie**, q.v., from fashion patterns seen in the dress of the day. Boyceau also worked on the Luxembourg Gardens for Louis XIII. See also **French landscape architecture**.

Brace, angle iron (irrigation) See **Angle iron brace**.

Bracket arm In light poles (luminaires), a protruding arm that supports a light or lights. Also **Mast arm**.

Brackish water Still or slightly flowing water that is salty, alkaline, or otherwise only partially fresh. Commonly found in deserts, where water recharge may take place slowly or not at all.

Bract A small modified leaf situated at the base of a flower or flower cluster. A bracteole is a tiny bract; a bractlet is found at the base of a **Pedicel**, q.v. Adjective: bracteate. See also **Glume, Spathe**.

Braided channel In streams, a broad channel course of intersecting rivulets often resulting from wholesale land-clearing in the surrounding watershed with the resultant large outwash of sediments into the stream bottom.

Brake A thicket of overgrown vegetation. Often **canebrake**, a reedy or shrubby thicket.

Bramble A very prickly shrub, especially a raspberry, blackberry, or the like.

Branch line In irrigation, small nonpressure lines within a section system supplying individual heads. See also **Lateral line**.

Brazilian landscape architecture
The venerable Portuguese **Praça** (square) dominated in Brazil until the 1930s. It was part of a very comfortable, very well-entrenched baroque tradition that also included the villa (quinta) and its Mediterranean courts and fountains, all planted in the riotous colors and forms of the flora of the New World jungles. From Baia (Salvador), the oldest of Brazilian cities, to Ouro Preto, the gold boom town in Minas

Brazilian landscape architecture. Cavanelas garden, Petropolis, 1954, by Roberto Burle Marx. Photo courtesy BBMSL, UNM.

Flamengo ("Waves Plaza" on Flamingo Beach, 1960s), in Rio de Janeiro.

Le Corbusier was intrigued by the local **Azulejo** tile, q.v. and there was a resurgence in its use after his visit. But none of the projects he inspired would have been possible without the rather despotic stability imposed on Brazil by Getulio Vargas (in office from 1930–45 and again from 1950–54), or the vision of his successor, Juscelino Kubitschek (1954–61). Kubitschek and his stubborn drive were responsible for the founding of Brasilia, the new national capital, by 1961. In Brasilia, landscape architects, including, among others, Burle Marx, had the opportunity to create public open space amid a dynamic series of interrelated International Modern structures. Brazilian architects and landscape architects gave the fledgling capital a new landscape and city form vastly different from the essentially Portuguese design idiom of the past.

Burle Marx's recent Sao Paulo Botanical Gardens are sophisticated, informative, and, of course, lushly planted. Sao Paulo, the industrial giant, is only a few hundred miles from Ouro Preto in distance. In time, it is centuries removed. The streets of Ouro Preto wind and plunge through the mountains, the tiled houses lining them like those of any Mediterranean hill town. The *chafarizes* (wall fountains) still spout tiny streams in quiet corners. Ouro Preto's Praça Tiradentes, like any church-bound square, is Old Brazil: cobbled pavements, baroque details, the only civic open space in a huddled mass of nearby structures. The

Gerais, the soft Portuguese formalism dominated Brazil for over 400 years.

Le Corbusier visited Brazil in 1936 to advise Lucio Costa, Affonso Reidy, and Oscar Niemeyer on the design of a new Ministry of Education building in Rio de Janeiro. His devotion to Cubism, his use of **Beton brut** as a radical new building material, and his views on the International Style and site-programming profoundly impressed his Brazilian hosts. The course of recent Brazilian architecture and planning and the future development of the new capital of Brasilia were set by Le Corbusier's visit.

Roberto Burle Marx, the founder of modern Brazilian landscape architecture, was working with Costa at the time of the 1936 Le Corbusier visit. Burle Marx, around 25 years old at the time, was a painter, jewelry-designer, botanist, and landscape architect of formidable talent. He had already begun to develop the flair for plant texture and color in landscape composition that would later make him famous. Encouraged in his early work by Lucio Costa, Burle Marx accepted the directorship of Parks and Botanical Gardens in the port city of Recife, Pernambuco, shortly after his collaboration on the Ministry of Education building. In his later work, Burle Marx has been noted for his curious ability to discover new species in the Brazilian hinterlands to satisfy the plant requirements for his commissions. Typical of his strikingly tropical designs are the Instituto de Ressegouros (1939), the Belo Horizonte Airport (1954), and his *Praça de Ondas na Praia do*

contradictions between Ouro Preto and Sao Paulo reflect the rest of the country: there is both pride in the strong, twentieth-century form and an abiding love and respect for the older Portuguese inheritance. These continue to delight, exasperate, and mix at every turn in Brazil. See also **Latin American landscape architecture**. See also **Burle Marx, Roberto**.

Break In botany, the new growth emerging from a plant bud or eye, especially after higher-growing tips or buds have been pinched.

Break, basal (botany) See **Basal break**.

Break, color See **Color break**.

Breaker, vacuum See **Vacuum breaker**.

Breaking Early budding, leafing out, or flowering. See also **Bolting**.

Breakwater See **Mole**.

Breeder seed See **Commercial seed classifications**.

Breeding of plants See **Plant breeding**.

Breeze, sea See **Sea breeze**.

Breezeway A covered walk between adjacent buildings or between a building and its carport or garage.

Brick A molded and fired, generally rectangular block of clay used in landscape paving, walls, and the like. Brick is called out by type, quality, finish, sand mold, and size. See also **Brick wall pattern, Paver brick pattern**.

Brick, economy See **Economy brick**.

Brick, jumbo See **Economy brick**.

Brick pattern See **Brick wall pattern, Paver brick pattern**.

Brick paver (paving brick) See **Paver brick**.

Brick, Roman See **Roman brick**.

Brick sand A very fine sand of maximum $1/8$ inch greatest-particle diameter in which brick patios or walks are laid. See also **Mortar sand, Sand**.

Brick, sewer See **Sewer brick**.

Brick, soft-mud See **Adobe**.

Brick wall pattern Brick courses in walls are laid in brick mortar in multiple patterns. Several of the most frequently found are these: **Common bond** (three or more **Stretcher** courses with a **Header** course following); **English bond**: a pattern of alternating header and stretcher courses; **Flemish bond**: alternating headers and stretchers in the same wall course; **Header bond**: wall courses of headers, with upper joints centered on the bricks below them. Also **Heading bond**. See also **Paver brick pattern**.

Brick, wire-cut Brick cut to size by wire before firing.

Brickwork See **Brick wall pattern, Paver brick pattern**.

Bridge A foot or vehicle span across a ravine, gorge, or watercourse. A footbridge is limited to pedestrian traffic. Stone bridges, overwhelmingly popular in landscape construction for the past two centuries, are often superseded by concrete or wooden bridges in the twentieth century.

Bridgeman, Charles (d. 1738) English nurseryman and landscape gardener, pupil of **George London** and partner of **Henry Wise**, q.q.v. Though noted for his use of formal French convention at Stowe and elsewhere, Bridgeman popularized the **Ha-ha** as an innovative landscape device. He often enclosed his developed garden areas with ha-has for ease of cultivation.

Bridgeman consulted at or planned out a multitude of early eighteenth-century English estates. He collaborated with John Vanbrugh (later the architect of Blenheim Palace) at Stowe, probably his most remarkable landscape. Also notable were the estates of Rousham and Chiswick. His successor at these sites, as well as at Stowe, was **William Kent**, q.v., who replaced Bridgeman's formal planning with the softer lines of the new **English School of Landscape Gardening**.

Bridgeman began the transition between formal and informal landscape design in England, and his work and influence are the subject of increasing critical study. See also **English landscape architecture**.

Bridging In landscape construction, a series of diagonally placed, sometimes overlapping reinforcements installed between overhead joists to prevent them from twisting and warping. See also **Blocking**.

Bridle path An urban riding trail. See also **Riding**.

British landscape architecture See **English landscape architecture**.

Broad spectrum control One of several herbicides that kill a number of different species of grasses or weeds. See also **Herbicide**.

Broad walk   In English and other gardens, a wide gravel path often bordered with lawns or planting beds.

Broadcast seeding   In horticulture, the planting of lawns or other areas by scattering seed. See also **Seed drill.**

Broadleaf (evergreen)   An evergreen plant with wide leaves, as opposed to needles. Generally mild-winter plants, broad-leaved evergreens do not produce cones.

Broderie (French)   See **Parterre** (de broderie).

Broker, plant   See **Plant broker.**

Bronze   An ancient alloy of copper and zinc still frequently used to produce busts and other sculptures for outdoor use. Often **Statuary bronze.**

Brook   A stream or course of running water. A rivulet.

Broom finish   A method of finishing concrete whereby delicate or strong roughly parallel brush or "broom" lines are scribed on a hardening surface. The finished texture will be apparently smooth to the eye. See also **Exposed aggregate** and **Smooth finish.**

Broom, witch's (plant growth)   See **Witch's broom.**

Brooming   See **Broom finish.**

Brown earth   A reasonably fertile soil developing beneath shortgrass on arid prairies or steppes, or in deciduous forests. May be alkaline or neutral. A kind of **Prairie soil.** Often **Brown forest soil.** Also **Chestnut soil.** See also **Black earth, Pedocal.**

Brown, Capability (Lancelot) (1716–83)   Brown and his compatriot and successor **Humphry Repton,** q.v., are probably the best known of the English landscape gardeners, but Brown was the more extreme in applying the principles of naturalism. In many of his estates, the informal "countryside" marches directly up to the manor door. Brown himself might have said that the house was merely set picturesquely in the countryside.

Brown was born in Kirkharle, Northumberland, and began working as a gardener at age 16 under Sir William Lorraine. He subsequently worked for Sir Richard Grenville and in 1740 was hired as an apprentice landscape gardener under **William Kent,** q.v., at Stowe. A phenomenal salesman, Brown developed a series of trademarks that became very popular: he created serpentine lakes by damming streams and laid out soft, isolated copses of trees in rolling sweeps of lawn. He used sun (when available in England) and shadow to great effect. Above all, Brown's aim was to substitute informal line and a strong contrast of texture for rigid geometry, multicolor flower beds,

and clipped masses of topiary. He mostly removed the incidental "ruins" set out at Stowe and elsewhere by Kent. Brown used Bridgeman's ha-ha in his estate designs, but his intent

Brown

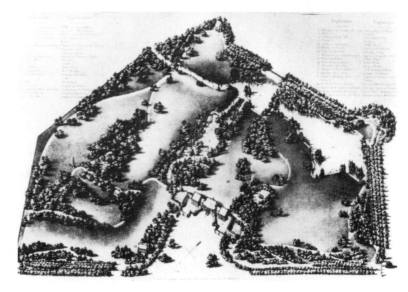

Capability Brown's design for the grounds of Stowe estate, England. Illustration courtesy BBMSL, UNM.

was still to set the manor house in a park—a modification of and improvement on nature itself.

Brown's deferential nickname sprang from his habit of pronouncing most proposed projects "capable" of immense improvement. It was deserved: during his lifetime he designed and supervised the construction of over 170 private parks and pleasure grounds all over Britain. Among the best-preserved of these are Bowood (1761), Warwick Castle (1750), and Blenheim (1765). Blenheim was redesigned from the original Vanbrugh-Wise and Bridgeman layouts. Brown was soundly criticized for his destruction of the Renaissance gardens of Blenheim and other estates by William Chambers and by **Uvedale Price,** whose *An Essay on the Picturesque* appeared in 1794. But Brown's highly stylized wildness had caught on during his own lifetime, and his apprentices and successors were in demand all over Europe. The natural garden also travelled to the colonies: Thomas Jefferson used naturalistic principles in his later estate design at Monticello.

After Kent's death in 1748, Brown became in a sense the Zen priest of Western landscape design. His landscapes were purer, more apparently casual, and cleaner than anything that had come before. He was criticized repeatedly for this, as **Le Notre** had been for his excessive formality. But Brown's recognition of the **Genius loci**—the spirit of place—in landscapes such as Chatsworth and Longleat distinguished his work from that of his predecessors and contributed to a fundamental change in English and European gardening.

Brown also designed several country houses in the Palladian style. See also **Charles Bridgeman** and **English landscape architecture.**

Brownline   A sepia reproducible drawing from which blue- or black-line prints may be made. See also **Sepia.**

Browse   Buds, leaves, and twigs eaten by animals.

Browse line   A rough "line" on the under-canopy of trees or shrubs that shows the highest point at which wildlife or livestock will browse an individual plant.

Brush dam   See **Check dam.**

Brush finish   1) In stone masonry, a rough, electric-brush, surface treatment. 2) In concrete construction, an extremely common slab finish obtained through the light, glancing strokes of a brush or broom.

Brush mat   Overlapping, uprooted small trees or shrubs placed with limbs facing downstream as a temporary method of gradient-stabilization in channels.

Bryophyte   A moss or moss-like plant; a wort. Bryophytes are relatively simple, spore-producing members of Division (phylum) II, *Bryophyta,* of the plant kingdom. See also **Botanical classification.**

Bubbler   In irrigation, a head that waters in a constant, easy flow without spraying. See also **Head.**

Bucolic   Pastoral; especially, dealing with a sense of rural tranquility or peace. See also **Pastoral landscape.**

Bud   A small protuberance or swelling of overlapping scales found at a leaf axil (axillary bud) or stem tip (apical bud) and containing a rudimentary blossom, leaf, cluster of leaves, or branch. The apical bud is

sometimes called the **Brown bud.** Also **Eye.** See also **Lateral bud, Terminal bud.**

Bud, crown (apical bud)   See **Bud.**

Bud, lateral   See **Lateral bud.**

Bud scale   A small, modified leaf surrounding a bud.

Bud sport   See **Sport.**

Bud, terminal   See **Terminal bud.**

Bud union   A grafting point. See also **Grafting.**

Budding   1) A type of grafting in which a live bud from a desired plant (scion) is inserted into a host plant (stock). 2) The emergence of immature leaves, flowers, or branches. See also **Grafting.**

Budget   A construction budget, or listing of items and costs necessary for the development of a landscape, is often set by an owner and followed by a landscape architect during the design process. The landscape architect may also prepare a budget for the owner's review and use if so requested. See also **Maximum allowable contruction cost.**

Budget, construction   See **Maximum allowable construction cost.**

Budget, project   See **Project budget.**

Buffer capacity of soil   The ability of a given soil to continue in its original pH condition after alkaline or acidic elements are added to it.

Buggy   In landscape construction, a rubber-wheeled cart used to transport concrete from a mixer to the forms. Also **Concrete cart, Georgia buggy.**

Building codes Regulations stipulating a type of construction, including height and materials standards, allowable in a specific project. Two basic sorts of codes exist: 1) **Form standard codes:** these standards call out a specific result and are the most common codes. Exact kinds of construction materials and methods of installation, among other items, will be found in form standard codes. 2) **Performance standard codes:** this kind of code designates the manner in which a construction design must work.

A **Housing code,** highly specialized, indicates acceptable standards for mechanical systems, numbers of doors, toilets, lavatories and sinks, fire safety, and the like.

An **Irrigation** or **Sprinkler code** lists backflow prevention devices (check valves or vacuum breakers) necessary to prevent contamination of a potable water system.

Building (construction) permit An authorization issued by a governmental agency allowing construction of a project according to approved plans and specifications.

Building-space ratio The amount of building area vs. the amount of remaining open space for a project area. The ratio is often strictly laid out by law and is an important zoning tool.

Bulb Normally, an underground, swollen stem ringed with fleshy, scale-like leaves that develops above-ground flowers in spring or summer. Onions, tulips, and irises are frequently occurring bulbs. See also **Corm, Tuber.**

Bulbil In botany, a special sort of axillary bud that may mature and separate from its parent to form a new plant. See also **Bud.**

Bulkhead In landscape construction, a crosspiece set in a form to contain freshly poured concrete, soil, water, or other construction elements.

Bull float (of concrete) See **Darby.**

Bump, speed See **speed bump.**

Bunchgrass A grass that grows in a clump and does not produce a mat by means of stolons or runners. See also **Grasses.**

Bundle, vascular See **Vascular system.**

Bunker See **Sand trap.**

Bur (burr) A seed casing covered with thorns or stickers.

Bureau of Land Management A U.S. Government agency charged with administering vast areas of public range and other land, much of it in the western states. Also **BLM.**

Bureau of Outdoor Recreation An agency of the Department of the Interior, United States government, formerly involved in the planning and funding of landscape architectural projects of an active or passive recreational nature. Also **BOR.**

Buried soil This unlikely term refers to well-defined soil overlain with lava, sediment, or windblown deposits (**Loess,** q.v.).

Burl An often round or oval woody lump on the bark of a tree.

Burle Marx, Roberto (1909–) An account of Burle Marx is equivalent to an account of twentieth-century landscape architecture in Brazil. Born in Sao Paulo, Burle Marx spent many of his formative years in Germany. He first studied Brazilian flora, ironically, in the Berlin Arboretum.

Back in Brazil, he composed one of his first gardens in 1933 for the noted architect Lucio Costa. Burle Marx was already accomplished in painting, set design, jewelry design, botany, and other fields, as well as in landscape architecture. Over the years he developed an acutely chromatic approach to garden design, reflecting his passions for Cubism and related geometries and for the beauty of unused Brazilian native plants.

Much of Burle Marx's design work has been developed in conjunction with the Modernist architecture of Affonso Reidy and Oscar Niemeyer, as well as Costa. His early work on the Ministry of Education Building in Rio de Janeiro and his compositions

Bulb

Roberto Burle Marx. Larragoite Hospital garden, Rio de Janeiro, 1957. Photo courtesy BBMSL, UNM.

Burn See **Bourne.**

Burn, fertilizer See **Fertilizer burn.**

Burnham, Daniel (1846–1912)
United States architect and city planner, and head of design for the World's Columbian Exposition of 1893 in Chicago, in which he collaborated with **Frederick Law Olmsted,** q.v., and others. Burnham built on L' Enfant's original plans for Washington to do extensive town planning for the national capital and the District of Columbia in 1902. His city planning for Chicago included loop roads, transportation systems, greenbelts, and extensive lakefront redesign, as well as the Columbian Exposition itself.
Burnham's later planning in the **City Beautiful** style, including civic redesign for San Francisco after the 1906 earthquake and plans for Manila and Baguio in the Philippines, was heavily monumental and somewhat overblown.

Bursting pressure In irrigation lines, about 500% to 1000% the rated pipe pressure.

Bus shelter A glass and steel or other shelter used to screen waiting bus passengers from the elements.

Bush 1) A short, low-branching shrub with multiple stems. 2) Back country or underbrush.

of the 1960s for the new capital of Brasilia have greatly influenced twentieth-century Latin American landscape architecture.
Burle Marx has also been a plant hunter. He has personally collected many of the plants for his compositions in the Brazilian forests, and, at present, has a thriving contracting and nursery business in addition to his design practice. His office has trained a considerable number of young Brazilian landscape architects. More than any other Brazilian, Burle Marx has been responsible for superseding the traditional, formal "Portuguese tropical" landscapes of the country with an intriguing twentieth-century landscape style.
Among his major works are Pampulha (in Belo Horizonte), the Civic Center of Curitiba, the Hospital Sulamerica, the Parques Este and Oeste in Caracas, Venezuela, and the Sao Paulo Botanical Gardens. The major work on Burle Marx is *The Tropical Gardens of Burle Marx* (1964) by P. M. Bardi. See also **Brazilian landscape architecture** and **Latin American landscape architecture.**

Bush hammering   A means of providing rough but consistent concrete texture through use of a) a special hammer with a grooved head, or b) a hammer-and-stone chisel process. The finish technique is used after the material has set.

Butt joint (landscape construction)   See **Wood and brick construction joints.**

Butte   A highly eroded mesa, much reduced in size.

Buttress root   A protruding part of a tree's trunk and root system that acts as a stabilizer or buttress for the main trunk mass. The American elm (*Ulmus americana*) and many tropical Ficus species are examples.

BWG   An abbreviation for **Birmingham wire gauge,** q.v.

Bye, A. E. (1919–)   Arthur Edwin Bye, American landscape architect, educated at Pennsylvania State University. Bye is noted for his acute eye for natural form. A prolific designer, he has executed projects throughout the United States and in Europe and the West Indies. His Soros estate on Long Island is one of the twentieth century's most refined exercises in **Naturalism,** q.v.

Bye's work has been widely exhibited throughout the U.S. in design schools and elsewhere. His publications include numerous articles and the lyrical book *Art into landscape, Landscape into art* (1983). Bye is also a lexicographer, having compiled the landscape architectural entries for the **Dictionary of Architecture and Construction.** He serves as a Visiting Professor at the University of Pennsylvania. Bye was elected a Fellow of the ASLA in 1971.

A. E. Bye. Photo courtesy A. E. Bye.

Bush hammering

Wall or fountain surface after forming

Hammer and bar used to break formed surface irregularly

Irregular surface with finished pattern for falling water or textured effect

Byzantine landscape architecture
An early medieval landscape architecture of no particular originality. The Byzantines, creators of the Eastern Roman Empire (330–1453 A.D.), are noted for their aristocratic baths, pleasure gardens, and monumental statuary. Flower gardens and great public market squares mark the period of the height of the empire (c. 500 A.D.). Although Greek and Roman civilization weighed heavily on Byzantium, Byzantine courtyards, colonnades, and wall-detailing all reveal stonework that has superseded classical forms.

Byzantine design in turn influenced the Italian architectural forms of the early Renaissance through Venetian and Genovese traders. See also **Greek landscape architecture, Medieval landscape architecture, Roman landscape architecture, Turkish landscape architecture.**

C

Cabinet An open space in the forest of a French formal garden. A small **Pergola,** q.v., in a garden.

Cadastral (map) A boundary or ownership map. Pertaining to a boundary or land ownership, as in cadastral map, cadastral survey.

CADD Acronym for Computer Aided (Assisted) Design and Drafting, a growing factor in landscape architectural plan production.

Cadmium coating (for steel members) See **Metal coating.**

Caducous In plants, early **Deciduous,** q.v. See also **Fugacious.**

Cairn Traditionally, a pile of memorial stones in a graveyard or elsewhere.

Caisson A **Cofferdam,** q.v.

Cal. See **Caliper.**

Calcareous soil Any soil which is highly alkaline due to a high concentration of calcium carbonate.

Calcium A common soil mineral and macronutrient, necessary in large quantities for plant and animal use. See also **Macronutrient, Soil minerals.**

Calcium carbonate A compound that is principally found in limestone, marble, chalk, coral, and many animal exoskeletons. It is readily dissolved and reappears as a deposit after the water bearing it has evaporated. Often occurring in caves.

Calcium chloride A chemical preparation used for dust control in relatively humid climates and for ice control on paths and roads.

Calendar day In construction specifications, a day allowed to a contractor for the completion of a project. Calendar days are sequential, and include Saturdays, Sundays, and holidays in the total amount of time allowed for the completion of a project. See also **Contract time** and **Weather working day.**

Calendar, garden See **Garden calendar.**

Caliche Crusted calcium carbonate, a kind of desert soil formed by calcite (or other soluble mineral crystallization) near the surface. A hardpan soil. See also **Hardpan.**

California garden (modern garden) A distinctive garden type developed in the United States in the 1930s, principally by **Thomas Church,** q.v. The California garden is suited to a moderate Mediterranean climate, and features outdoor "rooms," low maintenance, high livability, and, often, the use of local or native plants. The traditional courtyard landscapes of the Mediterranean basin are an influence, as is the Cubism of the early twentieth century.

Classic Japanese landscape architecture has also had an effect on the development of eclectic (posed, counterposed, offset, irregular) line in the California garden. The style emphasizes urban and suburban backyard living. Church's Donnell garden ("El Novillero") is a recognized masterpiece. In addition, Garrett Eckbo's work has generated many good examples of the style. **Lawrence Halprin,** q.v., Robert Royston, Theodore Osmundson, Courtland Paul, Douglas Baylis, and others have developed and contributed to the California garden, and it has been popularized by countless articles in *Sunset* magazine and other publications. See also **Eckbo, Garrett.**

Caliper In horticulture, a measurement of the diameter of a tree trunk taken at 6 inches (15 cm) above groundline for trees up to 4 inches (10 cm) in diameter and at 12 inches (30 cm) in diameter for larger trees. In forestry, caliper is commonly measured at 4¹/₂ feet (1.35 m) above groundline.

Callous In plants, hard and scruffy in texture.

Callus A tree scar, or any hard, swollen area on the trunk or limb surface.

Calyx The outer, leafy part of a flower consisting of individual (normally green) **Sepals,** q.v. See also **Corolla, Perianth.**

Camber In landscape construction, a bridge crown or the waterflow line in a pipe.

Cambium In woody trees and shrubs, the layer of tissue lying between the bark and the sapwood through which sap flows. Generative tissue.

Cam-driven head (sprinkler) In irrigation, a rotary head with a smoothly spinning nozzle driven by a cam. The cam is mounted directly over a rotor operated by water pressure. See also **Rotary head.**

Camel back hill Any hill with two knobs or peaks at its crest.

Camp A temporary living place constructed in a rural area, usually with a shelter, cooking facilities, and nearby water. The oldest sort of human settlement. A formal camping area used repeatedly by different groups of people is a campground, often furnished with quite sophisticated conveniences.

Campagna (Italian) Countryside. Also, a prairie or series of open fields.

Campanulate In plant (particularly flower) structures, bell-like.

Campo (old-fashioned, slang) Playfield.

Canadian landscape architecture. Robson Square, Vancouver, British Columbia. Arthur Erickson, architect; Cornelia Oberlander, landscape architect. Photo by author.

Campo(s) (Spanish, Portuguese) See **Savanna.**

Campus School grounds, or the grounds of a commercial establishment or other (nonschool) public institution. Originally, a parade or army drill ground.

Can, gallon See **Container plant.**

Canadian landscape architecture
 Canada's earliest landscapes are, of course, French. The French *place publique* is represented by the Place Royale in Basseville and the Place d'Armes in Hauteville, seventeenth-century Quebec. The church and monastic courtyard, or **Parvis,** was used to produce medical herbs, vegetables, and flowers. The Ursuline Convent (1642) in Quebec City still has its parvis, and the garden of the Sulpician Fathers in Montreal (probably mid-1600s), with its fountain, long reflecting pool, and **Casino** (summerhouse)—though neglected at present—is one of the oldest European gardens in North America. These French landscapes, following the style of the day, were quite formal, though much reduced in scale from their metropolitan counterparts.
 English landscape architecture in Canada in the eighteenth century

also followed the style of the late Renaissance and the naturalistic schools of the mother country. But the nineteenth century saw great changes and growth in Canadian landscape design. Public gardens for Halifax, Nova Scotia, were first proposed in 1836; they were to be a combination of pleasure ground and botanical garden. They were reorganized and expanded in 1872 by Richard Power, an immigrant who had worked for **Joseph Paxton,** q.v., in Ireland before coming to Canada in 1864. Power's design in typically Victorian fashion made use of an ornate bandstand and a huge number of planted species in beds. (The gardens bear a striking resemblance to their contemporary, the Government Gardens in Rotorua, New Zealand. See **New Zealand landscape architecture**.)

The grounds of Dundurn Castle, Sir Allan MacNab's estate in Hamilton, Ontario, date from 1833. Robert C. Wetherell (d. 1845), MacNab's architect, laid out the gardens near the house in a picturesque style. After Wetherell's death, the Scottish landscape gardener George Laing (1808–71) modified Dundurn extensively. Landscape gardening as a profession dates from about 1850 in Ontario and elsewhere in eastern Canada, with William Mundie (d. 1858) and Laing both establishing themselves in practice in Hamilton.

Many of Canada's greatest parks came into being in the second half of the nineteenth century. The U.S. landscape architect **Frederick Law Olmsted,** q.v., designed Mount Royal Park in Montreal in 1873. His sometime partner, **Calvert Vaux,** q.v., laid out the Parliamentary grounds in Ottawa the same year. Later Montreal public gardens, including the Parc Lafontaine (1888), were patterned on Olmsted's rich naturalism. Stanley Park in Vancouver was set aside by

legislative action in 1886. Its half-wild, half-sophisticated plan became the model for such later Vancouver parks as the Marine Drive Foreshore Park and Vanier Park. Quebec's Parc Jeanne d'Arc was laid out in formal French baroque style with parterres and bedding plants. The elegant public squares of the Place de l'Hotel-de-Ville, in Quebec, and the Place Victoria, in Montreal, also date from the nineteenth century.

The Canadian national parks movement roughly parallels the rise of national parks in the United States. Banff, the first national park, was created in 1886 through the efforts of William Pearce, a surveyor and engineer, and others. Pearce, an early environmentalist, was also instrumental in the planning and civic development of Calgary, Alberta. He managed his own estate of experimental plantings on the Bow River near Calgary and urged the fledgling city government to reserve parklands and to properly develop its public open space.

New town planning in Canada dates from 1854, when the "garden suburb" of Rosedale was constructed in Toronto. Other Toronto suburbs, including Wychwood Park (1888) and Kingsway (1912) followed. The Royal Botanical Gardens in Hamilton, Ontario, and other arboretums also date from the nineteenth century. Montreal's Jardin Botanique has developed one of the world's most extensive collections in the twentieth century, with over 20,000 species. It was founded in the 1930s by Fr. Marie-Victoria, author of *Laurentian Flora.* Butchart Gardens in Victoria, B.C. (1912), is perhaps the country's best Edwardian landscape garden, built on the site of an earlier stone quarry. Suitable plant species and landscape designs for nineteenth-century Canada were popularized by a pair of books, *The Beauties of Nature Combine with Art* by H. A.

Engelhardt, and the *Canadian Fruit, Flower, and Kitchen Gardener* by D. W. Beadle, both published in 1872. These volumes dealt with romantic naturalism as a landscape style and with the practical gardening experiences of early settlers in eastern Canada.

Thomas Mawson (d. 1933) and **Frederick G. Todd** (d. 1948), q.q.v., were the most influential landscape architects of the first half of the twentieth century. Mawson, an Englishman, had offices in Britain and British Columbia. An accomplished writer and speaker, his design was a good Victorian mixture of formal and informal line. He produced a great deal of work in the booming prairie provinces. His plans for the cities of Calgary and Regina featured integrated, green, open space, herbaceous borders near important buildings, and the use of hardy native plants. Mawson also completed master plans for the Universities of Calgary and Saskatchewan and for the city of Banff. Todd, born in New Hampshire, came to Canada about 1899 to supervise the construction of Mount Royal Park while working with the Olmsted office. Todd subsequently established an office in Montreal. Mount Royal, a Montreal suburb, was one of several "garden cities" or suburbs designed by Todd for the Canadian Pacific Railroad and other clients. Todd was the first landscape architect retained by the City of Regina, Saskatchewan, to design its Wascana Centre, a government-business-recreational area along the impounded Wascana River. His original plans, an effort to relieve the unrelenting flatness of the prairies, were later modified by Mawson, and the entire scheme was finished after two large construction efforts in the 1930s and the 1960s. Trees, a notorious rarity in the provincial landscapes of the early 1900s, were an essential element of

Todd's scheme for Wascana. The Wascana landscape, also encouraged by Malcolm Ross, the landscape architect for the province of Saskatchewan, influenced the grounds of the University of Saskatchewan at Saskatoon and numerous other northern prairie landscapes. Elsewhere in Canada, Todd was responsible for such diverse projects as Trinity College in Toronto and the restoration of the Ile d' Ste. Helene in the St. Lawrence River. His last work was a hillside garden, the Way of the Cross, for St. Joseph's Oratory in Montreal.

Rickson Outhet, a Montreal contemporary of Todd and Mawson, also practiced prairie landscape architecture. His Tuxedo Park in Winnipeg (c. 1900) was a garden suburb designed in the City Beautiful manner. The Scottish golf course architect Stanley Thompson began practice in Toronto in 1922. Later a partner of Robert Trent Jones (see **Golf course architecture**), Thompson designed, among others, the spectacular courses at Banff and Jasper.

The Canadian Society of Landscape Architects (CSLA) was founded in 1934. The Society has helped to establish comprehensive courses in landscape architecture at the Universities of Toronto, Guelph, Montreal, and elsewhere. The curriculum in Montreal is offered in French, unique in North America. In the late twentieth century, the Canadians have begun a serious effort to recognize and preserve historic landscapes. The Motherwell Homestead National Historic Park in Saskatchewan, dating from about 1882, is a recently restored example of a self-sufficient prairie farm with food and ornamental gardens. In the 1970s and 1980s, the province of Quebec conducted a survey of building types in the countryside to help determine the cultural patterns of the province. Edmonton's Capital City Recreation Park, a restoration and enhancement project along the North Saskatchewan River designed by Roman Fodchuk and others, was a cooperative effort between provincial and city governments. The landscape historians Sue Donaldson and Pleasance Crawford started a comprehensive study of historic Canadian landscapes in the early 1980s.

The Law Courts in Vancouver (Robson Square) are perhaps Canada's most sophisticated contemporary landscape. This polished urban design project, combining buildings, gardens, plants, and water in an effortless flow, was a product of the architect Arthur Erickson and the landscape architect Cornelia Oberlander in the 1970s.

Canadian Society of Landscape Architects (CSLA)   Founded in Toronto in 1934 and originally the Canadian Society of Landscape Architects and Town Planners.

Canadian Zone   See **Life zone.**

Canal   A large ditch constructed for improved drainage through an area or, formerly, for large-scale transportation of goods.

Canal garden   A medieval garden "pathway" consisting of a small canal extending from a house (castle) to an outbuilding (lodge) along a clear sightline.

Canaliculate   In plant structures, grooved lengthwise. See also **Fluted.**

Cancellate   In plant structures, cross-hatched.

Cane   1) The hollow, sectioned stems of bamboo, sugar cane, or similar plants. 2) Any slender plant stem of approximately walking-stick length.

Canebrake   See **Brake.**

Canephorus (canephora)   In classical and Italian Renaissance gardens, a statue with an urn, bowl, or basket on its head. Plural: canephori.

Canescent   In plants, pubescent and gray; displaying a dense covering of fine gray hairs. *Chrysothamnus spp.* are an example.

Canopy   In gardens or parks, an overhanging, roof-like frame structure or mass of shading limbs and foliage.

Cantilever footing   An offset, usually asymmetrically balanced footing supporting a tie beam.

Cantilever wall   A kind of **Retaining wall,** q.v., utilizing an extensive footing on its uphill side, with a heavy soil mass to insure its stability.

Cantilevered beam   See **Beam.**

Canyon   A deep, steep-sided valley with vertical and usually stony slopes. Commonly found in arid areas.

Cap   In landscape irrigation, a screw-on cover which keeps soil and debris from entering a watering system. Installed at the end of a riser or on a main, lateral, or service line.

Capacity, bearing (in soils)
   See **Bearing capacity.**

Capacity, buffer (of soil)
   See **Buffer capacity of soil.**

Capacity, carrying (of land)
   See **Carrying capacity.**

Capacity, field (irrigation)
   See **Field capacity.**

Capacity, invasion (of plants)
   See **Invasion capacity.**

Capacity (of a stream or river)
See **Stream capacity.**

Capillarity In soils, the rising of water vertically or obliquely above its underground source. Capillary action is normally good in silty soils and poor if the soil is dry. See also **Liquid limit** and **Permeability.**

Capillary In plants, hairlike in form.

Capillary action A force causing liquid to rise against a vertical surface or series of surfaces. Sap flow is a capillary action. See also **Capillarity.**

Capillary fringe In soils, the stratum or portion of stratum just above a water-saturated soil layer. It is kept very damp by capillary action. See also **Capillarity.**

Capillary porosity All the interstices or tiny voids found between soil particles affecting the amount of water available for plant use.

Capillary (available) water A thick film of water found around soil particles; a kind of **Pellicular water,** q.v. The surface tension of capillary water is greater than the pull of gravity. Most capillary and gravitational water is available to plants. See also **Capillarity** and **Hygroscopic water.**

Capillary wave A tiny wave, generally less than one inch (about 2.5 cm) in height. The limited movement of capillary waves is a function of the surface tension of the body of water in which the waves are generated.

Capitate Pertaining to structures in the tip or "head" of a plant.

Capsule A dry fruit that usually splits open at maturity. See also **Dehiscence, Valve.**

Captive contractor An "in-house" contractor. In landscape construction, a contractor retained by a developer or owner on a long-term basis to execute a firm's projects.

Car park A parking lot.

Carbohydrate A food and structural product of photosynthesis, consisting of sugars, starches, and cellulose.

Carbon The basic "building block" element of almost all plant and animal life. Carbon combines with oxygen and hydrogen in multiple forms that are present in and necessary to the functions of life.

Carbon cycle The biological system involving the ingestion of carbon into plants by photosynthesis, its subsequent use in the life processes of plants and the animals that consume them, and its return to the inanimate world through the decomposition of feces and urine and bodily decay. See also **Nitrogen cycle, Oxygen cycle.**

Carbon dioxide (CO_2) A common gas nevertheless found in minute ($\pm$ .03%) though growing amounts in the atmosphere. Carbon dioxide is utilized by plants in photosynthesis, a by-product of which is oxygen. Animals expire CO_2 as a waste product of their metabolism. Because of increased fossil fuel use in the twentieth century, atmospheric carbon dioxide is increasing. As the gas is capable of absorbing heat (infrared radiation) from sunlight, the atmosphere is slowly warming, thus raising the possibility, in the long-term, of the melting of polar ice and other drastic climatic changes.

Carbonate of calcium See **Calcium carbonate.**

Cardinal points (of the compass) The four principal directions of north, south, east, and west.

Carinate (carinata) In plant structures, with a keel. Keeled.

Carotene Orange-yellow plant pigment. See also **Plant pigments.**

Carotenoid See **Plant pigments.**

Carpel In flowers, the female reproductive organ. A single **Pistil,** q.v. Carpels collectively form a **Gynoecium,** q.v. See also **Stamen.**

Carpenter's work Renaissance trellises, arbors, and other garden woodwork.

Carpet bedding A type of Victorian bedding planting of low foliage plants or annuals in patterns similar to those found in carpet design. Also **Massed bedding, Mosaiculture.** See also **Bedding plants.**

Carport A shelter for automobiles that is exposed on three or more sides. The coining of the term is frequently attributed to Frank Lloyd Wright.

Carriage bolt A strong metal pin often used to secure two or more wood members in modern landscape construction. Originally used to fasten components of carriages or buggies.

Carrying capacity (of land) The amount of plant and animal life, agricultural or industrial production, or other activities or constructs that can be absorbed and sustained by an area of land without gross injury to its condition.

Cart, concrete See **Buggy.**

Cartography Map-making.

Caruncle A kind of hardened, protruding aril or seed coat.

Caryatid A sculpted, lyrical woman's figure used as part of an upright architectural member.

Caryopsis In plants, a kind of specialized, dry nonopening fruit with its seed grown fast to the seed coat. See also **Indehiscence.**

Cascade A small-scale waterfall or series of rushing falls.

Case, Wardian See **Terrarium.**

Cash allowance In a contractor's bid, an amount specifically set aside for an item of construction dealing with unforeseen circumstances, hidden obstructions, and the like.

Cash crops Farm produce cultivated for sale and not subsistence. See also **Subsistence crops.**

Casino In Renaissance Italy, a garden house used for social functions; a **Pavilion.** Also, a modest country house.

Cast-in-place concrete Concrete that is placed in forms at the site of a project. Also **CIP concrete.** See also **Precast concrete.**

Cast iron pipe A common kind of iron pipe sometimes used in sewer, irrigation, and other landscape construction. Formerly, often used in municipal water mains. Often abbreviated **CIP.**

Castrorum A Roman legion camp, square and gridiron in form, influential in town layout and planning in late Classical times and thereafter.

Catabolism A metabolic process involving the breakdown of large compounds by plants and animals resulting in a release of energy. See also **Anabolism, Metabolism.**

Cataract A large, often high, thundering waterfall.

Catch basin (CB) 1) An underground chamber constructed to collect suspended sediment in runoff water and then direct the cleared water into a conduit or storm sewer. Abbreviated CB on surveys or plans. 2) In general, any small cavity excavated below grade level to receive drainage water. See also **Manhole, Drop inlet.**

Catch crop In gardens, a quick crop grown at the side of one more slowly maturing. See also **Intercrop.**

Catchment basin See **Watershed.**

Catkin In deciduous plants, a drooping cluster of flowers resembling a segment of cat's tail in form, and typical of trees such as alder, willow, birch, and the like. Also **Ament.**

Caudate In plant structures, tail-like.

Caudex The point at the root crown of a plant at which the stem and roots join. Also, the base of a trunk or stem.

Caulescent In botany, exhibiting a definite, often leafy stem above the soil surface. See also **Acaulescent.**

Cauline (botanical) Stemmed, carried on a stem, or pertaining to a stem.

Caus, Isaac de See **Tudor garden.**

Caus, Salomon de (also **Solomon de Caux**) Designer, in the early seventeenth century, of the palatial gardens at Heidelburg (subsequently destroyed), an excellent example in Germany of Renaissance formalism. Relative of Isaac de Caus, designer of the formal gardens at Wilton in Wiltshire, England. See also **German landscape architecture.**

Causeway A raised-up walkway normally developed to provide access from a mainland shore to an island.

Cautley, Marjorie Sewell
Twentieth-century U.S. landscape architect, responsible for landscape planning at Radburn, New Jersey, with the architects Clarence Stein and Henry Wright. Cautley also followed Utopian (**Garden city,** q.v.) principles of design at Sunnyside Gardens, Queens, New York (c. 1928). See also **United States landscape architecture.**

Cavitation Pitting, gouging. 1) In irrigation pumps, overwhelming suction or low pressure at the pump intake can cause vapor pockets that in turn become exploding bubbles as water is pumped. The charged water from the bursting air pockets can pit or gouge the pump's impeller vanes. The process is cavitation. 2) In dams, lined channels, and other structures, excessive water speed or volume coupled with suspended particles can cause cavitation or pitting.

CB See **Catch basin.**

CBD Central business district; usually, a city's downtown.

C/C or CC An abbreviation for **Center to Center,** i.e., from the central point of one object to that of the next. A plan notation. See also **On center (OC).**

Cedar A common, tight-grained, outdoor building wood, durable and even-weathering.

Cemetery design. New Orleans,
Louisiana. Photo by author.

Cedar shake Split center timber,
useful in fencing or as shingles.

Ceilings in landscape A design
term designating an overhead cover
of tree branches, wooden or metal
framing, vines, or the sky itself.

Cellulose The essential component
of all plant tissues and fibers. A
white carbohydrate substance. See
also **Lignin.**

Cement 1) A powdered substance,
often calcined rock and clay, that
becomes an adhesive matrix when
mixed with water. A key element,
along with fine and coarse

aggregates, of concrete. 2) Asphaltic
and Portland cement mixtures are the
most common binders used in
landscape construction. However,
Lutes, q.v., which are elastic kinds
of cement and adhesive, have
specialized construction application.

Cement asbestos pipe
See **Asbestos cement pipe.**

Cement, asphalt See **Asphalt
cement.**

Cement, block See **Concrete
masonry unit.**

Cement, masonry See **Masonry
cement.**

Cement, neat See **Neat cement.**

Cement, soil See **Soil cement.**

Cemetery design Modern cemetery
design begins with **J. C. Loudon**
(1783–1843), q.v., and his studies
of graveyards and suggestions for
their wider social use as parks.
Loudon's pattern was early
duplicated in the United States by
Joseph Bigelow at the Mount Auburn
Cemetery, Cambridge, Massachusetts
(1830s).

   Victorian graveyards were
characterized by upright tombstones,
crypts, cast-iron fencing, and heavy
evergreen plantings.

   In the twentieth century,
graveyards are often located away

from churches and synagogues, feature flat monuments and fewer crypts, and, frequently, a more open planting. These design changes perhaps emphasize ease in lawn mowing as well as evolving social and religious taste.

Modern graveyards also suffer from euphemistic naming, as they are often places in which people "come home to rest" in a "memory garden."

Cenotaph   A tomb without a body; often, a tomblike monument erected to an absent hero.

Center to center (plan notation)
See **C/C.**

Center, shopping   See **Shopping center.**

Centerline   1) In surveying, a north-south or east-west line used to divide a section into quarters, a quarter into eighths, and the like. 2) In landscape construction, the center or midpoint of a post, fenceline, sidewalk, or other feature, often indicated on plans and in details as ₵. See also **Eighthline, Quarterline.**

Central Asian landscape architecture
It was in Central Asia, in the Middle Ages, that the classic formal landscape tradition of Islam met equally refined Chinese naturalism. Invading Muslim armies fought the Chinese at the Battle of the Talas River (c. 751 A.D.), and subsequent mingling of the two cultures produced, among other results, the remarkable gardens of Samarqand, in modern-day Soviet Turkestan, and of Kabul and Herat in Afghanistan.

Mongolia and China, unified in the early thirteenth century, began to trade as far afield as the Mediterranean. Chinese landscape paintings became known in the West after the time of Marco Polo (c. 1295 A.D.). In the Afghanistan of the thirteenth and fourteenth centuries, garden paintings were rendered in the Chinese informal style, but their descriptive notes or poems were in Arabic/Persian script. The gardens themselves were somewhat compact, with understated fountains and typical Central Asian plants: poplars, willows, cypresses, and stone fruits. Other specialty plants included roses, nut trees, and bulbs. Chinese design elements began to appear in Persia itself after the thirteenth century.

Samarqand was Tamerlane's capital. In the second half of the fourteenth century, he began to create garden parks in the city in emulation of the great Genghis Khan, his traditional ancestor. The large-scale Garden of Eram and the Plane Tree Garden were probably the best of these.

Tamerlane's successor Hussein Bayqara developed several notable gardens in Herat, Afghanistan. And in the early sixteenth century, King Babur built the Bagh-i-vasa in Kabul, a garden around a square water tank. Babur, a lover of the traditional, geometric Islamic garden form, carried the Central Asian garden with him to India when he invaded that country in the early sixteenth century. Babur subsequently became the first of the Indian Mogul emperors.

See also **Chinese landscape architecture, Indian landscape architecture, Islamic landscape architecture, Persian landscape architecture, Russian landscape architecture.**

Central business district (CBD)
A **Downtown.**

Central (I) and deflection (Δ) angle (road curves)   In road layout, the angle created by the two curve radius lines striking the PC (point of curvature) and PT (point of tangency). It is equal to Δ, or the angle of deflection, found at the PI (point of intersection) of the tangents of the curve.

Central pivot (center pivot) irrigation
In agriculture, a mechanical irrigation arm on wheels or skids that sprinkles a circular field from a central radius pivot. Common in the western United States.

Centrifugal direction (city planning)
A factor such as growth that indicates a flow or focus away from a downtown or other urban center.

Centrifugal pump (irrigation)
See **Booster pump.**

Centroid   In the geometry of landscape-plan layout, the center of gravity. A focal or starting point.

du Cerceau, Jacques Androuet (c. 1510–84)   French Renaissance architect and author of *Les Plus Excellents Bastiments de France* (1576 and 1579). In the *Bastiments,* the French garden is clearly emerging from the tight geometric enclosures of the Middle Ages into the open vistas and broader scale of the Renaissance. At the estate of Gaillon, an elaborate knot garden and water garden are the backbone of an extensive landscape. At Montargis, an elegant arcade of **Carpenter's work,** q.v., dominates the garden. Du Cerceau's book shows the clear influence of the Italian villa on the new French landscapes of the day, but the extent of his own design work is unclear. See also **French landscape architecture.**

Cereal   A flowering grass or member of the Graminae family, the seeds of which are harvested for human or animal consumption. Corn (maize), wheat, rye, rice, oats, millet, barley, and the like are examples. Cereals are an overwhelmingly important source of human food.

Certificate of compliance A notice of approval and conformity to regulation obtained from a governmental agency by a contractor during the course of project construction.

Certificate for payment See **Pay request.**

Certificate of survey A certificate prepared by a surveyor containing a legal description of a piece of property, the drafted survey results, and a verification of metes and bounds, topographical information gathered, and the like.

Certification, landscape architectural See **Landscape architectural registration.**

Certified seed See **Commercial seed classification.**

Cespitose (caespitose) In plants, tufted.

CF Curb face.

CFS Cubic feet per second, a measure of the volume of water in motion through a pipe or natural or man-made channel. See also **CPM, Discharge rate.**

Chabutra In Indian (Mogul) Gardens, a pavilion or garden house. In Persian gardens, often a small raised area.

Chadar In Indian (Mogul) Gardens, a water stair.

Chaff A thin dry plant scale or bract.

Chahar-bagh (Persian) In classic Persian and later gardens (up to the sixteenth century A.D.), a formal garden divided into four parts by cross-axial water channels. See also **Persian landscape architecture.**

Chain 1) An old English measurement equal to 66 feet, with 80 chains equaling 1 mile. 2) To measure distance by means of a chain of set length (obsolescent).

Chain, food See **Food chain.**

Chainlink fence A widely used metal fence made of a heavy interwoven mesh and such other standardized components as top and bottom rails, cross-braces, and the like.

Chalk A form of soft, white limestone.

Chalky soil An alkaline soil overlaying a chalk bed, often poor for growing cultivated plants until amended adequately.

Chambers, Sir William (1726–96) English architect and critic, born in Sweden, popularizer of **Chinoiserie,** q.v. Chambers designed the Chinese pavilion at Kew Gardens and wrote *A Dissertation on Oriental Gardening* (1772). His attacks on the landscape gardening style of **Capability Brown,** q.v., and others were perhaps motivated by jealousy: Brown had replaced Chambers as architect at Claremont estate shortly before the publication of the *Dissertation.* Chambers also wrote *Views of the Gardens and Buildings of Kew* (1763). See also **English landscape architecture.**

Chamfer A 45° or other cut-off edge of stone, concrete, wood, or other material. $3/4$ or 1 in. chamfers are widely used. See also **Arris.**

Chahar-bagh

Change, eustatic   See **Eustatic change.**

Change order   A written notice to a contractor after a contract for construction has been signed authorizing a change in a specific item of work, the scope of work, or an alteration in the amount of the contract or the time needed for its completion. See also **Field order.**

Chaniwa   A Japanese tea garden.

Channel   In landscape design, a stream bed or drainage course.

Channel, braided   See **Braided channel.**

Channel drainage   A flow of water as a concentrated mass in a gully, swale, brook or river. See also **Drainage** and **Sheet drainage.**

Channery (collective)   Flat plates of sandstone, schist, or similar stone.

Chaparral   A dense, shrubby, often evergreeen plant cover found in hilly areas with mild, temeprate (Mediterranean) climates. The Southern California chaparral is typical. Also **Macchia** (Italian), **Maquis** (French).

Character plant   See **Specimen.**

Charette or **Charrette**   A "marathon" or intensive design and drafting of a project by an individual or group, from the French **charette** or cart. In nineteenth-century France, the Beaux Arts school of design often required students' renderings (paintings) of an assignment to be completed on a rigid, abbreviated time schedule. A **charette,** or small cart, was sent around at the appointed hour to collect the finished work.

Check dam

Charmille   A formal French clipped hedge of hornbeams or other trees, dating from the seventeenth century.

Chart   A map, graph, diagram, or plan.

Chart, synoptic   See **Weather chart.**

Chart, weather   See **Weather chart.**

Chartaceous   In plant structures, papery or parchment-like.

Chase   A hunting ground or broad expanse of unfenced parkland.

Chase line (irrigation)   See **Sleeve.**

Cha-seki, cha-niwa (Japanese)   See **Tea garden.**

Chateau (French)   A country estate or castle.

Chattels   Personal or moveable property, as opposed to **Real property,** q.v.

Check boring   A boring made to determine soil or strata characteristics contributing to instability or other soil problems.

Check dam   A limited obstruction in a small watercourse made of any of several materials and intended to retard flow and divert water for agricultural purposes. Check dams may also decrease erosion damage from quick runoff or improve streams for fishing by creating pools. Also **Brush dam, Debris dam, Log dam, Loose rock dam, Masonry** or **Concrete dam, Woven wire dam.**

Check valve   In irrigation, an automatically controlled valve allowing water to pass through a line in a single direction only. The check valve is a kind of directional-control valve. Also **Back pressure valve, Reflux valve.** See also **Double-check valve, Reduced pressure backflow preventer, Valve,** and **Vacuum breaker.**

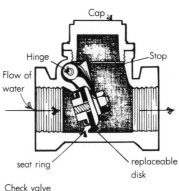

Check valve

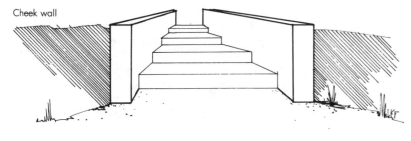

Cheek wall

Checkerboard sodding   See **Sod.**

Cheek wall   In landscape construction, a wall built alongside a series of steps to retain abutting earth. See also **Wing wall.**

Cheesecloth   A rather coarse cotton gauze used in temporary slope retention or as an insulating soil sheet.

Chelate of iron   See **Iron chelate.**

Chemical fertilizer   An intense fertilizer containing large concentrations of nitrogen, phosphorus, and/or potassium (NPK), trace elements, and inert filler. It is applied to a piece of ground to temporarily improve its productivity. Unlike **Organic fertilizer,** q.v., chemical fertilizers do not increase or augment the genuine quality of the soil or aid in drainage or water retention. They are principally derived from petroleum. Also **Artificial manure.** See also **Complete fertilizer, Fertilizer.**

Chemical gardening   In landscape irrigation, the direct addition of NPK or other nutrients to a water system for delivery to plants.

Chemotaxis   Chemical stimulation in plants. Often synonymous with **Chemotropism,** q.v.

Chemotropism   The tendency of a plant to respond to (usually) internal chemical stimuli. Often synonymous with **Chemotaxis,** q.v. See also **Geotropism, Haptotropism, Hydrotropism, Phototropism, Tropism.**

Chemier (French)   Sands laid down on top of the deposits of a river at its (usually swampy) delta.

Chernozem (Russian) soil   See **Black earth.**

Cherry-picker   A small A-frame crane with cable, winch, and hook frequently used in landscape construction.

Chestnut soil   See **Brown earth.**

Chiaroscuro (Italian)   Deep shade and strong, contrasting light in paintings, design, or finished landscape architectural product.

Children's Climber   A play structure, often of wood or wood and metal, provided for children's enjoyment and for the development of youthful muscles and coordination.

Chimaera (Chimera)   In botany, a growth of mutant tissues or of graft tissues on a plant at the point of joining of graft (shoot) and stock, composed of cells from both plants. Chimaeras are indicated by an addition sign before the generic name or following the botanical name of one donor and that of the second. See also **Hybrid, Sport.**

Chinampa   A floating garden common in the Valley of Mexico (Lake Texcoco and elsewhere) from the sixteenth century to the present. The Floating Gardens of Xochimilco are chinampas. See also **Mexican landscape architecture.**

Chinese landscape architecture   One of the world's great landscape architectures, developed over the course of thousands of

Children's climber

years in China's cities and in the rural gardens of the well-to-do. The Chinese prize the althea (*Hibiscus spp.*, one of which may be a legendary tree of immortality), the peach, and the orchid in their gardens. They have cultivated the chrysanthemum since at least the fifth century B.C. Plants with high symbolism, such as the plum, the pine, and the bamboo, emerge in ancient scrollwork. The Chinese thought the tree peony the most perfect and beautiful of all flowers.

Chinese gardens are noted for their meticulous and often decorative informality, and for their unparalleled continuity. They typically make use of reflecting pools, bridges, carefully selected trees and shrubs, pavilions, and marvelous, grotesque stones. Since Ming dynasty times (c. 1368–1644 A.D.), the finest stones have come from Lake Tai near Wuxi and Suzhou (west of Shanghai). The peculiar wave and current action of the lake has produced furrowed and hollowed-out boulders of much value to the Chinese. Often stones were placed in the lake to be retrieved by future generations of would-be rock users after time and the waves had suitably ground them into shape. The garden with the most famous rocks is perhaps the Lion Grove in Suzhou. It contains lion-like stones laid out in the courtyard of the monk Wei Zu about the year 1342 A.D.

One of the best known gardens of Chinese antiquity is the tomb of Confucius (c. 479 B.C.), in Shandong Province. Descriptions tell us that it was placed in a sacred grove and that its features were formal. Bamboo and pine were probably favorite garden plants of the time, as they were in later Chinese gardens.

In all Chinese landscapes, cut stone for building construction was often reserved for temples or royal structures; wood and screens were universal in most common buildings,

Chinese landscape architecture. Zigzag bridge in Suzhou. Photo courtesy BBMSL, UNM.

and they were mostly used in formal, symmetrical compositions. Enclosed gardens stood around them as counterpoints.

Early Chinese emperors began the tradition of immense imperial gardens, developed from earlier hunting parks and often taking dozens of years to build. The Zhou (Chou) dynasty King Wen built a pleasure garden for himself in the tenth century B.C. at his capital in Shaanxi province. Wen's garden contained terraces, fish pools, and a zoo. The Qin dynasty emperor Qin Shi Huangdi created an enormous hunting and pleasure garden with pavilions and exotic animals and plants on the Fan Chuan River (c. 210 B.C.). The emperor's garden, the Shang-lin Park, reputedly contained nearly 25 miles of covered passageways linking the garden pavilions. The Han dynasty, following the Qin about 207 B.C., praised the Shang-lin and continued its opulent example.

Sacred stone tortoises, which were common garden features and a persistent theme in Chinese landscapes, made their first appearance in the Han period. The first Han emperor, Han Gao Zu (r. 206–195 B.C.), established Confucian ethics and logic as the basis of the Chinese state. Confucius (about 550–479 B.C.) had suggested that agriculture should be the foundation of Chinese prosperity. Confucian simplicity and clarity were complemented by Taoism, mystical and intent on the connection between

Chinese landscape architecture.
Great stones in Shih-tzu Lin (the
Lion's Grove), temple grounds,
Suzhou, A.D. 1342. Photo courtesy
BBMSL, UNM.

essential garden construction elements of Wu's time, based on a knowledge of hydrology, transplanting and horticulture, pavilion layout and construction, and the creation of artificial mountains, were to become constants in Chinese garden design.

Buddhism, first entering China from India c. 58 A.D., began to influence the Chinese garden tradition in the fifth century A.D. Monastery gardens, richly furnished with ponds, flowers, selected trees, and intricate rockwork, added the rich landscape of the temple courtyard to the private royal garden heritage of China. The luxurious personal garden became, along with the contemplative, scholarly garden, one of the great subjects of Chinese landscape design. The Emperor Sui Yang di (r. 604–618), built a landscape park of some 75 miles in circumference in his capital, Loyang. Poetry, garden design, and landscape painting, as well as calligraphy, came to be complementary arts in China.

The Emperor Huizong (r. 1101–25) of the later Song dynasty (c. 960–1279) was among the greatest of Chinese outdoor painters, creating delicate scenes of birds, leaves, and flowers—and of garden visitors working on lines of poetry. Huizong was also a garden builder and rock collector of the first magnitude (see **Petromania**), constructing an enormous artificial rockery, the Genyu, at Kaifeng, the predecessor of Peking as China's capital. No complete Song gardens survive.

The Mongols began to assemble their own landscape gardens soon after they became masters of China in the early twelfth century. Marco Polo, in the employ of Kublai Khan from 1275 to 1291, visited Hangzhou, the old capital of the southern Song much renowned for its gardens, and took descriptions of

the human spirit and the landscape. The idea of the Taoist monk in isolation contemplating the world from a misty garden on a hillside became one of the great Chinese landscape themes. Landscape designers of the day attempted to create gardens in emulation of the Chinese legend of the Mystical Islands of the Blessed (or the Immortals), featuring man-made lakes with naturalistic groves on their shores. The Emperor Wu (d. 87 B.C.), also of the Han dynasty, enlarged the Shang-lin Park until it sprawled into some five counties from its original site. Wu extracted the necessary farmland from nearby peasants, and he expected a great deal from his park: horse racing, boating, scholarly contemplation, hunting, birdwatching, and floral display. In Emperor Wu's and other Han gardens, the stony hill, soon to be a hallmark of Chinese design, first made its appearance. The

Hangzhou's West Lake with its wonderful villas, temples, and public gardens back to Europe. Polo also witnessed Kublai Khan's monumental work at Peking, where the Khan had built the city on a large, Confucian grid, with the grounds around the imperial palace in the Forbidden City remaining calmly naturalistic. Kublai had flat land to work with. He excavated lakes and built a small island with a hill in the midst of his gardens. The hill was rigged with any rare exotic plant—always green—that caught the emperor's eye, and with great masses of greenish-blue lapis lazuli stone as a rip-rap. Kublai crowned the whole effort with a green palace on its summit.

Only bits remain of the thousands of these Chinese landscapes, dating from before the Han dynasty to the Mongol (Yuan). These were brought to life by the labor of millions over thousands of years. We know most of them through contemporary accounts and paintings. But the landscapes of the Ming (1368–1644) and the Qing (1644–1912) dynasties are close enough to our own time to have survived and are in some cases nearly intact. Beihai Park in Peking contains the remnants of Kublai Khan's Sea Palace Lakes, with lakeshore villas and other improvements made by both Ming and Qing rulers. Peking's great Tiananmen Square, over 100 acres (40.5 hectares) in size, is today a public plaza with Mao Zetong's mausoleum at one end. The Summer Palace grounds outside Peking and the Temple of Heaven in the city itself are now both public parks. These large-scale landscapes have remained in continual use since their creation in Ming times. The tomb of the last rebuilder of the Great Wall, the Ming emperor Yonglo (r. 1403–24), lies northwest of Peking, with its artificial hill planted thickly in trees and the sculpture-lined road leading

to it a much-visited historic passageway. Ming garden techniques were preserved in the *Yuan Ye (Book of Garden Building)* by the late Ming landscape designer Li Jicheng.

Qing dynasty landscapes include the Garden of Perfect Brightness (the Yuan Ming Yuan), often called the last great imperial garden, constructed by the Emperor Qianlong in the mid-eighteenth century near Peking. It contained some six square miles of pavilions, lakes, streams, and plantings and was mostly destroyed by the British in 1860. A section of this great park was furnished with European garden features created by Jesuit priests in the emperor's employ.

Suzhou, the "garden city" near Shanghai, is a place of canals and modestly scaled Qing landscapes. Many of its streets are lined with Oriental plane trees. In Suzhou's private gardens, grotesque topiary, fine grillework, outdoor rooms of limited space but endless complexity, exotic plantings, honeycomb rocks, moon gates and moon gardens (especially created for their night vistas) add to its charm. Chinese landscape design is notable for its stability, not its evolution, and Suzhou still seems fixed in time. As is true in most of China, a stationary population, present in the city and the surrounding countryside for nearly endless generations, has been essential to the continuity of Suzhou's gardens. Among the finest of these are the Wang Shi Yuan (Garden of the Fishing Nets Master), the Tiger Hill Garden, and the Garden of the Humble Administrator.

Chinese garden art, primarily in the form of scroll and other painting, certainly influenced the Western landscape architecture of some two centuries ago. The concept of formal, geometric buildings in the midst of informal gardens created as abstractions of nature had few

precedents in the West. However, China's real garden triumph may have been the wholesale export of its plant species. The country has one of the great temperate zone floras in the world, and the gardener in Dubuque, Iowa cultivating his crape myrtles rarely stops to consider their origin in continental East Asia. Similarly, the Chinese had exported their garden design along with Buddhism to Japan in the seventh century A.D., profoundly altering the course of landscape architecture in that country (see **Japanese landscape architecture**).

The ideal new garden in Suzhou or Peking will still contain a pavilion with one or two people sipping wine and talking quietly. The trees lining city streets nearby will be poplars or plane trees, grown in multiple rows like crops, and the streets themselves will lack cars but churn with bicycles. The city parks, oddly grassless but filled with willows or other graceful trees, will absorb enormous numbers of people, seemingly without effort. Tai chi classes, old men playing checkers, families eating ice cream and drinking tea out of thermoses all carry on a distinct landscape tradition most unusual in history for its vitality and unparalleled long life. See also **Landscape architectural theory**.

Chinoiserie In landscape design, European interpretations of Chinese (or Japanese) form popular from the seventeenth to the nineteenth centuries. Frequently found in early English Landscape Gardening School parks. Examples include the pagoda by **Sir William Chambers,** q.v., in Kew Gardens, and the Chinese Dairy at Woburn Abbey in Bedfordshire, England. See also **Japonaiserie, Sir William Temple.**

Chipper In landscape maintenance, a machine used to make chips of branches and tree trunks. See also **Shredder.**

Chlorination Treatment of water (ornamental pools, swimming pools, and the like) with chlorine to destroy vegetation and bacteria.

Chlorinator A regulating device controlling the quantity of chlorine and its release into a swimming or other pool.

Chlorine 1) An abundant nonmetallic element necessary in small amounts for plant (and animal) growth and health. A **Trace element,** q.v., or macronutrient. 2) A chemical added to swimming pools and fountains to reduce the danger of contamination and to impede plant (algae) growth. See also **Available nutrient, Soil minerals.**

Chlorophyll The cell bodies found in green plant tissue. Chlorophyll is responsible for photosynthesis, the manufacture of food (sugars) from carbon dioxide and water by action of sunlight. Also **Pyrrol.** See also **Photosynthesis.**

Chloroplast In botany, cell structures containing chlorophyll involved in photosynthesis—the manufacture of sugar and starch by means and carbon dioxide chemically reacting with sunlight. See also **Photosynthesis.**

Chlorosis A plant disease or deficiency, common in arid regions, in which the plant loses its normal green color, its leaves turning yellow. Usually due to an inability of the plant to use iron, magnesium, or zinc in the soil because of high alkalinity.

Choker aggregate Fine particles that fill the spaces between coarse aggregate pebbles or chips.

Chord The straight line drawn between any two points on the rim of a circle. Used in establishing curves for roads and driveways.

C-horizon See **Soil Horizon.**

Chorten (Tibetan) A small two-tiered Tibetan shrine dedicated to notable lamas and located at roadsides. Used for prayer.

Chozubachi In Japanese gardening, a stone basin used to provide fresh water for tea making or other purposes. An important accessory in the tea ceremony. See also **Japanese landscape architecture.**

Christmas tree Multiple irrigation valves installed next to one another, fed by the same main.

Chromatic Of or pertaining to color or color tone.

Chromatic color Pure color, excluding black, white, and gray, which are achromatic. Dull colors (shades) have low color "value"; tints or light colors have high "value." Matte or muted color can be successfully combined in design with glosses or brilliants to produce striking landscape effects.

Chromium (chrome) coating (for steel members) See **Metal coating.**

Chuckhole An erosion-formed pit in a roadway. Also **Pothole.**

Church, Thomas D. (1902–78) Prolific (over 4,000 projects) United States landscape architect and creator of the **California** or **modern garden.** Church was educated at Harvard and the University of California at Berkeley. He began his practice in the 1930s, concentrating on gardens. His **California garden,** q.v., was strongly influenced by Cubism, but it was also eclectic: it combined a tidy (and selective) formality, native plantings, and above all the pursuit of the "outdoor room" to produce its theme. Church was a master of **Occult balance** and of the uncanny use of tone—plant materials, cleanly irregular decks, the contrast of a glossy pool—to create a garden ambience not seen before in the United States.

Church's gardens were popularized by *Sunset* magazine, which carefully noted his attention to a client's particular requests, his intense studies of site conditions, the nature of materials and local maintenance requirements, and the unusual quality of site-specific "spatial expression." His approaches to design were also laid out in his book *Gardens are for People* (1955 and 1983), and in *Your Private World* (1969).

Church helped to steer American landscape architecture away from the heavy Beaux Arts tradition of the early twentieth century. The Donnell garden, "El Novillero" (1940s), is probably his best-known work. Church took a graceful California hillside with a fine view and added a perfectly scaled, curving pool, a sculpture, a deck, and highly responsive plant materials—including native trees pruned carefully in groves—to create his masterpiece. A beach house garden at Los Aptos, California, is also especially refined and dates from the late 1940s.

Thomas Church. Garden in Los
Aptos, California, 1948. Photo
courtesy BBMSL, UNM.

Church's other designs included
larger-scale housing, hospitals,
university campuses, and additional
specialty landscapes. Heavily
honored by the ASLA and the AIA
during his lifetime, Church influenced
the work of **Lawrence Halprin,
Garrett Eckbo,** q.q.v., and others.
See also **United States landscape
architecture.**

Chute   See **Paved flume.**

CI   A common abbreviation for
Cast Iron.

Ciliate (plants)   Hairy, downy, with
eyelash-like hairs. A plant structure is
ciliolate if it bears *tiny* hairs on its
leaf or other margins.

Cinereous   In plants, ashen gray.

Cinnabarine (cinnabarina)
Vermilion; deep red.

Cinquecento   The 1500s in Italian
art. A frequent Renaissance
reference.

Cion   See **Scion.**

CIP   An abbreviation for **Cast iron
pipe,** q.v.

CIP concrete   **Cast-in-place
concrete,** q.v.

CIPP   Cast-in-place pipe.

Circadian rhythm   The biological
rhythm, or pattern of function,
occurring in plants and animals each
24 hours or so. In plants, daily
rhythm, growth, flowering, and
other functions are set by circadian
rhythm. Also **Diural rhythm.**

Circinate   In plant structures,
pertaining to a leaf that is broad at
the base, narrow at the tip, and
spiralling. Coiling in form.

Circle, traffic   See **Roundabout.**

Circuit, irrigation (sprinkler)
See **Section system.**

Circulation The pattern and flow of foot and vehicle traffic in a landscape.

Site planners may successfully organize foot traffic in formal or informal layouts that respond to the particular requirements of a site. Vehicular circulation, however, is almost inevitably formal, and its very demanding nature is the single most important factor in twentieth-century city organization. The four commonest vehicular circulation patterns are: 1) **Curvilinear:** frequently found in new suburbs in the United States, Canada, and elsewhere. Characterized by an apparently casual but unbalanced quality, and highly capable of adaptation to terrain. 2) **Grid:** a checkerboard layout of streets and blocks dating from classical times. Also typical of cities in the United States, Canada, and elsewhere in the Western world. 3) **Linear:** a street or highway simply connecting two points with or without spin-off "loop" roads. 4) **Radial:** a series of streets fanning out from (converging on) a central point. Paris and Washington, D.C. are successfully oriented radial cities. These patterns are often mixed in the same city as it grows, with differing degrees of success.

Circumneutral In soils, exhibiting a pH between 6.0 and 8.0. Near-neutrality.

Cirque A glacial depression or basin, usually located at the head of a valley or beneath a crest or peak.

Cirrhus Tendril, q.v. Also **Cirrus.**

Cistern An underground tank for holding water.

Cité An often-cited French term for city.

Citriculture Citrus fruit raising.

City A large community of human beings requiring widespread physical and economic support from its neighboring or extended countryside and exhibiting a degree of self-government.

"Civilization" is developed and largely expressed in cities. The strident demand of the typical human city for raw materials has, in the late twentieth century, placed an immense claim on the countryside for satisfaction, resulting in multiple economic, environmental, and social problems.

City Beautiful movement A popular social concern of the late nineteenth and twentieth centuries. The City Beautiful idea began with the 1893 Columbian Exposition in Chicago. It originated with the architect Daniel Burnham and was popularized by the journalist Charles Robinson. Much romanticized, Cities Beautiful were laid out in a formal, Beaux Arts, semi-Garden City pattern, with Versailles rather than Central Park as a model. Burnham's redesigns for San Francisco, the Chicago Lakefront (loops, park systems, greenways, transportation), and multiple state capitol grounds are examples. The City Beautiful movement preceded the civic beautification efforts typical of the late twentieth century, as well as the attempts to "develop downtown" that are still quite popular in the United States. See also **Garden city.**

City, garden See **Garden city.**

City planning See **Planning**.

Cityscape The relatively large-scale landscape of a town or city. The overall form of a town or city.

CL See **Centerline**.

Cladding, glass (erosion control) See **Glass cladding**.

Cladophyll In botany, a plant displaying a stem that has taken over leaf function; i.e., a succulent or similar plant.

Clairvoyee Dutch Baroque garden feature. An iron grille implanted in a wall at the end of an allee of trees.

Clambering Vine or vine-like; dependent on other plants or structures for support. See also **Trailing**.

Clamp In gardens, a storage mound for root crops made of earth with straw or twigs.

CLARB The Council of Landscape Architectural Registration Boards (United States), formed in 1961 as a coordinating agency for state boards involved in licensing landscape architects to practice.

Clarification drawing A sketch or other graphic presentation of a portion of project construction documents prepared by a landscape architect as part of a change order, addendum, or other modification to the work.

Clasping Pertaining to a plant structure that wraps around all or part of a stem at its base.

Class 1) In irrigation, a normal standard given as maximum pressure of operation for pipes, fittings, and valves. Often expressed as a schedule. For example: Schedule 40

PVC. 2) In botany, a subphyllum or secondary classification of plant types. See also **Botanical classification, Schedule**.

Class of soil See **Soil class**.

Classical landscape architecture See **Greek landscape architecture, Roman landscape architecture**.

Classicism An architectural or landscape architectural style based on Greek and Roman models. Most useful as a design reference during the Renaissance. The **Adonis garden**, q.v., of Ancient Greece and Pliny's Villa near Ostia in Italy are examples. See also **Greek landscape architecture, Roman landscape architecture**.

Classification, botanical See **Botanical classification**.

Classification, horticultural See **Horticultural classification**.

Classification of land Because of increasing population pressure and consequent clamorous, endless demands for land of all kinds, it is necessary to classify various lands and, in many instances, to legally reserve their use for highly specific purposes.

Urban and rural land uses are recognized, and these are subdivided according to a number of factors. Climate, type of soil and vegetation, geography, and existing human activities must all be considered.

In the United States, the Bureau of Land Management, the Soil Conservation Service, and the Forest Service, among other agencies, have developed schemes of highly accurate classification that include soil depth and nature, degree of slope, amount of rainfall, altitude, and crop suitability as principal

considerations. This sort of evaluation helps in the allotment of primarily rural lands to logging, grazing, farming, housing, recreation, or other uses. Absolutely haphazard land use is prevented in this way, but rarely can all the conflicting interests be satisfied.

In cities, it is often necessary to restrict land use in a highly sophisticated way. This restriction is normally referred to as **Zoning**, q.v. As is true in planning for the countryside, good zoning is certainly no guarantee of an evolving, beautiful urban landscape with everyone's best interests perfectly synchronized. Urban land classification attempts to resolve housing, business, governmental, recreational, special use, and utility questions by reserving the use of particular properties. Noisy factories are not supposed to mix with sleepy bedroom neighborhoods. At the same time, governments or boards must plan for the integration of country and city at the margins of both—often the sites of the severest conflict. Attempting to preserve or even develop open space can also lead to long-term disagreement among planners, private interests (especially developers), and the public.

Perhaps the most difficult effort required of a twentieth-century society is that its people leave a piece of land—any land— in its original condition, untouched. "Wilderness" classification usually achieves this end, but it is increasingly harder to establish and arduous to defend once granted. See also **Planning**.

Classification of plants See **Binomial, Botanical classification**.

Classification of soil See **Soil classification**.

Classifications, commercial seed
See **Commercial seed classification.**

Clastics In soils, sediments representing the chemical erosion or weathered particles of rocks. Sand and clay, as well as sandstone and shale, are examples.

Claude (Lorrain) See **Claude Lorrain.**

Claude-glass In eighteenth-century England, a tinted convex mirror used to view landscapes. Claude-glasses "softened" and romanticized the English countryside seen through them.

Claudian garden or **Claudian landscape** An eighteenth-century English landscape garden or larger landscape designed "picturesquely," after the fashion of the landscape painter **Claude Lorrain,** q.v. Typical Claudian designs included artificial ruins, bucolic hills, romantic meandering streams, and other features of contrived informality. See also **English School of Landscape Gardening.**

Clause, bonus (contracts)
See **Bonus and penalty clause.**

Clause, "murder" (unfair advantage)
See **"Murder" clause (specification writing).**

Clause, penalty (contracts)
See **Bonus and penalty clause** and **Liquidated damages.**

Clavate In plant structures, shaped like a club.

Clay One of the three principal components of soils, the others being sand and silt. Clay is formed of the tiniest soil particles (smaller than .01 mm) and holds water exceptionally well. Clay is also fired for brick, tile, and pottery. It is extraordinarily plastic when wet and often finely powdered when dry. Clay is the only soil component that is chemically active. See also **Loam, Marl, Sand, Silt, Soil.**

Clay, boulder See **Till.**

Clay loam See **Loam.**

Clay masonry unit A pompous term for **Brick.**

Claypan See **Pan.**

Clay, varved (sediment)
See **Varved clay.**

Clay, vitrified See **Vitrified clay.**

Clean out (CO) A threaded pipe orifice, usually capped, available for pipe maintenance.

Cleaner (irrigation) A cleaning solution used on plastic pipe ends and fittings before **Pipe solvent,** q.v., is applied.

Clear sight "triangle" A clear sight (unobstructed) area where two streets abut at the corner of a property, adding to traffic and pedestrian safety.

Clearing A pocket of man-made or natural open, usually grassy space in a woodland.

Cleavage plane In flagstone and other stone used in landscape construction, the fracture line. A good cleavage will produce broad, flat, thin chunks of stone useful in pavement and wall building.

Cleistogamous Pertaining to certain small flowers that are often partly underground and/or self-pollinating. Violets sometimes produce cleistogamous flowers.

Clerk of the works An individual engaged by the owner of a project to act as a liaison with the contractor and to perform such duties as keeping of time, recording of job progress, processing of payments, and the like during the period of construction. See also **Contract manager.**

Cleveland, Horace W. S. (1814–1900) Pioneer United States landscape architect. Cleveland had accumulated considerable experience by the time he entered the competition to design Central Park in 1856. He lost the contest but wrote an incisive pamphlet about the benefits of the park, and later collaborated with **Olmsted** and **Vaux,** q.q.v., on the design of Prospect Park in Brooklyn. Born in Lancaster, Massachusetts, Cleveland was a member of an old New England family. He was trained in agriculture, civil engineering, and horticulture as a young man, and later worked as a surveyor. He formed an early partnership with Robert Morris Copeland before launching his own practice in the late 1850s.

Cleveland and such contemporaries as **Charles Eliot,** q.v., and Olmsted proposed fundamental changes in the form of American cities. They pressed for better sanitation, systems of parks, the development of public boards and commissions to insure good city planning, and the overall civilizing influence of landscape architecture on town and country alike. Cleveland thought of naturalism in open space design as a cure to growing urbanism. He was attracted to the burgeoning Midwest, locating first in Chicago in the 1860s, in Minneapolis in the 1880s, and finally back in Chicago in the mid-1890s. He developed a very broad practice, designing estates, state-capitol grounds, park systems,

private town residences, and suburbs—one of his special passions. Cleveland believed the suburb to be an unusual opportunity, part of a city-park-garden ideal in which squares and parks could be linked by means of landscaped boulevards. In a series of pamphlets, many of which were lost in the Great Chicago Fire of 1871, he also noted that, in a truly democratic society, the amenities of the estate should be available in the city for the enjoyment of all citizens. Cleveland's theories, which seem somewhat commonplace in the twentieth century, were radical enough in their day. They made him, along with Olmsted and Eliot, one of the foremost theoreticians of the new profession of landscape architecture.

Among his best known works are Roger Williams Park, Providence, Rhode Island, and the Minneapolis and Omaha park systems.

Cleveland took his son into practice with him in 1891. He later moved from Minneapolis, where he had carried on the bulk of his work for some years, back to Chicago, continuing his labors until nearly the end of his life.

Client In landscape architecture, the person, company, or agency paying for improvements to his, her or its property and therefore for the professional services of design and planning. The client is not necessarily the user—the person or entity who will utilize the landscape developments. See also **Owner, User.**

Climate The usual weather conditions of a region, influenced by latitude, altitude, physical geography, basic type of land mass (island or continent), proximity to the sea, and other factors. The most conspicuous aspects of any climate are temperature, rainfall, and winds. See also **Macroclimate, Microclimate,** and **Weather.**

Climate, community (of plants) See **Community climate.**

Climate, continental See **Continental climate.**

Climate diagram A climograph or hytherograph helpful in planning the successful use of outdoor space and the likelihood of survival of specific new plants in a region. See also **Climograph, Hytherograph.**

Climate, insular See **Insular climate.**

Climate, maritime See **Maritime climate.**

Climate, Mediterranean See **Mediterranean climate.**

Climate, mountain See **Mountain climate.**

Climate of soil See **Soil climate.**

Climate zone A geographical area exhibiting characteristic land and weather conditions which will support a recognizable range of plant associations.

Climatic factor An attribute of the climate of an area that influences the occurrence and lives of local plants and animals. Frost, rainfall, temperature and the like are common climatic factors. See also **Biotic factor.**

Climatic province A climate region, or area in which a uniform climatic pattern prevails. See also **Geographic province, Natural region.**

Climatic race In botany, a variety of a species that has made a genetic adaptation to a local photo (light) period or other significant climatic demand.

Climatology The scientific study of climates and their relation to environment. See also **Meteorology.**

Climax, biotic See **Biotic climax.**

Climax, edaphic (soil) See **Soil climax.**

Climax, fire See **Fire climax.**

Climax growth (climax community, climax vegetation) The normal plant association found on the typical undisturbed or restored topsoil of a region. Climax growth is relatively stable and quite long-lasting. Also **Natural vegetation balance.** See also **Consociation, Ecosystem, Plant growth, Plant succession.**

Climber, children's See **Children's climber.**

Climber (vine) In horticulture, a nonself-supporting plant, woody or herbaceous, which clings to a wall, trellis or other structure as it grows upward. See also **Creeper, Vine.**

Climograph A chart that indicates recorded temperature and humidity for an area. See also **Climate diagram, Hytherograph.**

Cline In botany, the continuous shading of physical or other differences found in a species as it occurs over a wide area.

Clinkers 1) Gravel, especially rough gray-green chips or pebbles. 2) Overfired, warped bricks or pieces of bricks.

Cloaca (Latin) In ancient Rome and elsewhere, a sewer or sewer inlet or outlet.

Cloche In gardens, a glass or plastic dome or similar construction (bell-jar or the like) used to protect crops and boost early growth.

Clock controller (irrigation)
See **Automatic controller.**

Clock, irrigation   See **Automatic controller.**

Cloister   An enclosed medieval courtyard with an encircling arcaded walk, often used for monastic horticulture, and similar to the ancient **Peristyle,** q.v. Cloister gardens were often "parterred" and formal in layout. See also **Ambulatory, Hortus conclusus, Medieval landscape architecture, Parterre.**

Clone (clon)   In horticulture, a vegetatively produced new plant, identical in all respects to its parent.

Closed bidding   See **Invitational bidding.**

Closed traverse (surveying)
See **Traverse.**

Closer   In decks, a detail member used at the edges of joist and surface-member construction to achieve a smooth appearance. A finish board.

Closure error   See **Error of closure.**

Closure, traverse   See **Traverse closure.**

Cloud   A mass of visible water vapor. Clouds add interest and drama to landscape, and are often used prominently as parts of "borrowed scenery" to achieve landscape effects.

Cloverleaf   A gauche traffic interchange characteristic of twentieth-century freeway systems, nearly impossible to integrate with local landforms. The interchange plan form is reminiscent of a four-leaf clover, but due to its immense scale it lacks altogether the plant's

simple gracefulness. The cloverleaf allows smooth traffic flows and direction changes to continue at a road junction of four principal directions by means of over-and underpasses and severely limited access. See also **Traffic interchange.**

Club, garden   See **Garden club.**

Cluster development   A common form of condominium, townhouse, or similar design in which several housing units are massed to allow vistas and recreation space and high density. A series of these "masses" is tied together to form the cluster development as a whole.

Cluster, flower   See **Inflorescence**

CMP   Corrugated metal pipe, q.v.

CMPA   A plan abbreviation for corrugated metal pipe arch.

CMU   See **Concrete masonry unit.**

CO   Clean out, q.v.

Coarse aggregate   In concrete mixtures, gravel from $1/4$ in. (4.76 mm) to 2 in. (38.08 mm) in size. See also **Aggregate, Fine aggregate.**

Coarse-grained soil   A soil containing an appreciable amount of gravel, sand, or stones. See also **Soil.**

Coarse texture (soils)   See **Soil texture.**

Coat, color   See **Stucco.**

Coat, finish (color)   See **Stucco.**

Coat, rough (scratch)   See **Stucco.**

Coat, scratch   See **Stucco.**

Cobalt   A metallic element utilized by plants (and animals) in small amounts as a nutrient. A **Trace**

element, q.v., or micronutrient. See also **Available nutrient, Soil minerals.**

Cobble   See **Cobblestone.**

Cobbled street   A street paved with rounded or cobblestones. See **Cobblestones.**

Cobblestone (cobble)   A water-rounded stone usually of small size used to pave streets or walkways.

Code, botanical   See **Cultivated plant code.**

Code (City)   See **Building codes.**

Code, Cultivated Plant
See **Cultivated Plant Code.**

Code, horticultural   See **Cultivated Plant Code.**

Code, housing   See **Building codes.**

Code, irrigation or sprinkler
See **Building codes.**

Codes, building   See **Building codes.**

Codes, form standard   See **Building codes.**

Codes, performance standard
See **Building codes.**

Coefficient of expansion   The amount of expansion of any sort found in a material due to a rise in temperature.

Coefficient, friction   See **Friction coefficient.**

Coefficient, pluviometric
See **Pluviometric coefficient.**

Coefficient of roughness   In pipes and channels, the degree to which water velocity is affected by rough inside surfaces. See also **Friction coefficient.**

Coefficient of run-off See **Rational formula.**

Coefficient of uniformity In irrigation, a measurement of the overall ability of a system to apply water.

Coefficient of wilting See **Wilting coefficient.**

Cofferdam A partially submerged structure used to keep water away from underground construction in progress. Also **Caisson.**

Coir screening A mesh woven from coconut fiber used to protect tender plants from wind or sun.

Cold mix (asphalt) An unheated mixture of aggregate and asphalt binder (cement) used as a patch or for other secondary asphalt construction. See also **Asphalt** and **Hot mix.**

Cold weather curing (of concrete) In concrete construction, the use of high early-strength mixtures, insulated coverings, heating of mixes, and other techniques during 40°F or colder temperatures to effectively cure a concrete pour.

Coldframe A framework of wood with a hinged and glass-covered top used to protect young plants during early growth outdoors in late winter. A coldframe that is electrically or otherwise heated is called a **Hotbed,** q.v. Also **Warming bed.** See also **Lath screen.**

Coliform A bacterium resembling a strainer, sometimes found in infected public waters, and often originating from fecal matter.

Collaboration (professional) A cooperative act of design or planning by several independent design firms. Codesign.

Collage Materials of various origins arranged in an artful pattern on a plane surface to form a composition. In landscape, a design of particularly disparate elements, especially if arranged on a flat surface.

Collar (roots) See **Crown.**

Collateral In botany, at one side.

Collected stock Trees, shrubs, or other plants dug up or otherwise removed from the wild for domestic landscape use. In the southwestern U.S. and elsewhere, this practice is extremely destructive of watersheds, wildlife habitat, and soils, and has resulted in the reduction of certain popular landscape species to an alarming degree. See also **Bareroot stock, Container grown stock,** and **Field grown stock.**

Collector A main street or walkway that receives traffic from multiple smaller "feeder" lines.

Colloidally held water See **Hygroscopic water.** Also **Unavailable water.**

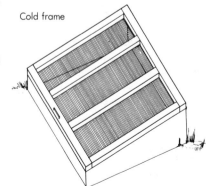

Cold frame

Colloquial landscape architecture See **Vernacular landscape architecture.**

Collusion affidavit See **Noncollusion affidavit.**

Colluvium A motley stone fragment or soil mass accumulation at the base of a slope.

Colonnade A row of columns connected by **Lintels.** See also **Arcade, Peristyle, Portico.**

Colonnette (French) A small column.

Color, achromatic and chromatic See **Chromatic color.**

Color, autumn See **Fall color.**

Color break A kind of **Sport,** q.v., in which the plant mutation consists of a variety of a new color.

Color coat See **Stucco.**

Color, cool See **Cool color.**

Color, fall See **Fall color.**

Color gardening Home gardening that develops a single color or series of colors as an overall theme, usually by means of careful flower selection and planting.

Color, warm (hot color) See **Warm color.**

Colors, complementary (accidental colors) See **Complementary colors.**

Colors, primary See **Primary colors.**

Colors, secondary See **Secondary colors.**

Columella   Roman writer of the first century A.D. Author of *De re rustica,* a long treatise. In its tenth book, "Of Horticulture," he describes in verse the joys of Roman gardening. His gardeners plan their yearly cultivation carefully and produce large quantities of familiar flowers and vegetables for their own use and for sale. See also **Pliny the Younger.**

Columnar   In horticulture, a slender, upright plant form. Italian cypress and Irish juniper are examples.

Coma   A tuft at the tip of some seeds.

Combined aggregate   Coarse and fine aggregate mixed for a concrete. See also **Aggregate.**

Commensalism   In botany, a form of plant symbiosis in which one species clearly benefits and the other is neither hurt nor helped. Virginia creeper vine growing on a large cottonwood is an example. Adjective: commensal. See also **Symbiosis.**

Commercial landscape   1) A landscape project installed by a professional landscape contractor. 2) The landscape surroundings of a business establishment.

Commercial seed classifications
   The following seed designations are used in the production and handling of commercial seed: 1) **Breeder seed:** a "patent" or proprietary seed. 2) **Certified seed:** seed derived from registered or foundation seed, "certified" as to source and purity. 3) **Commercial seed:** a generic term used for all kinds of generally available seed. 4) **Common seed:** a general use seed that is not certified. 5) **Dormant seed:** a viable seed that has not yet germinated. 6) **Firm seed:** a nonrotting, nongerminating seed under usual growing conditions. 7) **Foundation seed:** a pure seed stock used for further highly controlled seed production. 8) **Hard seed:** a seed that remains hard—i.e., does not germinate, even after soaking and placement in favorable growing conditions. 9) **Registered seed:** a highly pure basic seed that is used in the production of certified seed and as a foundation seed.

Commercial (manufacturer's) specifications   The specifications developed by a manufacturer for use with his product. See also **Specifications.**

Comminution   The smashing or grinding of stone or other substances into a powder.

Commission, planning
   See **Planning commission.**

Common   An expanse of land owned by the community as a whole. A paved or green public meeting place or square.

Common bond (masonry)
   See **Brick wall pattern.**

Common excavation
   See **Excavation.**

Common seed   See **Commercial seed classification.**

Common yard lumber   See **Lumber.**

Community   People in a set geographical area who think of themselves as a group and are ruled by the same government. Usually considered in terms of an area and its physical appearance. See also **Plant community.**

Community, bedroom
   See **Bedroom community.**

Community climate (of plants)   A small botanically created climate with its own characteristics that contributes to the larger climate. A forest plant association next to a prairie, a river-strip plant community, and an oasis are examples.

Community, climax   See **Climax growth.**

Community, plant   See **Plant community.**

Compaction   In soils, a lessening of volume due to the expulsion of air. Normally occurs following compression. In landscape construction, proper soil compaction of moved earth is accomplished by depositing fill in 6-inch layers (**Lifts**) and subsequent moistening, rolling, or tamping to achieve **Optimum density.** See also **Dry density.**

Company, bonding   See **Bonding company.**

Compensation point (in plants)   The point at which plant **Respiration,** q.v., or intake of oxygen and yielding of carbon dioxide, equals the rate of **Photosynthesis,** q.v.

Competition of plants   In botany, a "struggle" among multiple species in a given environment ultimately resulting in an evolved plant association or community in which the characteristic overstory (usually tree), understory (shrub), and ground-cover combination exactly fits an ecological niche.

Complementary colors   Accidental colors. Colors that produce a full spectrum, or white light, when mixed.

Complete fertilizer   Any fertilizer that contains enough nitrogen, phosphorus and potassium to take care of its own decomposition. See also **Chemical fertilizer, Fertilizer, Incomplete fertilizer, Organic fertilizer.**

Completion bond   See **Performance bond.**

Compliance, certificate of   See **Certificate of compliance.**

Compluvium   The central break in a Roman (or Greek) roof through which rainwater and melted snow poured, to be collected in an **Impluvium,** q.v., or floor cistern.

Composite landscape   In geography, a natural landscape containing forms that have developed through separate ages of erosion.

Composite wall   A wall in which two different materials—i.e., brick and concrete block—are used together.

Compost   A pulverized mixture of any kind of decayed organic material used as a fertilizer. 1) **Sheet composing** involves the placement of organic material directly into the soil. 2) **Windrow (Heap) composting** is the standard. Organic materials are heaped by themselves or placed in an enclosure and occasionally turned. 3) In **Mechanical composting,** the compost mixture is stirred or tumbled. 4) **Ventilated cell composting** is similar but the mixture is dropped and sifted through an arrangement of cells. See also **Fertilizer.**

Compound curve   A flat (plane) curve—often part of a driveway or lawn edge—consisting of two continuous arcs of differing radii joined at a common tangent.

Compound flower   See **Flower.**

Compound leaf   See **Leaf.**

Compound, rooting (hormone rooting compound)   See **Rooting compound.**

Compound, soil buffer   See **Soil buffer compound.**

Compressibility (of soils)   The degree of change in volume or shape of a soil due to compression and subsequent pressing out of water in the spaces between soil particles. See also **Compaction, Elasticity, Plasticity, Soil.**

Compression coupling   In irrigation, a fitting used to repair galvanized or PVC lines. Also, a connecting fitting to service lines.

Compression test (of concrete)   In concrete construction, a test of strength made by compressing a cylinder filled with a particular concrete batch at 7 and/or 28 days after the pour is made. See also **Slump test.**

Computer applications in landscape design   These, of course, increase almost exponentially with each decade. Computers may be used to compile background data for parks, commercial developments, or large-scale planning. They are helpful in producing specifications at very great speed, in assembling plant lists and cost estimates, in analyzing regional landscape characteristics (often from information produced by satellite observation or "remote sensing"), in plotting soils and their idiosyncrasies. Computers can aid in calculations for the design of irrigation systems and, in a limited sense, in the production of working drawings on mylar or vellum. This sort of computer-assisted design and drafting is often referred to by its acronym CADD. For the most part, however, such designs remain remarkably stiff and cold.

There are computers that can even create delightful and unexpected perspective drawings of a sort. They first generate line drawings; then, with multiple elevation views, a perspective can be developed. Computer-screen color "models" also now exist.

"BASIC" is the primary computer language in landscape architectural use. With it, programs may be generated that can help to calculate terrain, earthwork, and runoff, and to plot such project necessities as the Critical Path Method (CPM). "BASIC" may also assist in solar calculations, wind load projection, and the like.

Other essential functions of professional practice, such as accounting, payroll, and similar business necessities, may also be undertaken by computer.

The leading United States center for computer applications in landscape architecture is at the University of Massachusetts.

Conceit   In Renaissance France and elsewhere, any elaborately contrived garden element. Parterres, mazes, water gardens, and the like are examples.

Concentrated load   In landscape construction, the weight of a structure bearing down on a given point, used to calculate necessary structural strength.

Concolor (concolorous)   Of the same color.

Concourse   A large indoor or outdoor walkway designed to accommodate a great number of people.

Concret brut (French)   In landscape construction, concrete with a crude or unfinished surface displaying the patterns—often wood graining—of its formwork. Also **Beton brut.**

Concrete   A common construction material consisting of a cement matrix combined with water, fine aggregate (sand), and coarse aggregate (pebbles, gravel, stone chips) to form footings, walls, pavements, and other rigid features. When combined with steel mesh or rebar, plain concrete becomes reinforced concrete—a versatile and extremely strong structural material widely used in landscape construction. See also **Asphaltic concrete, Cement.**

Concrete, asphaltic   See **Asphaltic concrete.**

Concrete, bituminous   See **Asphaltic concrete.**

Concrete block   See **Concrete masonry unit.**

Concrete cart   See **Buggy.**

Concrete, ferro   See **Reinforced concrete.**

Concrete, glass-reinforced   See **GRC concrete.**

Concrete (GRC)   See **GRC concrete.**

Concrete, green   See **Green concrete.**

Concrete masonry unit (CMU)   A kind of concrete block, usually hollow, made of cement, aggregates, and water. Fly ash,. lime, and other elements may also be present in the block matrix. Also, commonly, **Concrete block.**

Concrete, monolithic   See **Monolithic concrete.**

Concrete nails   See **Nails.**

Concrete, precast   See **Precast concrete.**

Concrete, reinforced   See **Reinforced concrete.**

Concrete sand   A coarse sand of $^3/_8$ in. and less greatest particle diameter used, with coarse aggregate and cement, to produce concrete. See also **Sand.**

Concrete slump   See **Slump test.**

Concrete tile conduit   A runoff conduit used to carry flows of 10–20 FPS.

Concrete, warm tone   See **Warm tone concrete.**

Concrete-treated base (CTB)   In landscape pavements, a base paving of crushed rock or cinders containing an admixture of Portland cement, which, when rolled and moistened, adds a degree of stability and strength to a pathway.

Condemnation   See **Eminent domain.**

Conditional acceptance   In landscape construction, acceptance by an owner of work performed to complete a project, providing designated items of construction are completed or corrected within a specified period of time. See also **Acceptance, Final acceptance, Provisional acceptance.**

Conditioner, fertilizer   See **Fertilizer conditioner.**

Conditioner of soil   See **Soil conditioner.**

Conditions of the bid   See **Bid conditions.**

Conditions, general   See **General conditions.**

Conditions, special   See **Special conditions.**

Conditions, supplemental or supplementary   See **Supplemental conditions.**

Conduit   1) In landscape lighting or irrigation wiring, a protective pipe through which bundles of wires are passed. A **Sleeve,** q.v., found underground or above grade. 2) A **Culvert,** q.v. 3) In Elizabethan England, a garden fountain.

Conduit, concrete tile   See **Concrete tile conduit.**

Conduplicate   In plants, folded along the length of a structure or organ.

Cone   See **Strobile.**

Configuration   1) The form or lay of the land. 2) The **Habit of growth,** q.v., of a plant.

Confluence   A point at which streams merge. Also, the convergence point of pathways.

Conifer   A large and wide-spread order of **Gymnosperms,** q.v., composed of primarily evergreen, cone-bearing trees and shrubs. Some conifers, however, are deciduous (larches). *Pinaceae* (pine) and *Taxaceae* (yew) are two common conifer families. See also **Gymnosperms.**

Coniferales   Conifers, q.v.

Coniferous   In botany, pertaining to the coniferales order of angiosperms. These plants customarily bear naked seeds in cones, and include, among others, pines, spruces, larches, firs, and junipers. A conifer forest contains primarily needled evergreens.

Conker   In horticulture, the hard, spiny seed covering of the horse-chestnut.

Connate Referring to water captured in sedimentary deposits as they are formed.

Connection In irrigation, usually the link-up of a service line furnished for irrigation service.

Conquering capacity (of plants) See **Invasion capacity.**

Consequent stream A creek or river whose course is a direct result of the original lay of the land.

Conservation A private and public activity promoting the limited exploitation of natural resources, including minerals, soils, plants, and animals. Good conservation practices very often involve the selective cutting of timber and the regeneration of new forests through large-scale tree plantings. Conservation as a management approach limits the abuse of grasslands, seas, deserts, lakes,

Conservatory (20th century). Photo courtesy Leslie Allen.

Conifer

streams, and the Earth's supplies of wild animals and other resources. It also advocates the intelligent mining of mineral deposits. See also **Preservation.**

Conservation district See **Soil conservation district.**

Conservation tillage Seed-drilling of a crop directly into the mulch or stubble of the previous year's harvest to cut down on soil loss that would occur through traditional plowing.

Conservatory A glassed-in greenhouse or similar structure, usually attached to a house, used for plant propagation and display.

Consistency of soil See **Soil consistency.**

Consociation In botany, a **Climax growth,** q.v., with a single dominant species. The preponderant plant species is often a tree, as in oak forest, Ponderosa pine forest, and the like. See also **Climax growth, Plant succession, Society.**

Construction bond See **Performance bond.**

Construction budget See **Maximum allowable construction cost.**

Construction contract An agreement between an owner and a landscape contractor for the construction of a project landscape. Also **Agreement for site preparation.** See also **Specifications.**

Construction cost   The total amount necessary to install a project as per plans and specifications, not including land acquisition costs and design fee. See also **Project budget.**

Construction details (design)
See **Detail.**

Construction documents   Working or construction drawings and specifications. The plans and notes necessary to correctly install or construct a project. Also **Contract documents.**
Construction documents are often, but not always, equal to **Bid documents,** q.v. See also **Specifications** and **Working drawings.**

Construction documents phase
See **Working drawings phase.**

Construction drawings
See **Working drawings.**

Construction grade   See **Grade.**

Construction insurance   A general term covering the insurance carried by a landscape contractor and an owner during project construction against theft, storm and accident damage, fire, and the like. The term may include bonding as well.

Construction joint (concrete)   A joint installed between pours of concrete as a temporary measure when work is halted for a time. Often an **Expansion joint,** q.v. See also **Control joint.**

Construction, landscape
See **Landscape construction.**

Construction limit (construction boundary)   See **Limits of construction.**

Construction phase   A common term for what is usually the final portion of a landscape architect's services to an owner, including supervision or observation of a contractor's landscape installation.

Construction plans   See **Working drawings.**

Construction procedure outline
See **Progress schedule.**

Construction schedule   See **Progress schedule.**

Construction Specifications Institute
See **CSI.**

Construction, temporary
See **Temporary construction.**

Consultancy   An individual or group offering specific or general advice and information to a client, who may be a professional designer or other indivudal or organization. See also **Prime consultant.**

Consultant   See **Prime consultant** and **Consultancy.**

Container gardening   The planting of shrubs, small trees, and especially flowers and other small ground covers in pots, above-grade planters, boxes, or similarly confined contrivances. A form of small-scale gardening. Also **Tube gardening.**

Container grown stock   Trees, shrubs, or other plant materials grown in plastic or metal cans by a nurseryman. See also **Bareroot stock, Collected stock,** and **Field-grown stock.**

Container plant   1) A plant grown in a box, can, or other holder. Plants in metal or plastic cans most frequently come in one, two, five, seven, and fifteen-gallon sizes. Boxed plants are frequently found in 24 in., 36 in., or larger sizes. 2) A plant installed in an above-ground (above-grade) planter.

Contaminants, irrigation system
See **Irrigation system contaminants.**

Content, moisture   See **Moisture content.**

Continental climate   A climate found in the interiors of Asia and North America, extending in influence to the coasts in winter. It greatly modifies the effects of the oceans and their currents around each land mass. Extreme temperatures, prevalent seasonal winds, and, often, low humidity and rainfall typify continental climates. See also **Climate.**

Contingency (allowance)   A factor of (usually) 5% or 10% calculated in a landscape construction estimate to allow for unforeseen items of construction that may arise as the work progresses.

Continuous beam   See **Beam.**

Contour   The form of the land, existing or proposed—a part of its **Topography,** q.v. Often indicated by continuous map lines at intervals of one, two, five, or ten feet or metrically.
Proposed contours indicate the desired form of the land for project construction, and are often shown as solid lines; existing contours are dashed. The contour line, though imaginary, does indicate a continuous elevation above sea level or an assumed **Datum line,** q.v. See also **Grade, Grid.**

Contour and construction plan
See **Layout plan.**

Contour cultivation   See **Contour plowing.**

Contour furrow   See **Furrow.**

Contour interval   A vertical distance measured between contour lines.

Contour line   A map line connecting points of the same ground elevation above or below a fixed datum. Contours are plotted from **Stadia** or **Grid** survey layouts, q.q.v. See also **Grade, Topography.**

Contour plan   In landscape drawing, a plan showing existing and proposed grades for a landscape project. Contour plans are often combined with construction (hard landscape) plans in layout plans. Also **Grading plan.** See also **Layout plan.**

Contour planes method (earthwork)   See **Cut and fill.**

Contour plowing   An agricultural practice that checks erosion because the land is plowed at right angles to its slope, thus slowing surface runoff and encouraging percolation. Also **Contour cultivation.** See also **Land leveling.**

Contours, existing   See **Contour.**

Contours, proposed   See **Contour.**

Contract   A legally binding agreement made by two or more parties with each other. Also, occasionally, **Agreement.**

Contract bidding   In landscape architecture, the issuance of plans and specifications for open or selective bidding. The base-bid items are often accompanied by additive or deductive alternates. A recommendation of contract award to the owner will be made by the landscape architect after consideration of the merits of each bid submitted. See also **Specifications.**

Contract bond   See **Performance bond.**

Contract, construction   See **Construction contract.**

Contract, design   See **Design contract.**

Contract, divided   See **Divided contract.**

Contract documents   See **Construction documents.**

Contract drawings   Final design drawings with notes or specifications used to construct a project. **Working drawings,** q.v. Also **Construction drawings.** See also **Construction documents.**

Contract, express   See **Express contract.**

Contract, general   See **General contract.**

Contract, implied   See **Implied contract.**

Contract limit   See **Limits of construction.**

Contract, lump sum (design)   See **Lump sum contract.**

Contract manager   An owner's representative or a job superintendent (employed by a contractor) responsible for the coordination of trades and smooth flow of work necessary to complete a large construction project on time, within the budget, and in keeping with plans and specifications. See also **Clerk of the works.**

Contract, negotiated   See **Negotiated contract.**

Contract price   The awarded base and alternate cost for construction. With taxes and additional considerations added, it becomes the **Contract sum,** q.v.

Contract, prime   See **Prime contract.**

Contract sum   Adjustable only by change order, the contract sum is the amount agreed upon by the owner of a project and a landscape contractor as payable for the work stipulated in the construction documents. It often includes taxes and additional fees or considerations. The contract sum is usually quoted as a **Lump sum** or a total of **Unit prices,** q.q.v. See also **Contract price.**

Contract time   The number of calendar days or weather working days noted in a construction contract for finishing landscape improvements. Also **Period for completion, Time for completion, Time of construction.**

Contracting agency   See **Owner.**

Contraction joint   See **Control joint.** See also **Expansion joint.**

Contractor   See **Landscape contractor.**

Contractor, captive   See **Captive contractor.**

Contractor, landscape   See **Landscape contractor.**

Contractor's level   See **Level.**

Contractor's liability insurance   See **Liability insurance.**

Contractor's license   A certification granted by a government agency authorizing an individual or firm to contract for and install specified kinds of construction.

Contractual liability   The extent of responsibility for actions or outcome assumed by an individual or organization under the terms of a design or installation agreement.

Control, broad spectrum (herbicide or pesticide)   See **Broad spectrum control.**

Control joint   In concrete construction, a joint of about one-fourth the slab thickness struck between expansion joints to control slab cracking. A tooled or incised joint developed specifically for controlled cracking. Also **Contraction joint, Score joint.** See also **Construction joint, Expansion joint.**

Control, land use   See **Land use control.**

Control points   In surveying, established monuments used as references for further, more minute surveys. See also **Benchmark.**

Control, post-emergence   See **Post-emergence control.**

Control, pre-emergence   See **Pre-emergence control.**

Controller, automatic (irrigation)   See **Automatic controller.**

Controller box (irrigation)   See **Automatic controller.**

Controller, clock (irrigation)   See **Automatic controller.**

Controller, hydraulic   See **Hydraulic controller.**

Controller, irrigation   See **Automatic controller.**

Controller, primary (irrigation)   See **Automatic controller.**

Controller, satellite (irrigation)   See **Automatic controller.**

Control joint

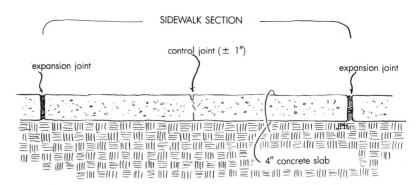

Conurbation   A growing together of previously distinct towns or villages into an urban mass. In general, urban sprawl.

Convection   A (fluid) motion of air or liquid essential to the distribution of heat and sound.

Convectional rainfall   Rainfall occurring when moisture-laden air rises and cools, forming clouds. Convectional rainfall is typified by summer thunderstorms. See also **Rainfall.**

Convent garden   See **Monastery garden.**

"Convivial" technology   Industrial-age technology that assists natural processes instead of hindering them. A term in occasional use since the 1970s.

Cool color   A blue, green, purple, violet, or shade of these. Cool colors are valuable in the landscape for the pleasant, untrammeled emotions they elicit. See also **Warm color.**

"Cool deck"   A cementitious paving product often installed around swimming pools and finished with a "sure-tread" texture to prevent slipping. "Cool deck" does not absorb as much heat as concrete or stone and can therefore be walked on comfortably even in the heat of the day.

Cool season plant   In horticulture, a plant at its growing and/or flowering best during spring or fall or, rarely, winter. See also **Warm season plant.**

Coordinates   In survey mapping, points of reference used to locate specific physical items (trees, structures, streams, streets, and the like) by means of exact measurement.

In surveying and site layout, the identification of a site point by use of two dimensions measured from a pair of **Base lines,** q.v., intersecting each other at right angles.

Polar coordinates utilize both angular and linear distances. A spherical coordinate system is used to determine the Earth's longitude and latitude.

Plane coordinates (rectangular coordinates) use a base line and reference meridian to determine the location of a desired point or object.

Physics makes use of three-dimensional coordinates for astronomical determinations.

Cop, silent See **Speed bump.**

Copeland, Robert Morris Pioneer U.S. landscape architect in partnership with **H. W. S. Cleveland,** q.v., in the late 1850s.

Coping A finish course of brick, stone, tile, or the like along the top of a wall or the edge of a pool. A coping often projects slightly to cast a shadow line.

Copper A metallic element utilized by plants (and animals) in small amounts as a nutrient. A **Trace element,** q.v., or **Micronutrient.** See also **Available nutrient, Soil minerals.**

Copper pipe In irrigation, a common kind of main supply line (type K) used for buildings and, occasionally, outdoor watering (type M). Copper pipe is tapped by means of attaching PVC, galvanized, or polyethylene lines to serve irrigation systems. Galvanized, PVC, or polyethylene pipe may also be used in place of copper. Also **Copper water tube.**

Coppice See **Copse.**

Coppice and tree forest In forestry, a wood that is grown for continual production by leaving larger trees for seed production but consistently cutting the underwood or lower tree association.

Copse Short version of **coppice,** a thicket or grouping of trees. A coppice may also be a wood that is grown for periodic cutting.

Cordate In leaves, heart-shaped. The eastern redbud, *Cercis canadensis,* is an example.

Cordon In fruit or other trees, a plant with a single trunk formed by careful pruning.

Cordonata (Italian) In Italian Renaissance gardens, a series of intertwined or chain falls in a garden cascade.

Coriaceous In leaves, leathery.

Corm A bulb-like, swollen underground stem sometimes found on monocotyledonous plants. See also **Bulb** or **Tuber.**

Cormophyte A **Pteridophyte,** q.v., or **Spermatophyte,** q.v. A plant with a stem or trunk, leaves, and roots.

Corneous or **corniculate** In plant structures, horny or rough and hard-textured.

Cornice 1) A generally horizontal, molded detail sometimes found in garden houses. 2) A walk along the edge of a cliff or embankment.

Cornute In plant structures, horned in form.

Corolla The circle of flower petals; normally, the most colorful part of a flower. Corollaceous, corrollate, adjectives. See also **Calyx, Perianth, Petal.**

Corporation, professional (PC) See **Professional corporation.**

Corporation stop In irrigation, a $^3/_4$ in. or other valve used to tie a service line into a public main.

Corps of Engineers A technical branch of the U.S. Army that has enormous powers of impoundment and water-flow control throughout the United States. The Corps is also responsible to a greater or lesser degree for land-related improvements at military installations across the country.

Corral In the United States and Spanish America, a cattle or sheep pen made of wood or metal uprights and stringers.

Corrasion A mechanical erosion occurring as suspended, loose, solid particles in air or water pass over a land surface or streambed. Also **Scour.**

Corrugated metal pipe (CMP) A commonly used pipe for culverts and other drains. Also **Corrugated steel pipe.**

"Corten" steel A patented process steel that weathers (rusts) at a calculated rate, with a protective rust coating forming on its surface.

Cortex (botanical) See **Bark.**

Cortile (Italian) A central courtyard in a building, flanked by loggias or arcades.

Corymb In plant structures, a kind of **Inflorescence** or **Raceme,** q.q.v., flattened or widened at its tip. Adjectives: corymbiform, corymbose.

Cost-benefit analysis In design programming, a study of the potential cost of site purchase, demolition, and improvement in comparison to the income or other benefit that is to be derived from site development. See also **Pro forma** and **Programming.**

Cost, construction See **Construction cost.**

Cost estimate See **"Ball park" estimate, Detailed estimate of construction cost,** and **Preliminary estimate.**

Cost estimate, construction See **Detailed estimate of construction cost.**

Cost, guaranteed maximum
   See **Guaranteed maximum cost.**

"Cost plus" fee (agreement)   A contract form which guarantees payment to a contractor or landscape architect on the basis of a bill submitted for direct and indirect costs plus a lump sum or percentage of total design or construction cost. Often, more specifically, cost-plus-fixed fee, cost-plus-percentage, or cost-plus-sliding-fee scale. See also **Professional fee.**

Cost, project   See **Project budget.**

Costa   See **Midnerve.**

Costs in use   All of the expenses incurred by an owner in maintaining his property and/or operating enterprises developed on it.

Cottage garden   A compact planting area around a small city or country dwelling used for the cultivation of flowers and herbs and, occasionally, vegetables. The modern cottage garden generally dates from the mid-nineteenth century in Britain and Holland, and is naturalistic and vernacular in form and very casual and easy in feeling. See also **Gertrude Jekyll.**

Cotyledon   An embryonic, primary leaf, thickened with food, that is, along with the stem, the first plant structure to emerge from a sprouting seed. See also **Dicotyledon, Monocotyledon.**

Coulee   In the northern Rocky Mountains (Montana and elsewhere), a draw or gully with or without water.

Council of Landscape Architectural Registration Boards (United States)
   See **CLARB.**

Count, germination
   See **Germination count.**

Country place. Hearst Castle, San Simeon, California. Photo courtesy Leslie Allen.

Counterfort wall   A wall set as a cantilever buttressed by a counterfort, or lateral, berm. The counterfort buttressing is often of heavy concrete. See also **Retaining wall.**

Counterscarp   In medieval military design, a ditch-wall facing a fortress.

Countersinking   A method of bolt insertion that depends on the bevelling of a wood or metal surface to allow a bolt head to be recessed. Generally, the recessing of a bolt head or its securing nut. Adjective: countersunk.

Country park   A romantic (nineteenth-century) English park at the edge of a city consisting of stylized, naturalistic hills, tree copses, lawns, and the like.

Country place   An American euphemism for an estate or villa, especially one built in the late 1800s or in the early twentieth century by an industrial magnate. Country places were often landscaped in a pleasant combination of formal and informal themes first made popular by **Charles A. Platt,** q.v.

County agent   A term used to identify agricultural extension agents in the United States. The county agent provides useful advice and good pamphlets to both private citizens and designers on specific agricultural and horticultural problems. Also **Extension Agent.**

Coupler key   In irrigation, a metal rod used to engage a quick coupler. See also **Quick coupler.**

Coupler, quick (irrigation)
   See **Quick coupler.**

Coupling, compression (irrigation)
See **Compression coupling.**

Course, base See **Base course.**

Course, belt (masonry) See **Belt course.**

Course, grade See **Grade course.**

Course, leveling (road or slab construction) See **Leveling course.**

Course, oversailing (brick or stone) See **Oversailing course.**

Course, soldier (masonry) See **Paver brick pattern.**

Course, stretcher (masonry) See **Stretcher course.**

Course, string (masonry) See **String course.**

Course, wearing (pavements) See **Wearing course.**

Course of masonry A single, horizontal layer of brick, stone, cinderblock, or the like, laid in mortar.

Coursed rubble See **Rubble.**

Coursed veneer (wall construction) See **Veneer.**

Court 1) A courtyard. 2) A hard surface used for games such as tennis, squash, handball, and the like. See also **Courtyard.**

Court, food See **Food court.**

Courthouse square In the United States, a public ground or park developed around a courthouse. A typically American landscape form. See also **Square.**

Courtyard An outdoor area of limited space enclosed by walls and attached to or contained within a house or other building.

Covenant An agreement or legal arrangement. Restrictive covenants often apply to **Planned unit developments,** q.v.

Cover, ground See **Ground cover.**

Cover crop In hillside retention or other erosion control, a grass or herb crop sown as a temporary cover. Cover crops are usually replaced during the course of normal plant succession in an area. Also **Nurse crop.**

Coverage, irrigation See **Sprinkler coverage.**

Coverage, land See **Land coverage.**

Coverage, mean (irrigation) See **Mean coverage.**

Coverage, sprinkler See **Sprinkler coverage.**

CPM See **Critical path method.**

Cracks, alligator (pavement) See **Alligator cracks.**

Cracks, frost (in trees) See **Frost cracks.**

Crannied-stone walkway A paved pathway made of flat stones, the spaces (crannies) between them being filled with mortar, sand, or the like.

Crazing Fine surface cracks in concrete or reinforced concrete slabs.

Crazy paving A type of flag- or other flat-stone pavement in which irregular or broken stones are fitted together to create a more or less informal walk or patio surface.

Creek 1) A brook or stream. 2) An inlet of the sea. Often a **Slough,** q.v.

Courtyard. Tikal, Guatemala. Photo by author.

Creep, hill　See **Hill creep.**

Creep, pipe　See **Pipe creep.**

Creep, soil　See **Soil creep.**

Creep, talus　See **Soil creep.**

Creeper　A woody or herbaceous plant that creeps along the ground or up walls, fences, trees, and the like. A vine. See also **Climber, Vine.**

Crenate　In leaf surfaces, saw-toothed with rounded tips.

Creosote　A common oily, very smelly **Wood preservative,** q.v., and waterproofing agent. Creosote is highly toxic.

Crepidoma　The stepped foundation of a Greek building, especially a temple.

Crescent (barchan) dune
　See **Dune.**

Crescent, wheat　See **Wheat crescent.**

Crest　A wall-top finish detail, often ornate or intricate.

Cribbing　In landscape construction, a series of tightly knit beams used for slope retention. Wire mesh may also be added to decrease the loss of smaller soil components. Cribbing produces **Crib walls.**

Crinkle-crankle wall　A zigzag or serpentine wall.

Crispate　In plant structures, curled, crispy, wavy in the vertical plane.

Critical path method　A kind of master planning which includes project scheduling as a critical element of design and construction. Also **CPM.** See also **Progress schedule.**

Crocks　Potsherds placed in the bottom of a container for good drainage.

Croft　In Britain, a tenant farm or any little field near a rural house.

Cromlech　Palaeolithic structure of one heavy uncut stone slab positioned horizontally on approximately three other stone uprights. Occurring in Britain and Ireland. See also **Dolmen, Menhir, Trilithon.**

Crop　Produce. See also **Cash crops, Subsistence crops.**

Crop, catch　See **Catch crop.**

Crop, cover　See **Cover crop.**

Crop, nurse　See **Cover crop.**

Crop, pulse　See **Legume.**

Crop rotation　A cyclical system of soil conservation and land replenishment practiced by farmers to maintain land fertility indefinitely. A representative temperate zone rotation includes a root crop such as turnips, a legume crop (alfalfa, clover, or the like), and a cereal crop such as wheat. A typical cycle may be from two to seven years, in which different crops are planted in succession. Modern crop rotation was pioneered by the Dutch and the Flemings during the early Renaissance.

Crop, smother　See **Smother crop.**

Crops, cash　See **Cash crops.**

Crops, strip　See **Strip crops.**

Crops, subsistence　See **Subsistence crops.**

Cross axial symmetry
　See **Symmetry.**

Cromlech

Cross fertilization　See **Cross pollination.**

Cross pollination　Fertilization of one plant by another, occurring when wind- or insect-borne pollen is successfully introduced in a seed-producing flower. Cross pollination often refers to the fertilization of one species or variety by another. See also **Fertilization.**

Cross section　See **Section (drawing).**

Cross section method (earthwork)
　See **Cut and fill.**

Cross slope　See **Pitch.**

Crossing, grade　A railroad crossing. See **Grade crossing.**

Crowe, Dame Sylvia (1901–)
　British landscape architect and writer. Dame Sylvia is the author of, among other works, *Tomorrow's Landscape* and *The Landscape of Forests and Woods.* She was educated at Swarley Horticultural College, 1920–21, and designed multiple private gardens in Britain until the outbreak of World War II in 1939. She resumed her private practice in 1945.

Dame Sylvia served as design consultant for Harlow and Basildon New Towns and prepared the master plan for Commonwealth Gardens in Canberra, Australia. She has also been Design Consultant to the British Forestry Commission. Her often visionary work has been cited by the British Government, by the Royal Institute of British Architects (RIBA), of which she is an Honorary Fellow, and by the Australian Institute of Landscape Architects (AILA).

Crown 1) The foliage-covered tip of a tree's branches and trunk (**Leaf crown**) or its roots and trunk (**Root crown**). The root crown is also known as the **Collar** or **Flare.** 2) A slight convex curve in a road or walk to allow for runoff to both sides.

Crown bud (botany) See **Bud.**

Crown land In Britain, Canada, and other British dominions, land owned by the national government in the name of the sovereign.

Cruciferous In botany, pertaining to a vegetable (cabbage) or other plant producing flowers with four petals arranged in a cross. Used with the mustard family.

Cruciform In plant parts, cross-shaped.

Crushed gravel Man-made pebbles with at least one fractured surface. See also **Gravel.**

Crushed rock See **Gravel.**

Crusher-run aggregate Gravel or aggregate prepared in a mechanical crusher and unscreened after processing. See also **Crusher-run base.**

Crusher-run base The base course for asphalt pavement, usually placed on top of a foundation course and/or compacted subgrade, consisting of crushed gravel.

Crustaceous Pertaining to a crusted or withered plant structure.

Crypt A subterranean cave, often used for burials.

Cryptogamous (plant) In botany, pertaining to a **Bryophyte,** q.v.—i.e., a moss or fern. Noun: cryptogam—a spore-producing plant. See also **Phanerogam.**

Crypto porticus (Latin) A partially or completely underground passageway. A covered passageway.

Crystal garden See **Terrarium.**

CSI Construction Specifications Institute (United States), an organization developing uniform national specifications for architectural, landscape architectural, and related projects.

CSLA See **Canadian Society of Landscape Architects.**

CTB See **Concrete-treated base.**

Cubage In measurements, the cubic volume of a structure or element.

Cube In landscape construction, a cubic foot, yard, or other quantity measurement.

Cubic feet per second See **CFS.**

Cubism A twentieth-century art movement founded about 1907 by the painters Braque and Picasso, based on an abstraction of physical form reduced to geometric shapes. Cubism early influenced sculptors and architects, and was introduced to U.S. landscape design during the "Harvard Revolution" of the late 1930s by **Garrett Eckbo, Dan Kiley,** q.q.v., Walter Gropius, and others.

Cucullate In plant parts, a hood-like form.

Cuesta (Spanish) In geology, a long, sloping ridge much like a **Hogback,** q.v. Also **Wold.**

Cul-de-sac A street with only one entry ending in an enlarged circular turnaround area.

Culling In horticulture, the selection for further growth of the best of a group of seedlings through elimination of poor specimens.

Culm A plant stem, especially a jointed grass stalk. Carpet grass (*Axonopus compressus*) and African bermuda (*Cynodon dactylon*) are typical examples.

Cultigen A plant species that has been cultivated by man for so many generations that it becomes distinct from all naturally occurring plant species.

Cultipacking A cultivation and planting operation in which the soil is mechanically cut in V-shaped rows, seeded, and firmed in place.

Cultivar (also Cultival) In botany, a plant variety that is bred to exhibit desirable characteristics from a wild or domesticated parent stock. Cultivars generally cannot maintain themselves distinctly outside of cultivation, as their main method of reproduction is asexual. In classification, they are listed in Roman typeface after the **Binomial,** q.v. See also **Species, Subspecies, Variety.**

Cultivated Plant Code An international code compiled under the auspices of UNESCO that establishes botanical names for cultivated plant varieties by common review and agreement. Also **Horticultural Code.** See also **International Code of Nomenclature for Cultivated Plants.**

Cultivation, contour See **Contour plowing.**

Cultivator A common garden machine used to till the soil for planting or to weed a vegetable or fruit row.

Cultural geography See **Landscape history.**

Cultural landscape See **Man-made landscape.**

Culture (plant culture) The care and cultivation of plants.

Culture, water See **Hydroponics.**

Culvert A drain under a roadway or an embankment constructed for ease of water flow. Often consisting of metal, reinforced concrete, or cement asbestos pipe. See also **Conduit.**

Cunneate In leaves, wedge-like in form.

Cupola A small, "capping" domelet built atop a garden house, belvedere, or similar structure.

Cupulate In plant structures, cup-like in form.

Curb A concrete, asphalt, or stone edging along a walkway or road. Often constructed with a gutter, and thereby offered for bid as "curb and gutter." British: **Kerb.**

Curb, bottom of See **Bottom of curb.**

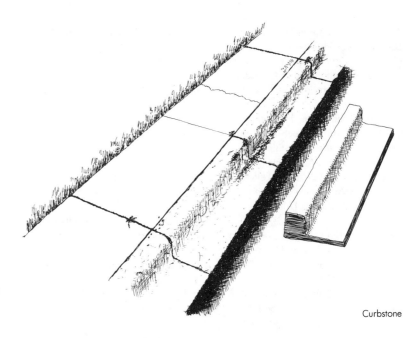

Curbstone

Curb elevation See **Top of curb.**

Curbstone A single monolithic section of poured curb or curb and gutter. Also **Kerbstone (British).**

Curb stop In irrigation, a valve, sometimes installed by a local government, supplying water at the curb to control a water supply.

Curb, top of See **Top of curb.**

Curing, cold weather (of concrete) See **Cold weather curing.**

Curing (of concrete) The process of hardening in concrete occurring because of chemical reaction between cement and water in which new compounds are formed with water in a definite ratio. Often called **Hydration,** q.v.

Curing, moist (of concrete) See **Moist curing.**

Curvature, point of (road design) See **Point of curvature.**

Curve alignment, horizontal See **Horizontal curve alignment.**

Curve, compound See **Compound curve.**

Curve, irregular See **Irregular curve.**

Curve, reverse See **Reverse curve.**

Curve, simple See **Simple curve.**

Curve, vertical (roads) See **Vertical curve.**

Curvilinear In design, curving or flowing in curves.

Cushion, pipe (irrigation) See **Pipe cushion.**

Cuspidate Referring to a sharp, hard leaf point, as in yucca and agave species and the like.

Cut (cut sheet) In landscape architecture, a selected sheet, taken from a manufacturer's brochure or

D

Dado   A square-sided groove routed cross-grain in a board.

Dale   A grassy valley, often possessed of picturesque qualities.

Dam, brush   See **Check dam.**

Dam, check   See **Check dam.**

Dam, debris   See **Check dam.**

Dam, log   See **Check dam.**

Dam, loose rock   See **Check dam.**

Dam, masonry or concrete
   See **Check dam.**

Dam, woven wire   See **Check dam.**

Damages, liquidated
   See **Liquidated damages.**

Damping down   In horticulture, watering the floor and woodwork of a greenhouse to humidify it.

Damping-off   A fungus disease of seedlings and cuttings in which new growth decays from the surface inward. Often derived from overwatering.

Danish landscape architecture
   See **Scandinavian landscape architecture.**

Darby (darbying)   In concrete finishing, the leveling of ridges and filling of voids left by a straight edge during screeding. Also **Bull float.** See also **Screed.**

Date, bid   See **Bid date.**

Date, "drop dead"   See **"Drop dead" date.**

Datum level   See **Datum line.**

Datum line   In landscape design, the basic plane of reference to which assorted landscape elements are referred. A **Datum point** is located on the datum plane or along the datum line. Mean sea level is often used as a basic datum line. Also **Datum level.**

Datum point   See **Datum line.**

Day, calendar   See **Calendar day.**

Day, weather working
   See **Weather working day.**

DBH   Diameter breast height, q.v.

Dead load   The weight of earth or permanent construction over a pipe or other underground object or beam. See also **Dynamic load, Live load, Snow load, Wind load.**

Dead man   In landscape design, a length of log or lumber buried horizontally underground to which a rope or cable is tied to secure a nearby tree trunk, post, etc. Also **Ground anchor.**

Deadweight   The weight of the materials comprising a landscape structure by themselves, with no live load included.

Dealer, package (project development)   See **Turnkey project.**

Dealkalization   In soils, alkali removal by soil amendment or leaching.

Debacle   In streams, the massive spring runoff that follows the winter thaw. Also, more broadly, any exceptional flood.

Deblossoming   In horticulture, the removal of fruit or vegetable blossoms to insure a more desirable crop—i.e., larger and better produce.

Debris   1) Left-over waste after construction or other activity. 2) A built-up mass of rock particles. Also **Talus.**

Debris dam   See **Check dam.**

Decibel   A measure of sound intensity equal to $1/10$ of a bel. Abbreviation: dB.

Deciduous trees, having shed their leaves in the autumn, often make dramatic winter profiles. Photo by author.

Deciduous   A classification of temperate zone tree and shrubs, mostly hardwoods, which shed all their leaves in autumn or in a dry season. Also **Caducous** (early deciduous). See also **Evergreen, Fugacious.**

Deck   A wooden platform, at or near grade or raised, much used in landscape construction for patios, terraces, or accent features. Originally, the flooring of a ship. Also **Timber terrace.** See also **Duckboards, Plank and beam construction.**

Deck tennis   A tennis-like lawn game played in an 18 ft. by 40 ft. space (approximately 5.5 meters by 12 meters).

Decomposed granite (DG)
   Crumbled granite, usually developed by erosion, commonly used in landscape construction as fill and for walks or other pathways.

Decorative tile   See **Tile.**

Decumbency   In grasses, low growth or a low-lying mat. Adjective: decumbent. See also **Recumbent.**

Deck

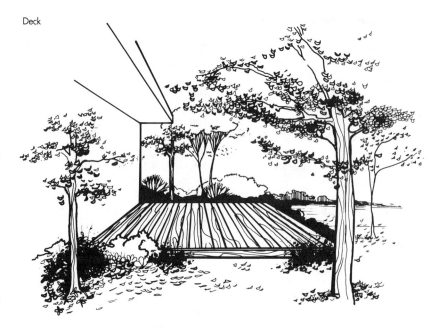

Decurved   In plants, reflexive or **Reflexed,** q.v.—i.e., curved downward. Also **Decurrent, Deflexed.**

Decussate   Pertaining to alternating pairs of leaves which grow at right angles to each other along a common stem.

Dedicated tax bonds   See **Financing for public works construction.**

Deductive alternate   See **Alternate (bid).**

Defects liability period
   See **Guarantee.**

Deflation   Wind turbulence carrying sand and dust. See also **Loess**.

Deflection   In landscape construction: 1) the twisting or deforming of a beam or other structural member because of stresses produced by loads dependent on it; 2) load stress on a surface and its resultant material distortion; 3) conduit or pipe distortion without cracking.

Deflection tolerance (support of upright members)   The ability of a structural wood, metal, or other beam or finish plant to withstand twisting or deformation caused by load stress.

Deflexed   In plants, bent down. Also **Decurved**. See **Reflexed**.

Defoliant   A chemical spray that causes leaves to drop from a tree or shrub.

Deforestation   A process in both temperate and tropical zones in which woods are cleared for crop planting or grazing. Frequently the appalling result of overpopulation or the collective avarice of real estate brokers.

Degradation   The natural process involving the wearing away of land along a streambed by running water and the corrosive action of its suspended particles. Degradation of slopes can also occur through **Soil creep,** q.v. See also **Aggradation**.

Degree of curve   In road layout, the curvature of a circular—not parabolic—arc.

Degree of slope (slope angle)   See **Gradient**.

Dehiscence   In flowering plants, the ability of an ovary structure to open of its own accord and release seeds. See also **Capsule, Indehiscence**.

Deliquescent growth (in trees)   A pattern of abrupt, staccato branching from a tree trunk.

Delta   At a river mouth, an area-wide deposit of sediments roughly resembling a large triangle.

Deltoid   In plants, sharply triangular. The cottonwood leaf is an example.

Demand, water   See **Water demand**.

Demesne   The land surrounding a mansion or comprising an estate, especially park land. Also **Domain**.

Demography   The study of populations and their characteristics.

Demolition   The destruction and removal of an existing site feature in anticipation of the installation of replacement or correlate elements.

Dendritic drainage   A very common drainage pattern resembling a tree and its branches, commonly occurring in mountain areas with level or near-level rock strata. See also **Drainage pattern**.

Dendrochronology   The specialized botanical study of tree growth as it relates to climatic history and other factors in a tree's environment. The study of tree rings to determine age.

Dendrology   The specialized portion of botany that deals with the study of trees.

Densification of soils   See **Soil densification**.

Deshooting   In horticulture, the removal of a tree or shrub shoot, usually by rubbing.

Density, dry (of soil)   See **Dry density**.

Density, optimum (soil compaction)   See **Optimum density**.

Density of population   See **Population density**.

Dentate   In leaves, a toothed margin. See also **Erose**.

Denticle   A minute "tooth" on the edge of a leaf or other plant structure.

Denudation   The stripping of vegetation and erosion of land by natural or artificial processes. A disagreeable form of earth sculpting. See also **Deposition, Erosion**.

Department of horticulture   A university division in which plant cultivation for food production, commercial or industrial use, or landscape improvement is taught. Often called a **Garden school**. See also **Education in landscape architecture**.

Department of Housing and Urban Development (U.S.)   See **Housing and Urban Development, Department of.**

Departure (surveying)   See **Latitude**.

Depauperate   Pertaining to ill-formed or stunted smaller plants growing under poor conditions.

Dependency   In the colonial eastern United States, a small outbuilding or service hut constructed near a house or government building. Often a garden service structure.

Deposit, siliceous   See **Diatomaceous earth**.

Deposition   The placement in new areas of transported sand, mud, dust, stones, and silt by such natural agents as winds, glaciers, rivers and the sea. A form of natural earth sculpting. See also **Denudation, Erosion.**

Depositional landform
   See **Landform.**

Deposits, eluvial   See **Eluvial deposits.**

Depth, effective soil   See **Effective soil depth.**

Depth of flow   In pipes or channels, the distance between the flowing water surface and the bottom, or invert, of its conduit.

Derelict garden   An abandoned or semi-abandoned garden plot lacking regular upkeep.

Derelict land   1) A portion of developed property allowed to revert to its prior condition. 2) A tract of defiled land, such as that left after strip mining or construction demolition, allowed to stay in a spoiled and useless condition through the irresponsible stewardship of its owner or user.

Derrick stone   In landscape construction, boulders that can only be handled by means of a light derrick or crane.

Desalination (desalinization)   1) A process of desalting brackish or salt water for agricultural or urban use. 2) A leaching or flushing process used to remove salt from soils.

Desander (irrigation)   A filtering device attached to wells or well pumps that removes sand, scale and other impurities from a water supply before the pumped water is put into an irrigation system or pool. Also **Separator.**

Descanso   In Spanish America and the southwestern United States, a small shelter under which a coffin rests while the gravesite is readied. Similar to a **Lych gate,** q.v.

Desert   An area that is generally barren because of climatic extremes, especially lack of rainfall. A region with less than 10 in. or 25 cm of annual rainfall. An arid region. Deserts of the twentieth century are expanding because of general climatic trends aggravated by generally poor land management and increased human population. See also **Desertification, Relief desert, Tropical desert.**

Desert garden   In the United States, a specialty garden often found in the Southwest that features succulents and other plants that tolerate low rainfall and extreme heat (and sometimes cold) well. Desert gardens often include stones and boulders as well.

Desert, high   See **High desert.**

Desert, intermediate
   See **Intermediate desert.**

Desert, low   See **Low desert.**

Desert, relief   See **Relief desert** and **Desertification.**

Desert soil   See **Gray earth, Red desert soil.**

Desert, subtropical   See **Tropical desert.**

Desert, tropical   See **Tropical desert** and **Desertification.**

Desertification   The progressive drying out and denudation of a region due to climatic processes and human misuse. Continent-building is a chief cause of desertification, as steadily rising mountain ranges prevent rain-bearing clouds from reaching the interior of large land masses. See also **Relief desert, Tropical desert.**

Desertification. Sultanate of Oman. Photo courtesy Steve Borbas.

Desiccation   In landscape architecture, the drying out of land or plant materials, especially by winds or sun.

Design   In landscape architecture, the creative laying-out and planning of outdoor space for the greatest possible amount of harmony, utility, and beauty.

Design, barrier-free   See **Barrier-free design.**

Design contract   An agreement between Owner and Landscape Architect, Prime Consultant and Landscape Architect, or Contractor and Landscape Architect outlining the basic provision of services and payments to be made for the duration of a project. Design contracts may be drafted as Letters of Intent, on ASLA (or other) standard forms, or on an individual basis to suit the needs of the work. See also **Letter of Intent, Professional fee.**

Design control drawing   The schematic design drawing of a specific project produced by a landscape architect for a client architect or engineer. The design control drawing is then developed as working drawings by the client designer.

Design development phase   A common term for the preliminary plan and estimate part of a landscape architect's services to an owner, including the preparation of detailed design sheets, specifications, and cost projections for the owner's review and approval. Followed by the **Working drawings phase,** q.v. See also **Bid phase, Construction phase, Schematic design phase.**

Design drawings   In landscape architecture, the drawings from which a project is constructed, usually augmented by **Specifications,** q.v. See also **Working drawings.**

Design, environmental
    See **Environmental design.**

Design, intuitive   See **Intuitive design.**

Design, landscape   See **Landscape design.**

Design life   The reasonably foreseeable, useful life of a design project.

Design pressure   In irrigation, the **Adjusted static pressure,** q.v., or highest pressure for which an irrigation system may be designed. See also **Flow pressure.**

Design, programming for
    See **Programming for design.**

Design, rational   See **Rational design.**

Design retainer   See **Retainer (design).**

Design, site specific   See **Site specific design.**

Design storm   In site planning, a projected storm of particular intensity used to compute conduit and channel sizes and capacities and to plan for floods. The intensity of the design storm is calculated by examination of local weather records. 10-, 25-, 50-, and 100-year storms are commonly used. See also **Drainage, Rational formula.**

Design theory   See **Landscape architectural theory.**

Design, urban   See **Urban design.**

"Desire" path   A path made casually by people finding the shortest route between two points. Desire paths are common occurrences in densely populated apartment complexes, on large school campuses, in parks, and in other heavily used public landscapes.

Detail   An enlargement drawing of a portion of a plan showing specific dimensions, components, and other intricacies necessary for successful construction in a given landscape area.

Detailed estimate of construction cost   A specific projection of project costs based on a breakdown of labor and materials charges for each item of proposed work. See also **"Ball-park" estimate.**

Detention water   Water held temporarily in a pond or basin before discharge into a drainage system. See also **Retention water.**

Dethatching   In horticulture, the process of vigorously raking an established lawn to remove accumulated layers of old grass, debris, and the like. Dethatching maintains or improves the health of a turf area. See also **Thatch.**

Detritus   Rock debris. Adjective: detrital.

Detritus load   See **Stream load.**

Development, cluster   See **Cluster development.**

Development, planned unit
    See **Planned unit development.**

Development, strip or ribbon
    See **Strip development.**

Dew   Early morning moisture, formed when cool night air causes droplets to condense in the lower layers of the atmosphere. The temperature at which condensation occurs is the dew point.

DF Douglas fir, q.v.

DG Decomposed granite, q.v.

D-horizon A distinct rock stratum underlying the A-, B-, and C-horizons often dealt with in landscape design.

DHV In traffic engineering and transportation projections, design hourly volume. See also **ADT**.

Diageotropism (in plant growth) See **Geotropism**. See also **Hydrotropism, Phototropism**.

Diagram, climate See **Climate diagram**.

Diameter 1) Concerning sprinkler discharge, the circle of coverage produced by a given head at a given pressure. 2) In irrigation piping, line size.

Diameter breast height (DBH) A sectional measurement of tree trunk size taken at 4.5 feet (1.37 m) above ground level used as a standard. See also **Caliper**.

Diaper work A repetitive pattern of small squares, ovals, inset triangles, or the like, in tile or other material on the surface of a wall.

Diaphragm valve In irrigation, a remote control valve utilizing either an electric or a hydraulically activated diaphragm for its operation.

Diary, garden See **Garden diary**.

Diastrophic landform See **Landform**.

Diatomaceous earth Soil that contains the silicon skeletal parts of diatoms, sometimes used in pump or irrigation line filters.

Diatoms Algae largely lacking chlorophyll but with glass-like cell walls containing silicon. Diatoms are basic to the Earth's food chain.

Diazo An ammonia duplication or reproduction process used with transparent original plan sheets. See also **Sepia**.

Dibble (dibber) A pointed spike with a handle used to punch holes in the soil for the placement of bedding plants.

Dichogamy In botany, the maturation of male (staminate) or female (pistillate) organs in sequence to prevent self-fertilization. See also **Protandrous** and **Protogynous**.

Dichotomous In plants, double-branched.

Dicotyledon (dicot) A member of the plant subclass *Dicotyledonae*. A flowering plant that produces two embryonic seed leaves or **Cotyledons**, q.v., at germination. An **Angiosperm**, q.v. Also **Exogen**. See also **Monocotyledon**.

Die-back Loss of leaves, buds, or flowers at branch or stem tips due to freezing, wind damage, drought, disease, and the like.

Digging, double See **Double digging**.

Digitate A leaf form in which leaflets all radiate from a common center. The horsechestnut leaf is an example.

Dike (dyke) A man-made bank of earth along a seashore or river that protects against flooding. See also **Levee**.

Diluent In concrete mixing, a "thinner" or a liquid or solid added to a mix as a filler.

Diluvium An old term for a flood deposit.

Dimension In design drawing, a precise measurement noted on a plan to aid in construction. A floating dimension ($\pm$) is an approximate measurement. Plans are most frequently "dimensioned" by offset, angular, grid, running, reference line, or modular systems (layouts). See also **Offset distance, Reference line**.

Dimension lumber (joists and planks) See **Lumber**.

Dimension stone See **Ashlar**.

Dimensioning (of plans) See **Dimension**.

Dimensioning, offset See **Offset distance**.

Dimorphism (sexual) In botany, a difference or differences in physiology between male and female plants. Sexual dimorphism is also a very common zoological phenomenon. See also **Allometry**.

Dioecious In botany, a species in which male and female flowers occur on different plants. See also **Hermaphrodite, Monoecious, Polygamous**.

Dip or soak wood treatment A light immersion (dipping) or rather lengthy immersion (soaking) of wood in a vat of chemical preservative. See also **Wood preservative**.

Diploid (plant cell) A cell with a normal quantity of properly paired chromosomes. See also **Polyploid, Tetraploid**.

Dira'a (Arabic) A common unit of measurement in Islamic gardens until its recent replacement by the meter.

Direct expense   In design or construction, any item of clearly related expenditure incurred in relation to a specific project. Such items are sometimes reimbursable to the landscape architect. Also **Reimbursable expense.**

Direction, centrifugal (city planning)   See **Centrifugal direction.**

Direction-control valve (irrigation)   See **Check valve** and **Vacuum breaker.**

Directory   In office and industrial parks, zoos, botanical gardens, and other public landscapes, a direction finder and self-help guide for visitors. Directories are usually located close to entry roads or main footpaths.

Disabled access   See **Handicapped access.**

Disbudding   In horticulture, the removal of the tender buds or new flowers of a plant. Also **Pinching back.**

Discharge rate   In irrigation, a measurement of the quantity of flow for a given time. Often measured as **GPM,** or gallons per minute. Discharge rate is calculated for sprinkler heads, water meters (GPM flow), pumps, and the like.

Disciform   In plant structures, disc-like in shape.

Discing   In landscape construction, soil cultivation with a disc harrow.

Discontinuous distribution   In horticulture, the dominance of single plant species in intermittent areas. Continuous and exclusive distribution of a single plant species is quite rare.

Dish garden   A small **Terrarium,** q.v., filled with potting soil and furnished with house plants—usually tender exotics.

Dispersal, wind (of seed)   See **Wind dispersal.**

Distance, offset   See **Offset distance.**

Distance, sight (roadway design)   See **Sight distance.**

Distance, travel (crown plotting of roads)   See **Travel distance.**

Distribution, discontinuous   See **Discontinuous distribution.**

District, assessment   See **Assessment district.**

District, conservation   See **Soil conservation district.**

Ditch   A long and somewhat narrow uncovered hollow or trench dug in the ground to receive and/or conduct water. See also **Trench.**

Ditch, boulder   See **French drain.**

Ditch, intercepting (drainage)   See **Intercepting ditch.**

Diurnal   In plants, day-opening; active or occurring during the day.

Diurnal range   In air temperature, the difference between the nighttime minimum and the daytime maximum of a single day.

Diurnal rhythm   See **Circadian rhythm.**

Diurnal variation   The fluctuation of temperature between day and night. Diurnal variation is greatest in deserts, in which there is little vegetation or water to prevent nighttime heat loss or provide daytime cooling.

Divaricate (Divaricata)   In plant structures, splayed or wide.

Divided contract   A series of prime contracts awarded to specialty contractors directly by an owner rather than through a primary or general contractor.

Divider   A **Mowing strip** or kind of **Edging,** q.q.v.

Division   1) A broad category of primary plant classification, sometimes referred to as a **Phylum,** q.v., See **Botanical classification.** 2) A kind of plant **Propagation,** q.v., by splitting clumps, cutting root sections, severing runners and the like. Frequently used with perennials and bulbs.

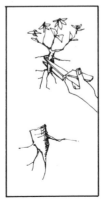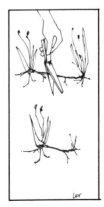

Division

DMD (Double meridian distance) A method of computing the area of a surveyed property with a closed traverse.

DMH A plan abbreviation for **Drop manhole.**

Documents, bid See **Bid documents.**

Documents, construction See **Construction documents.**

Documents, contract See **Construction documents.**

Dogleg A sudden oblique or right angle turn in a path, golf fairway, road, or the like.

Dog's tooth wall A brick wall in which at least one course is laid with its brick corners protruding.

Dogtrot In the southern U.S. and elsewhere, a sheltered area (an arcade or overhead) between two buildings, or a building and a garden structure.

Dolabrate In plant structures, hatchet-like in form.

Dolmen Paleolithic stone slab constructions of huge monolithic uprights and horizontal roof members. Precursor of lintel and post combinations. See also **Cromlech, Menhir,** and **Trilithon.**

Domain In New Zealand and elsewhere, public open space containing a museum, war memorial, park, or the like. Also **Demesne.**

Domain, eminent See **Eminent domain.**

Domestic water See **Potable water.**

Domestication The conversion of wild plant and animal species into organisms specifically suited for human use. Taming.

Dominant species In a wild or man-made landscape, the plant species that determines the character of an area.

Dooryard garden See **Kitchen garden.**

Dope, pipe (irrigation) See **Pipe dope.**

Dormant Not in active growth or development; in a state of dormancy. Often said of deciduous plants during winter or of their flower buds before blooming. Noun: dormancy. See also **Hardy (hardiness).**

Dormant seed See **Commercial seed classifications.**

Dot plant A relatively tall specimen or feature plant in a formal flowerbed.

Double check valve In irrigation, a double valve allowing water to pass in a single direction only. See also **Check valve.**

Double digging A garden operation in which the soil is spaded or forked once at the surface and once under the original turning. A double vertical digging.

Double flower In horticulture, flowers (mutants, hybrids and the like) that have a second or third row of conspicuous petals; especially, large, showy, multipetaled flowers. See also **Flower, Single flower.**

Double meridian distance (surveying) See **DMD.**

Douglas fir (DF) A wood of high strength and considerable durability frequently used in the construction of outdoor features. Often called out simply as **Fir.**

Dovecote A pigeon or dove coop, sometimes located in or near a garden.

Dowelling In concrete construction, the placement of steel connecting dowels between two separate pours for added strength.

Downing, Andrew Jackson (1815–52) United States nurseryman, landscape gardener, and writer, born in New York. Downing was the son and brother of nurserymen. He was an enthusiastic admirer of the English Landscape Gardening School, from the forms and writings of which he fashioned an early American approach to landscape design. He proposed to adapt the serpentine lines, soft grasslands, and copses of the naturalistic landscape to the more modest home grounds of the growing American middle class. The curving suburban front lawn is one of his legacies.

Downing was early influenced by the English painter Raphael Hoyle and, later, by his own travels in Britain. He published his *Treatise on Landscape Gardening* (full title: *Theory and Practice of Landscape Gardening, Adapted to North America, With a View to the Improvement of Country Residences*) in 1841. It was a widespread success. Later works included *Notes About Buildings in the Country* (1849), *The Architecture of Country Houses* (1850), and the posthumous *Cottage Residences: A Series of Designs for Rural Cottages and Cottage Villas, and Their Gardens and Grounds Adapted to North America* (1853), all of which consolidated his reputation.

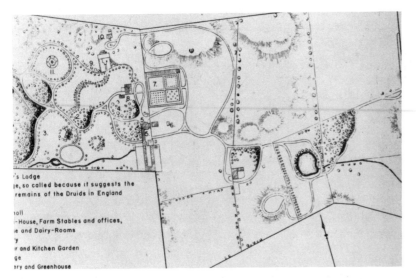

A. J. Downing. Garden at Springside for Matthew Vassar, early 19th century. Illustration courtesy BBMSL, UNM.

's Lodge
je, so called because it suggests the
remains of the Druids in England

oll
-House, Farm Stables and offices,
e and Dairy-Rooms
y
r and Kitchen Garden
ge
ry and Greenhouse

Downtown. Portland, Oregon. Many U.S. downtown districts have been revitalized in the 1970s and 1980s. Photo by author.

Among Downing's major concerns was the development of the **Genius loci,** q.v., of his sites. His designs included the grounds of Wodenethe, Fishkill, New York, and early plans for the White House and the Smithsonian Institution. Downing realized that the social effects of the Industrial Revolution were far-reaching and campaigned for public parks in American cities. His partnership with the English architect **Calvert Vaux,** q.v., begun in 1849, marks the beginning of the shift from the older American landscape gardening tradition of **Jefferson, Parmentier,** q.q.v., and Downing himself to the modern practice of landscape architecture. See also **United States landscape architecture.**

Downlands In Australia, temperate, grassy regions.

Downs Gently rolling grassed uplands.

Downtown A central business and cultural district in a town or city. Also **CBD** or **Central business district.**

Dragon's teeth In Britain, a row or rows of low bollards set along the edge of a road, used to control access to adjacent lands.

Drain A pipe used to collect and carry off storm, irrigation, or sanitary waste water. See also **Drainage.**

Drain, French See **French drain.**

Drain inlet See **Drop inlet.**

Drain, intercepting
See **Intercepting ditch.**

Drain, rubble See **French drain.**

Drain, trench See **French drain.**

Drain, trickle (pond overflow)
See **Trickle drain.**

Drain valve (irrigation) 1) Manual: a valve that is opened in the late fall to allow standing water to drain out of a system and air to enter it. 2) Automatic: a self-operating valve consisting of a gravity ball-, spring-loaded ball- or plunger-mechanism that opens to release supply line water at the low point(s) of a sprinkler zone. Not under continuous pressure.

Drain, yard See **Yard drain.**

Drainage The running off of water from a land surface or subsurface by various means and for differing purposes: 1) Sanitary drainage: see **Sanitary sewer.** 2) Site drainage: the patterns of existing or proposed water runoff in a given project area. 3) Storm drainage: runoff from snow, rain or other storms. See **Storm sewer.** 4) Subsurface drainage: sanitary and storm sewers, tile drains, overall water percolation through permeable soil, and the like. 5) Surface drainage: any movement of water from one area of land to another. 6) Underground drainage: see **Subsurface drainage.** 7) Interior drainage: a closed drainage, not emptying into an ocean.
See also **Channel drainage, Drainage pattern, Sheet drainage.**

Drainage, annular (pattern)
See **Trellis drainage.**

Drainage, antecedent
See **Inconsequent drainage.**

Drainage, dendritic (pattern)
See **Dendritic drainage.**

Drainage, inconsequent
See **Inconsequent drainage.**

Drainage, interruption
See **Interruption drainage.**

Drainage pattern

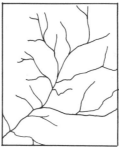 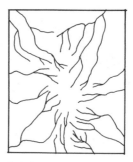 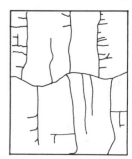

Dendritic   Radial   Trellis

Drainage pattern The forms streamcuts make in the surface of a watershed. Patterns include **Dendritic, Radial, Rectangular, Trellised,** and **Inconsequent** drainages, q.q.v., and their variants. Dendritic, radial, and trellis patterns occur most frequently.

Drainage, positive See **Positive drainage.**

Drainage, radial (pattern)
See **Radial drainage.**

Drainage, rectangular (pattern)
See **Rectangular drainage.**

Drainage, relief See **Relief drainage.**

Drainage, superimposed
See **Superimposed drainage.**

Drainage system In landscape architecture, a designed series of pipes, gutters, channels, and accessories used to develop good water run-off from a parcel of land.

Drainage, trellised See **Trellis drainage.**

Draw (United States) A small gulch or valley through which passes permanent or seasonal water.

Drawing, clarification
See **Clarification drawing.**

Drawing, design control
See **Design control drawing.**

Drawing, isometric See **Isometric drawing.**

Drawing, reference See **Reference drawing.**

Drawings, as-built See **As-built drawings.**

Drawings, construction
See **Working drawings.**

Drawings, contract See **Contract drawings.**

Drawings, design See **Design drawings.**

Drawings, preliminary See **Design development phase.**

Drawings, record or **drawings of record** See **As-built drawings.**

Drawings, working See **Working drawings.**

Dressed size (of lumber) The finished size or dimension of lumber after planing and/or sawing is complete. Usual finished sizes are $^3/_8$ in. (.95 cm) for thicknesses and $^1/_2$ in. (1.27 cm) for widths. Also **Cut down size.** See also **Lumber.**

Dressed stone Well-finished stone used in walls.

Dressing 1) Stone or lumber finishing. 2) An amendment added to soil. 3) The preparation of plant stock by pruning or selective removal of leaves, stems, and the like for use as cuttings or for grafting. Dressing also makes possible a desired kind or quality of blooming.

Dressing, top See **Top dressing.**

Drift In landscape design, a usually irregular mass of flowers or other plants positioned for effect.

Drift bolt A fastening rod or bolt used in heavy timber construction.

Drift pin In landscape construction, a long metal pin similar to a steel rebar used to anchor cast concrete or wooden bumper barriers or curbs.

Drill A seed trench made by hand or machine.

Drill, seed See **Seed drill.**

Drill seeding Planting seed by machine at close and regular intervals. See also **Seed drill.**

Drilling, fluid (horticulture) See **Fluid drilling.**

Drip A canale or other device projecting from an eave or the top of a wall, used to convey runoff water away from the wall surface.

Drip irrigation See **Trickle irrigation.**

Drip line An imaginary, roughly circular ground line indicating the maximum spread of the limbs of a tree or shrub.

"Drop dead" date In design contracts, a date given by the designer in hope, arrogance, or foolhardiness for the receipt of comments or plan changes by the

Drift of flowers. Photo courtesy Rosalind Menton.

owner. Often used to speed up the progress of reviews and general design work.

Drop inlet (drain inlet) A small underground box, usually of metal and concrete, to which surface water is directed. The drop inlet in turn directs water into an adjoining conduit. See also **Catch basin, Manhole.**

Drop manhole (DMH) A kind of access **Manhole.**

Drop, pressure See **Friction loss.**

Drop pruning In horticulture, the selective pruning or trimming of tree branches that protrude downward. Drop pruning is helpful along walkways or boulevards, where drooping limbs can be hazardous. Also called **Raising.**

Drop structure An engineering wall or run that controls water turbulence or velocity. Often a fall.

Drumlin A glacial hill, smooth, elongated, and low.

Drupe In botany, a fleshy stone fruit such as the peach, olive, or plum, originating in a single pistil.

Dry density (of soil) The weight of a given volume of soil when dry; its natural density. Dry density may be increased by **Compaction,** q.v.

Dry farming The technique of farming unirrigated land.

Dry landscape gardening A form of **Japanese landscape architecture,** q.v., in which "dry" features such as carefully raked gravel beds and stones represent, respectively, water and hills or mountains.

The dry landscape is a Zen form perfected in Japan after the seventh century A.D. The best example is perhaps the garden of Ryoanji in Kyoto. Also **Kare sansui.**

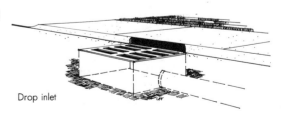

Drop inlet

Duckboards

Dry laying   In road and other pavement construction, the setting of stone, brick, block or like materials without mortar or grout.

Dry pressed brick   A brick made of barely damp clay molded under very high pressure.

Dry rot   An infection of woody plant tissue by fungus and/or bacteria.

Dry stone masonry   A kind of **Dry wall** construction, q.v., in which a low wall is constructed of loose, unmortared stones.

Dry streambed   In landscape design, a simulation of the bed of a creek, used when the effect of a watercourse is wanted but flowing water is not available or desirable. **Japanese landscape architecture,** q.v., is the most influential source of this kind of design. See also **Ephemeral streambed.**

Dry wall   A freestanding or retaining rubble wall without mortar joints. Most dry walls do not exceed three to four feet (1.0 to 1.35 m) in height and are found in informal gardens. See also **Rubble.**

Dry well   See **French drain.**

Dryad   An understory plant that prefers shade.

Duchene, Achille (1886–1947)
   French landscape architect noted for his restoration of the Vaux-le-Vicomte gardens, designed by Le Notre and originally constructed in 1661. Duchene was responsible as well for the new water gardens at Blenheim Palace, England.
   His father, Henri, was also a noted garden architect.

Duckboards (military)   A series of deck members set on stringers across a muddy stretch of ground to allow foot traffic to pass. Widely used in Europe during World War I and in the frontier American West, and now found commonly as garden walkways.

Duct, multiple tile   See **Multiple tile duct.**

Duecento   The 1200s in Italian art. A pre-Renaissance reference.

Duff   Pine needles, leaves, and other loose woodland litter. See also **Mor, Slash.**

Dummy joint   See **Control joint.**

Dump   A depository for the excess or temporarily useless products of human settlement. An obvious source of minable riches for the future, now euphemistically called **Sanitary landfill.**

Dune   A hillock made of particles of sand arranged by waves or the action of the wind. 1) **Barchan (crescent) dune:** a crescent-shaped dune typical of continental deserts, with a gently-falling windward slope and a steep leeward face. Barchan dunes constantly move in the prevailing wind direction. 2) **Gray dune:** a dune covered with small grasses. 3) **Mainland dune:** an inland dune lying at some distance from a shoreline. 4) **Marginal dune:** a seashore dune. 5) **Seif (longitudinal) dune:** a dune strung out in the direction of a prevailing wind. The windward end of a seif may be stabilized on a boulder or shrub. 6) **Transverse dune:** a very large barchan dune, or collection of barchan dunes, developed at a cross-angle to the prevailing wind. 7) **Whaleback dune:** an enormous dune formed at a parallel with the prevailing wind. 8) **White dune:** at a shoreline, a bare or sparsely vegetated dune built up continually by sand grains.
   See also **Erg.**

Dung   Animal waste. Manure.

Duodecimals (English measurement)
   A numbering system of twelfths, including inches and feet, commonly used in the United States and other English-speaking countries to calculate design items drawn in foot-and-inch scale ratios ($1/4$, $1/8$, $1/16$, and the like).

Duramen   See **Heartwood.**

Dust   Powdery soil particles, finer than sand. Often created from worn out, misused, and unprotected topsoil, and lost through wind erosion.

Dust, crusher   See **Crusher dust.**

Dust mulch   A surface deposit of very fine soil created by cultivation. Serves as an inhibitor to evaporation of soil moisture.

Dust palliative   A cretinous euphemism, primarily in military use, for soil compaction and the subsequent application of liquid asphalt to the soil surface. Common in the southwestern United States and other arid regions. Also **Asphalt soil stabilization.**

Dusting   The application of an insecticide or fungicide in the form of a fine powder.

Dutch garden   A popular nineteenth-century kitchen garden, usually formal and edged in low, trimmed hedges, developed in the Netherlands.

Dutch landscape architecture   Dutch gardens are renowned for their flower color and for their modest formalism. The first Turkish tulips reached Haarlem in 1571; by 1634, bulb growing and trading had reached the fever pitch of **Tulipomania,** q.v. The Dutch government stopped the excessive trading and a crash occurred in 1637, but the Dutch love of bulbs continued. The Keukenhof garden in Lisse, former hunting park of Countess Jacopa von Beyeren, has become the center of Dutch bulb cultivation. In its 62 acres (25 hectares) are some 80 separate show gardens, laid out formally with a wooded park and a lake as additional attractions.

The Dutch landscape has been carefully shaped since the Middle Ages. The small, square monastic gardens, laid out precisely in the even Dutch lowlands, had developed at the time of the Renaissance into axial gardens of great color and variety. The grounds of Het Loo, the palace of William of Orange, were designed in 1684 in the French style by Daniel Marot. They contained a great number of tulip beds and tracery parterres, bisected by small canals, and they were enormous in scope. The remarkable formal garden at Middachten, constructed between 1694 and 1697, also contained parterres intended for viewing from the chateau. Middachten's grounds, like those at Het Loo, were outlined by waterways in the Dutch tradition. A contemporary book, the

Dutch landscape architecture.
Canalside landscape, Amsterdam.
Photo courtesy BBMSL, UNM.

Gexantschap . . . an den grooten Tartarischen Cham of Jan Nieuhof (1665), notes the growing interest in and influence of **Chinoiserie,** q.v., in the late seventeenth century. This Dutch appreciation of things Oriental would soon cross the North Sea with William to influence the rising English School of landscape gardening. But Holland in the meantime was perfecting the stable agriculture and agricultural tools (such as improved horse harnesses) that would make large-scale landscape maintenance possible.

By the nineteenth century, topiary work, carpet bedding, and the English-style landscape garden had become popular in The Netherlands. The topiary garden at Kasteel Twichel, side-by-side with an English

garden and a lake, is typical of its day. At Weldam (c. 1900), the designer Edouard Andre laid out a castle with a moat, gardens, and canals along the property's edges. Andre's busy maze garden was intended for viewing from the castle itself. A contemporary, the similarly mixed formal/informal garden at Oostermeer, was designed by Leonard Springer.

Twentieth-century Dutch landscape style mixes traditional, tidy flower masses with informalism. Keukenhof has remained the principal display garden. The elegant contemporary landscape at Wildenborch castle combines a good vista with a landscape garden. Its long beech hedge is perhaps its most remarkable feature. A newer maze

was created at Tjaarda, Oranjewoud, in 1972. Sculpture gardens, such as Kroller-Muller at Hoge Veluwe, have become popular, and a **William Robinson,** q.v., wild garden, including a lake surrounded by woodlands, was designed at Wassenaar by C. M. Cremers and built between 1960 and 1970.
See also **Parterre, Wild garden.**

Duty of water (legal)   An amount of diverted water set aside for a specific use.

DW or **D/W**   Driveway.

Dwarf (dwarfing)   1) A healthy but genetically undersized plant. 2) Dwarfing involves a systematic effort by a gardener or several generations of gardeners to control and aesthetically shape the growth of a genetically normal pine, juniper or other plant. See also **Bonsai.**

Dwell   In rotary irrigation heads, the slight stationary watering of the sprinkler as it reaches either end of its coverage arc. "Dwell" allows outlying areas to be watered well despite the effects of wind drift on the spray of water.

Dynamic load   A pressuring force or weight producing compaction in a soil. See **Compaction.**

Earth   Soil, especially **Topsoil**, q.v. Dirt.

Earth basin   A circular depression around a newly planted tree or shrub used for improved watering. Also **Planting saucer, Soil saucer.**

Earth, black   See **Black earth.**

Earth, brown   See **Brown earth.**

Earth, diatomaceous
   See **Diatomaceous earth.**

Earth flow   See **Soil creep, Solifluction.**

Earth, gray   See **Gray earth.**

Earth pollution   The accumulation of noxious salts, radioactive wastes, toxic chemicals, contaminated water, the sloughed-off debris of construction, and civic decay that is left in the earth as a dubious legacy for plants, animals, and future generations of people. See also **Air pollution, Water pollution.**

Earth, prairie   See **Black earth** and **Brown earth.**

Earth, red and yellow   See **Podsol.**

Earth, surcharged   See **Surcharged earth.**

Earthscape   Landscape in the broad sense.

Earth science   The general term for the combination of geography, geology, meteorology, climatology, oceanography, and other specialized sciences that treats the earth as a whole.

Earthing up   In gardening, the mounding of soil around celery and other root crowns to block out light and whiten stalks. Also **Hilling up.**

Earthwork   1) Operations of grading, tamping, cut and fill, and the like associated with the moving of soil. 2) An embankment, berm, or other construction made of earth for strictly functional or sculptural purposes. Robert Smithson, Lloyd Hamrol, and others have contributed significant twentieth-century sculptural earthworks. See also **Cut and fill.**

Easement   The legal grant of right-of-use to an area of designated private property, utilized by public corporations (states, municipalities) and also made to companies providing public services such as gas, electricity, and telephone. See also **Scenic easement.**

Ebracteate   In plants, without **Bracts**, q.v.

EC   Plan notation for end of curve (roadway layout).

Earthwork. Denver Botanic Garden. Photo courtesy Rosalind Menton.

Ecclesiastical landscape architecture.
St. Catherine's Monastery and
grounds, Mount Sinai, 6th century.
Photo courtesy BBMSL, UNM.

Eccentric loading   The loading of
the weight of a wall off the center of
its footing.

Ecclesiastical landscape architecture
   The design of church, monastic,
mosque, or temple grounds or
gardens.
   In the West, medieval physic
gardens and the herbal and
horticultural gardens of monasteries
and convents formed the backbone
of the later Renaissance churchmen's
villas and botanic gardens.
   Modern ecclesiastical landscape
architecture is sometimes carried on
by professional church staffs, such as
those employed by the Mormon
Church and other denominations.
See also **Medieval landscape
architecture, Renaissance landscape
architecture.**

Echinate   In plants, covered with
spines; prickly.

Eckbo, Garrett   Twentieth-century
United States landscape architect,
theoretician, and professor, born in
New York and educated at the
University of California, Berkeley,
and at the Harvard University
Graduate School of Design. Eckbo,
Dan Kiley, and **James Rose,**
followed closely by **Lawrence
Halprin** and others, formulated the
Harvard Revolution in landscape
design of the late 1930s. Eckbo's
"new wave" drawings of the **Modern
garden** were the first ever to be
published, appearing in *Progressive
Architecture* magazine in 1937.
Eckbo's design was fresh, clean, and
eclectic; anti-Beaux Arts—indeed, a
reaction to excessive Beaux Arts
landscape ornamentation; an
exercise in the creation of functional
outdoor rooms. The landscapes that
Eckbo, Kiley, and Rose began to
produce were influenced by the
ideals of Cubism, by Walter Gropius
and the Bauhaus (Gropius had just
come to Harvard to teach), by the

quality of the classic Japanese intimate garden, and by **Thomas Church,** q.v., who had begun to design a new kind of temperate garden in California in the 1920s.

Eckbo went from Harvard to the design of migrant housing for the Farm Security Administration (1939–42), planning new communities and redesigning old ones for common people. Thus he became a restorationist of sorts, steering the profession away from its preoccupation with country places and back to the kind of responsiveness to public need that **Olmsted** had advised in the nineteenth century. He also produced a series of designs for the World's Fair of 1939.

Eckbo developed and refined the modern garden in California after World War II. His book *The Art of Home Landscaping* became, with Church's *Gardens are for People,* hallmarks of the style. Typical of Eckbo's design approach is the use

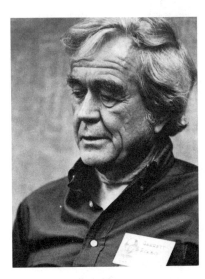

Garrett Eckbo at the California Shakespeare Festival. Photo courtesy Garrett Eckbo.

of offset forms **(Trompe l'oeil)** to change the apparent space of a garden. His gardens came to be enormously popular and his office, its range broadened with partners and associates, became highly influential throughout the country. The Fresno Mall, the grounds of Ambassador College in Pasadena, the Tucson Community Center, the Denver Botanical Gardens, the roof garden of the Union Bank in Los Angeles, the campus of the University of New Mexico in Albuquerque, and the master-planning for Shelby Farms in Tennessee are typical of his comprehensive projects.

Eckbo's standing as a twentieth-century theoretician is matched by only a handful of other figures. A good deal of his design work has been based on the rejection of preconceived form in the Beaux Arts style and on the sensitive employment of site-specific design. In such later books as *Urban Landscape Design* and *Landscape for Living,* he pressed for the integration of formalism with informalism, humanities with fine arts.

Eckbo's career spans the late Beaux Arts, the Harvard Revolution, and the period of the Environmental Movement in the twentieth century. He has been occupied in the 1980s with the development of a better aesthetic of ecology.

Eckbo taught at the University of Southern California in the 1940s and 1950s and served as Chairman of the Department of Landscape Architecture at the University of California, Berkeley, in the late 1960s. He also has lectured in Australia, Japan, Brazil, and elsewhere, and is a Fellow of the ASLA.

Eclecticism   In design, a free borrowing of styles, details, or features, and their combination into often inconsistent patterns.

Ecography   Ecological geography. The mapping or graphing of certain ecological factors such as vegetation or animal type, soil type, geology, or the like.

Ecological niche   That portion of an ecosystem for which a specific plant or animal is well-suited or well-adapted. Also **Microhabitat.**

Ecology   A branch of biology dealing with the relationships between organisms and their habitat. Coined by the biologist Haeckel about 1870, the term refers more to a point of view than to a classically defined discipline. See also **Autoecology, Human ecology, Phytoecology, Synecology, Zooecology.**

Ecology, animal   See **Zooecology.**

Economic Development Agency   An arm of the United States Department of Commerce, responsible in recent years for several federally funded public service programs, including many landscape architectural projects. Also **EDA.**

Economy (jumbo) brick   A brick fired at the nominal dimensions of 4 × 4 × 8 in.

Ecospecies   1) A plant species subdivision dependent on ecological barriers and genetic reinforcement to maintain its individuality among other varieties of the same species. 2) A plant species in its ecological context.

Ecosphere   The areas of the Earth involved with life and the ceaseless cycles of construction and decomposition that allow living things to alter the forms of inorganic matter. See also **Biosphere.**

Ecosystem   A community of living plants and animals typically found in a certain climate and locale. The well-being of any part of the community is dependent on the health of the system as a whole. Also **Biocenosis, Landscape type.** See also **Climax growth.**

Ecotone A transition area between differing plant and animal communities or associations. See also **Environmental gradients** and **Life zone.**

Ecotype In botany, a plant species that has made a genetic adaptation to a photoperiod or other climatic factor which distinguishes it from other members of its same species. An infraspecific category.

EDA See **Economic Development Administration.**

Edaphic Of or having to do with soils.

Edaphology The study of plant adaptation to a particular soil or soil series. See also **Pedology.**

Eddy A swirling pool at the side of a main current. Also, in landscape design, a quiet area to the side of a main path or walkway.

Edging 1) In concrete finishing, the smooth rounding off of a slab or wall with an edging trowel or stone. 2) In landscape construction, a vegetative or inorganic border between separate planting areas. Common edging materials are brick, stone, wood, and concrete. See also **Mowing strip.**

Edging plant Annuals, perennials, low-growing shrubs, or herbs used to accent the front of a planter or flower bed, or along the edge of a walk. Edging plants are often used for their seasonal color.

Education in landscape architecture

Landscape architecture is also called landscape gardening, landscape engineering, landscape planning, garden design, grounds design, and by other terms. Poets often practiced it in ancient China, and, indeed, gardens there were designed to provide settings for the composition and recitation of poems. The great English landscape gardeners of the eighteenth and nineteenth centuries learned their trade through traditional apprenticeships. **Bridgeman, Kent,** and **Brown,** q.q.v., all cut their teeth at the great estate of Stowe. Often they doubled as architects or painters: Repton's famous *Red Books* show several talents harnessed to a single purpose.

Thomas Jefferson, the leading (though still amateur) American landscape designer of the eighteenth century, was trained in liberal arts at the College of William and Mary, and informed himself through extensive reading, practical gardening, and travel in Europe. **Olmsted,** q.v., was a sailor, journalist, and farmer, influenced by the writings of **Downing** and by the public park designs of **Paxton,** q.q.v., which he observed firsthand in Liverpool. **Cleveland, Vaux, Jensen,** and **Eliot,** q.q.v., all received their training by means of travel, apprenticeship, and professional association. These American landscape architects heavily emphasized the public responsibilities of the profession.

Professional landscape architectural education began in earnest in the late nineteenth century. A course in landscape gardening was offered at the Massachusetts Agricultural College in 1868, just after the United States Civil War. In 1871, Iowa State College began a course of instruction in landscape architecture. P. H. Elwood was the pioneer instructor. In the same

period, Stanley White initiated courses at the University of Illinois. But the first full curriculum in landscape architecture was endowed at Harvard University in 1899 in memory of Charles Eliot.

Harvard's example has been copied throughout the United States, in Canada, and elsewhere. In the late twentieth century, the typical course in landscape architecture offers studies in plants, landscape design, construction drawings, landscape architectural theory and history, land use planning, ecology, irrigation design, soils, the design of landscape structures, light engineering, the use of computers, and related areas. Studies may take four to seven years, and result in the granting of bachelor's and master's degrees. Specialized postgraduate fields of study, such as regional planning or analysis, can lead to doctor of philosophy degrees.

Yet the profession is woefully lacking in careful research and general scholarship. Research into landscape architectural history has remained light and usually general; local historic landscape studies, as well as studies of such major geographic areas as Africa, Latin America, India, the Soviet Union, and others, are often nonexistent. Landscape architectural theory and the relationship of landscape architecture to cultural geography need much closer examination. There is a general lack of funding to allow such studies to be made and to apply them to landscape architectural education once they are completed.

A current emphasis in many of the more than 75 schools of landscape architecture in the United States is broad-scale planning. The fledgling landscape architect is taught to analyze the "sense" of a region to best determine how it might be developed and where it must be left in place. Computer use is new and growing quickly. The traditional relationship of landscape architecture with architecture and civil engineering is examined and reexamined. National groups such as CELA (the Council of Educators in Landscape Architecture) and the ASLA accrediting committees have begun to establish more uniform goals for the education of young people in the profession.

Landscape architecture is an art of connections: city and country, blossom and season, pool and lawn, stone and leaf. Yet many of the more important connections are difficult to describe, let alone teach. How do we reconcile ecological necessities with aesthetics? An understanding of the liberal arts is necessary for the landscape architect to know how landscape planning can serve modern civilization. Landscape design presents the designer with an opportunity to create art—it isn't art in itself. The student landscape architect needs to consider the broad implications of J. B. Jackson's landscape humanism: how does the popular or vernacular landscape relate to more sophisticated design?

The earlier professional approach of an apprenticeship coupled with field experience in horticulture, gardening, or construction has largely disappeared in the United States, having been replaced almost entirely by a period of formal schooling. Landscape architecture is taught in a similar fashion in Britain, Canada, and New Zealand. The profession is also flourishing in Australia, where the recent establishment of a landscape architectural program by Dean George Seddon at the Center for Environmental Studies, University of Melbourne, is serving as a model for other Australian programs.

Yet the pattern of education in most countries includes a training in related fields, such as civil engineering or botany, polished by an apprenticeship. As in the United States, would-be successful practitioners must then continue to work for older and more experienced landscape architects before they can become licensed or accredited in their own right.

The question facing a maturing profession, in practice as well as in education, is how landscape architecture is to give back to its contributing fields of horticulture, engineering, architecture, and the rest the benefits of its subtle and aesthetic-minded synthesis.

See also **J. B. Jackson** and **Landscape architectural theory.**

Eelworm   See **Nematode.**

Effect, strobe (lighting)   See **Strobe effect.**

Effective soil depth   In most cases, topsoil depth—i.e., the depth to which plant roots can penetrate to find adequate water and nutrients.

Effective span (of beams)   See **Span.**

Efficiency, irrigation   See **Irrigation efficiency.**

Efficiency of water application   See **Irrigation efficiency.**

Efflorescence   The white coating found on the outside surfaces of brick, mortared stone, or concrete block walls, caused by the presence of calcium or magnesium salts in the masonry unit or in the mortar used to construct the wall.

Effluent   A creek or river emerging from a lake; a channel of water emerging from an industrial source or sewage treatment plant. See also **Affluent, Influent.**

Egress   A way out, or exit. See also **Ingress.**

Egyptian landscape architecture

The plane (actually, the sycamore fig) and the palm were perhaps the greatest favorites of the ancient Egyptians. They formed the backbone of numberless gardens. Grapes were also widely cultivated. The Egyptians developed supporting structures for their grapevines to make harvest easier and as the millennia passed the supports became more elaborate **Pergolas,** still covered in vines but used in the shady recesses of estates for comfort and relaxation as well.

The ancient symmetry of Egyptian gardens was closely related to the axes and cross-axes of the irrigation channels supplying them. Surveying was highly developed in Egypt, and aristocratic villas up and down the Nile were well-supplied with elaborately regulated river water by 2500 B.C. Egyptian gardens were often designed around rectangular reflecting pools. Acacia, willow, papyrus, tamarisk, oleander, jasmine, and lotus were common garden plants. The Egyptians loved color, and poppies were among their favorite flowers.

The ancient form of the Egyptian house was based on a small, open courtyard surrounded by living quarters. This sort of house was common by 5000 B.C., predating similar dwelling forms in the rest of the Middle East. During the third dynasty, c. 2780–2680 B.C., the architect and minister Imhotep began to popularize building in stone. Rock tombs, raised temples in temple squares, stone terraces, obelisks, pyramids, and pylons all came to play important parts in the development of the public landscape of Egypt. Earlier organic structural materials, such as papyrus fasces used as posts, began to be replaced by stone columns that yet retained as

Egyptian landscape architecture.
Modern Deir el Bahari, Egypt:
Avenue of the Ram's Head Sphinxes.
Photo courtesy BBMSL, UNM.

surface treatment the form of the plants themselves. Among Imhotep's contributions during the reign of the Pharoah Zoser is the funerary complex at Saqqara, including the Step Pyramid of Zoser.

Thebes, the royal city in Upper Egypt, was laid out for processions and rituals. The nineteenth-dynasty Pharoah Rameses II improved the imposing roadway connections between the city and the nearby Valley of the Tombs of the Kings. Queen Hatshepsut's temple, c. 1500 B.C., reached via the Avenue of the Ram's Head Sphinxes, is perhaps the most spectacular surviving Theban monument. Its ramps, colonnades, and wide, dramatic terraces produced an entry to the temple as remarkable as the building and site themselves. The terraces are thought to have been planted originally in myrrh trees.

Scholars now note that the Egyptians were the first to develop topiary as a garden art. They also produced an early park in the third century B.C. at Philadelphia in the Fayum Oasis. The tradition of the garden **Mount,** q.v., begins in part with their temples on raised, flat platforms in the midst of cultivated fields and gardens. The Pharoah Amenhotep III, 1409–1379 B.C., is reputed to have developed quite complex formal gardens, including large water displays.

Egyptian influence spread not only through the Mediterranean but to the kingdoms of Kush (Meroe and Axum) and ultimately throughout much of the North African sudan. But the student of Egypt is struck again and again by the unwavering formality of line and tone in 5,000 years of Egyptian architecture and open space design. The striving for

perfection in axis and counterpoint seems to mimic the wish for assured immortality that preoccupied the entire society for so many thousands of years. Houses and gardens were temporary; the tombs were made for permanence.

In modern Egypt, the interpretation of traditional architecture made popular by the architect Hassan Fathy seems capable of breathing new life into ancient forms. Fathy's courtyards, patios, squares, wall treatments, and bathing pools, all developed inexpensively from local materials, have charm, character, integrity, and great promise.

See also **African landscape architecture, Islamic landscape architecture, Middle Eastern landscape architecture.**

Eighthline In surveying, a north-south or east-west centerline used to divide quarter-sections into eighth-sections. See also **Quarterline.**

El. or Elev. Elevation, q.v.

Elastic limit The point to which landscape construction materials or soils may be stressed or stretched and still return to original condition or position.

Elasticity, modulus of (structures) See **Modulus of elasticity.**

Elasticity (of soils) The capacity of a soil to go back to its original form after being compressed by a heavy weight. See also **Plasticity, Soil.**

Electric piston valve See **Piston valve.**

Electric thermal motor valve In irrigation, a kind of **Remote control valve,** q.v., activated by a heat motor.

Electrical surge protection
Lightning surging through automatic irrigation controls can trigger the operation of a system. A suppressor (or suppressors) is installed above the valves to protect against this kind of unwelcome occurrence.

Electro-horticulture The use of night-lighting or similar means to speed up plant growth or production.

Electrolysis In irrigation, a kind of corrosion by electrolytes (stray electric currents) that can damage steel piping.

Element, horizontal See **Horizontal element.**

Element, intermediate
See **Intermediate element.**

Element, minor See **Trace element.**

Element, trace See **Trace element.**

Element, vertical See **Vertical element.**

Elevation 1) A contour line or notation of relative altitude, useful in plotting existing or proposed plan features. 2) A side view of an existing or proposed feature. See also **Contour, Plan elevation, Spot elevation.**

Elevation, curb See **Top of curb.**

Elevation, finish floor (FF)
See **Finish floor elevation.**

Elevation, plan See **Plan elevation.**

Elevation, rim (site drainage)
See **Rim elevation.**

Elevation, spot See **Spot elevation.**

Elevation, super (of roadways)
See **Super elevation.**

Eliot, Charles (1859–97) The son of the president of Harvard University, Eliot received an A.B. degree in 1882 and began work with F. L. Olmsted in Brookline, Massachusetts the following year.

Eliot early recognized the depth and quality of English landscape-design influence in the United States. His travels in Europe and the eastern and southern United States further convinced him of the great need for naturalistic parks in gritty and burgeoning American cities. His work on the metropolitan park and open-space systems of Boston became his best-known achievement.

His interest in the preservation of landscapes led directly to his founding of the Trustees of Public Reservations in Massachusetts (1890), the first organization devoted to historic landscape preservation in the

United States. Eliot's strong sense of the social mission of landscape architecture carried on many of the ideals earlier expressed by **Jefferson, Downing,** and **Olmsted,** q.q.v. His death was also unusually noteworthy: in Eliot's memory, a benefactor endowed the first complete course in landscape architecture in the United States at Harvard, where classes began in 1900.

Eliot's father wrote the memorial biography, *Charles Eliot, Landscape Architect,* published in 1902.

Ell In irrigation, a pipe joint at a 90° curve in a line.

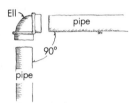

Eluvial deposits In geology, rock particles produced by weathering that are laid down near their place of origin. See also **Alluvium.**

Eluviation Leaching, q.v.

Emarginate In plant structures (particularly leaves), notched.

Embossing (concrete finishing) In concrete finishing, the stamping of a pattern into the surface.

Eminent domain The legal ability of a government body to condemn a piece of private property for public use, usually with adequate reason and compensation.

Emulsion, fish (fertilizer) See **Fish emulsion.**

Emulsion slurry seal (asphalt) A type of **Asphalt sealer,** q.v.

Encroachment The extension of a building or other physical improvement without authorization onto land belonging to a second party.

Encumbrance 1) A restriction on property use; a limitation. 2) A claim or liability attached to a property.

Endemic With plants, occurring naturally throughout a given area.

Endocarp In flowers, the inner lining (often bony) or layer of an ovary wall or its subsequent fruit. See also **Pericarp.**

Endogen See **Monocotyledon.**

Endogenous Pertaining to tissue growth under the bark of woody plants. Endogenous growth includes both wood and bark.

Endosperm In botany, a food-bearing substance found around a seed embryo.

Endwall See **Headwall.**

Enframement In landscape design, the use of plants, walls, fencing, or other materials to set off an element intended to be a feature. Surrounding or setting off a site element for emphasis.

Engineer, horticultural See **Horticultural engineer.**

Engineer, soil See **Soil engineer.**

Engineered fill In earthwork operations, carefully measured and graded fill installed to serve a highly specific function, such as foundation support, retainer wall backfill, and the like.

Engineering, value See **Value engineering.**

English bond (masonry) See **Brick wall pattern.**

English landscape architecture In Roman England, there had been scattered villas with their enclosed

English landscape architecture. Mansfield, Hardwick Hall, 16th century: view from Long Gallery. Photo courtesy BBMSL, UNM.

patios and orderly gardens as far north as Hadrian's Wall. But life in the English Middle Ages was life in a village: a cluster of modest houses, fields roundabout, a stream or river nearby, and a more or less wild forest beyond the domestic areas into which a tiny path or two disappeared. Monastic gardens, common throughout the country, kept up many ancient gardening traditions (see **Medieval landscape architecture**). In the late Middle Ages, enclosed castle courtyards and **Pleasances** developed slowly into the more open **Knot gardens** of the English Renaissance.

The early English Renaissance garden was at its prime during the reign of Elizabeth I (1558–1603). Haddon Hall, created c. 1470 south of Sheffield, was built with regular, squared-off terracing and elaborate knot gardens. Such typically English features as the **Forthright,** or broad path directly approaching a house, and the **Kitchen garden** were also found at Levens Hall in the North Lake Country (c. 1558) and Montacute in Somerset (c. 1547). Levens Hall (by the architect Beaumont for King James II) was noted for its topiary and bowling greens. **Water jokes** and garden

English landscape architecture.
Stourhead: landscape garden with
pantheon, first half of 18th century,
by Henry Hoare. Photo courtesy
BBMSL, UNM.

Mounts were popular at Montacute and other Elizabethan gardens, as was the typical cross-axial layout of the symmetrical gardens themselves.

The Elizabethan garden was more reserved than its Continental counterparts. But by the third decade of the seventeenth century, Italy and France had begun to influence the character of the formal garden. Palladianism, the adoption of neoclassical architectural orders from Italy, was popularized in England by Inigo Jones beginning in 1616. Hampton Court, owned by the English crown from the time of Henry VIII (1491–1547) onward,

was fitted out with the most elaborate of knot gardens. English writers from Shakespeare (Titania's realm in *A Midsummer Night's Dream*) to William Lawson (*New Orchard and Dream*) to Thomas Hill (*Most Briefe and Pleasaunt Treatyse,* 1563) began to arouse an interest in gardens as sources of pleasure. Perhaps the greatest landscape of the day was Wilton (begun 1615), the manor of the Earl of Pembroke. Its designer, either Isaac de Caus or **Salomon de Caus** (the designer of the grounds of Heidelburg Castle), created intricate formal gardens and excellent views—a typical

Renaissance novelty. Salomon de Caus is also said to have designed the grounds of Hatfield House, a Dutch-style Renaissance landscape in Hertfordshire.

Mazes, Allees, Ronds points and, above all, topiary work characterize the late Renaissance. Women spread out their washing to dry on the low, clipped hedges of the knot gardens and mazes, and collected herbs and vegetables from their kitchen gardens for home use. To this extent, at least, manorial gardens remained practical.

Much French style was perpetrated by **John Rose** (d. 1677), q.v., gardener to the Earl of Essex, possible student of **Le Notre,** and, finally, Royal Gardener to Charles II. Rose succeeded the **Mollets,** q.v., well-known French gardeners to the English crown. Charles himself brought the French regal style back to England during the Restoration (about 1660). Hampton Court began to appear more and more like a French vista garden under the hands of two of the Mollets; so did the grounds of Blenheim, Stowe, Castle Howard, and other baronial estates. Dutch gardening, nursery practices, and plants crossed the Channel with William and Mary (c. 1689); Hampton Court (again), Westbury Court, and other gardens were much affected.

The English seem to have become tired by this time (c. 1700) of 500 years or so of relentless formalism. Sir Francis Bacon had poked a bit of fun at topiary knot gardens and other garden extremities in his essays, including "Of Gardens," as early as 1625. For his own home in Gorhambury, Hertfordshire, Bacon prescribed simple flowers and herbs for their pleasant smells. **Sir William Temple** (d. 1699), q.v., sometime ambassador to the Hague, began what would become the English fascination with Chinese naturalistic design in his *Upon the Gardens of Epicurus,* 1685. Other English writers of the day elaborated on Temple's theme of informalism. Anthony Cooper, the Earl of Shaftesbury (d. 1713), proposed the idea of the "noble savage," and Richard Steele and Joseph Addison noted the great expense of formal gardens and their upkeep and the preferability of a softer and more natural landscape line.

The English countryside of the early 1700s had begun to show changes wrought since the late Middle Ages. The great forests had shrunk to mere windrows or hedgerows between fields in many

counties; cultivation of newly transformed forest lands was proceeding at a rapid clip to serve a growing population. Parliament, perhaps responding to the dawning of industrialization, had even created Richmond Great Park (1649) during the period of Cromwell's Commonwealth.

Against the backdrop of these rather fundamental alterations in the national landscape, an informed English gentry in a gardening mood welcomed the efforts of the nurserymen and estate designers **George London** (d. 1713) and **Henry Wise** (d. 1738), q.q.v. London, much influenced by John Rose, had established a nursery to compete with the Dutch by the 1680s. The partners created a series of French- and Dutch-inspired designs featuring topiary work, walled gardens, parterres, and other elements of the European formal standard of the day. The grounds of Melbourne Hall and Blenheim were among their best work.

Naturalism and the English School

The Romantic landscape paintings of **Lorrain, Poussin, Rosa,** and others deeply impressed the English landscape gardeners of the early eighteenth century, as did the irregular line of Chinese landscape painting and garden design. The Scottish golf course, a much underrated influence on naturalism, lurked in the background. Even writers created their own gardens in informal style. The poet Alexander Pope (d. 1744) is the best known of these; his five-acre gardens at Twickenham were an eclectic mix of bowling greens, wandering paths, evocative plantings, and a tomb for his mother.

The landscape gardener **Charles Bridgeman** (d. 1738), q.v., a protege of London and Wise, was

the first designer to use the naturalistic line in large compositions. His collaborations with John Vanbrugh at both Stowe (c. 1714) and Blenheim showed continuing strong formal paths and rides, but with casual tree masses in designated gardens. Bridgeman popularized the **Ha-ha,** making it possible to expand estate vistas without interruption and yet contain roving livestock. Bridgeman's opened-up gardens mark the beginning of the English Landscape Gardening School.

William Kent (d. 1749?), q.v., succeeded Bridgeman at Stowe and elsewhere. Kent had visited the Italian countryside and knew the work of Rosa and other picturesque painters of the 1600s. His landscapes were moodier than Bridgeman's, and his garden architecture was Palladian. Kent's gardens were a smooth mixture of formalism (near the mansion) and informalism as the distance between house and landscape park increased. Kent remodeled Stowe (c. 1769) and the grounds of Rousham, Oxfordshire, both previously designed by Bridgeman. At Stowe, the soft, rolling landscape with its scattered "ruins" began to look very picturesque indeed. Pope and Kent even collaborated on a design for Chiswick (c. 1736) and, later, on other estates. Though a popular designer and an evangelist of the new landscape gardening, Kent virtually erased a substantial number of earlier formal gardens with his redesigns, beginning a trend that was followed by his successors. By the twentieth century, only a handful of English Renaissance gardens had survived.

Lancelot (Capability) Brown (d. 1783), q.v., succeeded Kent as dean of English landscape gardeners. Brown began his gardening work as a teenager and finished his apprenticeship under Kent at Stowe.

His design trademarks became the symbols of the English School: the sinuous lakeshore, picturesque copses of trees, broad lawns with sweeping vistas. Brown started his "improvements on nature" at the foundation of the house; there were many ha-has and virtually no formal lines present in the works of this greatest purist of Western naturalism. Bridgeman's Blenheim, the Bridgeman-Kent Stowe, and Chatsworth in Derbyshire were among the best-known of Brown's many dozens of projects.

By the time **Humphry Repton** (d. 1818), q.v., had established himself, a large demand for new garden exotics had made itself felt in Britain. Repton early recognized their potential and began to design them into specialty gardens within his larger landscapes. With his sometime partner, the architect **John Nash,** q.v., Repton designed a very extensive series of large estates. Luscombe Castle in Devonshire is a good extant example. He carried on his later design work by himself or in collaboration with his sons.

Repton's design recognized a need for transitional, often formal spaces near the manor house that expanded gradually into the softer naturalism of wood, lake, and field. Repton consolidated many of the principles of the Landscape Gardening School in his *Observations on the Theory and Practice of Landscape Gardening* (1803), and in his other landscape writings, including his famous *Red Books*. Winpole Hall in Cambridgeshire (1801) and Attingham Park, Shrewsbury (1797—now under reconstruction by the British National Trust) are two of his best surviving landscapes.

Repton's contributions as a designer and theoretician notwithstanding, the English School was highly controversial in its own day. Sir **William Chambers,** q.v.,

the designer of the Chinese pagoda at Kew Gardens, had attacked Brown and his work as early as 1772. The writers **Richard Payne Knight** and **Uvedale Price,** q.q.v., thought the naturalistic style too bland; their proposals for **Picturesque** landscapes included more rugged scenery and less meticulous "manicuring" for effect. Nevertheless, naturalism had captured the imagination of gardeners throughout the British Isles. The amateur **Henry Hoare** completed Stourhead by 1783. **William Shenstone,** the poet, worked on the Leasowes (c. 1730) for more than 20 years; his Lorrain-like landscape helped to popularize the idea of the **Sublime,** q.v., in the English landscape. Certainly the largest of these melancholy naturalistic estates was Fonthill in Wiltshire, created by **William Beckford** and later popularized in Romantic literature by Edgar Allan Poe.

Victorians

The Industrial Revolution underlay many of the changes in landscape gardening that occurred in the nineteenth century. Nash's town planning at Regent's Park in London set the stage for the later design of suburbs, townhouses, and subdivisions. Suburban gardens for a growing middle class were emphasized by **J. C. Loudon** (d. 1843), q.v., the great garden writer and encyclopedist. Loudon was an early supporter of graveyard redesign for hygienic reasons and for light park use. His public park at Gravesend (1835) may be the first landscape of its kind in Britain. Loudon admired Repton and his theories and published a collected edition of many of Repton's works, but the problems of adapting Repton's naturalism to the scale of the bourgeois house were not quite

manageable. The **Gardenesque** (mish-mash) style resulted.

Meanwhile, Parliament continued the practice of systematically enclosing the open space of the country. The "hedgerowing" of England was essentially complete by 1850. Many former royal parks, the exclusive property of the crown, had been given over to public use even sooner, by the end of the 1700s. Overseas, the style of the English School had become immensely popular; from Marie Antoinette's **Ferme ornee** at Versailles to the Baltic lushness of Pavlovsk Park near St. Petersburg (See **Russian landscape architecture**), European monarchs and aristocracy scrambled to adopt it.

Color and a preoccupation with rustic details characterized the gardens of Victoria's time (1837–1901). Grottoes, iron railings and gazebos, columns of dead tree trunks, intricate flower beds, and fastidiously rustic cabins combined with the occasional "Chinese" bridge or pagoda in parks and private grounds. New and expanded botanical gardens brought more and more exotics and varieties of local species into cultivation. At Kew and Edinburgh alone, the collections comprised many tens of thousands of species. The **Wardian case** and lawn mower, both in wide use by 1850, were revolutionary technical advances in horticulture. So was the sophisticated greenhouse; **Joseph Paxton's** Crystal Palace at the London World's Fair in 1851 marked the early summit of its development.

Paxton (d. 1865) had first gained fame as the designer of Chatsworth, the estate of the Duke of Devonshire. His gardens for the Duke were neoformal, in the kind of revived Italian-French style that the Victorians found very appealing. Paxton was also the designer of Birkenhead Park near Liverpool, a public garden in the spirit of the English School that greatly impressed the young **Frederick Law Olmsted** and influenced the course of landscape architecture in the United States. Other nineteenth-century parks of note included Victoria Park in London's East End, designed by James Pennethorne; Queen's Park in Glasgow by Paxton (1853); and John Nash's earlier Hyde Park and Kensington Gardens in London. These planted urban open spaces, along with improved city sanitation, were Victorian attempts at improving the new social maladies of the Industrial Revolution.

Other attempts to the same end included Saltaire in Yorkshire (1853), the Cadbury Brothers' Bournville near Birmingham (c. 1879) and Port Sunlight near Liverpool (c. 1905) by Lever Brothers—all **New Towns** sponsored by philanthropic industrialists. These were precursors of the **Garden cities** later proposed by **Ebenezer Howard.**

Late Victorian eclecticism is best represented by **William Robinson** (d. 1935), the author of *The English Flower Garden* (1883). Robinson's ideal was a stylized English cottage garden landscape—innocent, popular, and a tantalizing step or two away from wildness. **Gertrude Jekyll** (d. 1932), the garden designer and proponent of the **Herbaceous border,** followed Robinson's lead in a highly successful career of her own. Nathan Cole, another Victorian designer, refined the **Carpet bed** in his revised layouts for Kensington and other London gardens in the 1870s.

The Modern Era

Naturalism had become very much a historic style in Britain by the twentieth century. Its influence was nonetheless broad and well-entrenched. The greatest modern English contribution to landscape architecture has perhaps been the garden cities of Ebenezer Howard and his successors and colleagues Raymond Unwin (d. 1940) and Patrick Geddes (d. 1932). These self-contained, self-limiting rural cities, characterized by greenbelts, good housing, good transportation, and local industry, were fresh models of environmental design for the twentieth century. Letchworth and Welwyn, constructed in the early decades of the century, were followed by Harlow, Stevenage, and other New Towns created by Parliamentary action after World War II.

An occasional scrap of the medieval countryside survived into the twentieth century, but the rural English landscape had become largely a uniform patchwork of fields set off by hedgerows. The landscape historian and cultural geographer **W. G. Hoskins** had produced a systematic analysis of the evolution of this landscape (with its accompanying villages) by midcentury. In addition, many of England's greatest domestic landscapes of the past several centuries have been preserved or reconstructed in this century by the National Trust and its over 800,000 members.

The work of the modern landscape architects Geoffrey and Susan Jellicoe and Dame **Sylvia Crowe** has been highly influential. Much sculpture by Henry Moore has dominated English specialty gardens of the past several decades. Brian Clouston and Derek Lovejoy, among others, have maintained far-flung international practices in the postwar years. The late **Nan Fairbrother** established herself as a leading contemporary landscape theorist in the 1960s and 1970s. These landscape architects and artists and other designers have worked within the framework of the English landscape tradition, probably the most magnetic in Western history.

The singular English devotion to landscape art was commemorated in a 1979 exhibition at London's Victoria and Albert Museum entitled "The Garden: A Celebration of One Thousand Years of British Gardening."

Also **British landscape architecture.** See also **Scottish landscape architecture** and bold-faced names and titles.

English landscape gardening
See **English landscape architecture.**

English Renaissance garden
See **Tudor garden.**

English School of Landscape Gardening   A naturalistic, romantic, and finally picturesque school of landscape design popular in Britain in the eighteenth and nineteenth centuries. The English School was founded by **Charles Bridgeman** and **William Kent,** q.q.v., as a reaction against prevailing European formalism. It was distinguished by its serpentine design lines, its lakes and copses of free-flowing trees, its ersatz ruins, and its reliance on texture and form instead of color. It was influenced by Lorrain, Rosa, and other painters, by Oriental principles of gardening newly introduced to Europe, and by the indigenous golf courses of Scotland.

The English School reached its zenith with the works of **Capability Brown** and **Humphry Repton,** q.q.v. Its forms have been preserved in the traditional British and North American city park, very popular even in the late twentieth century.

The grounds of Blenheim, Stowe, and Stourhead are examples of the English School.

See also **English landscape architecture.**

Enshu, Kobori (c. 1579–1647)
Cha-no-yu master of Japanese garden design. Enshu helped to develop a distinctly Japanese style from earlier Chinese models. Among his best known works is the Sento Gosho, an imperial garden in Kyoto. See also **Japanese landscape architecture.**

Ensiform   In leaves, sword-like in growth habit.

Entisol   A soil order with badly developed or absent horizons.

Entomophily   Plant pollination by insects. See also **Anemophily.**

Entropy   1) In botany, the loss of captive sun energy through natural plant processes, such as photosynthesis, transpiration, and seasonal change, which expend that energy. 2) In geology, a measure of the degree of uniformity of sediments. See also **Negentropy.**

Environment   1) All the world, natural and man-made, and its accompanying conditions and dilemmas. 2) The local surroundings in which a plant or animal must thrive or falter.

Environmental design   A twentieth-century term describing the conscious shaping of human and animal habitats through landscape architecture, engineering, urban planning, and architecture.

Environmental design professions
Landscape architecture, engineering, urban planning, architecture, and, often, agronomy.

Environmental gradients   In plant ecology, transition areas between **Plant communities,** q.v. See also **Ecotone.**

Environmental impact statement   In the United States, a thorough

analysis of and report on the effects of proposed site improvements, new federal or state legislation, and other governmental actions bearing on the quality of human, plant, or animal habitats. Required of all federally funded projects by the National Environmental Policy Act (1969).

Environmental planning   Planning for the intelligent management and use of land areas to assure proper habitat for people, plants, animals, and the resources upon which they depend. Also **Landscape planning.** See also **Planning.**

Environmental Protection Agency   A United States governmental division charged with the responsibility of environmental review, preservation, and rehabilitation in many federally funded projects. Also **EPA.**

Environs (Environ)   Surroundings.

EPA   See **Environmental Protection Agency.**

Ephemeral stream   A brook that flows partially on the surface and partially underground along the length of its watercourse. See also **Intermittent stream.**

Epidermis   In plants, the protective exterior layer of root, leaf, and stem or trunk cells.

Epigenetic   Pertaining to a geologic process taking place on the Earth's surface.

Epigeous (epigaeous)   In plants, ground-hugging, or with a habit of growth along the ground.

Epipedon   A **Soil horizon,** q.v., characterized by the presence of humus or **Fluvial deposits,** q.v.

Epiphyte   In botany, a plant growing on another plant but not

parasitic on it. An **Air plant.** The many varieties of orchids are common examples.

Epoch, Holocene (Recent)
See **Holocene.**

Epoxy aggregate rigid concrete   A form of concrete using rough aggregate and epoxy instead of lime as a binding medium.

Equal, approved   See **Approved equal.**

Equatorial forest   See **Rain forest.**

Erg   A Saharan landscape in which the desert surface is sand dunes. See also **Dune, Hammada, Reg.**

Erose   In plants, randomly toothed See also **Dentate.**

Erosional landform   See **Landform.**

Erosion   In land, the gradual deterioration and loss of surface soil and rock usually due to water with suspended solids in motion, or to the actions of wind. Often caused by improper human cultivation or other ill-informed use of the surface of the land. Also **Denudation.** See also **Gully erosion, Marine erosion, Sheet erosion, Wind erosion.**

Erratic   A worn boulder, often glacial and isolated, transported some distance from its source by ice movement.

Error of closure   In surveying, the dimension by which a "closed" traverse fails to complete itself.

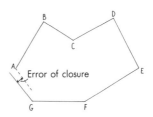

Errors and omissions insurance
Liability insurance secured by a landscape architect against mistaken or unincluded items of judgment or construction that are his responsibility while practicing professionally. See also **Malpractice insurance.**

Escape (escaped plant) A **Naturalized plant,** q.v. Also, a **Wildling.**

Escarpment A cliff-face at the edge of a mesa or plateau.

Espalier A kind of shrub trained on a frame to grow flat in a stylized form against a wall. See also **Quenouille training.**

Esplanade (French) A parade or excursion ground. See also **Mall** and **Promenade.**

Establishment period (landscape construction) See **Period of establishment.**

Estate A large parcel of privately held land with an imposing house.

Estate, life See **Life estate.**

Estate, real See **Real estate.**

Estimate, cost See **Preliminary estimate, Detailed estimate of construction cost,** and **"Ball park" estimate.**

Estimate, monthly (landscape contractor's) See **Monthly estimate.**

Estimate, preliminary See **Preliminary estimate.**

Estivation 1) An array of parts in a flower bud. 2) A state of hot-season dormancy in plants or animals.

Estoppel An old term for a dam or other natural or man-made obstruction in a watercourse.

Estuary The very lowest reach of a river at the edge of a sea. Estuaries are influenced by salt-water tides. Adjective: estuarine.

Etherization In horticulture, the use of ether to break the dormancy of a plant and begin its spring growth.

Ethnobotany The study of the culturally developed uses of plants of a given society.

Etiolation Plant growth in unusual dimness or darkness. A condition of blanched leaves or stems.

Euclidean zoning A common approach to **Zoning,** q.v., that defines land uses for residential, commercial, and industrial areas.

Euphony In gardens, the sound of flowing or falling water or the rush of wind through trees. Generally, a pleasant sound.

Euryecious (euryvalent) plant Any plant flourishing in a wide range of conditions and in many areas. A highly adaptable plant. See also **Stenoecious plant.**

Eustatic change A large variation in sea level with widespread effects.

Eutrophic Pertaining to water containing an optimum amount of dissolved plant nutrients.

Eutrophication 1) The aging process of a lake or pond, in which the body of water eventually becomes a swamp. 2) The accumulation of algae in a pond or lake.

Evaporation The process whereby water changes from a liquid to a gaseous state. Accelerated by sun, wind, lack of mulch, and the like. See also **Evapo-transpiration** and **Transpiration.**

Evapo-transpiration A compound of **Evaporation** and **Transpiration** indicating loss of water from soils or plant tissue through those two processes. Often expressed as the evapo-transpiration rate.

Evergreen A classification of tropical, temperate, and continental zone plants. Evergreens shed their needles or leaves slowly throughout the year, remaining for the most part green. They are customarily divided into conifer and broad-leafed types, and as a rule require substantial water to flourish. They are often used in landscape plantings for their winter color. See also **Deciduous, Gymnosperm.**

Evolution of plants See **Phylogeny.**

Excavation Earth removal, a hole resulting from earthwork, or material removed during earthwork. 1) **Unclassified:** a mixture of soil, gravel, and stone types in a common site. 2) **Common:** topsoil, subsoil with few rocks. 3) **Solid rock.** 4) **Borrow:** soil or fill material brought in to a site to complete earthwork operations.

Exedra (Exhedra) In an urban Greek or Roman courtyard house, an outside sitting room connected to the court, often shaded for summer use.

Exempt meter In irrigation, a meter that measures the amount of water that does not enter a sewer system or systems from a project or landscape area. A money-saving device.

Exfoliation 1) In trees, the peeling or scaling off of bark. Sycamores (plane trees) and Russian olives frequently exfoliate. 2) In geology, the splitting off of thin layers of rock from a matrix.

Existing contours See **Contours.**

Existing grade See **Grade.**

Exogen See **Dicotyledon.**

Exogenous Pertaining to tissue growth on the outside of a woody plant stem. See also **Endogenous.**

Exotic A plant that is not native to the area in which it is planted. An introduced plant. See also **Guest species, Native, Naturalized plant.**

Expansion coefficient See **Coefficient of expansion.**

Expansion joint A joint of standardized, fibrous material (celotex) or wood between abutting slabs of concrete or other pavement that allows expansion or contraction of the earth beneath a slab without cracking.
See also **Construction joint, Control joint.**

Expense, direct See **Direct expense.**

Expense, reimbursable See **Direct expense.**

Expert witness A legal term for a person testifying in an arbitration hearing or trial who is especially qualified to give a technical opinion on a matter relating to his expertise.

Exposed aggregate A concrete finish achieved by blowing off the outer surface of mortar with water spray before it hardens in order to expose the coarse aggregate. Also achieved by sandblasting after hardening. Sometimes an aggregate "seed" is added to the wet surface after floating for the desired effect. See also **Aggregate, Broom finish, Smooth finish.**

Exposure Site orientation, especially slope orientation, in regard to sun and wind.

Express (consent, agreement, contract, and the like) Direct or definite, but not signed. See also **Implied contract.**

Expressway A **Freeway,** or high-speed road with limited vehicular access.

Extension agent See **County Agent.**

Extensional landscape In landscape architecture, the landscape that must be considered outside the confines of a design area. The larger landscape. Sometimes, the **Borrowed landscape.** See also **Borrowed scenery.**

External grip (irrigation) A tool used to grasp a pipe to pull it underground. See also **Internal grip.**

Extreme fiber stress See **Stress.**

Extruded asphalt An asphalt concrete mixture extruded or spewed out of a machine to form a temporary curb or other asphalt structure.

Extruder In irrigation, a machine that manufactures various kinds of plastic pipe.

Extrusion (of brick and concrete) The emission by machine of unfired brick or wet concrete to be cut or formed in place.

Exurbs A recently coined word (1960s) used by Garrett Eckbo and others to indicate small clusters of houses or other buildings in the countryside beyond the suburbs of a twentieth-century city. Adjective: exurban.

Eye In botany, a flower's center; also, as in potatoes, a very young **Bud,** q.v.

Eye-catcher In English romantic landscapes, a prominent or incidental false ruin, often used as a focal point. See also **Follies.**

"Eyewash" Designers' slang for a sketch or plan created primarily to impress a project client or user.

F

F₁ (hybrid) In horticulture, the symbol for a first-generation plant variety obtained from a cross of two purebred parents. See also **Hybrid.**

Fabric, aluminum-coated (wire fencing) See **Aluminum-coated fabric.**

Fabric, galvanized (chainlink fencing) See **Galvanized fabric.**

Fabric, woven wire See **Woven wire fabric.**

Facade In structures, an applied front or surface.

Face planting In landscape design, the positioning of lower plants (shrubs, flowers, ground covers, or the like) in front of trees, tall shrubs, or structures.

Factor, biotic See **Biotic factor.**

Factor, climatic See **Climatic factor.**

Factor, pH See **pH factor.**

Fairbrother, Nan (d. 1971) Also Nan McKenzie. Twentieth-century English landscape theorist, born in Coventry. A graduate of the University of London, Nan Fairbrother became interested in landscape architecture in middle age. Her probing and brilliant books, *The Nature of Landscape Design* and *New Lives, New Landscapes,* attempted to develop a new landscape aesthetic for postindustrial Britain. She was a member of the British Institute of Landscape Architects.

Fairway In golf, a long, open lawn usually flanked with trees and "roughs" leading to the green.

Fairy ring A circular ring of fungi on a lawn surface.

Falcate See **Falciform.**

Falciform In leaves, a sickle-like growth habit.

Fall **Gradient,** q.v.

Fall color The deciduous leaf tones of autumn, an important element in landscape design. Also **Autumn garden.**

Fall garden See **Autumn garden.**

Fall, rock See **Rock fall.**

Fallow Applied to land left undisturbed after earlier cultivation. Fallow land soon regenerates itself and may be used again for crops. Verb participle: fallowing.
   Summer fallow land is cultivated during the growing season to suppress weeds and produce a supply of **Green manure,** q.v., to improve the soil.

Family In botany, a suborder or classification of plant type occurring beneath order and above genus. The family is a grouping of closely related genera. The *Gramineae,* or grasses, and *Leguminosae,* or peas, are examples. See also **Botanical classification.**

Family, soil See **Soil classification.**

Family (fruit) tree A fruit tree onto which several varieties of the same fruit species have been grafted, allowing a maximum of fruit production in a very limited space.

Fan, alluvial See **Alluvial fan.**

Fancy (flower) Parti-colored or striped; variegated.

Fancy farm An artificial "farm," purposely rustic, created as part of an English or other naturalistic landscape. See **Hameau.** See also **Ferme ornée.**

Fannie Mae The **Federal National Mortgage Association.** See **FNMA.**

Farina See **Bloom** and **Pubescence.**

Farinose In plant structures, covered with **Bloom,** q.v.

Farm An area of more or less fertile land used for the raising of crops or livestock. The farm is the irreducible pillar of modern human

Fertilizer, organic See **Organic fertilizer.**

Fertilizer, starter See **Plant starter.**

Fescue See **Grasses.**

Fetid Putrid-smelling; putrescent.

FH A common plan abbreviation for fire hydrant. Also, an abbreviation for **Feet of head,** q.v.

Fiberglass Glass spun into tiny filaments while molten. Sometimes used as reinforcement for plastic sheeting, concrete, and other materials. Also **Fibrous glass.**

Fibonacci number See **Proportional harmony.**

Fibrillose In botany, pertaining to fine hairs on leaf margins.

Fibrous glass See **Fiberglass.**

Fibrovascular system (of plants) See **Phloem** and **Xylem.**

Fidelity bond A bond that warrants personal or business honesty or contract performance. See also **Bond.**

Fief In the Middle Ages, an estate granted by a lord and held in trust by his vassal.

Field capacity In soils, a measurement (usually in inches or centimeters) of the amount of water remaining in a saturated soil after surface run-off has stopped. See also **Percolation rate.**

Field, leaching See **Leaching field.**

Field order In landscape construction, a minor change requested of the contractor in materials or implementation of work. See also **Change order.**

Field, playing See **Playing field.**

Field stone 1) In landscape construction, rough stones of irregular form and character used for walls, riprap, paving, and the like. Rubble. 2) Stones scattered across a ground or soil surface.

Field supervision See **Site inspection.**

Field-cured cylinder In concrete testing, a cylinder of concrete cured, as much as possible, under the same conditions as the batch for the slab, wall, or other concrete structure from which it was taken.

Field-grown stock Trees, shrubs, or other plant materials grown in a wholesale nurseryman's field. Also **Nursery stock.** See also **Bareroot stock, Collected stock, Container-grown stock.**

Filiferous In plants, threadlike.

Filiform In botany, referring to a leaf with a threadlike form.

Filigree work Arabesque tracery in medieval courtyards (cloisters). See also **Mushrabiyeh.**

Fill See **Cut and fill.**

Fill, engineered See **Engineered fill.**

Filler In fertilizers (chemical), a nonresponsive substance added to balance out active nitrogen, phosphorus, potassium, or other elements.

Fillet In landscape construction, the curving edge of a walk or roadway.

Final acceptance A statement of complete project acceptability made by the owner after notification from the landscape architect that the work has been finished in compliance with plans and specifications. Final acceptance is usually confirmed by a final payment to the landscape contractor and marks the start of the warranty period. See also **Conditional acceptance, Final inspection, Final payment, Punch list, Provisional acceptance.**

Final inspection The final review of a project by the landscape architect, landscape contractor, and others before a certificate for final payment to the landscape contractor is issued. See also **Final acceptance, Final payment, Punch list, Site inspection.**

Final payment The last payment made by an owner to a landscape contractor at the end of project construction. The owner makes final payment after receipt of a final certificate for payment from the landscape architect. See also **Pay request.**

Financing for public works construction Credit financing is usually necessary for the construction of parks, swimming pools, golf courses, streetside landscapes, and other public works. Three sorts of bonds are often utilized to provide for this sort of construction:

1) **Dedicated tax bonds:** This kind of bond is funded from a special assessment district tax or other restricted tax. It provides for street construction, right-of-way landscaping, or similar improvements on public lands adjacent to the primary beneficiaries of those improvements.

2) **General obligation bonds:** Probably the commonest kind of public-improvement bond, secured by real estate or chattel taxation. General obligation bonds are also low interest bonds.

3) **Revenue bonds:** These public bonds are issued subject to pay-back from the rent, admission, toll, or

other proceeds generated by the bond improvement after its construction. One of their primary features is often a long debt retirement.

See also **Bond, Municipal bonds.**

Fine aggregate   In concrete mixtures, sand up to ¹/₄ in. (4.76 mm) in size. See also **Aggregate, Coarse Aggregate.**

Fine (finish) grade   See **Grade.**

Fine texture (soils)   See **Soil texture.**

Fine-grained soil   A soil composed primarily of silts and/or clays. See also **Soil.**

Finial   An ornament or elegant cap at the top of a fence slat or post.

Finish, broom (concrete)
   See **Broom finish.**

Finish, brush   See **Brush finish.**

Finish (color) coat   See **Stucco.**

Finish, float   See **Float finish.**

Finish floor elevation (FF)   In construction, the ultimate grade at which a structural floor will be constructed. All landscape finish grades must drain water away from the finish floor elevation.

Finish grade   See **Grade.**

Finish, rubbed (masonry)
   See **Rubbed finish.**

Finish, smooth   See **Smooth finish.**

Finnish landscape architecture
   See **Scandinavian landscape architecture.**

Fir   A useful wood in landscape construction. Fir is a softwood and a conifer. The usual construction fir is **Douglas fir,** q.v.

Fire climax   In forests and grasslands, the kind of typical plant growth that has developed as a result of frequent fires. Fire can be a dominant influence on the form of the landscape, but its effects on forests and grasslands are still not completely understood.

Fire pit   In landscape architecture, a shallow hole excavated for purposes of cooking or warming, usually located in a residential patio or other private area, and lined with brick, sand, metal, or concrete.

Firebreak   A cleared trail or ribbon of land used for fire control in forests and on rangelands. Firebreaks, though sometimes effective, are difficult to maintain and often contribute to erosion.

Firm seed   See **Commercial seed classifications.**

Fish emulsion   An organic fertilizer comprised of fish parts, normally used in residential gardens.

Fissility   In slate, the quality of separation into flat sheets.

Fitting (irrigation)   In piping, any mechanical attachment that connects lengths of pipe or valves to pipe, allows changes in direction, attaches heads, makes changes in pipe size, or the like. Common types include adapters, elbows, clamps, flare fittings, ells, tees, threaded and compression fittings, inserts, and others.

Fixation   A process of chemical combination in soils that makes nitrogen, phosphorous, and potassium largely unavailable for plant use. Commonly occurring in alkaline soils in arid areas.

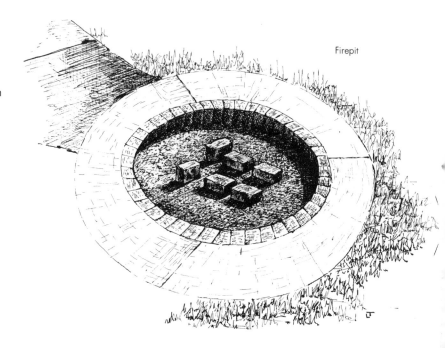

Firepit

Fixation, nitrogen　See **Nitrogen fixation.**

Fixed head (irrigation)　See **Stationary head.**

Fixed retaining wall　See **Retaining wall.**

Fixed spray nozzle　In irrigation, a head component that emits from a set (nonrotating) position.

Fixed spray sprinkler　See **Fixed spray nozzle.**

Fixture, lighting　See **Luminaire.**

FL　In (civil engineering) surveying, an abbreviation indicating **Flowline,** q.v.

Flabellate, flabelliform　In plant (especially leaf) structures, fan-shaped.

Flaccid　In plant structures, limp or relaxed.

Flagstone　A flat paving stone of shale, limestone, sandstone, or the like, set in sand or mortar.

Flagstone, iron　See **Iron flagstone.**

Flange plate　A plate attached to the protruding edge of a metal post or to a pipe for a strong mechanical linkage.

Flare　See **Crown (root crown).**

Flashing　A metal or other lining or covering used at the joints of various roof lines to preclude leaking.

Flat　1) In housing, an apartment. 2) In topography, a stretch of land with a grade of zero %—i.e., with no slope whatsoever. 3) In horticulture, an open-topped, low box in which bedding plants are raised, transported, and sold.

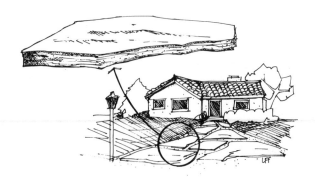

Flagstones

Flat fee　A professional fee of a lump sum paid for design work of a given scope. See also **Professional fee.** Also **Stipulated sum fee** or **Stipulated sum agreement.**

Flat spray head　In irrigation, a set spray sprinkler that emits water in a pattern almost parallel to the ground surface. Also **Flat spray sprinkler.**

Flat spray sprinkler　See **Flat spray head.**

Fl.El.　See **FF.**

Flemish bond (masonry)　See **Brick wall pattern.**

Flexible pavement　In landscape construction, generally low-cost sorts of pavement that include plain soil mixtures, sand-clay stabilized surfacing, and surface courses consolidated with lime or soil cement. Flexible pavement may also consist of **Asphaltic concrete,** q.v. See also **Lime, Rigid pavement, Soil cement.**

Flexible pipe　See **Polyethylene pipe.**

Flexuous, flexuose　In plant structures, bent backward and forward; undulating.

Float finish　A rough concrete-finish texture obtained by darbying or bull-floating.

Floating (concrete finish)　See **Float finish.**

Floating dimension　See **Dimension.**

Floating spray　In irrigation, a mist of fine droplets developing over a spray head operating under too much pressure.

Flocculation　1) The clumping together of clay or other tiny soil particles. 2) Clumping of cement particles.

Flood irrigation Sheet water coverage of a cultivated plant area. Flooding is the oldest kind of irrigation, possibly dating to 10,000 B.C., but it uses the greatest amount of water to produce plant growth.

Flood lighting A uniform, nearly shadowless illumination for night sports or the emphasis of special landscape features.

Flood, standard project See **Standard project flood.**

Floodplain In a river or stream basin, the area occasionally or frequently inundated by high water flows, which leave sediments contributing to its build-up as they recede.

Flora 1) The characteristic plant life of an area. 2) The classical goddess of flowers. 3) A list of plants for a given area that usually shows families, genera and species, and identifying characteristics. See also **Fauna.**

Flore-pleno A term describing flowers with a very large number of petals. Carnation and narcissus are examples. Sometimes abbreviated **Fl.pl.**

Floret In horticulture (especially in roses), multiflowered.

Floribunda Plant cultivation for flower production. Also, in a larger sense, **Ornamental horticulture,** q.v.

Floristic Pertaining to the characteristics of a part or all of the vegetation of a given area.

Flow adjustor (irrigation) A water control mechanism on a **Nipple,** q.v.

Flow, earth See **Soil creep, Solifluction.**

Flow, laminar See **Laminar flow.**

Flow pressure (irrigation) An essential line pressure used to design an irrigation system. The flow pressure is calculated for moving water in the system that is to be maintained as a constant during system operation. Also **Design pressure.**

Flow time, overland See **Overland flow time.**

Flow, uniform See **Uniform flow.**

Flow velocity In irrigation, the speed measured in **FPS** (ft/s) or **Feet per second** at which water flows through a line. Flow velocity is directly proportional to water volume, measured in **Cubic feet per second (CFS,** q.v.) or **Gallons per minute (GPM,** q.v.). See also **FPS.**

Flower The sexual structure of a seed-bearing plant, often colorful and pleasantly scented, and a source of great interest and satisfaction in landscape design. A perfect flower contains both male (staminate) and female (pistillate) organs. An imperfect flower contains only male or female organs.

Pollination may be carried out by wind or by insects. Rarely, a flower may pollinate itself. Generally, the more primitive the flower (i.e., the earlier it evolved), the more primitive the insect that pollinates it. Beetles and magnolias are an example. A great deal of flower evolution has been accomplished to better attract insects for successful pollination. Bees are the most common contemporary pollinators.

Flowers may be compound, composed of numerous, smaller **Florets,** or single, consisting of only one floral structure.

A **Single flower** consists of one row of petals. Wild rose is an example. A **Double flower,** such as a marigold, has two, three, or more rows of visible petals.

See also **Annual, Biennial, Bulb,** and **Perennial.**

Flower bubbler (irrigation) See **Bubbler.**

Flower cluster See **Inflorescence.**

Flower, double See **Double flower.**

Flower garden A garden arranged for the display of annuals, perennials, and bulbs, often with background evergreen accent plantings. Plantings in this sort of garden are best arranged in sympathetic and contrasting masses, with changes in color proceeding with the seasons.

Flower, monovular See **Monovular.**

Flower, plurovular See **Plurovular.**

Flower receptacle A structure at the apex of a flower stalk containing the flower's reproductive organs. Also **Thalamus, Torus.**

Flower show An exhibition of annuals, perennials, and bulbs—and often vegetables and fruits and flowering trees or shrubs—held during the growing season. Flower shows are important sources of new plants, bloom types and colors, and general horticultural information.

Flower societies In North America and elsewhere, garden clubs that are dedicated to the culture and exhibition of a favorite flower. They are named after their flower of choice—i.e., Iris Society, Rose Society, and the like.

Flowering ornamental A tree or shrub grown for shade, beauty, and bloom but not necessarily for the food it may produce. In landscape plantings, a generally small-scale, deciduous tree that produces spring or early summer flowers.

Flowline (FL) A series of connected points of mean elevation above sea level, often found as bottom of curb (B.C.) indications or low points in a swale, showing the basic direction of water flow. See also **Bottom of curb (BC)**.

Fl.pl. Abbreviation for **Florepleno,** q.v.

Fluid drilling A British horticultural technique utilizing already-sprouted seeds in a gel base for cool-temperature, early season crop planting.

Flume An inclined channel.

Flume, paved See **Paved flume.**

Flume, vegetated See **Vegetated flume.**

Fluorescent lamp Seldom used outdoors, fluorescent light is produced when electric cathodes excite the phosphorus-coated inside of a glass tube. A "low pressure" **Mercury vapor,** q.v., or fluorescent lamp has a partial pressure below 0.001 atmosphere. A "high pressure" lamp will measure approximately one atmosphere.

Fluorescent lighting
  See **Fluorescent lamp.**

Fluorine A nonmetallic element necessary in small amounts for plant and (principally) animal health and growth. A **Trace element,** q.v. See also **Available nutrient, Soil minerals.**

Flowering ornamentals. Pear (*Pyrus* sp.). Photo by author.

Flush head In irrigation, a sprinkler head (discharger) set at finish grade to irrigate lawn or shrub areas. Usually, not a pop-up head. See also **Pop-up head.**

Flush spray sprinkler See **Flush head.**

Flushing a system In irrigation, cleaning by removing heads and running water through a valve circuit to wash out dirt or other impurities.

Fluted In plant structures, distinguished by grooves. See also **Canaliculate.**

Flux, slime (tree disorder)
  See **Slime flux.**

FNMA ("Fannie Mae") **Federal National Mortgage Association,** an agency that deals with mortgage (federally insured) loans. Fannie Mae is a secondary mortgage market, set up to help insure a wider national availability of primary loan money through banks and savings and loan institutions.

Fog Water droplets in suspension in cold or cool air near the Earth's surface which obscure vision. Often apparent immediately after sun-up.

Fog mist In plant propagation, a light mist used to root softwood and herbaceous cuttings.

Fog seal (asphalt) A kind of **Asphalt sealer,** q.v.

Foggara See **Qanat.**

Foliaceous Leafy, leaf-shaped.

Foliage The collective leaves of a plant or plants.

Foliage crown See **Crown.**

Foliage, juvenile See **Juvenile foliage.**

Foliage plant An ornamental plant grown chiefly for the color and texture of its leaves.

Foliar feed In horticulture, a fertilizer applied to leaves and stems.

Foliate In horticulture, of leaves rather than leaflets.

Foliolate In horticulture, pertaining to leaflets rather than leaves. Commonly bifoliolate, trifoliolate, and the like.

Foliose Leaved.

Folly An outlandish and generally useless incidental garden structure designed into early eighteenth-century English landscapes. Often a bogus ruin. See also **Eye-catcher**.

Food chain A term describing the series of botanical food producers (green plants), zoological consumers (herbivores and omnivores; carnivores), and mixed decomposers (bacteria, fungi, and others), and their relation to each other. Food production and consumption are to some degree a function of sun energy storage, transformation, and transfer. Formerly balanced food chains are increasingly interrupted by human population growth and human tampering.

Food court In enclosed shopping malls, outdoor shopping plazas, and elsewhere, a courtyard with tables and chairs near fast-food shops. Usually an important adjunct to normal shopping-center retail trade.

Foods, plant See **Plant foods**.

Foot A measurement of 12 inches used in the English-speaking world, equal to .305 meters.

Foot head See **Feet of head**.

Foot, lineal (linear foot) See **Lineal foot**.

Foot valve A common valve in centrifugal pumps, used to maintain a water column and thus a pump's prime in the draw pipe.

Footbridge See **Bridge**.

Footcandle A measure of light radiation. An illumination unit of one lumen per square foot.

Foothill woodland community An association of mixed evergreens and deciduous intermediate and tall-plant species common to northern California and other temperate zones.

Footing A device used to extend the foundation area supporting a column, wall, post, structure. A footing transmits weight or structural loads to the earth. See also **Foundation**.

Footing, branch See **Haunch footing**.

Footing, cantilever See **Cantilever footing**.

Footing spread Footing movement due to inadequate soils under or adjacent to a load.

Footpath A strictly pedestrian path, often a principal garden or park feature.

Forb In botany, any small, broad-leafed, flowering understory or ground-cover plant. Forbs are usually mixed with grasses.

Force account A term describing an owner's "in-house" work crews as well as materials purchased by the owner to be used in a landscape project.

Force majeure (French) In contracts, pertaining to acts of war or switches in government that block or limit contract execution or performance.

Forcing In horticulture, causing a plant to bud or flourish out of (and especially before) its proper season by artificial means. See also **Retarding** and **Vernalization**.

Ford A shallow stream crossing, sometimes employed as a landscape device.

Forecourt An entry court.

Foreshortening In design drawing, an apparent distance or apparent depth as illustrated in a two-dimensional sketch or rendering.

Forest A woodland, especially tall-tree woods.

Forest, equatorial See **Rain forest**.

Forest garden See **Savage garden**.

Forest, high See **High forest**.

Forest, park See **Park forest**.

Forest Service An agency of the United States Department of Agriculture, primarily responsible for planning and overseeing the proper utilization of national forest lands by private, commercial, and governmental users. It is the Forest Service's task to care for plants and, indirectly, soil; state governments and the U.S. Fish & Wildlife Service are responsible for the animals in national forest areas.

Forest soil, brown See **Brown earth**.

Forest soil (evergreen) See **Podzol**.

Forest, thorn See **Thorn forest**.

Forest, virgin See **Virgin forest**.

Forestation The conversion into woodland of an area not previously covered by trees. Also **Afforestation**. See also **Reforestation**.

Forestry The science, management, and cultivation of woodlands for human use. See also **Silviculture.**

Forestry, social See **Social forestry.**

Forestry, urban See **Urban forestry.**

Form In botany, the most minute classification for plants, including slight color and textural differences and the like within a species.

Form, bid See **Bid form.**

Form standard codes See **Building codes.**

Formal garden A symmetrical garden laid out on an axis or axes, and projecting a strong geometric form and feeling in its hard and soft landscape elements. Somewhat old-fashioned in the late twentieth century. Origin: Middle East via Europe.

Formalism in landscape design The use of a linear axis or radial central point and its accompanying strong symmetry produce formalism. A careful, clear, and geometric balance of forms and qualities is typical of formalism. See also **Asymmetry** and **Occult balance.**

Formation, plant See **Plant association.**

Formation, sclerophyll See **Sclerophyll formation.**

Formation of soils See **Soil formation.**

Formed invert See **Invert.**

Formula, fertilizer See **Fertilizer formula.**

Formula, Manning (runoff) See **Manning formula.**

Forthright

Formula, rational (for runoff) See **Rational formula.**

Formula, Steel (for design storms) See **Steel formula.**

Formwork The system of wood and metal forms into which plastic concrete is placed to form a slab, wall, or other landscape element. Sometimes reusable. Also **Shuttering** (British).

Forthright In English Renaissance gardens (c. 1558–1750), a wide, straight path leading out of a manor house or running parallel to one of its sides. The forthright was also typical, on a smaller scale, of New England's house-garden layout.

Forum (Latin) A central open-air public space and principal public feature of Roman towns. A place of assembly for marketing and governmental activities. See also **Agora.**

Fosse (Archaic) A moat or ditch. See also **Ha-ha.**

Fossil plants See **Paleobotany.**

Foundation A footing device used to transmit a structural load to the soil, normally below grade. Foundations spread loads over an extended area. See also **Footing, Substructure.**

Foundation planting An old-fashioned massing of shrubs, flowers, ground covers, and—to a lesser extent—trees along the foundation lines of a building. Also **Base planting.**

Foundation seed See **Commercial seed classifications.**

Fountain. French Quarter, New
Orleans, Louisiana. Photo by author.

Fountain block. Portland, Oregon.
Lawrence Halprin, landscape
architect. Photo by author.

Fountain   A man-made spring of
water, often emerging from a jet,
used for drinking or amenity. At
Government Gardens in Rotorua,
New Zealand, several of the world's
most unusual fountains emit *steam*
escaping from bores probed into the
ground beneath them.

Fountain block   A man-made spring
concept pioneered by Lawrence
Halprin and others in twentieth-
century North America. The fountain
block is a grouping of stylized
concrete boulders over which water
cascades at a thunderous rate to
create an urban feature of distinct
excitement and beauty.

Fountain, trick   See **Water joke.**

FPS   Feet per second (linear), a
measure of the rate of flow of water
in a channel or pipe. Also ft/s.

Fragipan   See **Pan** and **Hardpan.**

Free water   Water percolating
through the soil due to the attraction
of gravity. Also **Gravitational water**
or **Gravity.**

Freeform   In design, informal in line
and displaying **Occult balance,** q.v.

Freehold   An estate held for life,
including a house or houses,
gardens, and undeveloped lands.
See also **Fee simple.**

Freestanding wall   Any wall or
fence that is nonloadbearing—i.e.,
that supports only its own weight.
Also **Nonloadbearing wall.**

Freestone   A limestone, sandstone,
or other stone that can be easily
shaped in any direction. Also, a kind
of peach.

Freeway   A limited access, tax-
supported, high-speed, multilaned
highway used for quick transit in

twentieth-century—especially North American—cities. Also **Expressway.** See also **Turnpike.**

French drain   A ditch, trench, or—occasionally—pit filled with stone, broken brick, gravel, rubble, or the like used for collection of runoff. A **Dry well.** See also **Sump.**

French landscape architecture   At the Chateau Gaillon, owned by the Cardinal d'Amboise, an early formal garden stretching out from the battlements of the castle was constructed c. 1500. We have a description and plan from **Jacques du Cerceau** (b. 1585), q.v., an architect and writer of *Les Plus Excellents Bastiments de France,* published in 1579. Gaillon contained a moat, a knot garden, a fountain, and extensive carpenter's work; but its most remarkable characteristic is the landscape itself as it leaves the castle fortifications and opens up to the broader world beyond. What du Cerceau describes is the first breath of the Renaissance in France.

French Renaissance design was derived from Italian models. Louis XII, intrigued by the landscapes he had seen in Italy, imported the noted *giardiniero* Pasello da Mercogliano in the early sixteenth century to design the grounds at his Amboise

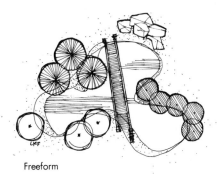
Freeform

estate and the enclosed courtyard gardens at Blois. Henri II (r. 1547–59) employed Philibert de l'Orme to plan a garden in the Italian style at his Chateau Anet. **Jacques Boyceau** developed the quintessentially French **Parterre de broderie,** q.v., for Henri IV, expanding on earlier clipped Italian formal gardens.

The French regal style gained in forcefulness and expanse as the sixteenth century wore on. **Claude Mollet,** q.v., head gardener at the Tuileries and second-generation royal gardener, began large-scale formal compositions for Henri IV (1553–1610). Etienne du Perac, trained in Italy, designed the grounds of St. Germaine-en-Laye for Maria dei Medici and collaborated with Claude Mollet on other projects. The French were able to make better use of flat bodies of water than the Italians because of their topography. But, as was true in Italy, their Renaissance landscapes were full of color and life, and arranged axially or radially to generate complete artificial vistas.

Writers such as Charles Estienne aroused a lively interest in the new French **Vista gardens.** Estienne's *Praedium Rusticum* (1554) and *Agriculture et Maison Rustique* (1570) stimulated the planning of pleasure gardens. Boyceau's parterres, usually laid out in boxwood at the center of an ornamental garden, were intended for viewing from the nearby second story of a house.

The French *place publique* became a popular national landscape form in the early seventeenth century, serving as a core for radial town planning. Early Parisian examples include the Place des Vosges and the Place Dauphine. Henri IV sponsored the construction of many of the *places* of Paris, and his initiative was followed by Louis XIV (1630–1715) and later kings. Louis developed his own ebullient Place des Victoires at Versailles and engaged **André Le**

Notre, q.v., the designer of Vaux-le-Vicomte for the king's finance minister, Fouquet, to design the great gardens at Versailles.

Le Notre, whose father Jean had also been Royal Gardener, based his design approaches on precedents set by Cardinal Richelieu (1585–1642) in his own estate. Richelieu, the minister of Louis XIII, had hired J. Le Mercier to produce a comprehensive plan for his chateau: village, castle, gardens, and forest were designed as a unified series. Le Notre had created his early masterpiece, Vaux-le-Vicomte (c. 1661), for Fouquet in much the same manner. But at Vaux-le-Vicomte, Le Notre's ability to conceive and execute landscapes at a grand scale became fully apparent. Le Notre used fountains, canals, parterres, lines of trees, and the tremendous power of a strong axis to achieve his effects. Le Notre's work was also much influenced by the principles of the French formal garden set forth in the book *Jardin de Plaisir* (1651), by **André Mollet,** q.v., royal gardener to Louis XIII.

Louis XIV employed Le Notre in an endless series of improvements and embellishments at Versailles, but the basic plan for the grounds had been approved by the late 1660s. Le Notre employed a massive 1-mile axis, cross-axes, and radial avenues as the basis for the design. Forty or more sculptors were employed to produce statuary for the grounds; as at Vaux-le-Vicomte, Le Notre used the *parterre de broderie* as a refined specialty garden. Hornbeams, boxwood, and other plantings were utilized for special topiary effects. Le Notre's fountains, canals, and pools created a theme of special water effects throughout the grounds. He painstakingly developed regal vistas and—as at Vaux-le-Vicomte—these became principal attractions of the gardens. Louis himself wrote a visitors' book for Versailles and

French landscape architecture.
Chateau de Marly, 1679, view from
north. J. H. Mansart, architect;
André Le Notre, landscape designer.
Illustration courtesy BBMSL, UNM.

sometimes had himself wheeled along in a *roulette* (small chariot) as he showed off the grounds to his guests. Versailles's architect, Le Vau, and court painter, Le Brun, were hard put to match Le Notre's landscape, which became the European standard for a century or more.

The Trianon (late 1670s) was a related, smaller chateau on the grounds of Versailles designed with somewhat more intimate gardens; it featured some 2,000,000 annuals in pots changed out for seasonal color. At the king's chateau of Marly, also dating from the 1670s, a series of pleasure gardens was created with an enormous cascade (the *Rivière*) at the heart of the landscape. Other architects and garden designers, including Mansart, Claude Desgots (a nephew of Le Notre), the Francinis (father and son), Gabriel, Jean de la Quintinie, and Claude Denis added to the development of Versailles, but by Le Notre's death in 1700 he was universally renowned as Europe's greatest garden designer. Versailles remains the most popular of French baroque landscapes; however, Le Notre's work at Chantilly, St. Germain, and elsewhere has also been carefully preserved or restored. European imitations of Versailles included the Bellbrun and Schonbrunn in Salzburg and Vienna, respectively; Drottningholm in Sweden; the Peterhof in St. Petersburg (Leningrad); the Nymphenburg in Munich and Sans Souci in Potsdam; and Hampton Court in England. In the United States, much of L'Enfant's plan for Washington, D.C. (1791) was derived from Versailles (see **Pierre L'Enfant**).

Today considered the ultimate Renaissance gardens, Vaux-le-Vicomte and Versailles may be traced to the successive development and refinement of large-scale landscape design by the Royal

Gardeners Jacques Boyceau, Claude Mollet, Jean Le Notre, and, at the pinnacle, André Le Notre. Their sixteenth-century work was codified and explained in the classic *La Théorie et la Pratique du Jardinage (Theory and Practice of Gardening, c. 1709),* possibly by Le Notre's disciple Alexandre Le Blond (see **Russian landscape architecture**) but probably by the botanist A. J. D. d'Argenville. The *Theory* was used as a guide to landscape design in the French style all over the Continent.

The naturalistic gardens of the English School gradually influenced French landscape design in the eighteenth century. The architect Nicolas Le Doux (d. 1806) designed an English landscape garden at the Hotel Thelusson, Paris, and a series of new residences, the Hosten houses, in an informal garden in the second half of the century. Rousseau's tomb is located on the grounds of Ermenonville, an estate filled with temples carefully sited in a rolling, wooded landscape. Ermenonville was designed for the Marquis de Girardin (c. 1766). The architect Carmontelle laid out a *parc* at Monceau for the Duc de Chartres (c. 1774), and a melodramatic "gothic" landscape was finished at Betz for the Princess of Monaco (c. 1780). See **Sublime.**

Naturalistic plans were predominant in Britain and on the Continent by 1800, but focus in landscape design was shifting from estates to city planning. Flaubert and other writers ridiculed early bourgeois attempts to understand the principles of good landscape design and to incorporate it in often-modest middle-class gardens. At a larger scale, however, Baron **von Haussmann** (d. 1891), q.v., remodeled Parisian boulevards and created new parks and vistas. Haussmann's radial roadways were tree-lined, with plenty of pedestrian space and roundabouts **(Ronds-points)** at critical intersections. Haussmann's deputy, **Jean Charles Alphand,** (d. 1891), was responsible for much open space redesign in the English naturalistic manner (Bois de Boulogne and elsewhere). Alphand also wrote *Les Promenades de Paris,* today a standard reference on nineteenth-century urban design.

In our own century, Le Notre's grand landscape at Courance (1690s) has been restored by **Achille Duchene** (d. 1947). Duchene also produced a new fountain garden at Blenheim Palace, England, and designed other new landscapes in high Renaissance style. The landscape architect A. Guy-Otin carried on Alphand's "greening of Paris" with additional proposals to tie together the green spaces of the city by means of parkways, gardens, and squares. Among modern exhibition gardens, the Parisian Bagatelle, first proposed in the eighteenth century, is renowned for its rose, narcissus, and other specialty gardens. See also **Canadian landscape architecture.**

Paul Friedberg. Photo courtesy M. Paul Friedberg and Partners.

Frenching   In landscape construction, the placement of a **French drain** (dry well) or drains to accept surface runoff.

Frequency of watering
   See **Watering frequency.**

Fresco   A wall painting executed on wet plaster. Frequently found in Roman and Italian Renaissance villas.

Freshet   A small, tumbling stream, especially a stream that appears after a hard, quick rainfall.

Friable (soil)   Crumbly or easily pulverized. Noun: friability.

Friction coefficient   In pipe-sizing calculation, the resistance of a pipe or channel wall to the flow of water through it. See also **Coefficient of roughness.**

Friction loss   In irrigation, a decrease in line or system operating pressure due to the passage of water through valves and piping. Generally, **Pressure loss** through the friction of water movement. Also **Pressure drop.**

Friedberg, M. Paul (1931–)
   United States landscape architect and teacher, born in New York City and educated at Cornell University. Friedberg is well known for his innovative playground and recreation area design. He has noted his playground development ideas in the books *Playgrounds for City Children* (1969), *Creative Play Areas* (1970), and *Handcrafted Playgrounds* (1975). His most celebrated book, however, is *Play and Interplay* (1970), written with

Ellen Perry Berkeley, in which he develops his themes of modular play equipment put to imaginative use in tight urban open spaces.

Friedberg has also specialized in downtown revitalization. In a series of "urban block" designs, including the Monroe Center in Grand Rapids, the State Street Mall in Madison, Peavey Plaza in Minneapolis, and others, Friedberg has refined a particularly lively Cubism to bring fountains, pathways, seating, trellises, plants, and other detail elements into harmonious compositions. Riis Plaza, a housing development landscape compositiion in New York City, has become perhaps the most celebrated of Friedberg's urban blocks.

Friedberg's work has included projects with such eminent twentieth-century architects as Skidmore, Owings and Merrill, I. M. Pei, Victor Gruen and Associates, and others. He founded and served as chairman of the Department of Urban Landscape Architecture at the City College of New York. Friedberg has also served on the faculties of Columbia University, the New School for Social Research, Pratt Institute, and elsewhere.

The majority of Friedberg's design work has been in the East and the Midwest. His recent compositions, such as the Winter Garden conservatory in Niagara Falls (1976) and Pershing Park on Pennsylvania Avenue in Washington, D.C. (c. 1980), are designed as sophisticated interludes in the city fabric. Pershing Park is sunken, with snack tables next to a reflecting pool and a forest of honey locusts roundabout at street level. The park is within sight of the White House, and acts as an "eddy" in the stream of pedestrian traffic passing by on Pennsylvania Avenue.

Fringe, capillary (in soils)
See **Capillary fringe.**

Frits Translucent pellets containing **Trace elements,** q.v., used to provide a slow, supplemental fertilizer in a planted area.

Frog A brick surface-panel.

Frond A kind of feathery compound leaf found commonly in ferns and palms.

Front end loader A mechanical scoop rigged to two arms on the fore end of a tractor, used for earthwork, site clean-up, and the like.

Front setback See **Setback.**

Frontage road See **Access road.**

Frost A white surface covering of small ice crystals that forms when air temperature falls below 32°F (0°C). Frost determines plant growing seasons and is a limiting factor of plant range.

Frost action Changes in ground condition due to the formation of frost or ice in the soil, including frost boil (soil subsidence) occurring as the soil thaws, and frost heave, the expansion of freezing water under or next to a plane surface. This water expansion, if occurring in stone, concrete, or asphalt cracks, for example, can cause extensive damage.

Frost boil See **Frost action.**

Frost cracks 1) In horticulture, deep fissures in tender bark tissue resulting from the action of warm daytime temperatures followed by a freezing cold night. See also **Winterburn.** 2) Deterioration of stone and soil caused by frozen water expansion in structural fissures.

Frost, ground See **Ground frost.**

Frost, heave See **Ground action.**

Frost seeding In lawn planting, the sowing of grass seed on prepared but frozen soil in very late winter.

Frostline In cold climates, the depth to which the soil freezes in winter.

Fruit A ripened, often edible plant ovary. A main human food. See also **Berry, Ornamental,** and **Vegetable.**

Fruit room (Roman)
See **Oporotheca.**

Fruit, stone See **Drupe.**

Fruit-bearing In horticulture, a term often used to distinguish a fertile shrub or tree from a sterile cultivar of the same species.

Fruiting spur In plants, a short bud or shoot that bears fruit.

Fruitless In horticulture, a term used to describe an ornamental variety of a normally fruit-bearing tree or shrub.

Frutescent Shrub-like.

Fruticose Bearing multiple small branches; bushy. See also **Suffruticose.**

Fugacious Of plant parts that drop off early—i.e., flower petals, sepals, and the like. See also **Caducous, Deciduous.**

Full head In landscape irrigation, a lawn sprinkler emitter that broadcasts a spray in a 360° direction.

Full-way valve See **Gate valve.**

Fulvous Pale yellow.

Fumarole   A gaseous vent, especially a steam vent in a volcanic region. In New Zealand (Rotorua), fumaroles are featured in parks as steam fountains.

Fumigant   A gas or droplet spray used to kill unwanted plants or animals in a limited area. See also **Insecticide.**

Functionalism   Design for ease of operation and maintenance, and for the expression of function in structure or landscape. A predominant aspect of twentieth-century design.

Fungicide   A copper- or sulfur-based or other preparation used to treat fungus attacks in plants.

Funicle   In botany, the stalk of an **Ovule,** q.v. Adjective: funiculous.

Furnishings, outdoor   See **Outdoor furniture** and **Street furniture.**

Furniture, outdoor   See **Outdoor furniture** and **Street furniture.**

Furniture, street   See **Street furniture** and **Outdoor furniture.**

Furring   The combination of materials (laths, wiring, and the like) that is used to build up a construction surface for stuccoing, plastering, or similar operations.

Furrow   A trench cut by a plow or other instrument. A **Contour furrow** runs on perpendicular to the slope of the land and is laid out to increase percolation, prevent erosion, and allow for irrigation.

Fuscous   Deep grayish brown.

Fusiform   In plants, a form like a spindle.

G

Gabion   A more or less rectangular wire mesh container filled with stone and installed on hillslopes, river banks, and elsewhere in a continuous series for stabilization and erosion control.

Gall   A kind of plant "wart" or cyst caused by bacteria, fungus, or insects. Often found on willow, oak and other tree trunks.

Gallery   An arcade, or covered walk. A veranda.

Gallet   A chip or stone sliver impressed in concrete or mortar to create a special effect. The process is galleting.

Gallon can (for plants)   See Container plant.

Gallons per minute (GPM) (irrigation)   See Discharge rate.

Galvanized fabric   In landscape construction, a galvanized steel mesh used in chainlink fence construction. See also **Galvanizing.**

Galvanized nails   See **Nails.**

Galvanized pipe   A wrought-iron or steel pipe used in landscape irrigation that is electrically coated with a layer of zinc or other metal for corrosion resistance. See also **PVC pipe.**

Galvanizing   A process bonding a zinc coating to a steel member, applied electrically or by a cold procedure. See also **Metal coating.**

Gamete   In flowers, a male or female sex cell, consisting of a grain of pollen or an ovule. See also **Ovule, Pollen.**

Gametopetalous   Pertaining to a unified mass of flower sepals.

Gamosepalous   Pertaining to a unified mass of flower sepals.

Ganat   See **Qanat.**

Gang mower   A reel or rotary lawn-mowing attachment of several units pulled by a small tractor.

Gap   In geology, a pass through a string of mountains or a ridge.

Garden   A planted or cultivated area of land, usually of limited size and near a house or other building, used for vegetable, fruit, or ornamental plant production. Gardens are often developed solely for pleasure and are usually enclosed.

Garden, allotment   See **Allotment gardens.**

Garden, alpine   See **Alpine garden.**

Garden, Anglo-chinois   See **Anglo-chinois garden.**

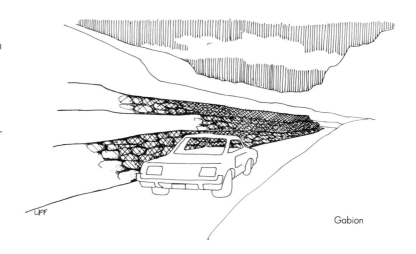

Gabion

Garden architecture   In Europe, a term describing the (often formal) design of gardens and garden structures.

Garden, autumn   See **Autumn garden.**

Garden, Bible   See **Bible garden.**

Garden, blue   See **Blue garden.**

Garden, bog   See **Bog garden.**

Garden book   A book of garden essays, a plant listing, or a series of suggestions for plant cultivation, popular in the West since the time of the ancient Greeks.

Jefferson's meticulous notes on the planting, development and management of Monticello comprise the best known of eighteenth-century American garden books. Washington's diaries included garden notes on Mt. Vernon. *The Gardener's Kalendar* of about 1779 by Martha Logan of Charleston, South Carolina gave detailed planting instructions for the American South. William Yong of Philadelphia wrote the *Catalogue d'Arbres, Arbustes et Plantes Herbacees d'Amerique* in 1783—an early American **Herbal,** q.v.

The classical *History of Plants* and *Causes of Plants* by Theophrastus of Erasus (b. 370 B.C.) is one of the earliest of all botanical works. It was influential as late as the Renaissance. The herbal *De Simplicium* by the Greek physician Claudius Galen (b. 130 B.C.) and *Materia Medica* by Dioscorides were also consulted well into the Middle Ages.

Pliny's *Letters* describe Roman horticulture and the joys of villa gardening, as does **Columella,** q.v., in his *De Re Rustica* of the 1st century A.D.

The *Opus Ruralium Commodorum* of Pietro Crescenzi (1471) reflected

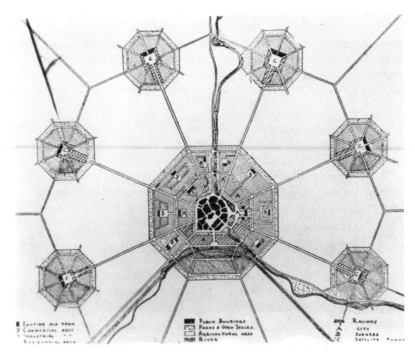

Garden city with satellite communities by Raymond Unwin (see **English landscape architecture**). Illustration courtesy BBMSL, UNM.

the new-found Renaissance delight in gardens. William Turner, John Gerard, and other garden writers popularized the herbal once again in late sixteenth-century England.

The massive *Cyclopedia* of Liberty Hyde Bailey (1900) was for many years perhaps the most widely used garden book in the United States. More recently, *The Education of a Gardener* by Russell Page and the *New Western Garden Book* have continued the popularity of the garden book into the late twentieth century.

Garden, bottle   See **Bottle garden, Terrarium.**

Garden calendar   A monthly or yearly list of cultivations, plantings, fertilizing, watering, prunings, harvesting and the like used for good garden culture. See also **Garden tables.**

Garden, California (modern garden)   See **California garden.**

Garden, canal   See **Canal garden.**

Garden city   A self-contained **New town,** q.v., comprised of a well-thought-out mixture of city elements with green space, good transportation, and local commerce and industry. First proposed in *Garden Cities for Tomorrow* (1902), by **Ebenezer Howard,** q.v. Letchworth and Welwyn in Britain were the first garden cities. See also **City Beautiful movement.**

Garden, Claudian   See **Claudian garden.**

Garden club   In North America, Britain, and elsewhere, a club organized for the promotion of gardening and improved horticultural practice. Garden clubs may be general or concerned only with the cultivation of certain plants (roses, irises, carnations, cacti, and the like).

Garden, convent   See **Monastery garden.**

Garden, cottage   See **Cottage garden.**

Garden, crystal   See **Terrarium.**

Garden, cutting   See **Cutting garden.**

Garden, derelict   See **Derelict garden.**

Garden, desert   See **Desert garden.**

Garden diary   A garden journal used to keep yearly track of cultivation, planting, blossoming, fruiting (fruit-setting), fertilizing, and harvest times.

Garden, dish   See **Dish garden.**

Garden, dooryard   See **Kitchen garden.**

Garden, Dutch   See **Dutch garden.**

Garden, fall   See **Autumn garden.**

Garden, flower   See **Flower garden.**

Garden, forest   See **Savage garden.**

Garden, formal   See **Formal garden.**

Garden furniture   See **Outdoor furniture** and **Street furniture.**

Garden, glass   See **Terrarium.**

Garden, gray and lavender   See **Gray and lavender garden.**

Garden, green   See **Green garden.**

Garden, hanging   See **Hanging garden.**

Garden, herb   See **Herb garden.**

Garden house   A casino or open shelter in a garden used for dining, viewing, or relaxation. See also **Gazebo.**

Garden, informal   See **Informal garden.**

Garden, kitchen   See **Kitchen garden.**

Garden, knot   See **Knot garden.**

Garden of love (medieval)   See **Pleasaunce.**

Garden, marsh   See **Marsh garden.**

Garden, maze   See **Maze.**

Garden, miniature   See **Miniature garden.**

Garden, model   See **Model garden.**

Garden, modern   See **California garden.**

Garden, monastery   See **Monastery garden.**

Garden, moss   See **Moss garden.**

Garden, naturalistic   See **Naturalistic garden.**

Garden, night   See **Night garden.**

Garden, pan   See **Miniature garden.**

Garden, paradise   See **Paradise garden.**

Garden, parlor   See **Parlor garden.**

Garden, peat   See **Peat garden.**

Garden, penthouse   See **Penthouse garden, Roof garden.**

Garden, philosopher's   See **Philosopher's garden.**

Garden, physic   See **Physic garden.**

Garden, pink   See **Pink garden.**

Garden plot   See **Plot.**

Garden, public   See **Public garden.**

Garden, purple   See **Gray and lavender garden.**

Garden, red (maroon)   See **Red garden.**

Garden, restaurant   See **Restaurant garden.**

Garden, rock   See **Rock garden.**

Garden, roof   See **Roof garden.**

Garden, room   See **Outdoor room.**

Garden, rose   See **Rose garden.**

Garden, sand   See **Sand garden.**

Garden, Saracen   See **Moorish landscape architecture.**

Garden, savage   See **Savage garden.**

Garden school   See **Department of horticulture.**

Garden, seaside   See **Seaside garden.**

Garden, seasonal   See **Seasonal garden.**

Garden, shady   See **Shady garden.**

Garden, Shakespeare
   See **Shakespeare garden.**

Garden, sink   See **Sink garden.**

Garden, spring   See **Spring garden.**

Garden, stroll   See **Stroll garden.**

Garden suburb   See **Garden city.**

Garden, summer   See **Summer garden.**

Garden, sunken   See **Sunken garden.**

Garden tables   Handy references for gardeners, including quantities of plants to be placed in beds of given dimension, tree and shrub growth statistics, seed characteristics, crop yields to be expected, and the like. See also **Garden calendar.**

Garden, tea   See **Tea garden.**

Garden, theatrical   See **Theatrical garden.**

Garden, trough   See **Trough garden.**

Garden, Tudor   See **Tudor garden** and **English landscape architecture.**

Garden, victory   See **Victory garden.**

Garden, vista   See **Vista garden.**

Garden, wall   See **Wall garden.**

Garden, white   See **White garden.**

Garden, winter   See **Winter garden.**

Garden, woodland   See **Woodland garden.** See also **Uvedale Price.**

Garden, yellow   See **Yellow garden.**

Garden, zoological   See **Zoo.**

Gardenesque   Garden-like in quality. Often, homey or informal. Gardenesque qualities were first generally proposed by Humphry Repton in the early nineteenth century. In the United States, **Andrew Jackson Downing,** q.v., proposed gardenesque design as the standard for an evolving nation of prosperous bourgeoisie.

Gardening, chemical   See **Chemical gardening.**

Gardening, color   See **Color gardening.**

Gardening, container
   See **Container gardening.**

Gardening, market   See **Truck farming.**

Gardening, organic   See **Organic gardening.**

Gardening, pin-money   See **Pin-money gardening.**

Gardening, soilless
   See **Hydroponics.**

Gardening, tank   See **Hydroponics (Soilless gardening).**

Gardening, tub   See **Tub gardening.**

Garden, prehistoric or primitive
   See **Prehistoric gardens.**

Gargoyle   A grotesque or caricatured animal or human form serving as a canal or water spout protruding from a roof. A frequent feature in medieval architecture.

Garigue   A savanna-like occurrence of low shrubs dotted across an arid landscape with little ground cover in between. The creosote deserts of southern New Mexico are an example. Also **Batha.**

Garth   An enclosed area next to a building serving as garden, yard, or pasture.

Gate   A hinged structure in a fence or wall serving as a landscape door.

Gate, lych (lich gate)   See **Lych gate.**

Gate valve   In irrigation, a valve normally installed between a vacuum breaker and a water meter which allows full or limited water passage to an underground sprinkler system. A gate valve is a general (not specific) sort of flow control. Also **Stop and waste valve.**

Gatehouse   A small house located near the entry to a park or an estate, especially in British gardens.

Gatehouses at Hidgate

Gazebo

Gauge, wire   See **Wire gauge.**

Gazebo (Dutch)   A covered and often elevated open-air pavilion with a view, often found in parks or squares. Gazebos are used for political speeches, band concerts, trysts, and other public and private functions. Nineteenth-century (Victorian) gazebos were often made of cast iron. Also **Garden house.**

Gear-driven head (sprinkler)   In irrigation, a rotary head with a slow-spinning nozzle driven by a turbine (rotor)-to-gear mechanism operated by water pressure. See also **Rotary head.**

Geminate (plant structures)
Occurring as twins or pairs.

Genecology   The scientific study of the genetics of plant populations as related to plant habitat.

General agency   A legal relationship between principal and agent established for a number of purposes and unlimited in scope and duration. See also **Agency.**

General conditions   A part of project specifications that lists many overall provisions or instructions to the landscape contractor necessary for the successful completion of installation work. Found in the General Specifications for the project.

General conditions are issued in standard form by the ASLA, APWA, and other organizations. They are often modified by **Special conditions,** q.v., and are sometimes called **General provisions.**
See also **Specifications.**

General contract   An agreement between an owner and a landscape contractor for the installation of a specific, complete project. See also **Prime contract.**

General obligation bonds
See **Financing for public works construction.**

General provisions   See **General conditions.**

General requirements   The introductory portion of project technical specifications, including a specific description and summary of work, notes on bid alternates, payment, construction schedules, submitted procedures, substitutions, project testing, temporary facilities, the method of closing out the work, and like items. See also **Specifications.**

General specifications
See **Specifications.**

Generic name (of plants)   The name in Latin of a plant's **Genus,** q.v., always capitalized. Example: *Ceratostigma plumbaginoides.* See also **Binomial, Botanical classification,** and **Species.**

Genesis, soil   See **Soil genesis.**

Genetics   The science dealing with heredity. Founded by Gregor Mendel (1822–84), Oskar Hertweg (1849–1922) and others, it deals with issues of botanical (and geographical) inheritance that are central to the development of new and better-adapted plants.

Geniculate   Pertaining to a plant joint similar to a knee in structure; a bent joint.

Genius loci (Latin)   A term referring to the particular spirit or flavor of a site; a sense of place. Frequently used by **A. J. Downing,** q.v., and other U.S. naturalistic designers.

Genotype   See **Phenotype.**

Genus   In botany, a group of closely related plants distinguished by species. The capitalized generic name always precedes the usually lower-case specific name. Several genera make up a family. The genus is the first half of a plant **Binomial,** q.v. Example: *Acer saccharinum.* Plural: genera; adjective: generic. See also **Botanical classification, Binomial, Generic name.**

Geobotany   The study of the relationship between plants and geology.

Geodetics (geodesy)   The scientific study of the shape and character of the earth.

Geoglyph   A relatively large human, animal, or other figure etched or formed into the ground by prehistoric tribes in North and South America. Geoglyphs are often thought to be religious in origin or intent. The Atacama Desert of Peru and Mojave Desert of California contain major quantities of geoglyphs.

Geographic climax vegetation   A plant association limited by a geographic factor such as a mountain range, seashore, dune series, or the like. Also **Physiographic climax vegetation.** See also **Climax growth.**

Geographic province   A distinct land region that is characterized by mountains, rivers, lakes, deserts, steppes, or prairies, and often rock strata. Also, loosely, a physiographic or geologic province. See also **Climatic province, Natural region.**

Geography   The study of the Earth's surface, its physical characteristics, weather and climate, soils, vegetative cover, kinds of people and the like.

Geography, cultural
   See **Landscape history.**

Geography, plant
   See **Phytogeography.**

Geologic province   See **Geographic province.**

Geology   The science or study of the Earth's crust and its underlying mantle and core.

Geomancy   An ancient art of divination popular in China. The geomancer would commonly throw a handful of earth on the ground and determine the shape of the future from the patterns it made. Tombs, parks, gardens, houses, and other land features were often sited by the dictates of geomancy.

Geometric   In landscape design, features pertaining to points, planes, or lines, and especially to physical items and design that tend to be obviously formal. Square, round, triangular, rectangular, and the like.

Geomorphic   Pertaining to a natural land form.

Geomorphology   The study of topography of land forms. Sometimes **Physiography,** q.v.

Geoponics   Earth gardening. See also **Hydroponics.**

Georgia buggy   See **Buggy.**

Geotaxis   See **Geotropism.**

Geotropism   Plant development or growth influenced by the presence of gravity. **Diageotropism** is horizontal gravity or climate-induced growth. **Plagiogeotropism** is gravity-induced growth at an acute angle. See also **Chemotropism, Haptotropism, Hydrotropism, Phototropism, Tropism.**

German landscape architecture

   The enclosed monastic garden and the market square were prominent medieval landscape forms in Germany. The highly formal castle garden of the late Middle Ages was best represented by the extensive grounds of Heidelburg Castle, laid out across a hillside with a river view. **Salomon de Caus,** q.v., the author of *Les Raisons des Forces Mouvantes* (1615) and *Hortus Palatinus* (1620), refined Heidelburg's raised gardens in the early seventeenth century. They were never properly completed because of the Thirty Years' War. The botanical garden at Breslau also dates from the seventeenth century.

   Narrow city streets with fountains or planters at prominent intersections dominated Renaissance Germany. Statuary was widely used in baroque gardens. The designer Francois Girard created the large formal grounds at Schloss Nymphenburg, near Munich, in the mid-seventeenth century. Schloss Nymphenburg was laid out in the French style, with great axial lines of statues. The German gardener Joseph Effner (1687–1745) added pavilions to the Nymphenburg Park and developed gardens for other German estates as well. The knot garden, with topiary resembling fruit or the forms of leaves, also dates from the 1600s; the garden at Idstein, Frankfurt-am-Main, is an example.

   Multiple influences dominated the German gardens of the eighteenth century. The Frenchman Zacharias Longueline (1684–1748) designed a formal park at Gross Sedlitz in 1726. Johann Prokop Mayer created a whimsical rococo garden for the Graf (Prince) von Hohenlohe at Weikersheim (c. 1720). Sculptures and fountains in an imposing perfect symmetry sprawled on Weikersheim's hillside above nearby Wurzburg. Mayer's Hofgarten at Wurzburg is

today Germany's best surviving formal garden. Georg Wenzeslaus von Knobelsdorff (1699–1753) laid out royal parks and courtyards for Frederick the Great. Louis XIV's Versailles was echoed at Karlsruhe near Baden; the palace gardens here were constructed with an elegant radial symmetry (c. 1715). Perhaps the best of the late formal designers was the French-trained Nicholas de Picage (1723–96), who executed the garden pavilion, allees, and parks at Schloss Benrath, near Dusseldorf (c. 1755), and the Elector's Garden at Schwetzingen (1750s ?), which included a theatre and follies in rococo style. Voltaire is thought to have written *Candide* while in residence at Schwetzigen.

Goethe (1749–1832) designed various royal parks at Weimar, all of which reflected Europe's growing fascination with the soft romantic landscape. Indeed, by 1800, German, French, and English gardens had all become "naturalistic." Sanspareil estate near Bayreuth had mixed a formal garden near the palace with a wilder garden in the distance as early as the 1740s. Hermitages, newly popular in the eighteenth century, had also fed German romanticism. Wilhelmshohe with its great cascade, Lowenburg, and Worlitz, an English landscape park, all had **Sublime** gardens, q.v., by the turn of the century. The Scot Thomas Blaikie designed a wild garden for Dych Castle, Dusseldorf. The island gardens of Mainau Castle, including extensive plantings of subtropicals and other exotics, were essentially complete by the mid-nineteenth century. However, Germany's greatest landscape garden was the estate at Muskau, designed by the Furst **von Puckler-Muskau** in the style of the **English Landscape School,** q.q.v. Von Puckler-Muskau laid out his grounds at Branitz in the same manner, though these were incomplete at the time of his death.

The first public parks in Germany (at Munich and Frankfurt) also date from the nineteenth century and were done in the English style. Fritz Encke (1861–1931), a landscape architect in the tradition of **Olmsted** and **Paxton,** q.q.v., designed parks and public open spaces throughout the country. Klettenbergpark, Cologne (1905–06) is a good remaining example of his work. The Bauhaus of the 1920s and 1930s, with its radical design theory displacing the Beaux Arts tradition, profoundly affected modern landscape architecture. Its director, Walter Gropius, headed the Design School at Harvard University after 1938 and influenced the work of **Eckbo, Rose, Kiley,** q.q.v., and others.

Modern, postwar German landscape architecture has followed international patterns. The Lower Castle gardens in Stuttgart, for instance, combine formalism and naturalism. The stepway and court of the new Pilgrimage Church in Cologne are an exercise in the elegant expression of contours. The influential Central Association of Landscape Architecture sponsors the annual German Garden Show. New botanical gardens, relatively rare in the twentieth century, have been designed in Hamburg (1980), and in Dusseldorf (1970s), where the landscape architect Franz Joseph Greub has created a modern plant museum at the University that combines Renaissance and twentieth-century styles.

See also **English landscape architecture.**

Germination   The process of sprouting in a fertile seed or a spore beginning its development into a plant. See also **Fertilization.**

Germination count   In landscape seeding, the actual percentage of plants that sprout and grow.

G-horizon soil   See **Glei soil.**

Giardino segreto (Italian)   A secret garden. A well-hidden and small private garden found in Italian Renaissance landscapes. Plural: giardini segreti.

Gibberd, Sir Frederick (1908–)   English town designer and architect. Gibberd designed the new Town of Harlow (1949). Author of *The New Towns.*

Gibberellin   A common plant growth hormone found in the fungal parasite *Gibberella fuyihuroi.* See also **Auxin.**

Gibbous   In plants, bulging or swelling on a single side.

Gilgai   Tiny troughs and ridges in the surface of a soil high in clay content.

Gilsonite   A naturally occurring asphalt, found in veins in harder rock strata.

Girdle, stem   See **Stem girdle.**

Girdling   In horticulture, the stripping of bark around a section of tree trunk or limb.

Girdling root   In nursery use, an extensive overgrown root circling inside a container that threatens a young plant with strangulation. Also, a root circling the lower root crown of a tree or shrub in the field.

Girt   In a sidewall, a lesser horizontal member used to increase wind resistance.

GL   A plan abbreviation for **Ground line,** q.v.

Glabra (botany)   See **Glabrous.**

Glabrate   In plant structures, becoming glabrous or smooth.

Glabrous   In botany, a smooth and hairless plant surface or structure.

Glacial erosion   A presently limited form of erosion caused by the grinding action of ice rivers. See also **Erosion.**

Glacial till   See **Till.**

Glaciofluvial   Referring to the icy streams emerging from mountain glaciers or their sedimentary deposits.

Glacis   A soft slope, especially a rampart or battlement slope, or a riverbank.

Glade   A forest opening.

Glass, bell   See **Bell glass.**

Glass cladding   In erosion control, a spun fiberglass mat applied to a hydraulic seeding and spot tacked with bitumen. Plants grow through the mat and eventually cover it.

Glass, fibrous   See **Fiberglass.**

Glass garden   See **Terrarium.**

Glass-reinforced concrete
   See **GRC concrete.**

Glauca   See **Glaucous.**

Glaucous   Referring to a waxy or powder-like coating on the surface of fruits such as plums or grapes, or on a leaf surface. **Bloom,** q.v. See also **Pubescence.**

Glazier   An installer of glass windows. See also **Glazing.**

Glazing   The placement of a glass window or window pane into an opening or compartment, or the glass fixture itself. See also **Glazier.**

Glei (gley) soil   A soil characterized by very bad drainage, with a high water table and a series of gray or red soil horizons. Saturated glei soils are often found between A, B, and C horizons. Glei soils are a kind of **Intrazonal soils,** q.v. **Humic glei soils** are found in bogs or soggy meadows. Also **G-horizon soil.** See also **Soil horizon.**

Schematic design for a new golf course, western U.S.
Illustration courtesy Morrow and Company.

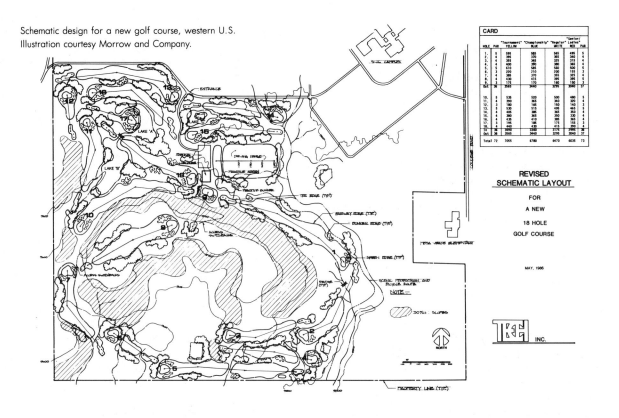

Glen   A small valley with high, steep sides.

Globe valve   A simple valve commonly used to control individual sections of an irrigation system. See also **Angle valve, Manual system.**

Glochid   A spine with a barb. The prickly pear cactus spine is an example. See also **Uncinate.**

Glorieta (Spanish)   A **Gazebo,** q.v., or park bandstand.

Gloss   A shining, reflective, or glossy finish. See also **Matte.**

Glume   In grasses and other plants, a **Bract,** q.v., that is particularly stiff or chafflike at its base.

Gnomon   The blade of a **Sundial,** q.v.

Golden mean ratio
   See **Proportional harmony.**

Golf course   Links. Nine, 18, 27, or 36-hole layouts.

Golf course architect   A designer whose work consists mainly of the design of golf courses and the supervision of their installation.

Golf course architecture (golf architecture)   A highly specialized and refined form of recreational landscape architecture developed over some five centuries from beginnings in the seaside dunes of Scotland. Scottish links were typically laid out over a series of sandy hills with grassy tops and many hollows. Early courses had no set number of holes, and as the land they occupied was marginal and public, their summer use from about 4:00 A.M. to 10:00 P.M. was democratically determined by the duffers themselves. St. Andrews, the oldest of all courses, was laid out in 1414, and it was here that greens were introduced into the game in the eighteenth century.

The 18-hole tradition also started at St. Andrews. A typical 18-hole course consists of more than 100 acres (41 hectares), but holes are not designed to set dimensions. Instead, two basic course design approaches have prevailed. The first, or "penal" approach, includes hazards which must be played. The second, or "strategic" approach, allows the player to skirt hazards, with a slight penalty exacted in strokes. Strategic design also allows direct play by more skillful golfers.

As the game has grown in popularity in the nineteenth and twentieth centuries, the number of courses has mushroomed. Research into turfgrass development, irrigation design, and landscape maintenance has been beneficial not only to the courses themselves but to landscape architecture in general. Course design as well has become increasingly sophisticated.

H. S. (Harry Shapland) Colt (1869–1951), an Englishman, was the first nonprofessional golfer to involve himself in course architecture. He was trained as a lawyer but began his design career before World War I with some limited modifications to the links at St. Andrews. Colt became an international designer, laying out courses in Britain, continental Europe, Canada, and the United States. Colt's plans were accurate and well drafted (very modern in that sense), and contained the first tree layouts devised for golf courses. Colt codified his ideas in the book *Golf Course Architecture* (1920).

The Scot Donald J. Ross (1872–1948) became the course manager at Pinehurst, North Carolina after immigrating to the United States in 1898. Ross had learned golf-club making and greens care as a young man, and developed his skill in course design on the job. The informality or naturalism of his approximately 600 layouts was a strong influence on golf course architecture in the United States. Ross was a founder and president of the American Society of Golf Course Architects (ASGCA).

Stanley Thompson (1894–1952), another Scot, began his practice in 1922 in Toronto. He was responsible for at least three masterpieces: the courses at Banff and Jasper, in the Canadian Rockies, and the course at Cape Breton Highlands. These are among the best in the world. Thompson was the mentor and later the partner of Robert Trent Jones, perhaps the best known of all golf course architects.

Jones, born in Ince, England in 1906, immigrated to the United States with his family in 1911. A golfer since boyhood, he devised his own course of study at Cornell University to prepare himself for a career in golf course design. By 1930, he and Thompson had developed a thriving partnership based in Toronto and New York City. They concentrated on strategic course design, and soon were carrying out commissions throughout North America. Jones later designed courses in the Soviet Union, Spain, Japan, Portugal, and elsewhere. Among his most noted projects are the Broadmoor in Colorado Springs, Spyglass Hill in Pebble Beach, California, and the Pevero Golf Course on the Costa Smeralda, Sardinia. His sons Rees and Robert Trent Jones, Jr. have also become practicing golf course architects.

Jones and Thompson, perhaps more than any other modern golf course architects, have set the tone of twentieth-century course design. Their courses are laid out to present both obvious and subtle obstacles to good play at each hole, and to make all the holes of a course function as a logical, attractive sequence.

Recently, the "executive (shorter) course," devised by William Amick and others, has become popular in the United States. It is designed for play in 2–2$\frac{1}{2}$ hours and has a par of 60–66.

"Good neighbor" fence A fence constructed to be equally attractive on both sides of a property line.

Goosefoot See **Patte d'oie.**

Gorge A canyon or valley with imposing vertical sides.

Gothein, Baroness Marie Louise Astute German landscape historian of the early twentieth century. Baroness Gothein was one of the earliest modern critics to note the influence of Eastern landscape-design principles on the gardens of Europe. She is the author of *A History of Garden Art* (1913).

Gothic A monumental building style of the high Middle Ages recreated in lesser proportions in the nineteenth century by Victorians eager to supply their gardens with "ancient" ruins.

GPM (irrigation) Gallons per minute. A measure of the volume of water moving through a channel or pipe. See **Discharge rate.**

Grade (gr) The slope or lay of a plot of land as indicated by a related series of elevations. 1) **Natural grade** consists of the contours of the unmodified natural surface. 2) **Rough grade** is established from **Existing** (or preconstruction) **grade** before planting, irrigation, and hard landscape items are installed. 3) **Finish grade** is accomplished after installation of landscape items is complete, and is shown on plans as proposed contours. Finish grade is also **Construction grade.** Also **Construction grade, Existing grade, Finish grade, Natural grade, Preconstruction grade, Proposed grade, Rough grade.** See also **Contour, Contour line, Gradient, Topography.**

Grade, construction See **Grade.**

Grade crossing   In vehicular and/or pedestrian circulation, the crossing of one road or pathway by another at the same ground level. Grade crossings are often referred to as railroad crossings.

Grade course   In wall construction, the first course—i.e., the course laid at or near finish grade.

Grade, existing   See **Grade.**

Grade, fine (finish)   See **Grade.**

Grade, finish   See **Grade.**

Grade, natural   See **Grade.**

Grade, preconstruction (existing)   See **Grade.**

Grade, proposed (finish)   See **Grade.**

Grade, rough   See **Grade.**

Grade separation   In vehicular and/or pedestrian circulation, the creation of a bridge or an underpass at a junction of ways to safely allow passage in cross directions at different levels. First used in the United States by **Frederick Law Olmsted,** q.v., at Central Park.

Grade stake   In landscape grading, a stake driven to show comparative elevations or areas to be cut or filled.

Grade valve   In irrigation, a valve used to regulate water flow because of its normally low friction loss.

Graded aggregate   Any aggregate containing an assortment of particles of uniformly varied sizes. See also **Coarse aggregate, Fine aggregate.**

Graded line (irrigation)   A sprinkler line graded to drain properly for the prevention of winter freezing.

Graded stream   See **Mature stream.**

Grades of sediment   See **Sediment grades.**

Gradient   The degree of slope of a pipe invert or road or land surface. Often expressed as a ratio (3:1, 6:1) in feet or meters, or as a percentage (2%, 30%). The gradient is a measurement of the slope height as related to its base. Also **Fall.** See also **Incline, Slope.**

Gradient, hydraulic (of pipes)   See **Hydraulic gradient.**

Gradient, moisture (soils)   See **Moisture gradient.**

Gradients, environmental   See **Environmental gradients.**

Grading   In landscape construction, the movement of earth to establish smooth finish contours for a project. Grading creates good drainage and sculpts the land to suit the intent of the landscape design.

Grading calculations   See **Cut and fill.**

Grading, heavy   See **Heavy grading.**

Grading plan   See **Contour plan.**

Grading (grade) tolerance   1) The amount of variation from absolute accuracy allowed in rough or finish site grading. 2) The variation allowed in quality or character of plant stock.

Graft hybrid   See **Chimaera.**

Grafting   In horticulture, the placement of a scion from one plant on the growing stock of another, with cambium layers in direct contact. The plants eventually fuse into a single tree or shrub. Grafting is useful in reproducing plants that would not breed true if propagated by seed. See also **Scion, Stock.**

Grain   A hard seed or kernel, usually found in cereal grasses such as wheat, millet, rye, and the like. A principal human food. See also **Caryopsis, Cereal.**

Grandfathering   A colloquial term describing admission of an individual to the practice of landscape architecture on the basis of work or education completed prior to the enactment of a registration law. See also **Landscape architectural registration.**

Granite   An igneous rock of great strength and durability used in landscape construction and for sculpture. Granite is generally composed of feldspar, quartz, and biotite or muscovite (mica). See also **Decomposed granite.**

Graphic scale   In landscape-plan or detail drawing, the ratio of the items depicted to their actual size. The graphic scale is always indicated on the drawings. The architect's scale, calibrated in sixteenths, eighths, quarters, or other portions of an inch, the engineer's scale, calibrated in decimals of an inch, and the metric scale are commonly used.

Graphics   Drawings. Designs.

Grasses   Useful landscape and food plants that characteristically have jointed stems, sheaths, and narrow blades (leaves). There are nearly 8,000 species. Among others, Indian corn, wheat, millet, oats, barley, and rice are important grass food crops.

Cultivated landscape grasses in temperate areas are often divided into cool-season and warm-season types according to their usefulness.

They are typically spreading, rather than bunch-growers.

Common cool-season grasses: 1) Bentgrasses (*Agrostis* species)—useful in golf greens; 2) Fescues (*Festuca* species); 3) Kentucky bluegrass (*Poa pratensis* varieties); 4) Orchard grass (*Dactylis glomerata*); 5) Redtop (*Agrostis alba*); 6) Ryegrasses (*Lolium* species); 7) Smooth bromegrass (*Bromus inermis*); 8) Wheatgrasses (*Agropyron* species).

Common warm season grasses: 1) Bermuda (*Cynodon dactylon*); 2) Bluestems (*Andropogon* species); 3) Broomsedge (*Andropogon virginicus*); 4) Buffalo grass (*Buchloe dactyloides*); 5) Carpet grass (*Axonopus compressus*); 6) Centipede grass (*Eremochloa ophiuroides*); 7) Dallis (*Paspalum dilitatum*); 8) Gramas (*Bouteloua* species); 9) Saint Augustine (*Stenotraphum secundatum*); 10) Zoysia (*Zoysia* species).

The largest grasses include sugar cane, river cane, and the bamboos, all of which may become woody.

Grasses, sod See **Sod grasses.**

Grassland A geographical area in which grass predominates. Called **Savanna** in the tropics, **Pampas, Plain, Prairie,** or **Steppe,** q.q.v., in temperate regions.

Grassland, tropical See **Savanna.**

Grassplot See **Lawn.**

Grate (grating) A grillework of metal or wood bars used as a fitting over drains at inlet points to allow the free passage of air and water while screening out large objects.

Grate, tree See **Tree grate.**

Grate, trench See **Trench grate.**

Gravel Water-worn or crushed pebbles or rock in a loose mixture. Gravel is generally larger than 2 mm in size. Also **Metal.** See also **Crushed gravel, Pea gravel, Sand.**

Gravel blanket A subgrade layer of gravel used to collect and transfer water to an underground drain or other outlet through porous backfill or chimneys.

Gravel soils Topsoils or subsoils containing a large amount of pebbles or gravel. Gravel soils often drain well but may lack the silt, clay, and humus necessary for healthy plant growth.

Gravel pit A pebble quarry.

Gravelboard In Britain and elsewhere, a horizontal, finish "stringer" along the base of a fence.

Gravitation Downward attraction and movement. A primary structural factor in the growth of plants (determining ultimate height, upright character, and the like) and in the ability of animate creatures to move through and affect the landscape in myriad ways.

Gravity outlet See **Outlet.**

Gravity retaining wall A large, heavy wall, usually of concrete, which is kept from overturning by the inertia of its sheer weight. See also **Retaining wall.**

Gravity, specific (in soils) See **Specific gravity.**

Gravity transport Fast or slow movement in the soil. See also **Soil creep, Solifluction.**

Gravity or gravitational water Water flowing freely down through the soil. **Free water,** q.v.

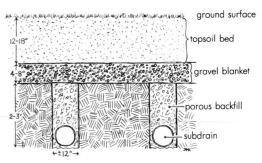

ground surface
topsoil bed
gravel blanket
porous backfill
subdrain

Gravel blanket

Gray earth A humus-free, neutral or alkaline soil found in semiarid or desert regions. A **Desert soil.** See also **Red desert soil.**

Gray-brown earth A temperate, humid, somewhat-acidic forest soil, with a relatively dark A horizon and modest B horizon. See also **Brown earth, Gray earth.**

Gray dune See **Dune.**

Gray and lavender garden A usually private garden designed with gray-leaved plants and purplish flowers as the primary feature. Stone outcrops or walls are often used as a backdrop to this kind of garden. Also **Purple garden.**

Gray water Used water—i.e., water tainted by dishwashing, clothes-cleaning, or other domestic or industrial use. Gray water is useful for irrigation, rinsing, or other purposes without first being filtered or purified.

Grazing The consumption of grasses and other foliage by animals. The grazing of domestic animals has caused the emergence of distinct landscapes in the countryside, and may thus be said to be a tool of man's social and cultural evolution and influence.

GRC concrete   Glass-reinforced concrete. A concrete strengthened with fiberglass reinforcement. See also **Asbestos cement pipe** and **Reinforced concrete.**

Greasebanding   A type of crawling-insect control developed for tree trunks. The stem of the tree is bound securely with a strip of paper, over which grease is spread to stop and trap insects.

Great groups (soil)   See **Great soil group, Soil classification.**

Great soil group   A collection of soils sharing like characteristics and developed in similar climates. The two primary groups are **Pedalfers** and **Pedocals,** q.q.v., and their many divisions. Also **Great group.**

Greek landscape architecture   A Persian influence made itself felt in the Greek landscape after the Persian Wars in the fourth century B.C. Oriental plane trees (sycamores) were planted in city agoras, and recent discoveries in **Landscape archaeology,** q.v., show that poplars were common trees near seeps on urban hillsides. Many of these city trees were watered by runoff carried in stone channels from the main market areas. The Acropolis itself was planted, adding to the drama of its hilltop location in Athens.

The Greeks developed public landscape forms and attitudes that have served the West now for millennia. Playing fields are among the most outstanding of these, and the idea of nonmurderous athletics that accompanied them. There were also Aristotle's Lyceum and Plato's Academy, outdoor schools conducted in groves and vineyards at the Athenian city walls. The Greek amphitheatre became an unparalleled vehicle for dramatic expression. In the conduct of

Greek landscape architecture. Ruins at Delphi. Photo courtesy Leslie Allen.

democracy as well, carried on amid boisterous discussion in semiopen meeting spaces, the Greeks made many political and social decisions essential to the subsequent makeup of Western culture.

Climate, of course, contributed to the evolution of an active outdoor public and private life in Greece. Our best idea of the smaller Greek

garden comes to us from literary sources. In the *Odyssey* we have the garden of Alcinous, about 4 acres, on Corfu. It was a courtyard close to a vineyard and an orchard. Laertes, the father of Odysseus, gave up his crown to work in his gardens and fields. The grape and the olive, of course, are at the heart of the ancient Greek landscape. And

Homer also notes that the Greeks thought of the Elysian fields as a kind of paradise after death for Achaean heroes. Still, the usual private garden seems modest: it characteristically contained a small basin of water in a courtyard or patio abutting the house, sometimes surrounded by fragrant flowers. Vines were frequently supported by trellises, and there may have been painted garden scenes on the interior courtyard walls. **Herm** statues, q.v., were popular features, and in the **Adonis garden,** q.v., the Greeks invented a Mediterranean classic: a geometric, central fountain, low-walled, warmed by small pots of seeds or newly planted flowers to welcome the coming of spring. Adonis, the handsome beau of Aphrodite, is the semideity whose rebirth the Greeks thus celebrated as winter passed. Unlike the larger and more permanent public landscapes, virtually none of these early gardens has survived intact; our idea of them must be reconstructed from pieces.

The Greeks excelled in city planning. As early as 1700 B.C., in Knossos and Phaestos, the Minoans had begun to develop the colonnaded walk or **Stoa** that would so characterize later Greek cities. The Minoans also devised shaded courtyards and hanging gardens for their palaces. Their courtyard pillars and walls were painted in lively colors. After the Mycenaean accession of about 1400 B.C., stone sculpture, one of the crowning glories of Greek culture, began to appear in the public and private landscape. The Mycenaeans developed the fortified acropolis and the central axis as key components of their cities. **Hippodamos** of Miletus, called the "father of city planning" by Aristotle, expanded and developed the Greek principle of gridiron planning (c. 500 B.C.). Deinocrates, an architect, worked out a town plan for Alexandria in

the fourth century B.C.; his religious and official projects emphasized good line and ideal proportion, and he laid out the city in a logical grid pattern.

The scientist and philosopher Theophrastus, in the fourth and third centuries B.C., systematized plant studies and created an early botanical garden. His *History of Plants* and *Etiology of Plants* were classical botanical studies. Greek botany formed the basis for Roman botanical and horticultural science and lasted as a principal source of information into the Middle Ages.

After Alexander's conquests in the third century B.C., a synthesis of Greek and Persian design developed in Macedonia and in Greece proper. Grottoes were sometimes built as a relief from summer heat in larger gardens, and villas and other Persian luxuries were widespread in the Greek city states. Greek sculpture continued as the standard of the ancient world. The **Hippodrome,** q.v., an oval outdoor racecourse, became popular. Alexandria grew into the jewel of the eastern Mediterranean, with a huge library and great parks and gardens. These late Greek (or Hellenic) forms continued in an unbroken evolution into Roman and Byzantine times. See also **Byzantine landscape architecture, Persian landscape architecture, Roman landscape architecture.**

Green (sports) 1) A closely shorn oval, round, or free-form area reserved for final strokes with a putter to finish a hole of golf. 2) Bowling green: a flat, grassy area some 120 feet (± 35 meters) square, lined with gutters on all sides, used for lawn bowls. The bowling green is popular in Britain and the former British colonies. 3) A common or public open space customarily planted in grass. See also **Village green.**

Greenbelt In nineteenth- and twentieth-century landscape and city planning, a mass of unspoiled, often treed, farm or other "country" land used to separate or ring urban areas. Greenbelts are usually designed as permanent features.

Green brickwork Just-finished brickwork in which the mortar has not set.

Green concrete Concrete that has just been placed or that has set but not completely cured.

Green garden A garden mostly dependent on leafy green foliage rather than fruits or flowers for its principal effect.

Green manure A vegetative cover of crop plants (grasses, clover, and the like) or weedy plants that is turned under to add humus-producing materials to the soil. Leguminous green-manure plants such as clover and alfalfa are valuable for the nitrogen-fixing properties of their roots. Also **Green crop fertilizer.** See also **Soil amendment.**

Green theatre In Italian villas, a formal open space usually bounded by evergreens and developed as a setting for plays or other presentations. See also **Theatrical garden.**

Greenhouse A glass-paned, wood- or metal-framed structure used for the rearing of delicate or young plants under controlled conditions throughout the year. Also **Glasshouse, Hothouse.** See also **Lath house.**

Greenleaf, James Leal (d. 1933)
Trained as a civil engineer, Greenleaf was a prominent designer of country places in the mid-Atlantic states after the turn of the century. His most notable gardens are at Killenworth, on Long Island. He served as president of the ASLA from 1923–27.

Greenstone In landscape construction, a metamorphic rock tinged green by traces of chlorite, actinolite, or similar materials.

Greensward A plot of lawn or turf.

Greenway (system) Advocated by the urban designer Edmund Bacon, among others, the "greenway" is a series of vegetative ribbons primarily within a city helping to give it coherence and life, and mitigating the effects of overdeveloped hard landscape items such as buildings and roads.

Greene, Guy Twentieth-century United States landscape architect and professor. Greene's Southwest (Arizona) landscapes in the **Modern garden,** q.v., style are elegant and polished, and evocative of the nearby harsh desert-mountain countryside.

Greenough, Horatio (1805–52)
United States design theorist, born in Boston, and colleague of the great Transcendentalist Ralph Waldo Emerson. Greenough spent approximately twenty years in Italy and elsewhere in Europe studying design and natural form. He theorized that nature was the ultimate source of functionalism; his idea that "form follows function" was later taken up by Frank Lloyd Wright and other twentieth-century "functionalist" architects and landscape architects. Greenough was the author of *The Travels, Observations, and Experience of a Yankee Stonecutter* (1852).

Grex In botany, a term used to define a closely related group of subspecies that can barely be individually distinguished.

Grid A crosshatch of intersecting, perpendicular points (roughly north-south and east-west) established by surveying as a basis for spot elevations. Used also for the preparation of existing and proposed contour plans (topographic maps). See also **Contour, Contour line, Grade, Stadia, Topography.**

Grid method (earthwork) See **Cut and fill.**

Grid pattern See **Gridiron.**

Gridiron A kind of city layout common in the United States that uses a square or rectangular cross-pattern of streets and blocks to provide for systematic roadways, paths, and the like. The gridiron concept is credited to Hippodamos of Miletus, a Greek city planner of the fifth century B.C. Also **Grid pattern.** See also **Circulation, Hippodamian scheme.**

Grille (grill) A series of metal bars welded together to form a screen or a support for cooking fresh food over a fire.

Grip, external (irrigation) See **External grip.**

Grip, internal (irrigation) See **Internal grip.**

Groin A sea wall constructed perpendicular to the shoreline to reduce sand movement and counter erosion. Also **Groyne.**

Groover In concrete construction, a tool used to create a **Control joint,** q.v. Also **Grooving tool.**

Grotto A natural or man-made cave—a primary feature of French Renaissance and early English Landscape School gardens from about 1500 A.D. onward.

Ground anchor (trees) See **Dead man.**

Ground cover Usually applied to plantings. Ground covers are the lowest and most horizontal level of vegetation in the landscape, and are usually installed as the final part of landscape construction.

Ground frost A land surface temperature below 1°C (33°F).

Ground line (GL) The surface of the ground as shown on a plan. See also **Datum line.**

Ground, parade See **Parade ground.**

Ground plane See **Base plane.**

Ground water Rain and snow water accumulated in the porous rock of the Earth's mantle. Also, if found below a water table, **Phreatic water.** See also **Aquifer, Water table.**

Groundflora Ground cover(s), or low-growing plants.

Grout A watery, fine mortar used to fill masonry and concrete cracks and to repair spalling on "honeycombing."

Grove A small grouping of trees. See also **Sacred grove.**

Growing medium Rich soil or artificially prepared soil used for plant culture.

Growing on The practice in the nursery industry of acquiring small plant stock and growing it to larger size for a season or two before resale.

Ground cover (sweet woodruff).
Detail at Dumbarton Oaks,
Washington, D.C. Photo by author.

Growth, deliquescent
See **Deliquescent growth.**

Growth habit (of plants) See **Habit of growth.**

Growth, juvenile See **Juvenile foliage.**

Growth, primary See **Plant growth.**

Growth region, plant See **Plant growth region, Hardiness zone.**

Growth rings In trees and other woody plants, the wood produced in one year by plant functions. Growth rings are composed of a wide, light-colored area (spring wood) and a thin, darker area (summer wood). Also **Annual rings.**

Growth, secondary See **Plant growth.**

Groyne See **Groin.**

Grubbing In site preparation, the digging or rooting out of stumps, old pipes, stones, and the like to make way for new development.

Grus Decomposed bits of igneous rock in a deposit.

Guano A special kind of highly concentrated organic fertilizer comprised of decomposed bird or bat excrement. Guano contains a high percentage of nitrogen and phosphates and has traditionally been a valuable export in the Pacific Basin and other areas of the world.

Guarantee (Guaranty) In contracts, an assurance on the part of the contractor that his materials and workmanship will last or perform as specified for a given period of time.
   The guarantee or defects liability period of a contract begins on the date of the contract final acceptance and normally lasts at least a year.
   Also **Warranty.**

Guarantee, bid See **Bid bond.**

Guaranteed ceiling fee See **Upset fee.**

Guaranteed maximum cost ("upset" cost) In landscape construction, a ceiling price guaranteed to an owner by a landscape contractor for project construction. The guaranteed maximum is calculated by including labor, materials, and overhead multiplied by a percentage factor for profit.

Guaranty bonds In landscape construction, bid bonds, labor and material payment bonds, and/or performance bonds required by the contract for construction. See also **Bond.**

Guard, tree See **Tree guard.**

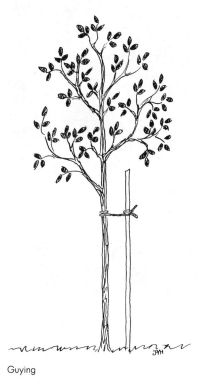

Guying

Guest species   An exotic plant that is introduced into a landscape for stabilization or some other functional purpose, or because of its aesthetic quality. See also **Exotic.**

Gully erosion   Erosion through quick-cutting channels in unvegetated or overgrazed land following heavy rain or snow melt. Gully erosion generally indicates abused land.

Gunnite   A kind of concrete applied by pneumatic pressure through a hose.

Gutter   A man-made, hard-surfaced swale or channel for water runoff.

Gutter, valley   See **Valley gutter.**

Guying   The stabilization of a young tree by means of wire or rope placed loosely around its trunk and then secured tautly to a stake or dead man in the ground. See also **Staking, Dead man.**

Gymnosperms   Conifers. One of the two primary subdivisions of seed-bearing plants (spermatophytes). Common woody evergreens in landscape design, gymnosperms bear naked seeds and often exhibit elongated needles as foliage. See also **Angiosperms, Conifer, Spermatophyte.**

Gynodioecious   In botany, referring to the existence of female and hermaphroditic flowers on separate plant specimens. See also **Gynomonoecious.**

Gynoecium   In flowers, the carpels or female reproductive organs collectively. See also **Androecium, Carpel.**

Gynomonoecious   In botany, pertaining to the occurrence of hermaphroditic and female flowers on the same plant specimen. See also **Gynodioecious.**

Gynophore   See **Pistil.**

Gyo   Japanese intermediate garden style. Generally less cluttered than the **Shin,** or formal, elaborate style, gyo develops the essence of the garden by use of both formal and informal landscape objects and forms. See also **Shin, So,** and **Japanese landscape architecture.**

Gypsum   Calcium sulfate. A mineral commonly used as an additive to improve the quality of clay soils and to reduce the alkalinity of any soil by replacing existing sodium with calcium. Gypsum is also used as a filler in insecticide dusts. Adjective: Gypsiferous. Also **Landplaster.**

Hand level   A small unmounted surveying instrument with a limited radius used in rough elevation and ground-level checking. See also **Level, Survey, Theodolite,** and **Transit.**

Handball   A modern (twentieth-century) outdoor or indoor game played by two opponents who bat a bouncing rubber ball vigorously against a high wall.

Handicapped access   Landscape design for disabled or handicapped people includes curb cuts, special seating, adequate paving with slight gradients, proper railing, specially constructed drinking fountains, and the like. It has been growing in popularity in the late twentieth century and is now often obligatory by law.

Hanging garden   In modern times, a roof or penthouse garden. The most famous hanging (building terrace) gardens of antiquity were those of Nebuchadnezzar at Babylon, c. 600 B.C., one of the Seven Wonders of the Ancient World.

In the twentieth-century U.S., a West Coast "hanging gardens" style has evolved featuring Cubistic concrete box planters, pendulous shrubbery, cascading water, and good pedestrian paths. See **Dan Kiley** and **United States landscape architecture.**

Haptotropism   The response of a plant to a specific local presence or object. A normally symmetrical tree curving away from the nearby wall of a house is an example. Also **Thigmotropism.** See also **Chemotropism, Geotropism, Hydrotropism, Phototropism, Tropism.**

Hard landscape   In landscape architecture, the nonliving components of the design, especially walls, walks, overhead structures, stones, benches, playing courts, and the like. Also **Inanimate landscape, "Hardscape."** See also **Soft landscape.**

Hard pinch   Pruning not at a plant tip but in hard wood further down a branch or stem.

Hard seed   See **Commercial seed classification.**

Hard water   Any water high in mineral salts.

Hardening off   The process of decreasing the amount of water a young plant receives and increasing its exposure to extremes of temperature, winds, and sun in preparation for locating it outside a lath house or other shelter. Also **Acclimation,** q.v.

Hard landscape. Note the contrast of wood, brick, and block with turf where the hard and soft landscapes meet. Photo by author.

Hardiness zone (plants)   A recognized geographic area in which specific plants may commonly grow and thrive. Approximately ten such zones exist in North America, ranging from Arctic (or Alpine) to subtropical. Also **Plant growth region.** See **Lifezone.**

Hardpan   An impervious, cemented layer of subsurface soil. A **Fragipan** is a soil layer that is hardened by compaction. See also **Alkaline soil, Caliche,** and **Pan.**

Hardwood   The timber or lumber of deciduous trees. Some of the most common temperate zone hardwoods are ash, oak, aspen, maple, and walnut. See also **Lumber** and **Softwood.**

Hardy (hardiness)   Said of plants that can withstand below-freezing temperatures. Many plants remain dormant and will not grow if air temperatures do not exceed approximately 43°F (6°C). Hardiness is a function of a plant's ability to become and remain dormant in a given locale or climate. See also **Dormant (dormancy).**

Hammada

Hare and Hare   United States landscape architects from Kansas City, Missouri. Sid J. Hare, father, and S. Herbert Hare, son. Hare and Hare gained wide renown for their design of roadways, houses, and accompanying gardens in the Country Club district of Kansas City, on which project they worked from 1913 to 1933. They are remarkable for their early use of the restrictive covenant as a means of controlling development.

Herbert Hare was the chief designer of the firm. Among the partners' notable projects outside Missouri were the new lumber town of Longview, Washington (begun 1922) and the Waite Phillips Estate (now Philmont Scout Ranch, c. 1926) in Cimarron, New Mexico. Hare and Hare also collaborated with the Olmsted office in the design of Forest Hills gardens in 1911.

Harmony (as an element of design)   In landscape architecture, the consistent recurrence of form, line, color, shape, texture, or the like in a composition. Landscape harmony is punctuated by **Rhythm,** q.v., or incidental counter-point.

Harmony, proportional
  See **Proportional harmony.**

Harp, Aeolian   See **Aeolian harp.**

Harrow   A metal or wood frame set with teeth or tines and pulled over a land surface to cultivate or cover a new seeding. A **Spring tooth harrow** is especially designed to cultivate hard-compacted surfaces. Harrowing is machine-raking.

Harvard Revolution   A design movement away from predetermined Beaux Arts form and toward site specific design. The modern movement in landscape architecture, occurring as an unlikely academic design "revolution" at Harvard University in the 1930s carried out by **Garrett Eckbo, Dan Kiley, James Rose,** and others. Somewhat superseded in the late 1960s by an "Environmental Movement."

Haulm   In gardening, the "useless" leafy upper part of a potato, pea, or other crop plant.

Haunch footing   In landscape construction, a footing and slab combined, with reinforcement, in the same pour.

Haussmann, Georges Eugene von (1809–91)   French lawyer and public official from Alsace-Lorraine, responsible for vast changes in the face of Paris. Baron von Haussmann served as Prefect of the Seine Department from 1853–70 under the Emperor Napoleon III.

Von Haussmann followed the traditional French design principles first established during the reign of Louis XIV. He attempted to unify Paris by planning long, formal boulevards, sewerage improvements, and impressive urban vistas. He developed multiple roundabouts or **Ronds-points** at arterial intersections to speed traffic flow. Many old Parisian structures were obliterated to carry out von Haussmann's schemes.

With his assistant, **Jean Charles Alphand,** von Haussman created the modern **Jardin anglais** form of the Bois de Boulogne, the Bois de Vicennes, and multiple other open spaces. The airy *places,* soft parks, and tree-lined boulevards of modern Paris are largely the work of von Haussmann and Alphand.

See also **French landscape architecture.**

Hazard (water, etc.)   In landscape design, a site feature such as a long pool, strong bank, or the like developed to quietly exclude people from an area.

Haze   A "clouded" air condition that develops as natural or artificially generated particles or gases mix with clear air. Haze may worsen with sunlight as it precipitates chemical reactions between atmospheric gases and pollutants. See also **Air pollution** and **Smog.**

Hazard

Hazen and Williams formula   A computation used to calculate flow loss in pipes. Usually expressed as $V = 1.318 \, Cr^{.63}S^{.54}$. V = velocity in feet per second (FPS), C = coefficient of roughness, r = hydraulic radius in feet, S = hydraulic slope.

Head   1) In irrigation, a water emission fixture containing a nozzle that is installed in shrub or lawn areas or elsewhere to deliver water at a fixed rate determined by pipe size, water pressure, and other factors. See also **Feet of head.** 2) In botany, a flower head in the composites.

Head, ball-driven   See **Ball-driven head.**

Head, cam-driven (irrigation)   See **Cam-driven head.**

Head, feet of (irrigation)   See **Feet of head.**

Head, fixed (irrigation)   See **Stationary head.**

Head, flat spray   See **Flat spray head.**

Head, flush (irrigation)   See **Flush head.**

Head, full   See **Full head.**

Head, gear-driven   See **Gear-driven head.**

Head, half (irrigation)   See **Half head.**

Head, high-pop   See **Pop-up head.**

Head, impact   See **Impact head**

Head, jet action (irrigation)   See **Rotary head.**

Head, lawn   See **Lawn head.**

Head, line (irrigation)   See **Strip head.**

Head, mist (irrigation)   See **Mist head.**

Head, one-fourth (irrigation)   See **Quarter head.**

Head, one-third (irrigation)   See **One-third head.**

Head, part circle (irrigation)   See **Part circle head.**

Head, pop-up (irrigation)   See **Pop-up head.**

Head, quarter (irrigation)   See **Quarter head.**

Head, rotary   See **Gear-driven sprinkler.**

Head, rotor   See **Gear-driven sprinkler.**

Head, shrub-spray (irrigation)   See **Shrub-spray head.**

Head, spider (irrigation)   See **Spider head.**

Head, spray   See **Spray head.**

Head, static   See **Feet of head.**

Head, stream-jet   See **Spider head.**

Head, stream-spray   See **Spider head.**

Head, strip   See **Strip head.**

Head, suction friction (irrigation)   See **Suction friction head.**

Head, three-quarter (irrigation)   See **Three-quarter head.**

Header   1) A landscape border, usually of wood timbers, brick, or poured concrete, installed to indicate a lawn or planter boundary. See also **Mowing strip.** 2) In walls, a brick course in which only the ends of the individual bricks are visible on the wall surface. See also **Brick wall pattern.**

Header bond (masonry)   See **Brick wall pattern.**

Header-stretcher courses (bricklaying)   Planter or other brick walls laid in alternate vertical courses of exposed short sides (headers) and long sides (stretchers). Usually, **English bond.** See **Brick wall pattern.**

Heading back   A pruning technique in which plant tips are bobbed to stimulate bushiness.

Heading bond (masonry)   Header bond. See **Brick wall pattern.**

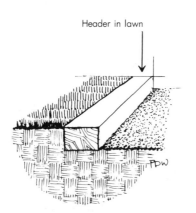

Header in lawn

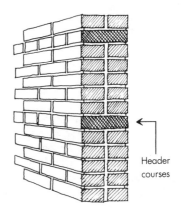

Header courses

Hedge

Hedgerow

Heavy grading Large-scale operations of cut and fill used to produce finish (proposed) contours.

Hectare A metric measurement of land of 100 meters by 100 meters. A hectare is equal to approximately 2.47 acres or 100 **Ares**, q.v.

Hedge A number of shrubs or trees planted closely together in a line. A hedge may be formal (if sheared and shaped often) or informal (if allowed to assume it natural shape). Also **Screen planting.**

Hedgerow A row of small trees or shrubs forming a break or boundary at the edge of or between fields. See also **Fencerow, Windbreak.**

Heel (of a cutting) In horticulture, the base of a cutting.

Heeling in In horticulture, the temporary storage of balled and burlapped or bareroot stock in a holding area of deep, wet sawdust, bark, or similar material. Heeling in protects **Feeder (hair) roots** q.v., from drying out.

Heliotropism See **Phototropism.**

Hemera A period of geologic time distinguished by a species of plant or animal in its heyday or full flower.

Herb In horticulture, an annual plant with a nonwoody or fleshy structure. Certain herbs are highly useful in cooking. Adjective: Herbaceous.

Herb garden A New England garden dating from colonial times (seventeenth century), used to produce cooling herbs and other small-scale fresh produce. A distinctive minor form of U.S. and related landscape architectures. See also **Knot garden.**

Herbaceous (adjective) See **Herb.**

Headwall (storm sewer) A wall used for retention at a sewer or culvert entry. An **Endwall** is used at the conduit outlet.

Heap composting See **Compost.**

Heartwood The inner part of woody plant tissue, essential for plant support. Heartwood is usually tougher and more durable than **Sapwood**, q.v., and darker in color. Also **Duramen.** See also **Wetwood.**

Heat, bottom See **Bottom heat.**

Heat of hydration (concrete) See **Hydration.**

Heath 1) A kind of waste land found in northern temperate regions; characteristically, a flat or rolling area covered with small shrubs and some herbaceous plants. 2) Heather, a shrub found in moors or heaths. See also **Moor.**

Heave, frost See **Frost action.**

Herbaceous border   In gardens, a planter or flower-bed edge that features annuals or other leafy, nonwoody foliage plants. An early advocate of the herbaceous border was **J. C. Loudon,** q.v., in the 1830s.

Herbage   Collectively, grasses and leafy plant parts.

Herbal   1) An archaic term for **Herbarium.** 2) A classical or medieval listing of plants.

Herbarium   A collection of dried plants arranged to form a scientific or horticulture display, or a room or building used to house such a collection. Also *hortus siccus* (Latin).

Herber   A garden, arbor, or orchard (antique English).

Herbicide   A chemical weed or plant killer. Translocational (applied to leaves, carried internally to roots), foliage contact, and root contact preparations form the three main kinds of herbicides. A "natural" herbicide of sorts is **Mulch,** q.v. See also **Broad spectrum control, Insecticide.**

Herbivore   An animal that eats only plants.

Herbularius   See **Physic garden.**

Hereditament   1) In property law, a right that accompanies the ownership of land. For example, the right to cut wood on a forested tract may be a hereditament. 2) An inheritance of land or other property.

Herm   In classical Greece, a small column, rectangular, supporting a small statue. Herms (after the god Hermes) also served as boundary markers, mileposts, and the like. See also **Greek landscape architecture, Terminus.**

Hermaphrodite   In botany, a species producing bisexual flowers in the same specimen. See **Flower.** See also **Dioecious, Monoecious, Polygamous.**

Hermitage   An isolated retreat or dwelling. The "home of a hermit." Popular in picturesque eighteenth-century English gardens.

Herringbone   In brick or tile pavements, diagonal coursework with adjacent rows laid in opposing directions. A zigzag pattern. See also **Paver brick pattern.**

Heterogamous   1) Referring to flowers in which the male and female organs may or may not occur. 2) In general botany, pertaining to an alternation of sexual and parthenogenetic generations. See also **Homogamous, Parthenogenesis.**

Heterogeneous   In botany, pertaining to related plants with certain unlike characteristics. See also **Homogeneous.**

Heteromorphous (heteromorphic)   In plants, many-formed. Noun: heteromorphy. See also **Homomorphic.**

Heterophylly   In botany, the occurrence of leaves of different shapes on the same plant in its young and adult stages. Eucalyptus and box elder are examples.

Heterosis   In horticulture, the rapid, robust growth of a hybrid plant. Also **Hybrid vigor.**

Heterotrophic plant   Any plant that must use organic portions or products of other plants as the basis of its metabolism. Usually parasites, fungi, or the like. See also **Autotrophic plants.**

Hewn stone   Ashlar, q.v.

Hickey   In concrete construction, a tool used in the bending of steel rods or rebars.

High desert   In the southwestern United States, a relief desert with harsh climatic extremes. Many temperate-zone plants will not grow well in the high desert (New Mexico, Arizona, Utah, Nevada) due to alkaline soil, high winds, low humidity, and scanty rainfall. Also applied to certain Middle Eastern and Central Asian deserts. See also **Intermediate desert, Low desert.**

High forest   A tall-tree woodland, usually grown or recognized as a source of lumber.

High point (HP)   In surveying, a hilltop mark.

High-early-strength cement   A cement with the necessary properties to age and strengthen a concrete mixture exceptionally quickly.

High-pop head (irrigation)   See **Pop-up head.**

Highway   A public road providing fast transit between town or cities. A scenic highway is specifically laid out to emphasize pleasant countryside—mountains, rivers, and the like—with minimum disturbance to existing landscape.

Hill creep   A movement of surface material, soil, or stone, down a hillslope. Similar to **Soil creep,** q.v.

Hill, Thomas   Noted as the first true English garden writer. His books *A Briefe and Pleasaunte Treatise* (1563), *Proffitable Arte of Gardening* (1568), and *Gardeners' Labyrinth* (1577) aroused widespread interest in garden design and gardening for pleasure. Hill's nom-de-plume was Didymus Mountain.

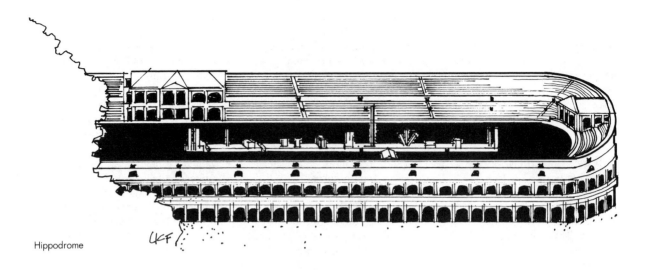

Hippodrome

Hilling   Mounding of earth around the base of a plant principally for frost protection or structural support.

Hilling up   See **Earthing up.**

Hinterland   Backwoods, boonies, sticks, bush.

Hip   In botany, a fruit of the Rose family, particularly as found on rosebushes after blooming.

Hippodamian scheme   In urban planning, a method of layout that uses two large cross-axial roads to divide a city into four parts that are further subdivided into blocks. So-called after Hippodamos of Miletus, a Greek city planner of the fifth century B.C. Also **Milesian scheme** or **planning.** See also **Gridiron.**

Hippodamos (Hippodamus) of Miletus (c. 500 B.C.)   Aristotle called Hippodamos the father of town planning. Hippodamos believed that good urban planning could help refine society, and his development of the gridiron became the standard of the Greek world. His ideas were especially influential in the Athens of Pericles and its dependencies.

The ideal Hippodamian city contained some 10,000 citizens, including artisans, soldiers, farmers, and other free citizens of various occupations. Its land was carefully divided into residential (private), business, public, and sacred areas.
Hippodamos's influence in Rome, Byzantium, and the developing United States of the eighteenth, nineteenth, and twentieth centuries was profound.
See also **Gridiron.**

Hippodrome (Greek, then Roman)
An oval track for chariot racing with multiple tiers of seats for spectators. The Circus Maximus in Rome is perhaps the greatest example.

Hira-niwa   A Japanese flat or level garden, formally described by Kitamura Enkin in the *Tsuki-yama Teizoden* (*The Creation of Landscape Gardens*), c. 1735.
Tsuki-yama (hillside garden), q.v., and hira-niwa are always laid out in **Shin, Gyo,** or **So** styles, q.q.v.
See also **Japanese landscape architecture.**

Hispid   In plants, covered with hard, bristlelike hairs.

Histisol (histosol)   A swampy soil containing a large amount of humus or humus-producing material. See also **Peat.**

Histology   The study of plant (or animal) tissue.

Historic preservation   Historic preservation and value in landscape architecture date from the late nineteenth century. **Charles Eliot,** q.v., the pioneer Massachusetts landscape architect, founded the Trustees of Public Reservations in Boston in 1890. Eliot intended to provide for open space development and conservation in Boston, Brookline, and other nearby towns. The Trustees, a quasipublic association, were also charged with preserving areas of special scenic quality around Greater Boston.
The idea of historic preservation was more strongly affixed to architecture than to gardens or other landscape almost at once, and perhaps rightly so. Plants, the basic materials of man-made landscapes, change seasonally as well as with the years, causing basic differences in garden appearance over time. It is very difficult indeed to replace original plant varieties in old

gardens, even if the preservationist is sure of what they were through descriptions or drawings. Modern plant varieties have all but completely superseded even the most commonplace specimens of earlier centuries. Weed or pioneer species will also have succeeded original plantings by natural processes in many gardens after a half century or so. In addition, changes in landscape scale due to plant growth must be taken into account, as must drastic pruning, successive landscape styles imposed one on top of the other, erratic maintenance, and other difficulties involved in determining an owner's original intent.

Natural human forgetfulness and the human fondness for good stories are prime factors in the investigation of old landscapes for preservation. The garden owner, the designer, the contractor, and the maintenance staff all become mixed in confusion after 10 or 20 years, often making it impossible to determine who was responsible for which aspect of the work. And fanciful stories by the handful arise about the origin of the landscape in question, all the events leading to its creation, and anything that happened in it through the years.

Despite these drawbacks, the twentieth century has seen several major efforts mounted toward historic preservation. Williamsburg, Virginia has been painstakingly restored to its 1740 condition. The chateau and estate of Villandry, France, have been carefully pieced back together, beginning in 1906. Franklin Delano Roosevelt's New Deal of the 1930s put huge numbers of artisans and laborers to work building, rebuilding, and expanding such American cultural treasures as the numerous state park systems. Roosevelt's Civilian Conservation Corps (CCC) camps constructed many of today's historic landscapes in the process.

In 1949, the United States Congress created the National Trust for Historic Preservation, modeled on the British National Trust. The National Trust became the first Federal agency to officially promote historic preservation. The Trust's influence has increased since the early 1970s, replacing "urban renewal" (the mass destruction of downtowns) with the lighter and more elegant approaches of "renovation" or the "maintenance of historic character" of city areas.

Currently, good historic preservation practice requires a definition of the traditional character or flavor of a city or region before individual landscapes are analyzed. In studying prairie landscapes, Professor Robert Harvey of Iowa State University has made use of the techniques of **Landscape archaeology,** q.v. He has applied his findings in the restoration of the Victorian grounds of Terrace Hill, the Iowa governor's mansion in Des Moines. Harvey's work, as well as that of **J. B. Jackson,** q.v., the cultural geographer, has contributed to an understanding of the American farm as a type of historic landscape. Ongoing excavation and renovation at Mt. Vernon and Monticello have built on techniques begun at Williamsburg in bringing back to life landscapes important in American social history. In France, Monet's gardens are being restored largely by means of reference to his accurate paintings of them, created during the last century.

The idea of the historic landscape as gardens or grounds contributing to the cultural history of their times is slowly taking hold in the late twentieth century. State or regional historic landscape surveys are contributing to its acceptance. Among these are landscape or garden studies in California, Arizona, and New Mexico. In New Mexico, a Registry of Historic Landscapes has been devised under the auspices of the State Historic Preservation Division. Directed by Morrow and Company, Landscape Architects, the Registry has performed a general survey of the state's historic landscapes and divided them by type (park, plaza, courthouse square, garden) into several overlapping categories. Among these are Precolumbian, Spanish colonial, Territorial, New Deal, Railroad Era, Frontier Pastoral, Route 66, and other useful divisions. The landscapes are then studied in detail for potential nomination to national or state registers of historic places, for inclusion in a state historic landscape system, or for various kinds of preservation and restoration.

Modern preservation may include, among other approaches or considerations: 1) preservation proper, or maintenance in a relatively static condition; 2) conservation of a site as part of a larger area or facility of historic importance; 3) restoration to a given date or quality; 4) renovation for ongoing use; 5) interpretation of a vanished landscape represented by only a fragment of its original condition or simply by knowledge of its whereabouts.

The emerging product of nearly a century of intensive interest in historic preservation has been a much-expanded knowledge of the regional landscapes of the United States and other nations and of the rich heritage they represent to landscape architecture as an art and a function of culture.

See also **Landscape archaeology, Landscape history.**

History, landscape   See **Landscape history.**

HMAC   Plan abbreviation for hot-mix asphalt concrete. See **Hot mix.**

Hoare, Henry Eighteenth-century English banker and designer of his own landscape gardens at Stourhead estate (1740–50). Stourhead became one of the finest (and earliest) picturesque landscapes, designed to reflect many of the classical events depicted in the *Aeneid*. Hoare's efforts helped to popularize the new **English School of Landscape Gardening** of his day. See also **English landscape architecture**.

Hoarfrost A kind of frost found on ground surface objects when ice crystals form directly from vapor. See also **Frost**.

Hoary An adjective describing a plant leaf or stem showing short white or gray hairs.

Hochmoor A mountain bog containing a large number of spongy mosses (peat moss). A raised bog.

Hogback (hogsback) A prominent ridge with two steeply declining sides. See also **Cuesta**.

Hogring In landscape construction, a strong metal ring used to hold chainlink-fence fabric to tension wires.

Hold harmless agreement A legal arrangement in which one party agrees to hold a second party harmless (i.e., not responsible) for the second party's negligent actions. Sometimes involved in design or construction contracts.

Holding tank A special tank to which water is pumped and stored, and in which particles are allowed to settle, before the water is filtered and repumped for irrigation use.

Hole, swallow See **Sinkhole**.

Holford, Sir William (1907–) English town planner, responsible for various postwar plans for London and for urban planning in Canberra, Australia.

Holocene The Recent, or current, geologic epoch, part of the **Quaternary** period, q.v.

Holotype In botany, the typical example of a species, especially the first example to be described and named. Also **Type specimen**.

Homestead A small, family farm carved out of a wilderness. A mainstay of United States land settlement in the nineteenth century, consisting by law of 160 acres of public land claimed and occupied by a family or an individual. The homestead is strongly engrained in the American character as a symbol of the resolute development of the country.

Homochromous All the same color.

Homo-ecology See **Human ecology**.

Homogamous Pertaining to flowers that are capable of fertilizing themselves, and in which the stamens and pistils mature together. See also **Heterogamous**.

Homogeneous In botany, pertaining to related plants with quite similar characteristics. See also **Heterogeneous**.

Homomorphic (homomorphous) In plants, the same in texture, form, appearance, size or the like. Noun: homomorphy. See also **Heteromorphous**.

Honeycombing In concrete finishing, gaps and cavities left on the surface or in the interior of a pour after forms have been removed.

Hood, sprinkler See **Sprinkler hood**.

Hook A sea **Spit**, q.v.

Horizon, agric (soils) See **Agric horizon**.

Horizon, albic (soils) See **Albic horizon**.

Horizon line In design or perspective drawing, the basic horizontal plane of reference.

Horizon, salic (soils) See **Salic horizons**.

Horizon, soil See **Soil horizon**.

Horizontal alignment (of streets) See **Alignment of streets**.

Horizontal curve alignment The road tangents and length of curve that combine to make a horizontal road curve.

Horizontal element In design layout, any animate or inanimate object or form that is flat or which tends to draw a vista out horizontally. See also **Intermediate element, Vertical element**.

Horizontal shear See **Shear**.

Hormone (plant) A substance manufactured by a plant to stimulate growth, the orientation of the plant to light, specialized sap flow, or similar functions, usually carried by the plant's vascular system to a point removed from its origin (i.e., roots to leaves or the like). See also **Auxin, Gibberellin**.

Hormone rooting compound See **Rooting compound**.

Horti pensiles (Latin) In classical times, gardens of lush extravagance such as the hanging gardens of Babylon, or Cyrus's paradise at Sardis.

Horticultural classification   The sorting out of various plants according to type—i.e., tree, shrub, ground cover, vine, and the like. Any basic cultivated plant type. See also **Botanical classification.**

Horticultural code   See **Cultivated Plant Code.**

Horticultural engineer   In several Eastern Bloc countries, a title used to describe a person graduating from a course in agricultural engineering, horticulture, and landscape design.

Horticultural variety   See **Variety.**

Horticulture   The cultivation of plants for food, practical, or ornamental use.

Horticulture, department of
See **Department of Horticulture.**

Horticulture, ornamental
See **Ornamental horticulture.**

Horticulturist   A cultivator or student of plants and the principles of their growth.

Hortorium   A botanical institution devoted to the scientific study, classification, and documentation of garden plants.

Hortus (Latin)   In the Middle Ages, a vegetable garden.

Hortus conclusus (Latin)   In the Middle Ages, a small "enclosed garden" dedicated to the Virgin Mary. See also **Cloister.**

Hortus inclusus (Medieval Latin)   A small, very formal, enclosed medieval garden.

Hortus siccus   **Herbarium**, q.v.

Hosebib   See **Bib.**

Hoskins, W. (William) G. (1908–)
British historian and pioneer, with the American **John Brinckerhoff Jackson,** q.v., of landscape history (cultural geography) as a new field of the liberal arts.

Hoskins was born in Exeter and began his work as a historian while still young. He taught English local history at the University of Leicester and also taught at Oxford. His special interest—a field analysis of local landscapes leading to an idea of the continuity of local history—is a novel break from the broader and more commonplace concentration of histories on political and royal themes.

Hoskins's groundbreaking study, *The Making of the English Landscape,* was published in 1955. His other works include *Exeter in the Seventeenth Century* and *The Midland Peasant,* as well as "English Landscapes," a companion publication to the BBC television series of 1973 and 1978 featuring studies of the English countryside.

Hoskins and Jackson both are regarded as cultural geographers, intensely involved in reconstructing settlement and cultural patterns from meticulous observation. Hoskins's analyses, however, normally end with the coming of the twentieth century, an event he regards with summary distaste. He was made a Fellow of the British Academy in 1969.

Hotbed   A planter or plant propagation bed warmed by the bacterial action of decaying manure or by artificial means. See also **Coldframe, Warming bed.**

Hothouse   See **Greenhouse.**

Hot line   In irrigation, any pipe under "live" (continuous) or static pressure.

Hot mix (asphalt)   A heated mixture of fine and coarse aggregates and asphalt binder (cement) which is applied to a dry, prepared base as asphalt pavement. Abbreviated **HMAC.** See also **Asphalt** and **Cold mix.**

Hot soil   Any soil with excessive capacity for corrosion. A grossly unbalanced soil.

Hourly fee   A professional fee charged on the basis of a set rate per hour for principal's time and for professional, technical, and secretarial time. See also **Professional fee.**

House, garden   See **Garden house.**

House, lath (slat)   See **Lath house.**

House, moss   See **Moss house.**

House, palm   See **Palm house.**

House, tea (Japanese)   See **Tea house.**

House, temperate   See **Temperate house.**

Housing code   See **Building codes.**

Housing and Urban Development, Department of (HUD)   A U.S. government agency responsible in recent years for multiple federally funded public service programs, especially in housing, and including many landscape architectural projects.

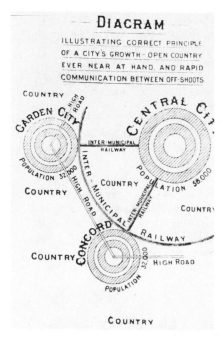

Ebenezer Howard. Principle of a city's growth, c. 1902. Illustration courtesy BBMSL, UNM.

Howard, Ebenezer (1850–1928)

British planner of **New towns** and **Garden cities,** q.q.v. Howard was a law clerk whose interest in urban planning was inspired by the ideals of Edward Bellamy's parable, *Looking Backward,* by the American Transcendentalists Walt Whitman and Ralph Waldo Emerson, and by the attempts at better workers' housing mounted by the British industrialists Cadbury, Lever, and others in the late nineteenth century.

Howard's classic *Garden Cities of Tomorrow* was published in 1902 after years of writing and revision. Howard's theories of the garden city as a permanent combination of exciting town and bucolic countryside immediately became popular. He proposed a city of some 30,000 people on approximately 6,000 acres (2,428 hectares) with ward or neighborhood

divisions, planned rail access, a central public park, and complete development planning. His garden city was essentially circular; when it had reached its maximum population it would not expand, and a second city would be built nearby. The social system of the garden city was to be egalitarian, and a greenbelt would keep its residents in constant touch with nature. The garden city was independent, looking to its own industries and shops to keep it employed.

The first New town to be modelled after Howard's garden city was Letchworth, designed by Raymond Unwin and Barry Parker in 1903. It was followed by Welwyn, some 12 miles away, in 1924. The success of these cities led after the war to the British New Towns Act (1946). Harlow, Stevenage, Crowley, and other New towns have since been established.

Many of Howard's ideas were adapted in the twentieth century to produce garden suburbs around existing cities, perhaps not the happiest of interpretations. In the United States, true New towns have included Radburn, New Jersey; Columbia, Maryland; and Reston, Virginia. In Germany, the work of Howard's contemporary, Richard Riemberschmid (1868–1957), was important in the redesign of Dresden.

HP See **High point.**

Hubbard, Henry V. (1875–1947)

United States landscape architect and professor. Hubbard was a partner in the Olmsted office in Brookline, Massachusetts, before assuming a teaching post at Harvard in 1906. As an early educator, he was known for his innovative use of actual design problems in the classroom. Hubbard was the author of *Landscape Design* (1917) with his wife, Theodora Kimball. From

1929–41, he chaired the School of City Planning at Harvard, and he was president of the ASLA from 1931 to 1934.

HUD See **Housing and Urban Development, Department of.**

Hudsonian zone See **Life zone.**

Hue A color, specifically red, orange, yellow, green, blue, and violet, or, more generally, any shade of these.

Huerta Orchard land (Spain, Latin America, and southwestern U.S.).

Human ecology The relationship of man to his physical surroundings. Also **Homo-ecology.** See also **Ecology.**

Human scale In design, composition intended to make people comfortable and well-satisfied emotionally; design that provides carefully and well for individual needs. In general, design that is scaled to the human body. See also **Monumentality.**

Humanism, landscape See **Landscape history.**

Humic glei soils See **Glei soil.**

Humidity The amount of water vapor in the air. **Absolute humidity** is the real amount of vapor measured at any one time; **Relative humidity** indicates a percentage of total saturation at a given temperature.

Hummock A knoll or ridge.

Hums Little, isolated limestone hills, often signs of Karst erosion. See also **Sinkhole.**

Humus   A deep brown or black mass of decomposing vegetable or animal matter that is a source of nutrients in soil. Also, loosely, any organic material applied to soil to improve it.

Hungry soil   An alkaline soil, low in humus, that quickly absorbs most soil amendments worked into it. Hungry soils are thin and often take massive applications of organic materials before reaching a neutral or near-neutral pH.

Hunter, plant   See **Plant hunter.**

Huntsman-Trout, Edward
   Twentieth-century American landscape architect, designer of Scripps College grounds, Claremont, California, and multiple other **California** or **modern gardens,** q.v.

Hurdle fence   See **Rail fence.**

Husbandman   A farmer or cultivator. See also **Husbandry.**

Husbandry   Agriculture. Care of cultivated crops or plants. See also **Husbandman.**

Hyaline   In plant structures, pertaining to a membrane that is thin and transparent.

Hybrid   In botany, any plant produced from breeding parents of different species or varieties. Hybrids are often indicated with a multiplication sign ($\times$) following the generic name. For instance *Platanus* $\times$ *acerifolia* (London plane tree). Certain hybrids (some varietal crosses) may be referred to as **Polybrids.** See also **Chimaera, F_1.**

Hybrid, bigeneric   See **Bigeneric hybrid.**

Hybrid, graft   See **Chimaera.**

Hybrid, vigor   See **Heterosis.**

Hydrant, lawn   See **Lawn hydrant.**

Hydration   The formation of a compound such as concrete in which water is contained in a definite ratio. Part of the curing process of concrete. The chemical reaction of water and cement during curing produces heat **(Heat of hydration)** as a by-product. See also **Curing.**

Hydraulic (automatic) controller   In irrigation, a kind of **Automatic controller,** q.v., that activates valves with hydraulic pressure. Obsolescent. See also **Automatic controller.**

Hydraulic diaphragm valve   In irrigation, a kind of **Piston valve,** q.v.

Hydraulic gradient   In storm-sewer layout, the grade or slope of the surface of water running through a pipe. A maximum capacity of 0.8 is the usual design criterion. See also **Self-cleaning velocity.**

Hydraulic limestone   A lime c e containing aluminum and si ion and yielding a cement that sets under water.

Hydraulic piston valve   See **Piston valve.**

Hydraulic radius   The wetted cross-section of the bottom of a ditch channel, or pipe **(wetted perimeter),** indicating design capacity or actual volume of flow. Hydraulic radius is expressed as the ratio $r = a/p$, in which **a** is the cross section area, *p* the wetted perimeter, and **r** the hydraulic radius.

Hydraulic ram   A water-powered pump usually charged from a brook.

Hydraulic seeding   The application of grasses, flowers, ground covers, or even trees to a slope or other area as a mixture of seed, fertilizer, and mulch (usually shredded cellulose fiber) shot out of a water cannon. Also **Hydroseeding.**

Hydraulics   The science of water mechanics and behavior. Also **Hydro-dynamics.**

Hydric   In soils, wet. See also **Moisture gradient.**

Hydrocarbon   A carbon-hydrogen compound constituting oil, coal, and like materials. See also **Carbon.**

Hydro-dynamics   See **Hydraulics.**

Hydrogen ions (in soil)   See **pH scale.**

Hydrogeology   The scientific study of water as a part of the Earth's geology.

Hydrography   A science dealing with the distribution and mapping of ce waters.

Hydrologic cycle   See **Water cycle.**

Hydrology   The science dealing with the laws, properties, and distribution of water. See also **Hydraulics.**

Hydrolysis   A chemical action combining water with a soluble element or elements, necessary for the intake of nutrients by plant roots.

Hydrophobia   In horticulture, the inability of a soil to absorb water.

Hydrophyte   A water-loving plant, found in or along streams or in areas of extremely high humidity. Adjective: hydrophilous. Also **Hygrophyte.** See also **Mesophyte, Tropophyte, Xerophyte.**

Hydropneumatic pressure In irrigation, the pressure of compressed air resulting from water being pumped into an empty tank. Hydropneumatic pressure tanks eliminate water hammer in attached irrigation systems by means of continually pressurized mains.

Hydroponics The cultivation of plants, especially vegetables, in water or water and sand/gravel solutions containing necessary nutrients. Also **Soilless gardening, Water culture.** See also **Geoponics.**

Hydroseeding See **Hydraulic seeding.**

Hydrosphere The surface waters of the Earth, including seas, lakes, streams, and rivers, as well as water vapor in the air and underground water. See also **Atmosphere, Lithosphere.**

Hydrostatic pressure 1) In irrigation, the force or pressure exerted by nonflowing water within a system. Hydrostatic pressure indicates the height of a water source supplying a main. Also **Static pressure.** 2) Soil water pressure.

Hydrostatics A branch of hydraulics dealing with the study of the pressures and other forces present in nonflowing water. See also **Hydraulics.**

Hydrotropism The tendency of plant roots to grow toward a water source. See also **Chemotropism, Geotropism, Haptotropism, Phototropism, Tropism.**

Hygrophyte See **Hydrophyte.**

Hygroscopic water Water contained in a film around a soil particle, generally unavailable for plant use. See also **Pellicular water.**

Hypaethral Roofless; opening to the sky.

Hypnum moss See **Peat moss.**

Hytherograph A chart that indicates recorded temperature and rainfall for an area. See also **Climate diagram, Climograph.**

I

I (road design) See **Central and deflection angle.**

Iberian landscape architecture See **Islamic landscape architecture, Portuguese landscape architecture, Spanish landscape architecture.**

Ibn Khaldun Medieval Arabic writer on history and city planning, born in Tunis in 1332. Ibn Khaldun's masterwork is the *Muqaddimah,* published in 1377.

Ice erosion See **Glacial erosion.**

ID (inside diameter) In irrigation, a measurement of inside pipe width usually given in inches and decimals of an inch. See also **IPS, OD.**

Idyllic Romantic, bucolic, or rustic.

IFLA See **International Federation of Landscape Architects.**

Ikebana Japanese dry flower arrangement.

ILA The **Institute of Landscape Architects,** a British professional organization founded in 1929.

Illuviation Soil leaching and drainage from an upper horizon (usually the A) into a lower (usually the B). See also **Eluviation, Leaching.**

Imbricate In botany, referring to overlapping plant scales.

Immature soil A young or azonal soil with no developed profile. See also **Soil horizon, Soil profile.**

Imp A plant shoot.

Impact head (sprinkler) In irrigation, a rotary head normally used for lawn sprinkling in which a nozzle-generated stream of water strikes a spring-mounted arm, causing rotation of the head and spray coverage of a large area. A "rain bird." See also **Rotary head.**

Impact statement, environmental See **Environmental impact statement.**

Imperfect flower See **Flower.**

Impervious (impermeable) In soils, used to describe a layer or stratum that cannot be penetrated by water.

Implementation phase (of construction work) See **Construction phase.**

Implicate In plant structures, wrapped together or twisted.

Implied contract An agreement that remains informal—i.e., consists of an inferred offer and inferred acceptance—between two parties. See also **Express contract.**

Impluvium A collection basin in the floor of an atrium. An ancient Roman device. The impluvium is fed by a roof opening, or **Compluvium,** q.v.

Impressed concrete pavement Concrete finished with a metal stamp in a rhythmic pattern. Also, often, **Bomanite** (trade name).

Improvement, soil See **Soil amendment.**

In situ (Latin) Describes objects found "in place" at a site.

Inanimate landscape See **Hard landscape.**

Incanous In plant structures, hoary and covered with a soft, powdery substance.

Inceptisol An extremely young or undeveloped soil, usually without clear horizons. Common as glacial or volcanic aftermath, or as a development of certain humid forest conditions.

Inch A measurement of distance in English-speaking countries equal to $1/12$ foot or .025 meters.

Inch, miner's See **Miner's inch.**

Incline A slope.

Indian landscape architecture.
Mughal Gardens, New Delhi, 1911–
31, by Sir Edwin Lutjens. Photo
courtesy BBMSL, UNM.

Incomplete fertilizer   A fertilizer
that does not contain enough of the
primary elements nitrogen,
phosphorus, and potassium to
decompose itself. See also **Fertilizer.**

Inconsequent drainage   A drainage
pattern that is at odds with the
general topography of its area,
often cutting into rising landforms
(antecedent drainage) or across
newly laid strata (**Superimposed
drainage,** q.v.). See also **Drainage
pattern.**

Indehiscence   In flower ovaries, the
inability of the ovarian structure to
open of its own accord and release
seeds. Adjective: indehiscent. See
also **Dehiscence.**

Indemnify   In contracts, to secure
against harm or loss due to well-
defined causes. An indemnification is
a contracted responsibility, well-
defined, made by two or more
parties. Nouns: indemnity,
indemnification.

Index, plasticity   See **Plasticity (of
soils).**

Indian landscape architecture
Gupta, in Patna state, had well-
developed gardens by the fourth
century B.C. Megasthenes, a
lieutenant of Alexander, tells us that
in the grounds of the nobles there
were tame birds (peafowl?), shady
groves, a wonderful variety of
shrubs, and elaborate pleaching of

selected trees. These early Indian
gardens were well-tended by crews
of gardeners; the Indians were fond
of exotics, and these were planted
as curiosities. Some Indian
landscapes are even older than this.
From excavations in the valley of the
Indus (present day Pakistan), we
know that courts, squares, even flush
toilets were common as early as the
late third millennium B.C.

But it was the Mogul emperors
who gave the country its greatest
gardens. They invaded India from
the north, from Central Asia, in the
sixteenth century. Their
predecessors, the Ghorids of the
twelfth century, had been Afghan
Muslims who had made Delhi their
capital. The Moguls, also Muslims,
brought the Mongol tradition of
tomb gardens to the flat plains of
north India. They combined their
funerary landscape architecture with
the strict, four-segment garden
architecture of the Persians. Thus the
Chahar bagh, or paradise garden,
was often laid out in front of a royal
tomb positioned to great advantage
at its far end. The first Mogul
emperor, Babur, was the author of
the famous memoir *Babur-nama* and
the creator of the Bagh-i-Vasa in
Kabul. In India itself, Babur's Ram
Bagh in Agra made use of great
water channels, terraces, and
grottoes in its scheme to provide a
relief from the sun. Babur also
began the tradition of flowering
plant color that would mark the
work of his successors.

A love of geometry, great

Buddhist and Hindu temples of the
fourth century A.D. and later were
covered with incredibly detailed
sculptures and bas reliefs of gods,
humans, monkeys, and other figures.
The Buddhist **Stupa** was a familiar
sight along Indian roadsides, and
pools and courtyards were common
in both Buddhist and Hindu temples.
Ancient murals show that the lotus
was a sacred flower for people of
both religions.

attention to detail, and the employment of good materials on a monumental scale came to be hallmarks of the Mogul style. Shah Akbar (1556–1605) was noted for his public works projects and for the gardens of his palace. He is best known, however, for his four-story tomb, set in the center of a cloister with a formal garden roundabout. Akbar's successor, Jahangir, began a series of elaborate hillside gardens in Kashmir about 1610. The Verinag Bagh was laid out as a sunken court with an octagonal pool. The Nishat Bagh (later improved by Shah Jehan) and the Shalimar Bagh were monumental terrace gardens with water stairs and long pools, planted in classic Persian plane trees (chenars) roses, pines, palms, cypresses, zinnias, marigolds, and the bhor and Ficus trees.

The Mogul garden tradition was thus well established by the time Shah Jehan, the grandson of Shah Akbar, succeeded to the throne in 1628. Jehan completed and expanded the Nishat Bagh after 1633, opening up spectacular vistas of the nearby Himalayas and developing viewing balconies for greater enjoyment of the garden's compartments. Jehan also built the Red Fort, now incorporated as part of Delhi, as a "new town." The Red Fort was perched on bluffs overlooking a river, and it was developed with finely detailed interior pavilions, pools, and courts. Jehan built an evening garden in it, full of white daturas and poppies, and intended to be enjoyed in the light of pavilions and a mosque on islands surrounded by tranquil water.

Yet all these projects are preludes to the Taj Mahal in Agra. The buildings and gardens of the Taj Mahal may have taken over 20 years to complete, and were a memorial to Mumtaz Mahal, Jehan's wife. The formal gardens in front of the main buildings are a classical

Indian landscape architecture. Fountain garden (*bagh*) in Srinagar, Kashmir. Photo courtesy BBMSL, UNM.

Persian **Chahar-bagh,** or paradise garden. The tomb itself is the best example of the cryptic tradition of Jehan's Mongol ancestors, Genghis Khan and Tamerlane. Rectangular canals emphasize the four parts of the garden and play perfectly up to the building. The marble of the building is richly carved and frequently inlaid, enriched with Muslim **Mushrabiyeh (stone grillework)** and sayings from the Koran in flowing script. Although the plantings have been much modified since the seventeenth century, the garden and its buildings still make up one of the world's outstanding design unities.

Jehan was usurped by one of his sons as an old man, held prisoner, and finally buried with Mumtaz in the Taj Mahal. His building and

grounds have, of course, taken their place alongside the Bagh-i-Takht in Shiraz, Iran and the Alhambra in Spain as one of the greatest examples of Islamic art.

Sir Edwin Lutyens borrowed heavily from Shah Jehan's work in his planning for the new Indian capital, New Delhi, built between 1912 and 1931. More recently, modern Indian landscape architects such as Ravindra Bhan have begun a reinterpretation of the Indian landscape tradition. Bhan's elegant designs for the courtyards and other gardens of the Mughal Hotel in Agra won the Aga Khan Award in 1980.

See also **Central Asian landscape architecture, Islamic landscape architecture, Persian landscape architecture.**

Industrial park. Journal Center, Albuquerque, New Mexico. Langdon and Wilson, architects; Emmett Wemple and Associates and Morrow and Worley, landscape architects, Journal Building; Morrow and Worley, landscape architects, parkways. Photo by author.

Indoor plant Commonly, an evergreen plant from a tropical or mild-temperate climate zone grown in a controlled inside environment.

Indument In plant structures, a hairy or woolly covering.

Indurate In flower or plant structures, hard or tough.

Industrial park A grouping of light or heavy manufacturing or commercial buildings in a park-like landscape.

Infiltration (of water) Percolation, q.v.

Infiltration rate (irrigation) See **Percolation rate.**

Inflorescence In botany, a flower cluster at the apex of a stalk.

Influent A creek or river delivering much or all of its water into ground water strata. See also **Affluent, Effluent.**

Informal garden A garden consisting of forms that are apparently casual and random. A nonaxial garden. Most modern informal gardens are influenced directly or indirectly by occultly balanced Japanese patterns. See also **Occult balance.**

Indicator (plant) A species that shows by its presence that an environment is shaped by a specific climate attitude, fauna, human use, or other like factor. For example, the presence of snakeweed, *Gutierrezia sarothrae,* in rangelands of the southwestern U.S. indicates chronic overgrazing. In large cities, some indicator species monitor pollution. See also **Life zone.**

Indigene (indigen) A native plant.

Indigenous landscape architecture
Colloquial or vernacular landscape design or forms that are native and fitting to a place or people. Examples: hedgerows in Britain, kraals in rural southern Africa, Maori pas and maraes, jacales in montane New Mexico. Also popular landscape architecture. See also **Vernacular landscape architecture.**

Inflorescence

Information for bidders In landscape specifications, a notice to contractors contained in the general specifications section stating that bids for a project may be submitted and outlining the correct procedures for preparation and submittal. Also **Notice to bidders.**

Ingress A way in, or entrance. See also **Egress.**

Inlet, drain or drop See **Drop inlet.**

Inlet time In storm drainage, the time elapsing before storm water from the remotest part of a drainage area reaches an inlet. Also **Overland flow time.** See also **Time of concentration.**

Inodorous In flowers, not smelly.

Inorganic 1) Dead. Any compound not containing carbon. A noncarbon mineral substance. 2) In design, a form or plan that is contrary to living shape or substance. A heavily geometric or obviously contrived plan. See also **Organic.**

Insecticide (pesticide) A chemical preparation used to dispatch insects. Insecticides were originally devised to enable large-scale production of crops to feed an expanding human population. Although they are sometimes effective in the short term, they often kill beneficial as well as harmful insects and larger animals. In addition, most insects capitalize on their own short and prodigious reproductive cycles to effectively mutate around the chemicals that are expended on them.

Systemic insecticides are ingested by insects and attack internal organs. Various oil-based preparations are sprayed on insects to kill them by smothering. Other insecticides work as stomach poisons or are applied as dusts, smoke,

aerosol sprays, granules, or powders.

An ongoing problem arising from the use of chemical insecticides in North America, Western Europe, Australia, New Zealand, and other industrialized areas is the residual toxicity often found in soils and water even after insecticides have come under government regulation. However, the use of highly toxic, highly unregulated chemicals is still quite common in developing nations.

In general, the widespread use or abuse of chemical insecticides since World War II—formerly a simple problem of agricultural or health policies and economics—has become a moral issue. Sounder controls have recently become available. Many ecologists and agricultural experts note that a concentrated use of genetic mutations or introduced predator insects ("natural" controls) holds much promise for the near future.

See also **Broad spectrum control, Herbicide.**

Inselberg See **Mesa.**

Inside diameter (irrigation) See **ID.**

Insolation Sunshine.

Inspection, final See **Final inspection.**

Inspection, site See **Site inspection.**

Institiate (institia) Grafted.

Institute of Landscape Architects (British) See **ILA.**

Instructions to bidders In construction specifications, the detailed summary of steps a contractor must follow to fill out and submit a project bid proposal. See also **Specifications.**

Insular climate A mild island climate determined essentially by the presence of the sea. See **Climate, Maritime climate.**

Insurance, construction See **Contruction insurance.**

Insurance, contractor's liability See **Liability insurance.**

Insurance, errors and omissions See **Errors and omissions insurance** and **Malpractice insurance.**

Insurance, liability See **Liability insurance.**

Insurance, malpractice See **Malpractice insurance.**

Insurance, professional liability See **Malpractice insurance.**

Insurance, professional practice See **Malpractice insurance.**

Integration The careful weaving together and coordination of landscape elements in a harmonious and symbiotic fashion.

Integrifolia In plant structures, pertaining to uncut leaves.

Integument, seminal See **Seminal integument.**

Intent, letter of See **Letter of intent.**

Intercepting ditch A drainage ditch laid out perpendicular to the slope of a hill to catch surface runoff. Also **Intercepting drain,** especially if underground. See also **Seepage trench.**

Interchange, traffic See **Cloverleaf, Traffic interchange.**

Intercostal In botany, pertaining to the spaces between leaf veins or nerves—the internerves.

Intercrop In gardens, a fast-growing crop sown between the rows of more slowly maturing vegetables. Also, a crop grown between lines of orchard trees. See also **Catch crop, Kitchen garden.**

Interior drainage See **Drainage.**

Intermediate course, asphalt See **Asphalt tack coat.**

Intermediate desert In the southwestern U.S., a desert of some climatic extremes of heat and cold in which certain fragile subtropical plants may not be grown (southern New Mexico, Arizona, California). See also **High desert, Low desert.**

Intermediate element A landscape item not predominantly horizontal or vertical. Intermediates are landscape incidentals or furnishings and include shrubs, benches, tables, cars, hydrants, above-grade planters, short fences, dogs, cats, stones, and other objects, as well as people. See also **Horizontal element, Vertical element.**

Intermediate-grade, new-billet steel The most commonly used kind of steel reinforcing bar for concrete. See also **Rebar.**

Intermittent stream A brook flowing only at certain times during the year. See also **Ephemeral stream.**

Intermontane Lying between mountain masses.

Internal grip A self-threading, grasping implement used to pull or handle pipe underground. See also **External grip.**

International Code for Botanical Nomenclature First established at the Botanical Congress in London (1866). The Code establishes rules for naming plants by international agreement according to a Latin **Binomial** system, q.v. See also **Botanical classification.**

International Code of Nomenclature for Cultivated Plants First published in 1953 as a result of the International Horticultural Congress of 1952, and separate from the **International Code for Botanical Nomenclature.** The code deals mainly with the classification and naming of domestic hybrids, sports, and cultivars—plant varieties. An on-going international commission reviews proposed additions to or changes in the code. See also **Cultivated Plant Code.**

International Federation of Landscape Architects (IFLA) A multinational organization of landscape architects whose purpose is the promotion of landscape design and planning.

International style An architectural form characteristic of the twentieth century in which particular emphasis is placed on the individual building rather than on a structure and its relationship to the web of roads, open spaces, and other buildings around it.
  The severe but often attractive and expansive planes of the International Style have frequently generated equally formal and restrained associated landscapes.

Internerve (botany) See **Intercostal.**

Internode In horticulture, the piece of stem between leaves or stem-joints.

Interpolation In site grading, the drawing of sequential contours on a map connecting grid or stadia points (elevations) established by a surveyor.

Intersection, point of (PI) See **Point of intersection.**

Interspersion In plant communities, the blending of associations from two or more life zones.

Interval, contour See **Contour interval.**

Interval, terrace See **Terrace interval.**

Intraspecific Pertaining to the members of a single species (botany).

Intrazonal soil 1) A glei or other soil lacking definite horizons. 2) A soil with distinctive characteristics that reflect more the parent material of their composition than local vegetation or climatic factors. See also **Glei soil, Soil horizon.**

Introduced plant See **Exotic.**

Intuitive design An approach to landscape architecture that depends primarily on subconscious, emotional, and insightful solutions to problems of site design. Usually combined with aspects of **Rational design,** q.v.

Inv. **Invert,** q.v.

Invasion capacity (of plants) In bioengineering, a measurement of the disturbed soil area that a given plant species can move into and overgrow in a prescribed amount of time. Also **Conquering capacity.**

Invasion, plant See **Plant invasion.**

Inversion, temperature See **Temperature inversion.**

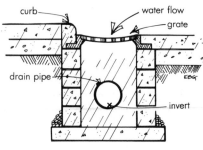

Invert

Invert (elevation) (IV) The low inside point of a pipe, culvert, or channel. A formed invert is made of shaped concrete or other material and is used to reduce water turbulence. Also abbreviated **Inv.** See also **Rim elevation.**

Invitation to bid In general project specifications, an announcement describing a project, requesting bids from contractors, and setting a specific date and time for bid proposals to be opened. Also **Advertisement for bids.** See also **Specifications.**

Invitational bidding In the letting of contracts, the admission and consideration of bids from selected contractors only. Invitational bidding is often used by private clients. Also **Closed bidding, Selective bidding.** See also **Open bidding.**

Involucre In plants, a ring of **Bracts,** q.v., or other structures found at the base of a compound flower.

Iodine A nonmetallic element needed in small amounts for plant (and animal) health and growth. Iodine is a **Trace element,** q.v. See also **Available nutrient, Soil minerals.**

IP A plan abbreviation for iron pipe.

IPS (iron pipe size) In irrigation, a measurement of nominal inside pipe diameter. IPS derives from the **OD,** q.v., of wrought iron pipe. See also **ID.**

Iranian landscape architecture
See **Persian landscape architecture.**

Irish landscape architecture Ireland was so green, and her abbey stones so gray, that the gardens of the Irish cloisters in the Middle Ages were among the most colorful of that pinched time in Europe. The learning of the Irish monasteries was legendary, as was the devotion of the monks to the preservation of classical horticulture.

The Anglo-Irish landscapes of the sixteenth, seventeenth, and eighteenth centuries followed the general, formal patterns of English and European Renaissance design. They were axial, with formal plantings. About 1768, the Earl of Belvedere laid out an early romantic garden at a small house in County Westmeath. The Belvedere garden opened up with a view to Lough Ennell. Among the delights of its grounds were follies, or ruins, and grottoes.

An extensive formal estate landscape, Powerscourt Garden, was laid out in the 1840s about 12 miles south of Dublin. The sweeping beauty of Powerscourt depends on its series of rhythmically descending terraces, with a framed lake in the middle landscape and soft hills in the distance. Like many other Irish estates, Powerscourt is widely planted in exotics. It uses **Perrons,** q.v., and Italian sculptures in high Victorian fashion. Its owner, Lord Powerscourt, was also its designer.

The landscape designer, journalist and critic **William Robinson** probably had the greatest say in the creation of the Irish landscapes of the nineteenth century. Robinson's

ideal was an improbably naturalistic "wild woodland garden," which he modeled on the common cottage gardens of the day. Mt. Usher, in Ashford, County Wicklow, is an example. Its roiling, exotic, "sublime" gardens were created by Frederick Moore, director of the Royal Botanic Gardens in Dublin. Anne's Grove in County Cork, by R. G. Annesley, was also extensive and very much in the Robinson mold.

The English architect Harold Peto designed all of Ilnacullin Island, the home of Annan Boyce, as a house with Italianate gardens in the best Edwardian style. Between 1910 and 1924, thousands of Southern Hemisphere exotics were imported and planted to flesh out Peto's plans.

Other twentieth-century landscapes include the remarkable Japanese garden at Kildare, created in 1906 by Tassa Eida, and the oddly picturesque grounds in Lord Orrery's park at Caledon, Tyrone, in which a wall of bones provides grist for conversation. The Killarney and Royal Dublin Golf Courses remain good examples of traditional links design. Other public landscapes of note include Phoenix Park and Zoo in Dublin and the botanic gardens in Glasnevin.

James Fehily is prominent among contemporary Irish landscape architects. His grounds for the Allied Irish Banks in Dublin make use of traditional Irish exotics, a strong axial design line, and cleanly understated fountains, reflecting pools, and sculpture.

Iron An important micronutrient for plants and animals, found widely in the Earth's crust. Iron is essential to photosynthesis, and its lack may cause **Chlorosis,** q.v., or poor growth and bud production. See also **Available nutrient, Soil minerals, Trace element.**

Irrigation. Irrigation flume near Chama, New Mexico. Photo courtesy Stevens Williams.

Iron chelate   An iron compound useful in treating chlorosis, the severe yellowing of leaves due to defective plant production of chlorophyll. Iron sulfate (an iron-sulfur compound) may also be used to treat chlorosis.

Iron flagstone   A kind of flagstone (pavement) made from bog iron in the Pine Barrens of New Jersey and elsewhere in the eighteenth and nineteenth centuries, highly resistant to rust.

Iron pan   A **Hardpan,** q.v., containing iron.

Iron pipe size (irrigation)   See **IPS.**

Iron, wrought   See **Wrought iron.**

Irregular curve   A two-dimensional curve that is not composed of arcs of circles. An erratic curve.

Irregular paving   A foot or vehicle pavement composed of odd blocks of stone or other incidentally sized concrete, brick, or similar pieces. See also **Pavement.**

Irregularity in landscape design   See **Informal garden** and **Occult balance.**

Irrigation   The application of water to a field or garden to support an intensive and regular growth of plants. Irrigation involves the use of overhead (sprinkling), underground (drip or the like), or flood systems and is among the most ancient civilized devices of mankind.

Irrigation, basin   See **Basin irrigation.**

Irrigation, central-pivot   See **Central-pivot irrigation.**

Irrigation circuit   See **Section system.**

Irrigation clock   See **Automatic controller.**

Irrigation code   See **Building codes.**

Irrigation controller   See **Automatic controller.**

Irrigation coverage   See **Sprinkler coverage.**

Irrigation, cutback   See **Cutback irrigation.**

Irrigation, drip   See **Trickle irrigation.**

Irrigation efficiency   A measure of the volume of applied water retained around the root system of a plant in relation to the amount of water applied at the ground surface. Also **Water application efficiency.**

Irrigation, flood   See **Flood irrigation.**

Irrigation head   See **Head.**

Irrigation loop   A system of closed sprinkler piping in which the line closes its own traverse to provide a series of heads with equal pressure from two directions.
    A loop system consists of smaller piping than a straight-line system, but it delivers an equal amount of gallons per minute at a comparatively high PSI to the demand point.

Irrigation pipe   See **Copper pipe, Galvanized pipe, Polyethylene pipe, PVC pipe.**

Irrigation, sprinkler   See **Sprinkler irrigation.**

Irrigation or sprinkler code   See **Building codes.**

Irrigation, surface   See **Surface irrigation.**

Irrigation system contaminants   The most common of these are: debris entering the system during connections or repairs, sand, rust flakes from municipal mains, and organic debris from lakes, ponds, rivers, or other primary water sources.

Irrigation timer   See **Automatic controller.**

Irrigation, trickle   See **Trickle irrigation.**

Irrigation water Water good for growing plants but not for drinking or other domestic purposes.

Irrigation zone See **Section system.**

Irrigation zoning The laying out of underground irrigation circuits (zones, sections) controlled by valves. Available water (GPM) and pressure (PSI), as well as kinds and sizes of pipe are primary considerations. See also **Section system.**

Irrometer A hybrid word for "irrigation meter," a device used to keep track of the ground moisture in a landscape and activate an automatic irrigation system to eplenish it.

Islamic landscape architecture The Persian garden of the first millennium B.C. was taken west to Spain and eastward to India with Muslim conquests after the seventh century A.D. It typically was located in a courtyard, and usually consisted of a central fountain with four radiating streams that also divided the garden into four parts. The Koran speaks of the Eden-like quality of Muslim paradise, also divided into quadrants. Thus the Persian garden, highly formal and with the fig and plane trees producing a lush shade, became identified with the letter and spirit of Islam.

The radiating streams or channels of a "paradise" garden are highly functional: they water the nearby planters. In the Qasr al-Mubarak, an eleventh-century garden in Seville, and in the grounds of the Generalife in Granada, the original flowerbeds may have been two feet (700 mm) or so below the garden paths. The original trees in these gardens were

probably oranges. It is remarkable that they have survived the centuries in good condition, but they have been planted many times over and today it is difficult to suggest the details of their original condition.

Garden ornament in Muslim countries is based on an intricate appreciation of geometry. Tiles, especially blue and yellow **Azulejos,** terra cotta, and the beautifully detailed stone screen or **Mushrabiyeh** are much employed. The austere Fountain of the Lions in the court of the same name in the Alhambra is a stylized oasis pool surrounded by a date "forest" of lean pillars and arches. This fountain, true to its Moorish tradition, uses a little water to great effect.

The Arabs studied the Greek and Roman villas in North Africa, Iberia, and the Levant and used them as models for their own country houses. Where the fountain courts of Baghdad, Cairo, or Delhi might be flat, the hillside villas of Andalusia

Irrigation design, including zoning

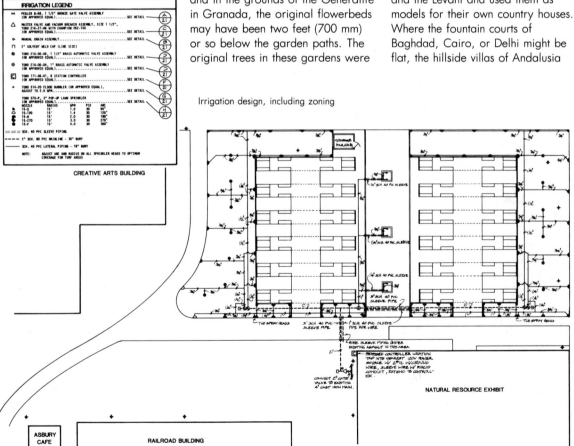

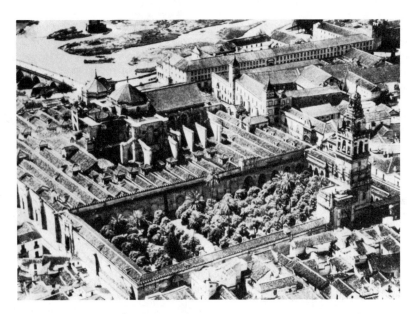

Islamic landscape architecture. Great Mosque of Córdoba, Spain, eighth century. Photo courtesy BBMSL, UNM.

or Kashmir developed impressive views while retaining formal gardens near living areas. There were perhaps 50,000 villas at the height of Moorish power in the Guadalquivir Valley; in Kashmir, the Shalimar and Nishat Baghs (Gardens) of the early seventeenth century also used hillsides to develop an intricate series of connected terrace and water gardens.

The Muslim garden in any location took careful advantage of sun and shade contrasts. There was an emphasis on light, airiness, and, above all, the quality of water. Of course, ritual ablutions at a bubbling courtyard fountain surrounded by shady arcades continue to be a primary feature of the mosque. The Great Mosque at Cordova, an Umayyad structure dating from c. 786 A.D., is one of the best current examples. Overall, the Moorish landscapes of Spain, constructed between 712 and 1492, form the most complete collection of historic

Islamic gardens in the world. They are certainly the finest medieval European gardens. There are accounts of other ancient Muslim landscapes, from Samarqand and Tashkent, in Soviet Central Asia, to the tiny walled gardens of Rabat and Fez in Morocco. But these, as a whole, are remnants and have not been kept in or restored to the best of condition. They do, however, present us with a remarkable unity in garden design over a vast expanse of time and land.

In the twentieth century, a landscape renaissance of sorts is underway in Saudi Arabia and the Gulf States. Large-scale gardens, public sculptures, and urban design and town construction are currently funded with oil revenues. A mosque entirely surrounded by water was constructed in the 1970s at Bandar Seri Begawan by Sultan Omar Ali Saifuddin. New national and city parks are under development in Saudi Arabia itself. Universities,

roadsides, public buildings, and squares are furnished with extensive green landscape. A new technology capable of supplying large quantities of plants, nutrients, and water has arisen. The American landscape architects T. L. Schnadelbach, Phil Harz, Guy Greene, John Moseley, and others have been responsible for much Saudi landscape architecture since the 1970s.

But parallel to the larger Islamic landscapes, and perhaps as important in the long view, is the vernacular garden tradition of the Muslim peasant. The terrace garden of the Panjshir Tajiks in Afghanistan is typical: A trickle of water from the Hindu Kush is granted by the ditchmaster to a farmer. In his garden surrounded by heaped stone walls, grass, mulberry trees, apricots and grapes will grow in profusion. There will perhaps be a streamside grove of poplars or willows for thick shade. And under a lattice screen a brass samovar will be more or less permanently rigged to brew tea. The Afghan pathside garden, like its ancient predecessor the Persian roadside garden, is used as a relief for the owner and the occasional traveler from the sun and wind that always lie just beyond its walls.

See also **Middle Eastern landscape architecture, Persian landscape architecture, Spanish landscape architecture.**

Isobar A line on a weather chart that links points of the same atmospheric pressure.

Isobath A line on a profile chart linking points at the same depth beneath a **Datum,** q.v., or surface line.

Isohyet A line on a weather chart linking points of equal rainfall.

Isometric drawing A type of perspective or three-dimensional stylized rendering in which the following occurs: 1) vertical lines and axes remain vertical; 2) horizontal lines are exaggerated at ±30° from normal; 3) base and overhead planes are drawn truly dimensioned and parallel to an established axis or axes. Also **Isometric projection.** See also **Perspective.**

Isopleth Any line on a chart or map linking points of the same interest or meaning. **Isobars** and **Contour lines,** q.q.v., are examples.

Isotherm A line on a weather chart that links several points of equal temperature.

Isotropic In landscape design, exhibiting the same appearance or properties on all sides without definite form in any direction.

Israeli landscape architecture
Modern Israeli landscape architecture has been inspired by several traditions: the ancient courtyards of the Middle East — small, enclosed gardens that serve as a verdant relief from the glare and heat of the region; the visionary gardens and farms of the kibbutzes, developed since the late 1900s as self-sufficient agricultural cooperatives and wasteland reclamation experiments; and the larger urban and landscape design traditions of the West.

In the twentieth century, the Israelis have pioneered broad-scale reforestation and desert agricultural development, including drip irrigation. Israeli public squares, tree groves, and vineyards tend to follow customary Near Eastern patterns. Israel has also developed "oasis" gardens as part of the system of national preserves created since World War II.

The Canadian architect Moshe Safdie, assisted by Gene Dyer and others, has been responsible for much of the current urban redevelopment planning of Jerusalem. The American landscape architect **Lawrence Halprin,** q.v., has also contributed to urban design efforts in Jerusalem. Halprin designed a graceful, shallow-water fountain courtyard at the Hebrew University.

Among modern Israeli designers, the architect and theoretician Michael Kuhn has helped to shape a contemporary aesthetic for Israeli architecture and urban design. The Israeli landscape architect Zvi Miller was elected president of the International Federation of Landscape Architects in the early 1980s.

See also **Middle Eastern landscape architecture, Trickle irrigation.**

Italian landscape architecture
See **Renaissance landscape architecture** and **Roman landscape architecture.**

Item of work In contracts, an individual item to be constructed (consisting of the installation of items or of procedures to be followed) used to prepare a **Bid list,** q.v.

Iwan (Persian) An airy corridor (often, a barrel-vaulted hall) opening into an interior courtyard. The iwan was adopted as a general feature of Middle Eastern architecture after the advent of Islam (seventh century A.D. and later).

Jabal　See **Jebel.**

Jacal　In the southwestern United States and in Spanish America, a wall, stockade, or corral made up of small, undressed timbers set upright and lashed together or connected by stringers. Also **Coyote fence.**

Jackson, John Brinckerhoff (J. B.) (1909–)　United States landscape historian, professor, writer, and pioneer cultural geographer, educated at Harvard University. Jackson's eminent counterpart in Britain is **W. G. Hoskins,** q.v.

　Very few men or women since the Renaissance can be said to have created a new branch of the liberal arts, or humanities. Jackson is one of these. He developed his unusual eye for the form of the common landscape as a young man on his uncle's ranch in New Mexico and refined it while poring over maps of the European landscape during World War II service in U.S. Army Intelligence. Jackson has made a specialty of the study of culture through its expression in the vernacular, or popular, landscape, and especially the small house in the small town.

　Jackson's journal, *Landscape,* of which he was the founder and editor (1951–68), has come to be, with Hoskins's *The Making of the English Landscape,* the guiding spirit of the idea of cultural geography or landscape humanism. His consistent view, expressed in his characteristic lucid and whimsical essays, is that American landscapes no longer are derived from European molds; that a cluster of houses erected by unsophisticated people for the purposes of everyday life will have dignity and meaning, even if only intended for a short existence; and that the vernacular landscape draws its life from a repertory of almost timeless forms.

　Jackson has been a professor at Harvard University, the University of California at Berkeley, the University of Texas at Austin, and, most recently, the University of New Mexico. His books include *Landscapes* (1971), *American Space* (1974), *The Necessity for Ruins* (1980), and *Discovering the Vernacular Landscape* (1984). Jackson was also a contributor to *The Interpretation of Ordinary Landscapes* (1979).

　See also **Landscape history.**

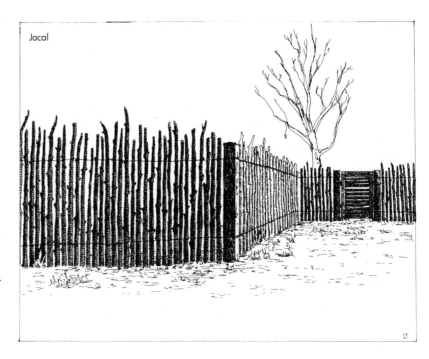

Jacal

Japanese landscape architecture

One of the world's most intricate and refined landscape architectures, developed from Chinese models over the course of centuries in a temperate climate moderated by maritime influences. Japanese landscape architecture is renowned for its near-perfect naturalistic gardens and for its stylized details, used in a religious and philosophic symbolism of great subtlety. Hill gardens, or **Tsuki-yama,** and flat gardens, or **Hira-niwa,** are the basic themes against which Japanese landscape design takes place. The most common garden types include the garden of movement, or domestic garden, usually of small scale and bordered by trees; the garden of contemplation, or **Kare sansui,** a rectangular, lean Zen Buddhist creation often found in monastery courtyards; and the **Sakkei** or garden of borrowed landscape, which attempts to merge man-made with more distant, natural scenery. Gardens are traditionally laid out in *Shin* (formal, elaborate), *Gyo* (intermediate), or *So* (abbreviated, informal) style, using local elements such as mountains, waterfalls, and seas as symbolic elements. Garden viewing is of great importance, and most Japanese gardens have been developed with views from the house or other structure, garden entrance vistas, or views from the garden itself to nearby buildings in mind.

The ancient Japanese garden ideal was the **Shima,** or misty island in a sea, often found with a **Torii** or Shinto arch nearby. By the Nara era (c. 646–794 A.D.), a vigorous trade with China had developed, and Chinese Buddhism and its accompanying garden design and nature painting techniques had begun to influence Japan. Stones, bridges, lanterns, and other garden elements took on greater meaning. Typical garden stones adapted by the Japanese from Chinese originals were the guardian stone, the stone of worship, and the stone of two deities. The Japanese simplified the elaborate, zigzag Chinese bridges into shorter and straighter stone or wood spans (*bashi*), and developed stepstones to invite the visitor to more remote parts of the garden. Garden lanterns, also of stone, indicated the rather obvious symbolism of light dispelling darkness; in later gardens, flat-topped lanterns were placed to catch snow for winter viewing. Water basins (*chozubachi*) and sleeve fences **(Sode-gaki),** used for screening, also developed into popular features.

Occult balance was a principal concern of the evolving Japanese garden. By the eleventh century, a series of rules for garden design had been listed in the *Sakuteiki* by Tachibana no Toshitsuna. Among the garden qualities prized most highly by the Japanese were lyrical beauty, mystery, and serenity. *The Tale of Genji* by Lady Murasaki, also dating from the eleventh century, is a novel set in a series of gardens. Its setting later inspired the grounds of the seventeenth-century Katsura Palace in Kyoto.

The best known of Japanese landscape architects is the Zen monk **Muso Soseki** (d. 1351), the designer of the Silver Pavilion in Kyoto, and of the Saihoji or "heart" garden. The fifteenth-century garden architect Soami is credited with the design of the rarified Ryoanji courtyard in Kyoto, an amazing garden consisting solely of swept silica particles, stone groupings, and a little moss, surrounded by highly formalized buildings.

Song Chinese influence continued to be strong in Japan into the sixteenth century; the priest-designer **Kobori Enshu** (d. 1647) is said to have made the naturalistic style a bit more Japanese. His masterpiece is

Japanese landscape architecture. Saihordi: landscape of temple garden. Photo courtesy BBMSL, UNM.

the garden at Katsura Palace. Typical Japanese refinements of his day included a banishing of most color from the garden, a growing fondness for waterfalls as primary garden elements, and the rise of the tea ceremony (and its garden tea pavilion) as a primary social function.

Night-viewing or moon gardens, snow gardens for winter use, and several forms of miniature landscapes such as *bonsai* also grew

Japanese landscape architecture.
Garden of the Ryoanji Temple,
Kyoto. Photo courtesy BBMSL, UNM.

in refinement and popularity from the period of the Shogunate (seventeenth to nineteenth centuries) to the present.

Timelessness continues to be an essential quality of the Japanese garden. Careful finger-pruning of evergreens (especially pines) and other trees has always been used to create a well-controlled style derived from picturesque models. In the late twentieth century, landscape architects such as Kanto Shigemori have attempted to reconcile the clamorous demands of a very heavy population with responses to the highly sophisticated, traditional garden heritage of Japan.

See also **Chinese landscape architecture, Landscape architectural theory.**

Japelli, Giuseppe (1783–1852) Italian landscape gardener and architect, working primarily in the Venetian countryside and in Rome.

Japelli's style was eclectic, but based on Palladian forms and the villa principles of **Alberti**, q.v. Japelli designed a number of villas with landscape parks in the English manner. Saonara and the Villa Torlonia are probably the best-known of these. See also **Renaissance landscape architecture.**

Japonaiserie A late Victorian garden fashion utilizing superficially Japanese elements in exotic plant settings. See also **Chinoiserie.**

Jardin anglais (French) An English naturalistic garden reproduced in France (late eighteenth century). See also **English landscape architecture** and **Naturalism.**

Jardinière (French) A ceramic planter. Most jardinieres serve as sleeves for other pots containing plants.

Jebel (Arabic) A common term in the Middle East for a single mountain or a range. Also **Jabal.**

Jefferson, Thomas (1743–1826) A preeminent figure in politics, architecture, science, diplomacy, and social philosophy, Jefferson was also the most influential landscape designer in the United States in the early years of the republic. His own estate at Monticello, Virginia, was precisely sited. Jefferson took great care with the essentially informal layout of the grounds, which he made over several times, and kept meticulous garden notes throughout his life. Among the plants he imported to Virginia were several pecan trees (*Carya illinoiensis*) from the Mississippi Valley, some of which he gave to George Washington. He records that they were planted at Mount Vernon on March 25, 1775; three of them are still alive.

As Minister to France (1785–89), Jefferson visited the famous old formal gardens of Louis XIV and his contemporaries. But they had been overtaken by the softer, more flowing naturalism of the **English Landscape Gardening School**, q.v., by the time Jefferson saw them. It was the **Anglo-Chinois** garden and the urbanity of Paris that made permanent impressions on Jefferson.

Jardiniere

Jefferson's Palladian architecture at Monticello, the University of Virginia (which he founded), and the new state capitol at Richmond, Virginia, set the tone for official government and institutional architecture in the United States. The **Quad,** q.v., at the University of Virginia includes a geometric open space bounded by Georgian structures that are connected by means of colonnades. Jefferson also worked with Benjamin Latrobe on the layout of the U.S. Capitol and its surrounds, burnt by the British in 1814.

The development of the grounds at Monticello, a lifetime project for Jefferson, reflected his awareness of the great change in landscape style that had occurred in his day. He began his gardens as an axial composition and as the years passed modified them to a softer and more naturalistic style. See also **United States landscape architecture.**

Jekyll, Gertrude (1843–1932)

British landscape designer and writer. Gertrude Jekyll loved the cottage garden and reinterpreted it in multiple medium and small-scale landscapes in Edwardian England. She was strongly influenced by the Anglo-Irish author and designer **William Robinson,** q.v.

Her books *Colour in the Flower Garden* (1908) and *Gardens for Small Country Houses* (1912) helped to popularize her ideas on "controlled" wildness and herbaceous borders. Much of her design approach was developed during visits to the Austrian Tyrol and the Swiss Alps. Her studies of the tiny formalism of the vernacular (or popular) gardens she found in them added to her design repertory.

Other books by Gertrude Jekyll are *Wood and Garden, Home and Garden,* and *Old English Household Life.* The recent work *Gardens of a Golden Afternoon* treats the lives

and work of Miss Jekyll and Sir Edwin Lutyens, with whom she shared a long collaboration.

Jensen, Jens (1860–1951) United States landscape architect, born in Denmark. Jensen immigrated to Florida in 1884. He also lived in Iowa before settling in Chicago in 1886. He began his career as a gardener in the Chicago West Parks in the same year. While a gardener, Jensen started the intense study of Midwestern native plants that he would later use with such artfulness in his designs.

Jensen rose rapidly in the Chicago park bureaucracy. Appointed superintendent of Humboldt Park in the 1890s, he was fired in 1900 for his outspoken opinions regarding graft and political meddling. He began a private practice in landscape architecture after his dismissal. His great gift was for creating a sprawling spaciousness in composition that he called the "prairie style." The prairie style ignored "hard" landscape construction to concentrate on plant massing. For effect, it depended greatly on broad lawns developed next to woodlands or tree copses. Jensen refined the use of local plants in his prairie composition and attacked any sort of formal line or

Jens Jensen

geometry in the landscape as wholly unsuitable. He was a friend and colleague of Frank Lloyd Wright during most of his practice, and the two exchanged ideas frequently. His best known commissions include Columbus Park in Chicago, the Ryarson Estate (now a seminary) in Lake Forest, Illinois, and the park system of Racine, Wisconsin. Jensen was also a founder of the Cook County Forest Preserve.

Although Jensen returned sporadically to public service with the Chicago park system, he had entirely broken off his association with the City by 1920. He belonged to the ASLA for a brief and knotty period. In 1935, he closed his practice in Chicago and retired to Wisconsin to run a casual school of landscape design. Jensen wrote *Siftings* (1931) after his retirement and published a second book, *The Clearing.*

Jest, water   See **Water joke.**

Jet d'eau (French)   Water jet.

Jet irrigator   See **Spider head.**

Jetting   See **Water jetting.**

Gertrude Jekyll

Jetty   1) Freshwater: A breakwater extending out from the exposed bank of a stream or river to cut the erosive force of the water; 2) Salt water: See **Mole.**

Job site   The place at which a project is constructed.

Jockey pump   In golf course and other large irrigation systems, an auxiliary pump used to maintain constant pressure in a line along with a **Main pump,** q.v., or pumps.

Joint   1) In landscape construction, the line along which concrete slabs, pipes, wood members, bricks, or other materials are connected. See also **Wood and brick construction joints.** 2) A crack in a rock stratum due to erosion or other natural processes. 3) A plant segment. See **Culm.** 4) In irrigation, pipe seams.

Joint, construction   See **Construction joint.**

Joint, contraction   See **Control joint.**

Joint, control   See **Control joint.**

Joint, dummy   See **Control joint.**

Joint, expansion   See **Expansion joint.**

Joint filler, asphalt   See **Asphalt joint filler.**

Joint, masonry   See **Masonry joint.**

Joint, score   See **Control joint.**

Joint, ship lap   See **Ship lap joint.**

Joint, stem (of grass)   See **Culm.**

Joint, struck   See **Struck joint.**

Joint, swing (irrigation)   See **Swing joint.**

Joint, tongue and groove (T and G)   See **Tongue and groove joint.**

Joint, tooled (masonry)   See **Tooled joint.**

Joint venture   In landscape architecture, a partnership between various individuals or firms formed to provide a specific result for a profit. Characteristics of short duration.

Jointer   A common mortar-finishing tool.

Joints, wood and brick construction   See **Wood and brick construction joints.**

Joist   In landscape construction, one of a series of closely spaced, parallel boards that rest on beams and support other smaller laths or act in themselves as finish members.

Joists and planks (dimension lumber)   See **Lumber.**

Joke, water   See **Water joke.**

Judgment lien   A lien established against an area of land by legal decision. See also **Lien.**

Jumbo brick   See **Economy brick.**

Jungle   A tropical rain forest; any dense mass of overgrowth. From the Sanskrit *jangala,* "desert." See also **Rain forest.**

Juvenile foliage   Young leaf and bud growth in plants, or the leaf growth of young plants. In trees such as *Eucalyptus gunnii* (cider gum) and others, the juvenile foliage may differ quite drastically from adult growth. Also **Juvenile growth.**

Juvenile water   In geology, water rising from volcanic vents. "New" water—i.e., water that was not previously present in the atmosphere or in surface streams, lakes, and the like. See also **Ground water.**

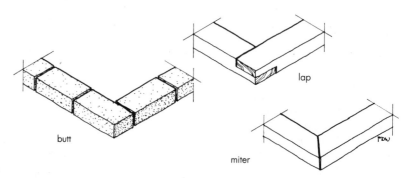

butt

lap

miter

Joints in construction

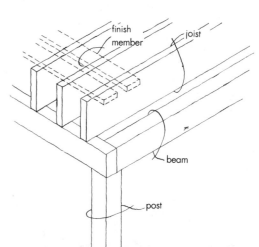

finish member

joist

beam

post

K

K   See **Potassium**.

Kare sansui (Japanese)   A dry rock garden, often highly stylized. See **Dry landscape gardening**.

Karst topography   See **Sinkhole**.

Keeper   A mechanism used in steel or other gates that automatically props them open.

Kent, William (1685–1748 or 1749)
English painter, furniture designer, architect, and landscape gardener. William Kent was an early master of the **English School of Landscape Gardening**, q.v., which he profoundly influenced through his work at Stowe and elsewhere.

Kent was a Yorkshireman, born at Bridlington. His early education included a stint in Italy, where he was exposed to the paintings of **Claude Lorrain, Poussin, Salvatore Rosa**, q.q.v., and others of the picturesque school. The typical Kentian landscape would later contain naturalistic lakes and vegetation and ornamentation in a Palladian style. Kent's central piece of luck was his introduction to Lord Burlington in Rome in 1716. Burlington guided his design development, employed him, and engaged him to edit the *Designs of Inigo Jones,* completed in 1727.

Back in England, many of Kent's landscape commissions were remodels of the work of his predecessor **Charles Bridgeman**, q.v. At Rousham, in Oxfordshire, and Stowe, Buckinghamshire, both of which had been landscaped in the formal style by Bridgeman, Kent redesigned to make the house an element in a larger composition. His gardens stayed somewhat formal near the manor house itself and became rustic in the ruin-strewn Italian manner beyond the garden wall or **Ha-ha**. A great popularizer of the new naturalistic style, Kent utterly destroyed many of Bridgeman's finest landscapes in the course of his work, eliminating the brilliant parts-to-whole relationship that characterized Bridgeman's best compositions.

Kent was not as successful an architect as he was a landscape gardener. However, his fanciful garden buildings, such as the "ruins" in the Gardens of Chiswick estate, were much celebrated. The Rousham grounds remain the best-preserved and best known of Kent's landscapes. Here, the woodland glades, the good vistas, the Praeneste arcade are still crisp and inviting.

The young **Capability Brown**, q.v., met Kent while working as an apprentice gardener at Stowe. Brown would later follow Kent's example and himself further refine and expand the grounds of Stowe. See also **English landscape architecture**.

Kerbstone (British)   See **Curbstone**.

Kerf, saw (landscape construction)   See **Saw leaf**.

Kettlehole   In geology, a pit left in the earth's surface by melting ice.

Key (sprinkler or valve)   In irrigation, a long-handled, metal, double-tined fork used to open and shut various globe valves.

Key, coupler   See **Coupler key**.

Kiley, Dan (1912–)   Daniel Urban Kiley, American landscape architect and urban designer, trained in the office of **Warren Manning**,q.v., and at Harvard University. Kiley is known for the keen geometry of his landscapes.

Perhaps the greatest of twentieth-century classicists, Kiley, **Garrett Eckbo, James Rose**, q.q.v., and others joined to produce the "Harvard Revolution" of the late 1930s, in which the Beaux Arts tradition in landscape architecture was supplanted by the general pursuit of more "site specific" design.

Kiley came into prominence after World War II for his collaboration with Eero Saarinen in the design of the Jefferson Memorial in St. Louis. Later commissions included the U.S. Air Force Academy in Colorado Springs with Skidmore Owings and Merrill, the Oakland Museum with

Dan Kiley. Photo courtesy Kiley Walker.

Kiley is a prolific lecturer. His design work has been critically reviewed in *Process Architecture, Inland Architect,* and elsewhere. His recent projects have included the National Gallery of Art, the Bank of Korea in Seoul, and Arcade Center, a new "urban block" in downtown Seattle.

Kiln-dried 1) In horticulture, a term used to define heat-treated and/or aged animal manure. Kiln-drying insures that weed seeds present in new animal wastes will be neutralized. 2) Of lumber, wood members that are systematically kiln-cured to reduce shrinkage, cracking, and warping.

Kilograms per square millimeter
KSMM, a measure of stress. See also **PSI, Stress.**

Kinesis See **Tropism, Taxis.**

Kiosk Originally Persian and Turkish, the kiosk, or small garden house, was adapted by the French from the nineteenth century onward for street use as a small multisided billboard or newstand. It has increased in popularity and usefulness and is now a common item of street furnishing the world over.

Kitchen garden In the twentieth century, a small garden handy to a home kitchen used to grow fresh vegetables for domestic consumption. In past centuries, this kind of garden often featured herbs and flowers as well. The historic kitchen was a well laid-out, rather formal, vegetable plot attached to the larger formal grounds of an eighteenth-century English estate. It often made use of an **Intercrop,** q.v. Also **Dooryard garden.**

Kevin Roche, and Dulles Airport in Washington, also with Saarinen. These projects show perhaps Kiley's greatest strength: the ability to create urbane and strongly architectonic outdoor space that still retains a lyrical quality. Kiley's residential work has included such polished gardens as the Miller house in Columbus, Indiana, planted in his trademark massed lines of trees and furnished with an elegantly sited Henry Moore sculpture.

The Oakland Museum (1963) was the first of the West Coast "Hanging Gardens." It is a study in the rhythm of steps and terraces, punctuated by water. Its lush plantings are reminiscent of the tropical gardens of the Brazilian **Roberto Burle Marx,** q.v. A regional public garden style has evolved since the Museum gardens were finished, and Portland, Seattle, Vancouver, and other Pacific coast cities now boast similar hanging gardens.

Kiosk

Kited   In landscape construction, formed or sawn at an angle.

Knaur (in trees)   See **Burl.**

Kniffen   A grape-support system using a series of horizontal wires much like fencing to train the plant.

Knight, Richard Payne (1750–1824)   English country gentleman, critic, and design theorist. Knight was a contemporary and friend of **Uvedale Price,** q.v., with whom he formulated an ideal of the **Picturesque** landscape. Knight's home, Downton Castle in Hertfordshire, was developed as a prototype of the picturesque country estate. His "The Landscape—A Didactic Poem" (1794) attacked **Capability Brown's** landscape gardening school. His later book, *Analytical Enquiry into the Principles of Taste* (1805), laid out the essentials of the picturesque landscape. See also **English landscape architecture.**

Knob   A small, sharply rising hill with a rounded top.

Knoll   A small, gently rounded hill.

Knot garden   A kind of **Parterre,** q.v., or Renaissance garden in which ground covers, low shrubs, or colored earths were designed in tenuous curlicues resembling knitted or embroidered knots. Also **Knot bed.** See also **Herb garden.**

Knuckling   In chainlink and other fence construction, the smooth linking together of two pieces of wire mesh by doubling back interlocking sets of wire ends on themselves. Wire mesh "looping."

Korean landscape architecture   The hapless last king of the Yi dynasty used the tiny Toksu garden in the palace of the same name in Seoul as his principal refuge. The Yi dynasty was one of history's longest, stretching from about 1392 to 1910. The Toksu garden, containing a pavilion and well-detailed, very green, intimate "nooks," is now surrounded by the skyscrapers of downtown Seoul. The Hyangwon pavilion, constructed about 1868 and a royal favorite, is a very small but refined late example of the Korean traditional garden style, sited on a circular island in a round pool.

Chinese garden style and Buddhism began to influence the Koreans after the fifth century A.D. The Kunjong-Jan reception hall in the Kyongbok Palace in Seoul is modeled after Peking's Hall of Supreme Harmony. In its courtyard is a square pool with square islands of cut stone and a pavilion. The Kyongbok Palace itself is about 500 years old. Its entries are guarded by *haet'aes*—guard lions, and it is famous for its many walks, courtyards, pools, and intimate gardens. The Piwon secret garden is a favorite among these, with ponds, streams, azaleas, pavilions, and flowering trees that have been nurtured for centuries. King Sun-Jo built a rustic cabin in the middle of the Piwon about 1828—the Yongkyongdong house, a royal copy of a simple Korean country dwelling. He used it as a retreat. Remarkably, it parallels similar European constructs of the same time, built with the same intent in mind.

The Ch'angdok palace in Seoul still houses the remnants of the Korean royal family. Here the old royal gardens with their numerous green and intimate spaces continue to reflect the painterly quality of the Yi dynasty landscapes that remains the Korean ideal.

Landscape architecture has become well established in South Korea in the late twentieth century. University curricula in landscape architecture, begun in the 1970s, have expanded rapidly. The Korean Federation of Landscape Architecture (KOFLA), founded as an amalgam of earlier organizations in 1981, now represents the profession throughout the country.

See also **Chinese landscape architecture, Japanese landscape architecture.**

Kraal (Zulu)   In Africa, especially southern and east Africa, a temporary village or settlement surrounded by a protective enclosure.

Kraft paper   See **Tree wrapping.**

Kremnophyte   In botany, a plant growing on a vertical face.

Krummholz   In forestry, the dwarf and distorted trees and shrubs found at the lower limit of alpine tundra on mountain slopes or near the Arctic Circle.

KSMM   Kilograms per square millimeter, q.v. See also **PSI** and **Stress.**

L

L (road design)   See **Length of curve**.

Label, stake   See **Stake label**.

Labor bond   See **Labor and materials payment bond**.

Labor and materials payment bond   A legal surety warranting that a contractor's bills and obligations under the terms of a contract will be paid. See also **Bond** and **Suretyship**.

Labyrinth   In landscape architecture (especially English landscape architecture), a garden **Maze**, q.v., formed of elaborately connected, hedged passages.

Lacerate   In plants, raggedly cut or incised. Usually descriptive of leaf margins.

Laciniate   Deeply and irregularly lobed.

Lacuna   An air cell in plant tissue.

Lacustrine   Pertaining to a lake or pond.

Lahar   In geology, a mud-flow or other soil movement on a volcanic slope. A form of **Gravity transport**, q.v.

Laitance   A light, chalk-like, inert, surface deposit often found on concrete after curing. Laitance can be increased by overfinishing a concrete surface.

Lake, ox-bow   See **Billabong**.

Lamina   The blade or wide portion of a leaf.

Laminar flow   A kind of water flow in which suspended particles move without scouring their channel. Nonabrasive flow. Laminar flow can also be found in air currents. See also **Uniform flow**.

Lamination   The bonding of several relatively thin and uniform wood pieces by dowelling and/or glue to produce a strong single member. Laminated wood benches and other kinds of street furniture are commonly used as landscape site features. Laminated timbers may also be used in the construction of gazebos or other outdoor structures.

Lamp, fluorescent   See **Fluorescent lamp**.

Lamp, mercury vapor   See **Fluorescent lamp**.

Lamp, neon   See **Neon lamp**.

Lanai   In Hawaii and elsewhere, an open-sided, roofed, outdoor sitting area.

Lanate   In plant structures, woolly or scruffily hairy.

Lanceolate (lanceolata)   In leaves, a lance-like form—pointed at the tip, wider at the base.

Land, crown   See **Crown land**.

Land, derelict   See **Derelict land**.

Land leveling   An agricultural practice usually found on nearly flat terrain in which the earth is reshaped to allow overall irrigation. See also **Contour plowing**.

Land, raw   See **Raw land**.

Land subdivision   See **Subdivision**.

Land surveyor   A professional surveyor who locates or plots boundaries, indicates existing land features on plans, locates and plots contours and gradients, and the like. The land surveyor's usual products are metes and bounds, topographical, and boundary surveys. See also **Survey**.

Land tile   Terra cotta or other butt-joint clay pipe used for underground drainage.

Land type, natural   See **Soil association**.

Land use Simply, any human activity on a piece of land. ***Land use map:** A more-or-less formal plotting of the existing uses of a given area. ***Land use plan:** A formal plotting of the proposed uses of a given area, often developed in reference to a land use map.

Land use control Zoning, or the application of restrictive ordinances or covenants regarding land use by governments or private companies. Heavily developed in the past 100 years to deal with expanding populations world-wide.

Landes (French) In Western Europe, a moor sometimes bordered by dunes.

Landfill An operation of depositing earth or other materials to raise the level of an expanse of ground. A dump. See also **Sanitary landfill.**

Landfill, sanitary See **Sanitary landfill.**

Landform A characteristic kind of terrain created by natural or artificial processes. Depositional landforms may be established by glacial action or by water and wind. Erosional landforms are created by the same forces but are remnants rather than deposits. Diastrophic landforms arise through twisting and pressure in the Earth's crust.

Landmark 1) A typical and widely recognized local landscape or architectural element that traditionally is identified with its place. 2) A boundary or property line mark.

Landplaster See **Gypsum.**

Lands, patent See **Patent lands.**

Landscape The surface of the Earth not covered by sea. Also, more narrowly, the amount of countryside and/or city that can be taken in at a glance. Landscapes include cities as well as countryside and wilderness, courtyards as well as parks, parking lots as well as the rooftop gardens of buildings, and are accordingly classified as either man-made or "natural." But there is really no twentieth-century landscape that has escaped the hand of man.

Landscape, animate See **Soft landscape.**

Landscape archaeology The emerging study of historic, man-made landscapes through archaeological analysis. The United States landscape architect Ralph Griswold completed a landscape restoration of the agora in Athens in the 1960s. In the United States, the pioneer work of Alden Hopkins in Virginia (1950s) and Robert Harvey in Iowa (1970s, 1980s) has also been noteworthy. See also **Historic preservation.**

Landscape architect A person who designs and administers the construction of landscapes useful to people and other creatures and who provides, in addition, related professional services. See also **Landscape architecture** and **Landscape gardening.**

Landscape architect as lienor In some states, the right of a landscape architect to file a mechanic's lien as a claim against real property improvement is recognized. The landscape architect may thus claim reimbursement for plans and specifications that he has prepared and/or construction that he has overseen. See also **Lien.**

Landscape architect's approval In landscape construction, a written acceptance of a contractor's methods, items of installation, or workmanship, or of a proposal made by the contractor in regard to the work. Items needing the landscape architect's approval are normally called out clearly in project **Specifications,** q.v.

Landscape architectural education See **Education in landscape architecture.**

Landscape architectural registration In the United States, a certification of individuals for the use of the term "landscape architect" or for the practice of landscape architecture or both, by means of a series of tests administered individually by most of the states. Since registration is relatively recent, many persons have been "grandfathered" or admitted to practice on the basis of their work or education prior to the enactment of certification laws. In theory, registration or certification establishes standards for practice to which landscape architects must adhere, and is controlled by a board or committee to which licensed landscape architects become accountable. Also Certification (for practice).

Landscape architectural theory A series of systematic assumptions and historic principles or rules applied to the design of a cultural landscape or garden. Most landscape architectural theory argues the relative propriety and application of formal layout or balance vs. occult or informal line and balance in outdoor design. Occult approaches are often identified with the Orient, in particular China and Japan. Formal or axial designs are usually Western or Middle Eastern in origin. Theory and style in painting, sculpture, and architecture also influence landscape architecture.

Hippodamos of Miletus, a Greek town planner of the sixth century B.C., is generally credited with the development of the gridiron as a standard of Western city design. Hippodamos theorized that a well-planned city was essential to social growth. The Roman writer **Pliny the Younger,** first century A.D., defined the design and uses of the well-managed estate (villa), setting a classical standard later copied by the Renaissance theoretician **Alberti** (fifteenth century). The Renaissance ideal of hilly, formal terraces or plots with a nearby "borrowed" landscape and a good vista has remained popular into the twentieth century.

Naturalism, a stylized "wildness" popular in Britain since the eighteenth century, was developed by **Bridgeman, Kent, Brown,** and **Repton.** A rolling lawn with a picturesque lake and copses of trees are its backbone. Lancelot "Capability" Brown, the true purist of these four, stylized the wild countryside right up to the manor door. The curving design line and the occasional artifical ruin were hallmarks of this style, the theory being that mankind could be improved if brought closer to untrammelled (yet idealized) nature.

The origins of landscape naturalism are primarily Oriental. The Chinese, Koreans, and Japanese had been refining an occult style throughout the Middle Ages—certainly several centuries before its rise to popularity in the West. But the golf links of Scotland, in use since medieval times, were striking local British examples of how a formal landscape purpose—the playing of golf with its distinct rules—could be combined with an informal, rambling design. The Scottish seashore dunes, with their scattered pockets of turf, lent

themselves casually but well to the actual form of the game itself.

Toward the middle of the nineteenth century, the landscape designer **Joseph Paxton** proposed that the naturalistic estate be adapted to public purposes inside cities. His landmark design for Birkenhead Park, constructed near Liverpool, was examined and admired by **Frederick Law Olmsted** during a walking tour of England in 1850.

In the United States, **Andrew Jackson Downing,** an ardent student of horticulture and landscape design, had proposed as early as 1841 that elegant, sturdy, naturalistic grounds should be developed around American houses as "democratic landscapes." Downing's theory was that each American family should have the quality to be found in a large estate, but at a smaller scale. Downing was also strongly in favor of public, tax-supported city parks—in particular, a large park for New York City. Olmsted, agreeing with Downing, proposed a plan with his partner **Calvert Vaux** for Central Park in 1858, was selected as designer, and with this and Prospect Park in Brooklyn established landscape architecture as a profession in the United States. Olmsted's design approach, best known for its ingenious "naturalism," also allowed axial, radial, or linear compositions, as the demands of a site might require.

From post-Civil War times into the Great Depression, landscape architects created **Country places** for a growing number of nouveau-riche entrepreneurs. **Charles A. Platt**'s small book, *Italian Gardens* (1894), set the tone for this work, redefining the design meaning of the Italian villa and demonstrating how easy it might be to combine formal "close-in" gardens with more informal work at some distance from the house. Platt's work proposed a careful

refinement of scale and color—not great, visionary garden treatments.

Later in the twentieth century, **Thomas Church** created the **California** or **Modern garden,** an eclectic combination of Eastern and Western historic styles, some local plant species, and above all **Site specific design.** The end product—the **Outdoor room**—is exemplified by Church's famous El Novillero (Donnell) garden. Other California landscape architects, **Edward Huntsman-Trout, Garrett Eckbo,** and **Lawrence Halprin** among them, have built upon the precedents established by Church. Typical of Eckbo's style is the inspired use of offset line to increase the apparent space of a garden. Eckbo has also helped to reestablish the social purpose and mission of landscape architecture through his writings and design work. Halprin has expanded the landscape architect's responsibilities to include unexpected areas of city and countryside: his fountain blocks, freeway parks, and design of monuments, all executed with a neo-Renaissance gusto, point to the twenty-first century. In the eastern United States, **Ian McHarg** has theorized that a careful regional or local analysis of all the physical factors of a site (grades, vegetation, waters, and the like) will lead to a proper site design. However, the problem of reconciling ecological worries with aesthetic necessities in a landscape design has not been completely solved.

Far East

The tomb of Confucius, built about 479 B.C. in Shandong Province, China, was located in a sacred grove. The plantings and burial garden structures were said by later Chinese to have been heavily "symbolic," though of precisely what we cannot be sure.

The ancient Chinese garden was a

place of repose, often designed by poets to be used for the composition of poems and the drinking of wine. Ideal gardens and parks were described by the writer Shang-lin in 179 B.C.: they were intended for day and night enjoyment, for moon-viewing, for the creation of reflections on water, for admiring a particularly comely tree or stone. In China, informal design involved an interpretation—not an imitation—of nature. By the time of Hui Yuan, a monk who established a Buddhist monastery in a wonderfully stylized garden in the late fourth century A.D., Chinese naturalism was very highly refined.

But it was the Japanese over the next several centuries who made it seamless. The Empress Suiko in the seventh century created a series of gardens in the Chinese style with artificial hills and ponds. Zen Buddhist influence simplified both Chinese and Japanese design: flowers were replaced by flowering and evergreen shrubs, texture and line were emphasized, fewer garden elements were permitted, and the tea ceremony became an important activity. The Zen garden began to use occult balance as an agent for understanding man's place in the universe. Ultimately, successive refinements led to the creation of the garden of Ryoanji in Kyoto (c. 1488), a nearly perfect, asymmetrical abstraction bounded by the severest formalism—one of the world's most remarkable gardens.

Perhaps the most ancient and venerable of Japanese landscape features was the *shima*—a more or less formless island in a pool. Both the water and the small bit of land became more stylized and particular in their functions as the centuries passed. The writer Tachibana no Toshitsuna (d. 1094) gives us a series of rules on their use and the function of other garden elements in his eleventh-century work, the *Sakuteiki.*

Another eleventh-century book, the *Tale of Genji* by Lady Murasaki, tells us of the early perfection of specialty gardens in Japan.

The ideal process for the tea ceremony was codified by the garden writer Sen no Rikyu (d. 1591). The ceremony was performed in the tea garden created specifically for the purpose. High Japanese landscape design also included hill gardens and flat gardens—both executed (as were tea gardens) in variations of *shin* (very full, complete), *gyo* (medium), or *so* (austere, simple) styles.

Of the most sophisticated of Chinese garden styles—that of the Song period, about 960–1280—we have no known extant examples in China. However, Song design can still be seen in Japan. The master landscape architect **Kobori Enshu** designed the Katsura Palace grounds in Edo (modern Tokyo) in the seventeenth century along classic Song lines. He used a lake as a focus, with carefully selected stepping stones, tea houses, and even riding and archery as garden attractions.

(Consult most boldface names or terms under their own headings.)

Landscape architecture   One of three broadly based professions (the others being engineering and architecture) dealing with the arrangement of animate and inanimate objects on land and the ties people have with those objects.

Landscape architecture as a science deals with the technical manipulation of objects and people in outdoor places. As an art, it expresses applied intelligence and human emotion, from anger to love, from compassion to aloofness, from frustration to nostalgia, in a compelling mixture of new and old ways, at its best linking people and landscape in a timeless, chromatic flow.

Landscape architecture, African
    See **African landscape architecture.** See also **Egyptian landscape architecture, Islamic landscape architecture.**

Landscape architecture, American
    See **United States landscape architecture.**

Landscape architecture, Australian
    See **Australian landscape architecture.**

Landscape architecture, Austrian
    See **Austrian landscape architecture.**

Landscape architecture, Brazilian
    See **Brazilian landscape architecture.** See also **Latin American landscape architecture,** and **Roberto Burle Marx.**

Landscape architecture, British
    See **English landscape architecture, Scottish landscape architecture.**

Landscape architecture, Byzantine
    See **Byzantine landscape architecture.** See also **Greek landscape architecture, Medieval landscape architecture, Roman landscape architecture.**

Landscape architecture, Canadian
    See **Canadian landscape architecture.**

Landscape architecture, Central Asian   See **Central Asian landscape architecture.** See also **Indian landscape architecture, Persian landscape architecture, Russian landscape architecture.**

Landscape architecture, Chinese
    See **Chinese landscape architecture.**

Landscape architecture, classical
See **Greek landscape architecture, Roman landscape architecture.**

Landscape architecture, colloquial
See **Vernacular landscape architecture.**

Landscape architecture, Danish
See **Scandinavian landscape architecture.**

Landscape architecture, Dutch
See **Dutch landscape architecture.**

Landscape architecture, ecclestiastical   See **Ecclesiastical landscape architecture.**

Landscape architecture, Egyptian
See **Egyptian landscape architecture.** See also (ancient) **Middle Eastern landscape architecture.**

Landscape architecture, French
See **French landscape architecture.**

Landscape architecture, German
See **German landscape architecture.**

Landscape architecture, Greek   See **Greek landscape architecture.** See also **Roman landscape architecture.**

Landscape architecture, Iberian   See **Islamic landscape architecture.** See also **Portuguese landscape architecture, Spanish landscape architecture.**

Landscape architecture, Indian
See **Indian landscape architecture.**

Landscape architecture, indigenous
See **Indigenous landscape architecture.**

Landscape architecture, Irish
See **Irish landscape architecture.**

Landscape architecture, Islamic
See **Islamic landscape architecture.**

Landscape architecture, Israeli
See **Israeli landscape architecture.**

Landscape architecture, Japanese
See **Japanese landscape architecture.** See also **Chinese landscape architecture.**

Landscape architecture, Korean
See **Korean landscape architecture.**

Landscape architecture, Latin American   See **Latin American landscape architecture.**

Landscape architecture, Medieval
See **Medieval landscape architecture.** See also **Renaissance landscape architecture, Roman landscape architecture.**

Landscape architecture, Mexican
See **Mexican landscape architecture.** See also **Latin American landscape architecture, Roman landscape architecture.**

Landscape architecture, Moorish   See **Islamic landscape architecture.**

Landscape architecture, New Zealand   See **New Zealand landscape architecture.**

Landscape architecture, Norwegian
See **Scandinavian landscape architecture.**

Landscape architecture, Oriental
See **Oriental landscape architecture** for various national and regional entries.

Landscape architecture, Persian
See **Persian landscape architecture.** See also **Islamic landscape architecture, Middle Eastern landscape architecture.**

Landscape architecture, Portuguese
See **Portuguese landscape architecture.** See also **Spanish landscape architecture.**

Landscape architecture, religious
See **Ecclesiastical landscape architecture.**

Landscape architecture, Renaissance
See **Renaissance landscape architecture.** See also **French landscape architecture, Medieval landscape architecture.**

Landscape architecture, Roman
See **Roman landscape architecture.** See also **Greek landscape architecture.**

Landscape architecture, Russian
See **Russian landscape architecture.** See also **Greek landscape architecture.**

Landscape architecture, Scandinavian   See **Scandinavian landscape architecture.**

Landscape architecture, Spanish
See **Spanish landscape architecture.**

Landscape architecture, Swedish
See **Scandinavian landscape architecture.**

Landscape architecture, U.S.
See **United States landscape architecture.**

Landscape architecture, vernacular
See **Vernacular landscape architecture.**

Landscape, borrowed
See **Borrowed scenery.**

Landscape character   The overall "feeling" or pattern of a landscape. The total effect of all the factors making up a landscape. Character is normally expressed as a positive summary of the quality of an area.

Landscape, Claudian See **Claudian garden.**

Landscape, commercial See **Commercial landscape.**

Landscape, composite See **Composite landscape.**

Landscape construction The modification of existing site conditions by earthwork, planting and/or structural installation to complete a desired landscape scheme.

Landscape contractor A professional builder or installer of landscapes. The landscape contractor's work may include the building of pathways, roads, outdoor structures, walls, patios, fences, retaining walls, planters and other like items. The landscape contractor also prepares soil, installs plants, irrigation systems, lighting and associated items of work. He or she may employ subcontractors to assist with certain technical phases of his or her work.

Landscape, cultural See **Man-made landscape.**

Landscape design 1) Any arrangement of objects or human activity outdoors. 2) "The poetry of space."—Dan Kiley.

Landscape, extensional See **Extensional landscape.**

Landscape garden The term used to describe a large-scale romantic landscape involving broad manipulation or transformation of extensive grounds. Especially applied to naturalistic eighteenth-century English gardens and their successors in the United States. See also **English landscape architecture, United States landscape architecture.**

Landscape gardening A popular term used to describe the product of the **English School,** q.v., of naturalistic gardening typified by the works of **Capability Brown, Humphry Repton,** q.q.v., and others in the eighteenth and nineteenth centuries. Landscape gardening replaced the earlier formal gardening. The landscape gardener served as a prototype for the modern landscape architect. Also, in a general and old-fashioned sense, the practice of landscape architecture. See also **English landscape architecture.**

Landscape gardening, dry See **Dry landscape gardening.**

Landscape gardening school See **English School of Landscape Gardening.**

Landscape, hard See **Hard landscape.**

Landscape history A kind of highly concentrated local history (micro-history) that analyzes land forms and settlement patterns, established as a new member of the liberal arts by the pioneers **J. B. Jackson** (U.S.) and **W. G. Hoskins** (U.K.), q.q.v. Landscape history focuses on the processes of cultural and natural history that produce vernacular (or popular) gardens and buildings. Also known as **Cultural geography, Landscape humanism.**

Landscape, inanimate See **Hard landscape.**

Landscape, man-made See **Man-made landscape.**

Landscape marble A limestone that shows "landscape scenes" when cut in clean planes. The "scenes" are the result of intrusive mineral action at the time of formation of the rock.

Landscape, mature See **Peneplane.**

Landscape, middle See **Middle landscape.**

Landscape, old See **Peneplane.**

Landscape, pastoral See **Pastoral landscape.**

Landscape planning See **Environmental planning.**

Landscape, rejuvenated See **Rejuvenated landscape.**

Landscape, residential See **Residential landscape.**

Landscape scheme A landscape plan, design, or concept.

Landscape study In landscape architecture, an early stage of design in which quick sketches for later plan and elevation development are made. This kind of design work is typically loose, imaginative, and fun, but it is soon succeeded by the refined tedium of working drawings production.

Landscape timbers Specialized construction timbers consisting of two flat and two rounded sides. Used in light planter and other landscape construction.

Landscape type See **Ecosystem.**

Landscape, wild See **Wild landscape.**

Landscape, young See **Young landscape.**

Landslip (slip) See **Solifluction.**

Lantern, stone See **Stone lantern.**

Lanulose In plant structures, wool-like, with short hairs or protuberances.

Lap joint (landscape construction) See **Wood and brick construction joints.**

Laps In landscape construction, an allowance calculated for the additional cost of material made necessary by overlapping wood or other joints.

Lapse rate The rate at which air temperature decreases as altitude or latitude increases. In terms of altitude, a drop of about 5°F/1000 ft. is normal. Also **Temperature lapse.**

Lapse, temperature See **Lapse rate.**

Larch A softwood of the genus *Larix,* usually species *canadensis,* with an excellent heartwood widely used in landscape construction. Larch sapwood may be treated with preservatives to extend its usefulness. Also **Western larch.**

Lateral line In irrigation, a line connected to a main supply, often leading to a lawn or shrub head. Normally, a line on the nonpressure side of the control valve. See also **Branch line, Main line.**

Lateral bud A side-bud on a plant stem. Also **Axillary bud.** See also **Terminal bud.**

Lath house

Lateral bud

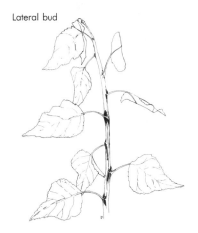

Lateral pipe See **Lateral line.**

Lateral soil load A measure of "sideways" soil pressure in PSF (pounds per square foot), with an allowance made for any existing **Hydrostatic pressure.**

Lateral and subjacent support See **Right of lateral and subjacent support.**

Lateral support, right of See **Right of lateral and subjacent support.**

Laterite See **Lateritic soil.**

Lateritic soil A tropical soil, rich in iron, and sometimes containing aluminum. Lateritic soil develops under heavy natural vegetation but its usefulness to agriculture and other properties is still being investigated. Amazonian and Equatorial African rain forest soils are often lateritic. Also laterite soil. See also **Pedalfer, Podzol.**

Lath A narrow, thin strip of wood used in the building of lath or plant storage houses and for plaster or stucco construction. Also a finishing member for a pergola (overhead) or trellis. See also **Lath house, Overhead, Pergola, Trellis.**

Lath house A plant storage building made of light wood framing, lath members, and plastic

sheets or glass panes as a weather covering. Often used by landscape contractors and nurserymen as a short-term holding shed. Sometimes **Slat house.** See also **Greenhouse.**

Lath screen A protective screen made of a sturdy frame and narrow lath pieces used to cover propagating stations such as **Cold frames,** q.v. Also a **Trellis,** q.v.

Latifundia Large Roman estates, first developed in the second and first centuries B.C. Latifundia were the predecessors of the medieval, Renaissance, and modern estate. Their form was one source of the modern park.

Latin American landscape architecture The earliest parks in the Americas were created not in the United States but in Mexico City, where Chapultepec Park (1530 A.D.) and the Alameda Central (1618) have served the public since the Spanish conquest. Chapultepec was developed from an earlier Aztec palace. Its grounds include museums, fountains, pathways, extensive tree and shrub plantings, and the bright flowers for which Mexican gardens are famous.

The Aztec gardens themselves reached their zenith in the late fifteenth century—remarkably, at the same time that the Renaissance villa gardens of Italy were created. They were usually very formal, with water, plant displays, and vista development as themes. The Aztecs used local plants and also imported exotics from the distant parts of their empire, frequently arranging their plantings scientifically. The world's first botanical garden may have been Huastepec, a palace garden of the Emperor Montezuma I constructed in the mid 1400s.

Aztec landscapes were often based on the public and private grounds of preceding empires. Of these, perhaps the Mayan was the most important. In Mayan cities clustered in the Mexican Yucatan, Guatemala, Belize, and Honduras, religious and public architecture mixed. Ball courts, platforms for holy cermonies, and the curious pentagonal Maya arch were common features. Often, buildings and pavement were of quarried limestone. In sculpture, there was a frequent use of figures and hieroglyphs to convey religious and historic ideas. The Great Plaza at Tikal, Peten, Guatemala, is perhaps the most striking of Maya public spaces. It is entered today as it was in the past, through narrow defiles between enormous pyramids and temples, still half-claimed by the jungle. The fine drama of the square is underlined by the rhythm of steps rising from its four sides, and by the pillars of the temples and the cockscombs of the pyramids set against the blue sky. The Mayas supported their great cities and towns with an intensive agriculture based on irrigation and the careful allotment of land. Evidence of the very broad extent of the Mayan civilization continues to be discovered.

In pre-Inca Peru, a widespread terracing of the western slopes of the Andes began about 500 B.C. It was continued by the Incas themselves and remained intact until approximately 1550 A.D. The Incas carefully channeled highland brooks to keep the fields productive. They also introduced into cultivation new plants, such as varieties of the potato, where some advantage might be gained. The palaces of the Incas were planted in elaborate gardens, often using flowering shrubs as special features. Their names have been preserved in Quechua, the language of the Inca Empire. Garden architecture included the elegant, mortarless masonry for which the Incas are well known. The Incas were fond of exotics and imported plants from Central America for their gardens. It is possible that they systematically planted street trees in Cuzco, Macchu Picchu, and others of their important cities.

Garcilaso de la Vega, the half-Spanish, half-Inca historian of the sixteenth century, tells us that the best of the Inca palaces were in Yucay, east of Cuzco. They boasted fountains, groves of trees, and special aromatic gardens. They also contained another curious Inca feature: reproductions of trees, shrubs, and flowers in gold and silver—with the living plants nearby.

In Mexico, Central America, and Peru, a European formalism was laid over the indigenous symmetry of gardens and public spaces. In Brazil, where no strong native landscape tradition apparently existed, the patio and **Praça** (square) in the Portuguese baroque style helped to establish the new pattern of European civilization in the late seventeenth century. The hot tropical climate of the Brazilian coasts, where the Portuguese first settled, provided great quantities of new plants for Brazilian gardens. In Baia (Salvador), Rio de Janeiro, and elsewhere, country villas (quintas) with courts and fountains brightened with azulejo tiles were common colonial landscape features.

The colonial landscape in Hispanic America followed the traditional Spanish pattern: private patios or courts, orchards, and kitchen gardens, often with fountains or pools, and usually enclosed on three or more sides; public plazas and parks, usually quite formal and very heavily used, with fountains, limited statuary, and (usually) plantings of local flora. In plazas, the style of both "hard" landscape and plantings was often baroque, with all the elements subservient to a strong geometric pattern and the plan symmetry radiating from a monument or gazebo in the center of the landscape. Plazas were constructed by royal edict on a given ratio of length to width (3:2), and were often paved in cobbles or other stone. Great **Atrios** or open courtyards were laid out by the Spaniards next to church entries to contain the large numbers of Indian converts won over by the padres in their early missionary work. Some of the best intact examples of colonial landscapes in Latin America may be found in Morelia, Michoacan state, Mexico, and in Antigua, Guatemala. Religious, private, and public landscapes combine in these cities in a rare unity.

Political independence in the early nineteenth century had little effect on landscape form in most of Latin America. The traditional baroque continued as a popular landscape style. In Buenos Aires, a boulevard-and-park remodeling based on Baron **von Haussmann**'s Paris was adopted after 1880, displacing the older Spanish colonial forms. Park development was particularly spectacular. The Brazilian rubber boom, lasting until World War I, brought tramways, new praças, new gardens, and an opera house to Manaus, the Amazon "capital." Theodore Roosevelt and other travellers remarked on the isolated wonders of this city some hundreds of miles from the mouth of the river. Meanwhile, the nitrate mines of Chile and the guano deposits of Peru and Ecuador helped to keep the

Latin American landscape
architecture. Tikal, Guatemala: main
plaza. Photo by author.

world's farms and Europe's gardens in prime condition.

In the early twentieth century, the Mexican muralist Diego Rivera and his colleagues, encouraged by the philosopher Jose Vasconcelos as Minister of Education (1920–24), began a series of large-scale outdoor wall compositions throughout Mexico depicting social revolutionary themes in bright color. In the years since, Rivera's murals have been influential in Latin

America and in the southwestern United States, which was the northern quarter of Latin America until 1846. Rivera's countryman, **Luis Barragan** (1901–), q.v., developed into a pivotal figure of twentieth-century landscape architecture. His work was influenced by Cubism, emphasizing a clear development of flat-surfaced vertical and horizontal planes in pavement and wall design, with water accents and strong plant masses as counterpoints. Barragan

mastered a simplification and stylization of traditional aqueduct, trough, garden wall, and landscape color design.

Roberto Burle Marx (1909–), q.v., has dominated landscape design in Brazil since 1936, when the Swiss-French architect **Le Corbusier** (Charles-Edouard Jeanneret, 1887–1966) visited Brazil and deeply influenced the course of architecture and landscape architecture in that country. An early

Cubist, Burle Marx later developed a new and flamboyant use of tropical Brazilian species in an occult landscape line of his own making, imitated now all over Brazil and the rest of Latin America. The São Paulo Botanical Gardens and Copacabana sidewalk landscapes are good examples of his style.

Two national capitals—Belmopan, Belize, in the Carribean, and Brasilia, the new Brazilian savanna city, have been created from scratch in the second half of the twentieth century following Utopian site planning methods. In both cities, with varying degrees of success, monumental buildings have been arranged in somewhat overbearing clusters with wide, empty spaces, motorways, and vague footpaths as connections.

See also **Brazilian landscape architecture, Mexican landscape architecture.**

Latitude 1) In geography, a north-south measurement set in degrees of distance from the equator, and often cross-referenced to **Longitude,** q.v. 2) **Latitudes and departures:** In surveying, latitudes are north-south line elements; departures are east-west line elements. They are calculated in a series of continued line segments that eventually must close on itself. The sum of all interior angles formed by the intersections of segments will equal 360°.

Latitudes, middle See **Temperate zone.**

Lattice A garden framework of open, interwoven wooden strips used as a vine support or by itself as a shade structure. See also **Pergola, Trellis.**

Latticework See **Lattice.**

Latticing See **Lattice.**

Law, "practice" See **"Practice" law.**

Law, "title" See **"Title" law.**

Law, "title and practice" See **"Title and practice" law.**

Lawn A mown green or plot of grass. A cultivated, grassy area preserved for its aesthetic quality and usefulness for play, outdoor eating, or other recreation.

Lawn head In irrigation, a stationary (fixed), pop-up, rotary, or impulse sprinkler that is specifically designed for grass areas.

Lawn hydrant (faucet, hosebib) A faucet in a metal or plastic container with a lid, usually installed flush with grade in a lawn.

Lawn mower Invented in the 1830s by the Englishman Edwin B. Budding, the lawn mower allowed growing numbers of middle-class gardeners to develop and maintain their own greens. It replaced sheep, cows, and scythes. Along with the **Ha-ha,** q.v., and **Wardian case** (see **Terrarium**), it revolutionized the gardens of the nineteenth century.

Lax In plants, applied to sagging branches, leaves, or flowering parts.

Layer, plow (soils) See **Surface soil.**

Layering In horticulture, a way of propagating plants in which a limb, stem, or shoot is partially covered with soil, vermiculite, or the like and kept damp in order to make it root. The "new plant" is then cut free from the parent. Also **Absenker, Marcottage.** See also **Air layering.**

Laying, dry (road and other pavement construction) See **Dry laying.**

Laying to bond In bricklaying, setting out an entire course without having to cut a brick.

Layout (irrigation) See **Spacing.**

Layout plan (contour and construction plan) In landscape drawing, a plan showing the existing and proposed locations of all site improvements, including earthwork, normally with emphasis on hard landscape features. Also **Staking plan.** See also **Contour plan.**

Leaching In soils, the separating out and deposition of mineral salts from a liquid solution through percolation. A common result in arid areas is the deposit of alkali (sodium or potassium compounds). Also **Eluviation.** See also **Alkaline soils, Illuviation.**

Leaching basin A kind of permeable **French drain,** q.v., or dry well lined with sand and/or gravel near its bottom.

Leaching field An area located downhill from a septic tank (sanitary drain) or other drain through which liquid and liquid-carried materials are slowly percolated.

Leader In plants, the section of stem or branch that holds terminal buds and extends growth upward or outward. In trees, the destruction of the leader may produce a deformed crown.

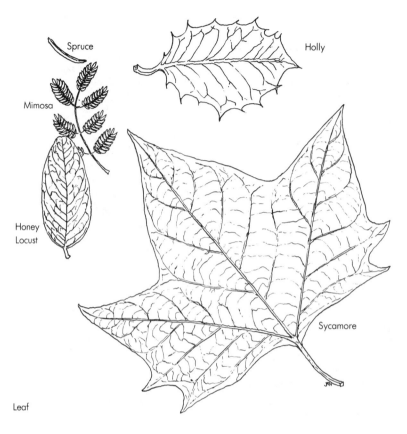

Spruce

Holly

Mimosa

Honey
Locust

Sycamore

Leaf

Leaf Normally, a green, flattened plant structure attached to a stem or suspended from a branch which contains chlorophyll and manufactures food through photosynthesis. 1) Simple leaf: a leaf of singular structure—i.e., sycamore, fig, elm, and the like. 2) Compound leaf: a leaf composed of several smaller structures, or leaflets. Locust, silk tree, and box elder are examples.

Leaf blade The flat and most obvious part of a leaf, simple or compound, usually responsible for photosynthesis.

Leaf crown See **Crown.**

Leaf mold The partly rotted, dark brown particles to which leaves are reduced on the ground with some moisture present. Leaf mold is an important source of **Humus,** q.v.

Leaf, true See **True leaf.**

Leaflet A single part of a compound leaf; literally, a tiny leaf.

Leaf-soil See **Leaf mold.**

Leasehold A form of land tenancy in which the occupant can use his leased land for limited purposes but may not drastically change its form. See also **Fee simple, Life estate.**

Leaves, alternate See **Alternate leaves.**

Le Corbusier (Charles-Edouard Jeanneret, Swiss, later French) (1887–1965) Twentieth-century architect, painter, and planner of riveting brilliance. Le Corbusier's visit to Brazil in 1936 to consult on the Ministry of Education building in Rio de Janeiro became a watershed for later Brazilian and Latin American landscape architecture. His structures were comprised of a lively Cubist-like style charged with his own occult balance.

Roberto Burle Marx, q.v., Lucio Costa, Oscar Niemeyer, and others were deeply influenced by Le Corbusier's style and by his approach to city planning. In Brasilia (c. 1961), many of the ideas were accomplished that Le Corbusier had first expressed in his book *La Ville Radieuse.*

His other large-scale planning effort was Chandigarh, the new capital of the Punjab (India) begun in the 1950s. **Concret brut** was the principal building material. Le Corbusier worked out a series of very strong, blunt buildings in a landscape of pools, parks, and groves—still somewhat unfinished.

The planning for Belmopan, the partially complete new capital of Belize in Central America, has Corbusian echoes but lacks the boldness and scale of Chandigarh and Brasilia.

Lectin A frequently occurring plant protein.

Lectotype (botany) See **Neotype.**

Le Doux, Claude-Nicolas (1736–1806) French neoclassicist, influenced by late Italian Renaissance form. Le Doux is noted for his popularization of the **English School of Landscape Gardening** style on the Continent. He designed naturalistic gardens to complement his neoclassic Hotel Thelusson in Paris and later set several houses designed for a M. Hosten in an informal garden setting. His writings and his interest in city planning are also widely recognized. See also **French landscape architecture.**

Legend   In landscape-design drawings, a plant chart indicating common and botanical names, quantities, sizes, and remarks on plant condition. The plant legend is typically shown on a planting sheet and indicates the items included on that sheet only. Also, any similar chart used on a plan.

Leggy or legginess   Said of spindly plants that have an excessive concentration of foliage at branch and stem tips, often caused by too much shade. See also **Spindling.**

Legume   1) A kind of plant generally valued for the ability of its roots to "fix" nitrogen in the soil, and characteristically displaying long seed pods with bilateral symmetry and a continuous suture-split line. Legumes belong to the pea family or *Leguminosae*. 2) The fruit of a *Leguminosae* plant. Also **Pulse crop.**

Leisure   Free time. Time not devoted to work. Especially, time used for relaxation and mental or physical recreation. Classically, time set aside for thought. Planning for leisure activity is an essential responsibility of the landscape architect.

L'Enfant, Pierre (1754–1825)   It can be argued that the Washington Mall is the most important of American public spaces. It is developed on an utterly gigantic scale that somehow accommodates hundreds or even thousands of simultaneous uses and that ties together a large number of the United States' most important public buildings in a logical and

quite pleasant way. The Mall effortlessly makes room for a congressional speech, several football games, thousands of speeding automobiles, and people gazing at the best modern sculpture.

L'Enfant, a French architect, city planner, and major of engineers in the Continental Army, was responsible for most of this. Mustered out of the army in 1784, the Revolution over, he was hired to remodel New York's old City Hall on Wall Street for the use of the first

Congress of the independent United States. President Washington and Secretary of State Jefferson subsequently engaged him in 1791 to draft plans for the new national capital.

L'Enfant's radiating avenues with their superimposed gridiron presumed a monumental Washington architecture fit in tone and style for the capital of a new republic. His vistas, most remarkable, perhaps, for the long holes they punch in the murky skies of the eastern seaboard,

Pierre L' Enfant. L' Enfant's plan for Washington, D.C., c. 1791. Illustration courtesy BBMSL, UNM.

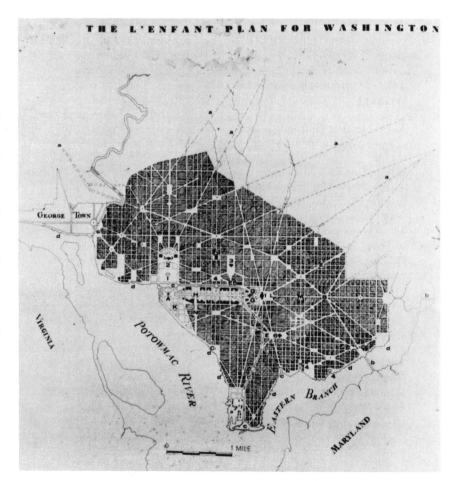

invariably terminate in a monument or an especially significant building. The Mall boasts the most important of these. L'Enfant came by his sprawling sense of scale honestly: his father had been court painter at Versailles and the young Pierre was raised in the royal village.

L'Enfant was extremely stubborn and uninterested in the political realities of the new capital. He was dismissed from his job and his elaborate plans lay on the shelf until 1889, when the Senate Capital Planning Commission brought them back to life. By 1901, actual construction of L'Enfant's design for Washington had begun. By the late twentieth century, with most of the mistakes and intrusions of the nineteenth century wiped away, Washington had become, essentially, L'Enfant's city.

Length of curve (L)   In road layout, curve distance as measured from **PC (point of curvature)** to **PT (point of tangency),** q.q.v.

Length, tangent (T) (road design)
   See **Tangent length.**

LeNotre, André (1613–1700)
   French formal landscape designer and trusted adviser to Louis XIV.
   Le Notre was the son of Louis XIII's Royal Master Gardener, Jean Le Notre, and was probably born at the Tuileries. André's grandfather had also been a gardener. Le Notre studied drawing with Vouet and architecture with Mansart, and by 1637 had succeeded his father as chief gardener at the Tuileries. In his subsequent career as royal landscape gardener, Le Notre developed and refined the French formal garden first codified by **André Mollet,** q.v., whose influence Le Notre had been exposed to since childhood. His reputation was established with the creation of

Vaux-le-Vicomte (1657), the chateau and vista garden of Louis XIV's finance minister, Nicolas Fouquet. Here he set the precedents that would guide him in his later work: a strong, central axis stretching out across a sheet of water into the far distance, with radiating or perpendicular paths, box and yew for hedge and topiary, and carefully framed vistas. Le Notre's **Parterres,** q.v., were designed for viewing from within the chateau itself. But it is the monumental scale of Vaux-le-Vicomte as much as the elegance of its details that still strikes the visitor. It is universally considered a masterpiece, and its designer at the very least the greatest of all formal landscape designers.

However, its owner, M. Fouquet, came to a bad end, and his designers, including André Le Notre, were appropriated by Louis XIV for the design and construction of the new palace and grounds at Versailles. Le Notre's Versailles gardens, begun in 1661, changed the course of European landscape design for a hundred years and more. Water in canals, cascades, pools, and fountains abounded; statuary was freely used; goosefoot allees, **Treillage,** mass flower plantings, parterres, fountain arbors, and vegetable and fruit gardens were developed as special features. Where Vaux-le-Vicomte was tight, intimately detailed, and intended to be viewed as a "single unit" **Vista garden,** Versailles was designed to sprawl, impress, overwhelm, and amaze. These it did in unmatched measure.

Le Notre's work for Louis was extended to designs for grounds at Marly, Trianon, St. Germain, Fountainebleau, Clagny, and, of course, the Tuileries. He also laid out gardens at St. Cloud, St. Germaine-en-Laye, Sceaux, and at Chantilly, the home of the Prince de Conde. The English court of Charles

II may have made note of Le Notre's work while the king was in exile in France, but there is no conclusive evidence that Le Notre designed any landscapes in England itself.

The grounds of Vaux-le-Vicomte and Versailles became the most talked about in Europe, imitated from St. Petersburg to Madrid, and they made Le Notre the most copied and celebrated landscape designer in Western history.
   See also **French landscape architecture.**

Lense   In soils, a coating of silt or clay on sand or gravel particles or on cobbles.

Lenticel   A lens-shaped, somewhat "corky" outgrowth of tender bark tissue. The lenticel is a kind of raised plant pore.

Lenticular   In plant structures, a shape like a doubly convex lens.

Lepidote   In plant structures, scurfy, or exhibiting tiny scales. See also **Scurf.**

Letter of agreement   See **Letter of intent.**

Letter of intent   A letter written by a landscape architect to a client, or by an owner to a contractor, indicating: 1) the scope of a project; 2) the scope of services to be performed; 3) the client's responsibilities; 4) the project schedule; 5) the requested reimbursement for services rendered and when it is to be paid.
   The letter of intent serves as a brief and concise legal contract, and should be prepared by the landscape architect in consultation with his or her attorney.
   Also **Letter of agreement.**

"Lettering" In landscape architectural drafting, printing or plan labeling usually executed in a typical style in capital letters.

Levee A river bank formed from the deposition of sediment in a flood plain which gradually raises the river level above the surrounding countryside. The Mississippi consistently builds levees in its lower valley. Levees may also be man-made, in which case they are constructed parallel to a river's course to prevent flooding. Also **Dike.**

Level 1) Displaying an even plane or surface. 2) A surveying instrument consisting of a tripod and a telescope containing an enclosed liquid "level" on a rotating mount, used to check elevations relative to a given horizon or reference plane. Also **Contractor's level.** See also **Hand level** and **Transit level.**

Level, base See **Base level.**

Level, datum See **Datum line.**

Level, hand See **Hand level.**

Level of saturation See **Water table.**

Leveling course In roadway, utility slab, and play-court construction, a semifinal layer of gravel or other material smoothed out and readied in final structural configuration for a surfacing course.

Leveling of land See **Land leveling.**

Ley farming The seeding of agricultural land in grass, which is allowed to stay as a cover crop for several years.

LF An abbreviation for lineal foot.

Liability, contractual See **Contractual liability.**

Liability insurance A form of insurance often secured by contractors for the duration of a project, covering acts or accidents involving physical injury or property damage and unforeseen hazards (public liability insurance). Landscape architects may secure the same sort of insurance for protection in their offices of operation. Additional coverages include automobile liability, broader contractual liability, and products and completed operations liabilities. Multiple liability insurance is often called comprehensive general liability insurance.

Liability insurance, contractor's See **Liability insurance.**

Liability insurance, professional See **Malpractice insurance.**

Liability insurance, public See **Liability insurance.**

Liane or liana Any of a number of tropical climbing vines. Sometimes a generic term for these and other vines.

Liber In botany, plant tissue used to transport sap descending to the roots. Sometimes incorrectly called inner bark. Source of woody plants' yearly growth rings. Also **Bast.**

License, contractor's See **Contractor's license.**

Lichen A tough, unusual form of plant life found on stone surfaces and tree trunks, presently thought to be a kind of fungus living as a parasite on an alga. The process is essentially symbiotic or commensal. A "character" plant on stone surfaces.

Lien An impediment upon or claim to property, arising from a failure to pay taxes **(Tax lien)** or to pay for goods and services that have been provided for property improvements **(Mechanics lien). Mortgage liens** are claims against real property made as loan security. See also **Judgment lien, Release of lien.**

Lien bond Similar to a **Labor and materials payment bond,** q.v., the lien bond specifically indemnifies a project owner against loss that may occur from unpaid labor or material claims filed during the course of construction. See also **Bond.**

Lien, judgment See **Judgment lien.**

Lien, release of See **Release of lien.**

Life cycle In plants, the course of life beginning with a fertile seed and ending with the maturation of the sexual organs that will produce a new generation of fertile seed. Also, in asexual reproduction, the course of cell division that ends with two new individuals capable of reproducing themselves sexually or once again by division (self-cloning).

Life, design See **Design life.**

Life estate A form of land possession in which an owner has control of a property for life and may make only limited improvements on it. See also **Fee simple, Leasehold.**

Life zone A geographic area in which a characteristic plant and animal life will flourish. In temperate or continental climates, an increase in altitude is analogous to a greater latitude: a high mountain in New Mexico will have roughly the same climate as a hilly forest or even steppe in Canada. Merriam's life-zone scheme of North America is widely used, though it does not perfectly distinguish between the zones. Various **Ecotones,** q.v., exist in valleys and on the slopes of mountain ranges with north-south orientations, and these are difficult to define accurately. The accepted North American zones are these: Arctic-alpine (Boreal), Hudsonian, Canadian, Transition (wet, dry), Upper Sonoran (Upper Austral, Alleghenian), Lower Sonoran (Lower Austral, Carolinian), Tropical. See also **Climatic province, Geographic climax vegetation, Geographic province, Soil region.**

Life-zone indicator (plant)
See **Indicator plant.**

Lift A layer or course of material—earth, gravel, asphalt, or the like—used to produce a finished surface.

Lift (pump) station A pump protected by a small housing structure, used to lift sanitary or storm sewage to a higher level so that it can continue to flow at the proper gradient through a long pipe.

Lift, suction (pumps) See **Suction lift.**

Lifting 1) Digging and removal of tree or shrub specimens to be transplanted. 2) The removal of tree underbranches for walkway or other clearance.

Light standard The post or pole used to support a **Luminaire,** q.v.

Light table An underlit wood and glass or metal and glass table, used for viewing of slides, plans, designs, and the like.

Lighting fixture See **Luminaire.**

Lighting, flood See **Flood lighting.**

Lighting, fluorescent
See **Fluorescent lamp.**

Lighting, outdoor See **Outdoor lighting.**

Ligneous In plants, referring to woody parts.

Lignin Along with **Cellulose,** q.v., the principal material of woody plant tissue. Lignin is a cell binder.

Ligorio, Pirro (c. 1500 or 1520–83) Designer, with Orezio Olivieri, hydraulic engineer, of the Villa d'Este (1550) in Tivoli, a whimsical and masterful Renaissance water garden commissioned by Cardinal Ippolito d'Este. Ligorio also was responsible for the casino or garden house of Pope Pio IV in the Vatican gardens. See also **Renaissance (Italian) landscape architecture.**

Ligulate In plant structures, formed like a tongue.

Ligule A portion of a grass blade. A thin extension found where leaf and stem join.

Lily pond A shallow garden pool, often stagnant, with a mud bottom or constructed boxes in which aquatic plants, especially lilies, are grown.

Liman (Hebrew) A dryland "tank" with a flattened bottom used to collect runoff in arid regions. Often planted in vigorous trees.

Lime 1) Calcium oxide (CaO). A term generally used for crushed or ground limestone. See **Limestone.** 2) Crushed limestone used as a stabilizer in warm areas for granular and other road surfaces. See also **Flexible pavement.**

Limestone A sedimentary rock composed of lime carbonate, often used in landscape construction or, when crushed, as the principal component of cement. Once pulverized, limestone is also an amendment used to correct acidic soils in both its calcareous (calcium carbonate) and dolomitic (magnesium calcium carbonate) forms.

Limestone, argillaceous
See **Argillaceous limestone.**

Limestone, hydraulic See **Hydraulic limestone.**

Liming The addition of lime to acidic soils to make them more alkaline, thus preparing them for better plant growth. See also **pH factor.**

Limit, contract See **Limits of contruction.**

Limit, elastic (landscape construction) See **Elastic limit.**

Limit, liquid See **Liquid limit.**

Limit, plastic (PL) See **Plastic limit.**

Limited agency A legal relationship between principal and agent created for a specific reason and of limited duration. See also **Agency.**

Limits of construction The boundary or limit of work shown on the construction drawings of a project, within which a contractor must confine all his activity. Also **Contract limit.**

Limnic Pertaining to fresh-water lakes and ponds. See also **Paralic.**

Lindero (Spanish) Minor ditch.

Line In irrigation, a pipe.

Line, base See **Base line.**

"Line of beauty" (in a garden) See **Serpentine.**

Line, branch (irrigation) See **Branch line.**

Line of Browse See **Browse line.**

Line, chase (irrigation) See **Sleeve.**

Line, contour See **Contour line.**

Line, datum See **Datum line.**

Line, graded (irrigation) See **Graded line.**

Line, ground See **Ground line.**

Line, head (irrigation) See **Strip head.**

Line, horizon See **Horizon line.**

Line, hot (irrigation) See **Hot line.**

Line, lateral (irrigation) See **Lateral line.**

Line, lot See **Lot line.**

Line, main See **Main line.**

Line, nozzle (irrigation) See **Nozzle line.**

Line pressure (irrigation) See **Main, Main line.**

Line, property See **Property line.**

Line, reference See **Reference line.**

Line, skinner (irrigation) See **Nozzle line.**

Line, springing See **Springing line.**

Line, strand See **Strand line.**

Line, valley See **Valley line.**

Lineal foot A foot as measured in a direct line. Also Linear foot. Abbreviated **LF.**

Lineament Any large, natural, linear landscape structure. Narrow valleys, hogbacks, coastlines, and the like are examples.

Linear perspective See **Perspective.**

Lineation A flat, plane surface on a stone or rock stratum.

Liner In nursery use, a small, potted plant. **Liner stock** is often field-planted for one to three years to produce marketable trees.

Lingulate In plant structures, tongue-like in form.

Links Golf course. From the *links,* or sandy, seaside, natural courses where the game began in Scotland in the fifteenth century. See also **Golf course architecture.**

Linnaean system (of plant names) See **Botanical classification.**

Linnaeus, Carolus (1707–78) Carl von Linne, the father of the Linnaean system of scientific plant classification. Linnaeus originated the binomial Latin delineation (genus, species) commonly used since to identify plants the world over. His major works are *Species Plantarum* (1753) and *Genera Plantarum* (1754).

Typical Linnaean classifications:

Fraxinus	*velutina*
genus	species
Forestiera	*neomexicana*
genus	species

See also **Botanical classification.**

Lintel A cross-beam or cross-stone bridging two columns or a doorway or window.

Liquid limit (LL) The minimum amount of water present in soil that will allow soil to move under its own weight. See also **Capillarity** and **Permeability.**

Liquid manure Horse or cow manure mixed with water and used for concentrated plant feedings. Also **Tea.**

Liquidated damages In landscape construction, an amount assessed the contractor on a daily basis for failure to complete specified work on time. Often specified in a **Bonus and penalty clause,** q.v.

List, short See **Short list.**

Lithosol An azonal soil composed of unconsolidated rock bits. Sand dunes and certain highly pitched hillsides are examples. See also **Azonal soil, Regosol.**

Lithosphere The solid-rock and soil-surface layer of the Earth, projecting through the **Hydrosphere,** q.v. See also **Atmosphere.**

Litmus A pigment made from lichen extract and added to paper for convenient pH testing. A red test color indicates acidity, or a pH of under 7.0; blue litmus color indicates alkalinity, or a pH greater than 7.0. See also **pH scale.**

Litter Leaves, branches, twigs, bark forming a mat over forest or other soils. Litter eventually adds tremendously to soil quality. See also **Duff, Mor, Slash.**

Litterbug   A popular 1960s term for an irresponsible reprobate who dribbles garbage whenever he appears in public and is incapable of understanding the simplest requirements of civil behavior.

Littoral   That part of a seacoast lying between high and low tide. Loosely, a coastline.

Live load   The weight of a vehicle, snow, or other temporary object or construction over a pipe or other underground object or a beam. Wind pressure may also be a kind of live load on a beam or other structural component. See also **Dead load, Dynamic load, Snow load, Wind load.**

Live pipe (irrigation)   An irrigation line carrying water, or in use.

"Live" water pressure   See **Water pressure.**

LL   See **Liquid limit.**

Llano (Spanish)   A plain or prairie. A savanna.

Load, axial   See **Axial load.**

Load, concentrated
   See **Concentrated load.**

Load, dead   See **Dead load.**

Load, detritus   See **Stream load.**

Load, dynamic (soils)   See **Dynamic load.**

Load, live   See **Live load.**

Load, snow   See **Snow load.**

Load, stream   See **Stream load.**

Load, wind   See **Wind load.**

Loading, eccentric (wall and footing design)   See **Eccentric loading.**

Loam   A rich soil type (texture) that is not overwhelmingly sandy, silty, or clay-laden. Normal loam contains about 40% sand, 40% silt, 20% clay (including a substantial amount of humus), and is fertile. Sandy loam contains more than 40% sand, silty loam more than 40% clay, and clay (clayey) loam more than 20% clay. See also **Soil, Subsoil, Topsoil.**

Locule   A specialized plant chamber containing a fruit or sexual organ.

Locus amoenus (Latin)   A pleasant spot or locale—i.e., a garden, especially a mythical or ideal garden.

Loess   In soils, a deposit of wind-borne silt or dust, usually porous, and fertile when mixed with humus and irrigated. Loess is often eroded topsoil. See also **Deflation.**

Log dam   See **Check dam.**

Loggetta (Italian)   Small **Loggia.** Several of the finest examples are in the Piazza San Marco, Venice.

Loggia   A roofed arcade or gallery, constructed along the wall of a house or other building, with at least one open-air side. See also **Gazebo.**

Logwood oil   A commonly used conditioner for outdoor timbers.

London, George (c. 1640–1713)
   London opened a nursery in the English capital to compete with the Dutch in 1681. He was a successful commercial nurseryman with a series of partners, the most important of whom was **Henry Wise.** London was influenced by the work of **John Rose,** q.v., royal gardener to Charles II, and by the grandiloquent style of **André Le Notre.** Topiary, parterres,

and walled gardens—all quite formal in layout—characterized his estate designs. In his gardens for Henry Compton, the Bishop of London, he pioneered the use of many new exotic species from North America. Melbourne Hall in Derbyshire is often considered to be London's masterpiece. See also **Henry Wise.**

Long.   Abbreviation for **Longitude** or longitudinal.

Longitude   In geography, an east-west measurement based on the Greenwich, England, prime meridian, and often cross-referenced to **Latitude,** q.v.

Longitudinal (seif) dune   See **Dune**

Loop, irrigation (sprinkler)
   See **Irrigation loop.**

Loose rock dam   See **Check dam.**

Loose yard   In landscape demolition, loose, unconsolidated earth or rock measured after grubbing or blasting.

Lorate   In plant structures, strap-shaped or tongue-shaped.

Lorrain, Claude (1600–82)   Lorrain is also known as Claude, Le Lorrain, and Claude Gelee or Gellee. Lorrain is the painter of the soft Italy of the Campagna. His frequent subject is the Temple of the Sibyl in highly romanticized surroundings.
   Lorrain, with **Nicholas** and **Gaspar Poussin** and **Salvatore Rosa,** q.q.v, was responsible for establishing landscape as a painting genre in its own right. His landscapes have a wonderful depth, seemingly achieved by contrasting color tones.
   Lorrain was a strong influence on the design style developed by the **English School of Landscape**

Gardening. The arcadian country estates of Kent, Brown, and others were derived in great part from Lorrain's moody, wild countrysides.

See also **English landscape architecture.**

Loss, friction (irrigation)
See **Friction loss.**

Loss, pressure (irrigation)
See **Friction loss.**

Lot line A property boundary, especially in cities.

Lot, parking See **Parking lot.**

Lot, play (Tot lot) See **Play lot.**

Loudon, John Claudius (1783–1843) British author, magazine editor, lexicographer, farmer, botanist, and landscape designer. Loudon moved to London in 1803 from Edinburgh, where he had worked for a landscape gardener and a nurseryman as a boy. A self-taught man, he was keenly interested in the problems and growth of the cities of the early Industrial Revolution. He pressed for greenbelts and parks as a means of making cities more habitable. His *On the Laying Out, Planting, and Managing of Cemeteries and on the Improvement of Churchyards* proposed the re-use of graveyards as public open space.

Loudon's remarkable series of encyclopedias brought him his greatest renown. These included the *Encyclopaedia of Gardening* (1882), *Encyclopaedia of Agriculture* (1825), *Encyclopaedia of Plants* (1829), *Encyclopaedia of Cottage, Farm, and Villa Architecture* (1833), and his *Arboretum et Fruticetum Britannicum* of 1830.

Despite terrible health, Loudon collaborated with his wife, Jane, in editing the *Gardener's Magazine* from 1826 until his death. He is thought to have coined the term

"landscape architecture," later popularized by **F. L. Olmsted.** His American contemporary, **A. J. Downing,** was heavily influenced by Loudon, from whom Downing borrowed freely for his own writings.

Louvers Sometimes referring to a horizontally slotted **Dovecote,** q.v., in a garden.

Love, garden of See **Pleasaunce.**

Low-angle nozzle In irrigation, a sprinkler-head nozzle designed to spray at an angle parallel or nearly parallel to the ground surface. Low-angle nozzles avoid wind deflection and keep spray off nearby walls, windows, and cars.

Low bidder See **Bidder.**

Low desert In the southwestern U.S., a desert with a high mean annual temperature in which many tropical and subtropical plants may be successfully grown (Southern California, Arizona). See also **High desert, Intermediate desert.**

Low point (LP) In surveying, a mark indicating the bottom of a depression.

Low voltage lighting, wiring
1) **Lighting:** normally domestic systems utilizing 24-volt components.
2) **Wiring:** use of 24-volt systems in automatic irrigation systems to operate electric solenoids.

Lower Sonoran (zone) See **Life zone.**

Lozenge (planter) In landscape architecture, a four-sided, diamond-shaped planter, sometimes with rounded corners.

LP See **Low point.**

Lug In metal connections, a nut, particularly a nut closed at one end to serve as a cap.

Lumber Timber sawn into boards, posts, or other finished pieces in uniform sizes for construction. In the United States and elsewhere, a board foot of lumber ($1/12$ of a cubic foot) is the standard of measurement. The dressed or cut down size of lumber is approximately $3/8$ inch smaller than nominal or prefinishing **(Rough lumber)** size.

All lumber is classified as **Hardwood** (deciduous) or **Softwood** (evergreen or coniferous). It is further characterized as either **Heartwood** or **Sapwood,** q.q.v. Structural lumber **(Common yard** or **Stress-graded)** used in landscape construction is separated as follows:

1) **Dimension lumber** (joists and planks): Any lumber nominally 2 inches or more wide and 2 inches to under 5 inches thick.

2) **Beam and stringer lumber:** Any lumber nominally 8 or more inches in width and 5 inches or more thick.

3) **Posts and timbers:** Nominally square-sectioned lumber of 5 inches $\times$ 5 inches or greater.

Overall dressing is indicated as:
S1S: Plane surface on one side.
S2S: Plane surface on two sides.
S1E: Plane surface on one edge.
S2E: Plane surface on two edges.
S4S: Plane surface on two sides and two edges (all surfaces dressed).

In addition, lumber is graded by number from 1 to 5, with 1 indicating the highest quality. Stress or other grading qualities are sometimes called out by lumber manufacturing associations.

Among the most common woods used in outdoor construction are **Cedar, Cypress, Douglas fir, Larch,** and **Redwood,** listed under their own headings.

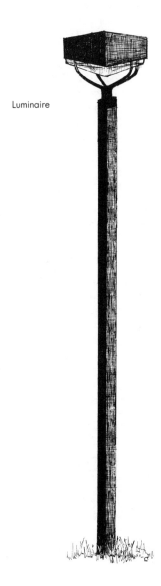

Luminaire

Lumber, B or better See **B or better lumber.**

Lumber, off grade See **Off grade lumber.**

Lumber, yard See **Yard lumber.**

Lumen A standard measurement or unit of light flux, equal to a flow of one (international) candle.

Luminaire An outdoor post, pole, or standard containing a lamp or lamps and protective panes or other covering, hoods, wiring, and additional components necessary to form a complete lighting unit. Also **Luminary.** See also **Light standard.**

Luminary See **Luminaire.**

Lump sum In a contract bid form, the cost of all labor and materials necessary for the construction of a project as quoted by a contractor. See also **Contract sum, Unit prices.**

Lump-sum contract In design or construction contracts, a set general cost agreed upon to perform an amount of work. See also **Contract.**

Lunate In plants, crescent-like in form.

Lute In landscape construction, an elastic adhesive or cement used for ceramic binding, pipe joints, metal-masonry connections, the adhesion of organic materials, and the like. Common lutes include epoxy resins, latexes, red lead, glycerol, and pitch. See also **Cement.**

Lutene (lutein) Yellow **Plant pigment**(s), q.v.

Lych gate (lich gate) A small, roofed gate at the edge of a churchyard. Traditionally, pallbearers pause with the corpse briefly at a lych gate while awaiting the final words of a parson.

By extension, a lych gate is also any small, covered entry to a garden.

See also **Descanso.**

Lycopene Red plant pigment. See **Plant pigments.**

Lyrate In plant structures, formed like a lyre.

Lysimeter A measuring device for ground water, used to make note of quantities of percolation and water quality.

M

M 1) Plan abbreviation for one thousand. 2) Plan abbreviation for meter or middle.

Macadam **Asphaltic concrete**, q.v., or **Asphalt macadam.** A pavement of aggregate bound together by tar or asphalt. Originally, crushed rock applied to road surfaces and rolled with water. Also **Tarmac, Tarmacadam.**

MACC See **Maximum allowable construction cost.**

Macchia (Italian) See **Chaparral.**

Macroclimate The weather and growth conditions of a large but distinct geographic area, as opposed to a **Microclimate**, q.v. See also **Climate.**

Macrolandscape The larger landscape; the landscape as a whole. See also **Microlandscape.**

Macronutrient A widely distributed, dissolved-in-available-form soil mineral or mineral compound that is necessary in large quantities for plant (and animal) growth and health. There are nine metallic and nonmetallic macronutrients. **Nitrogen, Phosphorus,** and **Potassium,** q.q.v., are the three principal soil macronutrients. Carbon, hydrogen, and oxygen, found universally in air and soil, are also macronutrients, as are calcium, magnesium, and sulfur. See also **Soil minerals, Trace elements.**

Magnesium A metallic element required in relatively large quantities for plant and animal health and growth. See **Macronutrient.**

Maiden In horticulture, a recently grafted fruit or other tree still being trained in size and form.

Main In irrigation, the municipal or other water-supply line under continuous pressure. See also **Main line.**

Main line (of irrigation system) In irrigation, a pipe or pipes downstream from the control valve supplying water to lateral lines and heads and/or additional service lines. Usually under continuous pressure. Also **Pressure line.** See also **Lateral line.**

Main pump In golf course and other large irrigation systems, a pump used in conjunction with another main pump and an auxiliary pump to provide a constant pressure in a main line.

Mainland dune See **Dune.**

Maintenance The performance of such duties of upkeep and care as mowing, pruning, fertilizing, watering, trash pick-up, oiling, painting, raking, and the like to ensure that a landscape develops and stays in good and serviceable condition. Maintenance should begin immediately following project completion. Better project maintenance is assured by careful planning; a maintenance schedule provided by the landscape architect may often help an owner in establishing good landscape care.

Malee scrub In Australia, a savanna-like vegetation of low shrubs found in arid areas. See also **Mulga scrub.**

Mall 1) A central, axial promenade or long formal passage through a landscape. Prominent examples exist at Central Park, New York City, and at Versailles. 2) An enclosed or open shopping promenade flanked by service and goods stores, booths, and the like. A shopping center. See also **Esplanade.**

Mall

Malpractice insurance A broad form of liability insurance secured by the landscape architect at the insistence of public agencies or private clients to protect him (her) and them in case of accident or injury resulting from faulty design. Also **Professional liability insurance.** See also **Errors and omissions insurance.**

Management, soil See **Soil management.**

Management of water See **Water management.**

Manager, contract See **Contract manager.**

Manganese A metallic element necessary in small quantities for plant health and growth. A micronutrient. See **Available nutrient, Soil minerals, Trace element.**

Mangum terrace A wide earth ridge constructed to follow existing contours on very gentle slopes to prevent erosion and slow runoff. Also **Ridge terrace.**

Manhole (MH) An underground chamber large enough for a person to enter to maintain an existing sewer pipe or pipes. Abbreviated **MH** on plans or surveys. See also **Catch basin, Drop inlet.**

Manifold In irrigation, a consolidated pipe assembly containing several valves at one location.

Manipulation of space In landscape design, the organization of areas of land for specific aesthetic or functional purposes. The landscape architect may manipulate a lengthy, narrow space to make it seem wider, for example, or reform an expansive, amorphous area into comprehensible smaller compartments.

Man-made landscape (cultural landscape) The manipulated, artificially created landscape of the face of the Earth, including farms, ranches, estates, roads, cities, gardens, parks, pastures, and other areas. Man-made landscape is always an expression of society, culture, and local geography, and is traditionally the basic area of concern for the landscape architect. The cultural landscape may also be the larger, regional landscape in which a society traditionally finds its home, develops its myths, and imagines its future.

Man-made soil See **Anthropic soil.**

Manning formula In run-off and other calculations, a formula used for computing the pipe size necessary to accommodate a given flow. Expressed as N = 0.012, indicating a coefficient of pipe smoothness, and usually graphically illustrated by a chart showing flow in cubic feet/second (CFS) related to velocity in feet per second (FPS) and pipe diameter.

Manning, Warren H. (1860–1938) U.S. landscape architect, born in Massachusetts. Manning was an apprentice in the Olmsted office before opening his own firm in 1896. His practice included a great deal of city planning and estate and park design. A founder of the American Society of Landscape Architects (ASLA), Manning became its president in 1914.

Manual drain valve (irrigation) See **Drain valve.**

Manual, project See **Specifications.**

Manual system In irrigation, sections of heads operated by hand-turned (manual or angle-control) valves. The sections collectively form the manual system. See also **Automatic system.**

Manual valve (irrigation) See **Manual system.**

Manufacturer's (commercial) specifications The specifications recommended by a manufacturer for use with his product. See also **Specifications.**

Manure 1) Raw, processed, or aged animal waste from stockpens, often mixed with sawdust or straw. 2) Any kind of fertilizer. See also **Fertilizer.**

Manure, artificial See **Chemical fertilizer.**

Manure, green See **Green manure.**

Manure, liquid See **Liquid manure.**

Manure, poor-man's (snow) See **Poor-man's manure.**

Map A two-dimensional scale drawing of a part of the Earth's surface. A relief map gives scaled features of the earth in three dimensions so that topographic qualities can be appreciated by touch as well as sight.

Map, base See **Base plan.**

Map, cadastral See **Cadastral map.**

Map of land use See **Land use.**

Map, photo See **Photo map.**

Map, soil See **Soil map.**

Map, topographic See **Topographic map.**

Mapping The process of map or chart research and drawing.

Maquis (French) See **Chaparral.**

Marble A metamorphic rock of great beauty and limited outdoor durability used occasionally in landscape construction and often for sculpture. Marble is crystalline limestone.

Marble, landscape See **Landscape marble.**

Marcescent In botany, referring to leaves, buds, or stems that remain on a plant after withering. Especially said of young plants that hold their browned foliage through the winter.

Marcottage Layering, q.v.

Marginal 1) In horticulture, pertaining to a plant that is only somewhat adapted to a local climate and its vagaries and thus susceptible to extremes of weather or siting. 2) Pertaining to a plant growing only in wet soil at the edge of a pool or stream. 3) Regarding land that has been eroded or depleted or that is too acidic or alkaline to support normal plant growth. See also **Submarginal.**

Marginal dune See **Dune.**

Marina A dock with boat facilities, usually constructed to handle light recreational craft.

Marine erosion The erosion of a shoreline by the sea, often aided by particles of stone or shells and other debris suspended in waves as they hammer the land.

Maritime climate A climate moderated by the influence of the sea, especially a mild, temperate zone climate with cool winters and summers. New Zealand and Southern California have maritime climates. Also **Insular climate, Oceanic climate.** See also **Climate.**

Market gardening See **French farming.**

Masonry (pattern). Casa Rinconada, New Mexico: view of walls, c. 13th century. Photo courtesy BBMSL, UNM.

Mark-up In drafting, a red-line or blue-line correction, usually on a print sheet, of a preliminary or working drawing. Used as a basis for smoothly finishing an original sheet.

Marl A valley clay containing substantial calcium carbonate.

Maroon garden See **Red garden.**

Marsh A low, boggy area often flooded in winter or spring and normally watery and mucky year-round. Reeds or grasses are usual marsh vegetation. See also **Bog, Salt marsh, Swamp.**

Marsh garden A small garden of selected wetland plants developed at the edge of an artificial pool.

Marsh, George Author of *Man and Nature* (1864). Marsh was an early conservationist and advocate of the preservation of forest and other wild

lands for future generations. See also **United States landscape architecture.**

Marsh, salt See **Salt marsh.**

Marshland See **Marsh.**

Marx, Roberto Burle See **Burle Marx, Roberto.**

Masonry Brickwork, stonework, or concrete blockwork. The product of a mason constructing with mortar.

Masonry cement The dry, cementitious material to which fine aggregates are added to make **Mortar**, q.v. Two types are common 1) **Type I:** Non-high-strength. 2) **Type II:** General masonry cement.

Masonry or concrete dam See **Check dam.**

Masonry, dry stone See **Dry stone masonry.**

Masonry joint The narrow space between stone surfaces or bricks. Joints may be mortared or dry. If mortared, they may be formal and regular (concave), or somewhat irregular and carefully compacted. Normal joint width is approximately $1/2$ in.

Masonry, modular See **Modular masonry.**

Masonry rubble Wall construction using raw, irregular stones. See also **Rubble.**

Masonry unit A building unit, usually standardized, which may be brick, stone, gypsum, glass, or concrete. See also **Concrete masonry unit.**

Masonry unit, concrete
See **Concrete masonry unit.**

Mass A unit or body of matter that stands as an opposite to and complement of **Void,** q.v. Mass defines space.

Massed bedding See **Carpet bedding.**

"Massive" soil A structureless soil that is also "bound." Clay pan and **Fragipan,** q.v., soil are examples. See also **Pan, Soil structure.**

Mast Fallen acorns, beechnuts, or similar fruits which accumulate on the ground in a woodland and make useful fodder for wild or domestic animals.

Mast arm (light pole) See **Bracket arm.**

Master plan 1) In landscape design, a highly detailed preliminary plan showing proposed ultimate site development. Master plans often comprise site work that must be executed in phases over a long time

and are thus subject to drastic modification. 2) Any comprehensive plan.

Master specifications Standard specifications prepared for landscape architectural or other projects. Master specifications are always modified slightly or extensively to suit a project, and are often set up for easy computer or automatic-tape typing.

Master (rain) switch In **Automatic (irrigation) controllers,** q.v., an override switch that allows a preset watering program to be shut off without cancelling the entire irrigation sequence.

Mastic, asphalt See **Asphalt mastic.**

Mat 1) (Horticulture): See **Thatch, Dethatching.** 2) (Design): See **Matte.**

Mat, brush See **Brush mat.**

Material, parent See **Parent material.**

Material, plant See **Plant material.**

Material supplier In landscape construction, a provisioner of materials who does no installation or construction.

Materials bond See **Labor and materials payment bond.**

Materials payment bond See **Labor and materials payment bond.**

Materials specifications
See Technical Specifications at **Specifications.**

Matrix 1) In landscape construction, a grout or cement-base material in which tile, mosaic, and the like are placed. 2) In geology, a principal rock mass in which additional minerals or rocks are embedded.

Matte (Mat) A dull, lackluster finish. See also **Gloss.**

Mature landscape See **Peneplane.**

Mature soil A well-developed, stable soil with A, B, and C horizons. A zonal soil or soil series. See also **Soil horizon.**

Mature stream A noneroding, old, stable stream or river that wanders through its landscape and deposits a great deal of silt in its flood plain. Also **Graded stream, Old stream.**

Mawson, Thomas H. (1861–1933)
English landscape architect of the late nineteenth and twentieth centuries. Mawson divided his time and practice between England and Canada, with offices in London, Lancaster, and Vancouver, B.C. He is well known in North America for his pioneer Canadian landscapes. He produced designs for public grounds in Regina, Saskatchewan beginning in 1912, and masterplans for the Universities of Dalhousie and Calgary. Mawson consulted on civic improvements for Ottawa and proposed modifications for Coal Harbour at Stanley Park in Vancouver. In England, Mawson was responsible for, among other projects, Port Sunlight near Liverpool (c. 1905). A celebrated lecturer, Mawson also wrote two popular books, *The Art and Craft of Garden Making* (1900), and *Civic Art: Studies in Town Planning* (1910). See also **Canadian landscape architecture** and **Frederick G. Todd.**

Maximum allowable construction cost   An amount established by the owner of a project as the allowable limit of construction spending. Often stipulated as a given element in an agreement between owner and landscape architect. Also **Construction budget, MACC.** See also **Budget.**

Maximum allowable slope
   See **Maximum slope.**

Maximum slope   A slope established at a very steep angle, beyond which its surface covering (gravel, stone, grass, or the like) will slide off or become impossible to maintain. See also **Angle of repose** and **Slope ratio.**

Maximum "upset" fee   See **"Upset" fee.**

Mayline (straight-edge)   A sliding straight-edge mounted on cables run through pulleys used for landscape architectural drafting. See also **T-square.**

Maze (maze garden)   In English (especially Tudor) and derivative landscape architectures, a garden **Labyrinth** composed of elaborate, intricate, topiary hedges.
   English mazes, often of *Ligustrum* species, are usually taller than their Italian predecessors.
   See also **Turf maze.**

McHarg, Ian   Scottish and United States twentieth-century landscape architect and ecological planner. McHarg emigrated to the United States after World War II and developed a highly original means of "overlay analysis" incorporating geographic, climatic, vegetative, and use studies of a given landscape area. He maintained an extensive private practice for many years and was founder and chair of the program in landscape architecture at

Maze. France: Villandry Gardens. Photo courtesy BBMSL, UNM.

Maze (English)

the University of Pennsylvania. He is perhaps best known for his book *Design with Nature*, 1972.

Meadow   Land mainly covered with grass, especially a low-lying grassy area bounded by hills.

Meal, bone   See **Bone meal.**

Mealy   In plants, covered with **Bloom** or strong **Pubescence,** q.q.v., or insect deposits.

Mean coverage (irrigation)   A mean line drawn as a measurement of water coverage parallel to a row of sprinkler heads. Often used to measure fairway precipitation in golf courses.

Mean sea level   An average sea elevation established by multiple calculation and used as a base of **Datum,** q.v., for determining land elevations. An average level is often calculated to lie between low and high tides.

Mechanical composting
   See **Compost.**

Mechanical pencil   See **Technical pencil.**

Mechanics   In physics, the behavior of materials under stress.

Mechanic's lien   See **Lien.**

Mechanomorphosis In botany, a change in normal plant form due to the influence of environmental stress. For example, modified tree form due to constant wind shearing, lightning-damaged leaders, air-rooting, and the like.

Mediacid Referring to a highly acid soil with a pH of about 5.0. See also **Acid soil, Minimacid, pH.**

Median In twentieth-century multilaned highways, a divider strip separating traffic travelling in opposite directions.

Medieval landscape architecture (500–1300) Gardeners in the Middle Ages took care to follow the moon: they tilled, planted, and harvested by it. Their gardens were enclosed, much like their world, but also curiously unlike the inward-facing courtyards of their contemporaries, the Moors. Moorish gardens were full of vivid, geometric structural detail, colorful plants, tinkling water—a warm, Mediterranean liveliness. The gardens of northern Europe were more sober and utilitarian, with a pace and form set by St. Benedict in the sixth century. Benedict's monastic grounds typically made use of a **Cloister** or cloister **Garth,** a pond, a **Hortus,** an orchard, a vineyard, a **Physic garden** (the precursor of the modern **Botanical garden**), grain fields, and a graveyard in their scheme. The monks also produced flowers for their altars and cultivated local forests for lumber and firewood. The study and practice of horticulture were as much a part of monastic life as reflective religion. Clerics continued the cultivation of ancient fruits and vegetables that might otherwise have been lost. Perhaps the best idea we have of the medieval monastery and its layout is found in the plan for St. Gall, Switzerland, in which trees and

Medieval landscape architecture. Castle of Sandsee, Germany. Photo courtesy BBMSL, UNM.

other plants are carefully noted. The Roman *villa rustica* and *villa urbana* (see **Villa**) were its probable models, and a formal, highly rectangular geometry, suitable for the contemplation of God, its design goal. The Certosa di Pavia, in Italy, is a good extant example of the quality of the medieval cloister.

We know from Charlemagne's *Capitulare* (c. 795) that the emperor wished specific trees, shrubs, and other plants to be grown in his

realm for their contributions to society. The poet Walafrid Strabo (809–849) talks about raised beds—the standard structures of medieval vegetable gardening—in his poem *Hortulus.* This Swiss work is also perhaps the best **Herbal** of medieval times, with an emphasis on the utility of horticulture.

But monastic grounds began to be supplemented after the Dark Ages by newly developed castle gardens and public squares. A stable agriculture was founded in Western Europe on rotating crops of cereals, grasses, root crops, and legumes. Crusaders home from the Middle East began to whet the European appetite for exotic plants (bulbs, oranges) and new garden forms (kiosks, pleasure gardens). Rising commerce stimulated the development of towns, and city squares, muddy and formless since the days of the Romans, began to come to life with decorative pavements, statuary, and houses of business. The Piazza del Campo in Siena and the Piazza della Signoria in Florence survive intact as good examples of the best squares of their day.

The formal castle garden included a place to romance ladies—the **Pleasance,** in which grass, often laid out in curious **Turf seats,** and chivalry had become popular by the mid-thirteenth century. Shakespeare mentions these as he sets the stage for Titania, the queen of the fairies, in *A Midsummer Night's Dream.* Trellises, copied from Roman models, also reappeared. Garden **Mounts,** or hummocks of earth, were used as vantage points to survey the pleached bowers, herbaries, orchards, and massed flowers in the mostly enclosed medieval garden. Grafting, a much-cultivated craft in the Middle Ages, was often fancifully pursued, with a variety of fruits grown on the same host stock.

By the time of the *Roman de la Rose* and Boccaccio's *Decameron* (c. 1350), the medieval ideal of a closed world of fantasy gardens was waning. Boccaccio's refugees from the plague told stories of faraway Crete and Babylon, and of May gardens created by magic in January. The real gardens of the day were also leaving the confines of their castle battlements and beginning to hint at the openness that would soon characterize the Renaissance.

See also **Renaissance landscape architecture** and **Roman landscape architecture.** For contemporary design in other parts of the world, see **Chinese landscape architecture, Indian landscape architecture, Islamic landscape architecture, Japanese landscape architecture,** and **Spanish landscape architecture.**

Mediterranean climate A mild, generally warm climate with dry summers and wet winters largely determined by a weather-modifying sea. Southern California, the Cape Province of South Africa, and the Mediterranean basin itself are examples.

Medium, growing See **Growing medium.**

Medium texture (soils) See **Soil texture.**

Medulla (botanical) See **Pith.**

Medullary rays In botany, tissues developing radially from pith to bark that transport nutrients uniformly within root, trunk, or limb parts of a plant.

Megalith A massive stone or slab of stone. Adjective: megalithic. See also **Monolith.**

Megalopolis (from the Greek) A term used to describe vast urbanized tracts, especially one city merging into another over a large area. Examples: Tokyo-Osaka, New York-Boston.

Mellow soil A good quality, friable, agriculturally useful soil with a neutral or near-neutral pH value. See also **Soil, Topsoil.**

Menhir A Paleolithic upright stone slab, especially as part of a series of stones laid out in a circle (France) for a religious purpose. See also **Cromlech, Dolmen, Trilithon.**

Mercury vapor lamp A type of outdoor lamp that, although in common use, is not as efficient or cost effective as high-pressure sodium lighting.

Mere (Old English) A pond, boggy area, sea creek, or land boundary.

Meridian A great circle of longitude passing through both poles. Extensively used as part of base data in surveying.

Meristem area In plants, a grouping of cells in bud, leaf, or vascular tissue capable of reproduction.

Mesa (Spanish) 1) An isolated, small plateau with cliff-like or steep sides, resulting from a hard cap-stratum resisting erosion. 2) (Southwestern United States) A short grass prairie or flat expanse of land.

Mesh, woven wire See **Woven wire fabric.**

Mesic In soils, moist. See also **Moisture gradient.**

Mesophyte A temperate zone plant requiring moderate rainfall or moisture. See also **Hydrophyte, Tropophyte, Xerophyte.**

Metabolism The series of complex organic, life processes occurring in plants and animals. See also **Anabolism, Catabolism.**

Metal In Britain, New Zealand, and elsewhere, gravel used for road surfacing. See **Gravel.**

Metal coating (for steel members) A finish applied to structural steel consisting of zinc (by galvanizing), chromium, nickel, cadmium, or other metals. See also **Galvanizing.**

Meteoric water Water that seeps into rock strata from the air or the surface. Hail, rain, snow, and the water of streams are examples. See also **Ground water.**

Meteorology The science of the weather. See also **Climatology.**

Meter A standard unit of measurement worldwide, equal to 39.37 inches, and divided into centimeters ($1/100$) and millimeters ($1/1000$).

Meter, electric See **Electric meter.**

Meter, exempt (irrigation) See **Exempt meter.**

Meter, water See **Water meter.**

Metes and bounds survey See **Survey.**

Methods of earthwork, including **Contour planes, Cross section, Grid,** and **Parallel planes** See **Cut and fill.**

Metropolitan Of a large city.

Mexican landscape architecture

The Aztec designer Itzcoatl laid out Tenochtitlan—the ancient Mexico City—c. 1427–40 A.D. The city was an island built in Lake Texcoco and reached by causeways. It was located in the high Valley of Mexico and ringed by mountains, some of them, such as Ixtaccihuatl and Popocatepetl, volcanoes. Cortes himself was amazed at the design of the city in 1520: the streets were each half-road, half-canal, with elegant bridges at intersections. There were roof gardens in the residential neighborhoods and great plazas for commerce and ceremony. Most houses had interior courts planted with flowers in a riotous display of colors. There were ballcourts, massive if grim sculpture,

bathing pools, and palaces with sparkling fountains fed by aqueducts.

The Aztec kings surrounded their grand homes with gardens. At Iztapalapa, the sprawling grounds contained aviaries, arbors of carpenter's work covered with vines, fruit trees, and a huge reservoir stocked with fish and faced with stone finished in bas-reliefs. Built by Montezuma I, Iztapalapa had a water's-edge casino that was approached by boat from Lake Texcoco. Its form was rigidly symmetrical.

The local king Netzahualcoyotl created several gardens during the high period of Aztec garden design in the late 1400s. He planned and developed his cypress garden, the Bosque del Contador, and his villa, Texcotzinco, at the northeast shore of Lake Texcoco. The Contador garden was enclosed by a double row of bald cypresses and featured shrub and flower plantings traversed by walkways and long still pools. Texcotzinco was a hillside villa created around the play of tumbling water, with formal gardens and a fine view of the lake. Netzahualcoyotl staged plays and held philosophical discussions at Texcotzinco. He planted tight groves of pines and masses of different flowers. The Texcotzinco bas-reliefs, depicting Aztec history, were eventually destroyed by the first Bishop of Mexico as idolatrous.

Aztec interest in botany was so keen that the first Montezuma created a botanical garden— possibly the first in the world—at his palace of Huastepec between 1440 and 1468. His plantings were systematically organized, and included specimens from the tropical lowland provinces of the Aztec empire. Montezuma I also imported gardeners from the lowlands who were familiar with the plants to care for them. Huastepec was expanded

by Montezuma II and included a zoological garden at the time of the coming of the Spaniards.

Montezuma's summer palace on Chapultepec Hill, with Lake Texcoco lapping at its feet, is probably the most famous of Aztec gardens. It has been in continuous use since its construction in 1440. It contained the basic Aztec royal garden elements: plenty of water, a well-developed symmetry, a multitude of tree (bald cypress), shrub, and flower plantings, a good view of the lake and mountains, and an animal collection. After the conquest in 1530, Chapultepec was dedicated as a public park to the people of Mexico City by the Spanish King Phillip II—the first such park in the Western Hemisphere. Its gardens were redesigned by the Emperor Maximilian (c. 1864). Today, Chapultepec contains extensive water works, museums, an amusement park, paths, fountains, and the sprawling plantings for which it first became famous.

Its sister park, the baroque Alameda Central, was constructed (c. 1618) on a very formal European design. The Alameda and Chapultepec have served for centuries as models for other Mexican parks.

The Aztecs' curious floating gardens, the **Chinampas,** used to supply Tenochtitlan with flowers and vegetables in pre-Columbian times, still occur in the twentieth century. Once common on Texcoco, Chalco, and other lakes in the Valley of Mexico, they are now found at Xochimilco, near Mexico City. But the Aztecs' legacy to later landscape design is centered in the love of strong wall color, bright flowers, and formal garden composition that persist in Mexico today. The Aztecs built a civilization based on precedents set by the Olmecs, Mixtecs, Zapotecs, and Mayas who preceded them. When they ceded it

Mexican landscape architecture. Chapultepec Park, Mexico City: Netzahualcoyotl's fountain. Photo courtesy BBMSL, UNM.

in turn to the Spaniards who would create New Spain, it is remarkable indeed that their very formal gardens were so similar to the symmetrical landscapes of Renaissance Europe. Both villa garden and focused **Piazza** were high points of contemporary Renaissance design.

Public open space became as important in the Mexico of the Spanish Empire as it had been to the Aztecs. The ancient Mexican city of Teotihuacan had featured great squares, terraces, and statuary as early as 200 B.C. Monte Alban, in Oaxaca, had a developed central square on a mountaintop by 300 A.D. The great plaza of the colonial period came to be El Zocalo—the *Plaza de la Constitución*—in Mexico City, established on an Aztec square. Most plazas in the country were developed by Spanish royal edict on a 2:3 ratio of width to length, following the theories of the Italian **Alberti,** q.v. They were often paved in rough cobbles, but they did not contain substantial plantings until the time of the Emperor Maximilian (1860s). The best-preserved of these plazas is perhaps at Patzcuaro, Michoacan (ancient Tzintzuntzan, capital of the Tarascan Indians). A recent movement has encouraged their restoration. But whenever they may occur, and whatever their condition, they continue to be the focus of Mexican social life and are thus intensively used.

The **Atrio,** or entry court in front of a church, was widespread in colonial Mexico. It was often planted in olives. It continues in use in the southwest United States as well as in Mexico itself.

Patios, the semienclosed house gardens of Moorish Andalusia, became enormously popular in Mexico. They were most frequently surrounded by archways, sometimes opening over a wall on one side to vineyards, orchards, or additional gardens beyond. Their layout was formal, with a centered fountain in tiers as the usual feature. Glazed tiles, religious figures, wall niches, and colorful plantings were commonly developed in the national Baroque style, which has remained popular into the twentieth century. Often a **Mirador,** or second-story viewing window, was designed to look out over the central axis or best viewing line of the patio garden.

Wrought iron, incorporated in grilles, benches, handrails, balustrades, gazebos, and other landscape details, was widespread in gardens and parks by the end of the nineteenth century. The dahlia, petunia, cosmos, zinnia, and other highly colorful indigenous flowers continued to be popular.

But the Mexican Revolution that began in 1910 ended in the 1920s with calls for more and better design of public squares, parks, and other recreational spaces. A series of sometimes brilliant interpretations of the old Aztec/European Renaissance landscape design tradition resulted. The comprehensive quad/open space system of the University of Mexico in the Pedregal, near Mexico City, is a new sort of landscape design that has responded to public need. The Chamizal Park and new Cathedral Plaza in Ciudad Juarez, Chihuahua, are recent open spaces developed for the use of a growing public. The clean lines of the walls and courts of the architect Ricardo Legorreta, along with the striking water gardens, aqueducts, *bebederos* (troughs), and contrasting plant masses of **Luis Barragan,** q.v., Mexico's premier twentieth-century landscape architect, have helped merge the public and private landscapes of the country into a new unity based on an abstraction of traditional form.

The designer Arturo Pani has developed luxuriant courtyard gardens, ponds, and fountains in Cuernavaca, Morelos. In Acapulco, perhaps the country's best contemporary terrace garden overlooks the Pacific at the home of the sculptor Victor Salmones. The modern painters Siqueiros, Orozco, and Rivera developed a mix of politics and color in their highly political murals of the 1920s and 1930s.

Color and boldness of form in multiple media strike the eye as Mexican landscape architecture continues to reinvent itself. Cortes wondered at its lushness and variety when he first saw Tenochtitlan and the palatial gardens of Chalco over four centuries ago. The current challenge in Mexican outdoor design is to maintain the graceful national connection between man and nature in the face of perhaps the world's most burgeoning population growth.

See also **Latin American landscape architecture.**

MH See **Manhole.**

Michelozzi, Michelozzo (c. 1400s) Designer of the Villa Medici at Fiesole (c. 1453), near Florence, for Cosimo dei Medici. Michelozzi's design was based on Pliny the Younger's writings and villa designs. Michelozzi used neoclassical techniques popular in his day to create a formal house and grounds in a hillside setting. See also **Renaissance landscape architecture.**

Microclimate The highly specific weather and growth conditions of a limited area, influenced by local geographic and atmospheric factors. The opposite of a **Macroclimate,** q.v., the larger-scale, usual climate conditions of an area. A microclimate exists in the ground air layer—the lowest level of air in the atmosphere. See also **Climate.**

Microcosm Literally, a universe in miniature. A small-scale environment or system which is typical of a larger environment or system.

Microhabitat See **Ecological niche.**

Microlandscape A relatively small landscape (courtyard, kitchen garden, and the like) with well-defined limits. See also **Macrolandscape.**

Micronutrient See **Trace element.**

Microphyllous In plants, showing typically small leaves.

Microrelief The small-scale flux and shape of the land.

Microspecies In botany, a number of plants, such as blackberries, raspberries, and the like, which may be distinguished but which nevertheless are so closely related that they are classified as one species.

Microsporophyll In botany, the male organ or stamen of higher plants.

Midden A garbage pile or dung heap. See also **Tell.**

Middle Eastern landscape architecture The ancient gardens and landscapes of the Middle East, with the exceptions of the great ziggurat at Ur and a public square or two in Harappa on the Indus, are known to us from literature. The Book of Genesis, of course, is quite familiar, and its Eden a very old story indeed. Older yet in Asia Minor is the *Epic of Gilgamesh,* the long narrative of the king of Sumerian Erech and his search for a friend lost in the afterworld. The tale itself is perhaps 5,000 years old, and it is our first clear picture of the haven the garden must have been to the Mesopotamians of the day, broiling in their mud cities on the flat plain.

In *Gilgamesh* there are cedar forests and a garden of the sun by the sea. The secret of eternal life is kept on the island of Dilmun (modern Bahrein), which lies in the Persian Gulf where the sun sets—and Dilmun itself is a paradise. There is a longing for Eden in *Gilgamesh* that appears again and again in Mesopotamia as the millennia roll slowly by.

The ziggurat at Ur (c. 2300 B.C.),

beautifully detailed with terra cotta ornament and bas reliefs, was one of the first hanging gardens, set off by its tiers of plants watered from a sophisticated tank-and-pipe system set up on the roof of the tower. The Babylonians would later copy it. At Harappa and nearby Mohenjo-Daro, the Indus Valley people laid out brick pavements in their squares and installed flush toilets in their houses in the third millennium B.C. And the Egyptians (see **Egyptian landscape architecture**) developed the most refined of early Middle Eastern gardens with the rise of sophisticated irrigation along the Nile. Their enclosed courtyards, laid out along purely formal axes, used sycamore figs and palms for shade, the grape, oleander, willow, and poppy for accents. The Egyptians, like the Sumerians, also made early use of the reflecting pool in an enclosed house space. The Sumerians and Egyptians oriented their dwellings to gain advantage over their hot climate, utilizing shade, breezes, and surrounding vegetation as well as pools in the design of their houses.

Sumerian architecture had been thoroughly developed, employing baked brick, the vault, arches, and domes, by the fourth millennium B.C. Careful Sumerian city design extended even to public gardens, if we are to believe a cuneiform fragment from about 1500 B.C. showing canals and a park for the city of Nippur.

By 1300 B.C., the Assyrians, successors of the Sumerians, had developed hunting parks. These great expanses of forests and other vegetation were watered by the **Qanat,** q.v., a sophisticated underground water ditch still in use in Oman and capable of transporting mountain stream water unbelievable distances with little or no evaporation. The hunting park, always tied to royal prerogative,

Middle Eastern landscape architecture. Great ziggurat of Ur, c. 2100 B.C. Above, an illustrative reconstruction, and below as it appeared in the early 20th century. Illustrations courtesy BBMSL, UNM.

Middle Eastern landscape architecture. Babylon: hypothetical reconstruction of Hanging Gardens. Illustration courtesy BBMSL, UNM.

became common in Assyrian cities along the Tigris and Euphrates. King Tiglath-Pileser I (1116–1078 B.C.), imported exotic plants for his park. By the time of Sennacherib (705–681 B.C.), extensive "straight-line" irrigation for hunting parks had been perfected and large-scale land development for this sort of royal landscape was common.

In the Babylon of 600 B.C., hollow columns were used to support essential parts of the famous hanging gardens, one of the Seven Wonders of the Ancient World. King Nebuchadnezzar's gardens were said to be arranged in tiers, with intricate plantings and "water engines," derived from Sumerian models, as part of their mechanical systems. The *Epic of Gilgamesh* continued to define the importance of the garden to society, as the Assyrians and the Babylonians themselves added new chapters to the already-ancient legend and

brought its many pieces together to form a good story.

Persian gardens and hunting parks, prominent after 500 B.C., were much refined (see **Persian landscape architecture**). The **Chahar-bagh,** q.v., was a garden style usually represented by a fountain in the center of a courtyard tumbling into streamlets radiating in the four cardinal directions and dividing the garden into quadrants. Pavilions in the garden's center and great reflecting pools were also popular in Persian landscape design. The *chahar-bagh* and its consistent use of geometry were adapted after the Muslim conquest into the Islamic garden that was built as far west as Cordoba and Granada in Spain. Darius, Xerxes, Cyrus, and other Persian emperors also made use of the hunting park as a royal relief from the harshness of the Persian and Mesopotamian countryside. It is remarkable that the familiar patterns

of the Persian carpet still faithfully reflect these ancient concepts of landscape design.

The Greeks learned from the Middle Eastern peoples who preceded them. Greek Antioch in Asia Minor was known as a garden city in the late first millennium B.C. It boasted street trees, elegant porticoes, fountains, pavilions, and lush gardens backed up against the foot of the mountain behind the city. But here, as elsewhere, Greek outdoor design concerned itself more with the creation of the public landscapes—the agoras, amphitheaters, and playing fields—which the Greeks pioneered in the Western world.

See also **Greek landscape architecture, Islamic landscape architecture, Israeli landscape architecture.**

Middle landscape   Historically, farms, ranches, and other quasi-settled land between a city and the wilderness.

Middle (mid) latitudes
See **Temperate zone.**

Midnerve or midrib   The largest vein or rib of a leaf. A **Costa** is an enlarged midrib.

Mies van der Rohe, Ludwig (1886–1969) Immensely influential German and American architect. As an originator of Modern Architecture, Mies's clear sense of line and its function when expressed in basic industrial materials—as well as his lifelong attention to detail—have had a strong effect on twentieth-century urban landscape architecture. The campus of the Illinois Institute of Technology and the Farnsworth House (hard elements in a soft prairie landscape) are typical of Mies's U.S. work.

Mil ¹/₁₀₀₀ of an inch. Used in landscape construction to measure the thickness of plastic and other sheeting.

Mile A measure of length equal to 5,280 feet or about 1,610 meters.

Milesian plan A **Gridiron**, q.v., layout in city planning, after the Greek city of Miletus. See also **Hippodamian scheme.**

Military landscape architecture
  Parade grounds, ditches, fortifying earthworks, quadrangular temporary camp layouts, and athletic facilities at military bases are among the most common forms of this type of landscape architecture.
  In ancient times, hunting parks and royal forest preserves, patrolled by soldiers, were also frequently set aside for the use of a ruler and his commanders.
  See also **Chinese landscape architecture, Roman landscape architecture.**

Mimicry In botany, the resemblance of a certain plant to other plants or objects. Adjective: mimetic.

Mineralogy, soil See **Soil minerals.**

Minerals, soil See **Soil minerals.**

Miner's inch In the United States, primarily the montane West, an old measurement of water quantity taken from a piped stream discharge point.

Miniature garden Any tiny garden developed in a planter, window box, terrarium, basin, or similar container. See also **Model garden.**

Minimacid Referring to a lightly acidic soil with a pH of about 6.0. See also **Acid soil, Mediacid, pH.**

Minor element See **Trace element.**

Mirador (Spanish) A window or balcony with a view. Perhaps the most famous mirador is found in the upper gardens of the Generalife in Granada, with a sweeping vista of the city below and the nearby Sierra Nevada.

Mist, fog See **Fog mist.**

Mist head In irrigation, a spray head.

Misting In irrigation, a spray of very fine droplets at the sprinkler head caused by too high a line pressure. See also **Fog mist.**

Miter joint (landscape construction) See **Wood and brick construction joints.**

Miticide A pesticide specifically developed and used to control mite infestations.

Mitosis Basic cell division in biology in which a nucleus splits in half. The cell chromosomes duplicate themselves at the beginning of the process.

Mix, cold (asphalt) See **Cold mix.**

Mix, hot (asphalt) See **Hot mix.**

Mirador. Huning Castle, Albuquerque, New Mexico, 1882. Photo courtesy BBMSL, UNM.

Mix, plant (asphalt) See **Plant mix.**

Moat A ditch full of water traditionally used as a landscape hazard.

Mobilization time In landscape construction, the amount of time needed to order materials, organize crews, and ready equipment to begin work on a job.

Model garden A small-sized plan development exhibit showing a proposed landscape laid out to scale. See also **Miniature garden.**

Modern garden   See **California garden.**

Modular masonry   Loosely, any masonry work involving stones, bricks, blocks, or similar materials, united with mortar to form walls, slabs, pads, or the like.

Modular pavement   Loosely, any sort of pavement using brick, flagstones, cinderblocks, or similar materials set in mortar or sand.

Module   A standard unit of construction or construction material(s) repeatedly used in a design. An anthropomorphic or human module is a criterion for design based on the dimensions of the human body that has been used in varying contexts since ancient times.

Modulus of elasticity   In landscape construction, a measurement of deformation caused by load. The deformation of concrete pavement and asphalt pavement distorted by an equal weight is an example.

Mogul (Mughal) landscape architecture   See **Indian landscape architecture.**

Moist curing (of concrete)   In concrete construction, light sprinkling or wet coverings applied to a newly finished surface to ensure curing at a uniform rate. The weather must be warm for good results with this method. See also **Curing.**

Moisture content (of soil)   The weight of water present in a specific amount of soil.

Moisture gradient   A measure of soil wetness, usually ranging from very dry to very wet. Dry—xeric; moist—mesic; wet—hydric.

Moisture sensor   In irrigation, a mechanism that measures the water content of soil, including its suction. Often used to regulate watering in **Automatic controllers,** q.v. Also **Tensiometer.**

Moisture, soil   See **Soil moisture.**

Mold (mould)   A rich soil composed of fine particles with a large humus content.

Mole   A breakwater laid out from a shoreline to help screen a port or beach from rough seas. Also **Breakwater** and **Jetty.**

Mollet   Name of a French family of gardeners and formal landscape and garden designers of the sixteenth and seventeenth centuries.
  Jacques Mollet (c. 1500s): Chief landscape gardener at the Chateau d'Anet; much involved in the creation of early French formal gardens.
  Claude Mollet (c. 1563–1650): Son of Jacques and royal gardener. Claude designed extensive parterres, but his larger schemes involved layouts uniting house (mansion) and garden as a single composition. During his lifetime, Claude published *Les Jardins de France.* His *Théâtre des Plans et Jardinages* (1652) was published after his death.
  André Mollet, the son of Claude, wrote the highly influential *Jardin de Plaisir* (1651), in which the principles of the formal garden were laid out. Andre worked as royal gardener to both Louis XIII of France and Queen Christina of Sweden. He was the best known formulator of the French pleasure garden, and strongly influenced **Henry Wise** and **George London,** q.q.v, his English contemporaries.
  Claude and **Gabriel Mollet,** of André's generation and later, were also employed as gardeners of note by the English crown.
  See also **French landscape architecture, André LeNotre.**

Molluscicide   A pesticide used against snails and slugs.

Molybdenum   A metallic **Trace element,** q.v., found in most soils, necessary to plant health and growth. See also **Available nutrient, Soil minerals.**

Moment   In the physics of landscape construction, an expression of a force acting upon an object, such as the stress found in a beam responding to twisting or rotation.
  Overturning and **Righting moments** are calculated as necessary requirements for retaining wall construction.

Moment, bending (landscape construction)   See **Bending moment.**

Monastery (monastic) garden   A simple, enclosed garden of the Middle Ages in which herbs and flowers were typically grown. In its expanded form, vineyards, orchards, and field crops were also parts of the monastery garden. The **Convent garden** of the same period is nearly identical in formal layout and purpose. See also **Medieval landscape architecture.**

Monocarpic   In plants, blooming only once in a lifetime, as in the agave or century plant.

Monochromatic   Consisting of only one color. Noun: monochrome. See also **Polychrome.**

Monocolor   One color only.

Monocotyledon (monocot)   A member of the plant subclass *Monocotyledonae.* A plant that produces a single embryonic seed leaf or **Cotyledon,** q.v., at germination. Also **Endogen.** See also **Dicotyledon.**

Monoculture   In agriculture, the cultivation of a single crop, often for cash sale. Most monocultures require the intensive use of **Insecticide(s),** q.v.

Monoecious   In botany, a species in which male (staminate) and female (pistillate) flowers occur in separate structures on the same plant. See also **Dioecious, Hermaphrodite,** and **Polygamous.**

Monolith   A single, massive piece of stone set in a garden, court, or building. Also, a column. Adjective: monolithic.

Monolithic concrete   Concrete poured of a piece—i.e., with only **Construction joints,** q.v. From the Greek "one stone."

Monophyllous   In horticulture, one-leaved.

Monotypic   In horticulture, referring to a genus containing only one species. *Ginkgo biloba* (maidenhair tree) and *Metasequoia glyptostroboides* (dawn redwood) are examples.

Monovular   In flowers, containing a single ovary. See also **Plurovular.**

Montage   A picture or graphic presentation made by arranging different elements or components on a canvas or board.

Montane   Found or originating in the mountains.

Monthly estimate   An estimate of construction work completed during the course of a project, prepared by the landscape architect or landscape contractor. The monthly estimate amounts to a **Pay request,** q.v.

Monthly pay request   See **Pay request.**

Monument   A permanent boundary or survey marker, often a metal stake. Frequently abbreviated Mon.

Monumentation   In surveying, the setting of property boundaries through placement of metal stakes, pins, or monuments.

Monumentality   The design of public works or private memorials on a grandiose scale. Any design whose major function is the evocation of awe or an exaggerated respect in the viewer. The opposite of **Human scale,** q.v.

Moor   An expanse of waste land found in northern temperate areas; a heath; a marsh. See also **Heath.**

Moorish garden or landscape architecture   See **Islamic landscape architecture.**

Mor   A compressed surface layer of forest litter. See also **Duff** and **Slash.**

Moraine   A stony alluvium found at the edge or end of a glacier. Often recreated at a smaller scale as the basis for rock gardens. See also **Rock garden, Scree.**

Morass   A swamp or bog.

Morgen (land measurement)   1) In the Netherlands, a land measure of about 2 acres. 2) In north Germany, Denmark, and Norway, an amount of land equal to approximately $2/3$ acre.

Morphology   In botany, the study of plant form or composition as distinct from function (**Plant physiology,** q.v.). The study of physical plant form.

Mortar   A mixture of lime or cement with water and fine sand, used to bond brick, concrete block, or stone. Also used to secure tile to a prepared, hard surface. See also **Masonry cement.**

Mortar (brick) sand   An extremely fine-grained ($1/8$ in. and less) and uniform sand used to make mortar or to bed bricks. See also **Sand.**

Mortgage lien   See **Lien.**

Mosaic   1) A design or motif often developed in atria and peristyles, especially in classical Rome, composed entirely of colored bits of tile or stone set in a grout matrix. 2) In botany, a viral disease of leaves resulting in spotting and other disfigurement.

Mosaiculture   **Carpet bedding,** q.v.

Moss garden   A small, shaded, humidified garden, usually a **Terrarium,** q.v., in which mosses are prominent.

Moss house   A rusticated Victorian **Garden house,** q.v., in which rough timber walls with live moss placed into the horizontal chinks were prime features.

Moss, peat   See **Peat moss.**

Moss, sphagnum   See **Peat moss.**

Motel   A motor hotel, usually small, relatively inexpensive, and located near heavily traveled roadways. Motel gardens became a new kind of twentieth-century landscape architecture, flourishing along such major U.S. highways as Route 66.

Motte   1) A grove or copse of trees on a plain. 2) In medieval times, a castle mound with steep sides.

Mottling   Patchwork-like in quality; spotted. The bark of the sycamore or plane tree is an example.

Mound   A small hill or bank of earth. Often called a berm in landscape design. See also **Berm.**

Mount   1) In medieval gardens, and in English Renaissance gardens, an artificial hill originally used for surveillance but later developing into a characteristic design feature. The mount is the predecessor of the twentieth-century **Berm,** q.v. Origin: ancient Egypt and Rome. 2) A mountain, usually a peak or dome with a proper name.

Mountain climate   A climate in which altitude and alpine geography are more important than latitude and maritime influence. Mountain climates are found in all regions of the Earth and can be isolates in areas of other types of general climate. See also **Climate.**

Movement, plant   See **Tropism.**

Mower, lawn   See **Lawn mower.**

Mowing strip   A border at grade at the edge of a lawn area designed as an aid to trimming. Mowing strips are often brick, concrete, or stone, and are wide enough to allow one wheel of a reel or two wheels of a rotary mower to pass over smoothly, thus eliminating much subsequent edge trimming. See also **Edging, Header.**

MTD   Abbreviation for **Multiple tile duct,** q.v.

Mucilaginous (plants)   Gluey and wet.

Muck   A combination of water and soil with a large humus content derived from decomposed peat.

Muckland   A peat or similar bog or former bog containing very large amounts of partially decomposed organic matter. Sometimes fertile.

Muck peat   See **Peat moss.**

Mulch   A top-dressing applied to a planting bed to retain moisture, suppress weeds, and provide good color or textural contrast to the rest of a landscape. Also, any naturally occurring layer of plant detritus found on the ground surface. Typical landscape mulches include peat moss, shredded or chipped bark, sawdust, ground corn cobs, pecan shells, grass clippings, pine needles, burlap, straw, and the like. See also **Dust mulch** and **Paper mulch.**

Mulch, dust   See **Dust mulch.**

Mulch, paper   See **Paper mulch.**

Mulch, stubble   See **Stubble mulch.**

Mulch tillage   A soil cultivation that leaves stubble or other cut plant parts as a surface mulch.

Mulga scrub   An acacia scrubland of Western Australia, South Australia, and the Northern Territory. See also **Malee scrub.**

Mull   In a woodland, a composite of finely decomposed organic particles beneath a surface mulch and above the A horizon of soil.

Multiplier   In design contracts, a multiplying factor used with personnel and office expense to arrive at a standard rate of recompense. For example, 2.7 × labor/reimbursable expenditures (the factor 2.7 is commonly used).

Multiple tile duct (MTD)   A kind of duct or pipe made up of joined tile sections.

Mowing strip

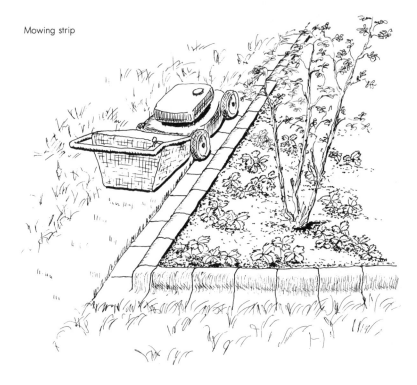

Multitrunk   In trees, having two or more stems. Multitrunk trees are often used as **Specimen** plantings, q.v.

Mumford, Lewis (1895–)   Eminent United States historian and an originator of Radburn planning, an ideal plan of town layout that completely separates pedestrians and vehicles (after the development of the New Town of Radburn, New Jersey following World War I).

Mumford, a prolific author, is a widely read authority on urban planning. He was born and educated in New York City. Among his best-known works are *The City in History* and *The Culture of Cities*.

Municipal bonds   Tax-exempt bonds, often issued by municipalities, to provide funding for capital improvements projects. See also **Financing for public works construction.**

Municipality   A town or city, usually incorporated.

"Murder" (unfair advantage) clause   In specifications or contracts, a sentence or paragraph intended to give an owner or designer unfair advantage over the contractor for a project. A form of lazy or inept specification writing.

Muromachi period (c. 1333–1573)   A nearly prime period of Japanese landscape architectural development, much concerned with the expresion of symbolism and philosophical ideas in the man-made landscape. See also **Japanese landscape architecture.**

Mushrabiyeh (Arabic)   In **Islamic landscape architecture,** q.v., a lattice-screen of wood or stone, often intricately carved.

Muskeg   An arctic or alpine bog, frozen during most of the year, in which mosses, lichens, and similar plants survive in a sodden landscape that cannot drain itself because of permanently frozen subsoil.

Mutagenic   In botany, causing mutation. Noun: mutagenesis.

Mutant   See **Chimaera.**

Mutation   In botany, any plant or plant part that diverges from the norm. Often called a **Sport.**

MW brick   A grade of brick used in landscape construction for wall veneer. See also **SW brick.**

Mycorrhiza   In soils, a beneficial symbiosis of fungi and plant roots.

N

N See **Nitrogen.**

n The coefficient of friction, or resistance to flow, in a channel or pipe.

NAA See **National Arborist Association.**

Nadir The projected low point of arc of the sun's trajectory or angle in the sky. See also **Zenith.**

Nails Multiple nail sizes and types are used in landscape construction. A two penny nail (1 in.) is the smallest commonly used; the 6 in., 60-penny nail is the longest. **Concrete nails** are used to fasten construction items to concrete.
Galvanized nails or **Alloy nails** are most useful in landscape construction because they do not rust and stain.

Name, botanical See **Botanical name.**

Name, generic (of plants) See **Generic name.**

Name, specific (of plants) See **Specific name.**

Name, varietal (of plants) See **Varietal name.**

Names of plants See **Botanical classification.**

Nash, John (1752–1835) English architect and town planner. Nash was a partner of **Humphry Repton** until 1802. His designs include, among others, Buckingham Palace, several seaside pavilions at Brighton, and a house for **Uvedale Price.** However, his greatest fame rests on his pioneering remodel of Marylebone Farm near London into Regent's Park. The idea of developing a series of villas around a naturalistic park foreshadowed the later subdivisions of the nineteenth and twentieth centuries in England and the United States. Regent's Park, with the Prince of Wales as client, generated tremendous popular interest in the picturesque qualities of large-scale planning. See also **English landscape architecture.**

National Arborist Association (NAA) A U.S. organization of consulting arborists.

National Crushed Stone Association (NCSA) A United States landscape supply organization often involved in efforts with the ASLA and other groups aimed at landscape reclamation of quarries and other mining sites.

National Labor Relations Board A United States government agency serving as an intermediary in the settlement of disputes and questions regarding labor and management, including landscape construction problems. Also **NLRB.**

National park In the United States and elsewhere, a large, public park—often highly scenic and isolated—belonging to and operated by the national government.
National parks in the United States are located mostly in the West. They owe their existence largely to the work and influence of Thoreau and of **Frederick Law Olmsted,** q.v. Yosemite and Yellowstone National Parks, both dating from the post-Civil War era, remain the most famous examples.
The modern National Park system was established through the vision and guidance of Stephen Mather, its first director, early in the twentieth century.
See also **State park.**

National Parks Service An agency of the U.S. Department of the Interior charged with the planning and administration of all parks and monuments in the federal park system. Also **NPS.**

Native A plant indigenous to a peculiar locale. See also **Exotic.**

Natural grade See **Grade.**

Natural land type See **Soil association.**

"Natural landscape" 1) A term which implies a land area untouched by the hand of man. No such landscape exists. 2) A rural or wild landscape. 3) A landscape design based on informality of line and tone.

Natural or self-pruning In trees, the natural dying and subsequent loss of branches due to snow weight, wind, decay, and other factors.

Natural planting 1) A planting of curvilinear or informal lines and compositions. 2) A planting using species native or natural to an area.

Natural region A region determined by natural physical and climatological characteristics rather than human political boundaries. See also **Climatic province, Geographic province, Natural vegetation.**

Natural revegetation See **Plant succession, Revegetation.**

Natural vegetation The normally occurring plants of a region unmodified by human tampering.

Natural vegetation balance See **Climax growth.**

Naturalism In landscape design, an attempt to imitate the flow, foliage, and apparent casualness of unspoiled countryside. Modern naturalism arose in eighteenth- and nineteenth-century England, and was partially inspired by newly discovered Chinese and Japanese garden stylizations. Among its most famous practitioners were Kent, Brown, and Repton, who created "natural" large estate plantings. The common modern park form has its origins in their work. See also **English landscape architecture.**

National Park. Grand Teton, Wyoming. Photo by author.

Naturalism. Soros residence, Long Island, New York. Design and photo by A. E. Bye.

Naturalistic garden An informal garden in the English naturalistic style of the eighteenth century. This sort of garden makes use of curvilinear line, tree masses and lawns, water, and careful, soft land shaping. See also **English landscape architecture, Naturalism.**

Naturalized plant In horticulture, a plant not native to a given area that has succeeded by natural means in establishing itself and filling an ecological niche through displacement of an existing species or coexistence with it. An escaped plant **(Escape)** or **Wildling.** See also **Exotic, Native.**

Naturalizing The growing of bulbs and other plants in new environments resembling their natural habitats.

Nature The physical world, including plants, animals, and all the worldly forces that act upon them.

Nature Conservancy A United States conservation society that purchases and protects plant and animal habitat in North America and elsewhere.

Navicular In plant structures, especially leaves, shaped like a boat.

NCSA (United States) The **National Crushed Stone Association,** q.v.

Neat cement Cement and water only in a mixture.

NEC National Electrical Code.

Necropolis (Greek) A graveyard. Especially, a cemetery of Egypt or Greece in antiquity.

Nectary In flowers, the nectar-producing gland or glands.

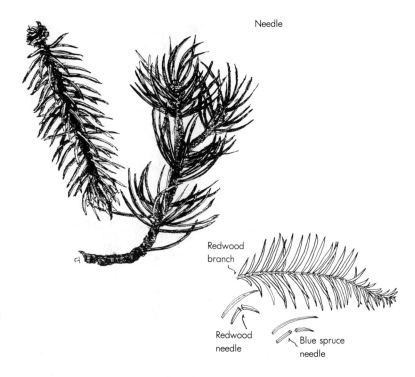

Needle

Redwood branch

Redwood needle

Blue spruce needle

Needle (tree) In botany, a specialized sort of conifer leaf characterized by a roughly cylindrical, long, usually pointed form. Needles are usually shed year-round.

Negentropy In botany, the prevention of the direct loss of captive solar energy by conversion to matter and other processes. See also **Entropy.**

Negligence In landscape architecture, failure to exercise adequate care or precaution to protect the health, safety, and welfare of another person. See also **Tort.**

Negotiated contract In landscape construction, an agreement for site preparation between an owner and a landscape contractor, reached: 1) through discussion and without formal bidding, or 2) after bids have been opened but when a contract may not be awarded by use of standard procedures. The two parties then arrive at an acceptable contract through negotiation. See also **Construction contract.**

Neighborhood 1) A community of people living a large part of their lives in proximity to each other and knowledgeable of the fact that they and their homes and grounds form a special—usually self-protective—group and area. 2) A community of other animals or plants. See also **Community.**

Nematicide An insecticide used against **Nematodes,** q.v., or eelworms.

Nematode In plants, a minute parasitic worm of the class *Nematoda* often found on roots or in surrounding soil. Nematodes are present in almost all soils and are a very common cause of tissue damage. Also **Eelworm.**

Nematology The study of the **Nematode,** q.v., and its effects on plant growth.

Neolithic New Stone Age. A time of the beginnings of agriculture and settlement currently estimated at 10,000 years before the present. The beginnings of the Neolithic coincide with the end of the last Ice Age.

Neon lamp A cold-cathode form of outdoor lighting in which the illumination is produced by electric current shot through neon gas.

Neotype In botany, the typical specimen of a newly-described plant that is used to replace an earlier **Holotype,** q.v., that has vanished or is not available for study. Also **Lectotype.**

Nesfield, William Andrews (1793–1881) British painter and post-Reptonian landscape gardener. Nesfield planned the garden of the Royal Horticultural Society in South Kensington and refined the plan for the great Kew Gardens. In collaboration with the architect **Charles Barry,** q.v., he also designed a large number of Victorian country estates.

Net fill, adjusted See **Adjusted net fill.**

Net positive suction head (NPSH) In irrigation pumps, the positive inlet pressure necessary to ensure a specified pump discharge.

Netting A natural twine or other fabric used as a mesh overlay in planting areas to keep seed in place until germination.

Neutral soil A soil that is neither alkaline nor acidic, with a pH value of about 6.6 to 7.3.

New town A nineteenth- and twentieth-century planned community. New towns are built from scratch, and traditionally feature careful mixes of housing, landscaping, commercial activity, and recreation.

Examples include Radburn, Reston, and Columbia in the United States, Harlow and Stevenage in Britain, and Belmopan in Belize. See also **Ebenezer Howard.**

New Zealand landscape architecture
New Zealand's finest parks are Victorian, dating from the period of intense European settlement beginning in 1840. Christchurch, the modern "garden city" of the South Island, was planned in 1850 to include a botanical garden, a greenbelt, and a **Domain.** Hagley Park, a great central public garden in Christchurch, was planned in 1864. It contains over 200 hectares of greenspace. The botanical gardens themselves, recognized as among the finest in the Southern Hemisphere, have excelled in their propagation and display of the primarily evergreen native plants of the country. Iron bridges over the River Avon and the soft romanticism of the parks along its banks added to the nineteenth-century character of the city. However, most Victorian park and garden plantings in New Zealand were of exotics. Norfolk Island pines, date palms, California

New Zealand landscape architecture. Albert Park, Auckland. Photo by author.

New Zealand landscape
architecture. Albert Park, Auckland.
Photo by author.

redwoods, Australian gums, and
roses were popular on both islands
in the gardens of the day.

The earliest European visitors,
including Captain Cook, had found
well-cultivated Maori gardens in the
Bay of Plenty in the late eighteenth
century. The first orchard in New
Zealand was laid out in the Bay of
Islands near Auckland by the
Reverend John Butler in 1819. By
1835, Darwin was able to describe
widespread plantings of exotics by
missionaries. Tradesmen, government
officials, and plantsmen were not far
behind. John Edgerley, one of the
first nurserymen in the country,
arrived in 1836. George Matthews,
a botanist trained at the botanical
gardens in Edinburgh, settled in
Dunedin (c. 1850). Gardening had

reached a fever pitch of popularity
in Britain at that time, and the
settlers, anxious to plant and
"civilize" the fertile new lands before
them, rapidly created a series of
private and public landscape
gardens on both islands.

A. W. Buxton, who arrived in
1866, was the first landscape
gardener of note to settle in New
Zealand. He designed gardens on
the North and South Islands. He also
established a commercial nursery on
the South Island. Mansion House, a
large estate on Kawau Island, was
created by Sir George Grey starting
in 1862. Sir George was the
governor general of New Zealand,
and he developed his grounds in a
rather eclectic Victorian style and
furnished them with exotic plants and

animals imported from Australia,
South Africa, and elsewhere. His
estate later passed through many
hands and suffered from often
indifferent maintenance; by 1950 it
was in ruins. Restoration and
preservation have been undertaken
in recent years by the New Zealand
Deaprtment of Lands and Survey
and by the Ministry of Works to put
the buildings and gardens back in
condition.

Botanical gardens were also
established in Wellington and
Dunedin in the nineteenth century.
Epsom, the old Government House in
Auckland, had elegant gardens
which perhaps served as an example
for the rest of the country. Auckland
had originally been largely treeless.
Albert Park was laid out on the

grounds of the old Auckland military barracks in 1870. Its iron gazebos, stately fountains, files of Mexican fan palms, and English oaks made it arguably the best example of Victorian park design in the country. Auckland University, its campus lined with plane trees and oaks in the open spaces amid neo-Gothic buildings, handsomely adjoins the park to one side. Old farm gardens, such as those at Chesterhope in Hawke Bay and Holmslea, Rakaia, also preserve the English landscape garden tradition.

The eclectic Government Gardens in Rotorua, arranged around a Tudor-style series of main buildings, have been kept in first-rate condition since the nineteenth century. The fountains in this public park are *steam* fountains, fed by pipes sunk to boiling geyser water beneath the city. Lawn bowls are the great recreation of the park. A larger than life-size statue of Sergeant Fred Wylie of Galatea, killed at Hartebeestefontein in South Africa in 1901 during the Boer War, adds a touch of stony Edwardian poignance to an aloe garden at one side.

Statues of explorers, political figures, or war heroes have continued to be popular in New Zealand's public landscapes in the twentieth century. Whether Queen Victoria or Captain Cook, they are often decked out in the country's ubiquitous white seagulls. But landscape design since World War II has been heavily influenced by the "outdoor room" ideal of the **California garden,** q.v., and by the necessity of training increasing numbers of landscape architects to meet a rising social need. A course in landscape architecture was established in the early 1970s at Lincoln College, Christchurch, by Charlie Challenger and Frank Boffa. The New Zealand Institute of Landscape Architects (NZILA) was founded in 1973. The Queen

Elizabeth II National Trust, a countrywide institution devoted to open space preservation and planning, was also set up in the 1970s. Development of national parks, including the many roadside camps and the tourist village at Mount Cook in the Southern Alps, has proceeded at a rapid clip in the past two decades.

Boffa, Jackman, Miskell and Marsh, Christchurch and Wellington landscape architects, have established the first nationwide practice in New Zealand, receiving commissions in Australia and Malaysia as well. The landscape architect Diane Lucas has concentrated on the rare specialty of rural farm design, with clients primarily in the South Island. In the 1970s, the Australian fountain designer Bob Woodward finished a set of dandelion fountains with pools in front of the Christchurch Civic Hall, a stone's throw away from the Victorian cabbage palms along the Avon. The nature of the work that these landscape architects and others have undertaken indicates an urbanizing New Zealand as interested in the open space quality of its cities as it is proud of the legendary loveliness of its countryside.

See also **Australian landscape architecture.**

Newton, Norman T. Twentieth-century landscape architect, professor, and historian. Newton's comprehensive study of European and United States landscape architecture, *Design on the Land* (1971) has become a standard. Among his projects is the general development plan for the Statue of Liberty National Monument, New York (c. 1937).

NAS A plan abbreviation for National Geodetic Survey (United States).

Niche. Rome: S. Ivo Sapienza Street, fountain and niche. Photo courtesy BBMSL, UNM.

NIC A construction abbreviation indicating that an item is Not In Contract—i.e., not to be included in the contractor's price quotes or items of work.

Niche A recess in a wall in which statuary, a vase, an urn, flowers, or similar objects may be placed. See also **Ecological niche.**

Nickel coating (for steel members) See **Metal coating.**

Night garden A domestic or public garden laid out for the moonlight-and-shadow or lamp-and-shadow effects of nighttime use. A garden designed for night use or enjoyment.

Night soil Human waste used as manure. In the United States and elsewhere, treated as (sewage) **Sludge,** q.v., before use.

Nigrescent In plants, a color shift to black.

Nilus Common classical term for a garden water feature—often a long reflecting pool. From the renowned River Nile. Roman emperors, including Hadrian and others, were fond of this device in their villas.

Nipple In irrigation, a short length of pipe connected to and rising above a service line to feed water to a sprinkler head.

Nitrification The formation in soils or by artificial means of nitrites and nitrates from ammonia.

Nitrogen (N) A nonmetallic element predominant in the atmosphere. One of the three most essential elements for plant growth and health, the others being phosphorus and potassium. Specifically aids in vegetation growth. See also **Complete fertilizer, Macronutrient, NPK.**

Nitrogen cycle The endless fixing and release of nitrogen in the earth's stony crust, its atmosphere, and the plants of sea and land. See also **Carbon cycle, Oxygen cycle.**

Nitrogen fixation A process whereby leguminous or other plants "fix" free atmospheric nitrogen in the soil by means of symbiotic soil organisms, thus making it available for plant use. Lightning and chemical catalysts can also "fix" nitrogen, forming NO or NH compounds. See also **Fixation.**

Nivation In soils, erosion by snow, including freezing and cracking. See also **Solifluction.**

NLRB See **National Labor Relations Board.**

Nocturnal In plants, blooming at night.

Node 1) In horticulture, a stem joint, often swollen, from which new buds, leaves, and limbs will develop. 2) In city planning (loosely), a cluster of activities or physical forms, as in a pedestrian or sidewalk "node," a "node" of houses, and the like.

Noise pollution A severe disturbance caused by traffic or airplane din, the loud operation of machines, poor but clangorous singing, or the like. Sometimes alleviated by **White noise,** q.v.

Noise, white See **White noise.**

Nomenclature, botanical
See **Botanical nomenclature.**

Nomenclature, plant See **Botanical classification, Botanical nomenclature.**

Nominal size 1) Given dimensions of sawn timber or lumber before surfacing and drying. 2) In specifications, the usual or standard measurement for tree caliper, fence height, gate width, irrigation line size, or other items of construction. "Nominal" implies the understanding that individual variation in size may occur but must approximate the measurement given. 3) Reference size. See also **Lumber.**

Noncollusion affidavit In contracting, a sworn statement by a bidder or contractor that he has not connived or colluded with any other contractor or individual in submitting a bid or in obtaining a contract for construction. Also **Collusion affidavit.**

Nonconforming work In landscape specifications and construction, any work that does not comply with project plans and/or specifications.

Nonhabitable structure In landscape architecture, an overhead trellis, colonnade, arbor, gatehouse, gazebo, or other item of building that is not used to house people.

Nonloadbearing wall
See **Freestanding wall.**

Nonpoint pollution Water, soil, or air pollution coming from an unknown source.

Nonpotable water Undrinkable water.

Nonpressure treatment (of wood) Any wood preservative applied by brushing, soaking, spraying, or similar means. Usually a "light duty" treatment. See also **Wood preservative.**

Nonsaline, alkaline soil A soil containing large amounts of exchangeable sodium. The sodium interferes with plant growth, but lacks soluble salts. pH usually 8.5–10.0. See also **Alkaline soil** and **Soil.**

Nonselective herbicide or pesticide A chemical preparation that indiscriminately destroys multiple species of plants or insects.

North American Indian landscape architecture See **Mexican landscape architecture, United States landscape architecture.**

Norwegian landscape architecture See **Scandinavian landscape architecture.**

Not-to-exceed fee See **"Upset" fee.**

Not-to-Scale (NTS) A note sometimes found on landscape construction detail drawing.

Notice of award In landscape construction, a written notice supplied by an owner to a successful bidder stating the owner's intention to enter into a contract for construction with the contractor as soon as the contractor fulfills the appropriate conditions regarding bonding, insurance, and the like set forth in the project specifications.

Notice to bidders See **Information for bidders.**

Notice to proceed A written notification to a landscape contractor prepared by an owner or the owner's landscape architect after a construction contract has been signed. The notice to proceed formally requires the landscape contractor to begin work on a project, and is usually the starting date of the construction contract. Also **Work order.**

Novation The substitution of a different agreement between two original parties to a contract or between an original and a third (or more) party.

Nozzle In irrigation, a spout attached to a hose or the discharger inside a sprinkler head.

Nozzle, fixed spray See **Fixed spray nozzle.**

Nozzle line In irrigation, an above-grade steel or other metal line that is punched or drilled for nozzle inserts. Also **Skinner line.**

Nozzle, low-angle (irrigation) See **Low-angle nozzle.**

Nozzle pressure See **Flow pressure.**

NPK Scientific abbreviations for nitrogen, phosphorus, and potassium, the three elements chiefly responsible for plant growth and health. See also **Nitrogen, Phosphorus, Potassium.**

NPS See **National Park Service.**

NPSH (irrigation) **Net positive suction head,** q.v.

NTS An abbreviation for **Not to Scale,** often found on landscape construction detail drawings.

Nuisance Legally, a disruption which causes a physical discomfort to a landowner. See also **Tort.**

Nullah (India) A dry streambed. See also **Arroyo, Wadi.**

Nurse crop See **Cover Crop.**

Nursery In horticulture, a plant-growing and display house.

Nursery stock, planting stock Young plants raised and sold in nurseries. See also **Transplanting.**

Nut A relatively large, one-seeded, hard-coated, often edible fruit. See also **Indehiscence.**

Nutrient, available See **Available nutrient.**

Nutrient, plant See **Plant foods.** See also **Available nutrient, Macronutrient, Trace element.**

Nyctinasty In plants, a response to a systematic, artificial variation of light and dark periods.

Nymphaeum In classical Greece, a grotto sacred to nymphs. In Rome, a water garden with nearby **Casinos** or pavilions.

NZILA New Zealand Institute of Landscape Architects.

O

Oak   An extremely durable temperate-zone hardwood, sometimes used for outdoor furniture, fittings, and other construction. Oak trees are also widely planted in man-made landscapes and are slow-growing and long-lived.

Oasis   A fertile area in a desert, made productive by the presence of a spring or springs.

Oasis

Obelisk   An upright, plane-sided, tapering pillar, often monolithic and ending in a pyramidal point. Egyptian in origin.

Obovate   In leaves, an oval or egg shape, with the wider end near the apex. See also **Ovate.**

Observation site   See **Site inspection.**

OC   See **On Center.**

Occidental   Western.

Oceanic climate   See **Maritime climate.**

Oceanography   The study and exploration of the seas and oceans.

OD (outside diameter)   In irrigation and general landscape construction, an outside pipe measurement taken usually in inches and decimals of an inch. OD measurements are standard regardless of pipe material. See also **ID.**

Occult (informal) balance   In landscape architecture, an odd and subtle rhythm of object and line which is nevertheless perceived to be harmonious and beautiful. "Natural" or asymmetrical balance or design. Occult balance is a highly refined characteristic of Oriental landscapes and has been incorporated into Western landscapes with success in recent historic times. See also **Chinese landscape architecture, Freeform,** and **Symmetry.,**

Occupational Safety and Health Administration (or Act) (U.S.)   See **OSHA.**

Off-grade lumber   In landscape construction, any lumber not meeting designated quality standards. See also **Lumber.**

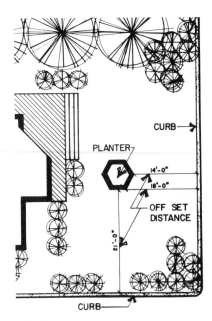

Offset distance

Offscape   Sometimes used to describe the area of which the local landscape or garden is a part. Sometimes the **Borrowed landscape,** q.v.

Offset   In horticulture, a new plant developing naturally from a side stem.

Offset dimensioning   See **Offset distance.**

Offset distance   A dimension recorded on a plan which shows the location of a site feature as measured from a curb, building wall, or other reference point.

Oil, logwood   See **Logwood oil.**

Oil, road   See **Road oil.**

Oil-borne preservative   Any of several wood preservatives useful in most landscape construction. Oil-borne preservatives are not

recommended for woods in contact with sea water. See also **Wood preservative.**

Old landscape   See **Peneplane.**

Old stream   See **Mature stream.**

Old wood   In horticulture, part of a tree, shrub, or vine that has aged at least a year and developed woody tissue.

Oldham, John and Ray   John Oldham, twentieth-century Australian architect and landscape architect, and Ray Oldham, writer, authors of *Gardens in Time* (1980), a history of landscape architecture in which they argue that Western landscape design is more fundamentally Asiatic in origin and continuing form than previously supposed.

John Oldham is a pioneer Australian landscape architect perhaps best known for his masterplan and detailed design of Perth Water (1954–present), an integrated series of botanic gardens, parks, zoological gardens, hospital grounds, parliamentary grounds, and freeway interchange landscaping at the Swan River estuary in Perth, Western Australia. John Oldham also designed the Australian pavilion at the New York World's Fair in 1939 and the grounds of multiple dam sites in Western Australia. Oldham supervised new town design for the Snowy Mountains Hydroelectric Authority and served as Government Landscape Architect in Western Australia from 1956–72. Oldham is a Fellow of the (British) Institute of Landscape Architects, and a Corresponding Member of the ASLA.

John and Ray Oldham are also authors of *Western Heritage I: A Study of the Colonial Architecture of Perth, Australia,* and of *Western Heritage II: George Temple-Poole: Architect of the Golden Years 1885–1897.* See also **Australian landscape architecture.**

John Oldham. Australian landscape architect. Photo courtesy John Oldham.

Ray Oldham. Australian landscape historian. Photo courtesy John Oldham.

Olericulture   Vegetable cultivation.

Olfactory   Pertaining to smell or the sense of smell.

Oligotrophic   A term describing lakes or ponds when they are low in available food and therefore only marginally able to support life.

Olmsted, Frederick Law (1822–1903)   United States landscape architect, journalist, and social visionary, founder of the profession of landscape architecture in North America, and designer of Central Park, the campus of Stanford University in California, and the pioneer "planned suburb" of Riverside, Illinois.

Olmsted was born in Connecticut, the son of a well-to-do merchant, and attended Yale University. He dabbled at different lines of work in early life, laboring as a farmer, a surveyor, a bookkeeper, and, remarkably, a journalist. His study of the antebellum South, *The Cotton Kingdom* (1861), became an American classic. Olmsted visited England with two friends in 1850, a journey he described in the subsequent *Walks and Talks of an American Farmer in England*. It was a turning point in his life. He toured the newly completed Birkenhead Park in Liverpool (see **Joseph Paxton**), observing first-hand the novel idea of a public garden serving the factory workers of the Industrial Revolution, and hiked at leisure through the English countryside, chatting with farmers.

Back in the United States, Olmsted formed a partnership with the English architect **Calvert Vaux,** q.v., in 1858 to prepare a plan for a new park in New York City. Vaux had previously practiced landscape gardening with **A. J. Downing,** q.v. Downing for years had lobbied for a new public garden in New York City with the journalist William

Frederick Law Olmsted

Cullen Bryant. The enabling legislation had finally been passed by the New York Board of Aldermen in 1853. The winning design for the new Central Park was Olmsted and Vaux's "Greensward." The park plan anticipated the city's future growth and made allowances for it. It separated pedestrians and vehicles by grade changes, provided playgrounds, parade grounds, and a mall for strolling and socializing, bridle paths, lakes for boating, and great expanses of woods and lawns. There was an endless variety of other activities as well—all laid out in a fresh mix of formality and naturalism determined by the nature of each park function. Central Park was a turbulent but instant success,

and the beginning of American landscape architecture. Olmsted himself was the first person in the United States to use the term (one or two Scots probably had employed it first) and to popularize it.

After Central Park, Olmsted produced a steady stream of often brilliant projects until the turn of the century. Prospect Park in Brooklyn, constructed between 1865 and 1888, is arguably the most lyrical of these—subtle, refined, and romantically aloof. It was designed in high English Landscape School style.

Olmsted's evolving urban park and open space criteria planning included systematic landscaping around public buildings, a large rural park on the city fringe, and a series of squares and small parks—as well as neighborhood and local parks—scattered throughout a city. Proper public garden development would also include a great "central park" and connecting avenues and parkways linking various sections of a city.

Olmsted served as Secretary of the U.S. Sanitary Commission (a predecessor of the American Red Cross) during the Civil War and became concerned with the growing problems of sanitation and sewage plaguing nineteenth-century cities. The development of Olmsted's public open spaces (some 1,000 or so parks in cities across the nation) as healthy answers to the basic difficulties of urban life paralleled the rise in sanitation engineering that contributed greatly to the improved public health of the day.

By 1865, Olmsted had proposed a series of national and state park systems, as well as wilderness, to be established as great reserves for the American future. Yosemite and Yellowstone National Parks were among the first products of this idea. Urban park and greenway systems were also among his best innovations. After moving his office from New York City to Brookline, Massachusetts in 1883, he worked on a unified scheme for the Fens and the Back Bay of Boston. (**Charles N. Eliot,** q.v., an associate in Olmsted's office, carried the idea of unification further by organizing the **Trustees for Public Reservations** in 1890 to preserve open space and historic landscapes in Boston and environs.) One of Olmsted's finest designs, the bucolic Franklin Park in Boston (1880s), was completed during his early years in Brookline.

Olmsted's collaboration with **Daniel Burnham,** q.v., and other designers of the World's Columbian Exposition in Chicago (1893) marked a shift in Olmsted's work from

"democratic naturalism" toward Beaux Arts formalism and monumentality. Olmsted's estate design at Biltmore, Asheville, North Carolina in 1896 set the standard for the design of **Country places,** q.v., through the 1930s.

Olmsted and his sometime partner Vaux were influential in Canada as well as the United States. Olmsted and Vaux designed Mount Royal Park in Montreal (1873–81) and the grounds of Parliament in Ottawa, 1873, for which Vaux was primarily responsible.

The Olmsted office itself continued to practice through J. C. Olmsted, Frederick's nephew, and other successors until 1954. Modern appreciation of Olmsted's work is growing. There is a National Association of Olmsted Parks contributing to the preservation and restoration of Olmsted's public projects. Multiple new biographies describe the man and his art. Unquestionably the most influential and arguably the most illustrious of American landscape architects, Olmsted is now perhaps more an institution than a man in American landscape architecture. See also **United States landscape architecture.**

On center (OC)   A term used to indicate the distance from center point to center point of posts, trees, shrubs, ground covers, irrigation heads, and the like. "OC" often implies triangulation of center points.

One-fourth head (irrigation)   See **Quarter head.**

One-third head   In irrigation, a shrub or lawn head that emits a nozzle spray of approximately 120°, covering 1/3 of a circle in area. See also **Head.**

On center

Ontogeny   In botany, the life development of a plant. Individual life history. Evolutionary history is **Phylogeny,** q.v.

Open bidding   In the letting of contracts, an arrangement whereby a project owner allows the submission of bids or proposals by all qualified contractors. Nearly always used in contracting for government work. See also **Invitational bidding.**

Open pollination   In horticulture, the production of seed through uncontrolled fertilization by wind, insects, or the like.

Open space   As a landscape design concept, a relatively clear or forested area left untouched in or near a city. Open space, unsullied by the stigma of a formally assigned function, is necessary for the physical and mental health of city-dwelling human beings.

Open traverse (surveying)   See **Traverse.**

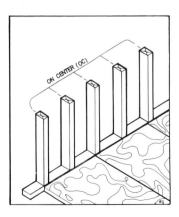

Operating pressure (irrigation)
1) The pressure at a given section within an irrigation system when the system is operating. 2) A recommended functioning pressure for an irrigation system. If operating pressure is exceeded, the system may be damaged by **Surge** or **Water hammer,** q.v. Also **Working pressure.**

Operating zone In irrigation, a section in use. See **Section system.**

Oporotheca (Greek) In classical Rome, a "fruit room" modeled on Greek originals.

Optimum, autoecological or synecological See **Autoecological optimum** or **Synecological optimum.**

Optimum density In landscape construction, the degree of soil **Compaction** required for landscape structures, planting, and the like. In the United States and elsewhere, expressed as a Modified Proctor rating, often of 90%–95% of maximum for pavement and structures and 85% for planted areas.

Opus sectile Angular but crazy-quilt pavements of cut marble.

"Or equal" specification Any specification that allows approved substitutions of contract items during project bidding or construction.

Orangery In seventeenth-century England, a stone or brick building with a translucent roof used as a greenhouse. Also **Orangerie.**

Oratorio In Spanish America and the southwestern United States, a small private chapel near or in a patio or garden.

Orbicular In plant—especially leaf—structures, circular.

Orchard A systematic plantation of fruit or nut trees.

Order In botany, a subclass or tertiary taxonomic classification of plant type. See also **Botanical classification.**

Order, change See **Change order.**

Order, field See **Field order.**

Order, soil See **Soil classification.**

Order, work See **Notice to proceed.**

Ordnance survey A highly detailed geographical survey made for government (specifically, military) use.

Ordnance survey datum line Mean sea level, q.v.

Organ, water See **Water organ.**

Organic 1) Containing plant or animal material—i.e., exhibiting hydrocarbons. 2) In design, a form or plan that utilizes wild or naturally occurring—especially informal—materials or shapes. See also **Inorganic.**

Organic fertilizer Animal manure or compost added to a soil to increase its fertility. See also **Chemical fertilizer, Complete fertilizer, Fertilizer.**

"Organic" gardening Gardening without chemical fertilizers, pesticides, or herbicides. Organic gardening uses the amendment of soil by humus-producing materials and animal manures as well as considerable surface mulching to improve deficient soils or increase the productivity of good soils and to hold in moisture, and is an ancient form of agriculture.

Organic material in the soil Any decomposing plant or animal remains found in soil. **Humus,** q.v., or humus-producing material.

Organic silt A silty deposit in which most of the particles are composed of animate matter. A lake or sea-bottom silt.

Organic soil A soil such as peat that is composed almost entirely of plant or animal material.

Oriental Eastern.

Oriental landscape architecture See **Central Asian landscape architecture, Chinese landscape architecture, Islamic landscape architecture, Japanese landscape architecture, Middle Eastern landscape architecture.**

Orifice In irrigation, the hole in a nozzle or fountain jet through which water streams.

Ornamental A plant generally employed for its design value or color. See also **Flowering ornamental.**

Ornamental, flowering See **Flowering ornamental.**

Ornamental horticulture The cultivation of trees, shrubs, flowers, and other plants, primarily for landscape amenity and not food-producing purposes. A plant thus grown is called an "ornamental."

Ornithon In Roman times, an aviary modeled after Greek originals. Popular in villa gardens for both profit and pleasure.

Orographic rainfall Rainfall caused by moisture-bearing clouds striking mountain ranges, particularly ranges standing at right angles to the winds carrying the clouds. A highly localized kind of rain. See also **Rain shadow, Rainfall.**

Ortet The parent plant of a variety or clone.

Orthogenesis The ongoing evolutionary tendency common to related kinds of plants or animals.

Orthogonal Right-angled.

OSHA An acronym and abbreviation for Occupational Safety and Health Administration (or Act), a U.S. government agency charged with ensuring on-the-job health and safety conditions nationwide.

Orthostichy (botany)
    See **Phyllotaxy.**

Osmosis The passage of pure water or water containing salts, sugars, or other substances in solution through cell tissue or membranes due to unequal pressure. The passage of liquid will continue until a balance is reached. Osmotic pressure is a principal basis of sap flow through plant vascular tissue.

Outdoor air conditioning A term used to describe the functional arrangement of trees, fences, lawns, shrubs, water curtains, pools, and the like for purposes of air cooling, wind control, and filtration of suspended pollutants and odors.

Outdoor furnishings See **Outdoor furniture.**

Outdoor furniture Items of furnishing in outdoor landscape, including many pieces of common street furniture plus chairs, tables, barbecue grilles, and other furniture generally found in residential landscapes. See also **Street furniture.**

Outdoor room. Strybing Arboretum. Photo courtesy Leslie Allen.

Outdoor lighting The illumination by means of luminaires of playing fields, streets, houses, parks, highways, and the like for safety, enjoyment, and extended usefulness.

Outdoor room A garden segment designed for casual dining, reading, companionship, or the enjoyment of a vista. Outdoor rooms are usually furnished with tables, chairs, shade structures or trees, and cooking accessories. The floor is brick, concrete, wood decking, stone, tile, or the like; the "walls" are fences, hedges, or screens; the ceilings are overhead structures, the underside of a leaf canopy, or the sky itself.

The outdoor room helps to make the landscape for which it is designed highly functional. It was popularized by **Thomas Church** as part of the **California garden,** q.q.v., in the 1930s and 1940s, and has since been refined by Garrett Eckbo, Douglas Baylis, Robert Royston, Theodore Osmondson, Guy R. Johns, and others.

Outdoor space Any area not enclosed by a structure; the basic raw material of landscape architecture.

Outlet   A point or structure of discharge for surface or piped water. There are two general types: 1) **Gravity outlet:** operates by a slight pipe gradient and the simple pull of gravity. 2) **Pump outlet:** gravity-collected water is pumped out of a cavity constructed at this outlet. See also **Access structure.**

Outline of construction procedure   See **Progress schedule.**

Outline specifications   Brief, "skeletal," general and/or technical specifications, often developed during the **Schematic** or **Design development phases,** q.q.v., of a project.

Outside diameter (of pipe)   See **OD.**

Ovary   In flowers, an enclosed cavity containing ovules or unfertilized seed structures. Ovaries become fruit after fertilization.

Ovate   In leaves, an oval or egg shape with the broader end toward the stem. See also **Obovate.**

Overburden   In landscape construction, the soil or rock strata lying on top of a proposed new grade (finish grade) to be removed during the course of site improvement.

Overhead   1) A trellis-like structure, often found in gardens or parks, that serves as an outdoor shelter from sun, glare, wind, rain, and the like. See also **Lath, Pergola, Post and beam construction, Trellis.** 2) In design office accounting, the costs of operation that must be included in the calculation of a fee.

Overhead plane   In landscape design, the lower side of a tree canopy, trellis, awning, or other construct that functions as the ceiling of an outdoor space. Sometimes the sky itself.

Overland flow time   In site drainage, the amount of time necessary for a quantity of water falling on the remotest part of a site to reach the collecting ditch, drain, or other central component of the storm collection system. See also **Drainage, Inlet time.**

Overlap   In irrigation, spacing distance between lawn or other heads that determines the efficiency of coverage. A percentage of the coverage diameter of single heads establishes the degree of overlap.

Overlay, asphalt   See **Asphalt overlay.**

Overpass   A sky bridge by means of which an elevated road or railway passes over a street or highway.

Overpotting   1) The placement of a small plant in a pot or other container too large for it. 2) In landscape construction, the furnishing of a smaller-than-standard plant in a container larger than necessary for its size in order to meet (incomplete) specification requirements.

Oversailing course   In a stone or brick wall, a course protruding beyond the course below it. Usually developed in a series.

Overstory   Trees or large shrubs. The large, dominant group of plants that forms the highest canopy in a plant community.

Overturning moment   See **Moment.**

Ovicide   An insecticide developed for use against insect eggs.

Ovoid   In horticulture, the egg shape of certain bulbs and fruits.

Ovule   In flowers, a tiny female reproductive structure that becomes a seed after being fertilized.

Owner   The person, persons, company, or agency by whose mandate plans and specifications are prepared or consultation is provided and for whom a project is executed. The owner is sometimes called the contracting agency (public works construction). See also **Client** and **User.**

Ox-bow lake   See **Billabong.**

Oxisol   A humid, aged, tropical soil, normally reddish; developed in rain forests.

Oxygen   The most important atmospheric gas to animals, produced by plant photosynthesis. Over 20% by volume of the atmosphere, and approximately 50% by weight of the rock in the Earth's mantle. It is widely thought that prehistoric oxygen was a poison given off by early plants, and that as its volume increased life forms of necessity began to use it in metabolism. Presently it is indispensable to 95% + of the Earth's life forms.

Oxygenator   In pools, an underwater plant grown for its oxygen-producing abilities. Oxygen production and subsequent infusion into the water is oxygenation.

P   See **Phosphorus.**

Package dealer (project development)   See **Turnkey project.**

Paddle ball   A court game similar to tennis but smaller in scale popular in the twentieth-century United States and elsewhere.

Paddock   A pasture, grazing field, or large corral.

Pagoda   An oriental temple with a pyramid-like form, or a garden structure similar in shape and feeling to such a temple.

Pair, stereo (aerial photography)   See **Photogrammetry.**

Pakistani landscape architecture   See **Indian landscape architecture.**

Paleaceous   In plant structures, chaff-like and thin.

Paled fence   See **Paling.**

Paleobotany   The study of ancient, or fossil, botany.

Paleoclimatology   The study of ancient climates through investigation of evidence found in sedimentary strata. See also **Climatology.**

Paleoecology   Ancient ecology.

Paleogeography   The study of ancient geographic conditions.

Paling   Vertical stave fencing; enclosure. Also **Paled fence.**

Palissy, Bernard   Seventeenth-century French garden designer, noted for his work at the Ecouen gardens of the Duc de Montmorency and at the Tuileries. Palissy's early French Renaissance design geometry would be refined to an ultimate expression by **André le Notre,** q.v.

Palladio, Andrea (1508–80)   Renaissance architect and author of the *Four Books of Architecture* (1570). The neoclassical stylizations of Palladio heavily influenced European architecture, and began to appear with regularity in the grounds of British and American estates from the eighteenth century onward. The style is Palladianism.

Palletized stone   Building stone carefully arranged on wood pallets for ease of sale, transport, and use.

Palliative, dust   See **Dust palliative.**

Palm house   A specially planned greenhouse used to display palms. The first palm house was erected at Kew Gardens in England by 1848. Modern palm houses are more generalized, and have been designed as portions of larger conservatories. The conservatory at the Denver Botanical Gardens in Colorado is an example.

Palmate   In botany, a leaf form of radiating divisions. Fan palms are typical examples. See also **Pinnate.**

Palmate form. Mexican fan palms (*Washingtonia robusta*) along the edge of a park. Photo courtesy Morrow and Company.

Parcourse

Palustrine   Pertaining to a plant of wetlands or marshy areas.

Palynology   Pollen analysis, q.v., especially of fossil spores. See also **Landscape archaeology.**

Pampa   A temperate South American grassland.

PAN (peroxyacetyl nitrate)   See **Air pollution.**

Pan   1) A shallow, hard earth basin that fills periodically with water. Often clayey. 2) An extremely hard soil layer. See also **Caliche, Hardpan.**

Pan garden   See **Miniature garden.**

Pan, iron   See **Iron pan.**

Pan, plow   See **Plow pan.**

Panicle   A more or less pyramidal flower structure with "branches" and blossoms emerging in sequence from bottom to top or outside to inside. Any multiple-branched, compound inflorescence. A kind of **Raceme,** q.v. Adjective: paniculate.

Pannose   In plants, displaying multiple tiny interlocking hairs.

Panorama   An expanded vista or view of wide proportions. Especially, a remarkable, broad view.

Pantograph   In design drawing, an extendable mechanical arm (measuring tool) used to proportionately increase or decrease (blow up, reduce) the scale of a plan or other item.

Paper, kraft   See **Tree wrapping.**

Paper mulch   Long strips of paper laid on the surface of a row or other planting to inhibit weed growth and hold moisture. See also **Mulch.**

Papilla   In leaf structures or stems, a small bump or projection. A typical papilla flower is the sweet pea.

Parade ground   An extensive, flat military marching or riding ground. Also **Campus.**

Paradeisos (Persian)   A hunting park—i.e., a royal garden. Source of the English "paradise."

Paradise (paradise garden)   1) A monastery garden or graveyard. See **Parvis.** 2) A courtyard with an **Ambulatory,** q.v., roundabout. 3) Paradise garden: In Moorish or Islamic gardens, a symmetrical courtyard divided into four parts by "streams" issuing from a central fountain. The four-piece arrangement represents the four sections of heaven, and is Persian in origin. See also **Persian landscape architecture.**

Paralic   Pertaining to tidewater pools or lagoons and their surroundings. See also **Limnic.**

Parallel planes method (earthwork)   See **Cut and fill.**

Parapet   A defensive or protective wall or other structure at the top of a rise or building.

Parasite   A plant species such as mistletoe that attaches itself to a tree or shrub and is sustained by the sap of its host. See also **Saprophyte.**

Paratechnician   In landscape architectural practice, a person with two years of study or its equivalent who serves a design office and its clients as a semiprofessional aide. Infrequently used.

Parcours or **parcourse**   In landscape design, a series of "exercise (gymnastic) stations" located alongside a running trail, allowing athletes to perform planned calisthenics in conjunction with their running. Also **Trim trail.**

Parent material   Solid stone or large fragments of it which weathers to produce, with other materials, a soil.

Parent stem   In woody plants, the main tree or shrub trunk.

Parge   In drop inlet, catch basin, and other construction, a cementitious or mortar coating over brickwork, concrete block courses, or the like. Also **Backplaster.**

Pargetting   1) An old and intricate form of scrollwork formerly used as building or structural decorations in rural Europe (medieval, Renaissance, modern). 2) The application of a **Parge,** q.v., to the surface of masonry courses. Also **Parging.**

Park   A distinct and pleasant natural or man-made area, usually with trees and some lawns associated, that is admired and used for its scenic and recreational qualities. Often, in Western thought, a small, idealized bit of paradise. See also **Frederick Law Olmsted** and **Humphry Repton.**

Park, car   See **Car park.**

Park, country   See **Country park.**

Park forest   An open forest with grasses as a conspicuous ground cover.

Park, industrial   See **Industrial park.**

Park, national   See **National park.**

Park, pocket   See **Vest pocket park.**

Park, provincial (Canada)
   See **Provincial park.**

Park, state   See **State park.**

Park, theme   See **Theme park.**

Park, trailer or mobile home
   See **Trailer park.**

Park, vest pocket   See **Vest pocket park.**

Parking   A paved or unpaved area set aside for the stationing of automobiles. An overwhelming twentieth-century design constraint.

Parking lot   The scourge of twentieth-century urban design. A surface area used for the temporary stationing of automobiles. Extremely difficult to integrate into a landscape, an adequately designed parking lot contains bays of about 10 ft. × 20 ft. (3.3 m × 6.7 m) in size as well as generous entries, exits, and back-up spaces.

Parking lots. Photos courtesy Morrow and Company.

Pargetting

Parkway. Photo by author.

Parkway 1) A low-speed road laid through a garden or park-like landscape, usually with median and roadside plantings. The first American parkways were developed by Olmsted and Vaux in Central Park, New York City, and elsewhere; their immediate European precedent is the shaded French boulevard. 2) More narrowly, a planted strip between a curb and sidewalk.

Parmentier, Andre (d. 1830)
    United States landscape gardener and nurseryman, born in Enghien, Belgium. Parmentier set up a successful nursery in Brooklyn in 1824. He included an essay on landscape design in his stock catalog of 1828 that promoted the development of the naturalistic garden.
    Parmentier designed the grounds of several estates along the Hudson River, including Hosack's Estate and, probably, Hyde Park. He founded an early botanical garden in Brooklyn in 1825. His informal landscapes influenced **Andrew Jackson Downing,** q.v., and are roughly contemporary with the design and development of Monticello, in Virginia. See also **Thomas Jefferson.**

Parlor garden In eighteenth-century New England, a small pleasure garden laid out for casual viewing from the dining room or parlor of a house.

Parquet A type of wood flooring consisting of short segments or blocks arranged in patterns. Sometimes, in landscape architecture, a patio or wood deck.

Parquetry Intricate stone pavements laid out in inset-block patterns of opposing grains.

Parsons, Samuel H., Jr. (1844–1923) U.S. landscape architect, educated at Yale University, from which he graduated in 1862, and partner of **Calvert Vaux** from 1880–1895. Parsons, a cofounder of the ASLA, was noted for his Beaux Arts parks design for the City of New York and other clients. Parsons described many of his projects in *Landscape Gardening Studies* (1910).

Part-circle head In irrigation, a spray head of 270° (three-quarter) or less. Most common sizes: 1) **Quarter head**—90°. 2) **One third head**—120°. 3) **Half head**—180°. 4) **Three quarter head**—270°. Special spray arcs are also obtainable from manufacturers.

Parterre (French) A formally laid out planter, often a box at ground level, but sometimes raised by means of masonry or wood borders. A **parterre de broderie** (French baroque) is an elaborate "curlecue" flower or clipped shrub bed. Parterre gardens were normally developed with gravel or other paths for circulation, and date from late medieval and Renaissance times. The rules of their creation were formalized by **André Mollet,** q.v., and brought to perfection by **Le Notre,** q.v. See also **Bedding plan, Knot garden,** q.q.v.

Parterre. Boboli Gardens, Florence, c. 1550. Photo courtesy BBMSL, UNM.

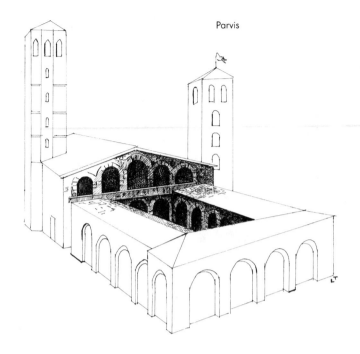

Parvis

Parthenocarpy The generation of infertile fruit—i.e., fruit without seeds. The banana is an example.

Parthenogenesis In botany, the very rarely occurring reproduction of a plant by means of a female flower producing fertile seed without male pollination. The common fig (*Ficus carica*) is an example.

Partnership In landscape architecture, a legally defined relationship in which two or more persons agree to jointly offer services and consultation as a business for profit.

Parts per million (PPM) A measurement of solutions.

Party wall A boundary wall set between two properties and common to both.

Parvis In medieval Europe, a church square or entry area, normally enclosed. Possibly from *Paradisus* or *Paradeisos*.

Passive space (in parks) An area used by park visitors for observation, conservation, quiet picnicking, reading, chess, or other quiet, inactive pastimes.

Pastoral Relating to rural life or settings and/or shepherds.

Pastoral farming The raising and breeding of hooved grazing animals for sustenance or profit. An ancient form of agriculture, often involving nomadic wandering from winter to summer or wet season to dry season pastures.

Pastoral landscape A romantic landscape of rolling hills, grassy slopes and dells, tranquil low-lying pools, and quaint structures, usually associated with the gardens of the eighteenth-century English Landscape School. A true pastoral landscape is used for grazing livestock. See also **English landscape architecture, English School of Landscape Gardening,** and **Pastoral farming.**

Pasture A field thickly covered with grass for grazing animals.

Patent lands Lands granted to a specific person or persons, or to a public agency, for an indicated use.

Pasture. A pasture in a gorge in the Sultanate of Oman. Photo courtesy Steve Borbas.

Patio. Garrett Eckbo, landscape architect. Photo by author.

Patent, plant   See **Plant patent.**

Path   A small trail intended for foot, bicycle, or horse traffic, or created by that traffic.

Path, bridle   See **Bridle path** and **Riding.**

Path, "desire"   See **Desire path.**

Patina   A film or light surface coloring or crust on metal surfaces, polished stone surfaces, glass, or the like.

Patio (Moorish>Spanish)   In Spain, Spanish America, the United States, and elsewhere, a fully or partially enclosed outdoor area—usually a courtyard—of a house or other building, used extensively for informal outdoor living.

Patio tree   A small-scale tree intended for shade, fruit production, or aesthetic enjoyment. Normally no taller than a single story.

Patte d'oie (French)   In French gardens or city design, a radiating goosefoot pattern of three streets or paths.

Pattern bond   The design pattern created by the combination of bricks or blocks and mortar seams in a wall or pavement.

Pattern, drainage   See **Drainage pattern.**

Pattern, grid   See **Gridiron.**

Pattern, pavement   See **Pavement pattern.**

Pattern, spray (irrigation)   See **Spray pattern.**

Pattern, sprinkler   See **Sprinkler pattern.**

Patulous   In trees or shrubs, referring to a spreading root or branch system.

Paved flume   An inclined, solid channel of concrete, masonry, or asphalt.

Pavement   Surfacing. A finish course of hard material used for walking, vehicle travel, structural support, and the like. Also **Paving.**

Pavement, flexible   See **Flexible pavement.**

Pavement, impressed concrete   See **Impressed concrete pavement.**

Pavement, modular   See **Modular pavement.**

Pavement pattern   A combination of pavement materials (brick, stone, concrete, gravel, and the like) and the visible design of their layout. Pavement patterns are used to suggest traffic flow, to emphasize larger landscape features such as statues or fountains, to unify a design, to create a pleasant walking sensation, and for other related purposes.

Pavement planting   In gardens, a planting of sedums, thymes, or other low herbs in the joints between flagstones or other pavement stones.

Pavement, rigid   See **Rigid pavement.**

Pavement, soft   See **Soft pavement.**

Paver brick   A hard-fired, tightly grained brick used for landscape paving because of its special resistance to weathering and wear.

Pavement pattern. Photo by author.

Pavilion 1) A fancy tent, especially a tent erected for jousting or celebration in medieval Europe. 2) A summer house or **Gazebo**, q.v.

Paving See **Pavement**.

Paving, asphalt See **Asphaltic concrete**.

Paving brick See **Paver brick**.

Paving, crazy See **Crazy paving**.

Paving unit A modular building material used to surface an area of ground. Brick, concrete block, and granite setts are common paving units.

Paver-brick pattern Paver bricks are laid in multiple patterns in sand or brick mortar. Among the most frequently found patterns are these: 1) **Soldier course:** Bricks laid as **Stretchers** with parallel lengthwise- and cross-joints. 2) **Running bond:** A stretcher bond layout with the joints of every other row occurring in the middle of the bricks of the adjacent row. Probably the most common paver pattern. 3) **Herringbone:** Diagonally laid coursework creating a zigzag pavement pattern. 4) **Basketweave:** A "pinwheel" pattern developed on a repeated system of four bricks laid at 90° to each other from a common center, thus creating a "woven" impression.

Brick headers are laid side-by-side with struck joints in a mortar base to create mowing strips or garden borders.

See also **Brick wall pattern**.

Paver-brick patterns

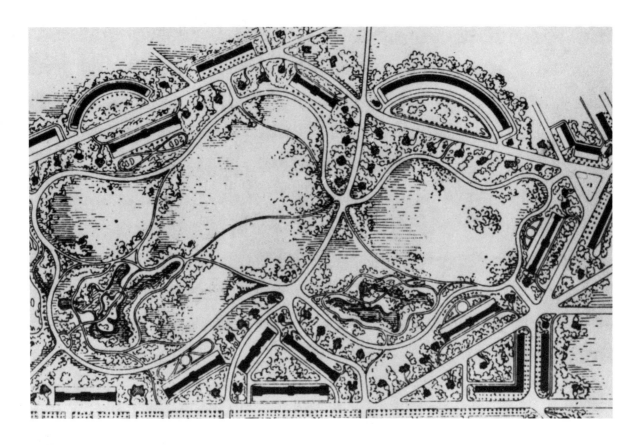

Joseph Paxton. Detail of Birkenhead
Park near Liverpool, plan, 1844.
Illustration courtesy BBMSL, UNM.

Paxton, Sir Joseph (1801 or 1803–
65)   English landscape gardener
and designer of Birkenhead Park
near Liverpool (1843–47), the first
nineteenth-century public garden
supported by taxes. Paxton was
born in Bedfordshire, the son of a
farmer, and gardened at Chiswick
as a boy. By 1826 his skill was so
great that he was appointed head
gardener at Chatsworth, the estate
of the Duke of Devonshire. Paxton
was an ingenious tinkerer; he
conceived the idea of building
prefabrication with his greenhouse
designs of iron and glass for the
duke. His vast Crystal Palace of

1851, some 1,800 feet (549 meters)
long, popularized modular glass
structures and was the star attraction
of the first World's Fair in London
that same year. His greenhouses
featured "ridge and furrow" roofs
and improved moisture-evaporation
capabilities.

Paxton was early in great
demand. As a successor of sorts to
Humphry Repton, q.v., he enjoyed
the friendship of **J. C. Loudon,** q.v.,
the most eminent writer on plants
and gardening of his day. In 1840,
Paxton declined an invitation to
become head gardener for the

crown at Windsor Castle. He served
briefly as a Member of Parliament
and designed several mediocre
country houses. But it was as
designer of Birkenhead Park that he
played his most important role—that
of linking the studiously casual
countrysides of the English School to
the overwhelming social needs of the
burgeoning cities of the Industrial
Revolution. Paxton was able to
successfully mix advances in
technology (i.e., glass and iron
greenhouses, modular construction)
and the softer garden traditions of
an earlier age.

F. L. Olmsted walked through England in 1850 and marveled at Birkenhead Park's agile design in a well-planned new suburb of Liverpool. The 120 acre (49 hectare) "people's garden" impressed Olmsted with its graceful form and quality and its public nature. Paxton was also responsible for the design of Prince's Park, Liverpool (1842); Kelvingrove; Queen's Park, Glasgow (1852); and Baxter Park in Dundee (1863). He consulted on the planning for St. James's and Hyde Parks in London, and designed Edensor—an early **New town,** q.v.

See also **Frederick Law Olmsted.**

Pay request   In contracting, the form submitted by the contractor to the landscape architect for payment of services, labor, and materials provided for a given period toward the completion of a project. All amounts are customarily verified by the landscape architect and forwarded to the owner for payment. The form is often referred to as a **Certificate for payment.** Also **Progress payment.** See also **Final payment, Monthly estimate, Schedule of values.**

Payment bond   See **Labor and materials payment bond.**

Payment, final   See **Final payment.**

Payment, progress   See **Pay request.**

PC   See **Point of curvature.**

PCC   See **Point of compound curvature.**

PC concrete   Portland cement concrete. Also PCC.

PCP   See **Porous concrete pipe.**

PE pipe   Polyethylene ("poly") pipe, q.v. A kind of **plastic pipe.**

Pea gravel   Small diameter (usually ¹/₂ in., 1 cm ±, or less) rounded pebbles in a loose mixture, commonly used for walkways, drives, mulching, and the like. See also **Gravel.**

Peat   A dark, partially decomposed and carbonized organic substance found in bogs, usually developing from reed-sedge or sphagnum moss. See also **Histisol** and **Peat moss.**

Peat garden   A usually hilly garden buttressed by or built up of cut blocks of peat. Plantings are made in the terraces between peat walls and in the spaces, or interstices, between the peat blocks themselves.

Peat moss   1) Sphagnum or hypnum moss found growing in peat bogs, used as an amendment to improve the organic content and tilth of a soil. 2) A peat-bog. Muck peat is a variety of peat more or less decomposed into basic organic compounds. See also **Peat.**

Peat pot   In horticulture, a small container made of moistened sphagnum or other material used to germinate and support a bedding plant seedling.

Peat pot

Peat wall   A small planter bed or terrace made of cut blocks of peat and ideal for plants such as azalea or rhododendron that need a highly acidic soil.

Pebble   A tiny stone, especially a river-turned or river-worn stone. See also **Rock, Stone.**

Pectinate   In plant structures, comb-like.

Pedalfer   A soil peculiar to a humid grassy or wooded area, often containing iron and aluminum but lacking in other soluble minerals. Often a leached soil. Pedalfers are divided into lateritic and podsol types, and are a distinctive **Great soil group,** q.v. See also **Lateritic soil, Pedocal, Podsol.**

Pedestal   The support base for a pillar, stela, obelisk, or the like.

Pedestal mount timer (irrigation) See **Automatic controller.**

Pedestrian walkway   See **Walkway.**

Pedicel   In botany, a small stem, particularly a stem supporting an individual flower. Part of a **Raceme,** q.v. See also **Peduncle, Umbel.**

Pediment   In dryland geography, an easy, boulder-strewn plain, often at the base of a mountain. See also **Pediplain.**

Pediplain (pediplane)   In geology, a large area composed of **Pediments,** q.v.

Pedocal   A distinctive **Great soil group,** q.v., with soils peculiar to arid areas, usually high in calcium and unleached. Pedocals may develop in steppes and semideserts or under grasses. Rich pedocals include **Black earth(s)** and **Brown earth(s),** q.q.v., which drain easily and develop strong horizons. Intrazonal soils with bad drainage and no distinct horizons (i.e., **Saline soil** and **Alkaline soil**, q.q.v.) are also pedocals. See also **Pedalfer.**

Pedogenesis   Origin and formation of soil.

Pedology   Soil science. See also **Edaphology.**

Pedon   A volume of soil of a given type that shows all the expected variations of that type. A representative mass taken from a **Soil profile**, q.v., of approximately 1 meter square.

Peduncle   In botany, a stem or stalk subtending a cluster of flowers. See also **Pedicel.**

Peening   In welding, the hammering out of a seam or matrix of metal.

Pegging of sod   In lawn planting, the hammering of small wooden pegs through sod into topsoil on slopes to prevent slipping.

Pelagic sediment   A fine, ocean-bottom sediment.

Pellicular water   **Capillary** and **Hygroscopic water**, q.q.v.

Peltate   In plant structures, a leaf shape in which the plane of the leaf (roundish) is attached to its stalk in the center and not at the margin. Nasturtium is a common example.

Peltate

Penal sum (contracts)   A penalty amount agreed upon by an owner and a landscape contractor, to apply in the instance of time overruns. More frequently, **Liquidated damages**, q.v. See also **Bonus and penalty clause.**

Penalty clause (contracts)   See **Bonus and penalty clause.**

Pencil-holder   See **Technical pencil.**

Pendant   In flowers or other plants, drooping.

Pendulous   Hanging; "weeping."

Peneplane (peneplain)   A geologically old region, worn down nearly to a flat plain. Also **Mature landscape, Old landscape.**

Penetrable plane   See **Vertical plane.**

Pentachlorophenol   A common oil-borne wood preservative. See **Wood preservative.**

"Penta-treated" (wood)   See **Wood preservative.**

Penthouse garden   A kind of **Roof garden**, q.v., found in apartment or condominium towers in cities.

Per diem   In design contracts, an amount stipulated as a reimbursement for travel, lodging, food, and other expenses. Normally, a "per diem" is collected in addition to the stipulated contract design fee. However, a flat per diem design fee may also be negotiated. See also **Professional fee.**

Per unit fee   A professional fee charged on the basis of a given rate of recompense per individual structure. Examples: X dollars per

apartment unit/complex, X dollars per house in a subdivision, and the like. See also **Professional fee.**

Percentage of construction cost fee   One of the commonest kinds of professional design fees, it is reckoned on the basis of a set percentage of actual construction costs. See also **Professional fee.**

Perched water table   See **Water table.**

Percolation   In soils, the slow downward filtering of water through soil particles. Also **Infiltration.** See also **Percolation rate.**

Percolation rate   The rate at which water filters into a specific soil area, usually measured at one hour of elapsed time. Also **Infiltration rate.** See also **Field capacity.**

Perennation   In plants, survival and vegetative growth lasting several years.

Perennial   In botany, a plant whose growth occurs for more than two years without replanting. The term is mostly used with herbaceous species. See also **Annual, Biennial, Bulb.**

Perfect flower   See **Flower.**

Performance bond   A legal surety guaranteeing that a contractor will execute his work in accordance with plans and specifications. Also **Completion bond, Construction bond, Contract bond.** See also **Bond, Labor and Material Payment Bond, Surety.**

Performance specifications   See **Specifications.**

Performance standard codes   See **Building codes.**

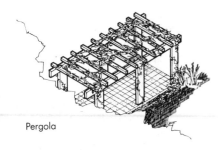
Pergola

Pergola An overhead wooden garden structure supported by posts of more or less even spacing and often covered with vines or other shade-producing plants. Pergolas normally shade walkways. See also **Arbor, Lath, Overhead, Trellis.**

Perianth In flowers, the **Calyx** and **Corolla**, q.q.v., collectively.

Pericarp In flowers, the outside layer or wall of an ovary or its subsequent fruit. See also **Endocarp.**

Perimeter, wetted (of a ditch, pipe, or creek) See **Hydraulic radius.**

Period for completion (landscape construction) See **Contract time.**

Period, defects liability See **Guarantee.**

Period of establishment In landscape construction, the length of time needed for lawns, shrubs, trees, or other plantings to clearly show root and foliar growth. A specific establishment period is usually written into project specifications.

Period, Quaternary See **Quaternary.**

Periodicity In plants, a cycle of active growth alternating with dormancy.

Peripaton (Greek) In classical Greece, a garden path or walkway.

Peripteros (Greek) A pergola, especially a pergola found in Roman gardens modeled on a Greek original.

Peristyle 1) A line of columns rimming a courtyard, building, or patio. See also **Arcade, Colonnade, Portico.** 2) **Peristylon:** In Roman times, a stylized colonnade, adapted from Greek models. The peristylon was a popular feature in Roman villa gardens.

Perlite A light-weight, spherical lava particle used in artificial soils, mulches, aggregates, and the like. See also **Vermiculite.**

Permafrost Permanently frozen arctic or alpine soil.

Permanent water table See **Water table.**

Permeability The ability of any porous or semiporous material to allow liquid water or water vapor to pass through it. Used especially in reference to soils. See also **Capillarity** and **Liquid limit.**

Permeable rock Porous rock strata which absorb percolating rainwater and snowmelt.

Permit, building (construction) See **Building permit.**

Permit, zoning See **Zoning permit.**

Peroxyacetyl nitrate (PAN) A noxious gas and major component of **Air pollution**, q.v.

Peristyle

Perron. Butchart Gardens, Victoria, British Columbia. Photo by author.

Perron   1) A series of steps leading up through a terrace or terraced lawn to a building or other landscape feature. 2) An imposing outdoor landing or the flight of steps leading up to it.

Persian landscape architecture

Persian gardens were always reliefs from the strain of harsh deserts and high plateaus. For millennia they have contained fountains in a soft, straightforward geometry, lapis-blue tiles, the characteristically splayed Persian columns, pavilions, and above all *chenars*—Oriental planes. Darius the Great (521–485 B.C.), developed a hunting park or paradise much envied by his satraps. A later Persian king, Cyrus the Great (d. 401 B.C.) built formal gardens of great expanse at Sardis. The Greek historian Xenophon (c. 430 B.C.) tells us that Cyrus's palace was set off by its broad terraces, its steps a dramatic, punctuating rhythm. Of course, the gardens of Cyrus's palace, like those of Darius's palace at Persepolis, were simply the most refined examples of the paradise gardens conceived as rest stops for any Persian king as he traveled. And the Persians came by much of the form of their gardens by inheritance: the Assyrians, the Babylonians, and the Sumerians before them had spent thousands of years refining their own outdoor design.

The **Chahar-bagh** or classic Persian garden was arranged in quadrants, with a tomb or fountain (or both) in its center. Four water channels usually radiated in the cardinal directions from a central pool of water. The plane tree was used to line and highlight the waterways, or to further divide the quadrants. Roses, planted in groups, were used to scent the garden, and figs, dates, and grapes were commonly planted for shade accent, or food. Spring tulips, daffodils, and crocuses were highlights. In ancient times, the water was often brought from a great distance in an underground conduit, or **Qanat.**

The classic Persian garden was always created as part of a larger building and grounds scheme. Its form was so refined, so productive of shade and relief from glare, that the desert tribes who brought Islam to Persia from the west in the seventh century adopted it immediately. The gardens of Cordoba and Granada in Spain became its direct descendants as early as the eighth century. Persian landscape design was as influential as Greek or Egyptian landscape planning, and as original.

Persian ideas penetrated to Central Asia as well. The gardens of Tamerlane and Babur in Samarqand, Kabul, and elsewhere are principally Persian but also influenced by China. They share a common objective with Persian landscape design: the creation of a colorful, enclosed, cool refuge from the vast southwest and central Asian wilderness.

A resurgence in Persian garden design began in Shiraz about the tenth century A.D., some 1,300 years after Alexander's conquest. By the late sixteenth century, the remarkable Shah Abbas had begun the construction of Isfahan, with its Imperial Square, a well-appointed public open space. His Bagh Mader-i-Shah (the Shah's Mother's Garden) was developed around a long, sycamore-lined, reflecting pool. The garden and nearby buildings were used as a school. Abbas also built the Chehel Sutun, a series of arched, blue-tiled buildings with pavilions, pools, water stairs, and lush gardens, in his palace at Ashraf, on the Caspian Sea. The Chehel Sutun was completed by about 1612.

The oldest extant gardens in

Persian landscape architecture. Royal Mosque with exterior gardens, Isfahan, Persia (Iran), c. 1627. Photo courtesy BBMSL, UNM.

Persia all date from the sixteenth century or later. Two particularly notable gardens from eighteenth-century Shiraz are the Bagh-i-Dilgusha (the Garden of Heart's Ease), featuring a long reflecting pool lined with orange trees, and the huge Bagh-i-Takht or Throne Garden, an amazing terraced landscape next to a lake that has survived, in somewhat ruinous condition, into the twentieth century.

Its long, niched walls and dusty cypresses against a stark hillside are brought to life by the "roostertail" of its cheerful jet, which spurts the lake's own water into the wind at the base of the garden stairs.

See also **Central Asian landscape architecture, Islamic landscape architecture, Russian landscape architecture,** and **Spanish landscape architecture.**

Persistent In botany, leaves, needles, flower parts, or fruit that remain attached to a plant for a considerable length of time.

Personal space The invisible but essential territory around each human being that is necessary to the normal functions of life. Gardens and larger landscapes are, at base, expressions of personal space or its analogues.

Perspective sketch. Gary Nolen, illustrator. Illustration courtesy Morrow and Company.

Perspective   In design and other drawing, a means of delineation that creates a sense of apparent depth and distance. Perspective attempts to make two dimensions appear as three. **Linear perspective** makes use of a vanishing point or points at which the lines of the drawing converge. In **Aerial perspective,** color sharpness and line quality blur as the landscape recedes, leaving the area of focused attention in good contrast and clear. **Aerial perspective** is also called **Atmospheric perspective.** See also **Trompe l'oeil.**

PERT (project evaluation review technique) schedule   A progress and activity chart prepared for a project.

Pervious rock   See **Permeable rock.**

Pesticide   See **Insecticide.**

Petal   An often colorful part of the corolla of a flower. See also **Corolla, Sepal.**

Petaline   Petal-like, or a plant structure attached to a petal.

Petiole   A leaf stalk. See also **Phyllode.**

Peto, Harold A. (1854–1933)   British architect and designer of formal gardens. Peto was a contemporary of the Victorian architects Reginald Bloomfield and Edwin Lutyens, and the partner of **Gertrude Jekyll,** q.v. Peto reestablished Italianate forms in his gardens, the best known of which are Iford Manor in England and Ilnacullin in County Cork, Ireland.

Petrography   The science of rock study.

Petrology   The study of the Earth's rock crust.

Petromania   The Chinese obsession with grotesque garden stones, probably at its greatest pitch during the Ming dynasty (1403–1644). Some of the finest garden stonework may be seen at the Lion Grove in Suzhou near Shanghai. See also **Chinese landscape architecture.**

pH factor or **pH scale**   pH is a chemical indication of hydrogen ion concentrations in solids or liquids. The pH scale is a common tool used to measure the acid-alkaline (hydrogen ion) balance of the soil. The pH scale ranges from 0.0 (pure acid) to 14.0 (pure alkaline), with 7.0 as neutral. Any soil tested at 4.5 or below is very acid, soils of 6.5 to 7.0 are effectively neutral, and any soil over 7.0 is alkaline. Landscape plants, generally speaking, grow best in neutral or slightly acidic soils. Also **Soil reaction.** See also **Litmus.**

Phanerogam   A plant reproducing by seed. An old-fashioned term, it is commonly replaced by **Spermatophyte,** q.v. See also **Cryptogamous.**

Phase, construction   See **Construction phase.**

Phase, design development   See **Design development phase.**

Phase, implementation (of construction work)   See **Construction phase.**

Phase, schematic design   See **Schematic design phase.**

Phase, working drawings   See **Working drawings phase.**

Phenology   The study of the influences of seasons on plant (and animal) life.

Phenotype   In botany, the sum total of a plant's characteristics as they exist in the living organism. Phenotype contrasts with **Genotype,** or the overall possibilities of development found in the plant's genes.

Philosopher's garden   An Italian Renaissance garden developed at a villa or similar location for conversation and pleasure. The earlier villa gardens of Roman times and the grove schools of the Greeks were used as models. See also **Renaissance landscape architecture.**

Phloem   In botany, the softer tissues of the vascular system of a woody plant conducting leaf- or stem-manufactured food towards the roots. See also **Xylem.**

Phosphorus (P)   A nonmetallic element essential, with nitrogen and potassium, for plant growth and health. Phosphorus is needed for good bud, flower, and fruit formation and for color. See also **Complete fertilizer, Macronutrient, NPK.**

Photo relief   A photograph of a relief model used to produce a map showing the significant physical forms of an area.

Photogrammetry   Land measurement from aerial photographs. Accurate photogrammetry depends on the superimposition of two photographs taken slightly apart (a stereo pair) and viewed in complementary red and green light. Highly accurate contour maps are produced by the process. See also **Aerial photography.**

Photography, aerial   See **Aerial photography** and **Photogrammetry.**

Photo-map   A composite map pieced together from a series of aerial photographs.

Photometrics   The measurement of light quality, intensity, and distribution.

Photonasty   In plants, a response to the coming of day or night. Usually observed in the opening or closing of flowers, curling of leaves, and the like. Similar to **Nyctinasty,** q.v. See also **Thermonasty.**

Photo period   The portion of a day or season during which a plant is exposed to light. Photo-periodism is a plant's response to the amount of daylight it receives.

Photosynthesis   The conversion of solar energy directly into carbohydrates by plants—a unique capability. Green (chlorophyll-containing) plant tissue manufactures sugars and starches from water and carbon dioxide by utilizing sunlight. The major by-product is oxygen, and it is to photosynthesis that we owe the current oxygen-rich atmosphere of the Earth. See also **Chloroplast, Compensation point, Respiration.**

Phototaxis (botany)
   See **Phototropism.**

Phototropism   The phenomenon of a plant's response to light through bending its leaves, stalk, or branches to best take advantage of it. Caused by a specialized hormone flow triggered by the direction of light. Adjective: phototropic. See also **Chemotropism, Geotropism, Haptotropism, Hydrotropism, Tropism.**

Phreatic water   See **Ground water.**

Phreatic zone   In soils, underground horizons or strata that are totally saturated. Also **Saturated zone.**

Phreatophyte   A plant that draws its water from very deep sources by means of long roots, especially an unwanted "water-grabbing" species in the process of naturalizing itself along a watercourse in an arid region (southwestern U.S.). The salt cedar (*Tamarix pentandra*) is a frequently occurring example.

Phyllode   A broad, usually flattened leaf stalk that assumes the form and function of the leaf itself.

Phyllotaxy (phyllotaxis)   The systematic occurrence of leaves or scales on a stem or other plant structure, or its study. Also **Orthostichy.**

Phylogeny   The origin and history of plants and animals. In botany, the study of plant evolution. See also **Ontogeny.**

Phylum   In botany, a very broad, primary classification of plants often referred to as a **Division.** The phylum is divided into a **Sub-phylum** or **Class,** q.v. Plural: phyla. See also **Botanical classification.**

Physic garden   In the Middle Ages, a small formal garden developed for the cultivation of herbs and other medicinal plants. Often found in the **Cloister,** q.v., of a monastery. Also **Herbularius, Physick garden.** In later centuries, the physic garden developed into the **Botanical garden,** q.v.

Physiographic province
   See **Geographic province.**

Physiogeographic climax vegetation
   See **Geographic climax vegetation.**

Physiography 1) Physical geography. 2) A description of nature in general or of a natural phenomenon. Also, often, **Geomorphology.**

Physiology of plants See **Plant physiology.**

Phytoecology Plant ecology, or the relationship of plants to their physical surroundings. See also **Ecology, Zooecology.**

Phytogeographic province A geographic area that is characterized by a distinct set of plants.

Phytogeography The scientific study of plant distribution. A division of **Biogeography,** q.v.

Phytology Botany, q.v.

Phyto-pathology Plant pathology, q.v.

Phytophagous In animals, herbivorous.

Phytosociology (plant sociology) See **Plant community.**

Phytotoxic gas A gas, normally a pollutant, that causes injury to plant cells and interrupts normal cell functioning and growth.

PI Point of intersection, q.v., or plasticity index. See also **Plasticity (of soils).**

Piazza (Italian) 1) A public or other square, or a rather wide, covered walkway next to a building. The piazza in its modern form developed during late medieval and Renaissance times (c. 1400–1700 A.D.). See also **Square.** 2) In New England, the South, and elsewhere in the U.S., a front porch.

Piazzetta (Italian) A small-scale, usually paved square or antesquare. A courtyard. See also **Piazza, Square.**

Picturesque Informal and bucolic; arranged to resemble a beautiful picture, but also rugged and "wild." The picturesque style of landscape gardening is based largely on the romantic landscape paintings of **Claude Lorrain, Nicholas Poussin,** and **Salvatore Rosa,** q.q.v., and was popularized in Britain by **Uvedale Price,** q.v., among others. See also **English landscape architecture.**

Piedmont The outwash area at the base of a mountain range; specifically, between mountains and the sea.

Pier A pillar or an upright made of masonry.

Pigeon cote Historically, an elevated bird house built on English estate grounds to supply fresh winter poultry (Renaissance and after).

Pigments, plant See **Plant pigments.**

Pilaster A common pier found in concrete block and other twentieth-century walls, used for stability.

Pile A pier, or built-up concrete, masonry, or stone structure, set in the ground to receive the weight of overlying building or other construction. Also piling.

Pilot valve In irrigation, a small, electric solenoid valve used to activate a section of heads.

Pimples In ceramics, tiny gas bubbles or popped bubbles left on ornamental tile surfaces after firing.

Pin drift See **Drift pin.**

Pinaceae (pine family) A large family of conifers, including the genera *Pinus* (pines), *Picea* (spruces), *Abies* (firs), *Tsuga* (hemlocks), *Pseudotsuga* (false hemlocks), *Larix* (larches), *Cupressus* (cypresses), *Thuja* (arborvitas), and others. Many of the *Pinaceae* are used as lumber in landscape construction or as plant specimens.

Pinch, hard See **Hard pinch.**

Pinching back See **Disbudding.**

Pinching off Stopping, q.v.

Pine A commonly used softwood in outdoor construction. Often treated with wood preservative, logwood oil, or paint for protection. See also **Softwood.**

Pine cone See **Strobile.**

Pine straw A mulch consisting of matted pine needles.

Pinetum A collection of planting of pines or members of *Pinaceae*—the pine family—for scientific study or other purposes. A pine arboretum.

Pink garden A (usually) private garden laid out with pink-flowering annuals, perennials, or shrubs as a primary theme line. Stone walls or gray-leaved background plants are often found in combination with the primary pinks.

Pin-money gardening The production of fresh fruit and vegetables and/or flowers on a small scale for sale along a roadside or at a local market.

Pinnate In plant structures, a compound leaf form in which leaflets extend from alternate or opposite points along a central axis. Black locust and frond or feather palms are typical examples. See also **Palmate.**

Pioneer species See **Plant growth.**

Pip 1) An apple, pear, or other relatively small seed found in a fleshy fruit. 2) A single root crown or stock distinctive in its root mass.

Pipe, ABS See **ABS pipe.**

Pipe arch A large-section conduit used as a culvert in engineering construction.

Pipe, asbestos cement See **Asbestos cement pipe.**

Pipe, cast iron See **Cast iron pipe.**

Pipe, cement asbestos See **Asbestos cement pipe.**

Pipe, copper See **Copper pipe.**

Pipe, corrugated metal See **Corrugated metal pipe.**

Pipe creep In irrigation, a stretching and weakening of plastic (PVC or Polyethylene) pipe material (walls) due to water hammer or operation under excessive pressure. See also **Pipe fatigue.**

Pipe cushion In irrigation, any material upon which a buried irrigation line is laid.

Pipe dope In irrigation, a lubricant used in joining pipe and fittings.

Pipe fatigue In irrigation, the failure of PVC or Polyethylene (plastic) pipe due to repeated **Pipe creep** or unrelieved **Water hammer,** q.q.v.

Pipe, flexible See **Polyethylene pipe.**

Pipe, galvanized See **Galvanized pipe.**

Pipe joint compound In irrigation, a sealer used on male threads at joints.

Pissoir. Paris, two stalls. Photo courtesy BBMSL, UNM.

Pipe, lateral See **Lateral line.**

Pipe, live See **Live pipe.**

Pipe, PE See **Polyethylene pipe.**

Pipe, plastic (irrigation) See **Plastic pipe, Polyethylene pipe, PVC pipe.**

Pipe, "poly" See **Polyethylene pipe.**

Pipe, polyethylene See **Polyethylene pipe.**

Pipe pulling In irrigation, a method of line installation by means of a line-pulling machine. The machine cuts a slit trench in the ground with a blade and pulls the pipe in behind it. Pipe pulling does very little damage to lawns or other existing landscape.

Pipe, PVC (polyvinyl chloride) See **PVC pipe.**

Pipe, rigid See **PVC pipe.**

Pipe saddle In irrigation, a mounted **Fitting,** q.v. Pipe saddles are very often used to connect new service lines into city mains.

Pipe solvent In irrigation, a glue used to bind and fuse PVC pipe sections. Normally, pipe solvent must be applied when the air temperature is mild.

Pipe, sprinkler See **Copper pipe, Galvanized pipe, Polyethylene pipe, PVC pipe.**

Pipe, steel cylinder concrete (SCCP) A kind of pipe sometimes used in public works.

Pipe, terra cotta See **Terra cotta pipe.**

Pipe, transite See **Transite pipe.**

Pipe, vitrified clay See **Vitrified clay pipe.**

Piscina (Italian, Spanish) A swimming pool, reflecting pool, or basin protruding from a garden wall.

Pise de terre (adobe block) See **Adobe.**

Pissoir (French) In France, a streetside urinal, partly screened and located for easy public access.

Pistil The stigma, style, and ovary of a flower—i.e., its female parts. A pistillate flower is seed-producing. The pistil stalk is the **Gynophore.** See also **Stamen.**

Pistillate A seed-producing or female flower, or female flower parts. See also **Staminate.**

Piston-valve In irrigation, a remote-control valve constructed with an internal piston that regulates water flow. Electric and hydraulic piston valves are the main varieties.

Pit, barrow See **Barrow pit.**

Pit, gravel See **Gravel pit.**

Pitch 1) The percentage of grade or overall slope of a piece of ground. Often applied to road verges or shoulders and rock strata. Also **Cross slope.** 2) Pitch as a wood preservative: see **Wood preservative.**

Pith In botany, a layer of plant tissue lying immediately beneath the bark of woody plants and containing the vascular bundles.

PIV valve (irrigation) See **Post indicator valve.**

PL In surveying, an abbreviation for **Property line,** q.v. See also **Plastic limit.**

Place of beginning (POB, surveying) The starting point for a boundary survey.

Place, country See **Country place.**

Place publique A French public square, especially a Renaissance square.

Place, roosting (Renaissance gardens) See **Roosting place.**

Placing (of concrete) The placement of concrete in forms for shaping and subsequent finishing. Often, incorrectly, **Pouring.**

Placita (plazuela) In Spanish America and the southwestern United States, a large private patio or the open space of a compound surrounded by related buildings.

Plaggen epipedon A thick topsoil created by the constant application and mixing of manure. See also **Epipedon.**

Plagioclimax In plant communities, a stable association of species that is nevertheless not the true climax growth of its region. Grazed or mowed natural pastureland is an example. See also **Climax growth, Plant community.**

Plagiogeotropism (in plant growth) See **Geotropism.**

Plain A level or mildly rolling area of land covered with grass. A rolling grassland. See also **Prairie, Savanna, Steppe.**

Plain, flood See **Floodplain.**

Plaisance See **Pleasaunce.**

Plan An outline, map, or other drawing, scaled or unscaled, locating objects in a defined space.

Plan, as built See **As-built drawings.**

Plan, base See **Base plan.**

Plan, contour See **Contour plan.**

Plan, contour and construction See **Layout plan.**

Plan dimensioning See **Dimension.**

Plan elevation In landscape detail drawings, a side view of a specific plan area drawn to scale and illustrating the construction of specific items. A side view, with notes, of a feature or features.

Plan elevation

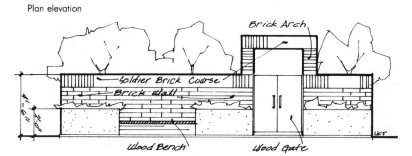

Plan, grading See **Contour plan.**

Plan, irrigation See **Irrigation plan.**

Plan for land use See **Land use.**

Plan, layout See **Layout plan.**

Plan, master See **Master plan.**

Plan, Milesian See **Milesian plan.**

Plan, planting See **Planting plan.**

Plan, plot See **Plot plan.**

Plan, site See **Site plan.**

Plan, staking See **Layout plan.**

Plan, utility See **Utility plan.**

Plane A flat surface. A visible or imagined level or smooth surface on which any two points may be connected by a straight line.

Plane, articulated See **Vertical plane.**

Plane, base See **Base plane.**

Plane, cleavage (stone) See **Cleavage plane.**

Plane coordinates In surveying, the establishment of an east-west line and a north-south meridian, to which all points on a two dimensional (plane) survey are related. Plane coordinate layouts are standardized for common reference throughout the United States and elsewhere. See also **Coordinates.**

Plane, datum See **Datum line.**

Plane, ground See **Base plane.**

Plane, penetrable See **Vertical plane.**

Plane, surface See **Base plane.**

Plane, vertical See **Vertical plane.**

Planimeter An ingenious measuring device (integrator) used to mechanically trace the outer limits of a map or map portion and calculate its area.

Planimeter method See **Cut and fill.**

Plank and beam construction A common kind of wood landscape construction in which a limited number of well-spaced beams supports finish planks that are very slightly sloped or spaced with narrow gaps for drainage. The end product is a deck. See also **Post and beam construction.**

Plankton Quite small, floating marine organisms, both salt and fresh water, which form one of the most basic links in the food chain.

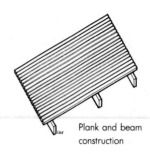

Plank and beam construction

Planned unit development (PUD) In zoning, a housing or commercial development composed of individual units that are regulated as a whole. Drainage, utilities, parking, and open-space requirements are applied to the entire development of which the units are parts.

Planned community. Tyrone, New Mexico, plan, 1917. Illustration courtesy BBMSL, UNM.

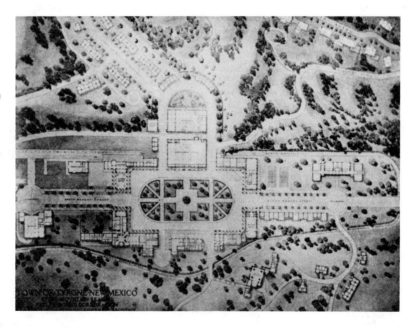

Planning. Defense-oriented city plan of Naarden, The Netherlands. Photo courtesy BBMSL, UNM.

Planner   Among the design professions, a person engaged in some form of land-use planning, especially an architect, landscape architect, engineer, or city planner involved in site or area development.

Planning (city or regional)   The laying out of problem statements and large-scale design solutions that concern extensive areas of land; the anticipation of problems that will be encountered as human use and "development" of land continue.

City or urban planning deals largely with zoning and code enforcement as they are related to the use of land. The overbearing influence of the private car spawns endless problems in this regard. Traffic and parking difficulties, as well as the encroachment of the car into traditional pedestrian reserves, must be resolved by planning decisions. Planners must also contend with conflicting governmental jurisdictions.

Regional planning considers many of the same questions dealt with in cities, but on a much broader and less tractable scale. As in city planning, an arduous data-gathering process is necessary. The regional planner must assess geography, climate, minerals, soils, existing land uses, water, sunshine, seasonal changes, and similar physical characteristics in his area and relate them to projected human demands for recreation, work, housing, circulation, and the like. The political consequences of proposed planning have to be considered. Comprehensive areawide planning will include contingencies for drainage, proper handling of sewage, the provision of water, new land-use restrictions, and well-developed circulation. Indirectly, it will attempt to limit population growth to a reasonable level and to properly channel potentially disruptive human activity.

Regional planning is, to a greater or lesser degree, a sophisticated attempt to cope with ever-rising human populations and to provide for the realities of the future. As is true of city planning, it is severely limited by social, political, and, perhaps more importantly, commercial restrictions.

"Planning" is also commonly used as a synonym for "design," which actually takes place when necessary data have been gathered to allow imaginative problem-solving to follow as a logical sequence.

See also **Site planning** and **Zoning.**

Planning agency   A public or quasi-public body, appointed or elected, concerned with single site, city, regional, or other forms of land use and related planning. Also **Planning board, Planning commission.**

Planning, environmental
See **Environmental planning.**

Planning, landscape
See **Environmental planning.**

Planning, urban   See **Planning.**

Planosol (plansol)   A humid climate soil with a hard clay B-horizon (subsoil) and a leached A-horizon (topsoil). See also **Soil horizon.**

Plans, construction   See **Working drawings.**

Plans, preliminary   See **Design development phase.**

Plant   A member of one of the two basic kingdoms of life (the other being animal), characteristically producing its own food through photosynthesis, developing cellulose cell walls, and lacking apparent sensors and any means of locomotion. Plants support all animal life and are responsible for the Earth's present atmosphere through their emission of oxygen as a metabolic by-product.

The plant kingdom is usually classified in four basic phyla, or divisions: 1) Divison I, Thallophytes; 2) Division II, Bryophytes; 3) Division III, Pteridophytes; 4) Division IV, Spermatophytes.

Spermatophytes or seed-bearing plants are the common flora of landscape architecture.

See also **Botanical classification.**

Plant, adventive   See **Adventive plant, Weed.**

Plant, air   See **Epiphyte.**

Plant, armed   See **Armed plant.**

Plant, association   See **Plant community.**

Plant, autotrophic   See **Autotrophic plant.**

Plant bed   A carefully prepared patch of ground used for vegetable, flower, or other planting.

Plant, bedding   See **Bedding plant.**

Plant, binomial (system of classification)   See **Binomial.**

Plant, boxed   See **Container plant.**

Plant breeding   Basic plant breeding utilizes field selection, crossing or hybridizing, and inbreeding. Hardiness, special color, growth rate, form, and unique character are attributes considered in selection for landscape design use. Careful hybridization and inbreeding produce many useful new varieties or even species each year. Stringent field selection culls poor specimens and produces a constantly improved breeding stock.

Plant broker   An independent agent handling sales of horticultural plants from several sources.

Plant, character   See **Specimen.**

Plant classification   See **Botanical classification.**

Plant, collected   In horticulture, a plant dug up in the wild. See **Collected stock.**

Plant community   A naturally occurring series of different species found associated with each other. Trees, shrubs, and grasses or herbs all occupy distinct ecological niches on the same piece of ground, creating a typical and mutually beneficial habitat. The study of these communities is **Plant sociology.** See also **Plagioclimax.**

Plant, container   See **Container plant.**

Plant, cool season   See **Cool season plant.**

Plant, dot   See **Dot plant.**

Plant, edging   See **Edging plant.**

Plant, escaped   See **Naturalized plant.**

Plant, euryecious   See **Euryecious plant.**

Plant evolution   See **Phylogeny.**

Plant family   See **Family.**

Plant, foliage   See **Foliage plant.**

Plant foods   Air and soil, with water added, are the sources of plant foods. 1) **Air:** the plant extracts carbon dioxide from the air through its leaf or stem surfaces for use in **Photosynthesis,** q.v. Sunlight is also necessary to food manufacture. 2) **Soil:** NPK, q.v., are absorbed with **Trace elements,** q.v., in water solution from the soil. These are also utilized by the plant's photosynthetic structures (leaves and/or stems) to make carbohydrates. An assured supply of water and soil minerals is necessary for continued plant growth. See also **Available nutrient, Macronutrient,** and **Trace element.**

Plant formation   A climatically determined regional **Climax growth,** q.v., of plants. Part of a **Biome,** q.v.

Plant geography
See **Phytogeography.**

Plant growth   In a man-made or man-disturbed landscape, the reclamation of a barren area by the invasion of plant species. **Primary growth** is composed of pioneer species (usually "weeds") which begin to hold and build soil and retain water. **Climax** or **Secondary growth** is the characteristic redevelopment of the species which normally would occur on the site as the permanent vegetative cover. In Rocky Mountain forests, the aspen is often the "pioneering" species in burned areas, to be succeeded later by pine and Douglas fir. See also **Climax growth, Plant succession.**

Plant growth region   In horticulture, a generally accepted **Hardiness zone,** q.v. See also **Life zone.**

Plant growth substance
     See **Hormone.**

Plant, heterotrophic
     See **Heterotrophic plant.**

Plant hunter   A plant explorer or collector. In Victorian times, plant hunters working for commercial English nurseries brought thousands of new species from Asia and the Americas into cultivation. Among the more famous nineteenth-century plant hunters are the British Lobb Brothers, Thomas and William, and David Douglas.

Plant, indicator   See **Indicator plant.**

Plant, introduced   See **Exotic.**

Plant invasion   In horticulture, a process of weed or other plant establishment in a new area. Plant invasions are often precipitated by disastrous human misuse of land areas.

Plant legend   See **Legend.**

Plant life scheme   The classification of different sizes and types of plants in groupings convenient for horticultural or landscape-design selection.

Plants may be grouped according to high-, medium-, or low-water use, or following their habit of growth as ground covers, vines, understory (shrubs), or overstory (trees) in a **Plant community,** q.v.

See also **Botanical classification, Hydrophyte, Mesophyte, Taxonomy, Tropophyte, Xerophyte.**

Plant material   In landscape architecture, plant species or specimens used as part of a design.

Plant mix (asphalt)   An asphalt mixture made up at a plant that consists of a uniform aggregate coated with asphalt cement or liquid at the correct ratio.

Plant movement   **Tropism,** q.v.

Plant names   See **Botanical classification.**

Plant, naturalized   See **Naturalized plant.**

Plant nomenclature   See **Botanical classification, Botanical nomenclature.**

Plant nutrient   See **Available nutrient, Macronutrient, Plant foods, Trace element.**

Plant patent   Reserved rights to the sale or use of a hybrid plant developed by an individual or organization.

Plant pathology   The scientific study of plant infirmities of any kind. Also **Phytopathology.**

Plant physiology   The study of the living processes of plants—transpiration, growth, flower production, and the like.

Plant pigments   Chemical substances responsible for the colors found in plants and their parts. Lutene and xanthophyll are responsible for much yellow coloring; lycopene is a red pigment found in berries, fruits, and elsewhere; chlorophyll is responsible for many green shades; carotene causes orange-yellow coloring. A **Carotenoid** is a **Carotene**-like pigment.

Plant, rampant   See **Rampant plant.**

Plant, resting   See **Dormant.**

Plant saucer   See **Earth basin.**

Plant society   See **Society.**

Plant sociology   See **Plant community.**

Plant starter   A very moderate fertilizing solution used to stimulate growth following transplanting. Often **Starter fertilizer.**

Plant succession   Natural changes in the characteristic vegetation of an area that occur due to modification of plant habitat. **Primary succession** occurs in barren landscapes devoid of vegetation. **Secondary succession** occurs when normal successive processes are interrupted by fire, construction, farming, timber operations, or the like. Plant succession normally progresses toward stability, or equilibrium, and the **Final succession** is the typical climax growth of an area. See also **Climax growth, Plant growth.**

Plant, vascular   See **Vascular plant.**

Plant, warm season   See **Warm season plant.**

Plant zero   The lowest temperature at which plant growth will occur. For the life zones of the Rocky Mountain West in the United States, 43°F (± 6°C) has been set as plant zero, but the rating does not hold true for all plants (i.e., lichens, mosses, and the like).

Plantation   1) A large-scale farm organized to produce cash crops. 2) A planting of ornamental or food species, especially trees.

Planter   In landscape design, a carefully defined area used for the cultivation of shrubs and flowers, as opposed to grass. Often located near, and complementary to, a lawn. Planters may be at ground level, raised, or below grade, and can be constructed of brick, stone, wood timbers, concrete, concrete block, or other materials.

Planting, base   See **Foundation planting.**

Planting basket   In horticulture, a bushel or similar basket used for the culture and transplanting of individual plant specimens.

Planting, face   See **Face planting.**

Planting, foundation
   See **Foundation planting.**

Planting, natural   See **Natural planting.**

Planting, pavement   See **Pavement planting.**

Planting plan   In landscape drawing, a plan showing existing and proposed plants for a project with a planting legend, details, and notes.

Planting saucer   See **Earth basin.**

Planting, screen   See **Screen planting.**

Planter

Planting, structural
   See **Bioengineering.**

Plants, fossil   See **Paleobotany.**

Plash   1) Splash, the striking of water on water. 2) A variant of pleach.

Plaster   A pasty (cementitious), highly plastic substance that is used as a wall coating. Plaster easily takes on the form or texture given to it in its wet state. See also **Stucco.**

Plaster sand   A medium grade sand (¼ in. and less particle diameter) used in plaster and stucco. See also **Sand.**

Plastic   Flexible, tractable, or malleable. Often applied to such common landscape features as concrete, asphalt, or epoxies which become rigid once set.

Plastic expansion tape (ribbon)   In planting, an expandable ribbon used for securing a branch or stem to a stake without harming the parent tree or shrub.

Plastic limit   The limit of plasticity, or stretching, that is typical of a construction material (soil and the like). Abbreviated **PL.**

Plastic pipe   Rigid (PVC) pipe or Flexible (polyethylene) pipe, q.q.v., widely used because of its cheapness, durability, and convenience in landscape irrigation.

Plasticity (of soils)   The ability of a soil to shrink or swell as moisture and temperature fluctuate without losing its basic character. Measured by means of an index (the *Plasticity index*) in which varying moisture and accompanying plasticity are correlated. See also **Elasticity, Soil.**

Plat The plan drawing of a selected property, usually indicating only site boundaries.

Plat book In survey recording, a book maintained by a government office showing the legal boundaries of all surveyed plats within a subdivision or other land area.

Plate, bearing See **Bearing plate.**

Plate, flange (landscape construction) See **Flange plate.**

Plateau A tableland; a large, flat expanse of ground or geological area rising above an adjacent area and bounded on at least one side by a vertical face or cliff. See also **Mesa.**

Platt, Charles A. (c. 1800s–1900s) Platt's book, *Italian Gardens,* published in 1849, dealt primarily with the Italian villa developed during the Renaissance. It demonstrated how formal and informal design could be combined to good effect in a country estate.

Platt began his professional career as a painter, studying in Paris and New York. As a landscape designer, he later applied his studies of the Italian villa to the grounds of several houses and country places in the eastern United States. The Faulkner Farm (1897) and the "Garden of Weld" (same period) both in Massachusetts, are examples of his early work.

Platt was also an architect of talent. His houses and gardens were unusually well-integrated. "Gwinn," the Mather estate on Lake Erie (c. 1908), is representative of his later designs.

Platy In soils, referring to laminated or flaky particles.

Play area A plot of ground set aside specifically for children's play. See also **Playground.**

Play equipment Traditionally, items of apparatus such as slides, swings, merry-go-rounds, teeter-totters, and the like installed in playgrounds for children's use. See also **Play area, Playground.**

Playground An area set aside for children's games and pastimes, usually formally designed. Formal playgrounds in the U.S. date from the 1880s; one of the very earliest appeared at Jane Addams's Hull House. Insurance worries and overrefinement in the late twentieth century work to make playgrounds dull. The best of the genre are located next to children's houses and/or are furnished by the youngsters themselves.

Playground, adventure See **Adventure playground.**

Play lot A tot lot, or children's play area.

Playing field Invented by the Greeks in the first millennium B.C., the playing field has been used for athletic ball games for nearly 3,000 years. In the twentieth century, seating for spectators has increased greatly.

Playa A shallow pan in a desert or arid area that becomes a lake only after rains. Often part of a **Bolson,** q.v.

Plaza (Spanish) 1) A town square, usually formal. 2) (U.S., 1970s) An office building, sometimes surrounded by parking and plantings. See also **Square.**

Plaza. Old Town Plaza, Las Vegas, New Mexico. Historic renovation early 1980s by Morrow and Worley, landscape architects. Photo by author.

Plaza. Ecuador: San Francisco
Plaza. Photo courtesy BBMSL, UNM.

Pleach   See **Pleaching.**

Pleached bower   A garden bower created by a mass of interwoven tree branches shading a path or sitting area. Also **Pleached allee.**

Pleaching   The training and interlacing of tree or hedge branches to form an arch or canopy over a walkway or road. Also, a similar training of growth producing a tall hedge pruned at the base. Also **Plashing.** See also **Pollarding, Stooling.**

Pleasaunce (pleasance)   A small medieval garden ("garden of love") enclosed within the ramparts of a castle, primarily used for entertaining ladies. Also, as a pavilion within an estate garden, **Plaisance.** See also **Medieval landscape architecture.**

Plicate   In plant structures, braid-like or occurring in folds.

Pleaching

Plinth   The square base of a pedestal or pillar.

Pliny the Younger (62–113 A.D.)
   Roman garden writer. It is to Pliny, the nephew and adopted son of Pliny the Elder, that we owe much of our knowledge of the Roman landscapes of the early Empire. Pliny's letters to Tacitus, the **Epistulae,** describe his villa at Laurentum, about 17 miles from Rome, in detail. Pliny mentions his favorite figs and mulberries, his kitchen garden, the summerhouse, terraces with flowers. There were formal gardens with topiary work, water in various guises, and a beautiful set of views. Pliny's second villa in Florence was much the same. The modern reader is struck by the very contemporary quality of the gardens Pliny describes.
   Pliny's letters and notes on gardening have made him the best-known writer on classical landscapes. His notions on villa design were copied liberally by the Renaissance theorist **Leone Battista Alberti,** q.v.
   See also **Columella, Roman landscape architecture.**

Plot   A small piece of land, especially one used for gardening or farming. Also **Garden plot.**

Plot plan   A precise drawing of a given location with significant features drawn to scale.

Plot, sample   See **Sample plot.**

Plow layer   Surface soil, q.v.

Plow pan   A type of hard-compacted, agricultural soil formed by the weight of farm machinery on layers beneath the plowed topsoil.

Plowing, contour   See **Contour plowing.**

Plug

PLS   Pure live seed, q.v.

Plug   Among turfgrasses or ground covers, a small section (approximately 2 in or 5 cm²) of plant, soil, and root mass installed in a prepared bed for vegetative reproduction and coverage of a landscape area. The installation itself is plugging.

Plumb (or plumb and straight)   Applied to a plant, post, stanchion, or other landscape item installed true to a vertical line.

Plumb-bob (surveying)   A weight in a plumb-line. An ancient instrument of surveying, it was used by the Egyptians some 4,000 years ago. The plumb-bob and plumb-line indicate verticality.

Plumose   In plant structures, feathery in appearance due to the presence of tiny hairs.

Plunge beds   See **Plunging.**

Plunging   The placement of a potted plant in the ground, pot and all. A technique sometimes used to protect or preserve indoor plants or to acclimate new outdoor specimens. Plunging also allows a change in display of seasonal color in the garden. Plunging is a technique often used in **Plunge beds.**

Pluriseriate   In plant structures, occurring in multiple series. See also **Uniseriate.**

Plurovular   In flowers, containing two or more ovaries. See also **Monovular.**

Pluvial   Having to do with rain.

Pluviometric coefficient   A percentage of the usual rainfall for a given region.

Ply   A layer of material, usually wood, bound with other layers in plies for strength and stability. Plural: plies.

Plywood   Thin sheets of wood glued together in laminations (arranged crossgrain layer by layer) to form a single thicker, larger sheet. A common form wood.

PMP   The **Probable maximum precipitation** expected in an area.

POB (surveying)   **Place of beginning,** q.v.

Pocket park   See **Vest pocket park.**

Pod   A dry fruit capable of opening to emit its seeds. See also **Dehiscence.**

Podere (Italian)   A Renaissance term used to describe the farmland from which a villa—house, vineyards, gardens, and fields—was developed.

Podium   1) The stone or concrete platform upon which a building is constructed. 2) A speaker's platform.

Podsol (podzol)   A **Pedalfer** soil, q.v., found in subpolar latitudes in coniferous forests. Podsol soil is characterized by heavy moisture content and little evaporation. Yet it contains distinct horizons, and is often leached. Its counterpart in the tropics is red and yellow or **Lateritic soil,** q.v.

Point of compensation (in plants)   See **Compensation point.**

Point of compound curvature (PCC)   In road layout, a point on a long curve at which one radius intersects another—i.e., the intersection of two arcs with different radii.

Point of curvature (PC)   In road layout, a point on a tangent (straight line) at which a radius intersects and a curve begins. See also **Point of tangency (PT).**

Point, datum   See **Datum line.**

Point of intersection (PI)   In road layout, a hypothetical point at a curve at which two road tangents (straight lines) intersect.

Point of relief (irrigation)   See **Water hammer.**

Point of reverse curvature (PRC)   In road layout, a point on a curve at which the curve reverses itself. An "S" curve intersection.

Point of saturation (soils, biological populations)   See **Saturation.**

Point of reverse curvature

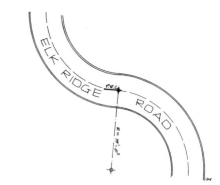

Point of stoppage (irrigation)
See **Water hammer.**

Point of tangency (PT) In road layout, a point on a tangent where a road curve ends. The curve-end counterpart of a **Point of curvature (PC)**, q.v.

Point, vanishing (drawing)
See **Vanishing point.**

Point of vertical curvature (PVC) In road layout, a point at the bottom or on the side of a hill or depression at which a vertical curve radius intersects a horizontal curve radius or tangent (straight line). The uplift point of a road. See also **Point of curvature.**

Point of vertical intersection (PVI)
In road layout, a centerline point at which intersecting slope lines (road gradients) meet.

Point of vertical tangency In road layout, a point on a vertical tangent at which a climbing or falling road curve radius ends. Also abbreviated **PVT.** See also **Point of tangency.**

Point of wilting See **Wilting point.**

Pointing, tuck (masonry) See **Tuck pointing.**

Points, cardinal (of the compass)
See **Cardinal points.**

Poison, soil See **Soil sterilant.**

Polar coordinates
See **Coordinates.**

Polder In the Netherlands, low-lying, fertile agricultural land reclaimed from the sea and protected by dikes.

Polis In ancient Greece, the city-state—an influential prototype of modern urban form.

Pollarding

Pollard See **Pollarding.**

Pollarding The practice of pruning the main limbs of trees to nubs, thus developing masses of small, "frantic" branches emerging from misshapen welts. Pollarded trees usually develop a compact, symmetrical crown. See also **Pleaching, Stooling.**

Pollen The tiny male grains produced by the anthers of flowers.

Pollen analysis The examination of pollen grains found in an ancient settlement to determine common plants used by its inhabitants. A highly effective tool of **Landscape archaeology,** q.v. Also **Palynology.** See also **Archaeobotany.**

Pollination See **Fertilization.**

Pollination, cross See **Cross pollination.**

Pollination, open See **Open pollination.**

Pollination, wind Anemophily. See **Wind pollination.**

Pollution, air See **Air pollution** and **Smog.**

Pollution, earth See **Earth pollution.**

Pollution, noise See **Noise pollution.**

Pollution, nonpoint   See **Nonpoint pollution**.

Pollution, water   See **Water pollution**.

Polybrid   See **Hybrid**.

Polychrome   Many-colored.
See also **Monochrome**.

Polyethylene   A plastic hydrocarbon film sometimes used as a surface mulch, as a lining for ponds, or as a component in flexible (polyethylene) pipe.

Polyethylene ("poly") pipe   In irrigation, an inexpensive, flexible, short-lived kind of tubing sometimes used as mains, laterals, and risers. Used with increasing frequency in drip irrigation. Also **PE pipe**. See also **Copper pipe, Galvanized pipe, PVC pipe**.

Polygamous   A plant species that produces both unisexual and bisexual flowers in the same specimen. See also **Dioecious, Hermaphrodite, Monoecious**.

Polygonal soil   In very cold regions, regular plane-sided soil-surface cracking developing from a sequence of freezing and thawing and related processes. See also **Tundra**.

Polyploid (plant cell)   A plant with a genetic makeup of more than twice the usual number of chromosomes in its cells. See also **Diploid, Tetraploid**.

Polyvinyl chloride (pipe)   See **PVC**.

Pome   An edible, fleshy fruit, usually with a core or seed-bearing center. Apples and pears, among others, are examples.

Pomology   Plant cultivation for fruit production.

Pompom (pompon)   In horticulture, a topiary treatment of juniper, privet, or similar shrubs or trees that produces a bare stem with a tuft-like ball at its end.

Pond   A body of water smaller than a lake.

Pond, lily   See **Lily pond**.

Pond overflow   See **Trickle drain**.

Ponga wall   In New Zealand, an informal garden fence made of the trunks of tree ferns lashed together.

Pool   A small pond or still body of water.

Poor-man's manure   Snow, so-called because of its ability to protect soil and then aerate it during a gradual thaw and melting.

Poorly graded soil   In engineering, a soil of even-sized particles, capable of little compaction. Sand is an example.

Pop-up head   In irrigation, a lawn spray head installed flush with finish grade and containing a pressure-activated nozzle which rises several inches above ground level to spray the surrounding vegetation. See also **Head, Spray head**.

Pop-up head

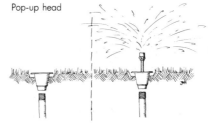

Pope, Alexander (1688–1744)
Pope is best known, of course, as a poet. His "Epistle to Lord Burlington" of 1731 celebrated the "wisdom" of nature and of natural design, and by means of this and other works Pope helped to trigger the change in British national taste that saw formal garden design give way to naturalism.

Pope's own estate at Twickenham is a pivotal garden: the tract of some five acres is one of the earliest examples in Britain of a romantic or poetic garden. It is an amalgamation of older styles, containing urns, a vineyard, an Italianate bosque, an orangery, a grotto, an obelisk, and a bowling green. As if this were not enough, Pope's garden also featured a prominent summerhouse, a kitchen garden, and his mother's tomb. Despite the hodgepodge, Pope's basic emphasis on the development of the **Genius loci** and on bringing the countryside into the garden profoundly influenced the **English School**, q.v., of the eighteenth and nineteenth centuries.

Popular landscape architecture   See **Vernacular landscape architecture**.

Population density   The ratio of a mass of people or other organisms to a specific area of land (i.e., 5,000 people/sq. mi.). Human population density increases wherever support mechanisms (resources available for use) are plentiful. Exhaustion of resources and intensification of technological means of exploitation occur in predictable cycles as population increases. See also **Demography**.

Population, soil   See **Soil population**.

Porch A covered, sometimes extensive, building entry. An elaborate, colonnaded porch is a **Portico**, q.v.

Porch stoop See **Stoop**.

Pore space Any space between soil particles. An interstitial space.

Pore water (in soils) See **Capillary water**.

Porosity In soils, a measure of the ability of a soil medium to allow air or water to pass into or through it. Porosity deals with the air spaces present in a given soil.

Porosity capillary See **Capillary porosity**.

Porrect In plant structures, extending at a right angle to a surface. Cactus or other spines are examples.

Portal In Spanish America and the southwestern United States, a verandah or long covered porch.

Porte-cochère (French) A carriage or car entrance and shelter.

Portico A walkway or arcade with a column-supported roof or overhang, often located in or next to a garden. See also **Arcade, Colonnade, Peristyle**.

Porticus (Latin) See **Portico**. The equivalent of the Greek **Stoa**, q.v.

Portland cement A common building cement named after a particular type of quarried stone in Portland, U.K., and consisting of calcium oxide, silicon oxide, and low percentages of other metal oxides. See also **Cement, Concrete**.

Portuguese landscape architecture. Queluz Palace grounds, Lisbon, c. 1760. Photo courtesy BBMSL, UNM.

Portuguese landscape architecture

Dolmens and other paleolithic monuments are still found in Portugal, but the Romans were the first historic people to develop distinctive gardens throughout the country. Roman villas with fountains, pools, formal gardens, mosaics, and extensive tilework flourished in Portugal's mild climate. The tiled baths of Condeixa remain from Roman times. The Romans also introduced the perforated wall in their patios and gardens, and the atrium in the center of their houses. The Roman villa eventually became the Portuguese **Quinta**, a country estate still popular in the twentieth century but little changed in form and intent from the first century A.D.

The quinta probably reached the height of its later development in the sixteenth century, when Portuguese caravels began to bring back spices and Eastern outdoor-design notions from newly accessible India. Tanks, or formal ponds, made their appearance in Portuguese palaces and country houses. The Quinta dos Torres, near Lisbon, had an Indian-style tank with a pavilion in its center; the Quinta Fronteira boasted reflecting pools and **Azulejo** tiles. The Quinta Bacalhoa, also near Lisbon, was designed with an Indian-inspired pavilion or temple in a pool. The stylized pool edges of this and other quintas also reflected the first influence of Mogul India on the gardens of Europe.

But Islamic gardens had been common in the country in the Middle Ages. The Moors were especially good at channeling water through tiny jets into jewel-like fountains. The whitewashed southern Algarve, with its windowboxes, courtyard alcoves, and *açoteias* or roof gardens, still feels very Moorish.

Medieval Christian gardens were primarily found in formal cloisters or *claustros*. Se de Coimbra, an excellent surviving example, is purely European in design. The very traditional cloister of the convent of Santa Cruz de Coimbra includes a central courtyard pavilion. The monastic gardens of the Mosteiro de Jeronimos in Lisbon are also in good condition. A medieval parterre survives at the Mosteiro de Batalha which is also notable for the play of light in its archwork. The designer of Batalha was the fifteenth-century architect Afonso Domingues, whose style influenced the country for the next several centuries.

The Renaissance in Portugal derives mostly from Italian models. Lisbon, Oporto and other cities were outfitted with new, large squares *(praças)* often centered around statues or monuments. Lisbon's Terreiro do Paco is typical. The *pelourinho*—a column marker or monument—is a common furnishing of this and other public squares. The Italianate **Loggia** or roofed arcade, sometimes facing a *praça,* was common in Portugal after the early sixteenth century. Paving was frequently of cutstone or cobbles. A surviving formal Renaissance garden, the Jardim de Santa Barbara near the Public Library in Braga, is notable for its fine topiary.

The baroque gardens of the Queluz Palace, the Praça Marques de Pombal, and the Parque Eduardo VII, with its enormous parterre hedges, still dominate Lisbon. Numerous statues and fountains and the Jardim de Neptuno (Neptune Garden), complete with petunias and clipped boxwood hedges, set off the Queluz. The landscape of the Praça Marques de Pombal, constructed in the late eighteenth century, connect neatly with the Parque Eduardo VII. These and other baroque landscapes profoundly influenced city form in colonial Brazil (see **Brazilian landscape architecture**).

There is a part of the Parque Eduardo VII that is designed naturalistically, but this is exceptional in Portugal. Most public and private landscapes throughout the country have remained quite formal and eclectic into the twentieth century. Benefactors continue to construct or inspire public gardens, which are then named after them. A recent example is the very formal Parque Dr. Manuel Braga in Coimbra. In streetside landscapes, the Alameda Affonso Henriques in Lisbon is the standard for national boulevard design. See also **Spanish landscape architecture.**

Positive drainage   The diversion of storm or irrigation water away from a building, paved surface, or lawn and into a ponding area, storm sewer, or other off-site area. The creation of positive drainage is a principal concern in landscape architecture. See also **Drainage.**

Post   An upright column or stake used for marking an area or for structural support. A pull-post, often used for wire fences, is reinforced with triangular or horizontal bracing at corners or intermediate points of tension.

Post and beam (post and lintel) construction   In landscape construction, a common pergola or trellis structure made of simple upright (vertical) and connecting horizontal members. Trabeated construction (see **Trabeation**). See also **Colonnade, Overhead, Pergola, Plank and beam construction,** and **Trellis.**

Postemergence control (treatment)   In horticulture, an herbicide applied to weedy areas after unwanted plants have germinated. See also **Preemergence control.**

Post, quarter   See **Quarter post.**

Pot, peat   See **Peat pot.**

Potable water   Clean, fit drinking water for domestic or other use.

Potash   Potassium hydroxide, potassium carbonate, or other potassium compounds. A kind of fertilizer. See also **Potassium.**

Potassium (K)   A metallic element that, along with nitrogen and phosphorus, is essential for plant growth and health. Potassium is especially important for the formation of healthy roots. See also **Complete fertilizer, Macronutrient, NPK.**

Potbound (plant)   Rootbound, q.v.

Pothole   1) A sinkhole in a Karst region. See **Sinkhole.** 2) A pit worn in rock by the revolving action of a stone propelled by water movement at the base of a fall. 3) A **Chuckhole,** q.v., in a road.

Potting   In gardening, the placement or replacement of a plant with soil in a container.

Pounds per square inch   A measure of stress, often designated as PSI. In irrigation, a measure of water pressure. See also **KSMM** and **Stress.**

Pouring (of concrete)   See **Placing.**

Poussin   The family name of two seventeenth-century landscape painters influential in the development of the English landscape garden: Nicholas Poussin (1573–1665), French, noted for his wild arcadian landscapes, and Gaspar(d) Poussin (Dughet) (1615–75), French but born in Rome, and either son-in-law or brother-in-law of Nicholas.

The Poussins are often confused or combined, as Gaspar Dughet took on the name of his famous in-law and also followed much the same subject matter, although his landscapes were more subdued than those of Nicholas. Many of the paintings of the Poussins were based on literary influences and on the older style of Titian. Typical, perhaps, is the *Arcadian Shepherds,* from Chatsworth, of about 1630. In this painting, ruins were scattered coyly throughout a bucolic forest scene. One of Gaspar's favorite topics was the Roman countryside executed as a fresco.

See also the Poussins' contemporaries **Claude Lorrain** and **Salvatore Rosa,** and the **English School.**

Powdery rot   See **Dry rot.**

Power of attorney   A legal enactment which permits one individual or body to serve as agent for another.

Power pole   An electrical utility pole. Sometimes abbreviated **PP** on plans or maps.

Power raking   A technique of deep surface raking by machine used to dislodge thatch that has built up in a lawn.

Pozzolanic admixture (in concrete)   Chemicals added to concrete to cut down permeability and improve resistance to sulfates.

PP   A common plan abbreviation for **Power pole.**

PPM   **Parts per million,** a measurement of solutions.

Praça (Portuguese)   A public square. See also **Square.**

Practice (in landscape architecture)   The delivery to society of landscape architectural services in an ethical manner.

"Practice" law   In U.S. landscape architecture, a state law which limits to licensed individuals the provision or advertising of landscape architectural services. See also **"Title" law** and **"Title and Practice" law.**

Prairie   A large expanse of gently rolling or flat land covered with multiple grasses and flowers but exhibiting very few trees. Formerly the dominant natural landscape of central North America. See also **Plain, Savanna, Steppe.**

Prairie soil (prairie earth)   A rich, productive **Great soil group,** q.v. See also **Black earth, Brown earth.**

Prairie topography   A landscape of softly flowing grassy hills, part of or resembling the prairies of central North America. Also **Rolling terrain.**

PRC   See **Point of Reverse Curvature.**

Precast concrete   A concrete monolith or member that is prepared beforehand and off-site for later use in construction. See also **Cast-in-place concrete.**

Precipitation   Water in any form that reaches the Earth's surface from the atmosphere.

Precipitation average (irrigation)   A calculation of the average amount of moisture necessary to adequately maintain a planted area that will be supplied by an irrigation (often sprinkler) system.

Precipitation rate   In irrigation, the amount of water supplied to a planted area in a set period of time, usually coordinated with a soil's **Absorption rate,** q.v. Often expressed as inches per square foot per hour or centimeters per square meter per hour.

Preconstruction (existing) grade   See **Grade.**

Preemergence control (treatment)   In horticulture, an herbicide applied to likely weedy areas before unwanted plants sprout. See also **Postemergence control.**

Prefabrication   In architecture and engineering, the manufacture of entire structures, modules, or components for delivery to a project site. In landscape architecture, irrigation elements, strips of sod for "instant lawns," benches, and similar items may be said to be prefabricated.

Prehistoric (primitive) gardens   Gardening probably became common with the onset of the Neolithic at the end of the last Ice Age, about 10,000 years ago, although recent archaeological evidence suggests that farming may have taken place in fertile pockets of Egypt's Western Desert some 17,000 years before the present. Ancient gardens were usually located near brooks and may have been surrounded by thorny hedges **(Zaribas)** to protect against marauding beasts. Their intensively cultivated vegetables and fruits allowed human communities to become more stable because of the greater assurance of consistent food. Gardening and farming (the cultivation of plants at a somewhat larger scale) advanced at an equal pace. And religion, a strong factor in human cultures since Neanderthal times, took on new meaning; by the time of the Greeks, gods and goddesses of fertility were much called upon to ensure the productivity of the soil.

New plants and beasts needed to work the ground and benefit from its bounty helped to develop intervillage and regional commerce. Hunting land dropped in esteem in human eyes; farm and garden land increased in value. Gardening contributed to the solid social base that allowed high cultures to flourish.

Few traces of early agricultural sites remain in the Middle East or elsewhere. Telltale signs include fire rings, shelter rings, and stone implements. There are also **Cromlechs, Dolmens, Menhirs, Trilithons,** q.q.v., and other remnants of early cultures that linked agriculture with hunting and gathering. It remained for the Egyptians, the Chinese, the Indus Valley people, and perhaps the ancient people of the Danube to take the next step to ornamental horticulture.

Preliminary drawings   See **Design development phase.**

Preliminary estimate   A projection of project costs submitted with schematic design or design development drawings based on current volume and area or labor and materials charges. See also **Detailed estimate of construction cost** and **"Ball park" estimate.**

Preliminary plans   See **Design development phase.**

Prequalification   In landscape contracting, the review of a bidder's or contractor's experience, qualifications, or bonding ability before the award of a contract. Prequalification is also used to limit the number of contractors bidding a job.

Preservation   A private and public activity promoting the continued existence of a wilderness or other primitive landscape in its unchanged condition. Preservation severely limits the use of a pristine landscape area to insure its intact survival. It is an all-inclusive kind of protectionism that is often complemented by **Conservation,** q.v., as a method of land management. See also **Historic preservation.**

Preservation, historic   See **Historic preservation.**

Preservative, oil-borne   See **Oil-borne preservative (wood).**

Preservative, wood   See **Wood preservative.**

Pressure   In irrigation, a measurement of water stress or force. Pressure is usually expressed as **Feet of head** (pump), q.v., or pounds per square inch. See also **PSI.**

Pressure, absolute (irrigation)   See **Absolute pressure.**

Pressure, atmospheric (irrigation)   See **Atmospheric pressure.**

Pressure, base (irrigation)   See **Base pressure.**

Pressure, bursting (irrigation)   See **Bursting pressure.**

Pressure, design (irrigation)   See **Design pressure.**

Pressure drop   See **Friction loss.**

Pressure, flow (irrigation)   See **Flow pressure.**

Pressure, hydropneumatic (irrigation)   See **Hydropneumatic pressure.**

Pressure, hydrostatic   See **Hydrostatic pressure.**

Pressure line (irrigation)   See **Main** or **Main line.**

Pressure loss (irrigation)   See **Friction loss.**

Pressure, nozzle   See **Flow pressure.**

Pressure, operating   See **Operating pressure.**

Pressure reducer (irrigation)   See **Pressure regulator.**

Pressure regulator   In irrigation, a valve installed in a system to maintain pressure at an optimum level. A pressure regulator often reduces pressure to an acceptable level. Also **Pressure reducer.**

Pressure, relief valve   See **Safety valve.**

Pressure, root   See **Root pressure.**

Pressure, static (irrigation)   See **Hydrostatic pressure.**

Pressure testing   In irrigation, an examination of the functioning of a main line under continuous "live" water pressure. Pressure testing is often carried out for a full day or longer.

Pressure treatment (of wood)   See **Wood preservative.**

Pressure vacuum breaker   In irrigation, a vacuum breaker operating under continual ("live") pressure. Often used in lieu of several **Atmospheric vacuum breakers,** q.v. See also **Backflow preventer, Vacuum breaker.**

Pressure, vapor (irrigation)   See **Vapor pressure.**

Pressure, water   See **Water pressure.**

Pressure, working (irrigation)   See **Working pressure.**

Prevailing wind   The usual wind for a certain season in a region.

Preventer, backflow   See **Backflow preventer.**

Priapus   In Greek and Roman mythology, the god of gardens. Possessed of enormous private parts, as he was also a god of fertility, Priapus carried a sickle or knife for pruning. His statues were placed in gardens to scare away birds, and are a source of the modern scarecrow. The rocket plant, *Erica sativa,* is named in his honor, and is considered an aphrodisiac. See also **Terminus.**

Price, contract   See **Contract price.**

Price per unit (landscape construction contracts)   See **Unit prices.**

Price, upset (construction)   See **Upset price.**

Price, Sir Uvedale (1747–1829)
English country gentleman and landscape critic; author of *An Essay on the Picturesque* (1794). Although Price is noted for his attack on the way in which the Brown-Repton naturalistic style had superseded and destroyed the late Renaissance formalism of Price's childhood, he is better remembered for his promotion of the "woodland" garden, modified ("improved") by a mass planting of naturalized rhododendron and other flowering shrubs. See also **English landscape architecture, Richard Payne Knight, Picturesque.**

Pricking off (out)   In horticulture, the first transplant of seedlings or cuttings.

Primary colors   Red, blue, and yellow. Mixed primary colors form all the other colors of visible light. See also **Secondary colors.**

Primary controller (irrigation)   See **Automatic controller.**

Primary growth   See **Plant growth.**

Primary succession   See **Plant succession.**

Prime coat, asphalt   See **Asphalt prime coat.**

Prime consultant   The key individual or organization responsible for project design and advice. See also **Consultancy.**

Prime contract   1) The agreement between an owner and a landscape contractor in which general responsibility for project installation is established. The prime contractor may then subcontract portions of the work to acceptable specialty contractors. 2) The agreement between an owner and a designer that establishes general design responsibility for a project. The primary designer may subsequently hire approved consultants to help complete the work. See also **General contract.**

Primer, purple and other   In irrigation, a chemical used in preparing PVC pipe ends for joining.

Uvedale Price. Frontispiece by Sir Thomas Dick Lauder from Sir Uvedale Price's essay "On the Picturesque." Illustration courtesy BBMSL, UNM.

Primitive gardens See **Prehistoric gardens.**

Principal 1) In legal contracts, a party who authorizes an individual or group to act as agent in its behalf. See also **Agency** and **Agent.** 2) A partner in a design firm.

Print In landscape architecture, a reproduction of an original plan, used for review, reference, and construction. See also **Blueprint.**

Probable maximum precipitation (PMP) The estimated greatest snow or rainfall for an area.

Probe, soil See **Soil probe.**

Procumbent An adjective used for low-growing or low-lying plants.

Produce A vegetable or fruit crop.

Productivity of soil See **Soil productivity.**

Professional corporation (PC) In landscape architecture, a legally registered entity formed to provide design services for a fee. Professional corporations somewhat limit the liability each designer must assume. In addition, a professional corporation may theoretically exist beyond the lifetimes of the individuals who have founded it. A professional association (PA) is similar.

Professional degree(s) In the United States and elsewhere, a 5- or 6-year first degree in landscape architecture or a second (master's) degree in the same or related fields. See also **Education in landscape architecture.**

Professional fee Reimbursement made to a landscape architect by a client (an owner) for services rendered. A professional fee may be set on a "cost-plus" basis, as a percentage of construction, on an hourly basis, as a lump sum (flat fee), or by other suitable methods. Compensation for such additional items as telephone calls, costs of plan and specification printing, travel, and the like is customarily made in addition to the stipulated fee.

A professional fee is normally part of a **Design contract,** q.v.

See also **Cost plus fee, Flat fee, Hourly fee, Per diem, Per unit fee, Percentage of construction cost fee,** and **Retainer.**

Professional liability insurance See **Malpractice insurance.**

Professional practice insurance See **Malpractice insurance.**

Professions, enviromental design See **Environmental design professions.**

Profile In design drawings, a longitudinal **Section,** q.v., showing a swale or road. Profiles usually indicate existing and proposed elements. The vertical scale is often exaggerated. Profiles are keyed to plan drawings.

Profile river See **River profile.**

Profile, soil See **Soil profile.**

Profile, stream See **River profile.**

Pro forma (Latin) Literally, "as a matter of form." A term used when a designer discusses a cost-benefit analysis with his client. Also the form used when preparing a cost-benefit analysis. See also **Cost-Benefit Analysis** and **Programming.**

Profile

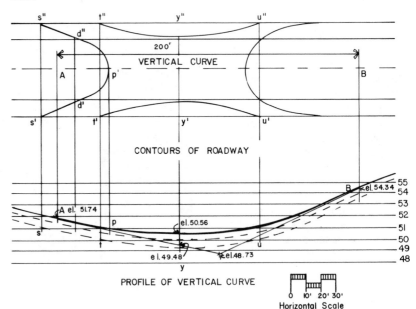

Programming In landscape architecture, an analysis of project requirements and the needs of the client, and an arrangement of goals set before design begins. Programming for design also includes the preparation of a schedule for plan production, review, and project construction. See also **Cost-benefit analysis** and **Pro forma.**

Progress payment See **Pay request.**

Progress schedule A program or chart prepared by a landscape contractor upon execution of a contract for construction that shows the installation of a project in proper sequence to the end of the allotted project time. Also **Construction schedule.** See also **Critical path method.**

Project budget A figure of total project expenditure established by the owner and/or the landscape architect, including professional fees, construction costs, financing costs, contingencies and the like. See also **Maximum allowable construction cost.**

Project cost See **Project budget.**

Project manual A book of **Specifications,** q.v.

Project, self-help See **Self-help project.**

Project, turnkey See **Turnkey project.**

Projection, axonometric See **Axonometric projection.**

Projection, isometric See **Isometric drawing.**

Projections Stones, bricks, or other units pulled partially out from a wall's flat surface for effect. See also **Oversailing course.**

Promenade An open public space used for walking or strolling. Often promenade ground(s). An **Esplanade** or **Mall,** q.q.v.

Promontory A high ridge or headland extending into a sea or lake.

Proof rolling In pavement construction, the passing of a weighted metal cylinder across a subgrade to check for highs and lows and to verify overall compaction.

Propagation The reproduction of plants by vegetative or sexual means.

Property line (PL) The property boundary, often staked, fenced, or otherwise indicated. A property line frequently forms the **Limits of construction,** q.v., of a project.

Property, real See **Real property.**

Property survey See **Survey.**

Proportion Usually, "Correct" proportion—i.e., the harmonious relationship of object sizes in a designed landscape or other human construct. See **Proportional harmony.**

Proportional harmony The establishment of an ideal size relationship among or within objects that appears in Western and Eastern approaches to design. In a golden section, the ratio is $1:\sqrt{2}$. In nature, the chambered nautilus displays ideal golden mean proportions. Also **Fibonacci number, Golden mean ratio.**

Propylaea

Proposal, bid See **Bid proposal.**

Proposal for site preparation See **Bid proposal.**

Proposed contours See **Contour.**

Proposed (finish) grade See **Grade.**

Proprietary specifications See **Specifications.**

Prospect A visible landscape, especially that specific part of a landscape vista seen from a well-defined point.

Propylaea (propylaeum, Greek) A kind of monumental and sometimes commemorative structure located in front of the gates to a city or a temple.

Prostrate In horticulture, flat and close to the ground.

Prostyle An extrusive, colonnaded **Portico,** q.v.

Protandrous In flowers, pertaining to the development of anthers before carpels. An act of **Dichogamy,** q.v. See also **Protogynous.**

Protection, electrical surge (irrigation) See **Electrical surge protection.**

Protogynous In flowers, referring to the development of carpels before anthers. An act of **Dichogamy,** q.v. See also **Protandrous.**

Prototype An **Archetype,** q.v.

Provenance (also **provenience**) In horticulture, the place of origin for plants—i.e., nursery, growing field, seed source, or the like.

Province, climatic See **Climatic province.**

Province, geographic
See **Geographic province.**

Province, geologic
See **Geographic province.**

Province, physiographic
See **Geographic province.**

Province, phytogeographic
See **Phytogeographic province.**

Provincial park In Canada, a public park—usually scenic and rural—administered by a provincial government. Comparable to the U.S. **State park,** q.v.

Provisional acceptance In landscape construction, acceptance by an owner of the majority of contract work performed to complete a project, with a certain sum (usually 10%) withheld to cover the cost of any replacement work required during the guarantee period. See also **Acceptance, Conditional acceptance, Final acceptance.**

Provisions, general See **General conditions.**

Provisions, special (specifications) See **Special provisions.**

Proxemics A term used by the anthropologist Edward Hall and others for the study of human social distance.

Pruinose In plants, referring to a white, powdery covering. See also **Bloom.**

Pruning The selective cutting of plant branches or stems to stimulate fruit production, provide for safety from low-hanging branches, create better form, and the like. Proper, wise pruning is necessary for continued plant health.

Root pruning is sometimes practiced to stimulate growth or to prepare a plant for transplanting.

Pruning, drop See **Drop pruning.**

Pruning, natural or self-
See **Natural pruning.**

PRV Pressure relief valve. See **Safety valve.**

PSF Pounds per square foot, a measure of stress used less frequently than **PSI,** q.v.

PSI Pounds per square inch—a measure of stress or pressure. See also **KSMM** and **Stress.**

PSY In landscape construction, an abbreviation for pounds per square yard, a measure of pressure.

PT A plan drawing abbreviation for **Point of tangency,** q.v.

Pteridophyte (pteridophyta) A spore-producing plant. A division of the plant kingdom including ferns, clubmosses, horsetails, and the like. See also **Botanical classification, Cormophyte, Spermatophyte.**

Pubescence A thin, powdery, downy leaf covering. Also **Farina.** See also **Bloom, Glaucous.**

Pubescent In botany, a plant or plant part covered with tiny hairs. Hairy.

Public easement See **Easement.**

Public garden A specialized kind of public park featuring intensive plantings of specimen trees, shrubs, flowers, and the like. Public gardens are sometimes combined with zoos. Some of the best-known examples in the United States include Founders Memorial Garden (Athens, Georgia), Dumbarton Oaks (Washington, D.C.), Bellingrath Gardens (Mobile, Alabama), Hershey Gardens (Hershey, Pennsylvania), the George Eastman House (Rochester, New York), and others. See also **Arboretum, Botanical garden.**

Public landscape A landscape developed for public purposes or with tax funds. Public landscapes include parks, street tree plantings, malls, campuses, rest stops, squares, the surrounds of tax-supported institutions, and the like.

Public liability insurance
See **Liability insurance.**

Public utility A company, usually a monopoly, licensed by a government agency to provide essential public services or goods. Often granted easements for the provision of its products. See also **Easement, Utility.**

Public way See **Right of way.**

Pueblo

Puckler-Muskau, H. L. H. von
(1785–?)   German prince (*fürst*) and
landscape gardener. Hermann
Ludwig Heinrich von Puckler-Muskau
inherited his father's estates at
Muskau, on the Neisse River, and
Branitz in 1811. A great student and
admirer of the English landscape
garden, he began the revamping of
his grounds at Muskau in 1815 and
kept at it until 1845. Muskau was
developed as a large park of native
plantings in naturalistic line with
multiple eclectic elements. Von
Puckler-Muskau's ideal was the
Sublime—a highly romantic,
gloomy, wild landscape of lawns
and forest. He also laid out a few
flowerbeds.

The prince conveyed his thoughts
on landscape gardening in his
Hints on Landscape Gardening
(*Andeutungen uber Lanschafters–
gartnerei*) of 1834.

By the time he was ready to
devote himself to his second estate,

Branitz, the enormous costs of the
Muskau estate had nearly
bankrupted him. The flat Branitz
terrain was swampy, but the
undaunted Puckler-Muskau designed
planters of flowers and a pyramid
near the Branitz castle. This second
estate never developed the high
quality of the first. But Puckler-
Muskau's work influenced the work
of such other nineteenth-century
designers as **Baron von Haussmann,**
q.v.

Today, the Muskau estate is half in
East Germany and half in Poland,
split by the Neisse. And the *fürst* is
buried in his own pyramid.
See also **German landscape
architecture.**

PUD   Planned unit development,
q.v.

Puddled soil   An unstructured clay
soil of great compaction when wet.

Puddling   In horticulture, the
dipping of the root system of a
bareroot tree or shrub into a messy
mixture of topsoil and water just
before planting. Useful in small-scale
garden plantings. Puddling coats the
hair roots (feeder roots) of the plant
and allows quick transplant recovery
and growth.

Pueblo   A unique, single or
multistory housing complex inhabited
by sedentary Indian tribes in the
southwestern United States combining
basic indigenous landscape materials
in indoor and outdoor design of
unusual harmony and usefulness.

Pugmill   A hot-mixing plant used to
combine aggregates and asphalt
cement to produce **Asphaltic cement.**

Pull-post (fencing)   See **Post.**

Pulling of pipe (irrigation)   See
Pipe pulling.

Pulse crop　See **Legume.**

Pulverization　Smashing into fine particles.

Pulvinate　In plant structures, cushioned or cushion-like in form.

Pumice　A very light volcanic rock, formed from lava "froth." Pumice floats on water and is sometimes used in man-made landscapes as a mulch.

Pump, booster　See **Booster pump.**

Pump, centrifugal, turbine, or submersible　Booster pumps, q.v.

Pump, jockey　See **Jockey pump.**

Pump, main　See **Main pump.**

Pump, outlet　See **Outlet.**

Pump station　See **Lift station.**

Punch list　In landscape construction, a listing of items yet to be completed to bring a project into full compliance with plans and specifications. Punch lists are usually prepared by the landscape architect and landscape contractor at a prefinal or final inspection. See also **Final acceptance, Final inspection, Final payment.**

Punching　In irrigation, the ramming, augering, boring, or water-jetting of a piece of pipe under a drivepad, sidewalk, or other solid surface to allow installation of a sprinkler line. Punches are the result of punching. See also **Water auger.**

Purification of water　See **Water purification.**

Pure live seed (PLS)　In horticulture, the percentage of a required species in a given quantity of seed, the remainder being weed seed or other impurities. The pure live seed amount is measured as the percentage of seed germination at a site added to the hard seed and the percentage of pure seed present in the mixture divided by 100.

Purity and germination (of grass seed)　See **Pure live seed.**

Purlin　In landscape construction, a horizontal beam supporting rafters or finish members in an overhead structure.

Purple garden　See **Gray and lavender garden.**

Pusztas (puszias)　Hungarian plains. See **Steppe.**

PVC　See **Point of vertical curvature.**

PVC (polyvinyl chloride) pipe　In irrigation, an extremely common sort of white (or brown) pipe often used as a replacement for galvanized pipe. PVC is durable but brittle and subject to deterioration from ultraviolet light, vibration, and other factors. It is sometimes called **Rigid pipe** or **Plastic pipe.** See also **Copper pipe, Galvanized pipe, Polyethylene pipe.**

PVI　See **Point of vertical intersection.**

PVT　See **Point of vertical tangency.**

Pylon　1) A gateway—especially the tapering gateposts of Egyptian monumental architecture. 2) A property or boundary marker.

Pyriform　Like a pear.

Pyrophyte　A plant species that is resistant to fire.

Pyrrol　See **Chlorophyll.**

Q Abbreviation for volume of runoff expressed as a rate of flow (Q = CIA). See **Rational formula.**

Qanat An Arabic term for an underground irrigation channel, often lined with stone, and constructed and maintained by means of stone chimneys. The quanat is a frequent feature in Persian **Paradise gardens** and **Chahar-baghs.** Also **Foggara.** See also **Persian landscape architecture.**

Quad, quadrangle 1) A campus square or courtyard. 2) The four boundaries of a surveyed plat of land. 3) A standard survey map.

Quadrat A square meter of random vegetation used for study or analysis.

Quadriga In statues, a stone chariot drawn by a team of four horses.

Quadrilateral Four-sided. Quadrilateral symmetry involves two crossed axes and the four equal divisions that they create.

Quadripartite Containing four pieces or parts.

Quagmire A sticky bog.

Quantity of water The measurement of water for specific uses. In the English-speaking world, the acre-foot is often used for agriculture and large-scale man-made landscapes; flow in cubic feet per second (CFS) is used with streams or rivers; water flow in gallons per minute (GPM) is computed for most urban landscapes.

Quantum meruit (Latin) In design and construction contracts, an implied agreement between the parties that the owner will pay the landscape architect or landscape construction a fair amount for services rendered. *Quantum meruit* applies when basic compensation has not been made contractually clear.

Qanat

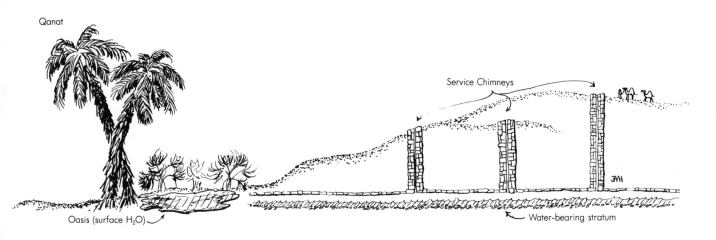

Oasis (surface H_2O)

Service Chimneys

Water-bearing stratum

Quaquaversal   Streaming out in radial directions from a central point.

Quarry   A kind of open mine from which stone is extracted in blocks for building purposes. Also, a gravel or sand mine.

Quarry tile   A popular paving and detail tile, usually larger than six square inches and thicker than one-half inch, made by extrusion, and often red or off-red in color.

Quarter head   In irrigation, a lawn or shrub spray head that emits a nozzle spray of 90° covering $1/4$ circle in area. See also **Head.**

Quarter post   In surveying, the intersection of a **Quarter-line,** q.v., with a section line boundary. North, south, east, and west quarter posts are recognized.

Quarter-line   In surveying, a north-south or east-west centerline used to divide a section into quarters. See also **Eighthlines.**

Quaternary   A geologic period consisting of the **Pleistocene** and **Holocene** (or Recent) epochs, q.q.v. The youngest period of the Cenozoic Era.

Quattrocento   The 1400s in Italian art. A common term of Renaissance reference.

Quay   A deepwater dock.

Quenouille training (French)   In horticulture, a kind of **Espalier,** q.v., in which the trained plant develops into a perfect cone. A time-consuming pruning of upper branches and staking-down of lower ones over a period of years is the common practice.

Quick coupler   In irrigation, a spring-seating valve, manually inserted, which is opened by a coupler key. A sprinkler (usually impact) head is then inserted into the valve. Quick coupling valves are usually under continuous line pressure and were formerly common in golf courses. See also **Coupler key.**

Quick coupling valve   See **Quick coupler.**

Quicklime   The product of superheated limestone. Burnt lime.

Quicksand   A usually watery area of unconsolidated sand at a river bank, bottom, or mouth, or along a seacoast. Hazardous to foot or vehicle passage.

Quickset   A hedge, or a stripling that will form part of a hedge (usually British).

Quiescence   In flowering plants, a state of hibernation or rest in preparation for flowering, leafing, or branching.

Quincunx   A formal, classical site design in which five statues, posts, or other features are laid out in a **Piazza,** q.v., with a statue or the like at each of the four corners and in the center.

Quinta   A Spanish or Portuguese villa, or country estate, derived from Roman models. See **Portuguese landscape architecture.**

Quintinie, Jean de la   Seventeenth-century French author and gardener. De la Quintinie worked on the development of Versailles, primarily in fruit and vegetable production. See also **French landscape architecture.**

Quoin   A right angle corner in a wall. The joint of two brick surfaces meeting at a corner.

R

R An abbreviation for **Radius,** q.v., in construction drawings.

R horizon A **Soil horizon,** q.v., which lies under the C horizon. Normally bedrock.

Race, climatic See **Climatic race.**

Race, geographic See **Climatic race.**

Raceme In botany, a simple inflorescence or flower cluster along an extended axis. Adjective: **racemose.** See also **Pedicel.**

Rachis In plant structures, the axis or "stem" of a compound leaf, or the axis of an inflorescence or individual flower cluster.

Radial drainage A drainage pattern associated with a solitary peak or closed basin with a single low point in which stream courses radiate out from or in toward a central area. See also **Drainage pattern.**

Radial symmetry See **Symmetry.**

Radiation, adaptive See **Adaptive radiation.**

Radiation, ultraviolet or UV See **Ultraviolet radiation.**

Radical 1) A kind of base leaf found in perennials and biennials at the ground. 2) Pertaining to roots.

Radicel A small plant root. See also **Radix.**

Radius (R) In landscape construction, used to lay out curves of roads, paths, mowing strips, and the like. The radius indicates the inside or outside of an arc from a given reference point.

Radius, hydraulic See **Hydraulic radius.**

Radix A plant root. Also **Radicel.**

Rafter In landscape construction, a plank that supports the roof of an overhead structure or greenhouse.

Ragnaia (Italian) Shrubbery for birds or bird-hunting.

Rail fence (hurdle fence) A rather open, rough-wood fence of semiuniform uprights and stringers.

Rain Individual drops of water which condense in clouds, gain in size, and are eventually brought to earth by gravity. See also **Rainfall.**

Rain, acid See **Acid rain.**

Rain forest A dense stand of trees and undergrowth found in tropical and temperate areas of high rainfall. Typical tropical rain forests (equatorial forests) are found in Brazil and Cameroon. Temperate rain forests include those of Westland, South Island, New Zealand, and the Cascade Range of the northwestern United States. See also **Jungle.**

Rain, orographic See **Orographic rain.**

Rail fence

Rain shadow A mountainous, hilly, or flat area of light rainfall on the leeward side of a mountain range. Orographic rain is deposited on the windward side, thus creating the rain shadow effect. See also **Orographic rainfall.**

Rain wash A rainwater-accelerated **Soil creep,** q.v.

Rainfall The total precipitation occurring in an area, including rain, snow, hail, and sleet. Dew, frost, and rime are also considered in rainfall calculation. Rainfall occurs as part of a convectional, cyclonic, or orographic cloud formation, and is directly related to prevailing winds. See also **Convectional rainfall, Cyclonic rainfall, Orographic rainfall.**

Raised bed A flower or vegetable planter set out above surrounding grade to provide for better drainage and ease of maintenance. See also **Parterre.**

Raised bog See **Hochmoor.**

Raising See **Drop pruning.**

Rake A long-handled, tined implement, hand or machine powered, used to gather debris, grass, hay or other materials. See also **Power raking.**

Ram, hydraulic See **Hydraulic ram.**

Ramble A wandering, informal garden path.

Rammed earth Pressed adobe in forms, often used in wall and other construction. Also **Pise de terre (French).**

Ramp An inclined plane. A common maximum for pedestrian and handicapped traffic is 12%; 6% or 8% is preferable.

Ramp, water See **Water ramp.**

Rampant (-growing) plant A vigorously growing or spreading plant, often a ground cover, used in low-maintenance landscape areas.

Rampart A low, rounded hillock or man-made ridge ringing a city or castle. Also, the crenelated stone parapets of a castle, used for observation and defense.

Rand An Afrikaans term for a low range or ridge of hills.

Range 1) Grazing area. Rangeland. 2) The geographic distribution of a plant or animal species. 3) A line of long mountain ridges or ridges and peaks.

Range, diurnal See **Diurnal range.**

Range management The art and science of planning and controlling the use of pasturelands and nearby areas for grazing and related agricultural purposes.

Range, tidal See **Tidal range.**

Ratchet An irrigation pipe-threading tool.

Rate of absorption (irrigation) See **Absorption rate.**

Rate of discharge (irrigation) See **Discharge rate.**

Rate of infiltration (irrigation) See **Percolation rate.**

Rate, lapse See **Lapse rate.**

Rate of percolation See **Percolation rate.**

Rate of precipitation (irrigation) See **Precipitation rate.**

Ratio, building/space See **Building/space ratio.**

Ratio, golden mean See **Proportional harmony.**

Ratio of slope See **Slope ratio.**

Ratio of void (soils, urban design) See **Void ratio.**

Ratio of water to cement (concrete) See **Water-cement ratio.**

Rational design An approach to landscape architecture that emphasizes the use of logic, codification, and applied intelligence to solve problems of site design. Often combined with **Intuitive design,** q.v.

Rational formula (for runoff) A reasonably accurate method for calculating runoff of watersheds up to two acres, or larger. Expressed as $Q = CiA$, in which: 1) Q is the volume of runoff in cubic feet per second; 2) C is the coefficient of runoff (the percentage of water not soaking into the site); 3) i is the intensity of runoff measured in inches per hour; and 4) A is the amount of land as expressed in acres.

Ravine A narrow, V-shaped valley or cut in the earth.

Raw land Undisturbed, undeveloped, and unplanned land.

Rays, medullary See **Medullary rays.**

RCP Reinforced concrete pipe, often used in landscape drainage.

Reaction, soil See **pH factor.**

Real estate Land and the structures erected on it; property. See also **Real property.**

Real property Land, the structures built upon it, and any rights which may pertain to its use or intended use. See also **Chattels, Real estate.**

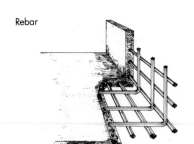

Rebar

Rebar   A ribbed steel reinforcement rod used to add tensile strength to poured concrete. Rebar is measured in numbers from 1 to 8. #3 rebar is ³/₈ inch, #5 is ⁵/₈ inch, and so on. Also **Bar, Reinforcing bar, Reinforcing rod, Rod.**

Recent (period)   See **Holocene.**

Receptacle, flower   See **Flower receptacle.**

Reclamation   Any attempt to restore or condition an area of agriculturally or otherwise unusable land so that fertility is improved, soil loss is minimized, and beneficial use results.

Reclinate   In plant structures, bent down.

Record drawings   See **As-built drawings.**

Recreation   Play or diversion. Design for private and public outdoor recreation is one of the landscape architect's principal tasks. Recreation is often divided into active and passive categories.

Rectangular coordinates   See **Coordinates** and **Plane coordinates.**

Rectangular drainage   A striking drainage pattern associated with geologic block fault areas in which streams follow fault and joint lines in angular courses. See also **Drainage pattern.**

Recumbent   In plants, resting on the ground. See also **Decumbency.**

Recurved   In plants, strongly flexing to a side or backward.

Recycling of water   See **Water reuse.**

Red desert soil   A reddish arid soil developing in hot, dry areas under sporadic, shrubby vegetation. See also **Gray earth.**

Red garden   A usually private garden laid out with red foliage plants or flowering annuals and perennials as a main theme. This kind of garden often uses white or blue accent plantings to offset the red central color. Also **Maroon garden.**

Red and yellow earth (red and yellow podsolic soils)   See **Podsol.**

Reduced pressure backflow preventer   In irrigation, a three-valve backflow preventer installed in a main. The central component is an atmospheric pressure differential relief valve which separates two check valves. See also **Backflow preventer.**

Reducer, pressure (irrigation)   **Pressure regulator.**

Redwood   A softwood of the genus *Sequoiadendron* or *Sequoia,* species *giganteum* (*gigantea*) or *sempervirens,* respectively, with an especially durable heartwood, widely used in North American landscape construction and, when uncut, as ornamental plantings.

Reed-sedge   See **Peat.**

Reed sods   Sod cut square from reed beds to about one foot (30 cm) by one foot (30 cm), used in revegetation.

Refectory   A room—often an outdoor room—in which meals are served.

Reference drawing   A drawing necessary for project construction but included in the contract documents only by reference. See also **Reference specification.**

Reference line   In design drawing, a baseline used to locate fixed landscape elements by dimensioned scaling. See also **Dimension.**

Reference specification   A specification necessary for project construction documents but included only by reference. APWA General Conditions are an example. See also **Reference drawing.**

Reflexed   Pertaining to plant parts, particularly branches or leaves, that show a distinct downward turn. See also **Decurved, Deflexed.**

Reflux valve   See **Check valve.**

Reforestation   The reclamation of woodland destroyed by fire or erosion through tree and understory planting. See also **Forestation.**

Refugium   In geography, a small land area, remnant of an earlier era, that shelters relic or relict species of plants. See also **Relic.**

Reg   A Saharan landscape in which a flat plain is covered by gravel or stones, all soil and sand having been carried off by the wind. See also **Erg, Hammada.**

Regeneration   In plants, the production of various organs or indeed an entire specimen from a root, stem, branch, leaf, or other part.

Regimen, stream   See **Stream regimen.**

Region, natural   See **Natural region.**

Region, plant growth   See **Hardiness zone, Life zone, Plant growth region.**

Region, soil   See **Soil region.**

Regional planning   See **Planning.**

Registered seed   See **Commercial seed classifications.**

Registration, landscape architectural   See **Landscape architectural registration.**

Regolith   In geology, the loose material of the surface of the Earth—i.e., unattached portions of rocks and minerals. Sometimes used as a synonym for soil.

Regosol (regsol)   A soil without true horizons that consists of a deep, loose mass of rock fragments. See also **Azonal soil** and **Lithosol.**

Regulator, pressure (irrigation)   See **Pressure regulator.**

Regur (regar)   An **Intrazonal soil,** q.v., that is dark in color, loamy, and high in clay content. A rich soil of India.

Reimbursable expense   See **Direct expense.**

Reinforced concrete   Concrete with steel rebars or steel mesh added for tensile and shear strength. Reinforced concrete resists bending and stretching, and is a highly useful, extremely common twentieth-century building material. See also **Shear strength** and **Tensile strength.** Also **Ferro-concrete.**

Reinforced concrete pipe   See **RCP.**

Reinforcing bar (steel)   See **Rebar.**

Reinforcing rod   See **Rebar.**

Rejuvenated landscape   A landscape uplifted by natural forces.

Relative growth increment   In horticulture or bioengineering, a measurement of plant growth as determined by a volume or weight increase of some kind.

Relative humidity   See **Humidity.**

Release of lien   The dropping of a claim against property for unpaid taxes, goods, or services upon satisfaction of the demands of the claim. See also **Lien.**

Relic (relict)   In botany, a plant, quantity of plants, or plant association surviving from a previous age. *Ginkgo biloba* is an example. See also **Refugium.**

Relief   The variations in elevation and contour of the Earth's surface. The pronounced lay of the land.

Relief desert   An arid or semiarid, often high altitude area, characteristically found in the interior of a continent, on which clouds formed over the sea are prevented from dropping rain by successive mountain ranges and great distances from the coast. The Gobi, North American, and Takla Makan deserts are examples. See also **Desert, Desertification,** and **Tropical desert.**

Relief drainage   A perforated pipe (or series of pipes) installed in a trench on relatively flat ground to provide improved drainage.

Relief, photo   See **Photo relief.**

Relief, point of (irrigation)   See **Water hammer.**

Religious landscape architecture   See **Ecclesiastical landscape architecture.**

Remolded soil   A man-made soil. Any soil changed or modified in structure by human activity.

Remontant   Of flowers or plant growth, a second blooming or budding in a single growing season.

Remote control valve   In irrigation, an automatic valve operated electrically from a distance. 1) **Normally open valve:** opens when electric power is suspended. 2) **Normally closed valve:** closes when electric power is suspended. Formerly, a hydraulically operated valve. Also **Automatic valve.**

Renaissance (Italian) landscape architecture   The ambulatories and cloisters of the Middle Ages were self-contained, all views inward, self-sufficient, suited to the contemplation of a very sober God. The Renaissance, developing in the **Quattrocento** (1400s) and lasting until the seventeenth century, was marked by outward views, the growing excitement of secular affairs, the definition of the Italian language in the works of Dante and Boccaccio, and by high art: painting, landscape architecture, building design, and sculpture that have remained the standard of the Western world ever since. In landscape architecture, two principal forms emerged in Italy: the piazza, or public square, and the Roman hillside villa, revived from its medieval slumber.

Medieval squares, though suitable for trading and moderate traffic, were often alternately dusty and muddy, fly-ridden, unpaved, unfocused. In the Renaissance, new mercantile fortunes made possible the construction of churches, fountains, and sculptures—all well displayed to the side or in the center of an open square, and all providing a focus, a conscious reason for the piazza to exist. Intricate pavements of tiles and cut stone kept down muddiness and carried off water. Medieval squares refined in the Renaissance include the Piazza della Signoria, Florence; the Piazza del Campo, Siena; the Piazza di San Pietro (St. Peter's Square), Rome; and the unmatched Piazza San Marco (St. Mark's Square) in Venice. These *piazze* depend on human activity and striking pavements for their liveliness; there are no trees. The Piazza Annunciata, in Florence, is generally thought of as the first "Renaissance square." The **Piazzetta,** or small piazza, was often designed for a private client to complement an imposing building or garden; Bernini's late Renaissance oblique piazza at the Vatican, constructed at the Spanish Steps, was a papal commission. In Rome, Siena, and elsewhere, the piazza with its radiating streets served as the core of the city.

The architect and theoretician **Leone Battista Alberti** (1404–72), q.v., set out a series of rules for the design of villas in his *De Re Aedificatoria* (1452). Most of these were taken from Pliny (see **Roman landscape architecture**) and, in keeping with the rising spirit of the Renaissance, were an interpretation of classical themes. A proper villa needed a good hill with a view and water. Around the house, a series of compartment gardens were to be laid out in terraces abstracted carefully from the slope. The design line was formal, and the display gardens nearest the house were intended for viewing from important inside rooms. Fountains and topiary work, including mazes, filled the gardens. Vineyards and a **Bosco,** or grove, were laid out at some distance from the house. Alberti's approach to the villa was winding

Renaissance landscape architecture. Piazza San Marco, Venice. Photo courtesy BBMSL, UNM.

and romantic, providing glimpses of the pleasures of house and garden as visitors rode up.

The open and joyous quality of Alberti's ideas proved very popular indeed. The usual Renaissance villa designer was an architect, a hydraulic engineer, a sculptor, or perhaps a painter. He worked with a new sense of systematic perspective developed by Filippo Brunelleschi (1377–1446), an early Renaissance architect who practiced in Florence. The designer's vision of an ideal garden was defined by the romantic and very long-lived monk Francesco Colonna (1433–1527), whose "garden of the imagination"

was described in *The Strife of Love in a Dreame* (*Hypnerotomachia Poliphili*), translated c. 1592. Colonna thought old ruins to be wonderful additions to a new garden. The definitive vocabulary of Renaissance building elements was provided by Andrea Palladio (d. 1580), whose neoclassical structures have influenced Western design into the twentieth century. Palladio was especially concerned with the integration of building and grounds into a single unit.

The Villa Medici at Fiesole (1453) was among the earliest and best of Renaissance villas. Commissioned by Cosimo dei Medici, it was designed

Renaissance landscape architecture. Boboli Gardens, Pitti Palace, Florence: Isolotto pond. Photo courtesy BBMSL, UNM.

also retained to create the highly unusual water effects, which included water tricks and a water organ as well as fountains and pools. Ligorio's ornate and highly geometric layout, based on Alberti's principles, has been subdued over time by great masses of overgrown plants.

At the Villa Lante (begun c. 1564) near Bagnaia, a nearly perfect Renaissance estate designed by **Giacomo Barozzi de Vignola,** q.v., thin rectangular terraces with water stairs suggest Moorish influence. **Casinos,** a maze, and excellent vistas have contributed to the charm of the Lante gardens over time, and their design and scale anticipate the great French gardens of the seventeenth century. The Villa Farnese (1560) at Caprarola, with its caryatids, hillside cascade, and moderate size, also suggests Vignola's mastery of scale and detail. In addition, Vignola designed the Villa di Papa Giulio (1555) in Rome and expanded on Michelangelo's work at St. Peter's.

Two curious villa gardens of the sixteenth century do not fit into convenient patterns. Giulio Romano's (d. 1546) Pallazzo del Te at Mantua displays an early use of **Chinoiserie,** q.v. The Villa Orsini at Bomarzo, a garden of huge, grotesque statuary carved out of boulders on a hillside, was completed in the 1560s by an unknown designer. The Villa Aldobrandini at Frascati (c. 1598)

by Michelozzo Michelozzi on a hillside with a splendid view of Florence. The Spaniards controlled a great deal of Italy in the fifteenth century, and some of the features of their own villas, such as water stairs and lively pools, began to appear in Italian hillside estates.

The Renaissance villa was fully developed in the sixteenth century. Bramante designed a **Belvedere** for the Vatican in 1503, a summerhouse in the midst of neoclassical gardens.

The Medici built another villa (c. 1540), this time in Rome, and filled it with parterres and great transverse allees of trees. The designer was Annibale Lippi, who sited the garden just above the Spanish Steps to take advantage of a good view of Rome. The Villa d' Este, perhaps the greatest of the world's water gardens, was constructed in Tivoli between 1550 and 1580 from a plan by **Pirro Ligorio,** q.v. Orazio Olivieri, the hydraulic engineer, was

was designed along more conventional Renaissance lines by Giacomo della Porta and Carlo Maderno. It is a transitional villa, furnished with a grotto, a water theatre, clipped hedges, and other baroque elements.

The great villa development of the sixteenth century was paralleled by the refinement of the piazza, the establishment of Europe's first botanical garden at Padua in 1545, and the extraordinary growth of Renaissance sculpture. Michelangelo Buonarroti (1475–1564), famous for such figures as "David" as well as for the creation of the oval piazza, set an almost impossible standard. His direct heir, the baroque master Gianlorenzo Bernini (1598–1680), nearly matched it. These and other first-rate sculptors furnished gardens and piazze with some of the finest sculpture the West has ever produced.

Much of the playfulness of the early Renaissance had disappeared by the time the baroque Isola Bella (c. 1632–70) was constructed in Lake Maggiore. Many favorite villa plants, such as acanthus, olives, plane trees, and cypresses, persisted; but the clean and highly charged garden line had vanished. Water tricks and ornate, superfluous detail characterize Isola Bella and such other seventeenth-century baroque estates as the Villa Garzoni and the Villa Gaspero Massini.

The architectonic quality of both villa and piazza in Renaissance Italy heavily influenced seventeenth-century France and the rest of Europe until the advent of the English Landscape Gardening School of the eighteenth and nineteenth centuries. Many baroque designs of great quality remain in the twentieth century, the most famous of which is probably Rome's Trevi Fountain, created between 1732 and 1762 by Nicola Salvi. In the nineteenth century, **Guiseppe Japelli,** q.v.,

Renaissance landscape architecture. Erice, Sicily: street pavement. Photo courtesy BBMSL, UNM.

produced a number of villa designs near Venice and in Rome in the landscape garden style. The best known of these is the Villa Torlonia in Rome. Milan's Galleria Vittorio Emmanuele (1864), by Guiseppe Mengone, is the prototype of the modern landscaped shopping arcade.

One of the most spectacular of contemporary Italian gardens is Ninfa, south of Rome, begun in 1922. The twentieth-century sculptor Arnaldo Pomodoro has produced outdoor pieces for clients in the United States, France, Australia, and

Brazil as well as his native Italy. Professor Pietro Porcinai (b. 1911) has established himself as a remarkable modern interpreter of villa design. In practice since 1935, he has built on Renaissance themes for his villas at Servardio, Fiorati, and elsewhere; his park work in Saudi Arabia and for the cities of Palermo and Milan has also brought him wide recognition. Porcinai's book *Giardini d'Occidente e d'Oriente* (1966) discusses his interpretation of the origins and meaning of the garden in human society.

Rendering. Illustration courtesy BBMSL, UNM.

Rendering. Entry, New Mexico State Fairgrounds. Arrison-Greer, architects; Morrow and Company, Ltd., landscape architects. Photo courtesy Arrison-Greer.

Rendering   A representational drawing, in color, pencil, black and white, or a combination of media, of a plan for design development.

Rendzina   A **Great soil group**, q.v., composed of an essentially calcium-rich material developed into a brown topsoil underlain by a lighter subsoil. Rendzina is found in grassy or forested areas with relatively humid climates.

Renewal, urban   See **Urban renewal.**

Reniform   In plant structures, a kidney-like form.

Repent   In horticulture, creeping or low-lying.

Repose angle   See **Angle of repose.**

Reproducible   In drafting, a sheet from which blue- or black-line prints may be made.

Reproduction, agamic (in plants)
See **Agamic reproduction.**

Reproduction, asexual (in plants)
See **Asexual reproduction.**

Reproduction, vegetative
See **Vegetative reproduction.**

Repton, Humphry (1752–1818)
English landscape gardener and writer. Repton and **Capability Brown**, q.v., are often mentioned in the same breath as the greatest of English landscape gardeners. Repton was better than Brown at creating a transition between house and grounds; he "softened" Brown's extremes, but he had a different aim in mind: he was fascinated with the large quantities of exotics coming into use at the time, and the courtyards and terraces of manor houses, treated somewhat formally, were ideal places to experiment with these new plants. Repton, who popularized the term "landscape gardening," mixed formal and informal elements in his designs as the needs of the site dictated.

Repton was born in Bury St. Edmunds, Suffolk, and lived in Holland and Ireland as well as England while a boy and young man. A contemporary of **Richard Payne Knight** and **Uvedale Price,** q.q.v., whom he influenced, Repton was a country gentleman until financial reverses squeezed him into a career as a landscape gardener in the 1780s. He announced his decision in letters to his friends. Repton was deeply influenced by Capability Brown, obtaining Brown's design notes from one of Brown's children. He later became a clear and convincing design theoretician: he noted well the difference between two-dimensional picturesque painting and the three-dimensional necessities of landscape design, in which the frame of reference changes constantly as the viewer moves through or past a garden.

Repton began the modern procedure of before-and-after sketches with his famous Red Books,

Humphry Repton

demonstrating his proposals to his clients in a series of fold-over drawings. He also used reports, maps, and cleanly drafted plans— all precursors of standard nineteenth and twentieth-century practice.

From 1792 to 1802, Repton was a partner in a country house-and-grounds practice with the architect **John Nash,** q.v., the creator of Regents Park in London. After 1802, Repton's sons did the bulk of the country house design required in his work. Repton's parks are very elegant, with broad, sweeping lawns, serpentine lakes, and massed trees in the best landscape gardening tradition. His landscape elements were frequently more refined and "natural" than any part of nature herself. Cobham Park in Kent, Welbeck Abbey in Nottinghamshire, Ashridge in Hertfordshire, and Holkham, Norfolk, are examples.

His *Sketches and Hints on Landscape Gardening* (1794) was the first of his books to state his theory of landscape design. Repton recognized that the changes in landscape taste in his day were closely related to the influence of the Industrial Revolution, and that an increasing interest in botany and botanical gardens was also part of the changing social and scientific conditions of the times.

He continued to write and design prolifically. His later works include: *Observations on the Theory and Practice of Landscape Gardening* (1803); *An Inquiry into the Changes of Taste of Landscape Gardening* (1806); and *Fragments on the Theory and Practice of Landscape Gardening* (1816). Repton also wrote a play, *Old Whims.* **J. C. Loudon,** q.v., later edited many of Repton's works, and Jane Austen pulled him into her novels.

Repton's influence on landscape architecture was profound. The style of his estate parks was adapted for

use in public parks by such later designers as **Paxton** and **Olmsted,** q.q.v. Of his more than 200 projects, a few remain in good condition. These include, among others, the Antony House at Torpoint in Cornwall and Plas Newydd on the Isle of Anglesey.

See also **English landscape architecture** and **English School of Landscape Gardening.**

Request, pay   See **Pay request.**

Requirements, general
See **General requirements** and Specifications.

Requirements, water   See **Water requirements.**

Reserve border   A small garden section utilized in growing replacement plant stock.

Reservoir   A man-made body of water created for any purpose.

Residential landscape   A house garden. Any garden or other surroundings around a private house, townhouse, or apartments.

Residential square   An English unit of town planning in the eighteenth and nineteenth centuries. An aristocratic, usually small-scale suburb. John Nash's Regents Park in London is an example. See also **John Nash.**

Residual soil   A local soil composed of decomposed rock generated in place. An early or incomplete soil.

Resources, water   See **Water resources.**

Respiration (in plants)   The intake of oxygen and output of carbon dioxide—a nighttime function. See also **Compensation point, Photosynthesis.**

Rest, roadside (safety rest)
See **Roadside rest area.**

Restaurant garden   A cafe landscape designed to enhance outdoor dining pleasure for patrons, with landscape elements chosen for color, texture, shade-producing and wind-breaking ability, and the like. See also **Sidewalk cafe.**

Resting (plants)   **Dormant** plants, q.v.

Resultant   In the physics of landscape construction, a downward and an outward force acting together on a wall or other structure. Any similar combination of forces.

Retainage   A sum held back by an owner from the amount due a landscape architect or landscape contractor during the progress of design or construction work. Normally does not exceed 10% of billed charges.

Retainer (design)   A fee paid by a client to engage the services of a landscape architect and ensure their availability for an agreed-on period of time. Retainer fees are often minimum charges for services rendered. See also **Professional fee.**

Retaining (retainer) wall   A vertical or tilted wall constructed to prevent hillside erosion. A fixed retaining wall is solidly held in place top and bottom by an additional structure or structures and can thereby be made more stable than a free-standing wall. See also **Cantilever, Counterfort,** and **Gravity walls.**

Retardant   See **Retarder.**

Retarder (concrete)   An admixture used to slow the hardening of concrete so that the material stays workable for a longer period of time. Also **Retardant.**

Restaurant garden. Hotel Amador, Las Cruces, New Mexico. Photo courtesy Bill Haghart.

Retarding of plants   Any gardening technique used to cause a late flowering or fruiting. See also **Forcing.**

Retention water   Water percolating into a site by natural means or through ponding. See also **Detention water.**

Reticulate or **Reticulated**   In botany, pertaining to leaves or other plant structures showing veins or a vascular network.

Reuse, water (water recycling)
See **Water reuse.**

Reveal   In landscape construction, a wall indentation or opening—usually a slit or channel in a flat plane surface. See also **Rustication strip.**

Revegetation   The regrowth of plant cover over a disturbed ground area. **Natural revegetation** takes place without human assistance, and ultimately results in a **Climax growth,** q.v.

Revenue bonds   See **Financing for public works construction.**

Reverse curve   A flat curve of two radii with opposite centers.

Reversion   1) In soils, the reaction of a mineral necessary for plant growth with the soil, resulting in the mineral's unavailability for use by plants. 2) In hybrid plants, a growth or reproductive pattern similar to that of its nonhybrid parent or parents. A "reversion to type." 3) In exotic landscapes, the return of the planted area to plant associations typical of its region due to vastly decreased watering, maintenance, or the like.

Revetment   A facing or covering of stone, masonry, sod, wood timbers, or the like installed on a ditchbank or hillslope, or at seaside, to support softer earth or sand and retard erosion. See also **Rip-rap.**

Revolute   In leaves, pertaining to the rolling or curling up of tips or margins.

Revolution, Harvard   See **Harvard Revolution.**

RGRCP   A sometimes used abbreviation for rubber gasket-reinforced concrete pipe.

Rhizobia   Bacteria found in the root nodules of legumes, useful in fixing nitrogen.

Rhizome (rhizoma)   A horizontal underground root or root-like stem, creeping out from a parent plant to produce new shoots. A **Rootstock,** q.v. See also **Stolon, Tiller.**

Rhizosphere   See **Root zone.**

Rhizoplane   The surface of a plant's root zone.

Rhythm (as an element of design)   In landscape architecture, an incidental occurrence of form, feature, or the like in an otherwise harmonious (homogeneous) composition. See also **Harmony.**

Rhythm, circadian   See **Circadian rhythm.**

Rhythm, diurnal   See **Circadian rhythm.**

Ria   A fjord or deeply cut bay (Ireland).

Rib   A leaf vein or a ridge on a stem.

Ribbon bedding   In gardens, bedding plants arranged in long lines or contrasting "ribbons" for textural, chromatic, or other effect.

Ribbon development   See **Strip development.**

Ricami (Italian)   An elaborate, interlacing plant pattern, usually consisting of bedding and other small plants. See also **Parterre de broderie.**

Ridge terrace   See **Mangum terrace.**

Riding   A green pathway or track cut through a park or forest. Sometimes, a riding trail or bridle path as well.

Right of lateral and subjacent support   Legally, the right of an owner to hold land supported by neighboring land. Excavation during construction of a project may remove such support and cause injury or damage to structures or the configuration of the land through hillside collapse, erosion, and the like.

Right of way (ROW, RW)   A public road, passageway, or easement bordering or bisecting public or private lands, in which utilities may be located and pedestrian or vehicular traffic may freely pass. A public way.

Righting moment   See **Moment.**

Rights, air   See **Air rights.**

Rights, riparian   See **Riparian rights.**

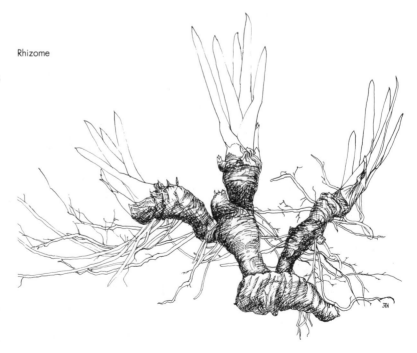
Rhizome

Rio Grande landscape architecture. "Frontier pastoral" style, Glorieta Baptist Conference Center, New Mexico. Photo by author.

Rigid pavement In landscape construction, solid-soil pavement containing Portland cement concrete as a finish course and/or foundation course. See also **Flexible pavement.**

Rigid pipe See **PVC pipe.**

Rill A tiny run of water usually generated by rainfall.

Rim elevation In site drainage, the elevation at the point of inlet of a drainage pipe, manhole, or other structure. The upper elevation of a drainage structure. The low inside elevation of the same structure is its **Invert,** q.v.

Rime Ice crystals formed on outside objects when supercooled droplets freeze on them. See also **Frost.**

Ring, fairy (lawns) See **Fairy ring.**

Rings, growth See **Growth rings.**

Rings, annual See **Growth rings.**

Rio Grande landscape architecture
A southwestern United States regional landscape architecture, eclectic but distinctive, begun in the modern era by C. E. "Bud" Hollied, the designer of Roosevelt Park in Albuquerque (1930s), Glorieta Gardens near Santa Fe (1950s), and other landscapes, and by Cecil Pragnell, designer of Los Poblanos gardens in Albuquerque (1930s) and codesigner of Glorieta Gardens.

Rio Grande landscape architecture incorporates a Spanish Mediterranean tradition of enclosed courtyards and fountains, English Naturalistic park conventions, and

irrigation systems, flagstone masonry, and adobe wall construction long used by Pueblo Indians in the area. Also typical are small-scale gardens developed by both Europeans and the indigenous people.

The evolving style has been much influenced by John Gaw Meem (d. 1983) and his Pueblo Revival architecture (Albuquerque: University of New Mexico; Santa Fe: St. Francis Auditorium, Museum of Fine Arts; and elsewhere), by the observations and notes of **J. B. Jackson,** q.v., by **Garrett Eckbo,** q.v., and others. Frequent elements are high-altitude plantings intended to withstand intensive ultraviolet radiation, oasis-style parks (Estancia, Roswell, Truth or Consequences, Las Cruces, and elsewhere), an increasing cultivation and use of native plants, a refined stylization of local landforms as landscape elements, and a developing sophistication in the use of local materials for outdoor landscape furnishings.

A series of estate and institutional grounds along the Rio Grande, mostly dating from the early twentieth century, best represent this distinctly regional landscape architecture. They include El Mirador near Espanola, Los Poblanos in Albuquerque, the Butte Gardens at Elephant Butte, and the original Carrie Tingley Hospital in Truth or Consequences.

See also **United States landscape architecture.** For the development of a similar high-altitude regional design, see **Persian landscape architecture.**

Riparian Referring to land along both banks of a (usually) nonnavigable stream. Also, any land adjacent to a streamcourse.

Riparian rights The rights of ownership and use of land along the banks of a nonnavigable stream. Also, the right of a landowner to use water flowing through his land. See also **Tort.**

Riparian vegetation Streamside plants.

Rippability The extent to which a stony soil may be removed or replaced by heavy mechanical equipment—especially a ripper.

Ripper In the United States and elsewhere, a toothed machine pulled by a tractor, used to loosen hardpan soil and rock. The process is called "ripping."

Rip-rap A slope-retaining cover of loose, irregular stone installed to retard erosion. See also **Revetment.**

Riser 1) The vertical face of a **Step** or **Stair,** q.q.v. See also **Tread.** 2) In irrigation, a vertical pipe extending above grade from a main or lateral line with a spray or bubbler head attached. See also **Head.**

Riser, adjustable See **Adjustable riser.**

River profile In geography, a lengthwise cross-section which shows the fall of a river from its source to its mouth. See also **Profile, Valley line.**

River terrace A flat or gently sloping escarpment or series of escarpments bounding a river channel.

Rivulet A brook or small stream.

Riwaq (Arabic) A **Peristyle,** q.v., or shaded walk rimming a courtyard. Especially, the shady arcade of a mosque.

Road, access See **Access road.**

Road, frontage See **Access road.**

Road oil A kind of heavy liquid asphalt used as a primer for gravelling and other road surface operations.

Road, traverse See **Traverse road.**

Roads, temporary See **Temporary roads.**

Roadside rest area (safety rest) In the United States and elsewhere, a turn-out along a roadway used as a public rest stop. Rest areas often have shade trees or shelters, toilets, picnic tables, hearths, and trash cans, but rarely accommodate overnight stays.

Robinson, William (1839–1935) Anglo-Irish journalist, critic, and landscape designer. Robinson was a strong influence on the career of his contemporary, the garden designer

William Robinson. Little Barrington, Gloucestershire, England. Garden by Robinson. Photo courtesy BBMSL, UNM.

Gertrude Jekyll, q.v. He stubbornly felt that the "wild woodland garden" was a high landscape ideal, and that his somewhat stilted Victorian naturalism was the key to successful garden layout. *Alpine Flowers for English Gardens* (1870) is perhaps his best-regarded book.

Robinson's garden ideas were partly based on his studies of the popular English kitchen garden. His *The English Flower Garden* (1883) reflects his fascination with "natural" design based on plants and their changing form. He thought of gardens as display spaces for "neat" plants. Robinson's early books *Gleanings from French Gardens* and *Parks, Promenades and Gardens of Paris,* were written from his experience on assignment in France for *The Times* of London. His later ideas regarding casual gardens were to a degree a reaction against the grandiloquence of French formal design.

See also **Irish landscape architecture.**

Rock   A solid mass of mineral or petrified matter. A stone. See also **Pebble** and **Stone.**

Rock blanket   A euphemism, primarily military, describing perfectly useful ground areas stripped of their cover (i.e., shrubs, grasses, and the like) and smothered in crushed stone. Vegetation is subsequently suppressed by heavy use of herbicides.

Rock, crushed   See **Gravel.**

Rock fall   A common kind of erosion in hills or mountains, caused by frozen water in rock fissures and the subsequent shattering of boulders on steep slopes.

Rock garden   A stony garden developed on a slope to resemble a glacial scree or moraine. The rock

garden uses low-lying and accent plants for texture, color, and contrast, carefully massed or singled out, but always integrated with the rocks to form a harmonious composition. Local stone, laid with a careful back tilt into the slope, will produce highly satisfactory results.

The Oriental garden compositions of the period of the late Middle Ages in Europe were the original inspiration for the rock gardens of the West. Alpine plants, their roots cooled in well-drained, very moist soil, and stylized waterfalls or pools are the customary features arranged with the stonework of the rock garden.

Also **Alpine garden,** q.v., developed as a small-scale imitation of a glacial **Moraine.** Rock gardens have been popular in English and American gardens since Victorian times.

See also **Scree.**

Rock, permeable   See **Permeable rock.**

Rock, pervious   See **Pervious rock.**

Rococo   A late **Baroque,** q.v., (sub) style of architectural and garden ornament. Shells, curlicues, leaves, bucolic bas-relief, and a general mixture of Oriental and European forms are typical of this eighteenth-century design fashion.

In landscape architecture, rococo is more light-hearted than baroque, beginning more or less with the death of the overshadowing Louis XIV of France in 1715.

Rod   1) A common measurement in fencing and racetracks of $16\frac{1}{2}$ feet or 5.03 meters. 2) A vertical bar, sometimes calibrated, used for surveying measurement. 3) **Rebar,** q.v.

Rod, reinforcing   See **Rebar.**

Rogue   A nontypical plant specimen. Roguing is the removal of poor specimens from a planting. See also **Chimaera.**

Roll, fascine   See **Wattling.**

Rolling (of soil)   In fill and paving operations and following lawn seeding, the compaction of earth or pavement layers or seed and top dressing by passing a weighted metal cylinder (roller) across the land surface.

Rolling, proof   See **Proof rolling.**

Rolling terrain   See **Prairie topography.**

Roman brick   A large (nominally 2 in. × 4 in. × 12 in.) brick sometimes used in walls or as a landscape paver in other constructions.

Roman landscape architecture
Priapus, the misshapen but fecund garden god, watched over Roman horticulture with a pruning knife and leering smile. His fellow god Terminus was set out on short posts at the garden's far corners to mark its boundaries. These eventually came to be property markers, or stakes. Priapus himself, always rougher as the later centuries of the empire wore on, turned into a familiar caricature of his old form— the scarecrow.

Of Roman public spaces and outdoor public works we know a great deal, as many of these are extant. The Roman forum, now a lumpy, grassy field in the center of the city with marble blocks lying roundabout, was an improvement over its predecessor, the Greek **Agora.** The forum was an open public market and gathering place, well paved, bounded by temples, merchants' stalls, the Senate, private houses, and, eventually, statues and

Roman landscape architecture. Roman forum.

victorious campaign arches. Roman amphitheatres, baths, roads, and aqueducts were creations of an innate permanence the twentieth century can only envy at a distance. Hippodromes, or horseracing rings, and the **Gestatio,** or strolling ground—popular for "constitutionals"—were common by the time of the late Republic. A visitor wandering through Rome in the first century B.C. would have noticed plane trees, olives, mulberries, figs, oleanders, palms, grapes, oaks, aspens, cypresses, and other familiar Western trees and shrubs planted in profusion. Violets, anemones, poppies, roses, crocuses, and other flowers were common as bedding plants or in formal parterres; boxwood, spruces, and laurels were available for topiary shaping. Roof gardens (sylvae in tectus) and windowboxes were also common throughout the city.

A series of large public gardens and parks had come into being along the Tiber by the time of Julius Caesar. Caesar himself donated a large estate garden to the citizens, setting an example followed by later emperors. Landscape art reached a high mark under Octavian (27 B.C.–14 A.D.), whose minister, Marcus Agrippa, is often credited with the development of the imperial villa at Tivoli (later completed by Hadrian) and with such landscape engineering works as the aqueduct (Pont du

Gard) at Mimes, France. In Rome itself, Nero's Golden House (c. 65 A.D.) was furnished with ponds, courts, specialty gardens, and a 120 foot (38 meter) statue of the emperor himself. This giant urban villa, notorious for its opulence and debauchery, was generally unpopular. The Emperor Vespasian built the Flavian amphitheatre (the Colosseum) in Nero's fish pond a short time after Nero's death. Other parts of Nero's pleasure gardens are today occupied by the Vatican.

Roman writers as well as the well-preserved ruins of Pompeii and Herculaneum have left us a detailed picture of Roman landscape design in its heyday. Dioscorides wrote an **Herbal,** Pliny the Elder *Historia Naturalis,* books on garden philosophy and natural history. We also have accounts of gardening and horticulture by Cato, Varro (market gardening), and Columella. The most influential of all, however, is Pliny the Younger (c. 100 A.D.), who described his villas at Florence and Laurentum in detail. Vistas were all-important in Pliny's gardens; walkways, trellises of carpenter's work, marble colonnades, good topiary gardens, sun-screening, fountains (including **Water jokes**), and lush plantings of figs, mulberries, grapes, stone pines, and flowers were staple garden features. Pliny's villas were perched on hillsides not only for views but for correct ventilation and ease of irrigation as well. His notes and ideas on Roman landscape design were lifted by the Renaissance theorist **Alberti,** q.v., who used them to devise his rules for villa planning in the fifteenth century. The first-century Pompeiian frescoes and other archaeological details of the destroyed city show a whimsical, almost romantic garden character: flowers, naiads, tiled alcoves, mosaics and fountains in classic Mediterranean courtyards shut off from the outside world. We also know that sycamores, willows, and olives were the usual street trees of the city. Truck gardens, vineyards, and orchards occupied much of the "open space" in downtown Pompeii. All in all, the slices of Roman life that we have from Pliny and from the ruins of Pompeii indicate sophisticated, formal Roman gardens and other landscapes that required a sustained and very high level of maintenance. This was frequently provided by slaves.

Hadrian's Villa at Tivoli (c. 118–138 A.D.) is the prime example of a Roman villa urbana, a country place developed in formal—usually axial—gardens. There are descriptions of it at its best from Spartian. Its 160 acres (65 hectares) of buildings strung together by promenades, colonnades, canals, topiary, excellent statues, and scenes recreated from the myths of antiquity have survived half-ruined but still fetching into the twentieth century. Hadrian's softly romantic Vale of Tempe became a source of inspiration for Western naturalism in the modern era. The other Roman villa style, that of the villa rustica, was not as polished and was still devoted to agriculture—to actual food production. Pliny the Elder found it comfortable and inspiring. Villa gardens flourished until c. 480 A.D., when Christian austerity and the raids of the Ostrogoths put them in decline. They became the model for the monastery gardens of the Middle Ages.

The wonderfully detailed palatial gardens of such designers as Rabirius, architect to the Emperor Domitian, were also examples of Roman propriety for the Renaissance. The new towns of Domitian and other emperors, including Jerash, Leptis Magna, and Timgad, among others, displayed the Roman passion for gridiron cities. Based on Greek originals, their axis/cross-axis layout became a standard for the Western world. Outside these, of course, were the **Castrorum**—the legionaries' camps. Here there were often great drifts of delicate madonna lilies, Roman favorites. Though creamy white, showy, and very beautiful in the early summer sun, they were a good remedy for corns and other sores of the feet.

See also **Greek landscape architecture, Medieval landscape architecture, Renaissance landscape architecture.**

Romanticism   In landscape architecture, a stylized—usually pastoral or rustic—approach to design typified by flowing hills, lawns, tree clusters, artificial ruins, and enhanced vistas. The development of **Picturesque,** q.v., quality. Usually associated with the English Landscape School of the eighteenth and nineteenth centuries.

Rond point (French)
    See **Roundabout.**

Rood   An old English measure of land equal to a quarter-acre.

"Roosting place"   In English Renaissance gardens, a bench or seat tucked into an arbor or other out-of-the-way place.

Roof garden   Popular in many twentieth-century metropolitan areas, roof gardens feature light-weight, usually shallow soils and plants that can thrive in them. They require good, quick drainage. They can be up to an acre in size (or larger) but are usually smaller to accommodate residential users.

Roof gardens have their origin in the temple structures of ancient Mesopotamia: the Sumerians, Assyrians, and Babylonians developed them along with terrace gardens in labor-intensive forms. In Rome they were common as *sylvae in tectus.*

Room, fruit (Roman)
See **Oporotheca.**

Room, garden See **Outdoor room.**

Root The specialized portions of a plant (usually underground) that serve as a support structure, store food, and take in water, minerals, and air for general plant use. Aerial or air roots are secondary roots that extend to the ground from the branches of certain tree species and in some cases allow the plant to spread over an extremely large area. Buttress roots begin on a tree trunk several feet above the ground and help support the tree in high winds or as the crown reaches a considerable height.

Root ball In horticulture, the highly concentrated mass of roots and earth dug and bound by burlap and wire or rope for tree or shrub transplantation. As a general rule, there should be approximately one transverse foot (.304 meter) of root ball for each inch (2.54 cm) of trunk caliper.

Root, buttress See **Buttress root.**

Root collar See **Crown.**

Root compound See **Rooting compound.**

Root crown See **Crown.**

Root, feeder or hair See **Hair root.**

Root, girdling See **Girdling root.**

Root pressure 1) The pressure exerted by a plant's roots to force water with dissolved substances into the xylem or woody tissue. 2) The

pressure exerted by expanding surface roots on sidewalks, foundations, and the like. Sometimes causes dislocation of surface landscape features.

Root pruning See **Pruning.**

Root run The area covered by the roots of a plant. Also **Rhizosphere, Root zone.** See also **Dripline.**

Root, tuberous See **Tuberous root.**

Root zone The soil area covered by plant roots. Also **Rhizosphere, Root run.**

Rootbound In horticulture, referring to an overgrown plant in a restrictive container with its roots massing around the edges of the ball. An unhealthy condition.

Rooting compound A plant hormone preparation—most usually a powder or liquid—in which a fresh plant cutting is dipped before its placement in sand or compost for rooting. Also **Hormone rooting compound, Root compound.**

Rootstock 1) A low-lying or underground branch or stem that roots to one side of the parent plant. A **Rhizome,** q.v. 2) The lower plant part (parent plant) that receives a **Scion,** q.v., in grafting. Usually **Stock,** q.v. See also **Grafting.**

Rosa, Salvatore (1615–73) Also Salvator Rosa. Neopolitan painter whose moody, picturesque landscapes strongly influenced the designers of the English Landscape Gardening School of the 1700s. **William Kent,** q.v., a central figure in the English School, became acquainted with Rosa's work while touring Italy. Rosa is most often lumped with the picturesque painters **Lorrain** and **Poussin,** q.q.v.

Rose garden A public or private garden or garden segment organized for the culture of roses— often selected hybrids. Also **Rosarium, Rosetum.**

Rose, James Twentieth-century United States landscape architect, educated at Harvard University, and an instigator of the "Harvard Revolution" in landscape design of the late 1930s. Rose was a classmate of **Dan Kiley, Garrett Eckbo,** q.q.v., and other avant-garde landscape architectural students whose careers began in the late Depression years. His work was highly publicized by the *Ladies' Home Journal* in 1946, for which he produced a series of modular gardens designed to suit suburban architecture and executed in the International Style.

Rose's highly imaginative gardens are inspired by Japanese informalism and by Cubism, in particular the work of Mondrian. His practice has been largely confined to the East Coast.

Rose has published three books that discuss his approaches to landscape design: *Creative Gardens* (1958), *Gardens Make Me Laugh* (1965), and *Modern American Gardens-Designed by James Rose* (1967).

Rose, John (1629–77) English Royal Gardener under Charles II, by whom he was appointed in 1666. Rose succeeded the eminent French gardeners the **Mollets,** q.v., in the king's service.

Rose was a well trained horticulturist, originally engaged by the Earl of Essex and sent to France to study under Le Notre. Whether he actually worked with Le Notre is unsure, but Rose did take many Continental plant species back to England with him when he ended his stay. His main responsibility as Royal

Gardener was the grounds at St. James' Palace.

Rose's work was centered on the rise of Dutch detail and the decline of French influence in English gardening. His plant knowledge was featured in John Evelyn's *The English Vineyard Vindicated* (1666). Rose's work influenced the popular London commercial gardeners and designers **George London** and **Henry Wise,** q.q.v.

Rose, wind   See **Wind rose.**

Rosette   In horticulture, a circular or radial, often basal, leaf growth from a center similar to the appearance of a rose.

Rosetum   A Rose garden, q.v.

Rosulate   In plant structures, rosette-like. Rosetted. See also **Rosette.**

Rot, basal   See **Basal rot.**

Rot, dry   See **Dry rot.**

Rot, soft   See **Soft rot.**

Rotary (sprinkler) head   Any of several kinds of pop-up irrigation sprinklers that rotate in a partial or full circle to water a relatively large lawn area. See also **Ball-driven head, Cam-driven head, Gear-driven head, Impact head.**

Roundabout (rond point). Rond point des Champs Élysées, Paris. Photo courtesy BBMSL, UNM.

Rotation of bloom   In landscape design, the succession of flowering and leaf change that is planned to provide color through most or all of the year.

Rotation of crops   See **Crop rotation.**

Rotor head   See **Gear-driven sprinkler.**

"Rough"   In golf, the relatively unkempt area lying to both sides of a fairway and, often, flanking a green.

Rough (scratch) coat   See **Stucco.**

Rough grade   See **Grade.**

Rough lumber   See **Lumber.**

Rough tillage   In wet or moderately wet areas, furrowing or plowing at right angles to the wind to keep soil from blowing away. A technique of doubtful usefulness advocated by the U.S. Army and other government agencies. See also **Tillage.**

Roundabout (French: Rond point)   A circular junction point in Renaissance garden paths, modern automobile traffic intersections, and the like, which eases the smooth circulation of vehicular and foot traffic. A **Traffic circle.**

Roughness coefficient   In channel design and pipe sizing, the unsmooth quality of conduit or ditch material reduced to a formula. The roughness coefficient indicates the degree to which water flow will be slowed.

ROW   In surveying, an abbreviation for **Right of way,** q.v. Also **RW.**

Row spacing (RS)   In irrigation, the regular line layout of sprinkler heads; the typical distance between heads.

Royston, Robert   Twentieth-century United States landscape architect, important in the development of the California garden and modern

Rotary head

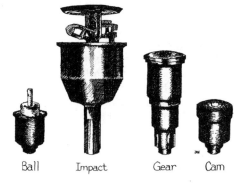

Ball   Impact   Gear   Cam

landscape architecture. See **Harvard Revolution** and **United States landscape architecture.**

RS   Row spacing (irrigation), q.v.

Rubbed finish   A common concrete or stone finish, accomplished by hand or with power tools.

Rubble   1) Chunks of undressed stone used in the construction of outdoor walls. 2) Waste pieces of rock or concrete, sometimes resulting from building or other structural demolition. **Coursed rubble** is carefully set in mortared walls brought to a more or less level top or finish elevation. See also **Ashlar, Masonry rubble.**

Rubble drain   See **French drain.**

Rufous   A dull reddish-brown.

Rugose   In plant structures, wrinkled or with a wrinkled surface.

Run   1) In streams, a channel or stretch of quick-flowing water. 2) In distance measurement, a given length—i.e., a run of 20 feet or 20 meters.

Run, root   See **Root run.**

Runnel   A small stream or run-off channel.

Runner   See **Stolen.**

Running bond   In masonry, a pattern created by laying stone or paver brick in lengthwise (stretcher) rows with the joints of one row striking an adjacent row midway between its own joints. Also **Stretching bond** and **Stretcher bond.** See also **Paver brick pattern.**

Running track   In sports, a built-up cinder or artificially surfaced oval racetrack used in formal track and field meets.

Russian landscape architecture. Modern park in Moscow. Photo courtesy R. Jack Meyers.

Runoff   Melted snow and rain flowing across a surface into streams and rivers. Immediate runoff reaches streams very shortly after it begins its flow; delayed runoff percolates into the ground but often reappears as springs and is thus reusable as surface water. The amount of runoff is determined directly by the size of a watershed, its slopes or gradients, and its ground cover. See also **Urban runoff, Watershed.**

Runoff coefficient   See **Rational formula.**

Runoff, zero   See **Zero runoff.**

Rural   Of or pertaining to the countryside or farms.

Russian landscape architecture   The Soviet Union lies in the center of the great Eurasian land mass, occupying a good half of both continents. Three strong influences have marked the landscape architecture of the country into the twentieth century. The first, and the strongest, was the early baroque formalism of seventeenth-century Versailles and Vaux-le-Vicomte, developed in a Russian Baltic variation near St. Petersburg (Leningrad) by Peter the

Great and his successors at Peterhof, Pushkin, and Pavlovsk. In the south, the ancient patio and villa traditions of the Mediterranean have been continued in the Crimea, Georgia, and eastward along the shores of the Caspian Sea. Thirdly, the market squares, blue tiles, shade trees, and mud bricks of Samarqand, Bokhara, and Tashkent in Soviet Central Asia date from the days of Tamerlane (fourteenth century) and exert a Mongol-Muslim influence on the region today.

Leningrad (St. Petersburg)

Peter the Great (1672–1725) began his new capital of St. Petersburg at the mouth of the River Neva on the Gulf of Finland c. 1703. His late Renaissance architectural and landscape architectural style was based on the work of Le Vau and especially **Le Notre,** q.v., at Versailles. Peter had lived in the Trianon of Versailles for some time during a visit to western Europe. Peterhof, his new estate near St. Petersburg, consisted of an elegant neoclassical palace with extensive grounds. Alexandre Le Blond, a student of Le Notre, was the landscape designer. Arriving in Russia in 1716, he laid out extensive formal gardens in Le Notre's style, including a lengthy axial prospect in the Lower Park looking out from the palace along a canal lined with trees to the Baltic. Fountains and statuary (often gilded in the Russian style) were liberally grouped along the Neva Prospect and other garden pathways. The French artisan Nicolas Pineau was responsible for many of the fountains in Le Blond's gardens. Le Blond's Upper Park was a more direct imitation of Versailles, with sweeping terraces, a Great Cascade, and an inspired sea view. Peterhof (now, more commonly, Petrodvorets) is arguably the finest and best-detailed of all Russian

landscapes. In the twentieth century it has become part of a commuter suburb for Leningrad (St. Petersburg).

Tsarskoye Selo (Pushkin), the eighteenth and nineteenth-century summer residence of the czars, was originally built for Catherine the Great (1729–96) about 35 km south of St. Petersburg. It consists of a palace surrounded by a park and lake, with numerous canals, bridges, and fountains mostly designed by Bartolomeo Rastrelli (d. 1771) between 1749 and 1756. Tsarskoye Selo's parterres, located near the palace, were arranged along strong axes with thick forests left as background. Three rococo pavilions, the most famous of which, perhaps, was "Mon Bijou," were part of Catherine's "personal touches" among the gardens' furnishings. Catherine intended to change the earlier royal style of French formalism to the soft irregularities of the English School at Tsarskoye Selo; she employed the Scotsman Charles Cameron to create various follies and other features and to selectively modify Rastrelli's formal Renaissance line. In addition, Cameron designed a Chinese "village" for Catherine in the *Chinois* fashion of the day. Field Marshal Grigori Potemkin (d. 1791), a court favorite of Catherine, also employed the English landscape gardener Gould, who had trained under **Capability Brown,** to design the grounds of his country estate.

Cameron designed the great palace and grounds of Pavlovsk for Catherine's son and successor, Paul I, beginning in 1777. His landscape park at Pavlovsk dates from c. 1782–86. Cameron's architecture was Greek revival; in the gardens, he made frequent use of follies, pavilions, statues, and a half-hidden Temple of Friendship to emphasize the landscape garden effect. Cameron laid out a number of parterres near the main house of

Pavlovsk; the park contains numerous other elements from contemporary French, Dutch, and Italian landscapes developed alongside its main English landscape garden theme. Its bosques of firs, birches, maples, and oaks, though typical of the valley of the Slavianka River (near Tsarskoye Selo) in which Pavlovsk is located, lent themselves well to the irregular line and balance of Cameron's naturalism. In later years, the architects and garden designers Quarenghi, Gonzaga, and Voronikhin embellished Cameron's work. As was true at Petrodvorets and Pushkin, many of the Greek and Roman statues in Cameron's gardens were gold-plated as the park was finished over a period of fifty years.

The Black Sea and Georgia

The poplars and red tile roofs of Tbilisi (formerly Tiflis), the capital of Soviet Georgia, could occur anywhere on the north shores of the Mediterranean. Under Russian rule since 1801, Tbilisi in the twentieth century is a notable city of parks and public gardens. In the Middle Ages, it was the capital of a much larger kingdom of mountains and vineyards that served as a commercial and cultural conduit between the Caspian and Black Seas. Perhaps its most remarkable feature is the long, tree-lined Rustaveli Avenue, ending in Rustaveli Square.

Joseph Stalin (né Dzhugashvili) undoubtedly its best-known native son, was honored into the early 1960s by a large statue in a prominent Tbilisi park; the pedestal base remains. The Georgian commercial ports of Sukhumi, Batumi, and the nearby Turkish Trebizond (source of the "Russian" olive, *Elaeagnus augustifolia* or Trebizond date) have doubled as spas and resorts since early modern times. The botanical gardens at Sukhumi have specialized in the twentieth century in researching the adaptability of tropical plants to temperate zones. Batumi is noted for its subtropical streetside plantings and for its very extensive botanical garden (begun in 1912), one of the most complete in the U.S.S.R.

In the Crimea, on the balmy northern shores of the Black Sea, resorts and spas such as Yalta and Alupka have been popular since the eighteenth century as retreats from the harsh Russian winter. The modern "Renaissance" gardens at Nikitsky Sad in Yalta are an example. Here a modest water stair and colonnades with a nearby collection of cedars, Chinese windmill palms, and Italian cypresses are watched over quietly enough by an outsized bust of Lenin. At Alupka, the Vorontsov Castle (completed c. 1846) museum is in the center of a large park planted in magnolias, cypresses, and other trees. The architecture at Vorontsov is a mixture of Palladian and Moorish styles. Somewhat further to the north, the botanical garden at the Ukrainian Research Institute in the village of Askama Nova has been developed on the grounds of a former estate and features local plane trees and catalpas as well as pines, birches, spruces, and other exotics of special interest.

Soviet Central Asia

Tamerlane (d. 1405) rebuilt Samarqand as his capital in the late fourteenth century. Mud brick, his primary building material, often faced with blue glazed tile, was used to create such masterpieces as the Shah-i-Zinda and the enormous Bibi Khanum, perhaps after the Hagia Sophia in Istanbul the largest mosque in Islam. Samarqand's streets were lined with trees and furnished with raised tea platforms constructed in their shade or

Russian landscape architecture. Statue of Lenin in Moscow park. Photo courtesy R. Jack Meyers.

cantilevered over the Zeravshan River for coolness. By local custom, the platforms were covered in carpets and the tea was served in translucent Chinese bowls. The Rigestan, Samarqand's public square, was surrounded on three sides by famous **madrasas,** or schools of specialized knowledge. Other trade and social squares were located nearby. Private homes and houses of commerce in Samarqand were constructed around central courts, shaded by porticoes and trees to cut the intense glare of the sun. Tamerlane's tomb, on a hillside near the city, lay along a narrow path lined with mosques and other tumuli, all tiled in multiple shades of blue.

The city, of course, is much older than Tamerlane: it first became known in the West after its conquest by Alexander the Great in the fourth century B.C. Alexander or his predecessors, the Persians, introduced the hunting park to the region. Great public squares have also distinguished Samarqand's companion cities of Bokhara and Tashkent. For centuries, the favorite street trees of these cities have been Oriental planes, poplars, oaks, and maples.

Modern Soviet urban centers in Central Asia have maintained many of the centuries-old landscape patterns of the region. In Dushanbe, capital of the Tadzhik S.S.R., street trees and squares as well as parks are irrigated by open channels in the ancient pattern. In Fergana, Uzbekistan, a network of parks has been developed along the Margilansai River. In Frunze, the capital of the Kirghiz S.S.R., broad-scale street tree and park plantings are watered by *aryks,* the Kirghiz version of Tamerlane's open channels. Alma Ata, the capital of Kazakhstan, is a gridiron city graced by poplars fed by surface flumes. These are older cities; but new towns constructed in the region (such as Ashkabad in the Turkmen S.S.R., rebuilt after an earthquake in 1948) are also furnished with street trees, squares, and public gardens irrigated in the traditional way. (See also **Central Asian landscape architecture**.)

The Contemporary Soviet Union

The founding and construction of St. Petersburg in the very early eighteenth century marks the beginning of modern civic design in Russia. St. Petersburg was built on the banks and islands of the Neva. A number of architects and other designers were hired by Peter and his successors to complete various of its important buildings and open spaces. Le Blond, the primary designer of Peterhof (Petrodvorets), was appointed architect-general of the city. The Nevski Prospect became one of his most important designs. Bartolomeo Rastrelli (d. 1771) had become the most influential architect in the city by midcentury; he is best known for his designs of the Winter and Summer Palaces. Giacomo Quarenghi (d. 1817) and V. I. Bashenov (d. 1799) created a number of gardens in St. Petersburg and its environs in the naturalistic style. Karl Ivanovich Rossi (d. 1849) was responsible for a great deal of the city's planning after 1815. Rossi's Lomonosov Square (created 1828–

34) is probably his best-remembered design.

St. Petersburg, its climate somewhat moderated by the Baltic, had become the "Venice of the North" after a century or so of existence. Among its finest features were Peter's Summer Garden (1704), designed to outshine Versailles, and the Admiralty Tower next to the Neva, with the city's streets radiating from its base. It became the Russian standard for centuries to come.

Russian nobles followed Peter's lead in their country estates. Uman, the Ukrainian estate of Count Pototsky, designed in the Picturesque style (c. 1793) and planted in multiple exotic species, is exemplary. In Moscow, the German district on the old outskirts of the city continued to be influential. Its tree-filled avenues, orchards, pavilions, and private gardens furnished in topiary plants and fountains had earlier impressed Peter as he created his new capital. The future Red Square was a bustling marketplace and gathering point dominated by an imposing Kremlin (fortress).

In the twentieth century, such design elements as the old Russian onion-domed churches, strong, broad pavements, and monumental scale have continued to flavor the landscape architecture of the country. The current Soviet trend is to emphasize growth in medium-sized—not large—cities. Squares in new cities, such as Novosibirsk in Siberia, tend to be designed with rough pavements, combinations of local deciduous and evergreen plantings, and traditional cast-iron fencing. Open-air vendors sell cut flowers as early in the season as possible as an antidote to long winters. Greenbelts are often left along rivers or created by urban planners as new towns develop. Parks in new cities throughout the country commonly have names such

as Gorky and Pushkin; officials frequently refer to them as "parks of culture and recreation," and they may be combined with squares to take best advantage of public open space. Kirov Square in Irkutsk (Lake Baikal), Pioneers' Park and the Park of the October Revolution in Rostov-on-Don, and the parks of Khabarovsk in the Soviet Far East are examples. Larger-than-life-size statues of prominent politicians are found in the squares and parks of most cities.

The Soviets have developed an extensive national park (reserve) system in the twentieth century. The Altay Reserve (2,135,485 acres or 864,219 hectares) in Soviet Central Asia, for example, is now one of the largest parks in the country. Since World War II, a growing series of motor camps for travelers has been constructed, mostly in the European portion of the country. A number of new arboreta have been created to solve problems of plant selection, adaptation, and acclimatization throughout the Soviet Union. Novosibirsk, Kiev, and Kharkov are among the cities that have recently benefited from the work of these highly specialized botanical gardens.

Modern Moscow is dominated by Red Square. Facing the Kremlin at the opposite end of its huge open space is the GUM Department Store, flanked by spruces. Wall niches around the square contain the ashes of departed national figures. A 10-kilometer-wide greenbelt runs around the city. Red Square's counterpart in Kiev, the country's third-largest city, is Kalinin Square. The contemporary Dnieper Promenade, also in Kiev, is the city's favorite strolling park.

Education and training in landscape architecture are provided by, among other schools, the Department of Landscape Architecture at the School for

Russian landscape architecture.
Grounds at Pushkin Palace, 1752–
57, by Rastrelli. Photo courtesy
BBMSL, UNM.

Architecture in Moscow, the Department of Decorative Garden Architecture at the Institute for Forest Technology in Puschino, Moscow, and the School for Garden and Landscape Architecture at the Academy for Forest Technology, Leningrad. Garden "technicians" follow a design course concentrating in landscapes for public housing at the Technical Institute for Communal City Administration in Moscow. In addition, correspondence courses in landscape architecture are offered by other schools in the country.

The restoration of the grounds and buildings at Pavlovsk, Pushkin (Tsarskoye Selo), and Petrodvorets (Peterhof) after their destruction in World War II has spurred a growing interest in historic preservation in the U.S.S.R. The parks and parterres at Pavlovsk, for example—the careful work of Cameron, Voronikhin, Gonzaga, and others in the early eighteenth century—have been researched and laboriously reinstated by the modern landscape architects George Kurovskoy, Nicolai Anufriyev, and Marina Vliet. The greatest restoration here is perhaps not so much trees and parterres as it is the lingering charm of the place, returning like a lost child as the gardens, forests, and fields are put back in good order.

Rustication   A stone masonry of rough, often fanciful surfaces and recessed (channelled) joints dating from the Renaissance.

Rustication strip   In concrete work, a wood or metal strip attached to the inside of a form to create a channel or groove in the concrete surface. Rustication stripping is sometimes the first step in **Bush hammering,** q.v. See also **Reveal.**

Rusticism   A design technique that calls for the purposeful creation of a romantic, old-fashioned, folksy, self-consciously rural form. Example: a contemporary "nineteenth century National Forest" cabin.

RW   An abbreviation for **Right of way,** q.v. Also **ROW.**

Rye   See **Grasses.**

S

Sabkha (Arabic) See **Salt marsh.**

Saccate In plant structures, sac-like.

Sacred grove In classical and later times, a tree grove near water, an altar, or a memorial dedicated to a spirit, god, hero, or event. Often **Sacro bosco** (Ital.).

Saddle A connecting ridge between two prominent peaks or rises along the crest of a hill or mountain.

Safety rest See **Roadside rest area.**

Safety valve In irrigation, a spring-loaded valve which opens when excessive pressure builds up against it.

Sagittate A plant structure resembling an arrowhead and sharply lobed at the base.

Sakkei (Japanese) A garden of borrowed landscape—.i.e., a garden arranged to take advantage of a nearby vista or landscape feature. See also **Japanese landscape architecture.**

Salic horizon A soil layer dominated by aluminum and silica salts.

Salina See **Salt marsh.**

Saline 1) Salty, as in salt-laden land. 2) A salt marsh.

Saline soil A slightly alkaline soil with its productivity limited by a heavy content of soluble salts. Also **Solonchak soil.** See also **Pedocal, Soil.**

Saline-alkali soil See **Alkaline soil.**

Salt marsh A briny marsh at the seaside or inland. Also **Sabkha, Salina, Saline, Shott.** See also **Marsh.**

Salt pan A dry, salty depression.

Saltation The motion of a heavy particle in air or water currents.

Salts The results, water excluded, of the reactions of acids with bases. Sodium and potassium salts are common in arid soils.

Salts, toxic (as a wood preservative) See **Toxic salts** and **Wood preservative.**

Samara A kind of winged seed, common in maples and other deciduous trees, dependent on the wind for its distribution. See also **Achene.**

Sample plot In horticulture, a small plantation established to observe soil or plant performance under carefully controlled conditions.

San S Abbreviation for **Sanitary sewer,** q.v.

Sand Small grains of decomposed rock or mineral (usually quartz) that form a major part of the earth's surface cover, either alone or in combination as soil. Sand is not as fine as dust but is coarser than gravel (.05 mm to 2 mm). See also **Clay, Dust, Gravel, Loam, Silt, Soil.**

Sand binder Marram and other grasses used to stabilize sand dunes along a shore or elsewhere.

Sand, brick See **Brick sand.**

Sand, concrete See **Concrete sand.**

Sand dune See **Dune.**

Sand garden A garden type common to sandy areas in which heat tolerance and the ability to resist rapid percolation are necessities for good plant growth. Many grasss, wildflowers, cacti, and herbs are suitable for use in a sand garden.

Sand, mortar See **Mortar sand.**

Sand, plaster See **Plaster sand.**

Sand seal (asphalt) A kind of **Asphalt sealer,** q.v.

Sand separator (irrigation)
See **Desander.**

Sand trap In golf, a sand-filled basin hollowed out near the green as a hazard for players. Also **Bunker.**

Sandblast In landscape architecture, a technique using violently air-propelled sand to produce a textural or finish effect on a masonry, concrete, or wood surface.

Sandstone A sedimentary rock of high permeability and relatively low resistance to weathering, used for paving, veneer, and other landscape construction purposes.

Sandy loam (soil) See **Loam.**

Sanitary drainage See **Drainage.**

Sanitary landfill A twentieth-century dumpground, or the operation of depositing rubbish in such a dumpground, with at least a minimum of earth cover deposited over the garbage. The term is a euphemism for the blunter "dump." See also **Landfill.**

Sanitary sewer An underground conduit or connected series of conduits collecting and channeling human and other wastes carried in suspension. The water is processed in a sewage treatment plant. Often abbreviated SAS or San S. See also **Drainage** and **Storm sewer.**

Sanitation In horticulture, the destruction or plowing under of diseased plants to prevent infection from spreading.

Sap The "blood" of plants—i.e., vital watery fluids carrying nutrients through plant tissue.

Sapling A young tree, especially a deciduous tree.

Saprophyte A plant species that gains its sustenance from decaying, dead plants. See also **Parasite.**

Sapwood The outer part of woody plant tissue, more prone to decay than **Heartwood,** q.v. Also **Alburnum.**

Saracen garden See **Moorish landscape architecture.**

SAS Abbreviation for **Sanitary sewer,** q.v.

Sasaki, Hideo (1919–) United States landscape architect and professor. Sasaki was educated at the University of California at Berkeley, at the University of Illinois, and at the Harvard Graduate School of Design.

Sasaki's work demonstrates a studied integration of building and landscape, highly polished and refined in detail. Among his best-known projects are the grounds of Deere and Company (John Deere) in Moline, Illinois and Greenacre Park in New York City. Sasaki was responsible for many landscape and urban design improvements on Pennsylvania Avenue in Washington, D.C. from the Capitol to the White House, and served on the U.S. Commission of Fine Arts through appointment by Presidents Kennedy and Johnson.

As a professor at the University of Illinois and later as professor and department chairman at Harvard, Sasaki pressed for originality of expression in landscape architecture. He helped shape and mature the art in the twentieth century by insisting that landscape architecture need not imitate its sister arts. He was an early and influential practitioner of regional planning, now common in

Hideo Sasaki. Photo courtesy Sasaki Associates.

schools of landscape architecture throughout North America.

Perhaps Sasaki's Boston Waterfront Park and Harbour Town at Sea Pines Plantation, Hilton Head Island, South Carolina, best show his talent for design integration. Both projects have a lively, "local" dynamism, and both consist of architecture and civil engineering, as well as planning and landscape architecture, generated in Sasaki's office. Hideo Sasaki was made a Fellow of the American Society of Landscape Architects and received the ASLA and AIA (American Institute of Architects) Medals in 1971 and 1973, respectively.

Satellite 1) A suburb. 2) A secondary high school or college campus still subordinate to a parent campus.

Satellite controller (irrigation) See **Automatic controller.**

Satellite town A secondary "village" or town that is commercially and/or culturally linked to a nearby city. Sometimes a **Bedroom community,** q.v.

Saturated zone (soils) See **Phreatic zone.**

Saturation 1) A condition of soil or air completely charged with water or water vapor. 2) A maximum population level of plants or animals in a given area.

Saturation level See **Water table.**

Saucer, planting or soil See **Water table.**

Savage garden (forest garden) A romantically wild garden, designed to reflect a minimum human influence; often, a minimal garden at the edge of a forest. See also **Picturesque.**

Savanna A tropical grassland dotted by occasional medium- or small-sized trees. See also **Prairie, Steppe.**

Saw kerf In landscape construction, the width of the blade used in calculating wood cuts.

Sawdust Wood grains created by the process of milling logs at a sawmill. A useful humus-producing material when mixed into the soil but slow to decompose, especially in dry climates.

Saxatile In botany, said of plants common to stony outcrops.

Scabbing In landscape construction, the adherence of concrete mixture particles to a form as it is removed, thus damaging a new concrete surface.

Scabbled In stone, rough-dressed.

Scabrous In plants, rough with a surface of multiple prickly points.

Scald See **Sunscald, Windburn,** and **Winterburn.**

Scale 1) The relationship of a design element or group of elements to the balance of the landscape— i.e., trees to buildings, roads to cities, mountains to plains, people to trees, and the like. The relative size of the elements of a landscape. 2) In plants, a tiny leaf often overlapping other leaves or plant organs, or a similar structure protruding from a plant's outer tissues.

Scale, bud See **Bud scale.**

Scale, graphic See **Graphic scale.**

Scale, human See **Human scale.**

Scale, pH See **pH factor.**

Scale reference In landscape architecture, the measuring or sizing unit used to develop the scale of a design. Normally, the human body in the form of client or user is the scale reference. See also **Graphic scale.**

Scalping In lawn care, mowing so low as to expose the root systems of grass. Scalping commonly occurs at the crest of a hill, especially a hill that has been badly graded during landscape construction.

Scandent A sprawling, climbing plant, often a vine scaling a wall, without tendrils.

Scandinavian landscape architecture
Monastic cloister gardens were typical of the Middle Ages in Scandinavia, as were the highly stable, sound, and efficient farms that developed in the Nordic countries as well as other parts of northwest Europe in late medieval times (see **Medieval landscape architecture**). Aspects of these ancient farms have been preserved and are on display at the Frilands Museet, near Copenhagen.

The Renaissance was slow and late in Scandinavia. When it came, it affected primarily Sweden and Denmark. French formal design appeared in Sweden in the mid-1600s with André **Mollet,** q.v., who became royal gardener to Queen Christina. The great formal gardens at Drottningholm Palace, Stockholm, were laid out by the palace architect, Nicodemus Tessin the Elder (1615–81). They were derived from the French formalism of **Le Notre,** q.v., and included well-detailed parterres, an outdoor theatre, and statuary. Tessin also designed a number of country houses with grounds in the French style. His son, Nicodemus Tessin the Younger (1654–1728), probably worked for Louis XIV in France. He returned to Sweden to design the Royal Palace and grounds in Stockholm. The younger Tessin created a country house for himself in Steninge (c. 1695), with grounds based on Le Notre's Vaux-le-Vicomte.

In Denmark, the royal gardens at Frederickborg Palace have been preserved as one of the best extant examples of North Renaissance landscape architecture. The sea is a principal element at Frederickborg; formal flower gardens, topiary work, and a refined, paved court with a fountain also distinguish this landscape. A regal late baroque Deer Park with hermitage was built (c. 1734) north of Copenhagen from Italianate plans by Laurits Thura (d. 1759).

Late formal gardens in Sweden include the landscape at Sturefors Castle, with its great axis, round "temple," and planters designed for viewing from the castle's main floor,

Scandinavian landscape architecture. Library Park, Stockholm, 1927–35, by Gunnar Asplund. Photo courtesy BBMSL, UNM.

Scandinavian landscape architecture. Tivoli Gardens, Copenhagen, 20th century. Photo Morrow and Company archives.

and the "Italian" landscape at Sandemar, begun about 1700, with its views of the sea, hedges, and collection of sculpture. Naturalism and **Chinoiserie** began to appear in the late eighteenth century. A new garden extension in the style of the English School was made at Sturefors. Frederick Magnus Piper (1746–1824) introduced the **Picturesque** landscape to Sweden in a number of estate designs, including a new landscape garden at Drottningholm Palace and a landscape park at Haga. Haga was remodeled with Oriental elements at the end of the eighteenth century by the Frenchman Jean Louis Desprez.

The Swede Carl von Linne (d. 1778) created the Linnaean system of plant classification—an invaluable contribution to horticulture and landscape architecture—in the mid-eighteenth century. Linne (see **Carolus Linnaeus**) also founded a famous botanical garden at Uppsala. Other notable Scandinavian botanical gardens were later established at Visby, on the Swedish island of Gotland, at Copenhagen, and, in the twentieth century, at Goteborg, Sweden.

Tivoli, the spectacular nineteenth-century amusement park and fantasy gardens in Copenhagen, has remained popular in the twentieth century. However, **New towns,** q.v. have been perhaps the great preoccupation of modern Scandinavian design. The Swedish architect and urban designer Sven Markelius (d. 1972) is noted for his careful work in the new Stockholm suburb of Vallingby. Swedish cemeteries, lyrical and displaying a lean naturalism, are among the most refined in the world. New planned cities such as Tapiola and Otaniemi in Finland show the pervasive influence of the architects Aalto and Saarinen.

The Swedes have constructed an outdoor sculpture garden for the work of Carl Milles in Stockholm. In Stavanger, Norway, the city parks, gardens, and lakes, remarkable for the strong texture of their cobble pavements, compete with the fjords for the visitor's eye. The feeling of stone, mountain, and sea is everywhere. In Oslo, a striking city at the head of a long, deep fjord, the large sculptures of Gustave Vigeland are displayed in Frogner Park, one of a series of more than 100 square miles (approximately 25,800 hectares) of parkland and recreation space scattered throughout the Norwegian capital.

Scape 1) A flower-bearing stalk rising directly from its roots, with leaves reduced to **Bracts,** q.v., or present only at the ground surface. 2) A landscape view, either general or of a particular feature. 3) (Slang) A landscape.

Scarification 1) The breaking or cultivation of the soil surface, usually without wholesale plowing. 2) The sanding or scratching of seed coats to speed germination.

Scarious Pertaining to thin, dry plant tissue.

Scarp In medieval fortifications, a ditch-wall facing the enemy. Also **Escarp.**

Scarp face See **Escarpment.**

Scatter-plant In seeding, to broadcast.

Scavenger A soil or other organism that feeds on the wastes of other organisms.

SCCP An abbreviation for **Steel cylinder concrete pipe,** a kind of pipe sometimes used in public works construction.

Scenery Aesthetically appealing natural or man-made landscape viewed from a point of reference.

Scenery, borrowed See **Borrowed scenery.**

Scenic easement A twentieth-century innovation, the scenic easement relies on the old precedent of restricting the specific use of a corridor of private land for the provision of a public service. A scenic easement provides for the protection of beautiful views and associated aesthetic quality along a roadway by restricting change in existing features without government approval.

Scenic highway See **Highway.**

Schedule In irrigation, a rating of pipe usefulness and sturdiness based on wall thickness. Usually listed with a number—e.g., Schedule 40 PVC line. General pipe schedules are based on an original measurement of wrought iron pipe. See also **Class.**

Schedule, construction or progress See **Progress schedule.**

Schedule, PERT See **PERT schedule.**

Schedule of values In some landscape construction contracts (lump sum), a schedule prepared by the contractor to show the value of individual items of work under a contract. The schedule is then used as a basis for comparison when pay requests are submitted. See also **Pay request.**

Schematic design phase A common term for the first portion of a landscape architect's services to an owner, including site review, an assessment of the owner's project requirements, programming, design and cost studies, and other work necessary to the beginning of design for a project. See also **Bid phase, Construction phase, Design development phase, Working drawings phase.**

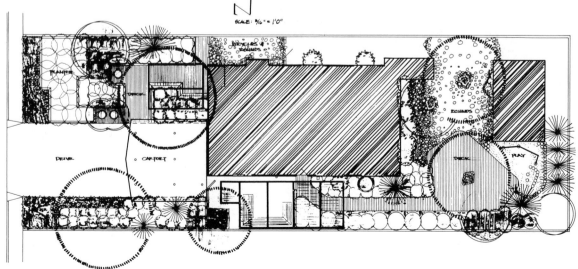

Schematic design. Illustration courtesy Morrow and Company.

Scheme, Hippodamian (city planning) See **Hippodamian scheme, Gridiron.**

Scheme, landscape See **Landscape scheme.**

Scheme, plant life See **Plant life scheme.**

School, garden See **Department of horticulture.**

School, landscape gardening See **English School of Landscape Gardening.**

Schools of landscape architecture See **Education in landscape architecture.**

Science, earth See **Earth science.**

Scientist, soil See **Soil scientist.**

Scion In grafting, a plant bud or sprout that is detached and inserted into the tissue of a stock or receiving plant. Also **Cion.** See also **Grafting, Stock.**

Sclerenchyma Plant tissue that provides physical support or protection—i.e., bast and wood fibers, stonecells (nut hulls), and the like. Adjective: sclerotic.

Sclerophyll formation A plant association containing both shrub and forest evergreen climax species. Occurs from Oregon to southern California and beyond, in the Mediterranean and elsewhere.

Sclerotic See **Sclerenchyma.**

Score joint See **Control joint.**

Scoria Loose lava clinkers or gravel.

Scottish landscape architecture The Scottish contributions to landscape architecture have been considerable, but they are often mixed with those of England and thus not fully acknowledged.

A Scot, G. L. Meason, was probably the first person to coin the term "landscape architecture," later popularized by another Scot, **J. C. Loudon,** and by the American **F. L. Olmsted,** q.q.v.

St. Andrews, the earliest golf course, was in use by 1414. Golf links are a true anomaly in Western landscape architecture. Their form is flowing, naturalistic, and an effective use of otherwise marginal sea dunes. The game played on the links is formal. But golf-course design itself stands against the entire Western tradition of symmetry and formalism. It is only in the landscape gardens of the eighteenth century that the venerable naturalism of the golf course becomes the *British* garden style. The **English School,** q.v., is often traced to the fashions of picturesque painting and to the influence of the Orient; yet the nearby Scottish golf links were a 350-year-old precedent at the time of its rise.

Loudon wrote a great deal about **Humphry Repton,** q.v., and his work. Loudon also understood and popularized the need for good landscape design to provide for the novel conditions of the growing cities of the Industrial Revolution. However, estate gardens in Scotland continued to be popular in Victorian and Edwardian times. The best of these include the formal gardens at Falkland Palace, Edzell, and Pitmedden, and the massive exotic plantings at Culzean Castle.

The Scotsman Patrick Geddes, an early twentieth-century landscape architect and town planner, produced park designs for cities from Scotland to India. T. H. Mawson, a twentieth-century

designer as well as writer, planned a number of campuses and practiced in Scotland and Canada. He helped to bring the term "landscape architecture" into common use in Britain.

The Edinburgh botanic gardens have contributed greatly to horticulture and landscape design in the nineteenth and twentieth centuries. Here, Scotland's maritime but northern climate has nurtured a very wide range of plants (more than 20,000 species), including the subtropical *Trachycarpus fortunei,* the Chinese windmill palm, cultivated outdoors.

The twentieth-century Scottish and American landscape architect **Ian McHarg,** q.v., has pioneered the technique of detailed land use analysis to determine the extent and character of site development for many projects in the United States and elsewhere.

See also **English landscape architecture, Golf course architecture.**

Scour The action of water in eroding soil at a culvert outlet apron, near other engineering structures, or more generally, along a stream bottom. See also **Corrosion.**

Scratch coat See **Stucco.**

Scree A mass of loose detritus on a hillslope, often recreated with pebbles or cobblestones in a garden as a bed for specialized plantings. See also **Moraine, Rock garden.**

Screed The removal of excess concrete from the forms immediately after a pour. Also **Strike off.** The screeding tool is also a screed.

Screen In landscape design, a vegetative or constructed hedge or fence used to block wind, undesirable views, noise, glare, and the like. Also, often, **Screen planting,** which follows.

Screen, coir See **Coir screening.**

Screen (irrigation) See **Strainer.**

Screen, lath See **Lath screen.**

Screen planting A planting of shrubbery or trees to hide a patio, courtyard, or other feature. A hedge. Also, a wind-screen planting.

Scrub Tight-growing, low-to-intermediate-height brush vegetation found in light-rainfall areas, often on poor soil. See also **Malee scrub, Mulga scrub.**

Scrubland An area covered with scrub brush.

SCS See **Soil Conservation Service.**

Sculptured plants See **Topiary.**

Scupper (drain) An opening or outlet in a curb or along a retaining wall to allow the passage of water.

Scurf In plant structures, the tiny scales found on leaves or stems. Adjective: scurfy. See also **Lepidote.**

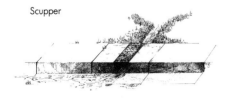
Scupper

SD Survey or map abbreviation indicating storm drain. See also **Drainage** and **Storm sewer.**

Sea breeze A daily sea-to-land breeze caused by the unequal warming of the two areas.

Sea level See **Mean sea level.**

Seal, aggregate (asphalt) See **Asphalt sealer.**

Seal coat, asphalt See **Asphalt sealer.**

Seal, emulsion slurry (asphalt) See **Asphalt sealer.**

Seal, fog (asphalt) See **Asphalt sealer.**

Seal, sand (asphalt) See **Asphalt sealer.**

Sealer, asphalt See **Asphalt sealer.**

Sealing In concrete finishing, the placement of a plastic sheet or tarpaulin over the finished, wet concrete surface to assure an adequate cure.

Seam weld A weld developed as a line of overlapping spot welds. See also **Ship weld, Tack weld.**

Seaside garden A beach or sea-cliff garden designed to protect against battering winds, excessively drifting sand, and wind-borne salt spray. Slope stabilization and evergreen windbreaks are common design concerns in this kind of garden, as is protection from occasional or frequent sea-fogs. Sandy soil is often built up by heavy **Soil amendment,** q.v., allowing an intensive planting if desired.

Season, growing See **Growing season.**

Seasonal color A kind of landscape planting which provides for flowering bloom in the spring and summer and bright leaf tones in the autumn. A typical temperate zone deciduous color sequence: Spring—Forsythia (*Forsythia intermedia*); Summer—Butterfly bush (*Buddleia davidii*); Fall—Bigtooth maple (*Acer grandidentatum*); Winter—Red osier dogwood (*Cornus stolonifera*).

Seasonal garden A garden planted to produce changing colors and/or textural effects as the seasons pass. See **Seasonal color.**

Seasons Yearly periods of approximately 3 months' duration in the temperate zones which exhibit special climatic conditions. Seasons are caused by the tilt of the Earth's axis during the revolution of the planet around the sun. Tropical seasons are characterized by wet and dry periods rather than by heat and cold.

Seat, turf See **Turf seat.**

Secateurs (French) Pruning shears.

Secondary colors All the colors developed from a mixture of two or more **Primary colors** (red, blue, or yellow), q.v.

Secondary growth See **Plant growth.**

Secondary succession See **Plant succession.**

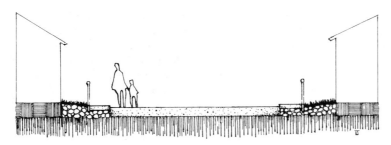

Section

Section (drawing) In design drawings, a "slice" through a wall, deck, parking area, planting area, or the like showing structure. Also **Cross section, Transverse section.** See also **Section system** for irrigation.

Section (surveying) In the United States, an area of land normally determined by east-west and north-south boundaries that contains 640 acres. A section is 1 mile square. There are 36 sections in a **Township,** q.v.

Section system In irrigation, a group **(Section, Zone)** of heads operated by a single valve. Also **Block system, Circuit, Zone.**

Section, transverse See **Transverse section.**

Secund Referring to a single-sided plant structure.

Security, bid See **Bid security.**

Sediment grades Waterborne mixtures of stones, pebbles, sands, silt, and clay deposited as detritus.

Sediment, pelagic See **Pelagic sediment.**

Seed A fertile plant embryo encased in a protective coat of varying hardness with nutrients in a cotyledon or mass of endosperm tissue. A seed will develop (sprout) given the correct amount of water, light, and warmth. The seed is a ripe ovule.

Seed binder An organic or inorganic mat used to hold seeds on a soil surface until they germinate.

Seed, breeder See **Commercial seed classifications.**

Seed, certified See **Commercial seed classifications.**

Seed, commercial See **Commercial seed classifications.**

Seed, common See **Commercial seed classifications.**

Seed, dormant See **Commercial seed classifications.**

Seed drill A mechanical planter that creates a straight, shallow furrow, plants seed, and then covers up the trench. The process is seed drilling. See also **Broadcast (seeding).**

Seed, firm See **Commercial seed classifications.**

Seed, foundation See **Commercial seed classifications.**

Seed, hard See **Commercial seed classifications.**

Seed, registered See **Commercial seed classifications.**

Seed types See **Commercial seed classifications.**

Seedbed In horticulture, a prepared planting area for seeding.

Seeding, broadcast See also **Broadcast (seeding).**

Seeding of exposed aggregate concrete See **Exposed aggregate.**

Seeding, frost (lawn planting) See **Frost seeding.**

Seeding, hydraulic See also **Hydraulic (seeding).**

Seedling A young plant germinated from seed or vegetatively reproduced with one unbranched stem or trunk.

Seepage Water traveling through soil or rock. Seepage can be a problem with retaining or other walls, footings, and other hard landscape features. **Weepholes,** q.v., are a common way of dealing with seepage or percolation.

Seepage trench A shallow drainage cut, often filled with gravel or the like, that catches and carries off seepage water. See also **Intercepting ditch.**

Segregation In plants, **Back-crossing,** or **Selfing,** q.q.v., in order to produce desirable new combinations of characteristics.

Seicento The 1600s in Italian art. Frequently used in reference to Renaissance art and design.

Seif (longitudinal) dune See **Dune.**

Select grade In lumber, a tight-grained and generally knotless and unwarped grading of finish-cut wood. Usually expensive. "C" and "D" are widely used grades of select lumber. See also **Lumber.**

Selective bidding See **Invitational bidding.**

Self-cleaning velocity In pipes, a water flow of 2.5 cfs is the minimum velocity needed to prevent damaging silt build-up.

Self-fertile A plant capable of producing fertile seeds without a pollinating agent.

Self-help project A community design or development project in which outside money and/or materials are matched by local labor, materials, or money. First popularized by the United States Peace Corps and VISTA in the 1960s.

Self-mulching soil A soil fed by a steady accumulation of leaves, clippings, or other debris; the opposite of a **Hardpan soil,** q.v. A pervious, friable soil.

Self-pruning (trees) See **Natural pruning.**

Self-sterile A plant that needs a pollinating agent to produce seed.

Selfing (in flowers) Self-fertilization of a plant.

Selva (Spanish and Portuguese) Jungle or rain forest. See **Jungle, Rain forest.**

Selvage In landscape construction, chainlink fence fabric.

Semiarid An adjective describing a regional climatic condition of somewhat limited rain- and/or snow-fall that limits general plant growth. In temperate or continental climates, semiarid regions receive from 10 inches (25 cm) to 15 inches (32.5 cm) of annual precipitation. See also **Desert.**

Semievergreen In botany, plants that retain their leaves until late in the winter season.

Seminal integument In botany, a seed casing or shell. A skin.

Sensor, moisture (irrigation) See **Moisture sensor.**

Sen-tei A Japanese water landscape.

Sepal A single part of the calyx of a flower, sometimes mistaken for a **Petal,** q.v. See also **Calyx.**

Separates, soil See **Soil separates.**

Separation, grade See **Grade separation.**

Separator (irrigation) See **Desander.**

Sepia An ammonia plan development process resulting in brownline reproduction. See also **Brownline, Diazo.**

Sere In plants, dry and withered.

Seriate In plant structures, set up in rows or spirals.

Sericeous In plants, structures exhibiting fine, gossamer hairs or down.

Sericulture Cultivation of silkworms for silk production.

Series, soil See **Soil classification.**

Serpentine Winding, snakelike—especially, a curved path or other line in a garden. Also serpentine wall. Usually associated with naturalistic landscapes.

Serrate or Serrated In leaves, having a toothed edge inclining forward.

Serrulate In plant structures, finely **Serrate,** q.v.

Service (utility) area In a residential or other landscape, an area set off for storage and miscellaneous use. Often established in an easement in which other landscape features would be impractical. Also **Service yard.**

Service line In irrigation, a valve supply line carrying water from a meter or main line around a house or other building or across an expanse of ground to an additional set of valves.

Service radius In public landscape architecture, the radial distance lying between the facility and the furthest reasonable point it can be designed to serve.

Services, basic See **Basic services (of the landscape architect).**

Sessile In plant structures, flat or low-lying; stalkless.

Seta A plant bristle. Adjective: setaceous, setiform.

Setback In zoning, a requirement stating the allowable placement of building walls, fences, bases of trees, or other objects behind a property line or within an easement (front setback). A sight-line setback states the distance a dense object (hedge, tree, wall, or the like) must be pulled back from a trafficked corner to allow a clear line of sight for drivers.

Sett, granite and other   A small, roughly wedge-shaped paving block often set in shell-like patterns in streets, walks, and the like.

Settling (settlement)   In landscape construction, the compacting action of fill soil resulting in a sinking or reduced grade level.

Sewage   The water, waste, or other material carried in a storm or sanitary sewer system. See also **Sewerage.**

Sewage sludge   See **Sludge.**

Sewer brick   An abrasion-resistant, fine-textured brick used in drains.

Sewer, sanitary   See **Sanitary sewer.**

Sewer, storm   See **Storm sewer.**

Sewerage (system)   A conduit system for sanitary or storm drainage. See also **Sewage.**

Shadow box   A box constructed with at least one glass viewing side for the exhibiting of cut flowers or foliage.

Shadow, rain   See **Rain shadow.**

Shadow, wind   See **Wind shadow.**

Shady garden   A heavily shaded garden or portion of a garden designed to make best use of shade-tolerant flowers, ground covers, vines, and shrubs. Often a feature in a larger garden, and characterized more by its foliage and texture than by a profuse bloom.

Shake, cedar (landscape construction)   See **Cedar shake.**

Shakespeare garden   A specialty Tudor or English Renaissance garden laid out with the plants noted in Shakespearean plays and poetry. Among the most notable are those in Central Park, New York City, and Golden Gate Park in San Francisco. See also **English landscape architecture** and **Tudor garden.**

Shale   A sedimentary rock composed of clay and traces of minerals. Shale has excellent cleavage and is highly useful in landscape construction.

Sharawadji   In garden design, an effect of graceful beauty achieved by a well-executed informal layout. A Chinese concept, its introduction in the West is credited to Sir William Temple in his essay "On the Gardens of Epicurus" (1685).

Shear   In landscape construction, pressure or force that applies at a right angle to the movement of the instrument of its origin. **Horizontal** and **Vertical shear,** both involving structural beam failure, are the most common forms of shear.

Shear strength   In concrete, wood, and other construction materials, the ability to endure or resist bending. See also **Tensile strength.**

Shearing strength (of soils)   A soil's ability to remain cohesive and support foundations or resist **Soil creep,** q.v. It is the consequence of particle friction as well as cohesion.

Sheath   An enclosing, partially or fully tubular plant part that surrounds a stem or other structure. Grass stems bear sheaths.

Sheep-tracks   See **Terracettes.**

Sheet composting   See **Compost.**

Sheet drainage   A flow of water occurring as a widespread, single-direction film over a ground surface. See also **Channel drainage, Drainage.**

Sheet erosion   The loss of soil from a plant surface through wind weathering (abrasive particles suspended in air) or water runoff (abrasive particles suspended in water). See also **Erosion.**

Shelter belt   A series of prairie windbreaks on a large scale.

Shelter, bus   See **Bus shelter.**

Shenstone, William (1714–63)   Shenstone, a poet, was an early influence on the English Landscape Gardening School and is credited with first using the term "landscape gardener." He studied gardening theory at Oxford in the 1730s and went on for the balance of his life to develop his 300-acre estate, the Leasowes, as a "play" farm or **Ferme ornée.** Shenstone admired the **Sublime,** q.v., as a garden development ideal. His gardens featured **Belt walks,** providing well-developed internal views. Much of the Leasowes remains as a modern golf course.

Shima   The island in a misty sea of Japanese legend. The *shima* evolved into part of an ideal garden. See also **Japanese landscape architecture.**

Shin   Japanese formal garden style. Consists of great and intricate articulation of a large number of landscape objects and forms. *Shin* landscapes are lusher and more complex than either **Gyo** or **So** landscapes, q.q.v. See also **Japanese landscape architecture.**

Shingle   Loose beach pebbles.

Ship weld   A weld using a continuous molten contact between two metal members to secure them. See also **Seam weld, Tack weld.**

Shoal   An undersea ridge of sand or rock barely beneath the water's surface.

Shoot   A robust new branch or stem.

Shop drawing   A drawing or other submittal prepared by a contractor during the course of landscape construction indicating a method of construction or a particular use of materials or supplies. A shop drawing is usually reviewed and approved by the project landscape architect.

Shopping center   A suburban twentieth-century form of the traditional "downtown" or clustered retail merchants' quarter, designed primarily to take advantage of automobile access.

Strip centers are small in relative size, lack transitions from streets and to adjacent housing areas, and are normally ugly and blatantly utilitarian in architecture and site layout.

Medium and large shopping centers may exhibit sophisticated soft landscaping and developed transitions, feature one or several department-store tenants, and must accommodate enormous quantities of cars. They sometimes call themselves "malls." One of their principal attractions is a "street life"—moving throngs of people engaged in leisure purchasing and people-watching as recreation. Large centers can produce considerable quantities of smog, noise, and concentrated traffic.

It is questionable whether a predominant urban feature such as a shopping center, based principally

on the trade of petroleum-powered clients, can retain its form or even survive as oil and fuel in general become scarcer.

Short list   The "select few." In the marketing of landscape architectural or other design services, the roster of three or four firms selected from all those applying for a design job to be interviewed for the work.

Short radius head (nozzle)   In irrigation, a head with a part-circle, limited-radius throw and a low trajectory.

Shott or Shaat (North Africa)   See **Salt marsh.**

Shoulder   A **Verge** or road edge.

Show, flower   See **Flower show.**

Shredder   In landscape (tree) maintenance, a machine used to make shreds of branches, leaves, and sections of tree trunks. See also **Chipper.**

Shrinkage allowance   In earthwork, a calculation of cut (see **Cut and fill**) at approximately 20% beyond the apparent amounts required for a grading (fill) operation to allow for shrinkage and compaction.

Shrinkage and swell (in soils)   A condition, common in high-clay soils, in which soil volume drastically increases as water content rises and then is greatly reduced as the soil dries out. See also **Elasticity** and **Plasticity.**

Shrub   A woody plant of low to medium height, deciduous or evergreen, generally having several stems. "Shrub" is normally used in preference to "bush" when referring to low woody plants for landscape architectural purposes (U.S.).

Shrub head   In irrigation, a spray, bubbler, or spider head used to water shrub and flower plantings.

Shrub-spray head   In irrigation, a head emitting a stream or mist used to water shrub and flower plantings. See also **Head.**

Shuttering (British)   See **Formwork.**

Sidewalk   A pedestrian pathway, most often paved in concrete or brick, and located just behind a streetside curb or slightly recessed from the street. British **Pavement.**

Sidewalk cafe   An outdoor restaurant set on the pavements alongside a boulevard, often under a street tree canopy. Its attraction lies in the mixture of exciting streetside bustle and the chance of good dining. See also **Restaurant garden.**

Shrub

Sierozem A kind of **Great soil group**, q.v., found in dry regions of scattered shrubs or grasses and exhibiting a shallow gray A horizon.

Sierra (Spanish) A sawtoothed mountain range.

Sieve test In construction, a sifting test made to determine the percentage of sand and fine gravel present in a sample of soil.

Sight distance In road layout, a measurement of the roadway view to be expected at a given point of measurement.

Sight-line setback See **Setback**.

"Silent cop" See **Speed bump**.

Silica A compound (SiO_2) of silicon normally observed as quartz or quartz particles (sand).

Siliceous deposit See **Diatomaceous earth**.

Silicon An extremely abundant nonmetallic element; as **Silica**, q.v., it is the primary mineral in sand.

Silt One of the three principal components of soil, the others being sand and clay. Silt is midway between sand and clay in particle size (about .002 mm to .05 mm), and is composed of fine rock or other sediments carried in and deposited by water. See also **Clay, Loam, Organic silt, Sand, Soil**.

Siltation The deposition of suspended particles by water action. Siltation in channels can occur wherever the water velocity is less than 2.5 feet (about .91 m) per second. See also **Silt**.

Silty loam (soil) See **Loam**.

Silviculture In forestry, the study and cultivation of the trees of a woodland. See also **Forestry**.

Simonds, John O. Twentieth-century U.S. landscape architect and writer, noted for his work at the Chicago Botanic Garden and elsewhere. Simonds's book *Landscape Architecture* (1961, revised 1982) is a penetrating study of the subtleties of landscape design, perhaps the weightiest work of theory in the field in the mid-twentieth century. Simonds edited *The Freeway in the City* and is also the author of *Earthscape*.

Simple (archaic English) Any plant grown for curative or other medical use.

Simple beam See **Beam**.

Simple curve (roads) A single plane arc of a circle connected to intersecting tangents at either end.

Simple flower See **Flower**.

Simple leaf See **Leaf**.

Single flower A flower with only one row of conspicuous petals. Often, the wild progenitor of hybrid species. See also **Double flower, Flower**.

Sink garden A small display garden, often of annuals or showy foliage plants, developed in a stone or masonry basin ("sink"). See also **Trough garden**.

Sinkhole 1) An underground basin or drain for wastes. 2) A cavity in the earth formed by natural action of water and other elements, especially a limestone hole geologically occurring as Karst topography in Yugoslavia, Yucatan, and elsewhere. In France, **Aven**.

Sinuous (sinuate) Pertaining to wavy plant tissue.

Siphon-breaker (irrigation) See **Vacuum breaker**.

Site 1) In landscape design, the area for which a development, conservation, or other plan is undertaken. 2) In botany, an area of specific vegetative or general ecological study.

Site analysis 1) A map of a proposed project area ahowing physical and psychological factors that will affect project design. 2) The process of inspecting and evaluating all pertinent factors before beginning site design. Site evaluation for design. **Site assessment**.

Site assessment See **Site analysis**.

Site drainage See **Drainage**.

Site inspection The landscape architect's supervision of the progress of job installation during the construction phase of a project. Also **Site supervision, Field supervision, Site observation**. See also **Final inspection**.

Site, job See **Job site**.

Site observation See **Site inspection**.

Site plan A dimensioned drawing indicating the form of an existing area and the physical objects existing in it and to be built or installed upon it.

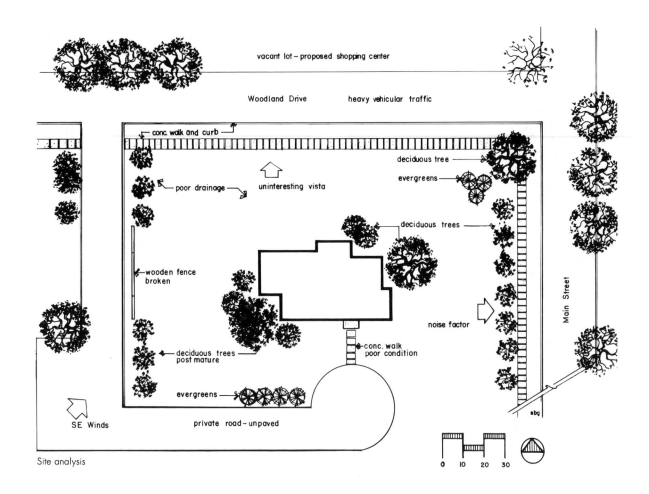

vacant lot – proposed shopping center

Woodland Drive   heavy vehicular traffic

conc. walk and curb

deciduous tree

evergreens

poor drainage

uninteresting vista

deciduous trees

wooden fence broken

Main Street

deciduous trees post mature

conc. walk poor condition

noise factor

evergreens

SE Winds

private road – unpaved

0 10 20 30

Site analysis

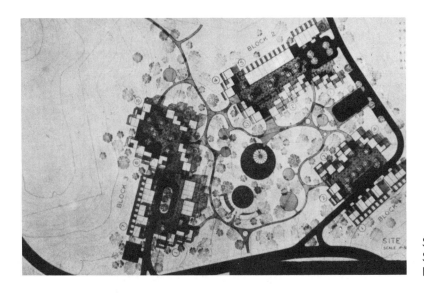

Site plan. U.S.A.: Reston, Virginia.
Site plan of the Hill Clusters.
Illustration courtesy BBMSL, UNM.

Site planning   The arrangement in detail of all elements to be incorporated in the development of an area of land. Site planning is both a conscious and intuitive process that considers social, economic, aesthetic, and geographic factors. Engineering, architectural, and landscape features are subsequently constructed following the site plan. See also **Planning**.

Site preparation, agreement for   See **Construction contract**.

Site specific design   In landscape architecture, the analysis of conditions peculiar to a given site and the development of design solutions (as opposed to the use of preconceived notions) for that site. See also **Harvard Revolution**.

Site supervision   See **Site inspection**.

Sitté, Camillo (1843–1903)
   Austrian architect, teacher, and town planner. Sitté served as Director of the Trades School of Salzburg from 1875 to 1893 and as Director of the Vienna Trades School from 1893 to his death. His feeling that the nineteenth-century city should take better advantage of open space to enrich the lives of its inhabitants is found in his book, *City Planning According to Artistic Principles* (*Der Stadtebau nach seinen kunstlerischen Grundsatzen,* 1889). Sitté proposed refinement of landscape and urban-design detailing rather than initiation of radical changes in city planning to accomplish his transformations. See also **Austrian landscape architecture**.

Situation (archaic)   Formerly used to refer to a landscape **Site**.

Size, cut down (of lumber)
   See **Dressed size** and **Lumber**.

Size, dressed or nominal (of lumber)   See **Lumber, Dressed size, Nominal size**.

Size, nominal   See **Nominal size**.

Skeleton soil   A soil composed of largely unconsolidated rock particles, usually occurring in extremely cold regions.

Skerry   A stony sea ridge, usually exposed only during low tide.

Skinner line (irrigation)   See **Nozzle line**.

Slab   A broad, flat horizontal or upright pour of concrete or piece of stone.

Slag, basic   See **Basic slag**.

Slash   Woody forest litter. See also **Duff, Mor**.

Slat house   See **Lath house**.

Slate   A blue or gray metamorphic building stone with highly useful horizontal cleavage. Slate stands up well to weathering and wear.

Sleet   A chilling mixture of snow and rain. An early-spring kind of precipitation.

Sleeve   In landscape irrigation, a pipe of larger dimension (conduit) in which a smaller live pipe is placed for protection from soil pressure, rock damage, and the like. Sleeves are most often used under walks or drives. Also **Chase line**. See also **Conduit**.

Sleeve fence (Japanese)   See **Sode-gaki**.

Slime flux   A tree disorder in which ooze from a suppurating wound is present on a trunk or branch. Often seen in Siberian elms and other trees that have been badly pruned. Also **Wetwood**.

Slip   1) In horticulture, a **Cutting**, q.v. 2) In geology, hillside soil movement. See **Soil creep** and **Solifluction**.

Slope   An expanse of rising or falling land, especially a hillside. See also **Gradient, Incline**.

Slope angle   See **Gradient**.

Slope, cross   See **Pitch**.

Slope drainage   See **Drainage**.

Slope, maximum   See **Maximum slope**.

Slope ratio   A proportion of horizontal to vertical distance. Five feet horizontal to two feet vertical would be 5 to 2 or 5:2. See also **Angle of repose, Maximum slope**.

Slope stabilization   In soil conservation, the prevention of vegetative and topsoil loss on sloping ground. Permanent slope stabilization is not achieved by building engineering structures; it comes as a natural result of good land management and the protection of climax-growth ground cover. See also **Angle of repose**.

Slough   A tidal creek or marsh.

Sludge (sewage)   A clean, excellent fertilizer and organic soil amendment obtained from sewage treatment plants, often sold or applied to municipal parks or other landscapes. **Activated sludge** is simply aerified wastes purified by the action of protozoa and bacteria. Some sludges are also irradiated during treatment.

Sluice A man-made water channel (ditch) with a valve or gate control.

Slum An impoverished town or city section in which large numbers of people live tightly together in grimy, decaying housing. Slums are a persistent social and economic problem throughout the world.

Slump block A sort of concrete block which bulges in the middle or enlarges at the base while curing. Widely used in the southwestern U.S. and in California, where some of its forms imitate local adobe block. See also **Concrete masonry unit (CMU).**

Slump, concrete See **Slump test.**

Slump test (concrete) In concrete construction, a test of mix and the water it contains through use of a 12-inch-high cone and fresh concrete. The cone is turned upside down and removed, and the drop in height or slump is measured. See also **Compression test.**

Smog A compound word (from smoke and fog) describing a mixture of smoke, soot, dust, and moisture suspended in the atmosphere. Characteristic of nineteenth and twentieth-century cities and injurious to plant and animal life. See also **Air pollution.**

Smooth finish 1) A glossy or extremely even overall method of concrete finishing used for shuffleboard and certain other playing surfaces. 2) A broom finish. See also **Broom finish, Exposed aggregate.**

Smother crop Soybeans, oats, rye, clover, or other crops sown thickly to form a dense cover that smothers weeds. Once established, smother crops and dead weeds are plowed under as **Green manure,** q.v.; desired plants are then introduced.

"Snaking" (of irrigation lines) In landscape construction, the placement of lines in "reverse curve" or winding alignment in trenches.

Snap tie In concrete surfaces, a cone-ended form-holder that leaves a tapering hole when forms are removed. Sometimes used as a means for introducing texture to a wall surface.

Snowline The lowest level of permanent snow in the upper reaches of a mountain range. See also **Timberline.**

Snowload The calculated weight of snow that may be successfully carried by landscape construction members (wood, metal, or the like).

Snow-seeding The placement of woody plant, grass, or herb seeds on snow, usually in late winter or early spring. The melting snow provides a good source of water for the sprouting young plants.

So The Japanese informal garden style. Uses distinctively sparse animate and inanimate landscape objects to create some of the leanest and yet most finely detailed of Japanese gardens. See also **Gyo, Japanese landscape architecture,** and **Shin.**

Soakaway In children's playgrounds, a shallow drain for a sand pit released into a drainage field or plot.

Sobole A sucker emerging from the ground at the base of a plant. Common in several palm species. Adjective: soboliferous.

Social forestry In India and elsewhere, the development of woodlots and forests near villages or towns for the production of fuel and fodder and for erosion control.

Societies, flower See **Flower societies.**

Society In plant associations, a small area within a **Consociation,** q.v., that exhibits distinct species. Societies occur in microclimatic pockets or because of hillslope orientation, human land development, or the like. See also **Climax growth, Plant succession.**

Sociology, plant See **Plant community.**

Sod Thick, established grass with roots and soil attached. Normally grown commercially for landscape use as a mixture of bluegrass and fescue, bluegrass and rye, or as bluegrass alone. Also **Turf.** Sodding produces an immediate, finished lawn. In addition to general sodding, checkerboard and strip sodding are common—both leaving intervening bare areas of prepared soil into which established grass will spread.

Sod cutter A sod-slicing machine used to cut and lift free grass strips for transplanting.

Sod grasses A variety of grasses forming a thick, smooth turf or sod from **Rhizomes** or **Stolons,** q.q.v.

Sode-gaki A Japanese screening fence, commonly used to create privacy or block off unwanted views. A sleeve fence.

Sodic soil A sodium (salt)-laden soil, unhealthy for most plant growth.

Sodium An extremely abundant metallic element sometimes considered to be a micronutrient because of its extensive presence in plant and animal tissue. See also **Alkaline soil, Available nutrient, Soil minerals, Trace element.**

Sods, reed   See **Reed sods.**

Soft landscape   Those portions of a landscape, both plant and animal, normally considered as living. Also **Animate landscape.** See also **Hard landscape.**

Soft pavement   Bark, sawdust, wood chips, leaves, clippings, or the like used to surface an area of foot or vehicular traffic.

Soft rot   A fungus and/or bacterial infection of the softer parts of a plant. Woody plant parts frequently suffer from **Dry rot,** q.v.

Soft water   Water containing a small quantity of dissolved mineral salts.

Soft-mud brick   See **Adobe.**

Softwood   1) The timber or lumber of evergreen trees, especially pine and fir. Other common temperate zone softwoods include Douglas fir, juniper, cedar, and spruce. See also **Hardwood.** 2) Immature, new wood.

Soil   A medium suitable for plant growth consisting of an admixture of air, water, organic material, and minerals. Soil is the loose, weathered, uppermost layer of the Earth's lithosphere mixed with dead organisms. It ranges in depth from less than an inch (2.5 cm) to several feet. The best soil for plant growth is a **Loam,** q.v., made of clay, silt, and sand with humus. See also **Subsoil, Topsoil.**

Soil, ABC   See **Soil horizon.**

Soil absorption   See **Absorption rate.**

Soil, acid   See **Acid soil.**

Soil additive   See **Soil amendment.**

Soil, alkaline   See **Alkaline soil.**

Soil amendment   Any addition to the soil the purpose of which is the improvement of friability, percolation, fertility, aeration, or general organic condition. Typical amendments: manure, chemical fertilizers, sawdust, bark, compost, leaves, peat moss, straw, gypsum, lime. Soil improvement also considers drainage, irrigation, green manuring, and the like. Also **Additive.** See also **Green manure.**

Soil, anisotrophic   See **Anisotrophic soil.**

Soil, anthropic   See **Anthropic soil.**

Soils, aridic   See **Pedocal soil.**

Soil association   A series of distinct soil types found in a similar and recurrent pattern throughout a region. Also **Natural land type.**

Soil auger   A small screw drill used to cut into soil to extract a sample for analysis. Similar to a **Soil probe,** q.v.

Soil, azonal   See **Azonal soil.**

Soil, basic   See **Alkaline soil.**

Soil bin   A laboratory container holding soil to be used for analysis or experimentation.

Soil binders   Ground covers, shrubs, or quick-growing trees planted on steep hillsides or cuts to hold the soil and prevent erosion.

Soil block   A small mass of soil, shaped in a flowerpot and then extracted. Soil blocks usually have a small, central planting hole and are used as mediums for such bedding plants as annuals and vegetables.

Soil, bog   See **Bog soil.**

Soil buffer compound   Any soil component that acts as a structural stabilizer, preventing significant changes in pH. Humus-producing material and clay are examples.

Soil, buried   See **Buried soil.**

Soil, caliche   See **Caliche.**

Soil cement   A soil pavement for generally light-use footpaths in sandy or gravelly areas. Portland cement at the rate of about 15% total soil volume is mixed with existing soil to a depth of approximately 4 inches to produce the finished product. The area to be paved must be finish-graded before soil cementing begins. After the mixture has begun to set, it is kept wet by spraying or the application of moistened burlap or similar materials for ten days to two weeks. Soil cement may also be used as a surfacing material for pools without steep slopes and as a subgrade preparation (often including caustic soda or sodium silicate) for roadways.

Soil, chalky   See **Chalky soil.**

Soil, chestnut   See **Brown earth.**

Soil class   A soil type. A soil group distinguished by its texture. The most widely used soil classes are 1) Gravel, 2) Sand, 3) Clay, 4) Loam, 5) Loam with some sand (Sandy loam), 6) Silt loam, 7) Clay loam.

Soil classification   A categorizing of various soils into appropriate groups and relationships. Overall and individual soil characteristics are used as the means of identification. The current United States categories are these:

1) Order: soil horizons, their presence and maturity.
2) Suborder: the characteristic moisture, temperature range, and general make-up of a series of horizons place it in a suborder within an order.
3) Great group (see also **Great soil group**): soils exhibiting identical or similar horizons in the same sequence form the great group of a region.
4) Subgroup: a division of a great group.
   a) Common properties subgroup: exhibits horizons with the typical characteristics of their great group.
   b) Intergrade subgroup: a subgroup that typically has the properties of two or more great groups.
   c) Atypical subgroup: a subgroup without the properties of any great group.
5) Family: a soil type that characteristically is identified by its ability to support agriculture or plant production.
6) Series: a sequence of similar soil horizons that occur in the same profile in a region.

Soil climate   Water, temperature, and air norms for a given soil.

Soil climax   A climax vegetation largely determined by soil type or character. See also **Climax growth.**

Soil compaction   See **Compaction.**

Soil conditioner   An organic or other amendment or operation which improves soil quality or friability.

Soil Conservation District   A recognized area defined by the U.S. government but under the legal jurisdiction of individual states. Over 3,000 soil (and water) conservation districts exist in the United States. They plan for the intelligent reduction of soil loss and for water use. Soil conservation districts were established during the dustbowl days of the 1930s.

Soil Conservation Service (SCS)   An agency of the United States Department of Agriculture that is involved primarily in the preservation and enhancement of farm and ranch lands. The SCS, established in 1935, has engaged in erosion control and conservation planning for virtually every farm and ranch in the United States since the 1930s.

Soil consistency   The substance or cohesiveness of the soil. Soil consistency depends greatly on **Soil structure,** q.v., and the presence of water.

Soil creep   The extremely slow and continual movement of soil downhill, caused by freezing and thawing, the impact of rain, and other natural processes. Sometimes **Slip.** Similar to **Hill creep,** q.v. See also **Solifluction.**

Soil densification   The application of a thickening filler (such as clays) to a loose soil to fill in its larger voids.

Soil, desert   See **Gray earth.**

Soil engineer   1) A horticultural scientist engaged in the analysis, preservation, and building up of soils. 2) A civil engineer engaged in grading design or construction supervision.

Soil family   See **Soil classification.**

Soil fertility   A measurement of soil quality involving the ability of any soil to sustain plant growth while maintaining itself in good condition. The stability of a soil depends on the continued growth of a good vegetative cover. Decomposing plant and animal tissue left on the surface or mixed in assures that valuable nutrients will be returned to the soil. Lack of soil humus can lead to alkalinity, the basic condition preventing nitrogen, phosphorus, and potassium, as well as other macronutrients and trace elements, from being incorporated by plant root systems.

In the United States, soil fertility has been taken for granted, although many thousands of acres of excellent land are lost each year to erosion caused by ignorant or greedy management. Soil use practices in most parts of the world do not meet the demands of burgeoning populations. Western European soils are currently considered to be the most stable and continue to be highly productive after centuries of intensive use. See also **Soil productivity.**

Soil, forest (evergreen)
See **Podsol.**

Soil formation   The slow weathering of the Earth's rocky crust produces particles suitable for soil formation. The addition of organic material to a greater or lesser degree completes the **Subsoil** and **Topsoil,** q.q.v., thus produced.

Soil genesis   The origin and development of soils.

Soil, G-horizon   See **Glei soil.**

Soil, glei   See **Glei soil.**

Soil group, great   See **Great soil group.**

Soil, halomorphic
See **Halomorphic group.**

Soil horizon   A layer of **zonal soil,**
q.v., differentiated by its color,
texture, structure, location, or other
characteristics. Topsoil (A), subsoil
(B), and a "parent rock" layer (C)
are typical horizons. Soil horizons
usually develop fully only in well-
watered regions, and are a
distinguishing characteristic of
Mature soils, q.v. A single horizon
may contain several smaller
divisions. In wetter areas, horizons
may also be divided by **Glei,** q.v.,
or intrazonal soils. Also **Soil zone.**
See also **Soil profile.**

Soil, hot   See **Hot soil.**

Soil, hungry   See **Hungry soil.**

Soil, immature   See **Immature soil.**

Soil improvement   See **Soil
amendment.**

Soil, intrazonal   See **Intrazonal
soil, Glei soil.**

Soil, lateritic   See **Lateritic soil.**

Soil load, lateral   See **Lateral soil
load.**

Soil management   All the
operations of conditioning,
cultivating, irrigating, harvesting,
and the like necessary to keep land
in a healthy and productive
condition.

Soil, man-made   See **Anthropic
soil.**

Soil map   A chart or map indicating
various existing soils in an area. The
map may also indicate particular soil
use.

Soil, "massive"   See **"Massive" soil.**

Soil, mature   See **Mature soil.**

Soil, mellow   See **Mellow soil.**

Soil minerals   Chemical elements
often useful to plants, occurring
regularly in most soils.
Macronutrients and **Trace elements,**
q.q.v. Soil minerals may be
unavailable to plants because of
high alkalinity. The watery medium
in which they are dissolved is the
Soil solution. Soil mineralogy
describes the exact minerals present
in a given soil. See **Available
nutrients, Soil alkalinity.**

Soil moisture   **Capillary water, Free
water,** and **Hygroscopic water,**
q.q.v., found in the soil.

Soil, mushroom   See **Mushroom
soil.**

Soil, neutral   See **Neutral soil.**

Soil, night   See **Night soil** and
Sludge.

Soil, nonsaline-alkali
See **Nonsaline-alkali soil.**

Soil order   See **Soil classification.**

Soil, organic   See **Organic soil.**

Soil organic matter   See **Humus**
and **Organic material in the soil.**

Soil, poison   See **Soil sterilant.**

Soil, polygonal   See **Polygonal
soil.**

**Soil, poorly graded
(engineering)**   See **Poorly graded
soil.**

Soil population   The plants and
animals (for the most part, tiny) in a
given soil area.

Soil, prairie   See **Black earth** and
Brown earth.

Soil probe   A hollow probing tube
used to penetrate soil to withdraw a
sample for analysis.

Soil productivity   The overall real
or expected ability of a soil to grow
a crop or crops when managed
under a given system. See also **Soil
fertility.**

Soil profile   A section showing a
series of soil horizons. See also **Soil
classification, Soil horizon.**

Soil, puddled   See **Puddled soil.**

Soil reaction   See **pH factor.**

Soil, red desert   See **Red desert
soil.**

Soil profile

Warm-wet climate

A horizon: little organic
matter, little silica,
contains much iron and
aluminum. Coarse texture.

B horizon: subsoil,
some illuvial bases,
accumulated laterite.

C horizon: parent material,
much soluble material lost
to drainage.

D horizon: bedrock.

ebg

Profile development in soil formation

Soil region   Any area with the same soil or soil series. Soil regions are related to plant **Geographic provinces** and **Life zones,** q.q.v.

Soil, remolded   See **Remolded soil.**

Soil, residual   See **Residual soil.**

Soil, saline   See **Saline soil.**

Soil, saline-alkali   See **Alkaline soil.**

Soil saucer   See **Earth basin.**

Soil scientist   An agronomist who specializes in the study of soils with the aim of putting them to best use in plant production.

Soil, self-mulching   See **Self-mulching soil.**

Soil separates   The principal components of a soil—i.e., sand, silt, or clay. Also, any individual mineral fragments in a soil.

Soil series   See **Soil classification, Soil horizon, Soil profile.**

Soil, skeleton   See **Skeleton soil.**

Soil, sodic   See **Sodic soil.**

Soil, solonchak   See **Solonchak soil.**

Soil, solonez   See **Alkaline soil, Solonez soil.**

Soil solution   See **Soil minerals.**

Soil, sour   See **Sour soil.**

Soil stabilization   Soils containing a high percentage of clay or certain other particles are subject to excessive swelling, shrinking, and displacement. Soil stabilization by means of conditioning with gypsum, cement, asphalt, tetrasodium

pyrophosphate, phosphoric acid, or like items alleviates many unwanted changes in soil conditions and increases overall soil strength. Temperature and rainfall are important factors in soil stability. For **Asphalt soil stabilization** see **Dust palliative.**

Soil sterilant   A chemical applied to soil to kill off plant life. Also, steam forced wholesale into soil to kill off latent fungi causing damage to plants. Soil sterilants are often called **Soil poisons.**

Soil sterilization   The application of steam to soil to kill off latent or active fungus diseases causing plant damage. Steaming can also control **Damping off,** q.v. See also **Soil sterilant.**

Soil structure   A term referring to the arrangement of organic materials, minerals, air, and water in a soil. Soils consisting of only one kind of soil particle (sand, silt, or clay) are structureless. If structureless soils are also bound, as with clay or fragipans, they are considered "massive." See also **Loam, Soil texture.**

Soil, subgroup   See **Soil classification.**

Soil suborder   See **Soil classification.**

Soil, surface   See **Surface soil.**

Soil survey   An investigation of typical soil samples or cores from an area to determine soil type, pH value, moisture and organic content, suitability for construction, and the like. The results of a soil survey may be plotted on a soil map, and are highly useful as data in landscape planning.

Soil testing   A determination by analysis of the pH balance (alkalinity vs. acidity) or fertility of a soil. Also, the testing of a soil to determine its suitability for construction. See also **pH factor, Soil fertility.**

Soil texture   A term referring to the overall composition of the mineral and organic materials in the soil. 1) **Coarse-textured soils** are high in sand content. 2) **Medium-textured soils** are loamy and contain moderate mixtures of sand, silt, and clay. 3) **Fine-textured soils** are high in silts and clays. The fertility of these soils is determined to a large degree by the amount of organic material present in them. See also **Loam, Soil structure.**

Soil, thin   See **Thin soil.**

Soil, tired   See **Tired soil.**

Soil trafficability   The characteristic traffic-bearing quality of a soil.

Soil, transitional   See **Transitional soil.**

Soil, tropical   See **Lateritic soil, Pedalfer.**

Soil type   A soil series. The surface layer or horizon should be representative of the strata beneath it for an accurate classification. See also **Soil series.**

Soil, virgin   See **Virgin soil.**

Soil water ratio   The amount of soil water vs. the quantity of soil in a given measurement.

Soil, zonal   See **Zonal soil.**

Soil zone   See **Soil horizon.**

Soilless gardening A kind of plant culture in tanks of water with dissolved nutrients. See also **Hydroponics.**

Soils, alpine meadow See **Alpine meadow soils.**

Soils, gravel See **Gravel soils.**

Soils, tundra See **Tundra soils.**

Solar adaptations in landscape architecture Landscape architects have always taken advantage of plant photosynthesis in their designs, depending on plants to grow, flower and fruit in normal sequence so that landscapes might be shadier, stiller, better-smelling, productive of food, self-perpetuating, and able to block or channel breezes as needed. The extensive use of cold frames and greenhouses extends delicate plant lives and crop periods. These functions depend utterly on a constant supply and use of the sun's energy. The sun may also be harnessed indirectly. Heat-retaining walls, pavements, and isolated objects such as stones help to make possible the use of outdoor areas during chilly nights and cold seasons. Well-placed trees, fencing, hedging, and other landscape items also prevent a great deal of winter heat loss in buildings. In summer, the same features can result in considerable cooling, thus reducing energy expenditure for air-conditioning in buildings and automobiles.

Soldier course See **Paver brick pattern.**

Solenoid In irrigation, an electromagnetic element that starts water flow through a valve, thus allowing water pressure to open it.

Solid rock excavation See **Excavation (types of).**

Solifluction (solifluxion) The comparatively rapid movement of soil downhill due to natural causes (usually underlying wetness), primarily in tundra regions. Solifluction is a quicker process than **Soil creep,** q.v. Sometimes **Slip.** See also **Nivation** and **Tundra.**

Solonchak soil A **Pedocal soil,** q.v., with a high percentage of soluble salts. See also **Saline soil.**

Solonez soil An **Alkaline soil,** q.v., containing some sodium. Also **Solonetz soil.** See also **Pedocal.**

Soloth A variety of **Great soil group,** q.v., featuring a leached A-horizon over a dark-colored lower horizon. Soloths develop in somewhat dry grassy or shrub-covered regions.

Solum A and B soil horizons. Genuine soil.

Solution, soil See **Soil minerals.**

Solution, starter See **Plant starter.**

Solvent, pipe (irrigation) See **Pipe solvent.**

Somatic Referring to all plant cells except those of the pollen grains or ovules—i.e., all cells with a full complement of chromosomes.

Sondage (French) In archaeology, a step-trench made in a mound to determine the whereabouts of layers of human habitation. A properly studied sondage can reveal an enormous amount of information regarding the successive landscapes and building patterns of a particular human settlement, and is a primary tool of the emerging discipline of **Landscape archaeology.**

Sono tube In the United States, a patented precast method of manufacturing concrete pillars.

Soseki, Muso (1276–1351) A Japanese garden architect, also known as Muso Kokushi. Soseki, a Buddhist priest, was the influential designer of various temple grounds in and around Kyoto, including the Koke-dera (Moss Garden) at Saihoji and the small but refined Tenryu-ji. See also **Japanese landscape architecture.**

Sour soil An extremely acidic soil (pH approximately 5.5 or below), usually sodden, lacking oxygen, and unsuited for plants. Bogs often contain sour soil. See also **Acid soil.**

Source (of a stream) Where a stream rises. The head of a stream.

South African landscape architecture See **African landscape architecture.**

Southern cypress (landscape construction) See **Cypress.**

Soviet landscape architecture See **Russian landscape architecture.**

Sp and **Spp** **Species,** q.v., singular and plural.

Space, open See **Open space.**

Space, personal See **Personal space.**

Space, pore (soils) See **Pore space.**

Spacing (irrigation) The design and layout of sprinkler heads to accurately and uniformly cover an area to be watered. Proper spacing takes into account water pressure, head capacity, wind drift, overlap among heads, and related factors.

Spacing, row (irrigation)   See **Row spacing.**

Spacing, square (irrigation)   See **Square spacing.**

Spacing, triangular (irrigation)   See **Triangular spacing.**

Spadix   In botany, a type of flower cluster or **Inflorescence,** q.v.

Spalling (concrete finishing)   1) The breaking off of fragments that have exceeded the forms to produce a desired surface effect. 2) The wasting away of a concrete surface to a rough and pitted condition due to weathering, excessive salting, and the like.

Span   In landscape construction, the distance a beam covers between supports. The **Effective span** is the distance from support face to support face.

Spanish landscape architecture
   Tarak and his Moorish armies invaded Spain in 711 A.D. from Morocco. The Jebel Tarak (Gibraltar) was named in his honor; and by 732 the Moors had taken most of Iberia, leaving only remnant Christian kingdoms in the north. The prophet Mohammed had decreed that, near human habitations, water should always be kept moving, and the perfect opportunity for just this was present in hilly Andalusia. The great garden of the Alhambra was begun in Granada in 712, the gardens of Alcazaba and Gibilfaro in Malaga even earlier, in 711. Well-contrived vistas and the playful but intricately geometric use of water were of primary importance in these gardens.
   By 755 A.D., Cordoba had become the center of a new caliphate that would endure until 1031. In Cordoba, as well as in Seville, Granada, Malaga, and the

Spanish landscape architecture. Granada: Court of the Lions in the Alhambra, c. 1391. Photo courtesy BBMSL, UNM.

rural Guadalquivir Valley, the enclosed courtyard landscape developed along the lines of the Persian paradise garden. Central fountains spewed a spare few gallons of water into four channels oriented to the cardinal directions. Orange trees or date palms lined the water channels and were irrigated by them. A lacy architecture of stone grilles **(Mushrabiyeh)** and slim columns under elegant arches helped to mix

indoors and outdoors. The Great Mosque at Cordoba, now a Christian cathedral, and its Patio de los Naranjos (Orange Court) is the most remarkable surviving Moorish landscape in the city. Inside, it is a "forest" of columns; outside, a forest of orange trees and palms, all laid on the same tight grid spacing.
   The villas of the Moors were scattered widely in Andalusia and were based on earlier Roman and Mediterranean models. In these, as

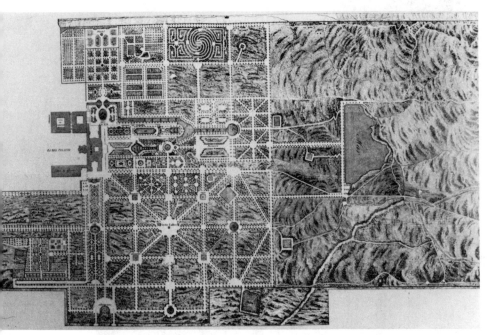

Spanish landscape architecture. Plan and photograph of La Granja, San Ildefonso, c. 1720. Illustration courtesy BBMSL, UNM.

in other Moorish landscapes, water, views, and geometry were principal elements. The Generalife in Granada, perched on a hillside in view of the Alhambra, is the best known of these. Its long pool gardens, water stair, and hillside terraces predated and influenced the great villas of the Italian Renaissance.

In Seville, the Moorish Casa de las Duenas and the Alcazar, a Moorish palace, contained beautifully detailed gardens. But the most widely celebrated of Moorish landscapes are probably the Court of the Lions and the Court of the Myrtles in the Alhambra, Granada. These patios were perfected in the thirteenth century. The Court of the Lions is a stylized oasis, with the slim pillars of its surrounding arcades embellished to resemble date palms and tiny streams of scarce water dripping from the basin on the lions' backs in the courtyard center. Much of the Alhambra has been restored to its fifteenth-century likeness.

The Italian Renaissance made itself felt in Spain as early as 1509, when the castle courtyard of the Calahorra was constructed. At Buen Retiro in Madrid, the formal gardens of a minister of Phillip IV were laid out in the expansive Renaissance style. The theatre garden at Buen Retiro was a great attraction, and the landscape as a whole anticipated the grandiloquent designs of Vaux-le-Vicomte and Versailles. Some of Buen Retiro survives transmuted as a public park. Versailles itself influenced the later gardens of La Granja (c. 1720)—a large, formal landscape created at San Ildefonso for Philip V.

But it is the gardens of medieval Andalusia that have remained the most influential in Spanish landscape design. They were exported wholesale to Spanish America, where they came to dominate a good half of the Western Hemisphere. They also became, despite their isolation and rarity, one of the two or three dominant forms of European landscape architecture in North America. Medieval Spanish landscape patterns, with their emphasis on air, light, and the geometry of courtyard space, remain especially popular in the southwestern United States.

The Parque Guell in Barcelona (c. 1900) by Antoni Gaudi is probably the best known of twentieth-century Spanish landscapes. The "Adonis garden"—planter pots with flowers around a pool or fountain—has remained a popular vernacular landscape, especially in Andalusia. A proposed riverway park in Valencia and a new series of plazas in Barcelona, all in a neoformalist style, continue the Spanish tradition of symmetry in landscape design. Other gardens in the late twentieth century have relied heavily on exotics. The formal-informal landscape of the Casa de Gallo on the coast south of Granada is perhaps typical: terraced, very well sited, and strongly planted in trees, shrubs, and flowers from anywhere but Spain.

See also **Islamic landscape architecture, Portuguese landscape architecture.**

Spathe   In plant structures, a **Bract,** q.v., that rings a flower cluster.

Spatulate   In plant structures, like a spatula in form. Spoon-shaped.

Special conditions   An auxilliary section to **General conditions** and/or **Supplementary conditions,** q.q.v., in the General Specifications portion of project specifications. Special conditions usually contain instructions to a landscape contractor regarding the peculiarities of construction at a project site. They modify general conditions. See also **Specifications.**

Special provisions   In certain general or boiler-plate specifications, a catch-all grouping of such items as the bid proposal, instructions to bidders, general conditions, bonds, insurance, and the like. See also **Specifications.**

Speciation   The rise of species.

Species   In botany, a recognizable, individual group of plants that can breed with like plants to produce fertile offspring with the characteristics of their parents. Species always follows **Genus,** q.v., in plant classification, and is normally not capitalized. See also **Binomial, Botanical classification, Cultivar, Subspecies, Variety.**

Species, guest   See **Exotic, Guest species.**

Specific gravity (in soils)   A measurement of weight consisting of a comparison of volumes: an air weight volume of soil particles in ratio to an equivalent volume of distilled water at 20°C.

Specific name (of plants)   The name in Latin of a plant's **Species,** q.v., always in lower case. See also **Binomial, Botanical classification,** and **Generic name.**

Specific surface (of soils)   A measurement of the complete surface area of the soil granules of a given volume.

Specification, "or equal"   See **"Or equal" specification.**

Specification, reference
See **Reference specification.**

Specifications   In landscape architecture, written instructions to a landscape contractor that act as a supplement to **Working drawings,** q.v.

A book of specifications usually consists of the following:

1) **General specifications:** instructions to the landscape contractor on the overall requirements of a project. General specifications include an invitation to bid (invitation for bidders), instructions to bidders, construction contract, bonds, general conditions, supplementary general conditions, special conditions, and other like items.

2) **Technical specifications:** specific instructions to the landscape contractor on the installation of items of construction and associated workmanship and materials. Technical specifications include the requirements of quality and performance necessary for successful project completion. If only quality and performance are called out, and only the purpose (not the manufacturer's name or model number) of a specific item is outlined, performance specifications are used. Performance specifications often refer to Federal, AASHTO, ASTM, or trade association standards as well. If exclusive commercial products or methods are necessary to a project, they are indicated in proprietary specifications. Most technical specifications are a mixture of both performance and proprietary specifications.

In the CSI (U.S. Construction Specifications Institute) Uniform System, technical specifications make up sixteen divisions. The APWA (American Public Works Association) has also composed a standard set of construction divisions that is sometimes used for the construction of public landscapes. However, these are generally not as adaptable to landscape construction as the CSI divisions.

The specifications and **Working drawings** of a project make up the **Construction documents,** q.q.v. A book of specifications is often called a **Project manual.**

Specifications, commercial or manufacturer's See **Commercial specifications.**

Specifications, master See **Master specifications.**

Specifications, outline See **Outline specifications.**

Specifications, trade association See **Trade association specifications.**

Specimen (plant) In landscape plantings, a particularly fine individual example of a species, often displayed for purposes of accent, form, color, size, or texture. Specimens are good-looking from all viewpoints, and are sometimes referred to as **Character plants.**

Specimen, type See **Holotype.**

Speed bump A rounded ridge of asphalt or earth constructed across a road to discourage fast traffic. Also "Silent cop."

Spermatophyte (spermatophyta) A seed-bearing or flowering plant. Most plants used in landscape architectural design are spermatophytes (from Division *Spermatophyta* of the plant kingdom). Spermatophytes are subdivided into **Angiosperms,** q.v., or flowering plants, and **Gymnosperms,** q.v., or conifers. Also **Phanerogam.** See also **Botanical classification, Cormophyte, Pteridophyte.**

Sphagnum moss See **Peat moss.**

Sphere, armillary See **Armillary sphere.**

Spider head In irrigation, a shrub sprinkler which discharges water from several perforations in the nozzle, forming "spider legs"—long narrow streams or jets of spray. Also **Stream spray head.** See also **Head.**

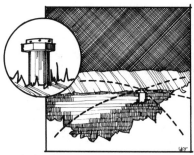

Spider head

Spider, wind See **Wind spider.**

Spike A long flower stem with short or nonexistent flower stalks.

Spiking Aeration by means of a manual or machine-driven tool, resulting in multiple holes punched over a lawn surface.

Spillway The outflow duct, channel, or other water passageway at a dam or in a fountain or aqueduct.

Spindling In plants, a leggy form of stem and intermittent foliage with few flowers or fruits. Often results from a plant growing in the shade. Also **Spindly.**

Spinney A little forest or shrubby woodland. Also **Spinny.**

Spiny In plants, covered with prickles or small thorns.

Spit 1) A metal bar or bars suspended over a barbecue. 2) A short, narrow gravel or sand projection from a shoreline into a sea or lake. 3) The approximate ten to twelve inch (.25–.35 m) depth to which the soil may be turned by a shovel or spading fork.

Splash pad (splash block) A concrete, wood, or masonry construction set in the ground beneath a roof canale or downspout to break the force of streaming water and moderate erosion.

Split face block In landscape construction, a concrete block (CMU) that is cleanly and mechanically fractured on one of its faces.

SPN Standard Plant Name(s): See also **Cultivated Plant Code** and **International code of Nomenclature for Cultivated Plants.**

Spodosol A soil developing in wet conifer forests, featuring a gray topsoil (A horizon) with a humus-rich B horizon.

Spoils See **Cut and fill.**

Spore A tiny, often air-launched, reproductive cell (or cells) of flowerless plants such as ferns, fungi, and the like.

Splash pad

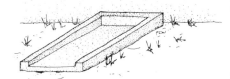

Sport 1) In gardening, a mutation. Also **Bud-sport.** 2) An active and usually somewhat stylized diversion or recreation. The provision of all sorts of grounds for formal and informal sports is one of the landscape architect's chief responsibilities. See also **Chimaera.**

Spot elevation In surveying and contour layout, an existing or proposed elevation noted as a dot or circle on a plan sheet. Normally called out in feet or meters with decimals—i.e., 416.9 or 231.3.

Spot zoning The granting by a zoning authority of a land use at odds with the generally coded uses of a specific area. See also **Strip zoning.**

Spray 1) A small bouquet. 2) An amount of water dispersed in fine droplets in a given area by a sprinkler head.

Spray, floating (irrigation) See **Floating spray.**

Spray head In irrigation, a sprinkler head emitting under pressure a circle or semicircle of fine water droplets. Spray heads are used principally for lawn irrigation and often for shrub and flower watering, and have no moving parts except screw adjustments. Also **Mist head.**

Spray pattern In irrigation, the characteristic coverage area of a particular head. See also **Sprinkler pattern.**

Spread, footing See **Footing spread.**

Spreader-sticker In plant sprays, an additive used to improve the distribution and adhesion of the solution on leaf and stem surfaces.

Spring garden. Garden of Gertrude Jekyll, England, 1925. Photo courtesy BBMSL, UNM.

Sprig A plant shoot or branchlet.

Sprigging Turf planting by means of placing live grass stems on a prepared bed. Sprigging of bermuda and other warm-season grasses is common.

Spring A flow of water emerging from the ground.

Spring color A euphemism for new flowers and foliage planted for their seasonal effect.

Spring garden A garden developed to feature the color and feeling of spring. A spring garden is often a feature in a larger garden, and is usually most successful when informally laid out in a grove of trees or as part of a shrub mass. Bulbs, early-spring perennials or annuals, and flowering shrubs or trees are key elements of most spring gardens.

Springhouse A **Summerhouse,** q.v.

Spring tooth harrow See **Harrow.**

Spring wood See **Growth rings.**

Springing line The widest horizontal dimension of a large pipe or culvert. Also, the point in an arch column at which curvature begins.

Sprinkle irrigation See **Sprinkler.**

Sprinkler In irrigation, a mechanical watering device fed by a hose or underground lateral line that releases water into the air in a series of broadcast droplets approximating rainfall.

Sprinkler code See **Building codes.**

Sprinkler coverage In irrigation, the area watered by a single head or an entire sprinkler system.

Sprinkler, fixed spray   See **Fixed spray nozzle.**

Sprinkler, flat spray   See **Flat spray head.**

Sprinkler, flush spray   See **Flush head.**

Sprinkler, gear-driven   See **Gear-driven nozzle.**

Sprinkler head (irrigation)
See **Head** or **Sprinkler.**

Sprinkler hood (irrigation)   In **Ball-driven** and **Cam-driven heads,** q.q.v., a partially cut-out cap that allows part-circle water coverage.

Sprinkler, impact   See **Impact head.**

Sprinkler irrigation   The watering of cultivated plants from perforated nozzles in sprinkler heads supplied by underground or surface lines.

Sprinkler or irrigation code
See **Building codes.**

Sprinkler key   See **Key.**

Sprinkler loop   See **Irrigation loop.**

Sprinkler pattern   The arrangement of sprinkler heads in an area to be irrigated and the resulting water coverage and its intensity. See also **Spray pattern.**

Sprinkler pipe   See **Copper pipe, Galvanized pipe, Polyethylene pipe, PVC pipe.**

Sprinkler, rotary   See **Gear-driven sprinkler.**

Sprinkler zone   See **Section system.**

Sprout   New plant growth, especially a bud or shoot.

Sprout, water   See **Water sprout.**

Square. Pioneer Square, Seattle, Washington. Photo by author.

SPS (irrigation)   Standard pipe size, q.v.

Spur, fruiting   See **Fruiting spur.**

Squamiform   In leaves, a scalelike growth habit.

Squamose   In botany, scaled.

Square   One of the most ancient urban forms. A gathering and focal point for human activity in the center of a village, town, or city, used for purposes of commercial sales, dining, strolling, resting, bird-watching and feeding, public addresses, courting, parades, art shows, and other displays, and for recreation limited only by tradition and human imagination. Occurring in paved, grassed, and unpaved versions, shady or open to the sky, in virtually every human society.

Square, courthouse
See **Courthouse square.**

Square, residential   See **Residential square.**

Square spacing   In irrigation, a 90° four-cornered layout of sprinklers.

Square, whirling (windmill)
See **Whirling square.**

Squash (game)   A popular racquet game played with a soft rubber ball.

S2S, S4S   In the United States, an abbreviation for a lumber measurement of two or four board sides, respectively. See **Lumber.**

Ssp   Subspecies, q.v.

St. Augustine   See **Grasses.**

St. Fiacre   A seventh-century patron saint of gardeners. Fiacre was a Celtic missionary to France, where he maintained a small garden in a forest. See also **St. Phocas**, which follows.

St. Phocas   A third-century Christian figure and patron saint of gardening. Phocas was a native of Sinope, a Black Sea town, where he kept a little garden. See also **St. Fiacre** above.

Stabilization   See **Slope stabilization, Soil stabilization.**

Stacked bond   In wall construction, brick or uniformly shaped stone with completely aligned horizontal and vertical joints. See also **Brick wall pattern.**

Stadia (surveying)   In topographical mapping, a series of spot elevations established on a **Traverse**, q.v., of a given site. The elevations are set by reading off the viewed increments marked on a vertical rod as the survey proceeds. See also **Grid.**

Stadium   A specialized "amphitheatre" constructed for sports and other public presentations.

Staggering   In landscape design, the placement of objects such as trees, shrubs, ground covers, and the like in a strictly alternating sequence offset from a centerline. See also **On center.**

Staging   Shelves or layout tables in a greenhouse used for the nurturing and cultivation of plants.

Stair   An elevated step which by itself or in a series provides a path between two or more elevations. The vertical stair face is a riser; the stepping (horizontal) surface is a tread. Effective outdoor stairs should have risers no higher than 5 in.

(12.7 cm) and treads no shallower than 15 in. (38.1 cm). See also **Step.**

Stair, water   See **Water ramp.**

Stake, blue (landscape construction)   See **Blue stake.**

Stake, grade   See **Grade stake.**

Stake label   A small, usually wooden stake driven in the ground to identify a single plant or a plant mass.

Staking   A method of securing a young transplanted tree to wooden or metal stakes by means of rope, wire, twine, lengths of hose, or plastic expansion tape in order to prevent damage to root tissue from vandalism, wind, rain, snow, or other elements. Stakes usually remain until the tree has matured sufficiently to support and defend itself. See also **Guying.**

Staking plan   See **Layout plan.**

Stamen   In flowers, the male reproductive organ. Stamens collectively form an **Androecium**. The **Anther**, q.v., is the tip of a stamen, and the **Androphore** is the stalk that supports a cluster of stamens. See also **Carpel, Pistil.**

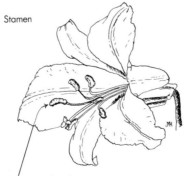

Stamen

Stamen and anther

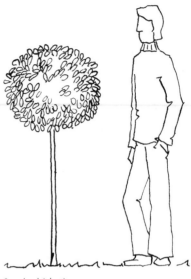

Standard (plant)

Staminate   Referring to male flowers or male flower parts. See also **Pistillate.**

Stanchion   An upright post or column.

Stand   A group of trees or other plants of the same species.

Standard (plant)   1) An informally shaped shrub pruned and trained to single-stem growth in the semblance of a small tree. 2) In plant structures, the protruding back or upper petal of a sweet pea or other leguminous flower. See also **Half-standard, Papilla.**

Standard atmospheric pressure (irrigation)   See **Atmospheric pressure.**

Standard codes of performance   See **Building codes.**

Standard, light   See **Light standard**.

Standard pipe size (SPS)   In irrigation, a pipe measurement of nominal inside diameter and wall thickness keyed to steel pipe standards.

Standard(ized) plant names   See **Cultivated plant code**.

Standard project flood   A flood of maximum size and duration provided for as a project is designed.

Stanzone (Italian)   A Renaissance conservatory basically intended for over-wintering garden citrus trees.

Starter fertilizer   See **Plant starter**.

Starter, plant (starter solution)   See **Plant starter**.

"State of the art"   A phrase commonly used in specifying proprietary items or expertise in landscape construction. A "state of the art" technique or material is the best and most modern available.

State park   In the United States, a public park—often in a rural or wild area—belonging to and administered by a state government. State parks include lakes, rivers, forests, deserts, mountains, and sites of historic interest. They have developed since the U.S. Civil War (1861–65) in conjunction with national parks, wildernesses, and U.S. urban parks, all of which owe perhaps their greatest debt to the designs and writings of **Frederick Law Olmsted**, q.v.

See also **National park**, **Provincial park**.

State registration of landscape architects   See **Landscape architectural registration**.

State wage rates   See **Wage rates**.

Static head (irrigation)   See **Feet of head**.

Static pressure (irrigation)   See **Hydrostatic pressure**.

Static water pressure   See **Water pressure**.

Station   1) In irrigation, a zone or section activated by an automatic controller. 2) In sewer and street construction, a 100-foot point or other designated interval between points. See also **Stationing**.

Station, lift or pump   See **Lift station**.

Stationary head   In irrigation, a lawn head of limited coverage with a non-rising nozzle. Now obsolescent. Also **Fixed head**.

Stationing   In road and sewer layout, a means of indicating distance from a starting point (0 + 00) by means of "stations" (reference points) at 100-foot intervals.

Statuary bronze   See **Bronze**.

Steel, corten   See **Corten steel**.

Steel cylinder concrete pipe (SCCP)   A type of public works construction pipe.

Steel formula   A formula used to plot intensity of rainfall for development planning. Expressed as $i = \dfrac{k}{t_c + b}$, in which i = rainfall quantity/intensity, k and b = known rainfall constants, t_c = **Time of concentration (minutes)**, q.v.

Steel, galvanized (pipe)   See **Galvanized pipe**.

Steele, Fletcher   Twentieth-century United States landscape architect, known for his highly functional designs. In the early decades of the century, Steele reversed a great deal of the prevailing romanticism in residential landscape design by developing service areas on the street sides of his projects. His backyards became expanded living areas. Many of Steele's ideas were presented in his book *Design in the Little Garden* (1924).

Steeping of seeds   In horticulture, the soaking of seeds with very hard exteriors as a means of encouraging germination.

Stele (Greek)   A standing slab or pillar with inscriptions or relief sculpture. Also stela.

Stellate   In flower structures, star-shaped. Applies to radiating flower hairs that resemble an asterisk.

Stem   The stalk or trunk of a plant.

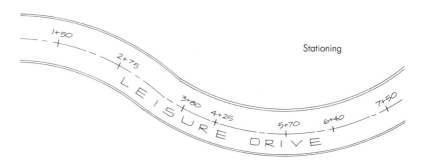

Stationing

Stem girdle   In horticulture, an injury to bark tissue which occurs when very high soil surface temperatures kill bark in contact with the ground surface.

Stem joint (grass)   See **Culm.**

Stem, parent   See **Parent stem.**

Stenoecious (stenovalent) plant   In botany, a plant species with a very limited range, growing successfully only under highly restrictive conditions. See also **Euryoecious plant.**

Step   1) A stair. 2) A treading stone in a path. See also **Riser, Stair, Tread.**

Steppe   A temperate- or continental-zone grassland, especially in eastern Europe and Asia. See also **Prairie, Savanna.**

Stepping stone   A smooth-surfaced rock set in a lawn or gravel bed as a component of a pathway. Well-developed in **Japanese landscape architecture,** q.v.

Stereo pair (aerial photography)   See **Photogrammetry.**

Sterilant, soil   See **Soil sterilant.**

Sterile   Describing plants incapable of setting seed.

Sterility (of land)   A condition in which severe lack of rain, the presence of salts or high alkalinity, or chemical herbicides prevent plant growth. Also, a condition of cities or installations in which the utter artificiality of an area produces a feeling of barrenness.

Sterilization of soil   See **Soil sterilization.**

Stigma   In botany, the female flower part at the tip of the style in which pollen grains are deposited. See also **Style.**

Stile   An A-shaped stepway over a fence.

Stippling   In landscape design, the emphasis of a plan area by means of pencilled or inked dots.

Stipulated sum fee   See **Flat fee.**

Stipule   In plants, a small, leaf-like structure found at the base of a leafstalk. Sycamores (plane trees), peas, and other plants commonly produce stipules, which often occur in pairs.

Stoa (Greek)   A colonnade. Perhaps the most famous was the stoa of classical Athens, along which the Stoic philosophers strolled and worked out the details of their views of life and humankind. See also **Greek landscape architecture** and **Portico.**

Stock   1) A tree trunk. 2) In grafting, the parent or original plant receiving a **Scion,** q.v., or new plant graft. Also **Rootstock, Understock.** See also **Grafting.**

Stock, bareroot   See **Bareroot stock.**

Stock, collected   See **Collected stock.**

Stock, container grown   See **Container grown stock.**

Stock, field-grown   See **Field-grown stock.**

Stock, liner (potted nursery plant)   See **Liner.**

Stock, nursery or planting   See **Nursery stock.**

Stoep (Dutch)   Porch or veranda. Equal of the English **Stoop.**

Stolon   A horizontal above-ground branch or stem produced by a parent plant. Stolons root and generate new shoots where they touch ground. Strawberries and blackberries are examples. Also **Runner.** See also **Rhizome, Tiller.**

Stoma   The breathing pore of a leaf or other plant structure. Collectively, stomata are all the pores controlling a plant's exchange of water vapor and other gases in photosynthetic tissue. Often found on the underside of leaves. See also **Transpiration.**

Stone   1) A solid form of mineral or aged earth. A rock or piece of rock. 2) A **Curbstone,** q.v. 3) The hard seed of a drupe, or **Stone fruit,** q.v. See also **Pebble, Rock.**

Stone, accent   See **Accent stone.**

Stone, bond (masonry)   See **Bond stone.**

Stone, border   See **Border stone.**

Stone, derrick   See **Derrick stone.**

Stone, dimension   See **Ashlar.**

Stone, dressed   See **Dressed stone.**

Stone, field   See **Field stone.**

Stone fruit   A **Drupe,** q.v.

Stone, hewn   See **Ashlar.**

Stone lantern

Stone lantern   A rough or finished stone sculpture or combination of stones used to house a candle or oil light in Japanese gardens. The stone lantern is a primary detail in the contemplative Japanese garden setting, but illumination is often its secondary function.

Stone, palletized   See **Palletized stone.**

Stone, stepping (stepstone)   See **Stepping stone.**

Stooling   The horticultural procedure of cutting trees or shrubs back severely to produce masses of young stems for propagation or massed foliage effect. See also **Pleaching, Pollarding.**

Stoop   A raised landing, sometimes shaded by an overhang, at the entrance to a house. Also **Porch, Porch stoop, Veranda.**

Stop, corporation (irrigation)   See **Corporation stop.**

Stop, curb (irrigation)   See **Curb stop.**

Stop and waste valve   In irrigation, a valve located behind a water meter that performs a control function similar to that of a **Gate valve,** q.v. Stop and waste valves are usually buried more deeply than gate valves.

Stop, water   See **Water stop.**

Stoppage, point of (irrigation)   See **Water hammer.**

Stopping   The removal of the terminal bud of a plant for growth or flower effect. Stopping encourages side shoots. Also **Pinching off.** See also **Disbudding.**

Storm, design   See **Design storm.**

Storm drainage   See **Drainage** and **Storm sewer.**

Storm sewer   An underground conduit or connected series of conduits designed to collect surface runoff from rainstorms, melting snows, and the like. See also **Drainage** and **Sanitary sewer.**

Stove   In romantic English landscapes of the eighteenth century, a greenhouse.

Straight-edge   1) A straight or uncurving plane surface used for line drawings in plans or maps. T-squares, Mayline bars, and the like are common straight edges in landscape architectural design and drafting. 2) A straight-sided board or bar of metal used for screeding poured concrete surfaces or for leveling.

Strain   In horticulture, a particularly desirable species or variety raised from seed.

Strainer   In irrigation, a mesh screen installed inside a line to filter impurities. Generally used with "raw" water systems. Strainer opening sizes are called out in micrometers or as meshes.

Strand   A beach or shoreline.

Strand line   A watermark in the sand of a beach, pond, or lake which shows the water's high point.

Strata   Plural of **Stratum,** q.v.

Stratification (of plants)   1) The arrangement of species in a plant community in an order ranging from greater to lesser dominance of resources and space. 2) Storage of seeds in layers of natural or artificial materials to retain freshness or encourage germination. 3) Chemical or mechanical treatment of seed hulls to allow plant germination.

Stratosphere A high layer of the atmosphere at the base of which the **Lapse rate,** q.v., ceases. The stratosphere begins approximately six miles above the Earth's surface.

Stratum A layer of rock ranging from millimeters to several meters in width. Plural: strata.

Straw, pine See **Pine straw.**

Stream 1) A brook. A flow of running water. 2) A spurt of water from an irrigation sprinkler.

Stream capacity A measurement of the suspended load (sediment) a river or creek can carry at a given flow.

Stream, consequent
See **Consequent stream.**

Stream, graded, mature, or old
See **Mature stream.**

Stream, ephemeral See **Ephemeral stream.**

Stream, graded See **Mature stream.**

Stream, intermittent
See **Intermittent stream.**

Stream-jet head See **Spider head.**

Stream load The suspended matter carried in the water of a creek or river. The stream load is usually deposited as silt. Also **Detritus load.**

Stream, mature See **Mature stream.**

Stream, old See **Mature stream.**

Stream profile See **River profile.**

Stream regimen (flow pattern) The usual scheme of high and low seasonal flow in a stream.

Streambed The bottom of a brook.

Streamcourse The bed a brook follows.

Stream-spray head See **Spider head.**

Stream, yazoo See **Yazoo stream.**

Stream, young See **Young stream.**

Street, arterial See **Arterial street.**

Street, cobbled See **Cobbled street.**

Street furniture Seating, lighting, fire hydrants, signs, bus stops and shelters, clocks, trash containers, drinking fountains, tree-protective wrought iron fixtures, bicycle racks, tree grates, clocks, kiosks, and the like found as incidental amenities within or next to a street right of way. See also **Outdoor furniture.**

Street furniture

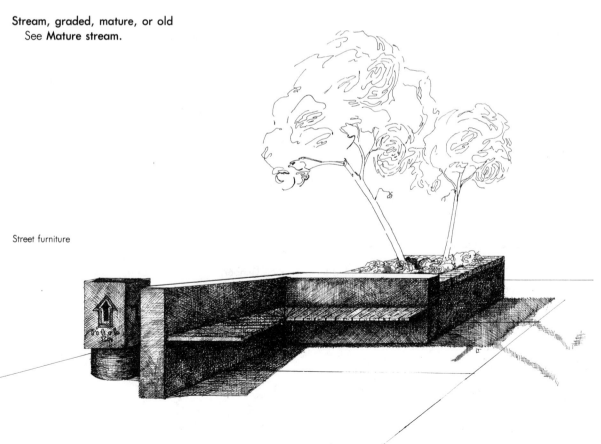

Street trees

Street tree A tree used architectonically along streets and boulevards, usually near sidewalks, to provide shade, shelter, color, diversion, air purification, air conditioning, and other useful services. Good street trees can resist drought, vandalism, cold, heat, neglect, erratic drivers, and other urban miseries. Good temperate-zone choices include ashes, trees of heaven, sycamores, elms, mulberries, ginkgoes, maples, honey locusts, locusts, lindens, and others. See also **Tree Grates.**

Strength, shear See **Shear strength.**

Strength, tensile See **Tensile strength.**

Stress Resistance of a material to pressure exerted on it by a force. Often shown as a measurement of kilograms per square millimeter (KSMM) or pounds per square inch (PSI). 1) **Extreme fiber stress** indicates wood beams bent to their maximum. 2) **Working stress** is the calculated, realistic design stress for a material.

Stress graded lumber See **Lumber.**

Stretcher bar In chainlink fence construction, a vertical steel bar "woven" through the mesh at posts and attached securely to crossrails and posts alike.

Stretcher bond (masonry) See **Running bond.**

Stretcher course (masonry) A row of bricks or stone laid lengthwise in a wall or as a pavement. See also **Brick wall pattern, Header, Paver brick pattern.**

Stretching bond (masonry) See **Running bond.**

Striate (striated) In plant structures, grooved or lined.

Strigose In plant structures, equipped with stiff hairs.

Strike A plant cutting that successfully "takes" or roots.

Strike off (of concrete) See **Screed.**

String course In masonry, a slightly protruding course of brick or block in a wall.

Stringer In fences, stairs, or other wood construction, a horizontal supporting member to which are attached finish members.

Strip crops In agriculture, the planting of different crops in long, extended rows that follow the contours of the land and often alternate with one another.

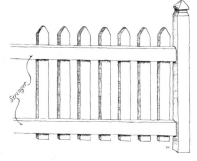

Stringer

Strip development A shopping center, housing, or other development that occurs as a lively but trashy and uninterrupted, amorphous mass along a road. Typical in suburbs. In Britain, **Ribbon development.**

Strip head In irrigation, a shrub or lawn head designed to sprinkle in a long narrow area. Also **Line head.**

Strip, mowing See **Mowing strip.**

Strip, rustication See **Rustication strip.**

Strip sodding See **Sod.**

Strip zoning In North America, the zoning of lands abutting a main street for commercial or industrial purposes. See also **Spot zoning.**

Stripling A young tree or shrub.

Strobe effect Alternating dimming and brightness in electric lamps, caused by current fluctuation.

Strobile In botany, the cone of a fir, spruce, pine, larch, or other member of the pine family (*Pinaceae*). The strobile usually displays well-developed fruits or flowers covered and protected by tightly arranged scales.

Stroll garden A garden designed for leisurely walking and contemplation, with well developed footpaths, points of interest, and seating areas. Stroll gardens are common in royal Oriental landscape architecture and in Renaissance and post-Renaissance aristocratic landscapes. They have also been developed in the more publicly oriented parks and arboreta of the nineteenth and twentieth centuries.

Struck joint A concrete, brick, or other joint that is struck with a trowel. A concave joint in brickwork.

Structural bond In masonry, overlapping courses of brick, concrete block, or similar materials distinguished by great strength and integration of material.

Structural planting
See **Bioengineering.**

Structure, access (drainage)
See **Access structure.**

Structure, drop See **Drop structure.**

Structure, nonhabitable
See **Nonhabitable structure.**

Strut In landscape construction, a diagonal brace member, usually of wood, sometimes used in trellis or overhead structures.

Stub out In landscape construction, an irrigation supply line brought into an area for future use. The stub out is capped after installation.

Stubble Grass or forb "stumps," especially the stubs remaining after a grain crop such as wheat or barley has been harvested. A stubble mulch is often left in place to control erosion. It may eventually be plowed under as **Green manure,** q.v.

Stubs, bleeder See **Bleeder stubs.**

Stucco A plaster or calcium (calcareous) cement used as a finish on walls. Two coats are common: 1) Scratch or rough coat: an uncolored first stucco coat laid over laths or a wire base. 2) Color or finish coat: the final, surface plaster coating applied over a scratch coat. Sometimes a **Brown** (or intermediate) **coat** is applied between the two.

The finest stuccoes were formerly made of gypsum and crushed marble.

Study, feasibility See **Feasibility study.**

Study, landscape See **Landscape study.**

Stumpery A Victorian garden creation consisting of an artificial clump of stumps or tree roots.

Stupa In south and east Asia, a mound or other roundish Buddhist monument—especially a roadside monument, sometimes containing holy relics.

Style 1) In botany, the elongation of the flower ovary that serves as a support for the **Stigma,** q.v. 2) The **Gnomon,** q.v., or upright time-marking blade, of a sundial.

Stylobate A continuous base upon which columns or pillars are set.

"Sub" See **Subcontractor.**

Subjacent support, right of
See **Right of lateral and subjacent support.**

Subalpine Applied to species native to a mountainous area just below the treeline.

Subbase In paving or other landscape construction, a preparatory course that is constructed over an inadequate **Subgrade,** q.v. Also, the formed and graded indigenous soil of a project site.

Subbidder A contractor who submits a proposal for the installation of a certain kind or kinds of specialty work to a bidder, or prime contractor. His proposal is a subbid. See also **Bidder.**

Subclass (botanical) See **Botanical classification, Order.**

Subcontract An agreement made by a general or prime contractor with another contractor for the provision of specialized construction items or work for a project. Subcontract work is performed by a **Subcontractor,** q.v.

Subcontractor In landscape construction, a specialty tradesman or installer who subcontracts with a prime contractor for the construction of a distinct portion of a project. The landscape contractor for the construction of a distinct portion of a project. The landscape contractor himself sometimes subcontracts to a general contractor. See also **Landscape contractor.**

Subdivision In city planning, a new or existing residential or other land development. Subdivisions constitute one of the primary land use problems of the twentieth century due to the vast increase in numbers of human beings and the tremendous demands they place on land and other resources.

Land subdivision in the general sense partitions virgin or already developed areas into parcels suitable for farming, ranching, residential, commercial, or public use. These parcels are often created with no reference to the existing type or quality of land use, and consequently are developed with commercial profit as their real basis. High public demand for land allows this ecologically unsound and essentially ignorant practice to continue as the norm in the United States, Canada, and elsewhere.

Subdrainage The removal by pumping or other means of quantities of underground water located relatively close to the surface of the land.

Subgrade Earth area beneath a finish or proposed grade that is compacted, moistened, or otherwise made ready to support a pavement, footing, structure, or plantings. See also **Subbase.**

Subgroup, soil See **Soil classification.**

Subhumid (climate) A partially damp, consistent atmospheric condition, typical of the usual climate of a region.

Subinjection irrigation A means of applying irrigation water through a generally level series of underground "ejector" tubes attached to pipe laterals. See also **Trickle irrigation.**

Subirrigation Underground watering, or water supplied to distribution points by means of a buried pipe system. See also **Irrigation.**

Sublime An adjective used by Edmund Burke, William Gilpin, and others in the eighteenth century to describe an idealized, highly romantic, gloomy, rough, wild landscape. Influential in the development of the English naturalistic landscape. See also **English landscape architecture.**

Submarginal (land) An area that is unfit for human habitation or cultivation. Frozen mountaintops, swamps, sandy deserts, and the like—though beautiful—are submarginal. See also **Marginal.**

Submersible pump (irrigation) See **Booster pump.**

Submittal During project construction, a presentation of delivery ticket, product invoice, manufacturer's literature, materials, or other items made by the contractor to the landscape architect to assure his compliance with contract documents. See also **Shop drawing** and **Specification.**

Suborder, soil See **Soil classification.**

Subphylum (botanical) See **Botanical classification, Class.**

Subrogation In contracts, a shift of monetary responsibility and the right of recovery (of money or damages) from a first to a second party.

Subshrub A small plant that is woody at its base and herbaceous in its upper parts. Adjective: **Suffrutescent.**

Subsidence Ground settling. Improper compaction under landscape structures may result in subsidence damaging to slabs, wooden structures, lawns, and the like.

Subsistence crops The produce of a farm only raising food for its own immediate use.

Subsistence farming Farming for the sole purpose of feeding the farm family involving in raising the crops.

Subsoil A type of soil found below topsoil. Subsoil generally is not friable and lacks the organic materials that support plant life. It is not as oxidized as topsoil. Most plant species cannot tolerate subsoil and will not live in it. Subsoil is often noted as the B-horizon. See also **Soil** and **Topsoil.**

Subspecies In botany, a recognizable member of a genus and species that nevertheless has distinct characteristics of its own. A subspecies can interbreed with other plants of the same species. Sometimes abbreviated **Ssp.** Also **Variety**, q.v. See also **Botanical classification, Cultivar, Species.**

Substructure An underpinning, footing, or foundation. A below-grade support construct. See also **Footing, Foundation.**

Subsurface drainage See **Drainage.**

Subtending In plants, supporting or underneath.

Subtropical Pertaining to plants or climates exhibiting both temperate and tropical characteristics. See also **Temperate zone** and **Tropical.**

Subtropical desert See **Tropical desert.**

Subulate In plants, like an awl in form.

Suburb A bedroom community. An urban spillover. Generally, any "urban fringe" development without a center of its own.

Suburb, garden See **Garden city.**

Suburbscape A term used by Garrett Eckbo and others to describe the landscape (buildings, streets, paths, and plant features) of Western suburbia.

Succession farming (cropping) Generally, the planting of a series of crops, one immediately following the other, thus allowing the land no time to regenerate itself.

Succession, plant See **Plant succession.**

Succession, primary See **Plant succession.**

Succession, secondary See **Plant succession.**

Succulent In botany, a plant such as cactus or sedum with rounded juicy leaves and stems that hold moisture as an adaptation for drought. Any juicy plant.

Sucker In botany, a shoot that comes up from the roots in addition to the main plant trunk. Suckers can prevent the development of a well formed tree. Also **Basal break, Thief (Thieves), Water sprout.**

Suction friction head **Feet of head,** q.v., in a well pump, with allowances for pipe entrance and exit pressure losses, and for losses due to changes in pipe sizes. Suction friction head also affects **Suction lift,** q.v.

Suction lift In pumps, the distance between a water table (water supply) and the pump at the head of a well shaft. 1) **Static suction lift:** Vertical suction lift calculated before friction loss in the pipe is taken into account. 2) **Dynamic suction lift:** Static suction lift and **Suction friction head,** q.v., calculated for a specific pump.

Suffrutescent See **Subshrub.**

Suffruticose Of or pertaining to a short shrub or **Subshrub.** See also **Fruticose.**

Sulcate Like a groove or trench in structure.

Sulfate A compound of sulfur and iron, aluminum, or other minerals, applied to soils as a fertilizer.

Sulfate of iron See **Iron chelate.**

Sulfur An element required in relatively large quantities for plant health. Sulfur is also widely used to reduce the pH of alkaline soils. See also **Macronutrient.** Also sulphur.

Sum, contract See **Contract sum.**

Sum, lump See **Contract sum, Lump sum.**

Sum, penal (contracting) See **Liquidated damages, Penal sum.**

Summer bedding See **Bedding plant.**

Summer fallow See **Fallow.**

Summer garden A garden planted for strong flowering effect in the summer and employing, in particular, cool-tone colors.

Summer house 1) A garden or park outbuilding constructed for coolness. Often of simple, unaffected character. 2) A summer estate or home in the country. 3) A cellar or grotto, often cooled by a spring, used to store vegetables and fruits in hot weather (U.S.). A **Springhouse.** See also **Tea house.**

Summer wood A **Growth rings.**

Sump 1) A pit or low area sometimes filled with stone, gravel, rubble, broken brick, or the like used for the collection of drainage. 2) A cesspool or septic pit. See also **French drain.**

Sundial A garden or terrace instrument, usually circular in form and marked off in hours, used to tell time by means of the sun's shadow falling across it. An ancient device. The sundial's blade is a **Gnomon.** See also **Armillary sphere.**

Sunk or sunken fence See **Ha-ha.**

Sunken garden. The Hirschhorn Garden on the mall in Washington, D.C., with its fine collection of sculptures. Photo by author.

Sunken garden   A garden or garden segment that by design is at a lower level than its surroundings.

Sunscald   In trees, the killing of bark tissue resulting from the effects of a warm winter day followed by a freezing night. Sunscald is caused by water (sap) flowing in subcutaneous trunk tissue, where it ruptures tender cells while crystallizing. See also **Windburn, Winterburn.**

Super   1) The superintendent of project construction. 2) A bid area expressed in square feet, yards, meters, acres, or the like. An abbreviation for **Superficial** (surface) **area.**

Superelevation   In roadway construction, an elevation point at the high paved edge of an outside curve that has been banked to accommodate fast traffic.

Superblock   In city planning, a large area composed of a number of combined blocks, often developed as a single concept or project. Robson Square in Vancouver, British Columbia, Canada is an example. The superblock was first proposed by Clarence Stein and Henry Wright at Radburn, New Jersey, in the late 1920s.

Superficial area (bidding)   See **Super.**

Superimposed drainage   In geography, a river and its tributaries that seem out of context because the lands they drain are old and have been worn away by erosion. See also **Inconsequent drainage.**

Supersedure   In contracts, a legal agreement or understanding that is made after a prior agreement and that takes the place of that agreement.

Supervision, field   See **Site inspection.**

Supervision, site   See **Site inspection.**

Supplementary conditions (supplemental general conditions)   In general project specifications, a series of project requirements that modifies the **General conditions,** q.v. See also **Specifications.**

Supplementary specifications   Any specifications issued as additions to an existing body of Technical Specifications for a project. Supplementary specifications modify the intent of the original specifications. See also **Specifications.**

Supplier, material   See **Material supplier.**

Supply bond   A kind of **Bond,** q.v., that warrants the provision of materials and equipment called out in a supply-only contract.

Surcharged earth   The portion of ground behind and above the top level of a retainer wall. See also **Surcharged wall.**

Surcharged wall   A wall built for slope or other retention which carries earth over its top level. See also **Surcharged earth.**

Surety   In contracts, a warranty or guarantee. Also, the person or agency guaranteeing payment or performance. See also **Bond** and **Suretyship.**

Surety bond   See **Surety.**

Suretyship   A legal relationship in which one party agrees to stand good for the debts of a second party. See also **Bond.**

Surface compaction (of soils)   See **Compaction.**

Surface course, asphalt   See **Asphalt surface course** and **Surface course.**

Surface drainage   See **Drainage.**

Surface irrigation   Surface watering by ditches or furrows, or by flooding.

Surface plane   See **Base plane.**

Surface soil   **Topsoil,** q.v., or the upper half-foot of topsoil that is normally cultivated. Also **Plow layer.**

Surface, specific (of soils)   See **Specific surface.**

Surface treatment of asphalt   See **Asphalt surface treatment.**

Surface water   Any water occurring on the ground surface.

Surge   See **Water hammer.**

Surge protection, electrical   See **Electrical surge protection.**

Surroundings (surround)   Environment.

Survey (surveying)   An instrumental determination of land-surface limits or elevations and their subsequent plotting on a plan or map. 1) **Metes and bounds** (property) **survey:** a plotting of the limits of an area and the structures and other items found on it from a point or points of reference, leading to an accurate property description. 2) **Topographic** (topo) **survey:** a plotting by grid, stadia, or other means of the existing contours or elevations of an area of ground. See also **Hand level, Level, Theodolite, Transit.**

Survey, ordnance   See **Ordnance survey.**

Survey, soil   See **Soil survey.**

Surveying rod   See **Rod.**

Surveyor   See **Land surveyor.**

SW brick   A grade of brick used often in specialized landscape construction (walls, footings, etc.). See also **MW brick.**

Swale   A moist, usually grassy area in low-lying land or an easy-sided drainage trench through a park or lawn.

Swallow hole   See **Sinkhole.**

Swamp   A wet, low-lying area that normally remains saturated year-round. Swamps are usually heavily vegetated and may occur when lake basins become silted and drainage is stifled. See also **Bog, Marsh.**

Sward   Any ground surface thickly covered with grass or herbage.

Swedish landscape architecture   See **Scandinavian landscape architecture.**

Swell and shrinkage   A term applied to soils during earthwork, when they swell during excavation due to aeration and shrink during placement and compaction. Swell and shrinkage of soil are also prime considerations in the design of landscape structures.

Swing check valve   In irrigation, a check valve with a hinged door or gate allowing water to flow through in only one direction. See also **Check valve.**

Swing joint   In irrigation, a common flexible riser joint that is used for large rotary heads. The swing joint can be easily adjusted to finish grade; it protects its supplying **Lateral line** by moving without breaking when run over by heavy equipment.

Switch, master or rain (irrigation)   See **Master switch.**

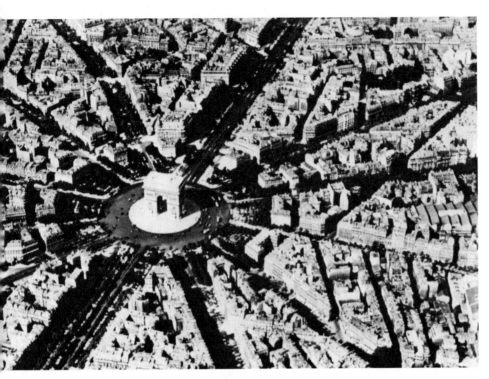

Symmetry. Radial symmetry: aerial
view of the Place de L' Etoile, Arc de
Triomphe, Paris, 1806–34. Photo
courtesy BBMSL, UNM.

Symbiosis   In botany, a relationship
of tight interdependence of growth
and metabolic function exhibited by
two genetically unrelated plants. An
alga and a fungus living together as
a lichen are an example. The plant
partners thus formed are symbionts.
Adjective: symbiotic.

Symmetry   A form of spatial or
structural organization that
demonstrates exactness of mass,
volume, or placement with opposing
balance. The following two varieties
of symmetry are quite common: 1)
**Axial or bilateral (two-sided)
symmetry:** in plant structure or
landscape design, an organization
of parts along both sides of an axis
or a series of parallel or intersecting
axes. 2) **Radial symmetry:** in plant
structures (particularly flowers) or
landscape design, a formal
geometry based on several axes
fanning out from a common center.

Symmetry, quadrilateral
See **Quadrilateral symmetry.**

Sympodial   In plants, pertaining to
growth by multiple branching.

Synecological optimum   In
horticulture, the best state of
reproduction, spread of range, and
growth habit achieved by a single
plant species mixed in its habitat
with multiple other species. See also
Autoecological optimum.

Synecology   Group ecology; the
environmental relationships of an
association of plants or animals. See
also **Autoecology, Ecology.**

Synoptic chart   See **Weather chart.**

System, automatic (irrigation)
See **Automatic controller.**

System, block (irrigation)
See **Section system.**

System, coordinate
See **Coordinates.**

System, drainage   See **Drainage**
system.

System, greenway   See **Greenway**
system.

**System, Linnaean (of plant
classification)**   See **Botanical
classification.**

System, manual (irrigation)
See **Manual system.**

System, section (irrigation)
See **Section system.**

System, transit   See **Transit.**

System, valve (irrigation)
See **Section.**

Systematic botany   Taxonomy, q.v.,
or the logical universal classification
of plants. See also **Botanical
classification.**

Systematic pesticide (insecticide)
See **Insecticide.**

T

T Tangent, q.v., or tangent distance.

Table, light See **Light table.**

Table, water See **Water table.**

Tableland See **Plateau.**

Table, garden See **Garden tables.**

Tack coat, asphalt See **Asphalt tack coat.**

Tack weld A weld using spot contacts between two metal members to secure them. See also **Seam weld, Strip weld.**

Tackifier In hydroseeding, a binding material that holds a hydraulically applied mulch together and helps to secure it to the soil.

Taiga Northern conifer forest lands, especially in Siberia. The forests are composed of members of the pine family. Taigas are often flooded in spring.

Talus See **Debris.**

Talus creep See **Soil creep.**

Talweg (Thalweg) See **Valley line.**

Tanbark Shredded bark, often used as a mulch or as a soft pavement in play areas.

Tangency, point of (road curves)
See **Point of tangency.**

Tangent (T) In landscape construction, a straight line leading into a road curve.

Tangent length (T) In road layout, the distance between PC and PI (point of curvature and point of intersection), and from PI to PT (point of intersection to point of tangency).

Tank 1) In arid parts of the United States, India, Australia, and elsewhere, a water-holding pond created by an earthen dam in a dry rivercourse. Tanks are often constructed to water grazing stock. 2) A square or round water-holding basin in Indian, Portuguese, and other gardens. A pond bounded by masonry.

Tank, holding (irrigation)
See **Holding tank.**

Tape, plastic expansion See **Plastic expansion tape.**

Tapisvert (French) An extremely close-cut ornamental green.

Taproot The central, vertical, anchoring root of many trees and some shrubs.

Tar (as a wood preservative)
See **Wood preservative.**

Tarmac See **Asphaltic concrete, Macadam.**

Tarmacadam See **Asphaltic concrete, Macadam.**

Tarn A small, high-mountain, glacial lake.

Tax lien See **Lien.**

Taxis Tropism, specifically movement or change in the position or stature of a plant due to a stimulus such as light. Also **Kinesis.** See also **Tropism.**

Taxon In botany, a group of related plants. See also **Botanical classification, Taxonomy.**

Taxonomy The systematic universal classification of plants or animals. See also **Botanical classification.**

t_c See **Time of concentration.**

TC In surveying, an abbreviation indicating top of curb. See **Top of curb.**

TD In road design, **Travel distance,** q.v.

Tea See **Liquid manure.**

Tea garden   In Japanese landscapes, a garden designed with precision for contemplation. The tea ceremony is incorporated as a prime landscape function. Also **Cha-niwa, Cha-seki.**
See also **Japanese landscape architecture.**

Tea house   In Japan, a small, partially or wholly enclosed garden house used in the customary tea ritual. Also, a light summer house of Oriental derivation in Western gardens. See also **Summer house.**

Technical pen   A mechanical-tipped pen with an Indian or other ink reservoir and a nib of exact size designed to produce a line of precise width. Sizes from 000 (.25 mm) to 4 (1.20 mm) are commonly available.

Technical pencil   A wood-encased or mechanically held pencil of good quality used for plan drafting.

Technical specifications.
   See **Specifications.**

Technology, "convivial"
   See **Convivial technology.**

Tee   1) A type of irrigation **Fitting,** q.v. 2) In golf, a flat, smoothly mown, elevated area from which golfers drive down a fairway with an iron or a wood.

Tell (or tel)   In the Middle East, a midden or mound—a site of former habitation. See also **Tumulus.**

Temperate climate   A middle latitude climate characterized by moderate temperature extremes and precipitation. Temperate climates are characteristically influenced by a body of water, favorable winds, and low altitude.

Temperate house   A greenhouse of moderate temperature.

Temperate zone   The middle latitudes north or south of the equator, falling between the Antarctic Circle and the Tropic of Capricorn (southern hemisphere), the Tropic of Cancer and the Arctic Circle (northern hemisphere). The interiors of Asia and North America experience continental weather and are not as truly temperate as the coasts. The Earth's temperate zones have been the historic setting for the development of landscape architecture.

Temperature inversion   A problem contributing to the concentration of smog over (primarily) urban areas. A layer of warm air overlies a concentration of cold air nearer the ground, thus preventing normal atmospheric circulation and trapping dust, smoke, exhaust gases, and the like in a stagnant mass. Temperature inversions often occur in winter over urban basins and are an increasing problem as the Earth's cities continue to grow.

Temperature lapse   See **Lapse rate.**

Temperature scale   The commonly used scales to determine relative temperature are Fahrenheit (principally U.S.) and Celsius (Centigrade). Conversions:
   Fahrenheit to Celsius: C = 5/9 (F-32)
   Celsius to Fahrenheit: F = 32 + (1.8 × C).

Template   A drafting tool, cut of standard shapes and forms from sheet metal or plastic, used to produce precision drawings.

Temple, Sir William (1628–99)
   English writer and ambassador to The Hague. Sir William gained an extensive knowledge of Chinese gardens through his contacts with the Dutch. He was one of the first

Europeans to realize the fundamental importance of naturalism—the lack of formal, symmetrical quality—in Chinese landscape design. His long essay, *Upon the Gardens of Epicurus* (1685), began the rage for **Chinoiserie** in Europe. Temple's coined word **Sharawadji** expressed his ideal of informal garden beauty gracefully achieved. His influence on the **English School of Landscape Gardening** of the eighteenth and early nineteenth centuries was profound. See also **English landscape architecture.**

Temporary construction   During the course of landscape construction, temporary items such as fencing; new, sheltered, or screened sidewalks; pavements; scaffolding; and the like may be used at a site. These are removed as permanent project construction is completed.

Temporary roads   In landscape construction, roads constructed to or within a project site during installation for the convenience of the contractor, usually under the landscape architect's supervision.

Tender   Applied to half-hardy plants incapable of surviving frost.

Tendril   In vines, a grasping support "arm" for climbing, consisting of a thin and tapering, coiling, twine-like appendage (a modified leaf or stem) that attaches itself to a wall, beam, trellis, or the like. Also **Cirrhus.**

Tennis   A popular sport played with a bouncing ball and rackets on a 36 × 78 ft. (11 m × 24 m) court. Courts may be of grass, clay, asphalt, concrete, or specially prepared commercial surfaces.

Tennis, deck   See **Deck tennis.**

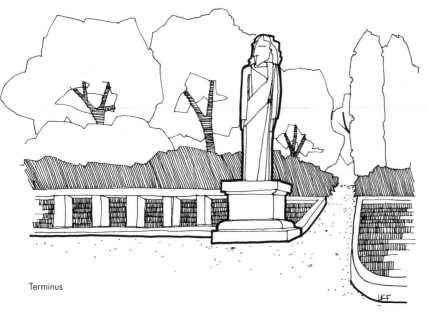

Terminus

Terra rossa (Italian)   In the Mediterranean, a red clay found in limestone areas.

Terra roxa (Portuguese)   Brazilian coffee-growing soil, violet or red in color, with a heavy humus content. Found in Sao Paulo state and elsewhere in eastern Brazil.

Terrace   1) A raised level area, usually attached to a house or other building and sometimes surrounded by planters, rails, or the like, used for outdoor recreational activities or for slope retention. 2) In agriculture, a shelf or narrow bench developed by farmers on a hillslope for the planting of crops **(Bench terrace)**. 3) A river terrace, or bench, formed by a river as it cuts its bed.

Terrace interval   The actual or proposed linear measurement between vertical terraces. Also, a horizontal distance occurring between two or more nearby terraces.

Terrace, mangum   See **Mangum terrace.**

Terrace, ridge   See **Mangum terrace.**

Terrace, river   See **River terrace.**

Terrace timber   A **Deck,** q.v.

Tensile bond   In masonry, the clinging together of cured mortar and brick, concrete block, rebars, or the like.

Tensile strength   In concrete, wood, or other construction materials, the ability to endure stretching. See also **Shear strength.**

Tensiometer   See **Moisture sensor.**

Tension bands and bars   Essential elements in the construction of chainlink fencing. Tension bars secure the fence fabric at gate, corner, and other posts, and are themselves attached to their posts by tension bonds.

Tension wire   In landscape construction, a steel wire set up between line posts to accommodate chainlink-fence fabric.

Teratology   The study of abnormal plant growth.

Terete   In plant structures, round in cross section.

Terminal bud   The tip or end-bud of a plant stem. Also **Apical bud.** See also **Lateral bud.**

Terminus   1) A Roman god of estate, garden, or national boundaries. His statues **(Terms)** have marked garden walkways and properties into modern times. 2) The end point or apex of an axis or other landscape feature. In Greece, **Herm,** q.v. See also **Priapus.**

Terms (term statues)   See **Terminus.**

Terra cotta   A very hard reddish or ochre clay often used in ceramic garden pots and figures.

Terra cotta pipe   A hard-fired clay pipe made in relatively short sections with overlapping ends.

Terra firma   Dry ground. Land.

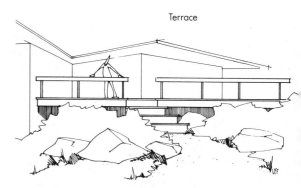

Terrace

Terracettes Tiny continuous ledges found on grazing slopes and used as paths by animals, possibly due to **Soil creep**, q.v. Also **Sheep tracks**.

Terrain A tract of the Earth's surface or its character.

Terrain, rolling See **Prairie topography**.

Terrane A rock formation or series of formations.

Terrarium A small-scale, glass-lined enclosure used to house and exhibit small animals or miniature gardens. A terrarium is sometimes called a **Bottle garden, Crystal garden, Fern case, Fernery, Glass garden, Moss garden,** or **Wardian case** (large scale). The invention of the Wardian case in the 1830s allowed large-scale transport of exotic plants from the far corners of the world to Europe and North America. See also **Model garden**.

Terrazzo (Italian) A kind of cultured-marble concrete in which marble chips are added as coarse aggregate to a cement matrix. Terrazzo is usually polished to a smooth finish and is often used in the form of precast benches and tables and in floors.

Terre tenant A person in possession of an area of land.

Terreplein (military) A wide, flat-topped embankment used for fortification.

Terrestrial Earthen, or pertaining to the land.

Terrigenous Pertaining to or originating in the land.

Tessellated (pavement) Composed of mosaic or small multicolor stone pieces.

Test, compression (of concrete) See **Compression test**.

Test, sieve See **Sieve test**.

Test, slump (of concrete) See **Slump test**.

Testa A (usually outer) seed coat. See also **Aril**.

Testing, pressure See **Pressure testing**.

Testing, soil See **Soil testing**.

Tetragonal With four angles.

Tetrahedral With four sides.

Tetraploid (plant cell) A cell with twice the normal number of paired chromosomes, often more vigorous than its parent cells. See also **Heterosis (hybrid vigor)**.

Texture The appearance of the structure and minute detail of the surface of objects as distinct from color.

Texture, soil See **Soil texture**.

TF See **Top of fence**.

T and G joint See **Tongue and groove joint**.

Thalamus In botany, a **Flower receptacle**, q.v.

Thalasso- (Greek) A prefix referring to the sea.

Thallophyte (Thallophyta) A member of the phylum (Division I of the plant kingdom) of simple plants, including, among others, algae, fungi, diatoms, seaweed, and possibly bacteria. There are approximately fifteen classes of thallophytes. See also **Botanical classification**.

Thalweg (Talweg) See **Valley line**.

Thatch In lawns, the build-up of fallen blades of grass and other detritus that can smother new growth. Treated by dethatching, which involves a stiff surface raking and removal of dead matter and, often, aeration and fertilizing. Also **Mat**. See also **Aeration, Dethatching,** and **Fertilizer**.

Theatre, green See **Green theatre**.

Theatre, water (Renaissance) See **Water theatre**.

Theatrical garden A formal, baroque garden in which plays and entertainments are presented. The Buen Retiro in Madrid, designed in the seventeenth century by Cosimo Lotti for the Count of Olivarez, is an example. See also **Green theatre**.

Texture. Photo by author.

Theca In botany, a sac found around the **Anther** (tip of the stamen, or male reproductive organ), q.v., of a plant.

Theme park A recreational park based on a historic or topical theme. The various segments of Disneyland, in California, or Smokey Bear Historical State Park, in New Mexico, are theme parks.

Theodolite A telescopic surveying instrument used to determine horizontal and vertical land angles. See also **Hand level, Level, Survey,** and **Transit.**

Theory, landscape architecture See **Landscape architectural theory.**

Thermal belt A hillside zone above the frost line in certain river valleys which stays green all winter.

Thermonasty In plants, a response to temperature. Often, growth or flowering in spring as the seasons change. See also **Nyctinasty, Photonasty.**

Thicket A dense, usually wild mass of small trees, shrubs, or undergrowth.

Thieves Profuse suckers emerging from a parent plant, usually a tree or large shrub. See also **Sucker.**

Thigmotropism See **Haptotropism.**

Thin soil A shallow topsoil, capable of supporting limited plant growth.

Thinning out In horticulture, the selective removal of the weakest of a group of recently germinated plants, or the selective pruning of limbs and foliage in trees and shrubs. Also, the removal of a portion of a fruit or flower crop at early growth to allow the remaining fruits or flowers to develop more fully.

Thorn A hard, pointed, modified plant structure used for protection. Uusally, a modified branch structure.

Thorn forest A typical savanna treeland featuring acacia or similar spiny species and thriving under conditions of modest rainfall (under 20 inches annually). See also **Savanna.**

Thoroughfare Any road, lane, highway, or other open-ended public way.

Three-quarter head In irrigation, a lawn or shrub head that emits a nozzle spray of 270°, covering three-fourths of a circle in area. See also **Head.**

Throttle In irrigation, the partial opening or closing of a valve to regulate water flow.

Throughway (thruway) A **Freeway** or **Expressway,** q.q.v.

Thrust In landscape construction, horizontal pressure exerted against a wall, post, or other structure. Thrust is generated by wind, (liquid) water, snow, or other elements and must be designed for carefully. Most often calculated for **Retaining walls,** q.v.

Tidal range The difference in elevation between a high and low tide.

Tie, snap (concrete) See **Snap tie.**

Tier (surveying) See **Town.**

Tierra caliente In tropical Latin America, the coastal and low-lying plains areas to approximately 1,000 meters above sea level. The climate is hot and wet and the normal vegetation is lush. Above the *Tierra*

caliente are the two other typical climate zones of the region, **Tierra fria** and **Tierra templada,** q.q.v.

Tierra fria In tropical Latin America, the highest climate zone of usual human habitation, normally occurring from about 2,300 meters to 3,400 meters or more above sea level. Temperate-zone crops may be grown in the *Tierra fria,* although normal vegetation is coniferous forest turning into scrub and grassland at the higher elevations. Below the *Tierra fria* are the **Tierra templada** and **Tierra caliente,** q.q.v.

Tierra templada The middle climate zone of tropical Latin America, found between 1,000 and 2,300 meters above sea level. The *Tierra templada* has a uniform, moderate climate with a tiny range of annual temperature. Rainfall is often light, but some crops are cultivated where the land has not been severely eroded due to misuse. The **Tierra fria** lies above and the **Tierra caliente** below the *Tierra templada.*

Tile Baked clay or similar material with a glazed or unglazed surface used as outdoor flooring or wall inlay, in drains, or as roofing.

Tile, land See **Land tile.**

Till Glacial debris. Also **Boulder clay** and **Glacial till.**

Tillage Cultivation. The operation of preparing ground for planting. See also **Rough tillage.**

Tillage, conservation See **Conservation tillage.**

Tillage, mulch See **Mulch tillage.**

Tillage, rough See **Rough tillage.**

Tiller A kind of lateral plant shoot or sprout usually upright (grasses). See also **Rhizome, Stolon.**

Tillering In grasses, heavy base or lateral sprouting due to mowing or cutting of the usual plant form.

Tilth The quality of tillage in soil. A good rich sandy loam that is moist and free of stones will have excellent tilth and may be worked easily.

Timber (log, overhead member) 1) Collectively, trees grown or wood cut for human use. 2) In landscape construction, an overhead beam or an upright supporting member in an arbor or other garden construction. See also **Lumber.**

Timberline The climatic limit on mountain slopes and at the Arctic Circle above which trees grow only as shrubs or not at all. In temperate areas, the boundary of the Arctic-Alpine Zone.

Timber terrace A **Deck,** q.v.

Time clock (irrigation) See **Automatic controller.**

Time for completion (landscape construction) See **Contract time.**

Time of concentration (TOC) In storm drainage, the time elapsing before water from the furthest point of a watershed (drainage area) reaches a drainage outlet. The time of concentration includes **Inlet** (overland flow) **time,** q.v., plus the time it takes for water to pass from the inlet to the outlet. Also t_c.

Time of construction See **Contract time.**

Time, contract See **Contract time.**

Time, inlet See **Inlet time.**

Time, mobilization (landscape construction) See **Mobilization time.**

Time, overland flow See **Inlet time.**

Timer, automatic (irrigation) See **Automatic controller.**

Timer box (irrigation) See **Automatic controller.**

Timer, irrigation See **Automatic controller.**

Timer, pedestal mount (irrigation) See **Automatic controller.**

Timer, wall mount (irrigation) See **Automatic controller.**

Tired soil In gardening, an exhausted soil.

"Title" law In U.S. landscape architecture, a state law that limits the use of the title "Landscape Architect" to certified individuals. See also **"Practice" law** and **"Title and Practice" law.**

"Title and Practice" law In U.S. landscape architecture, a state law restricting the provision of landscape architectural services and the use of the title "Landscape Architect" to certified individuals. See also **"Practice" law** and **"Title" law.**

TOC See **Time of concentration.**

Todd, Frederick G. (1876–1948) Pioneer Canadian landscape architect, born in Concord, New Hampshire, and educated at the Agricultural College, Amherst, Massachusetts. Todd worked for the Olmsted office from 1896–1900, moving to Montreal to superintend work on Mount Royal Park. He established his own office in Montreal in 1900.

Todd designed new "garden suburbs" for the Canadian Pacific Railroad in Montreal and elsewhere. He popularized the idea of a "necklace of parks" as linked open space in his designs. The City of Regina, Saskatchewan hired Todd in 1907 to design its Wascana Park, a lakeside recreation area near the proposed municipal government complex. Todd suggested a naturalistic landscape treatment with a great quantity of trees in shelterbelts and ornamental groves as a relief from the level contours of the prairie. Though greatly modified by **Thomas Mawson,** q.v., just before World War I, Todd's designs were constructed in the 1930s and 1960s. His other prairie work included Assiniboine Park in Winnipeg (1904).

Todd was a consistent popularizer of landscape architecture in his articles for magazines and newspapers. His practice was nationwide by the 1920s. Among his best known projects are the Parc des Champs de Bataille (Plains of Abraham National Battlefield, c. 1913) in Quebec City; site planning and design for Trinity College, Toronto; and Bowering Park, St. John's, Newfoundland (1913–18). During the Great Depression, Todd completed an extensive restoration of St. Helen's Island, Montreal, in the St. Lawrence River. He served as president of the Canadian Society of Landscape Architects from 1945 to 1946. Todd's last work was a garden design for the Chemin de la Croix at Montreal's St. Joseph Oratory (1945). An elegant exercise in naturalism, the grounds reached their young maturity and perhaps the height of their beauty in the late 1970s.

See also **Canadian landscape architecture.**

Toe of slope The very base of a hill or gradient.

Topiary. Green Animals, Portsmouth, Rhode Island, at the Brayton Topiary Gardens. Photo courtesy BBMSL, UNM.

Tolerance, deflection
See **Deflection tolerance.**

Tolerance, grading (grade)
See **Grading tolerance.**

Tombolo   A sandbar connecting an island to a mainland or other land mass.

Tomentose   In botany, pertaining to plants with stems, leaves, or flowers covered with downy and matted "hair." See also **Pubescence.**

Tonal border   A short gray or light-green massed border planting, often used as a garden accent by **Gertrude Jekyll,** q.v., and others.

Tongue and groove joint   In landscape construction, this male-female wood joint is mostly used in decking that requires no spaces between the planks. Also **T and G joint.**

Tool, arrising (concrete)
See **Arrising tool.**

Tool, grooving (concrete)
See **Groover.**

Tooled joint   In masonry, any joint shaped by means of a concave (round-edged) or V-form instrument.

Toot-hill   A look-out hill in medieval England, artificial or man-made.

Top of curb (TC)   A basic point of mean elevation, usually above sea level or relative elevation (datum), used for site construction information. See also **Bottom of curb.**

Top dressing   A landscape material, usually organic, and composed of shredded bark, bark chips, straw, manure, sawdust, peat moss, compost, or similar substance, which is applied to a planting area as a finish surface conditioner.

Top of fence (TF)   A surveying or site layout abbreviation.

Topiary   In landscape architecture, pertaining to (usually) evergreen shrubs or trees pruned into unnatural or purely geometric shapes. Topiary work is found almost exclusively in formal gardens. (Latin: *topiarus,* gardener.)

Topo (slang)   See **Topography.**

Topo map   See **Topographic map.**

Topographic map   A map displaying the physical features of an area, including elevations, roads, lakes, streams, woods, towns, and the like. Topographic maps are drawn with contours extrapolated from a 50-foot or other grid pattern, or from spot elevations established along a **Stadia,** q.v., traverse.

Top of curb / bottom of curb

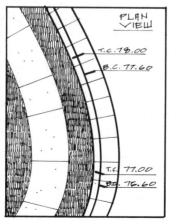

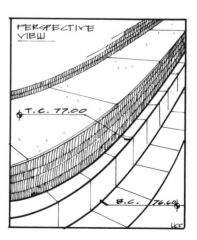

Topographic (topo) survey
  See **Survey.**

Topography   The lay of the land, existing or proposed. Plan contours and land features, often laid out on a **Grid,** q.v., with contour elevations. Also **Topo.** See also **Contour, Contour line,** and **Grade.**

Topography, Karst   See **Sinkhole.**

Topography, prairie   See **Prairie topography.**

Topology   A field within botany concerned with the areas or regions in which plants commonly grow.

Toposaic   "Topographical mosaic." A kind of photogrammetry in which contour lines are indicated. Similar to a **Quadrangle** map, q.v.

Topping   In tree or shrub pruning, an abrupt, flat-top cutting of end growth, often ending in needless disfigurement for ornamental trees.

Topsoil   The Earth's epidermis. This uppermost layer of soil rests on **Subsoil,** q.v., and contains minerals, water, and decomposed plant and animal matter. It is the basis for all land life and much of human economy and culture. Most of the civilizations of history have ultimately misused, not appreciated, or wasted it after using its bounty to flourish. One frequent by-product of a good topsoil is overpopulation.
  Relatively stable topsoils now exist in parts of Western Europe and East Asia. Topsoil is the A horizon.
  See also **Loam, Soil, Soil horizon.**

Top-working   An elaborate form of grafting in which a **Scion,** q.v., or bud is attached to the outer limb of a large shrub or tree. Sometimes the entire tip growth of a large tree or shrub is replaced by top-working.

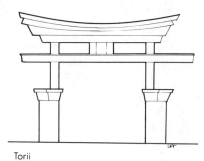

Torii

Tor   A weathered, oddly shaped, remnant rock mass. Tors continue to influence specialty landscapes, such as alpine gardens, and have been especially stylized in Oriental gardens.

Torrens system   A system adopted by various states of the United States to record land titles.

Torrent   A wild, steep, rough-flowing stream.

Town. Ancient town of the Arabian Peninsula. Photo courtesy BBMSL, UNM.

Torii (Japanese)   An originally ceremonial arch of stone, wood, or bronze found in larger Japanese gardens. Originally a feature of temple courtyards.

Tort   An injury to the property of another. In landscape architecture, the most common torts are nuisance, negligence, violation of lateral and subjacent support, violation of riparian rights. See also **Negligence, Nuisance, Right of lateral and subjacent support,** and **Riparian rights.**

Torus   See **Flower receptacle.**

Tot lot   See **Play lot.**

Town   1) A settlement that is larger than a village but smaller than a city. 2) In surveying, an alternate term for tier or township.

Town, new   See **New town.**

Town, satellite (planning)
See **Satellite town.**

Township   In the United States, a plat of land broken out of a 24-mile "control square" measuring approximately 6 × 6 miles. There are sixteen townships in a control square, the boundaries of which are usually surveyed east-west and north-south. Also **Town.** Also abbreviated **TWP.** See also **Section.**

Toxic salts (wood preservative)
See **Wood preservative.**

Trabeation   In landscape construction, the placement of long horizontal stone in a wall or as a substitute for an arch over a gate. Adjective: trabeated, or built with post and beam. See also **Arcuated.**

Trace element   An element necessary in small amounts for plant growth, health, and reproduction. Elements such as zinc, manganese, molybdenum, and iron, found in relatively minor quantities in the Earth's crust. One of the twelve **Micronutrients.** Other trace elements are boron, chlorine, cobalt, copper, fluorine, iodine, sodium, and vanadium. Also **Minor element.** See also **Available nutrient, Macronutrient, Soil minerals.**

Trachea   In botany, a vascular vessel found in xylem or wood.

Tracheophyta   A botanical group or division that encompasses all plants with vascular systems. See also **Pteridophyte, Spermatophyte.**

Traction   Surface friction. Good traction is important for safe foot traffic across decks, concrete pads, and other landscape surfaces.

Trade   In specification reference, a specialty contractor employed on a project.

Trabeation

Trade association specifications
   Technical specifications established by a construction trade or trades that are widely accepted as standard.

Traffic circle   See **Roundabout.**

Traffic interchange   In twentieth-century freeway systems, a highway junction of several directions, including access roads with entries, that allows smooth, continuous traffic flow and change of direction through a series of overpasses, underpasses, and multiple lanes. See also **Cloverleaf.**

Trafficability of soil   See **Soil trafficability.**

Trail, trim   See **Parcours.**

Trailer (mobile home) park   A twentieth-century industrial-housing area. Trailers (mobile homes, caravans) located on permanent or temporary grounds with utilities and, often, roads, plantings, a central office or community hall, washrooms, laundromats, and the like. The standardized nature of trailer construction and its usual unsympathetic form, among other factors, often make it difficult to integrate trailers and trailer parks with the surrounding landscape.

Trailing   In vines, growing flat against a ground surface but not usually rooting. See also **Clambering.**

Training   In horticulture, manipulation of plant growth by selective pruning, typing, espaliering, and the like to produce a desired form, fruiting habit, or other characteristic.

Training, arcure (of fruit trees)
See **Arcure training.**

Training, quenouille   See **Quenoille training.**

Transect (of vegetation)   A "study line" of plants established for purposes of review and analysis across an area of vegetation that is typical of its type and habitat.

Transhumance   The moving of livestock from lower to upper or drier to wetter pastures and back with changes in season, especially by settler farmers or graziers. The practice can contribute substantially to the development of a "cultural" landscape.

Transit   1) A basic telescopic surveying instrument used to determine horizontal and vertical elevation, distances, and directions. A specialized theodolite. See also **Hand level, Level, Survey,** and **Theodolite.** 2) Public or private conveyance, especially in an urban area. A transit system is a bus, subway, or streetcar network.

Transite pipe   A large diameter **Asbestos cement pipe,** q.v., used in municipal water mains.

Transition   1) In landscape architecture, an area whose elements serve as an intermediate space or spaces between one outdoor place or activity and another. Examples include step landings, porches, forecourts, and the like. 2) In environmental geography, an **Ecotone,** q.v.

Transplanting. Tree-lifting machine, French, 19th century. Illustration courtesy BBMSL, UNM.

Transition (zone)   See **Life zone.**

Transitional soil   Any soil with the qualities of two or more distinct soils and clearly related to or shading into them.

Translucent   Transparent but not completely so.

Transpiration   In botany, the loss of water from leaf and stem surfaces through evaporation. See also **Evaporation, Evapo-transpiration, Stoma.**

Transplanting   Moving a plant from its place of origin to a garden or landscape location.
   Transplanting is a completely unnatural process, never occurring in the wild, and it is a testament to the inherent hardiness and adaptability of green plants that they are able to survive it and even thrive with such regularity.
   Landscape plants are commonly transplanted from flats, pots, boxes, or metal cans. They may also be transplanted as bareroot or balled and burlapped specimens.
   See also **Bareroot stock, Collected stock, Container-grown stock, Field-grown stock,** and **Nursery stock.**

Transport, gravity   See **Gravity transport.**

Transverse dune   See **Dune.**

Transverse section   A cross-section. See **Section (drawing).**

Transverse valley   A valley which cuts perpendicular to its mountain range. Very typical of Rocky Mountain and other formations in the southwestern United States.

Trap   A debris or grease "catch" protecting a pipe, conduit, or sewer.

Tree grate. Photo courtesy Morrow and Company.

Travel distance (of contours)   In road layout, an allowance for contour plotting which graphically illustrates the crown of a road. The distance between road contours. Also **TD.**

Traverse (surveying)   A connected series of lines with determined and plotted bearings and angles. There are two common types: 1) **Closed traverse:** a kind of boundary survey consisting of a series of connected lines that begin and end at the same point, enclosing a plot of land. 2) **Open traverse:** a series of consecutive lines that do not close on themselves. The open traverse is often used for roadways or long path layout.

Traverse road   A vehicular way located over and usually perpendicular to a pedestrian or bicycle pathway.

Travertine   A silicaceous or calcareous rock formed by deposit of underground water, springs, and the like; **Tufa.** Travertine onyx is considered to be and is used as a low-grade marble.

Tread   The flat stepping surface of a stair or stairway. See also **Riser, Stair, Step.**

Treatment (pressure) of wood   See **Wood preservative.**

Trecento   The 1300s in Italian art. A common Renaissance reference.

Tree   A woody plant, generally taller than 6 feet (2 meters), with a discernible trunk or trunks below a leaf crown. Any woody plant a person can stand under.

Tree family (fruit)   See **Family (fruit) tree.**

Tree farm   A commercial or experimental farm used for the propagation and production of plant species for ornamental horticulture.

Tree grate   A useful metal grille, installed at the very base of a tree otherwise surrounded by hard pavement, that allows the free passage of air, water, and nutrients to tree roots, but does not interfere with foot traffic. Often used with **Street trees,** q.v. See also **Tree guard.**

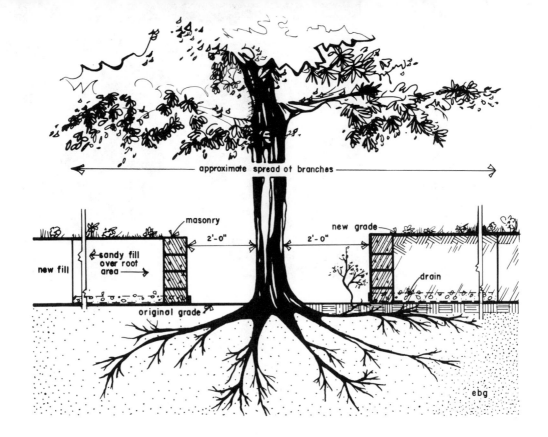

approximate spread of branches

masonry

new grade

2'-0"

2'-0"

new fill

sandy fill over root area

drain

new grade

original grade

ebg

Tree wells

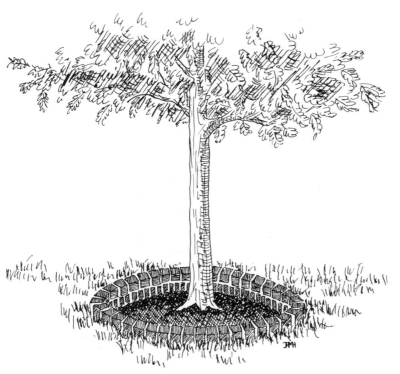

Tree guard An upright series of metal bars arranged around a tree and held together by metal bands. Tree guards deter vandalism and help to prevent involuntary damage by passing wagons, strollers, wheelbarrows, and similar vehicles. They are often used with **Tree grates,** q.v., in heavily urbanized areas. Also, an upright cone secured around a tree trunk to prevent animals from climbing.

Tree gum See **Xylan.**

Tree, street See **Street tree.**

Tree surgeon See **Arborist.**

Tree well A constructed "hole" around an existing tree that keeps the root crown from being covered when the nearby grade is increased during the course of site improvement. Tree wells are usually protected by upright retainer walls of varying construction.

Tree wrapping A thin brown (kraft) paper or burlap strip wound around young tree trunks to protect them against sunscald and windburn.

Treeline A mountainous or subarctic limit of forestation beyond which trees will only grow as shrubs or not at all because of the excessively harsh climate.

Treillage (French) An architectural pierced screen or latticework developed as a backdrop for nearby gardens. Common in the Renaissance work of Le Notre and others.

Trellis A garden structure consisting of light, often-overlapped or crossing laths or light wood or metal members used as an overhead or vertical sun-shade and plant support. See also **Lath, Overhead, Pergola.**

Trellis drainage A drainage pattern resembling a lattice, trellis, or tree with horizontal branching habits. **Annular drainage** is trellis-like but consists of curving "branch" tributaries around solitary, eroded individual mountains. See also **Drainage pattern.**

Tremie A movable chute or tube with a widened upper end, normally used to deposit concrete underwater.

Trench A long and narrow, often vertically sided excavation made for the placement of pipe, wire, and footings, or for the conduction of water. See also **Ditch.**

Trench drain In landscape construction, a narrow but lengthy light drain used to channel runoff from a paved patio, plaza, or the like.

Trench grate A kind of drainage grate designed to cover a narrow trench in an area of foot or vehicular traffic. See also **Grate, Tree grate.**

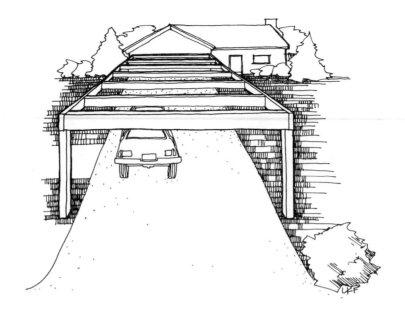

Trellises

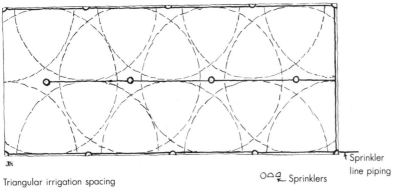

Triangular irrigation spacing

○□◁ Sprinklers

↑ Sprinkler line piping

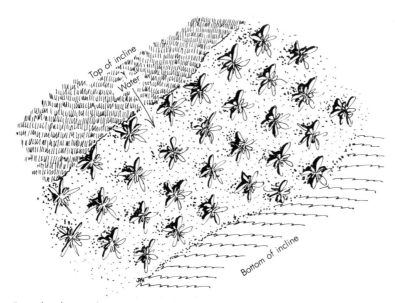

Top of incline

Water

Bottom of incline

Triangular plant spacing

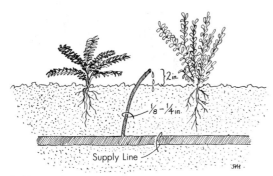

2 in.

⅛ – ¼ in.

Supply Line

Trickle irrigation

Trench, seepage   See **Seepage trench.**

Trenching, bastard   See **Bastard trenching.**

"Triangle," clear sight   See **Clear sight "triangle."**

Triangular spacing   In irrigation or planting, a three-point layout of sprinklers, shrubs, or ground covers in the form of an equilateral triangle. Also triangulation.

Tribe   In **Botanical classification,** q.v., a term used to organize related genera within a family of plants.

Trick fountain   See **Water joke.**

Trickle drain   A vertical pond overflow pipe, set with its open inlet at the same level as the pond surface.

Trickle irrigation   A method of watering farms and ornamental landscapes in which water is released through spaghetti-like strands supplied by low-pressure underground lines at a constant and highly specific rate. Trickle irrigation applies water directly to a plant's root zone. Also **Drip irrigation.** See also **Subinjection irrigation.**

Trifoliate or **Trifoliolate**   With three-part leaflets. See also **Foliolate.**

Trigonometry   In landscape architecture, triangular geometry applied in surveying and general land layout.

Trilithon   A type of Paleolithic stone construct in which a lintel or horizontal slab is placed on two upright slabs.

Trim trail   See **Parcours.**

Trompe l'oeil (French) In landscape architecture, foreshortening and other tricks of exaggerated **Perspective,** q.v., used to modify the apparent depth, length, or width of a landscape.

Tropical 1) Any plant naturally occurring between the Tropic of Cancer and the Tropic of Capricorn. 2) Of or pertaining to the tropics or torrid zone. See also **Tropics.**

Tropical desert A desert such as the Sahara of Africa or Great Sandy of Australia that lies more truly in the subtropics. High pressure zones, unfavorable winds and tides, difficult topography, and intense, continual sunshine are basic causes of tropical desert formation. The Kalahari and Atacama Deserts are also examples. See also **Desert, Desertification, Relief desert.**

Tropical grassland See **Savanna.**

Tropical rain forest See **Rain forest.**

Tropical soil See **Lateritic soil, Pedalfer.**

Tropics The area of the Earth lying between the north and south points of solstice—i.e., approximately 25° north and south latitudes. Climates within the tropics are characterized by "wets" and "dries" rather than by "hots" and "colds." See also **Tropical.**

Tropism Plant development, growth, or reaction triggered by an outside presence or influence. Plant movement. Also **Kinesis, Taxis.** See also **Auxin, Chemotropism, Geotropism, Haptotropism,** and **Phototropism.**

Tropopause A transition region of the atmosphere separating the **Stratosphere** from the **Troposphere,** q.q.v.

Tropophyte A plant adapted to dry periods succeeded by seasonal precipitation. Tropophytes drop their leaves during dry seasons and regrow them as rains come. The *Acacia spp.* of the savannas are examples. See also **Hydrophyte, Mesophyte, Xerophyte.**

Troposphere The turbulent lower regions of the atmosphere, varying in altitude from the Earth's surface up to a six-mile (9.67 km) maximum.

Trough garden Similar to a **Sink garden,** q.v. This sort of garden is a miniature, usually planted in annuals or foliage plants in a stone, brick, or concrete trough.

Trowelling In concrete finishing, a hand-rub process producing a smooth-grained surface by means of a metal trowel.

Truck farming The intensive raising of vegetable produce for shipment to town markets. Also **Market gardening.**

True leaf The typical leaf of a given plant.

True to type In horticulture, plants that are examples of the norm for their species. Good quality plants.

Truncate In leaves, spade-like or "sawed-off" at one end.

Trunk The main stem or bole of a tree.

(The) Trustees of Public Reservations In Massachusetts, an organization devoted to the preservation of highly valuable existing landscapes and open spaces for public benefit.

Founded in 1890 through the efforts of **Charles Eliot,** q.v., and by official act of the Massachusetts General Court in 1891, the Trustees became the prototype organization for landscape preservation in the United States.

T-square A drafting straight-edge shaped like a T, with the attached head rigid and slightly raised for smooth movement along the edge of a drafting table. See also **Mayline.**

Tsuki-yama A Japanese hill garden, dating from the fifteenth and sixteenth centuries A.D. Clearly elaborated in **Shin, Gyo** or **So** (Zen) style, q.q.v. See also **Hira-niwa.**

Tub gardening A kind of **Container gardening,** q.v., in which a whole or half barrel is used. Holes are bored in an end for drainage, and sometimes in tub or barrel sides to allow plants to spill out.

Tuber A swollen, fleshy underground root or plant stem with buds from which new plants develop. The potato is a common tuber. A small tuber is a tubercle. See also **Bulb, Corm.**

Tuberous root A tuber-like mass of root tissue found in yams and similar plants. Real **Tubers,** q.v., are formed of stem tissue.

Tuck pointing (masonry) A finish-joint method. The mortar or cement joint is carefully ground down and a second mortar fill is applied and tooled to finish the joint.

Tudor garden William Lawson, in his *New Orchard and Garden* of 1618, tells us that the typical English Tudor (Renaissance) garden consisted of a rectangle divided into squares. It was furnished with mounts, sundials, shelters, knot gardens, mazes, bowling greens, orangeries, fountains, and other delights. A little stiff in design, perhaps, but quite lively in execution.

Tudor gardens flourished in the sixteenth, seventeenth, and early eighteenth centuries, and are named after the monarchs during whose reigns they were built. Italian craftsmen, familiar with topiary massing, garden statuary, and courtyard composition were imported to develop the first of these gardens. Later, native English craftsmen were used. By the eighteenth century, the formal planters of the Tudor Garden were often filled with exotics unused in the late 1500s. The "Tudor" form was present as a shell in which newly created vistas, imaginative waterworks, and the use of classical motifs in whimsical ways would soon take over.

Wilton, Wiltshire (1615), probably by Isaac de Caus, was an early masterpiece of Tudor gardening. By combining medieval with new Italian forms, de Caus helped to popularize the Renaissance garden in England. The later modifications of Wilton by **Brown** and possibly **Repton**, q.q.v., indicate the general supplanting of the Tudor garden by the naturalistic Landscape Gardening School.

See also **English landscape architecture, Renaissance landscape architecture.**

Tufa A porous stone, sometimes sedimentary, often volcanic, used in building.

Tuff A light rock composed of compressed volcanic ash.

Tulipomania In seventeenth-century Holland, a fad involving an intense trading of and speculation in tulip bulbs. Tulipomania was brought to a close by the Netherlands government after a purported $10,000 was offered for a rare bulb at a 1630 auction, but the Dutch fondness for tulips and other bulbs continues.

See also **Dutch landscape architecture.**

Tumid In plant structures, swollen or enlarged.

Tumulus A mound over a grave. A common feature of old cemeteries. Plural: tumuli. Also **Barrow.** See also **Tell.**

Tundra A swampy, treeless plain or rolling mountainside area with a saturated soil and permanently frozen subsoil, covered largely in mosses, lichens, and grasses. Tundra is usually found north of the Arctic Circle. See also **Polygonal soil.**

Tunnard, Christopher (d. 1980)
British landscape architect and professor of city planning at Yale University. Tunnard's *Gardens of the Modern Landscape* was the first book to recognize the meaning of the "Harvard Revolution" of the 1930s. Tunnard favored and promoted the Modern or California Garden idea as a twentieth-century approach to landscape design. Among his other books are *American Skyline* (with H. H. Reed) and *Man-Made America* (with B. Pushkarev).

See also **California garden.**

Turbinate In plant structures, resembling a top.

Turbine pump (irrigation)
See **Booster pump.**

Turf Heavy, matted vegetative ground cover; usually grass. See also **Sod.**

Turf maze In Renaissance England, a garden maze consisting of high turf ridges carved into a lawn. See also **Maze.**

Turf seat In medieval and Renaissance gardens, a seat made of turf at the upper level of a small terrace. Turf seats were common features of the **Pleasaunce,** q.v.

Turgor In plants, a condition of swollen vascular cells caused by the presence of large amounts of fluid. Adjective: turgid.

Turkish landscape architecture The tulip was for centuries the favorite flower of the Turks. It grew wild in the hills of Anatolia and the Bosporus. The earliest of the Turks—the Seljuks—came to Asia Minor in the eleventh century, and their primary garden and architectural styles were Persian: fountains in secluded gardens, blue tiles for accents, cool lines of trees. The Seljuk Turks had been pushed out of central Asia by the expansionism of Genghis Khan. They were succeeded in Anatolia by the Ottoman Turks in the thirteenth century. The Ottomans eventually overwhelmed the crumbled Byzantine Empire, taking Constantinople in 1453.

The greatest of the Ottoman sultans, Suleiman the Magnificent, came to power in the mid-sixteenth century. Suleiman's kiosk in the sea, built along the shores of the Bosporus, was perhaps the most famous of Turkish garden houses. It was richly furnished in marble, porphyry, and bright tiles. Although enclosed, it had an entry from the sea, and its vistas of both Europe and Asia were spectacular.

The typical Turkish kiosk of Suleiman's time also featured **Mushrabiyeh** (lattice-screens, sometimes of carved stone), vines, and nearby fountains for coolness. The kiosk, of course, was later adopted by the French and other Europeans in a modified form. But it is remarkable that the Aztecs of Mexico had developed waterside casinos of equal sophistication and beauty during the same period, also approached by boat. See **Mexican landscape architecture.**

The architect of Suleiman's kiosk, Sinan, also designed the Suleimaniye complex, a series of garden courts and building links at the sultan's palace in Istanbul. He was responsible for the grounds of Topkapi Palace as well—now part of a Turkish national museum. Sinan's gardens were rather informal, and characterized by flowers, color, and a refined use of water. In these he set up the framework for later Turkish design, in which palaces or other public buildings are sited amiably in spacious gardens. Curiously, the form of many of these Turkish landscapes has been preserved in large-scale pastry models of sugar, marzipan, and the like.

See also **Byzantine landscape architecture, Persian landscape architecture.**

Turnkey project   A design project that is planned, designed, financed, developed, and constructed by a single company or agency. The responsible person, agency, or private firm is known as a **Package dealer.**

Turnout   A reasonably flat rest or repair area located along a highway or freeway.

Turnpike   A high-speed, limited access highway paid for by tolls collected from drivers as they enter it.

Tussie-mussie   Archaic English for a small bouquet from a garden.

Tussock   A clump or tuft of grass.

Twining   In vines, a climbing action in which the plant "spirals" about on another plant, a post, or the like.

Twisting and barbing   A term describing the connections and edging of chainlink fence mesh. See also **Chainlink fence.**

TWP   An abbreviation for **Township.**

Type, landscape   See **Ecosystem.**

Type, soil   See **Soil type.**

Type specimen   See **Holotype.**

Type, wild   See **Wild type.**

Types of landscape architectural contracts   See **Professional fee.**

Types, seed   See **Commercial seed classifications.**

Tyrannopolis   A term used by Garrett Eckbo and others to describe the overwhelming and banal form of an endless city sprawl, especially as advocated by irresponsible real estate "barons" and others.

Turkish landscape architecture. Suleiman's Mosque and grounds, Istanbul, sixteenth century. Photo courtesy BBMSL, UNM.

U

UD An abbreviation for **Underdrain,** q.v.

UF (irrigation wire) See **Underground feeder.**

Ultimate bearing capacity (of soils) See **Bearing capacity.**

Ultisol A soil type found in wet areas that contains large amounts of clay or **Hardpan,** q.v., and is relatively low in alkalinity. Some **Podsols** and **Lateritic soils,** q.q.v, are included in this soil type. See also **Alkaline soil.**

Ultraviolet (UV) radiation A form of invisible, radiant solar energy responsible for sunburn in humans and, at high altitudes, tissue damage in tender plants. See also **Sunscald.**

Umbel A flower cluster in which the individual pedicels spring from the same base and form a rounded or flat crown. Adjectives: umbellate, umbelliferous. See also **Pedicel.**

Uncinate In plant structures, pertaining to a barbed hair or spine. See also **Glochid.**

Unclassified excavation See **Excavation.**

Underbrush Low thickets beneath trees.

Underdrain A drain or set of drains located at the side(s) of a roadway for positive drainage in impervious soils. Abbreviated **UD.**

Underground drainage See **Drainage.**

Underground feeder (UF) In irrigation, a low-voltage buried wire used to activate electric valves.

Underpass A road or footway laid out under an obstacle for purposes of safe transit or passage.

Underplant 1) Verb, to install shrubs or ground covers under taller plants. 2) Verb, to design or install fewer plants than would normally be necessary to produce a desired landscape effect.

Undershrub A small semiherbaceous plant that is generally woody only near its base. See also **Subshrub.**

Understock **Stock,** q.v.

Understory An underlying, smaller-scale group of plants that lives beneath the dominant, larger **Overstory,** q.v. Shrubs.

Undressed (raw) stone Fieldstone. Rough, unfinished building stone.

Undulate In plant structures, wavy. See also **Flexuous.**

Unifoliate (botanical) Single-leaved.

Uniform flow In pipe and drain channel design, an acceptable, overall water velocity that will not cause scour or, oppositely, allow particles to fall out of suspension as sediment. See also **Laminar flow.**

Uniformity, coefficient of (irrigation) See **Coefficient of uniformity.**

Unimproved land A euphemism for undisturbed land. Often described by the avaricious as highly desirable, beautiful, and available for development.

Union (sprinkler pipes) A kind of **Fitting,** q.v.

Union, bud (botany) See **Bud union.**

Union wage bond A bond provided a union by a contractor warranting the payment of union scale wages and the provision of union benefits during job construction. See also **Labor and material payment bond.**

Uniseriate In plant structure, occurring in a single series. See also **Pluriseriate.**

Unit, masonry See **Masonry unit.**

Unit, paving See **Paving unit.**

Unit prices In contract
specifications, individual costs for
units or items of construction such as
a square foot or square meter of
pavement, trees, a given amount of
demolition, and the like. Unit prices
are quoted by the landscape
contractor and accepted by the
owner in a contract for construction,
and are the basis for change order
allowances during the course of a
project. They are indicated in the
unit price bid form of the general
specifications.

　　See also **Contract sum, Lump
sum.**

United States landscape architecture
　　At the time of the European
Middle Ages, in what would become
the southwestern United States, two
great public squares were
constructed in the towns of Tyuonyi
(Bandelier National Monument) and
Pueblo Bonito (Chaco Culture
National Historic Park), both in New
Mexico. These Anasazi commons
were partially paved and
surrounded by multistoried,
"condominium" dwelling units, and
they were used for many of the
same purposes as their European
counterparts: trading, defense,
refreshment, cooking, socializing.
Like medieval European squares,
they probably had no trees or other
plantings, and the quality of space
was derived from local topography
and the nature of the stone buildings
roundabout. Their liveliness and
usefulness were based on the success
of nearby agriculture, and, when the
exhaustion of local farmlands was
combined with an extensive drought
in the thirteenth century, they
withered.
　　Spanish settlements in North
America in the sixteenth century
were constructed around the plaza

United States landscape architecture.
Boston Common, modern view.
Photo by author.

United States landscape architecture.
Pueblo Bonito, New Mexico: the east
court as it may have appeared c.
A.D. 1050. Illustration courtesy
BBMSL, UNM.

or Spanish square. St. Augustine, Florida, founded in 1565, was laid out with the typical Iberian patio, or enclosed garden, as a common clerical and domestic feature. In Santa Fe, New Mexico, founded in 1610, the seat of government (Palace of the Governors, now a museum), complete with a large internal courtyard of its own, dominated a large plaza surrounded on its three other sides by houses and shops fronted with long porticoes to cut the intense glare of the sun. The usual Spanish hacienda of the day was a largely practical affair: a series of rooms laid out in the Mediterranean style on three sides of a patio, which was separated by a wall from neighboring orchards, grainfields, and pastures. The acequia, or local stream-fed ditch, was most often used as the source of water for both the household and the surrounding gardens. The Spaniards built great churches in the many pueblos of New Mexico after the conquest; the mission **Atrio,** or enclosed entry courtyard, was used to accommodate the overflow crowds of new converts attending services. At Gran Quivira in central New Mexico, a dry, lonely place of constant winds blowing between gray stone walls, a small waiting court for the priests' confessional survives to one side of the great mission church. Its benches are of much-weathered wood and stone. (See also **Mexican landscape architecture.**)

The Colonial Eastern Seabord

The colonial Dutch and English gardens of the seventeenth century were formal in design and full of flowers. The Dutch developed a number of estates along the Hudson River near New Amsterdam, which they furnished with large apple orchards (sources of cider) and bright gardens planted in roses, carnations, tulips, pot marigolds, lilacs, violets, and, of course, tulips and other bulbs. The gardens surrounding the Dutch houses in New Amsterdam itself were smaller in scale but also quite symmetrical.

The kitchen garden of New England was a very practical affair, located conveniently near Puritan sculleries to supply herbs and vegetables for home use. The Pilgrims brought hollyhocks, lilies, pinks, and other flowers with them after 1620, but their principal interest in the harsh New England climate was food production. Writers such as John Josslyn (*An Account of Two Voyages,* c. 1665) listed a growing number of vegetables, fruits, and even ornamentals in use in the colonies by the late seventeenth century. By the eighteenth century, the pattern of the New England garden was well set with vegetables and fruits at the rear of the house and ornamental trees, shrubs, and lawns in the "front yard." The gardens were often surrounded by a low, white picket fence. The Faneuil estate, an exemplary colonial landscape with a view of the Boston Common, reached its heyday in the 1730s: its hothouse, summerhouse, and wrought ironwork were much admired. The broad grounds of the Hancock House on Boston's Beacon Hill featured celebrated plantings of plums, tulips, yews, jasmines, and hollies—new exotics just brought into cultivation in the New World.

The landscapes of the warmer states further south were lusher and more intricate. Middleton Place (c. 1741) and Drayton Hall (now Magnolia Gardens) along the Ashley River near Charleston, South Carolina, boasted English garden mounts, bowling greens, radial flower gardens, statuary, and similar refinements. These have survived both the Revolution and the Civil War. The smaller-scale gardens of Charleston itself were developed along English Renaissance lines and influenced the course of landscape development in the rest of the South. In Virginia, Williamsburg grew to be a showpiece of colonial landscape design. The grounds of the Governor's Palace, laid out (c. 1713) included the classic parterres of clipped boxwood, maze, and bowling green of the English Renaissance garden. The other gardens of the town were also geometric, with little open lawn space. Williamsburg itself was laid out with a major axis, anchored at one end by the House of Burgesses, passing through some eight city blocks to the College of William and Mary. The Governor's Palace sat at the end of an intersecting minor axis. As in South Carolina, several estates with landscaped grounds were established up and down the James River near Williamsburg; Brandon, Shirley, and Berkeley are among the best known.

In Philadelphia, founded by William Penn in the seventeenth century, some half-dozen squares and gardens were established for public use. A number of estates with gardens were also established by the colonists in Philadelphia and the Pennsylvania countryside along the Schuylkill River. These were typically furnished with lawns, shrubs, statuary, kitchen gardens, and parterres. The Hills, the home of Robert Morris in Philadelphia, is probably the best of these. It came to be known as Lemon Hill and then Pratt's Gardens after the Revolution. Many Pennsylvania gardens were redesigned in the Naturalistic style in the late eighteenth and early nineteenth centuries.

Washington's Mount Vernon and Monticello, the home of Thomas Jefferson, are the most famous of late colonial landscapes. Washington acquired Mount Vernon from his brother Lawrence in 1754. Its layout was reminiscent of the work of **William Kent,** q.v., in England, with its flower and kitchen gardens, bowling green, greenhouse, and modified formal scheme blending gracefully into the wild Virginia countryside. Washington systematically developed the grounds between 1759 and 1775. Among his favorite trees were crabs, pines, dogwood, and weeping willow. The gardens were restored in the late nineteenth century. As passionate a gardener as Washington, Jefferson worked on his hilltop estate at Monticello from about 1766–1824, keeping meticulous notes all the while. Jefferson at first designed the grounds of Monticello as a formal complement to his Palladian house. After his service as U.S. Minister to France (1785–89), he returned to Virginia having observed firsthand the work of the new Landscape Gardening School in Britain. His subsequent modifications at Monticello softened his earlier formal lines. Among the many plants Jefferson experimented with at Monticello were pinks, pecans, poppies, anemones, and tulips. Jefferson also introduced the campus quadrangle **(Quad)** to the United States. It was a primary element of site design at his University of Virginia.

Naturalism and the Rise of Landscape Architecture in the Nineteenth Century

The landscape design of the Eastern Seaboard and the Southwest was essentially derivative from the time of European arrival through the Revolution and into the nineteenth century. Spaniards, Dutchmen, and Englishmen alike simply took along to the New World the prevailing formal garden and public landscape design of their day and reconstructed it wherever they could.

United States landscape architecture. Downing's plan for the Washington Mall, from a lithograph by B. F. Smith, Jr., c. 1852. Illustration courtesy BBMSL, UNM.

Naturalism first became popular in Britain in the eighteenth century and was a johnny-come-lately to colonial America. One of the first Americans to promote it was **Andre Parmentier** (d. 1830), q.v., a Belgian immigrant who by 1824 had set up his own nursery in Brooklyn. Parmentier designed estate grounds up and down the Hudson and contributed to a botanical garden in New York City.

Andrew Jackson Downing (d. 1852), the American nurseryman, landscape gardener, and writer, began to construct a popular philosophical basis for American landscape design in the 1820s. He admired Brown's and Repton's

graceful, informal lawn lines, their tree copses amid rolling landscapes, and their small curvilinear lakes. He also noted the more rugged aspects of the craggy hills, rustic bowers, and other constructs of the Picturesque school. But Downing thought all these could be provided at a more tractable scale for the common man, and that naturalistic design could serve as a true expression of American democratic intentions. Downing urged the adoption of the front lawn in a suburban setting—perhaps really a mowable chunk of the familiar Boston Common—as the democratic ideal. He also thought that each landscape should be carefully developed so as to best conform to the **Genius loci** or essential character of its site.

Downing's thought was much in keeping with the romantic notions of the day. Emerson, Thoreau, Melville, and the design theoretician Horatio Greenough were among the most luminous of Downing's contemporaries. These thinkers helped to establish a popular view of the United States as a country with a special social obligation. It was up to the Americans to tinker with the Industrial Revolution until it produced improved living conditions across the board, including paved streets, better sanitation, public education, and public gardens suitable for city workers. Downing's *Treatise on Landscape Gardening* of 1841 codified Naturalism as the national trend for many decades to come, and was an early high-water mark for what would become the East Coast landscape design tradition.

J. C. Loudon, q.v., the Scottish horticultural writer, lexicographer, and designer, had proposed the creative reuse of graveyards in Britain during Downing's time. Loudon's American contemporary, Dr. Joseph Bigelow, promoted much the same thing at Mount Auburn Cemetery near Cambridge, Massachusetts (c. 1831). Loudon helped spread the use of the term "landscape architecture." And Downing, in establishing a design partnership in 1849 with the English architect **Calvert Vaux,** q.v., also began the transition from landscape gardening to landscape architecture that was completed by **Frederick Law Olmsted** in the 1860s.

Olmsted remains the towering figure in American landscape architecture. He popularized the term itself in America, adopting it for his own use in his earliest park work with Calvert Vaux, for New York City. Central Park and Prospect Park in Brooklyn became the standards for American outdoor design for the nineteenth and twentieth centuries. Olmsted's idea was clear and straightforward: to provide as natural a series of landscaped places as possible in a growing city for the use of workers locked in gritty factory toil and for the public as a whole. He based his design work on a careful firsthand study of Birkenhead Park near Liverpool, England, the work of the landscape gardener **Joseph Paxton,** q.v. He was also influenced by other English landscapes observed during his travels and by his own experiences as a farmer, journalist, and surveyor. Olmsted's American Naturalism actually developed very late: it had been in its prime in Britain nearly a century earlier, and in the United States of the mid-nineteenth century it was overlaid with numerous Victorian elements, including iron bridges and railings, Beaux Arts buildings, and a general ornamentation that would not have been tolerated in Capability Brown's work.

Still, it was well in keeping with the raw and thumping industrialism of Civil War America. New arboreta and botanical gardens, such as the Arnold Arboretum in Cambridge and Shaw's Gardens in St. Louis, experimented with thousands of novel exotics from around the world. Greenhouses and their technology made plant propagation easier than ever. Lawn mowers, combines, mechanical cultivators, and sophisticated irrigation began to modernize ornamental horticulture, allowing landscape architectural projects of very great scope to be accomplished under difficult conditions. The growth of railroads and telegraphic communication made it possible for the first time for a brilliant designer like Olmsted to practice coast-to-coast. Olmsted even consulted on projects in Canada. Olmsted, by himself and in collaboration with Vaux, **Charles Eliot,** q.v., and other partners, was responsible for parks and park systems from Boston to Minneapolis to San Francisco; for campus planning at Stanford, Harvard, and at other universities; for country estates such as Biltmore in North Carolina; for the idea of a National Park system; for the redesign of much of Washington, D.C., and other cities; and for promoting landscape architecture as a new profession of equal stature with architecture and civil engineering. Olmsted designed "planned subdivisions" such as Riverside, Illinois, helping to popularize the idea in the United States. In the 1880s, he began to produce a series of designs for sports fields and other active recreation areas. His work inspired the creation of new schools of landscape architecture to train professionals in the field. And perhaps above all, he stated his design ideas and recorded his project experience in articles, books, and notes for lectures. Olmsted left an unparalleled legacy and set an example that has not yet been surpassed.

But he was not alone. George Perkins Marsh, the author of *Man and Nature* (1864) had based his arguments for conservation and preservation of the national "wild landscape" on scientific need. **Horace Cleveland** (d. 1900), q.v., another pioneer landscape architect, proposed Naturalism as a good civilizing influence on the gridiron mentality of nineteenth-century city planning. Cleveland became well-known for his park work in Chicago and Minneapolis. Like Olmsted, who had been Secretary of the U.S. Sanitary Commission during the Civil War, Cleveland noted that improved sanitation was as important in urban design as good open space planning. Olmsted also collaborated

United States landscape architecture. Central Park, New York City: view looking north, 1863. Illustration courtesy BBMSL, UNM.

on occasion with **Jacob Weidenmann,** q.v., the parks superintendent of Hartford, Connecticut, whose books on estate landscaping and cemetery design were widely read in the late 1880s. In 1890, Charles Eliot, who had been a partner in Olmsted's office, began a systematic analysis of older landscapes and open space in the greater Boston area. It was the beginning of organized historic preservation in the United States, and would lead to such twentieth-century institutions as the National Trust for Historic Preservation.

Olmsted and his contemporaries had consolidated their Americanization of landscape architecture by 1893, the year of the World's Columbian Exposition in Chicago. Based on an informal landscape line pulled into the service of democratic ideals, the orientation of the profession was that of art harnessed to public service—the park as "natural" creative expression in the national interest, albeit with a strong overlay of fastidious Victorian details. The exposition, however, was primarily an exercise in Beaux Arts grandiloquence, and in throw-away design. The buildings and grounds were razed soon after the great celebration was finished, setting a terrible precedent for the twentieth century. The focus of landscape design shifted strongly to the service of the rich, and the era of the "country place" was officially underway.

Italian Gardens (1894), by the painter and landscape designer Charles A. Platt, is the theme book for country places. In it, Platt studied Italian hillside estates and analyzed their unity of garden and structure. Platt's suggestions showed a way to integrate formal design (near a house) with increasingly informal grounds further afield. The "Italianate" villa became a popular American estate style. Olmsted's Biltmore was the largest of the genre; its elephantine grounds have since been used as a forestry and agriculture school and as part of a museum. Bryant Fleming, Marian Coffin, Fletcher Steele, Beatrix Farrand, and other turn-of-the-century landscape architects designed similar estates throughout the East and the Midwest. Country places were popular in other parts of the nation as well. Hare and Hare, known for their Country Club District work in Kansas City, also designed the grounds of the Villa Philmonte near Cimarron, New Mexico. The ancient Romans had copied the Greeks, the Egyptians, and the Persians; the Italians of the Renaissance had lifted their villa styles from the classical Romans; and when their turn came, the wealthy Americans of the Gilded Age joyfully mimicked the Italian Renaissance.

The Twentieth Century

Naturalism in the United States, as in Britain, had early allied itself to romantic writing; it was a literary as well as a design style. In a country founded largely on Utopian idealism, it struck a responsive chord. The Danish immigrant **Jens Jensen** (d. 1951) developed it in a Chicago variant that he called the "prairie style" as early as the 1890s. Jensen used Midwest natives

United States landscape architecture. Chicago, Illinois: Columbus Park, 1918, by Jens Jensen. Photo courtesy BBMSL, UNM.

extensively in his designs; his insistence on these and other elements of his widely heralded "soft landscapes" helped to educate the country to the value of local North American plants. Jensen's ideas predated by some 70 years the sharp calls for "local relevance" and environmental awareness of the ecological movement of the 1960s.

In Washington, D.C., Naturalism was downplayed in the late nineteenth century in favor of the expansive formalism of seventeenth-century France. The original plan (c. 1791) of **Pierre L'Enfant,** q.v., for the Washington Mall was resurrected and put under construction. One of the greatest open spaces in the country, its vast axial symmetry is curiously lost to the casual modern visitor: it simply seems to be a long, pleasant park full of baseball players and ice cream lovers with the Capitol at one end. Elsewhere in the city, the pioneer black landscape

architect David Williston designed the grounds of Howard University and other public buildings in the early decades of the century. Williston, who had studied with Liberty Hyde Bailey at Cornell University, was noted for his expertise in horticulture.

The Columbian Exposition had triggered an interest in ideal city form. The architect **Daniel Burnham,** q.v., with Olmsted one of the principal designers of the exposition, developed a countrywide practice of town planning on a Beaux Arts, "City Beautiful" model. The journalist Charles Robinson helped to publicize Burnham's work. Burnham redesigned many state capitol grounds along City Beautiful lines.

Ebenezer Howard's *Garden Cities for Tomorrow* (1902) influenced the architects Clarence Stein and Henry Wright, the designers of Radburn, New Jersey (1928)—a garden city created with the automobile in mind.

Housing at Radburn was arranged along culs-de-sac, with vehicles and pedestrians strictly separated. Marjorie S. Cautley was the landscape architect. Stein and Wright were also responsible for, among other projects, Sunnyside Gardens (c. 1925) in New York and Chatham Village (1937) in Pittsburgh. Later American New Towns (garden cities) have included Greendale, Wisconsin; Reston, Virginia; Columbia, Maryland; and Greenhills, Ohio. New towns and garden cities differed from City Beautiful constructs in their comprehensive scope and complete newness. Their basic premise was an accommodation of industry, commerce, aesthetic open space, and residential development in a pleasant setting. Burnham's City Beautiful work aimed more at the incidental, monumental effect of a building and landscape line in a limited area. But his influence, only slightly modified, is with us yet in the "beautification" efforts of cities throughout the United States.

Landscape architects began to be systematically educated after 1899, when Harvard University offered a full curriculum in the field. The American Society of Landscape Architects (ASLA), founded in the same year by Samuel Parsons, J. C. Olmsted, Beatrix Farrand, Warren H. Manning, and others, promoted professional standards of practice.

The abrupt arrival of the Depression after the stock market crash of 1929 changed the emphasis of American landscape architecture. There were few country places left to design, and many landscape architects began to work on public projects out of sheer necessity. A number of county and U.S. courthouses, with their accompanying courthouse squares, were built. New Towns such as Greenbelt, Maryland and Greendale, Wisconsin were created

by Elbert Peets, J. L. Crane, and other government landscape architects in collaboration with similarly employed architects and engineers. State park systems throughout the United States were founded or expanded through New Deal programs such as the Civilian Conservation Corps (CCC). The National Parks Act of 1916 had reserved large wild tracts of land of unusual scenic beauty as Federal preserves. The state parks that followed in the 1930s emphasized active recreation—often water sports—and the accommodation of growing numbers of cars. Another hallmark of the 1930s state park is first-rate stonework, usually in the form of retainer walls, picnic shelters, fireplaces, and the like. Landa Park in New Braunfels, Texas, and Elephant Butte State Park in central New Mexico are good surviving examples of New Deal landscape quality.

A curiosity of American landscape architecture is its pervasive but unconscious sense of moral purpose. This it shares with many other United States institutions, public and private. Jefferson was concerned with the right setting and atmosphere for education at the University of Virginia. Downing, while plagiarizing the English School wholesale, wanted to create a new kind of home landscape for the free (and prosperous) American citizen. Olmsted, of course, felt compelled to alleviate the dire social conditions of the growing cities of the Industrial Revolution with his park work. This harnessing of landscape aesthetics to serve the public good took a new turn in the late 1930s.

Garrett Eckbo, Dan Kiley, James Rose, q.q.v., and other students at the Harvard Graduate School of Design rejected landscape design as Beaux Arts ornamentation. Instead, they championed site-specific design, functionalism, and eclectic choice in

garden planning. They were influenced by Oriental landscapes, by **Thomas Church** and the developing **California (modern) garden,** q.q.v., by Professor Christopher Tunnard (*Gardens in the Modern Landscape,* 1938), by Cubism and the International Style. Eckbo, Kiley, and Rose were soon followed by **Lawrence Halprin, Robert Royston, Hideo Sasaki,** and others who by mid-century had established highly successful practices. Logical analysis of a proposed landscape site and the careful articulation of design elements to create "outdoor rooms" mark the work of all these practitioners. "El Novillero," the Donnell California garden of the 1940s by Thomas Church, is perhaps the best known of the genre, which continued uninterrupted for some 30 years.

An "ecology" movement sprang into being in the 1960s, concerned once again with landscape design as a moral tool to be used in the service of righting environmental wrongs. The landscape architect John Simonds, author of *Landscape Architecture* (1961), and others attempted to reconcile the "Harvard" style with this new ecological awareness. Though the efforts were well meaning, no strong aesthetic of ecological design has yet been devised to pull it into the mainstream of American landscape architecture.

Two new trends, supplanting the destructive **Urban renewal** of the 1960s and early 1970s, had emerged by the late 1970s. The first was a recognition that historic landscape preservation held great meaning for American landscape architecture. Secondly, there were efforts by several landscape architectural firms to develop regional or national practices, often with multiple branches. Paul Friedberg and Partners, Myrick Newman and Dahlberg, Johnson

United States landscape architecture. Harbour Town at Sea Pines Plantation, Hilton Head Island, South Carolina, by Sasaki Associates. Photo courtesy Bob Lancaster.

Johnson and Roy, EDAW, Lauri Olin, Peter Walker, and the Peridian Group have been typical of these offices.

Regional styles, though somewhat blurred, remained important. The Downing-Olmsted Naturalism of Harvard and the East Coast, the richly detailed California garden, and the landscape garden-plantation grounds of the Old South continued to be revered and copied traditions. **Rio Grande landscape architecture,** q.v., a high-altitude hybrid of Spanish colonial and desert reductionist elements, grew in use in the Southwest. The West Coast "Hanging Gardens" style, based on Kiley's Oakland Museum (1963), Halprin's Fountain Block and Downtown Plaza in Portland (1960s), and Erickson's Robson Square in Vancouver (1970s), attracted admiring visitors with its color, robust character, and water-splashed urban liveliness.

Unity   In landscape architecture, a well-developed design form in which all living and nonliving elements work together in visible and spiritual harmony. Unity can be found in repeated patterns, complementary plant masses and textures, a harmony between garden form and the surrounding landscape, and the like.

Upland   A highland area.

Upper Sonoran (zone)   See **Life zone.**

Upright   A post or column; a vertical timber.

Upset fee   A type of hourly fee with a set, cumulative, maximum limit. The landscape architect works up to the upset figure on a monthly or other billing basis and does not exceed its amount without first giving notice to the client. Reimbursable contract items are sometimes billed in addition to the upset limit. Also **Guaranteed ceiling fee, Maximum upset fee, Not-to-exceed fee.**

Upset price   A maximum construction figure allowed upon an upset price contract. The contractor may not exceed the upset price without an additional agreement with the owner.

Urban   Of or pertaining to cities or towns.

Urban design   The design of city patterns and places, often combinations of civil engineering works, architecture, and landscape architecture.

Urban forestry   The cultivation of trees in cities for aesthetic and functional purposes, usually carried on by an urban forester.

Urban planning   See **Planning.**

Urban renewal   In the United States, a process of demolition, pavement, and reconstruction of central cities begun by the Federal government in the late 1960s. The theory of urban renewal held that society's troubles could be resolved by new and better physical surroundings substituting for older and worse ones. The theory has not proven accurate to date.

In recent years, urban renewal has been superseded by **Historic preservation,** q.v., and adaptive reuse of old structures.

Urban runoff   Street gutter **Runoff,** q.v., sometimes containing a heavy concentration of asphalt oils, refuse, and other wastes.

Urbanization   Perhaps the twentieth century's most overwhelming problem. The making of rural areas into city; the making of city forms into ever more sophisticated or

intense versions of themselves. The metamorphosis of country to city thinking. A revolution in values of time. The removal of country influence anywhere; especially, the substitution of metal, concrete, asphalt, plastic, and glass for wood, stone, water, grass, and larger plants. Urbanization has been exacerbated in this century by the pressures of ever-increasing population.

Urea   A very effective high nitrogen fertilizer, synthesized from the urine of mammals.

Urn   In landscape architecture, a vase, often with an elongated stem or resting on a small column, used to hold flowers in a garden.

U.S. Army Corps of Engineers   See **Corps of Engineers.**

U.S. Fish and Wildlife Service   An agency of the United States Department of the Interior responsible for the management of certain game and fish species on both federal and nonfederal lands. Abbreviated **USFWS.**

Use of land   See **Land use.**

User   In landscape architecture, the person, company, or agency using landscape improvements made at a specific site. The user is not necessarily the **Client,** q.v.

USFS   See **Forest Service.**

USGS   United States Geological Survey, producer of innumerable excellent geologic maps of North America and elsewhere.

Utility   1) A privately held corporation that is publicly chartered to provide an essential good or service such as water, power, gas, or telephones. A public agency

Utility. Plaza del Rey, California: power plant. Photo courtesy BBMSL, UNM.

authorized to provide such services or goods or to furnish sanitary sewerage, storm drainage, and the like. 2) The public services outlined above in themselves. See also **Public utility.**

Utility area   See **Service area.**

Utility easement   See **Easement.**

Utility plan (map)   In landscape drawing, a plan showing existing and proposed public utility lines, including water, gas, telephone, electricity, sanitary and storm sewer, and the like. A utility plan may also show public easements.

Utility, public   See **Public utility.**

UV radiation   See **Ultraviolet radiation.**

V

V 1) Velocity, especially velocity of water flow. 2) **Variety (of plant),** q.v.

Vacuum breaker In irrigation, a common type of **Backflow preventer** or **Check valve,** q.q.v., installed above ground. A vacuum breaker prevents in-line vacuums from carrying water back to a main. Also **Antisiphon valve, Siphon-breaker.** See also **Atmospheric vacuum breaker, Pressure vacuum breaker.**

Vacuum breaker, atmospheric See **Atmospheric vacuum breaker.**

Vacuum breaker, pressure See **Pressure vacuum breaker.**

Vadose water Water found below the surface but above an aquifer. See also **Water table.**

Vale A small, wide valley.

Vacuum breaker

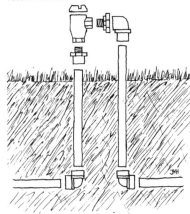

Valley An inclined depression or hollow on a flat plain or in a mountain range. There are streams or rivers in most valley bottoms.

Valley gutter A V-shaped, poured concrete flume designed to intercept and channel surface runoff.

Valley line A line connecting the lowest point of a valley from a river source to its mouth, thus forming a concave **River profile,** q.v.

Valley, transverse See **Transverse valley.**

Value, assessed See **Assessed value.**

Value of a color See **Chromatic color.**

Value engineering A review of project components and design approaches during the design period with the intention of producing the best design function at the very least cost. Value engineering is often conducted by a special firm contracted by an owner to offer a second opinion on the project designer's approaches and techniques.

Valve 1) In landscape irrigation, a device that starts or stops a flow of water. 2) In plants, part of the structure of a **Capsule,** q.v.

Valve, angle (angle-control) See **Angle valve.**

Valve, antisiphon See **Vacuum breaker.**

Valve, automatic See **Remote control valve.**

Valve, back pressure See **Check valve.**

Valve box A steel, wood, fiberglass, or concrete box built in the ground to hold and protect irrigation valves.

Valve, check See **Check valve.**

Valve, diaphragm See **Diaphragm valve.**

Valve, direction control See **Check valve** and **Vacuum breaker.**

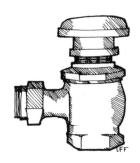

Valve

Valve, double-check   See **Double-check valve.**

Valve, drain   See **Drain valve.**

Valve, electric or hydraulic piston   See **Piston valve.**

Valve, electric thermal motor   See **Electric thermal motor valve.**

Valve, foot   See **Foot valve.**

Valve, full-way   See **Gate valve.**

Valve, gate   See **Gate valve.**

Valve, globe   See **Globe valve.**

Valve, grade   See **Grade valve.**

Valve key   See **Key.**

Valve, manual   See **Manual system.**

Valve, manual drain   See **Manual drain valve.**

Valve, pilot   See **Pilot valve.**

Valve, piston   A type of remote control valve. See **Piston valve.**

Valve, pressure relief   See **Safety valve.**

Valve, quick coupling   See **Quick coupler.**

Valve, reflux   See **Check valve.**

Valve, remote control   See **Remote control valve.**

Valve, safety   See **Safety valve.**

Valve, stop and waste   See **Stop and waste valve.**

Valve, swing check   See **Swing check valve.**

Valve system   See **Section.**

Valve-in-head   In irrigation, an automatic valve built into the head mechanism. See also **Valve-under-head.**

Valve-under-head   In irrigation, an automatic valve installed beneath a head, operated singly or in conjunction with other heads. See also **Valve-in-head.**

Vanadium   A metallic **Trace element**, q.v., necessary to plant metabolism. See also **Available nutrients, Soil minerals.**

Vandal   A person who disfigures or demolishes without reason public and private property.

Vanishing point   In drawing, a horizon point at which "parallel" lines come together. See also **Perspective.**

Vapor pressure   In irrigation, a pressure created by vapor existing near the free surfaces of line water. Vapor pressure rises with temperature.

Variance   In zoning, an acceptable deviation in land or structural use from the legal norm. In the United States, sometimes granted at the insistence of a developer.

Variation, diurnal   See **Diurnal variation.**

Variegated (variegation, variegata)   A mottled leaf texture or pattern with white or yellow streaks or patches running through the basic (green) leaf color.

Varietal name   In plants, the name of a **Variety** or **Subspecies**, q.q.v.

Variety   A subclassification of a plant **Species**, q.v. A **Subspecies**. Abbreviated **var.** or **V.** See also **Botanical classification, Cultivar.**

Varve   Annual lake bottom sediments deposited as rough silts in spring and summer and as fine clay particles in fall and winter.

Varved clay   A year's sedimentation visible as dried layers of silt and clay.

Vasca   In Italy, a basin or pond.

Vascular plant   A plant with a **Vascular system,** q.v.

Vascular system (in plants)   In complex plants, a series of tissues specialized to conduct nutrients and water up from the roots to the leaves, and manufactured foods from the leaves or stem tissues to the roots or other storage tissue. The collective ducts are often referred to as a vascular bundle. See also **Phloem** and **Xylem.**

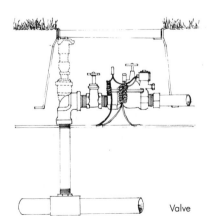

Valve

Vaux, Calvert (1824–95)   English and American architect and landscape architect. Vaux first came to the United States in 1849 or 1850 and entered into a partnership with the landscape designer and writer **Andrew Jackson Downing,** q.v. His subsequent partnership with the prescient **Frederick Law Olmsted,** begun in 1857 for the Central Park competition, lasted until 1872. Vaux and Olmsted laid most of the groundwork for and created many of the early masterpieces of American landscape and park design. Among their lasting contributions, aside from Central Park, were the designs for the subdivision of Riverside, Illinois, for Jackson Park in Chicago, and for the very lyrical Prospect Park in Brooklyn.

Vaux was later responsible for the design of the Parliament grounds in Ottawa—a strong influence on Canadian landscape design. Vaux's work and thought, though undeniably important, have been somewhat overshadowed by the earlier writings of Downing and by the towering figure of Olmsted.

VC   See **Vertical curve.**

VCP   See **Vitrified clay pipe.**

VCPI   Vertical curve point of intersection (plan notation).

Vega (Spanish)   1) Irrigated land producing one annual harvest. 2) A meadow (North America).

Vegetable   A plant grown for its edible roots, stalks, flowers, leaves, or seeds. See also **Berry, Fruit,** and **Ornamental.**

Vegetated flume   An inclined channel that is stabilized with grass and/or other vegetation. See also **Flume.**

Vegetation   Plant cover or plant life.

Vegetation, climax   See **Climax growth.**

Vegetation, natural   See **Natural vegetation.**

Vegetation, riparian   See **Riparian vegetation.**

Vegetative   Pertaining to herbaceous growth or to nonsexual plant reproduction.

Vegetative climax   See **Climax growth.**

Vegetative reproduction   The propagation of plants by cuttings, layering, clump division, or grafting, rather than by seeds. Also **Apomixis, Asexual reproduction.** See also **Agamic reproduction.**

Veld (Afrikaans)   In South Africa, rolling, open country marked with small mountain ranges, ridges, and valleys. Also **veldt.**

Velocity (of water)   In irrigation, an in-line flow rate measured in feet per second (FPS).

Velocity, flow (irrigation)   See **Flow velocity.**

Velocity, self-cleaning (of pipes)   See **Self-cleaning velocity.**

Velutinous   In plant structures, smooth and downy.

Venation   In botany, the network of veins in leaves, petals, or other plant structures.

Venation

Veneer   In landscape construction, a finish coat of stucco or paint or finish courses of brick or stone applied to a structural wall surface.

Venose   In plant structures, markedly veined.

Ventilated cell composting   See **Compost.**

Venting, automatic (irrigation)   See **Automatic venting.**

Ventricose   Pertaining to an unbalanced swelling of plant tissue.

Venturi   Generally, a narrow passage between buildings, tree rows or the like, through which a stiff wind habitually blows.

Veranda   A roofed-over porch. See also **Stoop.**

Verge   1) The shoulder of a road, especially in Britain. 2) A narrow line of lawn along a driveway or walkway.

Vermicide   A pesticide used against earthworms.

Vermiculite   A light, fluffy, scaled, and highly absorbent starting medium for plants consisting of hydrous silicate of iron, magnesium, and aluminum (mica). See also **Perlite.**

Vernacular landscape architecture   Landscape design or forms that spring from a local or regional tradition, use local materials, and are not produced by professional landscape architects or designers. Also **Colloquial landscape architecture, Popular landscape architecture.**

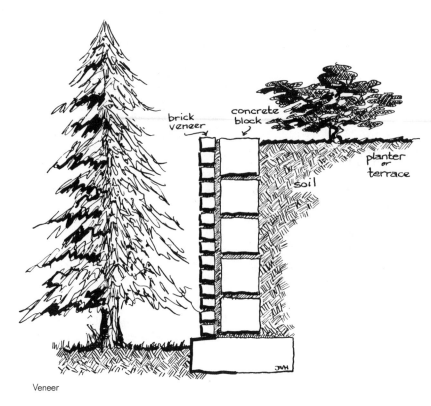

Veneer

Vesicular In soils, full of air pockets or considerable spaces between particles.

Vest-pocket park A tiny park built in a leftover space, usually in an older city neighborhood. Also **Pocket park.**

Vestibule In classical Greece or Rome, the semienclosed area in front of a building. Also, a court, especially an entry court. See also **Exedra.**

Vestigial Remnant (plant structures).

Viable In plants, able to grow and reproduce.

Viaduct An arched construction, usually of stone, supporting a road, bridge, or railway.

Victory garden In World War II, a home vegetable or fruit garden.

Vignola, Giacomo Barozzi da (1507–73) Italian architect and villa designer. His design for the Villa Lante at Bagnaia (c. 1560) is the best known of his compositions. A strong classicist, Vignola's work at Lante helped to establish the copse of trees **(Bosco),** series of terraces, and formal **Parterre** garden as the great elements of Renaissance villa planning.

Vignola, a student of Pliny, laid out the Villa Giulia in Rome (1550–55) along strict classical lines. His earlier plans for the giardini segreti (see **Giardino segreto**) at Caprarola (1547–49 and later) also reveal a Renaissance desire for personal expression and whimsical indulgence. See also **Renaissance landscape architecture.**

Vigor, hybrid See **Heterosis.**

Vernalization A method of partial seed germination during a cold season to allow full plant growth and flowering the following year. A type of seasonal "bypass." Often used with cereals. See also **Forcing.**

Vernation In botany, the leaf sequence found in a bud.

Verrucose In botany, warty.

Vertical alignment (of streets) See **Alignment of streets.**

Vertical curve An up-and-down—as opposed to horizontal—curve.

Vertical element In landscape design, any upright and especially tall or dominant living or nonliving feature or item. Trees and high walls are examples. See also **Horizontal element, Intermediate element.**

Vertical plane A wall, cliff, or other upright element of outdoor space. 1) **Articulated plane:** a plane surface made of multiple smaller pieces. A brick wall or natural cascade are examples. 2) **Penetrable plane:** an interrupted plane surface, defining the edge of an area but not solid. A row of trees or a line of power poles are examples.

Vertical shear See **Shear.**

Verticil A Whorl, q.v.

Vertisol A soil very high in clay, resulting in great swelling or lifting when wet and in pronounced cracking upon drying.

Vespertine In plants, blooming at dusk or in the evening.

Villa A country estate. A resort. A country house. 1) **Villa rustica:** a Roman or Renaissance Italian villa in the countryside. 2) **Villa urbana:** a large house and grounds in a Roman city.

Village A tiny, usually unconsolidated settlement. Originally, a collection of dwellings on an estate or near a villa.

Village green An American commonholding, especially prevalent (formerly) in the New England and Middle Atlantic states, used as common grazing grounds. The direct forerunner of the American front lawn.

Villeggiatura (Italian) The Roman and Italian custom of retreating from the summertime city to a country villa or resort.

Villose or villous In plant structures, covered with down or long, soft tiny hairs.

Vine A woody or herbaceous plant which typically must depend on a fence, wall, trellis, or adjoining tree or shrub for its support. See also **Climber** and **Creeper.**

Virgate 1) In plant structures, rod-like, erect. 2) An old English measure of land of about 30 acres.

Virgin forest A forest in uncut, original condition. An unlogged woodland.

Virgin soil Lands untouched by cultivation or other human interference.

Viridarium A type of Roman courtyard containing a central pool.

Viscid In plant structures, resinous or sticky.

Vista A defined or refined scenic view. A focused view. Vistas may be closed (limited within a garden) or open—i.e., stretching to the distant landscape. The creation of good vistas is a primary aim of landscape design.

Vista garden In the Renaissance landscapes of France, a garden contrived with a grandiloquent, formal vista as its main feature. Vaux-le-Vicomte and Versailles are the best-known examples. See also **French landscape architecture.**

Viticetum A vine-planting. A vineyard.

Viticulture The care and propagation of grapes.

Vitreous In tiles and glass, exhibiting a glazed surface of fused pores with an extremely low absorption rate. Glassy.

Vitrified clay pipe (VCP) A rigid pipe made of glazed clay sections.

Vitruvius, Marcus Pollius Roman architect and city planner of the first century B.C. Vitruvius's book in ten volumes, *De Architectura,* profoundly influenced the architects of the High Renaissance. See also **Alberti.**

Viviparous In botany, referring to the unusual sprouting of seed or development of buds while they remain part of a parent plant.

Void Space. In landscape architecture, emptiness—the opposite of and complement to mass. See also **Mass.**

Void ratio 1) In soils, the ratio of empty spaces to solid particles in a specific area or section. 2) In urban design, especially downtown areas, the volume of open space to buildings or other structural masses.

Voile (French) 1) Originally, a thin fabric. Often used to describe a pierced screen wall. 2) An allee or long double hedge, pruned only on the interior.

Volunteer A plant that springs up unbidden in a domestic landscape from seed or underground runner.

Voussoir A wedge-shaped stone, typically an integral part of an arch.

W

Wadi (Arabic) In western Asia and Africa, a dry watercourse that runs briefly after rains or heavy snowmelt.

Wage rates (federal and state) A set of formal wage guidelines issued by a government agency (Federal or state department of labor) that a contractor must follow in paying workers according to their job classifications, experience, and technical competence. Also **Federal wage rates, State wage rates.**

Wale A wood or metal brace used in trenching.

Walk, belt See **Belt walk.**

Walk, broad See **Broad walk.**

Walkway (walk, pedestrian way) A paved or unpaved path developed to serve as a regular means of passage from point to point in a landscape.

The best walkways use gentle slopes of less than 3%, wide treads and short risers, easy-access ramps, rails where necessary, and good lighting for nighttime utility.

Also, incorrectly, *Pedestrian walkway.*

Wall An upright structure forming a rampart or boundary and consisting of wood, stone, concrete, concrete block, brick, or similar material. Walls are used for screening, defense, shade, slope retention, wind protection, or other purposes. See also **Retaining wall.**

Wall, cantilever See **Cantilever wall.**

Wall, cheek See **Cheek wall.**

Wall, composite See **Composite wall.**

Wall, counterfort See **Counterfort wall.**

Wall, crib See **Cribbing.**

Wall, crinkle-crankle (serpentine) See **Crinkle-crankle wall.**

Wall, dry See **Dry wall.**

Wall, freestanding (nonloadbearing) See **Freestanding wall.**

Wall garden A dry-stone, terraced garden with mortarless walls containing soil niches in which plants are placed.

Wall, gravity See **Gravity wall.**

Wall mount timer (irrigation) See **Automatic controller.**

Wall, party See **Party wall.**

Wall, peat See **Peat wall.**

Wall, ponga See **Ponga wall.**

Wall, retainer See **Retaining wall.**

Wall, retaining See **Retaining wall.**

Wall, surcharged See **Retaining wall** and **Surcharged wall.**

Wall, wing See **Wing wall.**

Wall garden

Wand A young branch of the *Salicaceae* or Willow family (poplar, cottonwood, willow, and the like), sometimes planted to root as a new tree.

Want In **Pay requests,** q.v., a payment deduction made from a contractor's overmeasurement of a quantity submitted for payment.

Wardian case See **Terrarium.**

Warm color A red, orange, yellow, or shade of these. Warm colors in the landscape are stimulating, strong, and sometimes agitating. See also **Cool color.**

Warm season plant In horticulture, a plant at its blooming or growing optimum in the heat of summer. See also **Cool season plant.**

Warm-tone concrete A form of concrete to which a beige pigment has been added as a permanent coloring.

Warming bed A small area of cultivated ground on the south side of a building used to raise young plants in late winter and/or early spring. See **Coldframe** and **Hotbed.**

Warranty See **Guarantee.**

Wash The slope of a step-tread, given in inches per foot (cm per meter)—usually $1/8$ to $1/4$ in. per foot.

Wash, rain See **Rain wash.**

Washboards Ripples in paved or unpaved road surfaces caused by heavy, bouncing vehicles traveling at speed over a period of time. See also **Chuckhole.**

Water A chemical compound of hydrogen and oxygen necessary for animal and plant life, and the single most important factor in the natural or man-made landscape. The availability or lack of water determines at base landscape form. Hydraulic erosion is the strongest factor in landscape aging, and a key factor in man-made landscape. Ignorance of its presence or character can easily destroy a designed landscape.

Water is used in streams, fountains, waterfalls, stairs, ramps, sprays, pools, sluices, lakes and in other ways to add to or determine landscape character.

In irrigation systems, water can be distributed effectively to allow intensive "cultural" landscapes to flourish in otherwise desert or plains regions.

Water as ice or liquid is widely utilized for recreation.

An amazing 5% or less of the Earth's water is present as fresh water; of this, city (designed landscape) plantings need water at the same rate required by agricultural crops. The application of water to serve smog-filtering, oxygen-producing city plants becomes more and more necessary as urban areas expand at the expense of timbered or grassed countryside.

Water application efficiency See **Irrigation efficiency.**

Water auger In irrigation, a water-jetting procedure used to dig out a small tunnel for a sprinkler line under a drive pad, sidewalk, or other solid surface. See also **Punching.**

Water, available See **Capillary water.**

Water balance In plants, the ratio of water absorbed versus water expended in metabolism.

Water bloom Quick-growing algae in fresh water.

Water, bound See **Hygroscopic water.**

Water, capillary See **Capillary water.**

Water culture See **Hydroponics.**

Water curtain In landscape design, a thin, often dribbling fall of water from the edge of a shade structure through vines, latticework, or the air, used for its cooling effect or pleasant sound. See also **Water wall.**

Water cycle The process by which water moves from air to surface to subsurface and again to air. Also **Hydrologic cycle.**

Water demand In irrigation, the quantity of water needed to operate a **Section,** q.v. See also **Operating pressure.**

Water, detention See **Detention water.**

Water, domestic See **Potable water**

Water feature In landscape architecture, a fountain, pool, water sculpture, canal, channel, waterfall, or other element used as a central part of the composition.

Water, free See **Free water.**

Water garden A pool or pool and stream garden featuring aquatic plants. One of the most ancient and useful of landscape design elements.

Water, gravity (gravitational water) See **Free water** and **Gravity water.**

Water, gray See **Gray water.**

Water, ground   See **Ground water.**

Water hammer   Potentially damaging shock waves within an irrigation system caused by a momentary increase in pressure when a flowing mass of water (surge) is stopped.

   To produce water hammer, a shock wave travels through the irrigation system to a **Point of relief** and then reverses itself to a **Point of stoppage.** This action may occur several times until the water's energy is expended. Also **Surge.**

Water hammer arrester   In irrigation systems, a "shock absorber" for **Water hammer,** q.v., that also reduces the noise of surging water.

Water, hard   See **Hard water.**

Water, hygroscopic
   See **Hygroscopic water.**

Water, irrigation   See **Irrigation water.**

Water jetting   A construction process using a forced spurt or stream of water to: 1) excavate a tunnel or trench, or 2) compact fill in an excavated trench. See also **Sleeve.**

Water joke   A classical or Renaissance squirter used to moisten or drench garden visitors. Often constructed as part of a larger water garden, water jokes were often built into statuary. Also **Trick fountain, Water jest.**

Water, juvenile   See **Juvenile water.**

Water main   See **Main.**

Water management   The careful and systematic control and use of available surface and ground water for agricultural and urban development purposes. Water management also includes planning for wildlife, forest, and other "wild landscape" uses.

Water, meteoric   See **Meteoric water.**

Water meter   In irrigation, a device to measure water flow installed in the main line supplying a property.

Water, nonpotable
   See **Nonpotable water.**

Water, pellicular   See **Pellicular water.**

Water, phreatic   See **Ground water.**

Water plant   In botany, any plant that lives in water or with its roots in water. Often found in landscape architecture as a feature in garden pools or streams.

Water pollution   Eroded soil, chemical discharges, human waste, or any other items affecting the clarity or purity of a body of still water or a stream. See also **Water purification.**

Water, pore (in soils)
   See **Capillary water.**

Water, potable   See **Potable water.**

Water pressure   In landscape irrigation, the amount of force exerted by an impeded or actual flow of water in a pipe, measured in PSI (pounds per square inch). See also **Live water pressure** and **Static water pressure.**

Water garden

Water purification   In nature, the removal of mud, debris, or dissolved salts from streams occurs when water passes over sand and especially gravel bottoms, or when water is allowed to stand for some time so that suspended debris may settle.

Human-generated pollution such as eroded soil, industrial waste, and sewage is more difficult to remove. It occurs in water in increasing quantities because of the expanding human population, and must be eliminated by the use of filtration, sedimentation ponds, exposure to sunlight, chemical treatment, bacterial action, distillation, or like means. See also **Water pollution.**

Water ramp (water stair)   In Italian Renaissance gardens and thereafter, a usually formal set of running pools spilling over into each other down an incline.

Water requirements   Plants require different quantities of water throughout the year. The spring needs of a growing plant are greatest, followed by a somewhat lower rate for summer growth, a large decrease as dormancy approaches in fall, and minimal moisture in winter.

Food crops must receive between two and four acre-feet of water per year from rain or irrigation. The requirements of most plants grown in cities as ornamentals match this. Approximately 45% of all urban water is devoted to domestic use (including gardens), schools, and parks; 40% is used for commercial or industrial purposes; 15% is wasted due to leaks, overflows, and carelessness.

Water does not percolate equally well in all soils. One inch (.025 meters) of water on more or less level ground will penetrate 3–4 in. in clay, 6–10 in. in silty loam, and

up to 12 in. in sand. But to irrigate five feet deep (1.53 m) on level ground, the gardener or farmer would have to use 3–5 in. of water for sandy soils, 6–10 in. of water for silty loams, and 12–15 in. for clay soils.

In cities, water use tends to increase with income levels. Part of this heightened consumption is due to more elaborate and extensive grounds or gardens; but a great deal of it is due to the acquisition of water-using devices, such as garbage disposals and extra bathrooms, *inside* the house. Most twentieth-century cities have made little provision for this phenomenon of rising use: water is simply utilized once for the matter at hand and turned into a storm or sanitary sewer. The general need to recycle and reuse **Gray water** is a challenge of contemporary urban science.

Water resources   The ground and surface water available for use in a project or region.

Water, retention   See **Retention water.**

Water reuse (water recycling)   The use of dishwater, washwater, and other forms of dirty water to irrigate crops or ornamental plants.

After intensive purification, recycled water may sometimes be put back into a supply system as **Potable water.**

Water rights   Legal authority acquired or exercised by a property owner to use surface water existing on or passing through a plot of land.

Water, soft   See **Soft water.**

Water sprout   A fast-growing but nonproductive plant shoot stemming from a latent bud, especially an upper-branch **Sucker,** q.v.

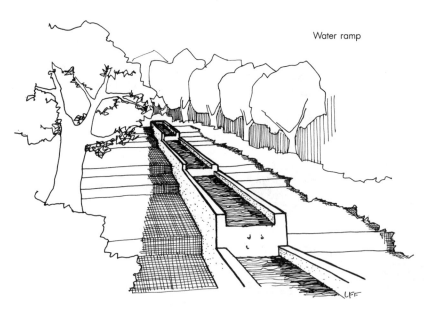

Water ramp

Water stop In landscape construction, a liner or diaphragm installed in a joint (usually concrete or stone) as a seal.

Water, surface See **Surface water.**

Water table A level of ground water, variable in elevation and fluctuating somewhat from dry to wet season, located at the meeting point of porous and impermeable rock strata.

A perched water table is located over a stratum of impervious rock that separates it from lower water tables.

See also **Aquifer** and **Ground water.**

Water theatre In late Italian Renaissance gardens, a semicircular court, built into a hillside, that features fountains, pools, cascades, statuary, bas-reliefs, niches, and other items of interest. Usually fed by diverted streams. The Villa Aldobrandini (c. 1600) in Frascati, Italy is an example.

Water tube, copper See **Copper pipe.**

Water, unavailable Water that cannot be taken up by plant roots in soil. See **Hygroscopic water.**

Water, vadose See **Vadose water.**

Water wall In landscape design, a specialized kind of fountain flowing off a vertical wall plane. See also **Water curtain.**

Water year A calculation of the flow of streams by means of monthly analysis from October 1st to September 30th.

Water-cement ratio In the making of concrete, the amount of water needed as compared to the quantity of cement in a mix. Aggregates are not considered in the ratio.

Water stop

Water wall. Caida de Agua Park, Albuquerque, New Mexico, by Morrow and Worley, landscape architects. Photo by author.

Watercourse   A stream or river channel.

Waterfall   1) In nature, a tumbling cascade in a watercourse caused by a softer understratum being worn away beneath a layer of hard rock. 2) In landscape architecture, a man-made cascade that imitates its natural counterpart in a garden setting, usually powered by a recirculating electric pump.

Watering frequency   In irrigated landscapes, determined by the slope of the land, the water required for plant health, the soil's percolation or infiltration rate, the local evapo-transpiration rate, and similar factors. See also **Water requirements**.

Watering zone (irrigation)   See **Section system**.

Water-organ   In the gardens of the Villa d' Este (c. 1560), Italy, and elsewhere, a hydraulic full-sound organ operated by means of valves.

Water-parting   See **Watershed**.

Watershed   A naturally occurring area in which surface water drains into a perceptible and definite system. Bounded by slope and ridge lines and, ultimately, basins. Also **Catchment basin, Water-parting**.

Wattle fence   A common medieval fence made of interwoven withes.

Wattling   An erosion-control method using bundles of live willow, cottonwood, alder, or similar wands that are commonly laid on hillsides or in gully channels perpendicular to the slope. The wattles are partially buried and sprout to form a living barrier to further erosion. Wattles are often laid in conjunction with boulders or rip-rap. Wattles are sometimes called **Fascine rolls**.

Wave, capillary   See **Capillary wave**.

Way, public   See **Right of way**.

Wearing course   In landscape construction, the top or finish course of asphalt or concrete pavement used for various kinds of traffic. Also **Asphalt surface course, Asphalt wearing course**.

Weather   A condition of climate. The state of the atmosphere at a certain season or during a particular time, including such factors as cloudiness, wind direction, windspeed, snow or rain, air pressure, humidity, and, in continental climates, altitude and exposure. See also **Climate**.

Weather chart   A map on which multiple regularly collected data are printed at various weather stations. Charts are plotted in a series and collected, at which time isobars are drawn and features such as high-pressure fronts and depressions noted. A forecast of upcoming weather can then be given. Also **Synoptic chart**. See also **Isobar**.

Weather working day   In some projects, a day suitable for landscape construction as determined by an owner or landscape architect and stipulated in the construction contract. Weather working days are usually fair-weather, Monday through Friday, normal working days. See also **Calendar day** and **Contract time**.

Weathering   The wearing away of surface soil and rock due to exposure to the atmosphere. In colder climates, frequent freezing and thawing are normal causes of weathering. In warmer areas, wind-borne sand and carbonic acid formed of rainwater and carbon dioxide are usual weathering agents. Severe solar heating followed by a drastic nighttime temperature (diurnal variation) is a factor in hot regions. See also **Denudation, Erosion**.

Wedge-tip   In landscape architectural drafting, an obliquely cut pencil or ink pen tip used for lettering.

Weed   Any plant that grows where people do not want it.

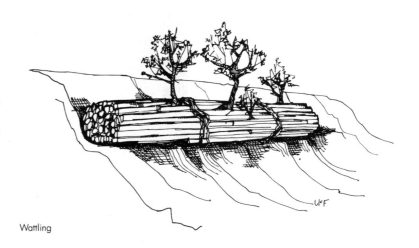

Wattling

Weedkillers See **Herbicide.**

Weep (roadside drain) An extended road shoulder foundation course creating percolation points through layers of impervious soil.

Weephole In retaining wall construction, a lined or unlined hole installed slightly above the footing to allow water drainage and relieve pressure buildup.

Weeping Applied to trees or other plants that have hanging crowns or foliage.

Weidenmann, Jacob (1829–93) A Swiss architect and engineer who emigrated to the United States in 1861. Weidenmann worked as the superintendent of parks in Hartford, Connecticut. He wrote two influential books: *Beautifying Country Homes: A Handbook of Landscape Gardening* (1870), and *Modern Cemeteries* (1888).

Weidenmann collaborated with **F. L. Olmsted** on a number of projects. He felt, as did **J. C. Loudon** and other nineteenth-century reformers, that cramped graveyards should be transformed into landscaped parks. Perhaps his most notable design was the Cedar Hill Cemetery in Hartford.

Weir A fence or wall placed across a brook to raise or lower water level and to improve fishing or catch fish.

Weld, seam See **Seam weld.**

Weld, ship See **Ship weld.**

Weld, tack See **Tack weld.**

Welding The process of metal joining through fusion caused by the controlled application of extreme heat. **Arc welding,** accomplished by the use of electrodes, is one of the most common welding methods.

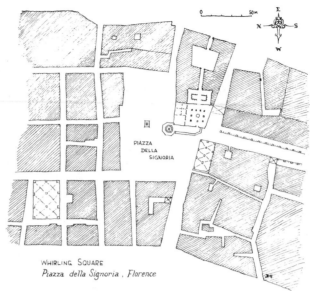

WHIRLING SQUARE
Piazza della Signoria , Florence

Whirling square

Well A bore-hole cut down to the water table, pumped for water.

Well, dry See **French drain.**

Well, tree See **Tree well.**

Well-log A systematic notation of soil and rock strata characteristics during well-drilling is made in a well-log. The direction of the bore is also noted, and specific measurements of resistivity, temperature, gamma rays, acoustic velocity, and the like may also be taken.

Western larch (landscape construction) See **Larch.**

Western yellow pine Ponderosa pine, a wood sometimes used in landscape construction.

Wetted perimeter (of a ditch, pipe, or creek) See **Hydraulic radius.**

Wetting agent A chemical used to improve liquid penetration into solid surfaces by reducing normal liquid surface tension.

Wetwood 1) Exceptionally saturated **Heartwood,** q.v. 2) **Slime flux,** q.v.

Whaleback dune See **Dune.**

Wheat belt An agricultural region of North America, east of the Rocky Mountains, and consisting of prairies and plains running from Texas to Alberta.

Wheat crescent An area lying east of the Andes, part of the Argentine pampas, in which wheat is the principal crop.

Whip In woody plants, a first year's growth of an unbranched shoot, especially the first growth of a graft.

Whirling square A town square in which four (or more) streets radiate from the square's corners in a pinwheel-like (whirling) fashion. Essentially medieval. The Piazza della Signoria, Florence, is an example. Also **Windmill.**

White dune   See **Dune.**

White garden   A (usually) private garden laid out with white-flowering annuals as a theme. Evergreens are often planted as a background. White gardens can be most effective when viewed at night in moonlight or under artificial lighting.

White noise   In urban landscapes, the sound of falling or splashing water, singing, the wind in the trees, or other pleasant resonances used to mask the harsher sound of traffic, loud machinery, or the like. See also **Noise pollution.**

Whorl   In plants, an occurrence of buds, flowers, leaves, and the like in a radial or circular pattern at the same level, especially around an axis. Also **Verticil.**

Wild garden   1) A casual landscape of forest with a selected undergrowth of flowering shrubs, ground covers, and flowers. Wild gardens need virtually no upkeep once they are established. 2) A Naturalistic garden including only native plants (North America).

Wild landscape   A term generally used to describe those landscapes that are relatively untouched by the hand of man. However, it should be noted that no existing landscape has escaped the influence of human beings.

Wild type   A plant chosen as typical because it exhibits the characteristic attributes of its species growing in a natural state. A sort of **Phenotype,** q.v. See also **Holotype.**

Wildflower   A native or naturalized plant—often an annual or perennial—noted for its colorful blooming habits.

Wilding (wildling)   A native or naturalized plant growing uncultivated in the countryside. A wilding may also be a cultivated plant that has escaped cultivation (an **Escape**). See also **Naturalized plant.**

Wilt proof   See **Antidesiccant.**

Wilting coefficient   In soils, a low percentage of moisture-holding capacity indicating the point at which water is no longer available for plant use from storage pores in the soil structure. A plant begins to wither once the wilting coefficient is reached. See also **Wilting point.**

Wilting point   The point at which plant growth stops and leaves and buds shrivel from excessive sun or wind, lack of water, or other factors. See also **Wilting coefficient.**

Wind dispersal   The scattering of plant seeds or spores by breezes.

Wind erosion   Erosion carried out by wind-blown particles of sand or silt. Common in arid or overgrazed, unprotected regions. See also **Erosion.**

Wind fertilization   See **Wind pollination.**

Wildflower. Many wildflowers are found scattered among field grasses. Photo courtesy Morrow and Company.

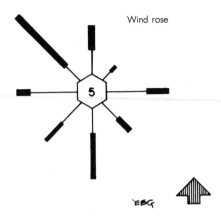

Wind rose

'EBG

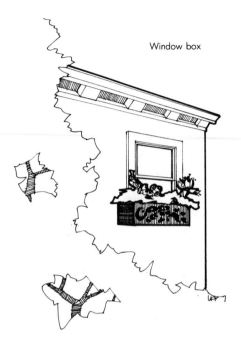

Window box

Wind load   The calculated pressure exerted by wind that may be successfully resisted without structural failure by trees or walls, fences, overhead frames, and the like (construction members). See also **Dead load, Dynamic load, Live load, Snow load.**

Wind pollination   Plant fertilization by airborne pollen. Also **Anemophily.**

Wind, prevailing   See **Prevailing wind.**

Wind rose   A graphic diagram showing the direction of winds blowing in a certain locality, with heavier lines indicating greater frequency and/or severity.

Wind screen planting   See **Screen planting.**

Wind shadow   An area of comparative calm on the leeward side of a windbreak.

Wind spider   A circle-shaped chart that indicates wind frequency and speed.

Windbreak   A hedgerow or tight planting of trees made in open areas to protect a landscape or building from drying, hot, or freezing winds. See also **Shelter belt.**

Windburn   In young trees and shrubs, damage to leaves, buds, bark, and other tissues caused by high or excessive winds. See also **Sunscald, Winterburn.**

Wind-cut or wind-formed (trees)
Trees or other plants characteristically shaped by the action of steady, high wind at a shore, mountain ridge, or elsewhere. See also **Mechanomorphosis.**

Windmill   A wind-powered pump or turbine used traditionally to draw water from boreholes and, increasingly, to generate electricity.

Windmill (square)   See **Whirling square.**

Window box   A small (often 8 in. × 8 in. × 36 in. or 20 cm × 20 cm × 1 m) box containing annuals, perennials, and/or other detail plants mounted beneath a window. The box is often gaily painted and is used as a cheerful accent in areas in which normal gardening space is limited or nonexistent. See also **Container gardening.**

Wind-cut trees

Windrow composting
See **Compost.**

Wind-shearing   See **Wind-cut or wind-formed trees.**

Wing wall   At bridge abutments, a short retaining wall. See also **Cheek wall.**

Winter annual   A kind of **Annual**, q.v., that is planted as seed in autumn, germinates, survives winter, and goes on to flower the following spring. Often a weed.

Winter garden   A cold-climate garden arranged to deflect chilling winds and provide enjoyment through the skillfully contrived contrasts of snow and evergreens, clear-running water and ice-skims, and early-blooming bulbs such as crocuses and snowdrops against a snowy or leafless background.

   Accent shrubs such as redosier dogwood and Oregon grape are also useful parts of the winter garden.

Winterburn In plants, damage caused by extreme fluctuation in winter temperatures. A warm winter day can cause sap to rise in a stem. If the thermometer drops below 32°F (0°C) after nightfall, the sap may freeze, thereby expanding in stem tissue and killing cells, usually on south and west sides of a trunk. Thicker bark at maturity can prevent winterburn. See also **Sunscald, Windburn.**

Winterkill In plants, death caused by exposure to severe cold or to quick and drastic changes in temperature.

Wire, annealed steel See **Annealed steel guy wire.**

Wire, barbed See **Barbed wire.**

Wire gauge A measurement of wire diameter. The smaller the number, the larger the diameter.

Wire, tension (chainlink fence construction) See **Tension wire.**

Wise, Henry (1653–1738) English commercial nurseryman and landscape gardener. Wise began a nursery partnership in London in 1681 with **George London**, q.v. Wise and London developed a very lively trade with a series of aristocratic clients. The gardens at Chatsworth and at Blenheim, arguably Wise's best work, were planned and installed by Wise after London's death in 1713. Wise developed Blenheim formally on a very large scale, with a somewhat awkward handling of detail. Blenheim was later modified by **Capability Brown**, q.v.

After London's death, Wise became royal gardener to Queen Anne. The Romantic School of landscape design (the **English School of Landscape Gardening**, q.v.) dates from Wise's death.

See also **Charles Bridgeman.**

Witch's broom In trees (or shrubs), an irregular mass of tight-knit, short, feeble branches developed as a result of fungus or insect infestation of the plant's vascular system.

Withe (withy) 1) A willow branch or slip. Also, generally, any slim twig. 2) A row of brick or other masonry courses in a wall.

Witness, expert See **Expert witness.**

Wold In medieval England, a **Cuesta**, q.v.

Wood or **Woods** 1) A small forest. 2) A specific kind of tree used as construction timber. 3) Tightly structured cellulose (xylem) cells.

Wood, autumn See **Autumn wood** and **Growth rings.**

Wood and brick construction joints In landscape construction, the joint surfaces at which wood members or bricks meet or are connected. 1) **Butt joint:** A 90° connection joint. 2) **Lap joint:** An overlap connection. 3) **Miter joint:** A 45° joint.

Other joints sometimes used in landscape construction are dovetail, rabbet, routed, and slotted joints.

Wood gum See **Xylan.**

Wood, old (horticulture) See **Old wood.**

Wood preservative Any preparation applied to outdoor wood timbers or lumber to prevent their weathering or destruction through decay. A preservative is especially useful on wood members placed on or in the ground. Common temperate-zone preservatives include paint (several kinds), creosote, pitch, tar, various toxic salts, **Pentachlorophenol (Penta)**, "Woodlife," and related

products. A common, useful wood conditioner is logwood oil. Pressure treatments are frequently employed to force preservatives into wood.

Wood, spring See **Growth rings.**

Wood, summer See **Growth rings.**

Woodland garden A kind of naturalistic garden consisting of light forest underplanted with rhododendron and other flowering shrubs. See also **Uvedale Price.**

"Woodlife" A common trade name **Wood preservative**, q.v.

Woolly In plant structures, covered with soft hairs. See also **Lanate.**

Work, alteration (landscape construction) See **Alteration work.**

Work, carpenter's See **Carpenter's work.**

Work, diaper (surface ornamentation) See **Diaper work.**

Work item (landscape construction) See **Bid list** and **Item of work.**

Work, nonconforming (landscape construction) See **Nonconforming work.**

Work order See **Notice to proceed.**

Working drawings Precise drawings and details used with specifications for the construction of a landscape project. Working drawings form part of the **Construction documents**, q.v. Also **Construction drawings, Contract drawings, Design drawings.** See also **Specifications.**

Working drawings phase A common term for the final design portion of a landscape architect's services to an owner, including

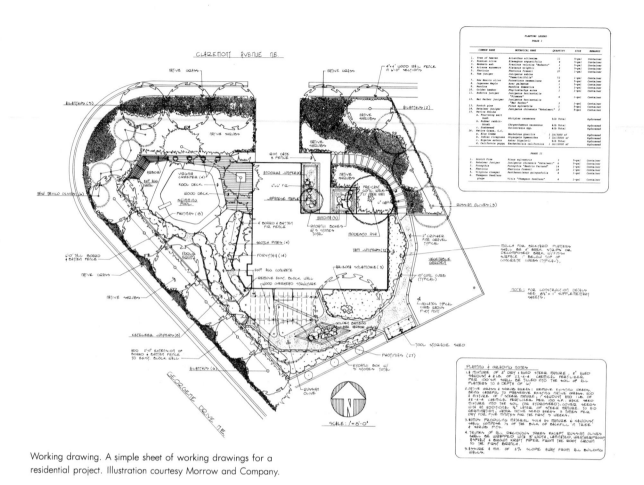

Working drawing. A simple sheet of working drawings for a residential project. Illustration courtesy Morrow and Company.

construction drawings and specifications, cost estimates, and other detailed information for the owner's use in awarding a contract for construction of a project. Also **Construction documents phase.** See also **Bid phase, Construction phase, Design development phase, Schematic design phase.**

Working pressure In irrigation, the force or pressure formed in a system in operation. Working pressure is less than static or **Hydrostatic pressure,** q.v., because of friction loss. See also **Operating pressure.**

Working stress See **Stress.**

Woven wire dam See **Check dam.**

Woven wire fabric (WWF) In concrete construction, a reinforcing mesh used in concrete slabs and columns, often expressed as WWF or WWM, with the mesh squares (i.e., 6 × 6, etc.) and wire gauge (#6, #10, etc.) given.

Wrapping, tree See **Tree wrapping.**

Wrought iron An extremely pure and malleable iron containing a very small amount of carbon, commonly used in outdoor fencing, grate, and other construction.

WWF See **Woven wire fabric.**

WWM See **Woven wire fabric.**

Wye In irrigation, a piece of connecting pipe linkage shaped in the form of a "Y."

Xanthophyll Yellow **Plant pigment,** q.v. See also **Carotenoid.**

Xenogamy In botany, cross-pollination or fertilization.

Xeric In general use, arid. Pertaining to an arid climate or habitat. Xeric farming, xeric landscape (xeriscape) are examples. See also **Moisture gradient.**

Xeromorphy In plants, exhibiting the characteristics of a **Xerophyte,** q.v.

Xerophilous Able to withstand drought or extreme aridity.

Xerophyte A plant capable, in extreme examples, of extracting the water and nutrients it needs from the air; in some cases, therefore, a soilless plant. A plant such as cactus or mesquite adapted by evolutionary device to life in a desert region. Adjective: xerophytic. See also **Hydrophyte, Mesophyte, Tropophyte, Xeromorphy.**

Xylan In botany, a gel found in wood tissue. Also **Tree gum, Wood gum.**

Xylem In botany, the harder parts of the vascular system of a woody plant. Wood. See also **Phloem.**

Xystus (xystos) 1) In classical Greece, an extensive portico often associated with games or athletics. 2) In classical Rome, a walkway or path lined with posts or trees.

Y

Yard, bank (earthwork)   See **Bank yard.**

Yard drain   A surface drain in an open landscape.

Yard, loose (landscape construction)   See **Loose yard.**

Yard lumber   General construction lumber of all kinds and sizes. Yard lumber is graded to indicate quality and use. See also **Lumber.**

Yard, service   See **Service area.**

Yazoo stream (geology)   A tributary that runs parallel to its main stream or river for some distance before joining it.

Year, water   See **Water year.**

Yellow garden   A usually private garden, often small, laid out with yellow or orange flowering annuals, perennials, and/or bulbs as the main theme. Accent plantings may include dark green hedges or tall, bulky deciduous trees or shrubs.

Yellow podsolic soil   See **Podsol.**

Yellows   In horticulture, a viral infection causing paleness or yellowing of plantstock.

Young landscape   A landscape newly emerged from the sea, created by volcanic action, or otherwise very recent. Characterized by sharp, uneroded landforms.

Young stream   A stream with a steep gradient that is speedily cutting its way down through its landscape.

Z

Zariba A thorn enclosure protecting a camp, garden, or animals. An ancient human construct. See also **Prehistoric (primitive) gardens.**

Zeitgeist (German) The spirit or sense of a time and generation.

Zenith 1) In regard to the sun's trajectory or angle in the sky, the high point of its arc. 2) The high point of the sky directly over the head of an observer.

Zero, plant See **Plant zero.**

Zero runoff In site drainage planning, the retention of all the water falling on a site.

Zinc A metallic element necessary in small amounts for plant (and animal) health and growth. A **Trace element,** q.v. See also **Available nutrient, Soil minerals.**

Zonal soil A complete soil, containing an ABC soil profile or series. See also **Soil horizon.**

Zone, climate See **Climate zone.**

Zone of hardiness (plants) See **Hardiness zone.**

Zone, irrigation See **Section system.**

Zone, life See **Life zone.**

Zone, phreatic (soils) See **Phreatic zone.**

Zone, saturated (soils) See **Phreatic zone.**

Zone, soil See **Soil horizon.**

Zone, temperate See **Temperate zone.**

Zoning A form of land-use control usually exercised by a city or county. Zoning involves the setting aside of distinct land areas for specific purposes, usually in and by a city. Commonly, zoning for industrial, commercial, agricultural, and housing uses is laid out by law. Public utilization of land for parks, utilities, bridle and bicycle paths, and the like must also be provided for in any zoning system.

A certain basic understanding of land types and compatibilities underlies zoning legislation and development. Compatible use, building sizes and setbacks, population concentration, and many other urban problems are regulated through zoning.

See also **Euclidean zoning, Planning, Spot zoning, Strip zoning.**

Zoning, Euclidean See **Euclidean zoning.**

Zoning, irrigation See **Irrigation zoning.**

Zoning permit An authorization granted by a city or county for a specific land use in a given area. See also **Zoning.**

Zoo (zoological garden) A sanctuary, or specially favorable place, in which various species of animals are kept for study, propagation, and exhibition. Successful modern zoos are havens for many animal species, combining thoughtful, interpretive landscape design with exhibit areas for a more effective overall habitat.

In the twentieth century, **Botanical gardens,** q.v., are often integrated with zoos to create more complete environments for public study and enjoyment.

Zooecology The relationship of animals to their physical surroundings. Also animal ecology. See also **Ecology.**

Zoogeography The scientific study of animal distribution over the surface of the Earth.

Zoophyte An animal, such as a sponge or a "walking twig," which appears to be a plant.

Zoo (zoological garden). Photos
courtesy Morrow and Co., Ltd.,
landscape architects.

A Dictionary of Landscape Architecture was designed by Emmy Ezzell, and set in Spartan with Memphis bold display, typefaces chosen for their quietness, versatility, and strong structural quality. The type was composed by the University of New Mexico Printing Plant on the Mergenthaler Linotron 202, and the book was printed and bound by BookCrafters on 50 pound Finch Opaque, an acid-free paper.